Economic Integration and International Trade

The International Library of Critical Writings in Economics

Series Editor: Mark Blaug

Professor Emeritus, University of London, UK
Professor Emeritus, University of Buckingham, UK
Visiting Professor, University of Amsterdam, The Netherlands

This series is an essential reference source for students, researchers and lecturers in economics. It presents by theme a selection of the most important articles across the entire spectrum of economics. Each volume has been prepared by a leading specialist who has written an authoritative introduction to the literature included.

A full list of published and future titles in this series is printed at the end of this volume.

Wherever possible, the articles in these volumes have been reproduced as originally published using facsimile reproduction, inclusive of footnotes and pagination to facilitate ease of reference.

For a list of all Edward Elgar published titles visit our site on the World Wide Web at
http://www.e-elgar.co.uk

Economic Integration and International Trade

Edited by

Carsten Kowalczyk

Associate Professor of International Economics
Tufts University, US

THE INTERNATIONAL LIBRARY OF CRITICAL WRITINGS IN ECONOMICS

An Elgar Reference Collection
Cheltenham, UK • Northampton, MA, USA

Published by
Edward Elgar Publishing Limited
Glensanda House
Montpellier Parade
Cheltenham
Glos GL50 1UA
UK

Edward Elgar Publishing, Inc.
136 West Street, Suite 202
Northampton
MA 01060
USA

A catalogue record for this book is available from the British Library.

Library of Congress Cataloguing in Publication Data
Economic integration and international trade / edited by Carsten Kowalczyk.
    (The international library of critical writings in economics ; 115)
    Includes bibliographical references.
    1. International trade. 2. International economic integration. I. Kowalczyk, Carsten,
1956- II. Series.

HF1379.E274 2000
382—dc21   99–049367

ISBN 1 84064 201 7   1 00 20 4 3 8 2 2
Printed and bound in Great Britain by MPG Books Ltd, Bodmin, Cornwall

Contents

C   Tariff Reform

PART III   RESULTS ON INTEGRATION AND WELFARE

A   Integration and National Welfare

B   Integration and Union Welfare

C   Integration and World Welfare

Acknowledgements

The editor and publishers wish to thank the authors and the following publishers who have kindly given permission for the use of copyright material.

American Economic Association for articles: Ronald W. Jones (1969), 'Tariffs and Trade in General Equilibrium: Comment', *American Economic Review*, **LIX** (3), June, 418–24; Paul Wonnacott and Ronald Wonnacott (1981), 'Is Unilateral Tariff Reduction Preferable to a Customs Union? The Curious Case of the Missing Foreign Tariffs', *American Economic Review*, **71** (4), September, 704–14; Gene M. Grossman and Elhanan Helpman (1990), 'Comparative Advantage and Long-Run Growth', *American Economic Review*, **80** (4), September, 796–815.

Blackwell Publishers, Inc. for article: Eric W. Bond (1990), 'The Optimal Tariff Structure in Higher Dimensions', *International Economic Review*, **31** (1), February, 103–16.

Blackwell Publishers Ltd for articles: John McMillan and Ewen McCann (1981), 'Welfare Effects in Customs Unions', *Economic Journal*, **91** (363), September, 697–703; Carsten Kowalczyk and Tomas Sjöström (1994), 'Bringing GATT into the Core', *Economica*, **61**, August, 301–17.

Canadian Journal of Economics for article: John Kennan and Raymond Riezman (1990), Optimal Tariff Equilibria With Customs Unions', *Canadian Journal of Economics*, **XXIII** (1), February, 70–83.

Carnegie Endowment for International Peace for excerpt: Jacob Viner (1950), 'The Economics of Customs Unions', in *The Customs Union Issue*, Chapter IV, 41–81.

Elsevier Science Ltd for articles: Murray C. Kemp and Henry Y. Wan, Jr. (1976), 'An Elementary Proposition Concerning the Formation of Customs Unions', *Journal of International Economics*, **6** (1), February, 95–7; Raymond Riezman (1979), 'A 3x3 Model of Customs Unions', *Journal of International Economics*, **9**, 341–54; Tatsuo Hatta and Takashi Fukushima (1979), 'The Welfare Effect of Tariff Rate Reductions in a Many Country World', *Journal of International Economics*, **9** (4), November, 503–11; Earl L. Grinols (1981), 'An Extension of the Kemp-Wan Theorem on the Formation of Customs Unions', *Journal of International Economics*, **11** (2), May, 259–66; Daniel Gros (1987), 'A Note on the Optimal Tariff, Retaliation and the Welfare Loss from Tariff Wars in a Framework with Intra-Industry Trade', *Journal of International Economics*, **23**, 357–67; Carsten Kowalczyk (1993), 'Integration in Goods and Factors: The Role of Flows and Revenue', *Regional Science and Urban Economics*, **23**, 355–67; Martin Richardson (1995), 'Tariff Revenue Competition in a Free Trade Area', *European Economic Review*, **39**, 1429–37; Eric W. Bond and Constantinos Syropoulos (1996), 'The Size of Trading Blocs: Market Power and World Welfare Effects', *Journal of International Economics*, **40**, 411–37.

Federal Reserve Bank of Kansas City for excerpt: Paul Krugman (1991), 'The Movement Toward Free Trade Zones', in *Policy Implications of Trade and Currency Zones: A Symposium Sponsored by the Federal Reserve Bank of Kansas City*, 7–41.

Keio Economic Society for article: Michihiro Ohyama (1972), 'Trade and Welfare in General Equilibrium', *Keio Economic Studies*, **IX** (2), 37–73.

Kluwer Academic Publishers, Inc. for article: Carsten Kowalczyk (1992), 'Paradoxes in Integration Theory', *Open Economies Review*, **3**, 51–9.

MIT Press Journals and the President and Fellows of Harvard College and the Massachusetts Institute of Technology for article: Luis A. Rivera-Batiz and Paul M. Romer (1991), 'Economic Integration and Endogenous Growth', *Quarterly Journal of Economics*, **CVI** (2), May, 531–55.

Review of Economic Studies Ltd for articles and excerpt: J. de V. Graaff (1949–50), 'On Optimum Tariff Structures', *Review of Economic Studies*, **XVII**, 47–59; Harry G. Johnson (1953–54), 'Optimum Tariffs and Retaliation', *Review of Economic Studies*, **XXI** (2), 142–53; Franz Gehrels (1956–57), 'Customs Union from a Single-Country Viewpoint', *Review of Economic Studies*, **XXIV** (1), 61–4; Tatsuo Hatta (1977), 'A Theory of Piecemeal Policy Recommendations', *Review of Economic Studies*, **XLIV** (1), 1–21; Konstantine Gatsios and Larry Karp (1991), 'Delegation Games in Customs Unions', *Review of Economic Studies*, **58**, 391–7; Richard G. Lipsey and Kelvin Lancaster (1997), 'The General Theory of Second Best', in Richard G. Lipsey (ed.), *Microeconomics, Growth and Political Economy: The Selected Essays of Richard G. Lipsey, Volume One*, Chapter 6, Cheltenham UK and Lyme NH: Edward Elgar, 153–80 [a revised version of an article originally published in the *Review of Economic Studies*, **XXIV**, 1956, 11–32].

University of Chicago Press for articles: Richard E. Baldwin (1992), 'Measurable Dynamic Gains from Trade', *Journal of Political Economy*, **100** (1), February, 162–74; Joy Mazumdar (1996), 'Do Static Gains from Trade Lead to Medium-Run Growth?', *Journal of Political Economy*, **104** (6), December, 1328–37.

University of Michigan Press for excerpt: Alan V. Deardorff and Robert M. Stern (1994), 'Multilateral Trade Negotiations and Preferential Trading Arrangements', in Alan V. Deardorff and Robert M. Stern (eds), *Analytical and Negotiating Issues in the Global Trading System*, Chapter 2, 27–85.

Weidenfeld & Nicolson, Orion Publishing Group Ltd for excerpt: Richard G. Lipsey (1970), 'Inter-Commodity Substitution with Constant Real Prices: 2 The Graham Demand Case', in *The Theory of Customs Unions: A General Equilibrium Analysis*, Chapter 6, 44–68, 158–61.

Every effort has been made to trace all the copyright holders but if any have been inadvertently overlooked the publishers will be pleased to make the necessary arrangement at the first opportunity.

In addition the publishers wish to thank the Library of the London School of Economics and Political Science and B & N Microfilm, London for their assistance in obtaining these articles.

Introduction

Carsten Kowalczyk

Global free trade has desirable properties. But how does one get there while minimizing the inconvenience of the journey?

The pre-amble to GATT was obviously written with the first proposition in mind. The rest of GATT, through its Articles and its many years of service as an international organization, has sketched a road map, and provided assistance to the travelers.

The most-favored-nation principle, central to GATT membership, became an important source of benefit for members, but it also presented a potential difficulty for trade liberalization if some GATT members were not willing or able to reduce their trade barriers, leaving the unappealing options of bringing multilateral liberalization to a halt, or of allowing 'free riding' on others' liberalization.

GATT Article XXIV addresses these concerns by providing for its members to exchange preferential tariff reductions through the formation of customs unions or free trade areas. The customs union provides for free trade between its members and stipulates that they set a common external tariff. The free trade area stipulates free trade between members as well, but permits them to set individual rates on trade with non-members. It is a constraint on both types of preferential arrangements that the average rate of protection on trade with non-members not increase. With the creation of the WTO and the accompanying Understanding on Article XXIV, it is also agreed that only in exceptional cases should the phasing out of intra-bloc tariffs exceed ten years.[1]

Already Viner (1950, Chapter 1 in this volume) demonstrated that a customs union, although constituting an apparent move towards global free trade, has the potential to reduce rather than raise welfare of the participants and of the world.[2] He argued that a customs union may cause a country to change source of production from high cost domestic firms to low cost union partner firms, and from low cost outside firms to high cost union partner firms. Viner labeled the first effect trade creation and the second effect trade diversion, and he argued that the welfare effect from customs union depends on whether trade creation, which he proposed raises welfare, or trade diversion, which he proposed lowers welfare, dominates.

In their celebrated paper, Lipsey and Lancaster (1956, revised 1997, Chapter 2 in this volume) state Viner's result on a welfare reducing customs union, and Meade's work on policy reform, as motivation for, and important examples of, their general theory of second best as they present it in the form of two principles of optimality and reform.

Meade (1955b) also lauds Viner for the insight that a move towards global free trade could be harmful, but he expresses doubt that trade diversion is necessarily welfare reducing since, in spite of the higher producer price, imports could increase due to the lower tariffs. Gehrels (1956, Chapter 3 in this volume) and Lipsey (1957) show this to be correct, establishing that trade diversion may raise rather than reduce welfare.[3]

Finally, because trade diversion is not a 'primitive' and the terminology not exhaustive even in simple competitive environments, Viner's approach gives little guidance to empirical researchers. This is problematic, given that the analysis of preferential trading arrangements quickly might involve the need to determine the net effect from several channels each raising or lowering welfare.

As discussed in Kowalczyk (1990, forthcoming), '[i]n spite of these difficulties, Viner's concepts have remained the pliers with which theorists and empirical researchers have attempted to solve the customs union problem.' But, since forming customs unions is nothing but a particular type of multi-country tariff reform, it would be surprising if the analysis of customs unions should have its own language in the first place. And, indeed, it shouldn't. In particular, the terms-of-trade and volume-of-trade approach to welfare analysis, which originates with Meade (1955a), and has been used in the theory of tariffs and their reform, constitutes a useful alternative to Viner's approach. Among its attractive features are that the terms-of-trade and volume-of-trade approach (a) is grounded in standard economic theory, (b) is exhaustive for competitive environments, and applies to members, non-members, and coalitions of countries, including the world, and (c) identifies relevant variables for the empirical researcher.

Applying the terms-of-trade and volume-of-trade approach as methodology and organizing framework, this volume presents the main contributions to the analysis of trade integration. After introducing formally the alternative approach with two papers, the selected articles present results on integration and welfare, on free trade areas versus customs unions, on the use of sidepayments to facilitate trade liberalization, and on growth and welfare from integration. This Introduction concludes with remarks on some work on integration not discussed in this volume, and with suggestions for further research.

Preliminaries

Assuming small tariff changes, Jones (1969, Chapter 4 in this volume) presents a brief derivation of the basic welfare expression from the nation's balanced trade constraint. He shows that the sum of changes in the world market prices, weighted by the initial trade volume, and changes in the trade volume, weighted by the initial wedge between domestic and world prices, constitutes an exhaustive measure of change in that nation's income. He shows also, as an intermediate step, that the income change can be expressed alternatively as the sum of change in consumer and producer surplus and tariff revenue.

Ohyama (1972, Chapter 5 in this volume) demonstrates that when tariff changes are large, the welfare calculus should be modified in two ways: some weights must be adjusted to reflect post-change values, and additional terms capturing substitution in consumption and production must be included. Ohyama also shows how the expression for the nation, under assumptions of lump-sum income transfers, can be aggregated to represent the welfare effects for groups of countries, or for the whole world. He applies the methodology to derive a large number of results, including the proposition that the formation of a customs union which sets its compensating external tariff, i.e., the rate which leaves trade with non-members constant, raises union and world welfare.[4]

It is a concern that members of preferential trading blocs may exercise market power and possibly harm non-members. While Article XXIV prohibits members of trading blocs from raising their average external tariff, there may be other outlets for such behavior, including various types of taxes or subsidies, or, for non-competitive environments, anti-dumping. De Van Graaff (1949–50, Chapter 6 in this volume) provides an early discussion of the proposition that the optimum tariff rate is the inverse of the trading partner's price elasticity of imports. Johnson (1953–54, Chapter 7 in this volume) shows, contrary to the conventional wisdom at the time, that the two-country tariff game need not be a Prisoners' Dilemma; one country may gain from tariff warfare relative to global free trade.

Bond (1990, Chapter 8 in this volume) derives the optimum tariff vector for a country that trades many goods, while Gros (1987, Chapter 9 in this volume) derives the optimum tariff with and without retaliation in a two-country version of the trade in varieties model that Krugman has employed so extensively.

These papers compare nations' payoffs across discretely different trading situations, but they do not consider how particular gradual changes in tariffs, i.e., tariff reform, affect welfare. Hatta (1977, Chapter 10 in this volume) introduces a technique involving assumptions on substitution in consumption and production, on income effects, and on policy parameters and rules for their change, which has become widely used in the reform literature.

Welfare Effects from Preferential Trading Arrangements

Should a nation engage in preferential trading arrangements with those countries that it already trades much with, or are better partners countries with which there is little initial trade? And is free trade still the best policy of a small country in a world of free trade areas and customs unions?

Lipsey (1970, Chapter 11 in this volume) argues that countries which already trade relatively much with each other are good candidates for a mutually beneficial customs union, while Riezman (1979, Chapter 12 in this volume) states that natural partners are those that trade little with each other initially. Kowalczyk (1990, forthcoming) shows that these statements can be reconciled since Riezman's is about trade levels while Lipsey's is about trade shares.

It is a widely held view that a small country has nothing to gain from joining a customs union beyond what it can achieve from a unilateral tariff elimination. Wonnacott and Wonnacott (1981, Chapter 13 in this volume) argue that this ignores the beneficial effects from the union partner's tariff elimination. Applying the terms-of-trade and volume-of-trade approach, Kowalczyk (forthcoming) shows that a large country's tariff elimination implies a terms-of-trade improvement for the small country, and that, not only may joining a preferential trading area be better for the small country than a unilateral tariff elimination, the small country may want to join many or even all of the world's free trade areas. If goods are substitutes, accession through mutual equi-proportionate tariff rate reductions ensures that the small country gains and that it can compensate the larger partners.

Kowalczyk (1993, Chapter 14 in this volume) presents a comparative analysis of the sources of welfare change when trade impediments are revenue-generating tariffs versus when they are not, as exemplified by administrative costs of crossing borders.

When investigating the effects from integration on the member countries, the question arises how the group of countries should organize itself if it strives to maximize its collective welfare. McMillan and McCann (1981, Chapter 15 in this volume) show that, for a small customs union whose members are not able to affect their terms of trade relative to non-members, the complete elimination of tariffs between members, required by Article XXIV, is generally not optimal. Focusing instead on the external tariff, Gatsios and Karp (1991, Chapter 16 in this volume) show that a 'timid' customs union member may want to have the 'aggressive' member set unilaterally the union's common external tariff rather than having both members determine the rate even if intra-union income transfers are possible.

The concern with how preferential trading arrangements affect world welfare is of vast importance. Indeed, if a customs union or a free trade area is harmful to world welfare, then a member or a non-member is hurt, and full compensation is not feasible.

Hatta and Fukushima (1979, Chapter 17 in this volume) apply Hatta's (1977, Chapter 10 in this volume) approach to analyzing the world welfare effects from multilateral tariff reform. Kowalczyk (1992, Chapter 18 in this volume) shows that the change in world welfare is given by a weighted sum of changes in bilateral price wedges, and that the effect from a customs union or a free trade area follows from this welfare expression as a special case of tariff reform.

Kemp and Wan (1976, Chapter 19 in this volume) present a proof of the proposition, shown also by Ohyama (1972, Chapter 5 in this volume), that a compensating customs union, i.e., one with no effect on trade with non-members, has the potential to raise world welfare.

Krugman (1991, Chapter 20 in this volume) shows, for a model of trade in varieties, that if the world economy moves toward global free trade through a sequence of enlarging symmetric customs unions, world welfare may fall until reaching a minimum at three blocs, and then rises to reach its maximum at global free trade. He argues also that transport costs may change the result. In particular, world welfare may increase monotonically if nations with low bilateral trade costs integrate, thereby expending fewer resources in high transport cost trade.[5]

Deardorff and Stern (1994, Chapter 21 in this volume) demonstrate, in a model with two types of countries and where trade is due to comparative advantage rather than variety, that if symmetric blocs are expanded by drawing bloc partners in random fashion then expected world welfare increases monotonically until free trade is obtained.[6]

Bond and Syropoulos (1996, Chapter 22 in this volume) investigate further the robustness properties of Krugman's findings, in particular, how the optimal external tariff of a trading bloc depends on the size of its trade, and whether free trade and the welfare-minimizing three-bloc situation are stable equilibria.

Other Results

GATT Article XXIV permits only two types of preferential trading arrangements. But which type of arrangement yields higher welfare, the customs union or the free trade area? In favor of the customs union is that its uniform external tariff structure does not create the need for possibly complicated and distortionary domestic content requirements within the trading bloc. On the other hand, it may be easier for a customs union to use its common external tariff to exercise market power in its trade with non-members.

Kennan and Riezman (1990, Chapter 23 in this volume) compare welfare of members and non-members under global free trade, non-cooperative Nash tariffs, customs unions, and free trade areas, for a calibrated three-country three-goods exchange model where countries set optimal tariffs against non-members.[7] Richardson (1995, Chapter 24 in this volume) shows that a free trade area creates an incentive for each member to reduce its external tariff to earn tariff revenue at the expense of its partners.[8]

While the assumption that income transfers between winners and losers from policy reform, whether within nations or between them, is made frequently (it is in most of this volume's papers, for example), it is rarely stated explicitly which transfers are required. Grinols (1981, Chapter 25 in this volume) identifies a transfer mechanism which ensures that no customs union member loses from expanding an Ohyama-Kemp-Wan customs union. Kowalczyk and Sjöström (1994, Chapter 26 in this volume) present a many country model of international trade in monopoly goods and, using cooperative game theory, derive an explicit expression for sidepayments between nations which will make the global trading club a core allocation.

With only few exceptions, the papers discussed so far have been concerned with the static welfare effects from integration for competitive economies. However, and as discussed by, among others, Harris and Cox (1984) for the Canada–U.S. free trade agreement, and by Smith and Venables (1988) and Cecchini, Catinat, and Jacquemin (1988), for the European Community's Internal Market, integration may lead to price and cost reductions in sectors with imperfect competition or scale effects, and therefore to substantially larger income gains, between 5 and 9 percent, than the approximately 1 percent gains derived for competitive environments.

Baldwin (1989) argued in a policy paper that increased income from Europe 1992 would lead to higher savings and capital accumulation which, he estimated, would lead to an increase in income of up to 15 percent. Baldwin (1992, Chapter 27 in this volume) proposes a theoretical framework and calibrations in support of these estimates. Mazumdar (1996, Chapter 28 in this volume) shows, however, that the model must contain at least two goods to generate capital accumulation and thus growth since, whether a nation experiences Baldwin's growth effect or not, depends critically on whether it imports or exports capital goods.

The final question considered in this volume is whether integration, besides raising a nation's income level and inducing medium-term growth, can raise its long-run growth rate. Grossman and Helpman (1990, Chapter 29 in this volume) show, in a model where technological spillovers are national in scope, that trade integration between countries with different factor endowments may raise or lower long run growth depending on whether resources relocate to or from the R&D-intensive sector in the capital-rich country. Rivera-Batiz and Romer (1991, Chapter 30 in this volume) propose that eliminating barriers to the international flow of knowledge would affect long run growth.

Other Work, and Extensions

The writings in this volume consider the theory of economic integration in a world where governments strive to maximize national income. Some approaches to integration are not included, therefore. There are also lines of inquiry which have received very little attention in the literature.

Recognizing that the effects from integration depend on economic structure and on type of integration, calibration analyses and more extensive computable general equilibrium models have found wide use in analyses of trade integration – sometimes with considerable impact on the public debate of proposed integration initiatives.[9]

This volume also does not include writings from the current research on the political economy of integration, a literature which adds to the concerns of the writings of this volume by modeling explicitly what are the consequences when national trade policy setting authorities respond to special interests.[10]

While the discussion throughout this volume has been cast in terms of trade in goods, the welfare approach applies also to trade in services and to international factor mobility.[11] There is, however, only little work on how investment and production location interact with integration, and multinationals have not been considered in any systematic fashion in the integration literature.[12]

Finally, the literature on preferential trading arrangements contains relatively few empirical papers. This is in part because of the difficulties implementing empirically the trade diversion and trade creation approach, in part because the need for quantitative analysis has been more a question of assessing effects from proposed integration than a perceived need to analyze effects from past integration. Preferential trading arrangements have proliferated in recent years and, as methodology changes, it should now become possible to draw lessons from completed agreements.[13]

Notes

1. Kowalczyk and Davis (1998) discuss the history, theory, and evidence on tariff phase-outs in both multilateral and preferential agreements.
2. As is standard in this literature, the terms welfare and income are used interchangeably throughout this volume, unless distributional concerns are the focus. This requires special restrictions on social welfare functions, or that income transfers within the nation are feasible.
3. Several writers, including Bhagwati (1971, 1973), Kirman (1973), Michaely (1976), Meade (1955a), Kemp (1969), and Collier (1979), tried to interpret or complete Viner's terminology. However, Meade (1955b, p. 34) also proposed what, in my view, 40 years of writing on integration using Viner's terminology has since borne out:
   '..., [Viner's] analysis is in my opinion incomplete; and when an attempt is made to complete it, it no longer remains as simple in its application as may at first sight appear to be the case.'
4. Ohyama credits Kemp (1964) and Vanek (1965) with the notion of the *compensating external tariff*, i.e., the rate that leaves trade with non-members unaffected. Kemp and Wan (1976, Chapter 19 in this volume), by application of the second welfare theorem, also present a proof of this statement, now known as the Ohyama-Kemp-Wan proposition.
5. He presents the basic argument and later discusses political economy properties of the model in Krugman (1991, 1993). Frankel (1997) explores further the role of transport cost for integration, and reports from joint work with Stein and Wei (in Frankel, ed.) that if there are also transport costs within regions, and if these costs are not much lower than inter-regional transport costs, then a U-shaped world welfare locus may reappear.
6. Haveman (1996) shows that if Deardorff and Stern's extreme assumption of no trade between blocs is relaxed, then a U-shaped expected world welfare locus re-emerges. Using a continuum-of-goods Ricardian framework, Srinivasan (1993) emphasizes that a given model may yield different world welfare paths depending upon whether blocs are formed in symmetric or asymmetric fashion.
7. Kennan and Riezman (1988) show how a country being large tends to induce benefits to it from a tariff war.
8. Bagwell and Staiger (1997a,b) show that tariffs will tend to increase during negotiation and implementation phases of a free trade area but fall during those phases of a customs union.
9. See, for example, Srinivasan and Whalley (1986).

10. Grossman and Helpman (1993) apply their recent general framework for optimizing interest groups and policy to free trade agreements.
11. If the environment is not one of perfect competition then additional terms capturing, for example, changes in profits must be added.
12. Puga and Venables (1997) consider location effects from integration.
13. Kowalczyk and Davis (1998) analyze the pace of tariff reductions in NAFTA.

References

K. Bagwell and R. Staiger (1997a), 'Multilateral Tariff Cooperation during the Formation of Regional Free Trade Areas', *International Economic Review*, **38**, 291–319.

K. Bagwell and R. Staiger (1997b), 'Multilateral Tariff Cooperation during the Formation of Customs Unions', *Journal of International Economics*, **42**, 91–123.

R. Baldwin (1989), 'The Growth Effects of 1992', *Economic Policy*, **4**, 247–81.

J.N. Bhagwati (1971), 'Trade Diverting Customs Unions and Welfare-Improvement: A Clarification', *Economic Journal*, **81**, 580–7.

J.N. Bhagwati (1973), 'A Reply to Professor Kirman', *Economic Journal*, **83**, 895–7.

P. Cecchini, M. Catinat, and A. Jacquemin (1988), *The European Challenge*, 1992, Brookfield, Vt.: Gower.

P. Collier (1979), 'The Welfare Effects of Customs Unions: An Anatomy', *Economic Journal*, **89**, 84–95.

J.A. Frankel (1997), *Regional Trading Blocs in the World Trading System*, Washington D.C.: Institute for International Economics.

G. Grossman and E. Helpman (1993), 'The Politics of Free Trade Agreements', *American Economic Review*, **85**, 667–90.

R. Harris and D. Cox (1984), *Trade, Industrial Policy and Canadian Manufacturing*, Toronto: Ontario Economic Council.

J. Haveman (1996), 'Some Welfare Effects of Sequential Customs Union Formation', *Canadian Journal of Economics*, **29**, 941–58.

M.C. Kemp (1964), *The Pure Theory of International Trade*, Englewood Cliffs, N.J.: Prentice-Hall.

M.C. Kemp (1969), *A Contribution to the General Equilibrium Theory of Preferential Trading*, Amsterdam: North-Holland Publishing Company.

J. Kennan and R. Riezman (1988), 'Do Big Countries Win Tariff Wars?', *International Economic Review*, **29**, 81–5.

A.P. Kirman (1973), 'Trade Diverting Customs Unions and Welfare Improvement: A Comment', *Economic Journal*, **83**, 890–3.

C. Kowalczyk (1990), 'Welfare and Customs Unions', National Bureau of Economic Research Working Paper No. 3476, October.

C. Kowalczyk (forthcoming), 'Welfare and Integration', *International Economic Review*.

C. Kowalczyk and D. Davis (1998), 'Tariff Phase-Outs: Theory and Evidence from GATT and NAFTA', in J.A. Frankel (ed.), *The Regionalization of the World Economy*, Chicago: The University of Chicago Press.

P.R. Krugman (1991), 'Is Bilateralism Bad?', in E. Helpman and A. Razin (eds), *International Trade and Trade Policy*, Cambridge, MA: MIT Press.

P.R. Krugman (1993), 'Regionalism vs. Multilateralism: Analytical Notes', in J. de Melo and A. Panagariya (eds), *New Dimensions in Regional Integration*, New York: Cambridge University Press.

R.G. Lipsey (1957), 'The Theory of Customs Unions: Trade Diversion and Welfare', *Economica*, **24**, 40–6.

J. Meade (1955a), *Trade and Welfare*, London: Oxford University Press.

J. Meade (1955b), *The Theory of Customs Unions*, Amsterdam: North-Holland Publishing Company.

M. Michaely (1976), 'The Assumptions of Jacob Viner's Theory of Customs Unions', *Journal of International Economics*, **6**, 75–93.

D. Puga and A.J. Venables (1997), 'Preferential Trading Arrangements and Industrial Location', *Journal of International Economics*, **43**, 347–68.

A. Smith and A.J. Venables (1988), 'Completing the Internal Market in the European Community', *European Economic Review*, **32**, 1501–25.

T.N. Srinivasan (1993), 'Discussion', in J. De Melo and A. Panagariya (eds), *New Dimensions in Regional Integration*, Cambridge: Cambridge University Press.

T.N. Srinivasan and J. Whalley (eds) (1986), *General Equilibrium Trade Policy Modeling*, Cambridge: MIT Press.

J. Vanek (1965), *General Equilibrium of International Discrimination: The Case of Customs Unions*, Cambridge: Harvard University Press.

Part I
Trade Diversion and Creation, and the General Theory of Second Best

[1]

IV

THE ECONOMICS OF CUSTOMS UNIONS

1. *Customs Union as an Approach to Free Trade*

The literature on customs unions in general, whether written by economists or non-economists, by free-traders or protectionists, is almost universally favorable to them, and only here and there is a sceptical note to be encountered, usually by an economist with free-trade tendencies. It is a strange phenomenon which unites free-traders and protectionists in the field of commercial policy, and its strangeness suggests that there is something peculiar in the apparent economics of customs unions. The customs union problem is entangled in the whole free-trade–protection issue, and it has never yet been properly disentangled.

The free-trader and the protectionist, in their reasoning about foreign trade, start from different premises—which they rarely state fully—and reach different conclusions. If in the case of customs unions they agree in their conclusions, it must be because they see in customs unions different sets of facts, and not because an identical customs union can meet the requirements of both the free-trader and the protectionist. It will be argued here that customs unions differ from each other in certain vital but not obvious respects, and that the free-trade supporter of customs union expects from it consequences which if they were associated in the mind of the protectionist with customs union would lead him to oppose it. It will also be argued, although with less conviction because it involves judgments about quantities in the absence of actual or even possible measurement, that with respect to most customs union projects the protectionist is right and the free-trader is wrong in regarding the project as something, given his premises, which he can logically support.

To simplify the analysis, it will at first be confined to perfect customs unions between pairs of countries; and the "administrative" advantages of customs unions, such as the shortening of customs walls, and the "administrative" disadvantages, such as the necessity of coordinating customs codes and of allocating revenues by agreed formula, will be tentatively disregarded. Also, to separate the problem of customs unions *per se* from the question of whether in practice customs unions would result in a higher or in a lower "average level" of duties [1] on imports into the customs union area from outside the area, it will be assumed that the average level of duties on imports from outside the customs area is precisely the same for the two countries, computed as it would be if they had not formed the customs union. It will at first be assumed that the duties are of only two types: [2] (*a*) "nominal duties," that is, duties which have no effect on imports because there would be no imports of commodities of the kind involved even in the absence of any import duties on them; [3] and (*b*) "effective protective duties," that is, duties which operate to reduce imports not only by making commodities of the specific kind involved more expensive to potential consumers and so lessening their consumption, but also, and chiefly, by diverting consumption from imported commodities to the products of corresponding domestic industries. The analysis will be directed toward finding answers to the following questions: in so far as the establishment of the customs union results in change in the national locus of production of goods purchased, is the net change one of diversion of purchases to lower or higher money-cost sources of supply, abstracting from duty-elements in money costs: (*a*) for each of the customs union countries taken separately; (*b*) for the two combined; (*c*) for the outside world; (*d*) for the world as a whole? If the customs union is a movement in the direction of free trade, it must be predominantly a movement in the direction of goods being supplied from lower money-cost sources than before. If the customs union has the effect of diverting purchases to higher money-cost sources, it is then a device for making tariff protection more effective. None of these questions

[1] Whether it is possible to give this concept of an "average level" of duties both some degree of precision of definition and economic significance is taken up later. See *infra*, pp. 66–68.

[2] "Revenue duties" are dealt with subsequently. See *infra*, pp. 65–66.

[3] Such duties, while they have no effect on imports, can have other effects of some economic importance, though these are not directly relevant here. In countries where an approach to perfect competition does not prevail, which means most countries, import duties may protect monopolistic or government-supported domestic price levels instead of protecting domestic production.

can be answered *a priori,* and the correct answers will depend on just how the customs union operates in practice. All that *a priori* analysis can do, is to demonstrate, within limits, how the customs union must operate if it is to have specific types of consequence.

The removal of "nominal" duties, or duties which are ineffective as barriers to trade, can be disregarded, and attention can be confined to the consequences of the removal, as the result of customs union, of duties which previously had operated effectively as a barrier, partial or complete, to import.

There will be commodities, however, which one of the members of the customs union will now newly import from the other but which it formerly did not import at all because the price of the protected domestic product was lower than the price at any foreign source plus the duty. This shift in the locus of production as between the two countries is a shift from a high-cost to a lower-cost point, a shift which the free-trader can properly approve, as at least a step in the right direction, even if universal free trade would divert production to a source with still lower costs.

There will be other commodities which one of the members of the customs union will now newly import from the other whereas before the customs union it imported them from a third country, because that was the cheapest possible source of supply even after payment of duty. The shift in the locus of production is now not as between the two member countries but as between a low-cost third country and the other, high-cost, member country. This is a shift of the type which the protectionist approves, but it is not one which the free-trader who understands the logic of his own doctrine can properly approve.[4]

---

[4] A third possibility should be mentioned. The import duty on a particular commodity may be so high in one of the countries that it is prohibitive of import, but domestic production may be impossible or excessively costly, so that there is no consumption. Upon formation of the customs union, the commodity in question may be imported from the other member country, where its cost of production may be high or low as compared to costs elsewhere but is assumed to be lower than outside costs plus the duty on imports from outside the customs union. The original duty thus served as a sumptuary measure rather than as a protective or revenue measure. Whether the removal of a sumptuary measure is of benefit for the country particularly concerned as potential consumer is not a type of question which the economist has any special capacity to answer. But if as the result of customs union country A removes a duty of this kind preferen-

44   THE CUSTOMS UNION ISSUE

Simplified as this exposition is, it appears to cover most of the basic economic issues involved. The primary purpose of a customs union, and its major consequence for good or bad, is to shift sources of supply, and the shift can be either to lower- or to higher-cost sources, depending on circumstances. It will be noted that for the free-trader the benefit from a customs union to the customs union area as a whole derives from that portion of the new trade between the member countries which is wholly new trade, whereas each particular portion of the new trade between the member countries which is a substitute for trade with third countries he must regard as a consequence of the customs union which is injurious for the importing country, for the external world, and for the world as a whole, and is beneficial only to the supplying member country. The protectionist, on the other hand, is certain to regard the substitution of trade between the member countries for trade with third countries as the major beneficial feature of customs union from the point of view of the participating countries and to be unenthusiastic about or even to regard as a drawback—at least for the importing country—the wholly new trade which results from the customs union.

From the free-trade point of view, whether a particular customs union is a move in the right or in the wrong direction depends, therefore, so far as the argument has as yet been carried, on which of the two types of consequences ensue from that custom union.

Where the trade-creating force is predominant, one of the members at least must benefit, both may benefit, the two combined must have a net benefit, and the world at large benefits; but the outside world loses, in the short-run at least, and can gain in the long-run only as the result of the general diffusion of the increased prosperity of the customs union area. Where the trade-diverting effect is predominant, one at least of the member countries is bound to be injured, both may be injured, the two combined will suffer a net injury, and there will be injury to the outside world and to the world at large. The question as to what presumptions can reasonably be held to pre-

---

tially for imports from the other member country, B, there is a clear loss for A as compared to the removal of duty regardless of source if B is a high-cost source of supply. There is an unquestionable benefit here, however, for the supplying country, and it does not injure outside countries in any direct way.

vail with respect to the relative importance in practice of the two types of effects will be examined subsequently.

To the reasoning presented above, there is one qualification in favor of customs union which needs to be made, on which both free-traders and protectionists can with reason find some common ground, although, in the opinion of the writer, they both tend to exaggerate its importance for the customs union problem. It has here been assumed hitherto that in so far as a customs union has effects on trade these must be either trade-creating or trade-diverting effects. This would be true if as output of any industry in a particular country increases over the long-run relative to the national economy as a whole, its money costs of production per unit relative to the general level of money costs also tended to rise. Economists are generally agreed, however, that there are firms, and consequently also industries, where this rule does not hold but instead unit costs decrease as output expands. From this they conclude that where a small country by itself, because of the limited size of its domestic market (and, it should be added, the prevention by foreign tariffs of its finding a market outside), may be unable to reach a scale of production large enough to make low unit-costs of production possible, two or more such countries combined may provide a market large enough to make low unit-cost production possible. If an industry which thus expands, whether from zero or from a previous small output, is in country A, and the other member of the customs union is country B, the diversion of B's imports from a country, C, outside the customs union to country A, may be a beneficial one for B as well as for A, and, moreover, there may be suppression of trade, namely, of the imports of A from C of the commodity in question, which may also be beneficial to A. Whether such diversion—and suppression—of trade will, from the free-trade point of view, be beneficial or injurious to A will depend on several circumstances. The cost of production in A of the commodity in question is now lower than it was before. There is gain, therefore, for A as compared to the precustoms-union situation with respect to that portion of its present output which corresponds to its previous output (which may have been zero), and there is clear gain on such of its additional output as is now exported to B. On additional output beyond this, however, there is loss to A if the new cost, though lower than the previous one, is higher than the cost (before duty) at which it is obtainable from C, but there is additional gain to A if the new cost is lower than the cost (before duty) at which it is obtainable from C.   For B, there is loss by the amount imported by B times the per unit amount by which A's price exceeds the price at which B's import needs could be supplied by C; there is gain to B only if A's price is now lower than C's price (before duty).   There is thus a possibility—though not, as is generally taken for granted in the literature, a certainty—that if the unit-cost of production falls as the result of the enlarged protected market consequent upon customs union there will be a gain from customs union for one of the members, for both the members, and/or for the union as a whole, but there is also a possibility—and often a probability—that there will be loss in each case.

It does not seem probable that the prospects of reduction in unit-costs of production as the result of enlargement of the tariff area are ordinarily substantial, even when the individual member countries are quite small in economic size.   The arguments for substantial econo-mies from increased scale of industry presented by economists rest wholly or mostly on alleged economies of scale for *plants* or *firms*, and on the assumption that large-scale plants or firms are not practicable in small *industries* and therefore in small countries.   It seems to the writer unlikely, however, that substantial efficiency-economies of scale of plant are common once the plants are of moderate size, and he is convinced that in most industries plants can attain or approach closely their optimum size for efficiency even though the industries are not large in size.   Were it not for trade barriers, moreover, even small countries could have large industries.

There are few industries, even in countries where large-scale pro-duction is common, in which there are not plants of moderate size which are as efficient, or nearly as efficient, measured in unit-costs, as the giant plants; and there are few giant firms which do not main-tain some of their plants, presumably at a profit, on a moderate scale. There are few manufacturing industries—and the economies of scale of plant or industry are generally conceded to be confined mainly or only to such industries—which have not been able to maintain them-selves on a low-cost basis in one or more small countries, such as Switzerland, Sweden, Denmark, or Belgium.   If the applicability of this argument is confined to products which nowhere are produced at a low unit-cost from plants which are quite small, either absolutely or as compared to the maximum size elsewhere, the scope of the argument is much more limited than is commonly taken for granted. It may be asked in rebuttal, how then explain the existence of giant plants and giant firms? It is at least a partial answer: (1) as to size of plants, that the survival of plants of moderate size in competition with the giant plants calls equally for explanation; and (2) as to size of firms, that there are in an imperfectly competitive world many incentives to growth in size of firm even at the cost of efficiency in production—firms of quite undistinguished records in efficiency of production have been known to grow by absorption of more efficient smaller firms and by the use of monopoly power in buying and in retention of customers, and, generally speaking, growth in size is more often the result of efficiency than contributory to efficiency.

The general rule appears to be that once an industry is large enough to make possible optimum scale—and degree of specialization of production—in plants, further expansion of the industry in a national economy of constant over-all size is bound to be under conditions of increasing unit-costs as output increases, in the absence of new inventions. To expand, the industry must draw away from other industries increased amounts of the resources it uses, and consequently must pay higher prices per unit for resources of the type which it uses more heavily than does industry at large, and must reduce the extent to which it uses them relative to other types of resources, thus bringing into operation the law of diminishing returns. It may be objected that this will not hold true in the case of a customs union, since this in effect increases the over-all size of the "national" economy. It is the supply conditions of factors of production, however, which are the relevant restrictive factor on expansion of output of an industry without increase of unit-costs, and unless customs union appreciably increases the inter-member mobility of factors of production it does not in this sense increase the "scale" of the "national" economy from the point of view of production conditions even if it does increase it from the point of view of the size of the protected market for sales.

Few free-traders have dealt with the economics of customs unions in any detail, and one must resort in some measure to inference from the implications of brief dicta to find the explanation for their general support of customs union as constituting an approach to their ideal of the territorial allocation of production in accordance with comparative costs of production. The major explanation seems to lie in an unreflecting association on their part of any removal or reduction of trade barriers with movement in the direction of free trade. Businessmen, however, and governments which have had to try simultaneously to satisfy both special interests seeking increased protection and voters hostile to protection, have long known of ways of making increased protection look like movement in a free-trade direction. They have known how, under suitable circumstances, protection against foreign competition could be increased by *reducing* duties and reduced by increasing duties. Let us suppose that there are import duties both on wool and on woolen cloth, but that no wool is produced at home despite the duty. Removing the duty on wool while leaving the duty unchanged on the woolen cloth results in increased protection for the cloth industry while having no significance for wool-raising. Or suppose that the wool is all produced at home, and sold to domestic clothmakers at the world price plus duty, but would be all produced at home even if there were no duty on wool, but would then be sold at the world price. Removal of the duty on wool again increases the protection for the woolen industry without reducing the volume of domestic production of wool.

When the customs union operates to divert trade from its previous channels rather than to create new trade, the partial removal of duties which it involves operates in analogous manner to increase the protective effect for high-cost producers of the duties which remain, not, however, by reducing imports into their own national territory but by extending the operation in their favor of the protective duty to the territory of the other partner of the customs union. It would in theory be possible that if two areas were joined in customs union, the customs union would have no trade-creating effect and only trade-diverting effect, i.e., no industry in either area would meet with new competition from the other area, while some high-cost industries, existing or potential, in each area would acquire a new set of consumers in the other area who would be placed at their mercy because the customs union tariff will now shut them off from low-cost sources of supply. A set of connected tariff walls can give more market-dominance to high-cost producers than a set of independent tariff walls, if the former set has had its internal sections knocked out.

This is well, though ingenuously, brought out in one of the leading treatises in favor of customs unions, where the author, after arguing that free-traders should like them because they eliminate trade barriers, proceeds to argue that protectionists should also like them because of the extension of the (protected) market area which they provide for producers within the territory of the customs union; "as for the internal competition, it will not be formidable if care is exercised in choosing as partners in customs unions countries which are complementary [in production] rather than competitive." [5]

Free-traders sometimes in almost the same breath disapprove of preferential reductions of tariffs but approve of customs unions, which involve 100 per cent preference, and this is the position at present of the United States Government and the doctrine of the Havana Charter.[6] If the distinction is made to rest, as often seems to be the case, on some supposed virtue in a 100 per cent preference, which suddenly turns to maximum evil at 99 per cent, the degree of evil tapering off as the degree of preference shrinks, it is a distinction as illogical, the

[5] L. Bosc, *op. cit.*, p. 98. He moves on to a perfect *non sequitur:* "Thanks to this judicious choice, *there will be established within the customs union a fecund division of labor*, while the customs frontiers thus extended further territorially will protect the internal market against the superiority of other countries." (Italics supplied.)

[6] Cf. Clair Wilcox, *A Charter for World Trade* (New York, 1949), p. 70: "Preferences have been opposed and customs unions favored, in principle, by the United States. This position may obviously be criticized as lacking in logical consistency. In preferential arrangements, discrimination against the outer world is partial; in customs unions, it is complete. But the distinction is none the less defensible. A customs union creates a wider trading area, removes obstacles to competition, makes possible a more economic allocation of resources, and thus operates to increase production and raise planes of living. A preferential system, on the other hand, retains internal barriers, obstructs economy in production, and restrains the growth of income and demand. It is set up for the purpose of conferring a privilege on producers within the system and imposing a handicap on external competitors. A customs union is conducive to the expansion of trade on a basis of multilateralism and non-discrimination; a preferential system is not."

There would seem to be little or nothing in what is said here about the *evils* of preference which is not potentially true also for customs unions; and equally little in what is said here about the *benefits* of customs unions which is acceptable further than as being potentially true if circumstances are right, and which, where true at all, is not also potentially true, if circumstances are right, of preferences.

50   THE CUSTOMS UNION ISSUE

writer believes, as this way of putting it makes it sound.[7] On the
legal side, the discussion of the bearing of the *degree* of preference on
its compatibility with most-favored-nation obligations has sometimes
led to the opposite conclusion, namely, that, on the principle *a majori
ad minus,* if a customs union with its 100 per cent preferences is compatible with the most-favored-nation principle, still more must frac-
tional preferences be compatible.[8] This seems plausible enough until
it is realized that acceptance of this reasoning would have the practical
consequence that 100 per cent preferences would be legal if incident
to customs union and lesser preferences would be legal because
greater ones were, so that *all* preferences would be legal. The moral
is that on both the economic and legal side the problem is too complex
to be settled by simple maxims.[9] A 50 per cent preference is economically either less desirable or more desirable than a 100 per cent preference according only as preference at all is under the circumstances
desirable or undesirable.[10]

There is one ground only on which, aside from administrative considerations, it can consistently be held that preferences are economically bad and are increasingly bad as they approach 100 per cent, but
that customs union is an economic blessing. Customs union, if it is
complete, involves a cross-the-board removal of the duties between
the members of the union; since the removal is non-selective by its
very nature, the beneficial preferences are established along with the

---

[7] One is reminded of Dryden's "My wound is great because it is so small,"
and Saint-Evremond's rejoinder, "Then 'twould be greater, were it none at all."
   [8] Sandor von Matlekovits, *Die Zollpolitik der österreichisch-ungarischen Mo-
narchie und des Deutschen Reiches seit 1868 und deren nächste Zukunft* (Leipzig, 1891).
   [9] The following illustration of the ambiguous working in practice of the *a
majori ad minus* principle is not, it is hoped, wholly without relevance:
   "It being made felony by an act of parliament to steal *horses,* it was doubted
whether stealing *one horse only* was within the statute: in construction of penal
law, the less number may not be included under the greater, but the reverse can
never follow.   Cf. the King of Prussia's error when he comments that, an
English law prohibiting bigamy, a man accused of having five wives was ac-
quitted, as not coming under the law." Daines Barrington, *Observations on the
More Ancient Statutes,* 4th ed. (London, 1755), p. 547. (Italics in the original.)
   [10] It is to be remembered that administrative economies are here disregarded.
If they were to be taken into account, a 100 per cent preference could be held
more desirable than say a 99 per cent one on the ground that it made the economic wastes of customs formalities unnecessary—if it did—even though otherwise the smaller the preference the less objectionable it would be.

injurious ones, the trade-creating ones along with the trade-diverting ones. Preferential arrangements, on the other hand, can be, and usually are, selective, and it is possible, and in practice probable, that the preferences selected will be predominantly of the trade-diverting or injurious kind. But aside from possible administrative economies, cross-the-board 100 per cent preferences without customs union are economically as good—or as bad—as customs union.

From the free-trade point of view, that is, the point of view that movement in the direction of international specialization in production in accordance with comparative costs is economically desirable, there can be formulated in accordance with the preceding analysis a series of propositions as to the conditions which need to be met to justify the presumption that the establishment of a particular customs union will represent a movement toward free trade rather than away from it.

A customs union is more likely to operate in the free-trade direction, whether appraisal is in terms of its consequence for the customs union area alone or for the world as a whole:

(1) the larger the economic area of the customs union and therefore the greater the potential scope for internal division of labor;

(2) the lower the "average" tariff level on imports from outside the customs union area as compared to what that level would be in the absence of customs union;

(3) the greater the correspondence in kind of products of the range of high-cost industries as between the different parts of the customs union which were protected by tariffs in both of the member countries before customs union was established, i.e., the *less* the degree of complementarity—or the *greater* the degree of rivalry—of the member countries with respect to *protected* industries, prior to customs union;[11]

(4) the greater the differences in unit-costs for protected industries of the same kind as between the different parts of the customs union, and therefore the greater the economies to be derived from free trade with respect to these industries within the customs union area;

[11] In the literature on customs union, it is almost invariably taken for granted that rivalry is a disadvantage and complementarity is an advantage in the formation of customs unions. See *infra*, pp. 73 ff., with reference to the Benelux and Franco-Italian projects.

(5) the higher the tariff levels in potential export markets outside the customs union area with respect to commodities in whose production the member countries of the customs union would have a comparative advantage under free trade, and therefore the less the injury resulting from reducing the degree of specialization in production as between the customs union area and the outside world;

(6) the greater the range of protected industries for which an enlargement of the market would result in unit-costs lower than those at which the commodities concerned could be imported from outside the customs union area;

(7) the smaller the range of protected industries for which an enlargement of the market would not result in unit-costs lower than those at which the commodities concerned could be imported from outside the customs union area but which would nevertheless expand under customs union.

Confident judgment as to what the over-all balance between these conflicting considerations would be, it should be obvious, cannot be made for customs unions in general and in the abstract, but must be confined to particular projects and be based on economic surveys thorough enough to justify reasonably reliable estimates as to the weights to be given in the particular circumstances to the respective elements in the problem. Customs unions are, from the free-trade point of view, neither necessarily good nor necessarily bad; the circumstances discussed above are the determining factors. As has been pointed out earlier, it would be easy to set up a hypothetical model where customs union would mean nothing economically except an intensification of uneconomic protection, an increase in the effectiveness of trade barriers as interferences with international division of labor. A universal customs union, on the other hand, would be the equivalent of universal free trade. Actual customs unions must fall somewhere between these two extremes.

The non-technical reader is again warned that this analysis not only takes for granted the validity—at least when only purely economic considerations are taken into account—of the argument for free trade from a cosmopolitan point of view, but that its results are much less favorable to customs union in general than the position taken by most free-trade economists who have discussed the issue.[12] One of the few exceptions is Lionel Robbins, whose formulation of the issue as here quoted is, in the opinion of the writer, excellent:

[12] For conclusions, by economists sympathetic to free trade, more favorable to customs union, see especially: Gottfried von Haberler, *The Theory of International Trade* (London, 1936), pp. 383–91 and *idem,* "The Political Economy of Regional or Continental Blocs," in Seymour E. Harris, *ed., Postwar Economic Problems* (New York, 1943), especially pp. 330–34, and other writings of Haberler; John de Beers, "Tariff Aspects of a Federal Union," *Quarterly Journal of Economics* (1941), 49–92; and *Customs Unions, 1947,* pp. 75 ff., which follows Haberler's treatment closely and uncritically.

The more favorable conclusions with respect to customs unions reached by these writers are the consequence, mainly: (1) of failure to give consideration, or to give adequate consideration, to the effect of customs union in extending the area over which preexisting import duties exercise a protective effect; (2) of confusing the problem of the effect on location of production of customs union with the different, and for present purposes inconsequential, problem of the "incidence of import duties," or the location of impact of burden of payment of import duties actually collected; and (3) of applying the standard techniques of partial equilibrium analysis, traditionally applied to the analysis of the determination of prices of particular commodities taken one at a time, to foreign trade as a whole and to the tariff problem where its findings are either totally without significance or of totally indeterminable significance.

The present writer's own questioning in print of the usual arguments for customs union began in 1931: see "The Most-Favoured-Nation Clause," *Index,* VI (1931), p. 11. Haberler and de Beers have in the writings cited above found fault with the present writer's treatment as unduly critical of customs union, in part on the basis of reasoning of the type commented on in the preceding paragraph, and in part on the ground that the possibility of increased division of labor within the area of the customs union was denied or overlooked. In the few sentences devoted to the problem in the above-mentioned *Index* article, the writer asserted only the *possibility* that preferential duties would mean a greater diversion of trade from its free-trade pattern than uniform protection. He did not discuss the possibilities more favorable to customs union. Nor can he find in that article anything corresponding to the proposition attributed to him by de Beers, that an increase of imports must come from the same sources as under free trade, if there is to be gain. De Beers, however, cites a statement made by the present writer in 1933: ". . . if a regional agreement, preferential as between the countries within that region, is beneficial to both those countries, it must necessarily follow that had it been extended to the entire world no substantial change would have resulted in the effect of the agreement." This *is* a faulty statement. It is taken from a non-verbatim report of an extemporaneous discussion which the writer had no opportunity to edit— and, may add, did not know until some years later to have been put into print. (See International Studies Conference, *The State and Economic Life* [Paris, 1934], p. 50). He makes no claim, however, to have been misreported, and is not now in a position to deny that it correctly represented the state of his thinking at that time.

. . . The purpose of international division of labour is not merely to make possible the import of things which cannot be produced on the spot; it is rather to permit the resources on the spot to be devoted wholly to the production of the things they are best fitted to produce, the remainder being procured from elsewhere. . . .

It follows, therefore, that the gain from regional regrouping or wider units of any kind is not a gain of greater self-sufficiency, but a gain of the abolition of so much self-sufficiency on the part of the areas which are thus amalgamated. . . .[13]

. . . From the international point of view, the tariff union is not an advantage in itself. It is an advantage only in so far as, on balance, it conduces to more extensive division of labour. It is to be justified only by arguments which would justify still more its extension to all areas capable of entering into trade relationships. . . . No doubt if we could coax the rest of the world into free trade by a high tariff union against the produce of the Eskimos that would be, on balance, an international gain. But it would be inferior to an arrangement whereby the Eskimos were included. The only completely innocuous tariff union would be directed against the inaccessible produce of the moon.[14]

Another exception, however, seems to go further than is justified. R. G. Hawtrey writes as follows:

The most-favoured-nation clause has been criticised in that it prevented a relaxation of tariffs between adjacent countries, by which at any rate a beginning might have been made in the removal of obstacles to trade. A reduction of import duties by Belgium and Holland in favour of one another's products would have involved discrimination against other countries, such as Great Britain. . . .

But to suppose that agreements of that kind would be a move towards free trade is a delusion. The preferential treatment that would have been given by Belgium and Holland to one another would have made their existing protective tariffs more exclusive against other countries. In fact the wider the extent of economic activity encircled by a tariff barrier of given height, the greater is its effect in excluding the goods of foreign producers. The break-up of the Austro-Hungarian Empire resulted in the creation of new frontiers, and the new tariff barriers obstructed trade between one succession State and another. But if the import duties had remained at the same level as before, the markets which the succession

  [13] Under customs union, there would be a decrease in the degree of self-sufficiency of each member area, but an increase in the degree of self-sufficiency of the customs union area as a whole.

  [14] Lionel Robbins, *Economic Planning and International Order* (London, 1937), pp. 120–22.

States lost in one another would have been more accessible than before to outside producers.[15]

Reduction of the extent of division of labor between the customs union area and the outside world is the major objective and would be a major consequence of most projected customs unions, and would be a consequence in some degree of *any* customs union with protective duties, unless the duties on imports from outside the customs union were drastically cut upon establishment of the union. But Hawtrey should not leave out of consideration the increase in the extent to which division of labor *within* the customs union area prevails as the result of customs union.

2. Customs Union and the "Terms of Trade"

There is a possibility, so far not mentioned, of economic benefit from a tariff to the tariff-levying country which countries may be able to exploit more effectively combined in customs union than if they operated as separate tariff areas. This benefit to the customs area, however, carries with it a corresponding injury to the outside world. A tariff does not merely divert consumption from imported to domestically produced commodities—this is, from the free-trade point of view, the economic disadvantage of a tariff for the tariff-levying country and one of its disadvantages for the rest of the world—but it also alters in favor of the tariff-levying country the rate at which its exports exchange for the imports which survive the tariff, or its "terms of trade," and within limits—which may be narrow and which can never be determined accurately—an improvement in the national "terms of trade" carries with it an increase in the national total benefit from trade. The greater the economic area of the tariff-levying unit, the greater is likely to be, other things being equal, the improvement in its terms of trade with the outside world resulting from its tariff.[16] A customs union, by increasing the extent of the territory which operates

---

[15] R. G. Hawtrey, *Economic Destiny* (London [1944]), pp. 135–36.

[16] The greater the economic area of the tariff unit, other things equal, the greater is likely to be the elasticity of its "reciprocal demand" for outside products and the less is likely to be the elasticity of the "reciprocal demand" of the outside world for its products, and consequently the greater the possibility of improvement in its terms of trade through unilateral manipulation of its tariff.

under a single tariff, thus tends to increase the efficacy of the tariff in improving the terms of trade of that area vis-à-vis the rest of the world.

The terms of trade of a customs area with the outside world can be influenced not only by its own tariff but by the tariffs of other countries. The higher the tariffs of other countries on its export products, the less favorable, other things equal, will be the terms of trade of a customs area with the outside world. But the level of foreign tariffs can be affected in some degree through tariff-bargaining, and the larger the bargaining unit the more effective its bargaining can be. The Balkans, for instance, could have secured better terms from Nazi Germany during the 1930's if they had bargained collectively with Germany rather than singly. This consideration has been an important element in fostering aspirations on the part of small countries for customs union. An abundance of historical evidence is available to show how significant has been its role in the movement for tariff unification, whether in the customs union form or in other forms, although not as a rule expounded in the sophisticated language of the "terms of trade" argument. A few historical instances will be cited.

The argument that under the Articles of Confederation, which left each state with its separate tariff, the United States was at a serious disadvantage in dealing with the commercial policy of Europe, and especially of Britain, was current among the founding fathers of the Republic and helped to create readiness on the part of the public to accept a closer federal union with tariff policy centrally controlled.[17]

In 1819–1820, France imposed heavy import duties on cattle. Baden, Württemberg, and some of the Swiss cantons which were hard hit by these duties thereupon negotiated an agreement whereby they were to engage jointly in retaliatory measures against France. The

[17] Cf. the reports of the Committee on Commercial Policy, September 29, 1783, October 9, 1783, U. S. Continental Congress, *Journals of the Continental Congress 1774–1789*, W. C. Ford and Gaillard Hunt, eds. (Washington, 1904–37), XXV, 628–30, 661–64; message to President Washington by John Adams, Benjamin Franklin, and John Jay, from Paris, September 10, 1783, in *The Revolutionary Diplomatic Correspondence of the United States*, Francis Wharton, ed. (Washington, 1889), VI, 691; President Washington, August 22, 1785, as cited in O. L. Elliott, *The Tariff Controversy in the United States, 1789–1833* (Palo Alto, 1892), p. 46; the *Federalist* [1777–1778], No. XI; Joseph Story, *Commentaries on the Constitution*, Sections 1056–1073.

agreement was operative from 1822 to 1824, when it lapsed because of the refusal of some of the Swiss cantons to give their adherence to the agreement and its consequent conflict with the customs provisions of the Swiss constitution, which prohibited separate action on the part of the cantons but provided no procedures for assuring concerted action. This demonstration that without more centralization of Swiss tariff authority no effective tariff-bargaining policy could be carried out helped in preparing the way for the Swiss Constitution of 1848, which put commercial policy under Federal Government control.[18]

The movement which sprang up in Europe toward the end of the nineteenth century for a "United States of Europe" arose in large part from the widespread belief that only through some form of European economic union could the "American menace" be satisfactorily dealt with. Often invoked in support of the movement was the doctrine, expounded especially by the German historical school of economists, that small countries are at a serious disadvantage in commercial competition with large countries. But the movement focused more particularly on the unfavorable impact of American competition and American tariff policy on disunited Europe. Many aspects of American-European commercial relations were pointed to as calling for concerted defensive action: effective American competition, first with European agriculture as overseas freight costs fell and the American West was opened up, next with European manufacturing industries as large-scale exports by the United States of manufactured products made their appearance; the high and ever-rising American tariff; the refusal of the United States to participate in the network of commercial treaties by which European tariffs were being lowered or at least their rise checked; the adherence by the United States to the conditional interpretation of the most-favored-nation clause, whereby it was able to withhold from third countries what tariff concessions it did make to particular countries in "reciprocity" agreements, while claiming successfully the extension to imports from the United States of the concessions which European countries were

---

[18] Cf. Joseph Litschi, "Das Retorsions-Konkordat vom Jahre 1822," *Zeitschrift für schweizerische Statistik*, XXVIII (1892), 1–22; Werner Bleuler, *Studien über Aussenhandel und Handelspolitik der Schweiz* (Zurich, 1929), pp. 35–36; *Mémoires et souvenirs de Augustin-Pyramus de Candolle* (Geneva, 1862), p. 313.

making to each other; [19] the emergence of talk of customs union between the United States and Latin America; the export methods of the new but lusty American "trusts"; and so forth.[20]

Since until the advent of the Roosevelt Administration there was no improvement from the European point of view in American commercial policy, and the severity of American competition in world trade was, if anything, more pronounced than ever before, the interwar phase of the movement for European union still retained, if less pronouncedly and less frankly than before, a distinctly anti-American orientation.[21]

3. *Administrative Economies of Customs Union*

(a) *The Removal of Internal Tariff Walls.*

The burdens on trade of a customs tariff, and its hindrances to trade, arise not only from the actual levy of duties—which for all the

[19] For an explanation of how this was achieved, see Jacob Viner, "The Most-Favored-Nation Clause in American Commercial Treaties," *loc. cit.*, pp. 119–20.

[20] No systematic study has apparently ever been made of the anti-American orientation of the movement for European union, 1880 and earlier to 1914. For comment by an American scholar, see George M. Fisk, "Continental Opinion regarding a Proposed Middle European Tariff Union," *Johns Hopkins University Studies in Historical and Political Science*, XX (1902), Nos. 11–12. The European source material is voluminous; the following items are representative: Henri Richelot, *L'Association douanière allemande* (Paris, 1845), p. 22; Michel Chevalier, "La guerre et la crise européenne," *Revue des deux mondes*, XXXVI² (1866), 758–85; Alexander Peez (an Austrian and a leader in the movement), *Die amerikanische Konkurrenz* (Leipzig, 1881), and "A propos de la situation douanière en Europe," *Revue d'économie politique*, V(1891), especially p. 138; Auguste Oncken, "L'Article onze du Traité de Paix de Francfort," *ibid.*, p. 602; Edmond Théry, *Europe et Etats-Unis d'Amérique* (Paris, 1899), the preface by Marcel Dubois; Ernst von Halle, "Das Interesse Deutschlands an der amerikanischer Präsidentenwahl des Jahres 1896," *Jahrbuch für Gesetzgebung, Verwaltung und Volkswirtschaft* ("Schmoller's *Jahrbuch*"), New Series, XX (1896), 263–96; Gaston Domerque, "Le péril américain," *La réforme économique*, May 26, 1901, February 2, 1902, June 15, 1902, etc.; Richard Calwer, *Die Meistbegünstigung der Vereinigten Staaten von Nordamerika* (Berlin, 1902); Rudolf Kobatsch, *La politique économique internationale* (Paris, 1913), pp. 375–89. Cf. also L. Bosc, *op. cit.*, pp. 428–86.

[21] See, e.g., the report of a speech in Vienna in 1926 by Reichstag President Loebe in M. Margaret Ball, *Post-War German-Austrian Relations; The Anschluss Movement, 1918–1936* (Stanford University, 1937), p. 72, and the comment of *Izvestia*, as reported in Kathryn W. Davis, *The Soviets at Geneva* (Geneva, 1934), p. 227, note, on Briand's plan for European union, as primarily a European defense against "American capitalist aggression on the one hand and Bolshevist revolutionary aggressiveness on the other."

countries concerned taken in the aggregate are, of course, exactly off-set, in monetary terms at least, by the revenues accruing to the levying government—but also from the costs involved, for exporter and importer, in meeting the customs regulations, and the costs involved, for the tariff-levying government, in administering the customs machinery. These costs are often, in fact, more important than the duties themselves as hindrances to trade,[22] so that if the duties were lowered to a nominal level but the customs administrative code remained as before, the tariff could still constitute an important restriction on trade. But the United States is an outstanding offender in this respect. In the case of most other tariffs, their removal would not involve comparable administrative economies.

If a customs union were "complete" or "perfect," so that the tariff wall were completely removed between its members, this would constitute therefore an important relaxation of trade barriers between members of the union aside from the removal of the duties themselves as well as a reduction of administrative expense to the governments of the member countries, since the frontier—or frontiers—between them would no longer have to be watched for customs purposes.[23] The more important economically, and the longer or more difficult to watch, the removed tariff frontier was, the more important per unit volume of trade would be the administrative economies resulting from its removal. Given the economic area of the customs union, the larger also the number of tariff frontiers eliminated as a result of the formation of the union, the greater, other things equal, would be the administrative economies resulting therefrom per unit volume of trade. Customs union, however, even if complete, results in the full elimination for administrative purposes of tariff frontiers only if and to the extent that the territories of the members of the union are contiguous territories. Even if no third country intervenes between

[22] Cf. *Monthly Review, The Bank of Nova Scotia,* New Series, No. 26, Toronto, July, 1948: "Nor are the barriers against imports into the United States a matter of tariff rates alone. Canadian exporters have long maintained that the difficulties connected with U. S. customs procedures, the complexity of the regulations, and the delays and uncertainties arising out of their administration are in some cases an even greater hindrance to trade than the tariff rates themselves." See also R. Elberton Smith, *Customs Valuation in the United States* (Chicago, 1948).

[23] This assumes that import duties are the only deliberate trade barriers, or that quantitative restrictions, etc., are also removed.

two members of a customs union, the existence between them of "high seas" is sufficient to cut down, perhaps drastically, the administrative economies of customs union. "The sea, it is said, unites and does not separate, which is true in a sense, but is not true for the purpose of a Zollverein." [24] Customs unions, actual or projected, however, appear invariably to include only contiguous territory.[25]

It would be a mistake, however, to assume that the administrative changes consequent upon customs union all involve economies. Where the administration of the customs union is not entrusted wholly to one of the members of the union, there are additional burdens of negotiation, of coordination of codes, and of mutual supervision which may substantially reduce the net economies as well as give rise to political frictions. The necessity of coordination and of mutual supervision may force a standardization and simplification of duties which on other grounds may be undesirable. It has been suggested, for instance, that the number of countries which had a right to participate in the administration of the German Zollverein made it necessary to confine the Zollverein tariff mainly to specific duties, since the administrative task of assuring that ad valorem duties would be uniformly interpreted and applied at all the frontiers of the Zollverein would have been an almost insuperable one.[26]

Where excise taxes are important and customs union does not carry with it standardization of excise taxes throughout the territory of the union, the "tariff wall" between the members of the union, moreover, cannot wholly be removed, since otherwise the excise tax systems would be undermined by the flow of commodities affected from the untaxed, or low tax, areas to the tax, or higher tax, areas. In the earlier days of customs unions, this was a major problem in the negotiation and administration of such unions, since excise taxes were then relatively more important than they are today as sources of government revenue, and the texts of earlier customs union treaties

---

[24] Sir Robert Giffen, *Economic Inquiries and Studies* (London, 1904), II, 393.

[25] If the relations of metropolitan France with those of its colonies which are "assimilated" to France for tariff purposes, and the relations of the United States with Puerto Rico may be taken to constitute "customs union," they provide illustrative instances of the administrative economies of customs union being only partially available because of the existence of high seas between the members of the union.

[26] W. O. Henderson, *op. cit.*, p. 278.

show how much attention had to be given to this problem, and how complex were the administrative measures required to deal with it. The complexity of the problem may, in fact, have been a significant factor in preventing customs union agreements from being reached.[27] Even today, moreover, especially given the revival of resort on a large scale to indirect taxation as a source of government revenue, a good deal of the possible administrative economy of customs union would be likely to be lost if the establishment of uniformity of excise taxes did not accompany the formation of the customs union.

It may be objected that American experience demonstrates that this is not an important problem, since the absence of tariff walls between the States has proved to be consistent with the levy by the States of non-uniform excise taxes. But state excise taxes in the United States, though growing in range and severity, are still levied as a rule only on a very limited range of commodities and at very moderate rates. They have not been unassociated, moreover, with the development of troublesome and irritating equivalents of state tariff walls, which have rightly become a matter of growing concern.[28]

Furthermore, the growth under "central planning" of disguised inflation, non-equilibrium exchange rates, price controls, subsidies, and so forth, makes it impossible today completely to remove trade barriers unless economic union is carried far beyond the customs union stage. But this applies, probably with greater force, to general as well as to preferential removals of trade barriers.[29]

[27] Cf. G. de Molinari, "Union douanière de l'Europe," *Journal des économistes*, 4th Series, 2d year, V (1879), pp. 314-15: "The most serious difficulty, and we can even say the sole genuinely serious difficulty which the formation of an international *Zollverein* will face, rests in the standardization of excise régimes. This difficulty has not yet been entirely overcome in Germany, where there has not been achieved a uniform tax on beer and spirits, which has made necessary the maintenance of a frontier (*ligne*) for the protection of the excises between the North and the South."

[28] Cf. Frederick E. Melder, *State and Local Barriers to Interstate Commerce in the United States* (Orono, Maine, 1937), and U. S. Department of Commerce, Bureau of Foreign and Domestic Commerce, *Bibliography of Barriers to Trade between States* (Washington, 1942).

[29] Cf. Etienne Mantoux, *The Carthaginian Peace* (New York, 1946), p. 189: "whatever increases the economic significance of the State will inevitably increase the economic significance of frontiers. How, in the present trend of economic policy, it is possible to make insignificant frontiers coexist with all-pervading states is utterly beyond the present writer's powers of imagination."

(b) *The Elimination of Taxes on Goods in Transit.*

One type of economy associated with customs union, namely, the elimination of transit duties, and of ordinary import duties on goods in transit, for members of the union, which was once of great importance, is now of little or no significance. In the early part of the nineteenth century, when transportation costs were high and the importance of using the lowest-cost route therefore great, heavy transit duties were common. Countries in a favorable geographical position exploited to the full the opportunity to levy toll on commerce crossing their territories. The exemption from transit duties on commerce crossing Prussian territory was a major inducement which Prussia could offer other German states to enter into customs union with her, since Prussian territory lay astride all the major routes for commerce between and through the German states to the north and the southern German states.[30]

Collection of duties on imported goods in transit to a third state, in conjunction with discriminatory railway rates, played an especially important role in the history of the movement toward customs union in South Africa. The Transvaal and the Orange Free State—later the Orange River Colony—were shut off from direct access to the sea to the south by Cape Colony and Natal and elsewhere by absence of railroads or even roads. The coastal colonies exploited their geographical position to the fullest extent which their rivalry with each

[30] A petition for customs union submitted in 1818 by a German group under the chairmanship of Friedrich List contains the following passage:

"To make a commercial shipment from Hamburg to Austria and from Berlin to Switzerland, one must cross ten states, study ten sets of customs regulations, pay six different transit duties. He who has the misfortune to reside at a frontier where three or four states touch each other, passes his entire life bickering with customs officials; he has not got a fatherland." Cited in J. Pentmann, *Die Zollunionsidee und ihre Wandlungen* (1917), p. 9.

Cf. also the dispatch to the Foreign Office from the British envoy to the German Diet, December, 1834, cited in Herbert C. F. Bell, *Lord Palmerston* (London, 1936), I, 159, from the British Foreign Office archives: ". . . hemmed in by a line of Custom Houses all round the Gates of the Town, its [Frankfort's] commercial intercourse with the interior of Germany was greatly harassed and restricted. . . . its commerce and trade had already fallen off considerably, and . . . great apprehensions were entertained that its Fairs would be irretrievably injured unless the Union with Prussia was speedily effected; . . . the British Houses . . . finding their old customers deterred from frequenting the Fairs and their buyers diminish, had themselves become the advocates of the Union with Prussia. . . ."

other permitted by levying their full import duties on imports from outside Africa passing to the interior republics through their territory and also by charging heavier rates for transportation on their railways of commodities coming from overseas than for competing commodities of their own production.[31]   At one time the Transvaal, under Oom Paul Kruger, sought escape from these exactions by building a railroad to Delagoa Bay in Portuguese East Africa and, to force traffic from overseas to take the Delagoa Bay route, imposed heavy freight rates on the portion of the Cape-to-Johannesburg railroad which lay within Transvaal territory.   The Orange Free State did not have even this alternative available, and its only defense was in its ability to thwart the railway-building plans of the coastal colonies by excluding their lines from its territory.   "But much as he [President Brand of the Free State] wanted the money, he wanted the railways more. The colonies knew it and continued to rob the republic." [32]

It might be supposed that these were just the types of evil in commercial relations for which customs union would provide an effective remedy.   But when the South African Customs Union Conventions of 1903 and 1906 were negotiated, the former Boer republics, defeated in war, had not yet been given responsible government, and were represented at the negotiations by British officials.   It was not until the establishment of political union between the four colonies in 1910 that the allocation of customs revenues and the structure of railway

[31] The treatment of sugar by Natal was a notorious example.   Cf. Transvaal, *Report of the Customs & Industries Commission* (Pretoria, 1908), p. 5: "Natal sugar is carried at a very much lower rate than sugar imported from oversea, the result being that the further inland the sugar travels the higher the protection afforded against the oversea traffic.   In consequence of this and of the fact that the production of sugar in Natal is far below the consumption of the Union, the bulk of the sugar produced is sent inland to the Transvaal, Orange River and Cape Colonies, while Natal very largely imports sugar from oversea for its own consumption; on these importations the Natal Government collects and retains duties amounting to a considerable sum, to a large proportion of which the Transvaal Government is fairly entitled."   Cf. also the Memorandum prepared by the Earl of Selborne, January, 1907, in A. P. Newton, *ed., Select Documents relating to the Unification of South Africa* (London, 1924), II, 418. This was *after* customs union was established, and was possible because the customs union agreement left to each territory, with some exceptions, the customs duties collected within that territory.

[32] Jean Van der Poel, *Railway and Customs Policies in South Africa 1885–1910* (London, 1933), pp. 11–12.

rates ceased to be patently unfair to the Transvaal and the Orange Free State.[33]

For European countries, the revolution in transportation which occurred in the nineteenth century resulted in shippers as a rule not being confined to single practicable routes and therefore deprived countries of the power of exacting as monopolists high tolls on transit trade, and, instead, caused them to eliminate transit duties and to compete for transit traffic by improving traffic facilities, lowering freight rates on railroads, and reducing administrative obstructions to economical transportation.   By the end of the century transit duties had almost wholly disappeared in Europe.   They were outlawed for signatory countries by the Covenant of the League of Nations, and by the Barcelona Conference on Communications and Transit of 1921.   Article 33 of the Havana Charter reproduces and strengthens the provisions for freedom of transit of the Barcelona Conference.

The elimination of transit duties is, indeed, the only significant nineteenth-century reform in the field of commercial policy which is surviving unimpaired in the twentieth century; to economic developments which make almost any country's departure from freedom of transit patently unprofitable to it, rather than to international diplomacy, the progress of economic enlightenment, or the will to international economic cooperation, belongs the credit.   The improvement of transportation facilities which, by opening up the possibility of competition between alternative routes for the transit business, led to the

---

[33] In addition to the references given above, A. J. Bruwer, *Protection in South Africa* (Stellenbosch, 1923), a University of Pennsylvania doctoral dissertation, can be profitably consulted.   There is an extensive bibliography in Bruwer of literature published up to 1921.

The fear that the United States would resume the collection of customs duties on traffic from Europe to the Province of Canada (i.e., Ontario and Quebec) was an important contributory factor to the formation of the Canadian Confederation.   An Act of Congress of 1845 provided for drawbacks of customs duties on through traffic to Canada across American territory and other legislation granted such traffic the privilege of transit in bond without payment of duties.   It was feared in Canada that, with the Southern states for the time being deprived of a voice in Congress and the North aggressive because of anti-British animosity and annexationist ambitions, these privileges would be withdrawn. Canadian Confederation would make possible construction of a railway route to the Atlantic wholly in Canadian territory.   Cf. Donald C. Masters, *The Reciprocity Treaty of 1854* (London, 1937), p. 229, and R. G. Trotter, *Canadian Federation* (Toronto, 1924), pp. 126 ff.   In this case, the duties on transit trade levied by one state operated to foster unification of *other* states.

elimination of transit duties, by intensifying competition between countries also led to a general raising of tariffs.[34] For the customs union question the significance of this development is that the formation of customs unions no longer has a major contribution to make to the freeing of transit trade from artificial burdens.

4. *Revenue Duties*

In the discussion so far, the question of revenue duties has not been dealt with. If the revenue yield of the tariff as a whole is substantial for one or more of the countries entering into customs union, this will complicate the problem of negotiation of the union. If the revenue yield of the customs union tariff is substantial, there will be the problem of how to allocate these revenues between the members. These problems will be considered in a subsequent section.

In so far as the effect of the formation of customs unions on international specialization in production is concerned, the existence of revenue duties raises no new question of principle. It is not easy sharply to distinguish between revenue duties and protective duties. For present purposes, revenue duties may be regarded as those duties productive of revenue which do not act as effective stimulus to the domestic production of commodities *similar* to those paying the duties. Even such duties, however, if they are not offset by general excises on commodities of domestic production, operate to increase the proportion of aggregate domestic consumption which is directed toward domestically produced commodities. The only differences, then, between revenue duties and protective duties which are significant for present purposes is that revenue duties have only a generalized protective effect, whereas protective duties have both this generalized effect and a specific effect in stimulating the domestic production of commodities similar to those subject to the protective duty, with the consequence that protective duties tend to be more effective than

---

[34] Cf. G. de Molinari, "Union douanière le l'Europe centrale," *loc. cit.*, p. 318: "Is it not absurd to pay at the same time engineers to facilitate the transport of persons and merchandise, and customs officers to make it more difficult?"

In a memorandum of 1815 to the Government of the Canton of Geneva, Sismondi argued that the widened range of transportation routes which had become available made it impracticable for Geneva to levy transit duties. See Jean-R. De Salis, *Sismondi 1775–1842; Lettres et documents inédits* (Paris, 1932), p. 23.

revenue duties as restraints on importation. Revenue duties can be regarded therefore as the equivalent of protective duties of slight effectiveness, or a high revenue duty may be regarded as the equivalent of a moderate protective duty, for present purposes.

The existence of revenue duties, therefore, does not make it necessary to change in any respect the conclusions as to the effect of customs union on international specialization reached on the basis of the assumption that there were no revenue duties. If a customs union should be established, however, between two countries which before had only revenue duties and if all the duties levied by the customs union continue to operate as "pure" revenue duties, the appraisal of the customs union would turn chiefly on its administrative economies or inconveniences, or on political aspects, and the foregoing analysis would be largely irrelevant for it. Some of the intercolonial customs unions are wholly or substantially in this category.[35]

5. The "Level" of the Customs Union Tariff

Whatever tendency the formation of a customs union may have to lessen the extent of international specialization, the lower the rates of duty in the customs union tariff, the less effect of this kind, other things equal, will it have.

Resolutions in favor of customs union often have a proviso that the customs union tariff should not be "higher" than the tariffs of the member countries prior to the formation of the union. The Havana Charter (Article 44, paragraph 2) sanctions the formation of customs union without the requirement of prior approval by the International Trade Organization provided the duties (and other restrictions) on imports into the union are "not on the whole . . . higher or more restrictive than the general incidence" of the duties (and other restrictions) on imports of the member countries prior to the formation of such union. What meaning can be given to such provisos?

There is no way in which the "height" of a tariff as an index of its restrictive effect can be even approximately measured, or, for that

[35] The fear that customs union would result in loss of revenues has sometimes operated for both the prospective members as a factor against proceeding with customs union negotiations. It is of course a probable result where the prospective members have a large volume of dutiable trade with each other before customs union, and also where customs union will divert a large amount of import trade from outside countries to member countries.

matter, even defined with any degree of *significant* precision.[36] It is possible to say that some proposed methods of measurement are less illogical than others. It may be possible to say, after careful examination and in the light of extensive background information, that one tariff is clearly higher than another. But it is scarcely possible to find a way of measuring the relative height in quantitative terms of two tariffs. An identical tariff might be high for one country or at one time and low for another country or at another time.

In the case of a customs union, if its tariff is made up of the highest rates on each class of imports previously levied by either (or any) of the member countries—and still more if the customs union rates are set even higher than this—the new tariff is clearly "more restrictive" of imports from outside the union than were the previous tariffs. But even if the new tariff is made up of the *lowest* rates previously levied by either (or any) of the member countries on each class of imports dutiable in both, it may still be "more restrictive" in fact, whether or not in the intent of the Havana Charter provision, than the previous tariffs, because customs union operates to convert revenue duties to protective duties.[37] Some part of an old higher rate may

[36] Cf. Jacob Viner, "The Measurement of the 'Height' of Tariff Levels," Joint Committee, Carnegie Endowment–International Chamber of Commerce, *The Improvement of Commercial Relations between Nations* (Paris, 1936), pp. 58–68.

[37] There is little likelihood that the Havana Charter provision will be given so exacting an interpretation. In the Benelux customs union, the new level of duties is commonly said to be about half-way between the (lower) rates of the previous Netherlands tariff and the (higher) rates of the previous Belgium-Luxemburg tariff, although this is true only in a limited sense. The Dutch tariff of 1934 comprised only 160 dutiable classes of items, and all unenumerated articles were exempt from duty. The Belgian tariff listed many more dutiable articles, and moreover made subject to duty all items not expressly exempted. In the Benelux tariff it is only on items which were common to the two tariffs that the new rates are half-way between the previous Netherlands and the previous Belgium-Luxemburg tariff rates, and all items not expressly exempted are made dutiable. The new tariff is therefore much closer to the previous higher Belgian tariff than to the previous Netherlands tariff. The relations between the old and the new tariffs are in fact more complicated than this indicates, because of changes in classification, the substitution of ad valorem for specific duties, and other factors. Examination of the old and the new tariffs by an American expert has resulted in the conclusion that "it may be stated generally that the Benelux Tariff is more protectionist than the Netherlands tariff, and that it apparently is not less protectionist than the Belgo-Luxembourg tariff." W. Buchdahl, "The New 'Benelux' Union—Western Europe Tariff Pattern?"

have been ineffective for the country levying it because even a lower rate would have been completely prohibitive of imports, while the lower rate of the other country may previously have been low enough to permit imports from third countries, whereas now, because of preferential treatment of imports from the other member country, it operates to exclude imports from third countries completely, or at least more completely than before. Thus a customs union tariff which, in the interpretations commonly given to "level of tariff," is lower than the average level of the previous tariffs of the member countries, and even one which is lower than either (or any) of these tariffs, may still be "more restrictive" of imports into the customs union territory from outside that territory than were the previous tariffs of the member countries. But customs union tariffs have not typically been "low" even in these senses of the term.

6. *Increased Tariff Protection as the Major Economic Objective of Customs Unions*

The tariff unification movement, in the nineteenth century and since, in so far as it culminated in actual arrangements or at least reached the stage of serious negotiations on an official basis, was primarily a movement to make high protection feasible and effective for limited areas going beyond the frontiers of single states, and to promote self-sufficiency for these larger areas because self-sufficiency for single states was clearly impracticable or too costly; it was not a movement to promote the international division of labor. It would be exceedingly difficult to demonstrate this, partly because clear definition and statement of objectives is often not essential for nor even helpful to effective negotiation, partly because there were obvious and weighty reasons why it would have been inexpedient to attract attention to

---

U. S. Department of Commerce, *Foreign Commerce Weekly,* October 11, 1947, pp. 3–5, 32. Since the increase in protection is not overt and unambiguous, however, there has been no suggestion from any quarter that this involves any conflict with the Havana Charter. An American Congressional Subcommittee has commented: "This procedure of establishing new common tariffs at, roughly, the average of the old tariffs is in accordance with the draft chaı ter of the International Trade Organization." U. S. Congress, House Select Committee on Foreign Aid, Subcommittee on France and the Low Countries, Preliminary Report Twenty-Four, *The Belgian-Luxemburg-Netherlands Customs and Economic Union* (1948), p. 2.

this phase of the movement. There is nevertheless no lack of circumstantial evidence to support this interpretation. This objective becomes explicit here and there in the literature of advocacy of customs unions,[38] and underlies all of the nineteenth century literature favoring European Economic Union as a means of coping with American competition. It reveals itself in the special provisions in customs union agreements intended to check the intensification of competition between the member areas which would otherwise result from the arrangement.[39] The aversion to opening their markets to the competition from each other's industries has been the chief factor economic in character which was responsible for so few customs unions actually being consummated when so many projects were launched.

Where of two potential members of a customs union one is predominantly free-trade or low-tariff in interest and sentiment while the other is protectionist and provides only a negligible market for the staple exports of the first, the low-tariff territory will not voluntarily enter into the union except as part of a political union and for predominantly political reasons, and even after it has entered it is likely to find the union economically irksome because the chief economic consequence of the union is to make its territory an additional field of operation for the tariff protection of its partner's industries. Such has been largely the case for the Transvaal and the Orange River Colony vis-à-vis the South African Customs Union, for the Prairie Provinces of Canada vis-à-vis Canadian Confederation, for Western Australia in relation to the Australian Commonwealth. Such was also the case for

---

[38] Cf. especially Henry Masson, "Les unions douanières," an extract from the Report of the Congrès International d'Expansion Economique Mondiale, held at Mons, Belgium, 1905.

[39] The role of the "Zwischenzoll" in the history of the Austro-Hungarian Customs Union is especially pertinent here. The major difficulty in keeping the customs union intact arose out of the insistence of the members, and especially of Hungary, that the customs union should not remove the barriers to competition between the members. Cf. Rudolf Sieghart, *Zolltrennung und Zolleinheit: Die Geschichte der österreichisch ungarischen Zwischenzoll-linie* (Vienna, 1915); Ivor L. Evans, "Economic Aspects of Dualism in Austria-Hungary," *The Slavonic Review*, VI (1927–28), 529–42; Louis Eisenmann, *Le compromis austro-hongrois de 1867; étude sur le dualisme* (Paris, 1904); Joseph Grunzel, *Handelspolitik und Ausgleich in Österreich-Ungarn* (Vienna, 1912), especially pp. 115, 224, 237. For the manipulation of railway rates within Austria-Hungary, as a substitute for internal import duties, see Ivor Evans, *op. cit.*, p. 539.

the Southern States in relation to the American Federal Union prior to the industrialization of the South. Such was for a time at least the case with respect to the Swiss Federal Union.[40] It was largely true also in the history of the German Zollverein, although Prussia for a variety of reasons—partial conversion to free-trade views, willingness to make economic concessions in order to establish a base for eventual political unification, readiness to keep the Zollverein tariff low in order to lessen Austrian determination to obtain entrance to it—for a time supported a low-tariff policy for the Zollverein.

The Tanganyika-Kenya Customs Union provides a striking instance where a territory was brought into a customs union by external authority in order to provide an expanded field for the tariff protection of the industries of another territory.[41] Tanganyika, captured by the British from the Germans in World War I, is a mandate territory. The British first introduced a new tariff in Tanganyika in 1921, higher than the German one, and then in 1923 changed the tariff again, making it identical with the still higher tariff of the Kenya-Uganda customs union, while abolishing the customs barriers between the three territories, all in preparation for full customs union. In 1927 full customs union was established, despite questioning from the British Governor of Tanganyika as to its suitability to the mandate's economic interests. The customs union operated to create a protected market in Tanganyika for the produce of the small colony of British planters

---

[40] Cf. Werner Bleuler, *Studien über Aussenhandel und Handelspolitik der Schweiz* (Zurich, 1929), p. 37, with reference to the situation in Switzerland in the 1830's:

"These free-trade traditions, in conjunction with the hereditary federalist views were an obstacle to the tariff unification of the land; for the economic controversy, Free Trade versus Protection, stood in the then prevailing opinion and circumstances in close connection with the political issue Federalism versus Centralization. The attitude was widespread that a unified Swiss tariff policy would at the same time be a protectionist one. People said to themselves, a unification of the customs would work in two ways: first it would reduce the political autonomy of the Cantons and would make openings for centralizing activities in other spheres, and second it would have the consequence that they would be gradually drawn into the channel of protectionist politics. Thus both the convinced Free traders and the extreme Federalists were opposed to the unification movement."

[41] The relation of the Transvaal and the Orange River Colony to the South African Customs Union provides an analogous earlier instance. See *supra*, pp. 62 ff.

in Kenya, for whose welfare the British Government has shown a constant and marked solicitude. To reinforce the tariff in providing a preferential market for Kenya produce in Tanganyika, a system of preferential rates on the railways, under which commodities of external origin paid higher rates than customs-union produce, also was introduced. After an investigation of the operation of the customs union on behalf of the British Colonial Office, Sir Sydney Armitage-Smith, an economist of repute and an objective civil servant, reached the conclusion that "Tanganyika should take steps forthwith to levy customs import duty at the same rates on foodstuffs imported from Kenya and Uganda as those chargeable on foodstuffs imported from foreign parts, and should cease to deplete her revenue and impoverish her citizens by protecting the products of her neighbours." [42]

The progressive contraction in range of application and decline in efficacy of the most-favored-nation clause have increased the range of special commercial arrangements which permit concerted action to restrict imports from countries outside the arrangement without involving either the removal of the barriers to competition between the members or sharp conflict with most-favored-nation obligations to third countries. A significant illustration is provided by the Argentine-Brazil commercial treaty of November, 1941, and the Argentine-Chile trade agreement of August, 1943, both designated as providing a base for eventual customs union, and both clearly and frankly designed to extend the effective area of protection from external competition of the industries of the participant countries without increasing the competition between the industries of the two countries. The crucial provisions in the Argentine-Brazil treaty are the following:

ARTICLE I.—1. The High Contracting Parties undertake to promote, stimulate and facilitate the installation in their respective countries of industrial and agricultural and livestock activities as yet not in existence in either of the two, mutually undertaking:

[42] "Report by Sir Sydney Armitage-Smith, on a Financial Mission to Tanganyika, 26th September, 1932. Presented by the Secretary of State for the Colonies to Parliament, October, 1932." British Parliamentary Papers, Cmd. 4182, 1932, p. 25. See also Charlotte Leubuscher, *Tanganyika Territory; A Study of Economic Policy under Mandate* (London, 1944), pp. 101-20, for an excellent treatment of this problem. Miss Leubuscher criticizes the League of Nations Mandates Commission for not giving sufficient attention to the economic effects of the customs union.

(*a*) Not to collect import duties during a period of ten years from the date of the entry into force of this Treaty on the products of such new activities;

.   .   .   .   .

(*c*) To arrive at protective measures with respect to competition by similar products from other sources when these can be classed as "dumping."

2. For the purposes of this Treaty industrial and agricultural and livestock activities described as non-existent are those not installed in either of the two countries at the date of the signature of this Treaty.

3. In order to enjoy the advantages provided for herein, the articles not included in the list referred to in Article IV will be considered not produced in either of the two countries.

ARTICLE II. With respect to the articles produced in one of the two countries or which are of little economic importance in one of them the High Contracting Parties undertake not to apply, during a period of ten years from the date of entry into force of this Treaty, duties of a protectionist nature on imports, but rather, on the contrary, to grant them special preference, not to be extended to other suppliers.

.   .   .   .   .

ARTICLE III. The High Contracting Powers mutually agree to extend the benefits of the preceding Article to those products of economic importance customs tariffs on which may be gradually reduced or eliminated without affecting present production or national economy.

ARTICLE IV. In order to put into effect the preceding provisions, the High Contracting Parties undertake to draw up, within a term of six months from the date of the signature of this Treaty, a list of all the articles already produced in each country, indicating the economic importance of such production, that is to say: the number of factories, capital invested, value and volume of present production, maximum capacity of production, total consumption of such products in the country, and other facts of interest for the study of the form in which free trade may be established between the two countries without affecting existing production and national economy.

ARTICLE VIII. The High Contracting Parties will appoint, once the lists referred to in Article IV have been exchanged, the organisms in charge of putting into practice the provisions of the present Treaty.[48]

The Argentine-Chile treaty was similar in character. The essential feature of both treaties was that they provided for removal or relaxation of trade barriers on a preferential basis only for such commodities

---

[48] *Customs Unions, 1947*, pp. 92–93. The Spanish text corresponding to the words "special preference" in Article II reads: "*favores especiales de países limítrofes.*" *Informaciones argentinas,* December 15, 1941, p. 3.

as involved little or no competition between themselves, and to effectuate this, provided for the non-competitive development of new industries.   Later, apparently, Chile closed with Brazil an agreement by which Brazil undertook not to establish a domestic nitrate industry, and with the Argentine an agreement by which the Argentine obligated itself for a minimum period of ten years to use only Chilean nitrates [44]—developments in the same direction.

The development of quantitative restrictions on imports has facilitated the removal of tariff barriers between pairs of countries without involving the opening of each other's territory to full competition from the industries of the other.   The Benelux Customs Union Agreement, signed at London September 5, 1944, which as revised by the Hague Protocol of March 14, 1947, came into operation on January 1, 1948, provided for removal of tariff duties between the members and a common tariff against imports from the outside world, but left intact, except as subsequently to be altered by mutual agreement, the whole machinery of import quotas, import licenses, special license dues and administrative fees, and subsidies, both with respect to imports from outside the Union and with respect to the intra-Union trade.   These devices can, in principle, be so operated as to make an economic union confined to ordinary tariffs operate in such a way as to involve no over-all relaxation in the effective barriers to competition between the industries of the member countries.

In the planning for further economic unification now in process, distinction is being made between "complementary," "parallel," and potentially or actually "rival" industries, and it seems clear from press reports that it is intended on both sides to provide, at least for a lengthy transition period, obstacles to free competition within the customs union area of rival industries.

For an important list of industries,[45] the governments must consult in the Council of the Economic Union before they sanction expansion. Likewise, there is a Committee for Industrial Development in which representatives of the three governments sit with delegates of trade

[44] *New York Times*, April 24, 1943, dispatch from Santiago.
[45] Window glass, carbonic acid, copper sulphate, explosives, coal and coke, sodium carbonate, steel, ball-bearings, steel balls, chains, plywood, furniture, strawboard, cement, rubber manufactures, sugar manufactures, rice-hulling, vegetable oils, flour-milling, beer, nitrogen.

organizations to deal with the same problem.   There will also be, on a third level, reliance on government-sanctioned cartel agreements to restrain competition within the customs-union area between rival national industries.[46]

The negotiations for a Franco-Italian Customs Union now in progress are following similar lines.   The First Joint Commission, acting in accordance with instructions received in September, 1947, in its Report of December 22, 1947, stated in unexceptional if vague terms the function of a customs union:

> The purpose of a customs union is essentially to permit, by virtue of the establishment of a more extensive economic territory, a division of labor more developed, better adapted to the existing natural and economic conditions, and consequently a more abundant and lower-cost production destined for a greater market.[47]

As the Report proceeds to examine particular products, however, it finds difficulties everywhere except where the economies of the two countries are "complementary" (that is, where customs union would operate to extend the area of effective protection against competition from outside) ; and where industries are parallel or are rival, it emphasizes the need for regulation and understandings for coordinated export of their products and for coordinated import of their raw materials, to avoid competition in trade with the outside world.   To avoid "dangerous competition" *within* the Union, allocation of capital and raw materials, industrial agreements, and other unspecified measures are suggested, but the general drift of the discussion of this problem, though vague at crucial points, indicates that full economic unification of the area, with competition between the areas as free—or as restricted—as within each area, is the long-run goal.[48]

The Second Joint Commission, set up in June, 1948, has recently submitted its report, and negotiations are proceeding toward an even-

[46] See "Benelux . . . An Example of Unity in a Divided World," *Rotterdamsche Bank Quarterly Review*, 1947, No. 4, pp. 5–42, and "Benelux and Industrial Development," *Amsterdamsche Bank Quarterly Review*, No. 80, April, 1948, p. 15.

[47] Commission Mixte Franco-Italienne pour l'Etude d'une Union Douanière entre la France et l'Italie, *Rapport final* (Paris: Imprimerie Nationale, 1948), p. 6.

[48] *Ibid.*, pp. 48–49.

tual customs union on the basis of the procedures recommended by this report. Here also the problem of "rival" industries receives emphasis. An interim period is contemplated when competition between the industries of the two countries will be restricted by compensatory taxes in the country of lower costs, by cartel agreements, and by regulated specialization in types of products. For the long run, however, the issue of rival industries is more frankly faced and competition between them within the Union accepted as unavoidable:

Certainly the Customs Union between France and Italy will derive its chief interest from the competition which this Union will establish between the two economies, which are only, as is known, very partially complementary. It is to be expected that there will result from this competition a more developed specialization, either because each country extends its production of those commodities for which it is better situated naturally, or because within the same category of products the two countries agree to specialize on specified types.[49]

7. *Cartels in Relation to Customs Unions*

There has long been an association of sorts between the tariff union idea and the international cartel idea as remedies through international cooperation for the problems arising in European countries from "excessive competition" in their markets from other countries, usually the United States.[50] This association has perhaps most often taken the form of rivalry, but frequently enough the two ideas became combined to constitute joint elements in a single plan for lessening the severity of international competition. Beginning with the preparatory work for the Geneva Economic Conference of 1927, proposals came from many sources for sponsorship of international cartelization, both as a method of international economic cooperation which would lessen the need for attempts to lower tariff barriers by multilateral agreement and as a method of making tariff reduction safe for high-cost domestic industries. The French were most prominent in furthering these ideas, but they received more or less qualified support

[49] *Compte Rendu de la Commission Mixte Franco-Italienne d'Union Douanière, Paris, le 22 janvier 1949* (Paris: Imprimerie Nationale, 1949), p. 96.
[50] See Harry D. Gideonse, "Economic Foundations of Pan-Europeanism," *Annals of the American Academy of Political and Social Science*, CXLIX (1930), for the early association of these ideas.

from the International Chamber of Commerce and from League of
Nations committees and conferences. M. Louis Loucheur, French
Minister of Commerce, who was the original sponsor and one of the
main participants in the Geneva Economic Conference, was an enthu-
siastic protagonist of international cartels and of international tariff
agreements to facilitate their operation as means of lessening international competition, and the documentation and proceedings of the
conference show that his ideas received substantial support. But for
the most part the discussion remained on an abstract level.[51]

With the coming of the depression, the search for means of allevi-
ating its impact on Europe through international collaboration led to
a revival of the discussion, under League of Nations auspices, of
cartels in relation to European "economic union." Various committees and conferences of the League of Nations gave support simultaneously to international cartelization and to multilateral agreements to
lower trade barriers, but there was apparently only one definite proposal to link the two together as related parts of a single project.

This proposal was made by the French Government to a meeting
of the League Commission of Enquiry for European Union in May,
1931. A strengthening and extension of international cartel agreements was to be sponsored. Since strong cartels reserve the national
markets for the domestic producers of the respective acceding countries and limit imports to agreed quotas and prices, tariffs become unnecessary to protect national industries. The lowering of tariffs,
therefore, becomes possible without adversely affecting the national
economies. However, "the producers in countries which were not

---

[51] Some of the references to the idea that the multiplication of international
cartels would facilitate the reduction of tariffs by reducing the need for them
made in the course of the Geneva Economic Conference apparently were related
to expositions of the idea which M. Loucheur had made outside the conference.
After a series of eulogies of international cartels had been presented in the
meetings of the Industry Committee of the conference, a Soviet delegate, Mr.
Sokolnikoff, made the following pertinent comment:

"Industrial and commercial ententes would not lead to social and economic
peace. The danger of a rise in prices was only too real. This was shown by
the fact that it was being proposed to replace Customs Tariffs, the object of
which was to maintain prices at a high level, by cartellisation, which enabled
the same result to be attained by more modern methods." League of Nations,
Report and Proceedings of the World Economic Conference, Geneva, 1927
(Document C.356.M.129.1927.II), II, 152.

disposed to take part in international agreements would not be allowed to benefit from Customs exemptions." Moreover, the tariff reductions would amount to a bounty to all who voluntarily accepted the discipline of the cartel.[52] The French proposed that the League and the governments take the cartel agreements under their sponsorship and stimulate the private efforts in this direction. These agreements would be less difficult to negotiate than a simultaneous multilateral reduction of tariffs, and would be better than a customs union. Tariffs would be retained, since they would be needed to forestall dumping, but the duties collected could be refunded with respect to all products carrying a cartel certificate.[53]

Nothing came immediately from the French proposal of 1931, but the idea it expounded did not die.[54] In the negotiations for the further development of Benelux, and in the negotiations for the formation of a Franco-Italian customs union, it is clear that much reliance is being placed on cartel agreements, sanctioned and probably also participated in by the member governments, both to eliminate competition in the import and export trade with non-members and to keep within bounds the rivalry for the customs union market between the industries of the respective member countries.[55]

There seems likelihood, therefore, that in the framing of future customs unions and in the development of existing ones, cartel agreements or their equivalent will be used as supplement or substitute for other means of assuring that the removal of the tariff wall between the members of the customs union shall not result in more increase of

[52] It is not clear to the present writer how a bounty would result for cartel members in non-exporting countries.

[53] League of Nations, Commission of Enquiry for European Union, *Minutes of the Third Session of the Commission,* May 15–21, 1931 (Document C.395. M.158.1931.VII), pp. 16–24; 79–88.

[54] In a 1937 Report, the Economic Committee of the League of Nations drew attention to the possibility of using cartel agreements as a substitute for prohibitive tariffs in dealing with competition from low-cost producers. "It may be pointed out that this difficulty could be met if arrangements could be reached between the industries concerned which would give an assurance against such excessive competition. Quotas applied solely as guarantees for these arrangements are not open to criticism." League of Nations, Economic Committee, *Remarks on the Present Phase of International Economic Relations,* September, 1937 (Document C.358.M.242.1937.II.B), pp. 14–15.

[55] See *supra,* pp. 73–75.

competition between the industries of the respective member countries than is desired. It is also likely, on the basis of the past record, that a minimum of increase in such competition will be desired. This is a reasonable forecast, I think, despite the fact that the Havana Charter contains the statement (Article 44, paragraph 1) that the members "recognize that the purpose of a customs union or free-trade area should be to facilitate trade between the parties and not to raise barriers to the trade of other Member countries with such parties."

8. *The Allocation of Customs Revenues*

Whenever customs revenues are important, the method of their allocation as between members of a customs union is almost certain to become a major issue,[56] which has a close counterpart in the controversies which have always arisen in federal unions over the distribution of revenues, or the allocation of taxation rights, as between the central and the regional political authorities. The greater the disparity in economic levels between the members, and the greater the differences as between the members in the customary consumption of imported commodities, the greater is likely to be the difficulty in finding a formula for allocation of customs receipts which will be mutually acceptable.

In the German Zollverein the simplest possible formula of allocation, namely, according to population, was found generally practicable, but modification was necessary in at least two instances for members with relatively high per capita income levels and with specially important trade relations outside the Zollverein; the City of Frankfort was allotted a share in the Zollverein customs receipts approximately four and a half times what it would have been entitled to on a population basis, while the rural districts of Frankfort received a lesser supplement; Hanover also was allowed a supplement. The problem of allocation of revenues as between Germany and Austria arising out of the different economic levels of the two regions was stated by Bismarck in 1864 to constitute an insurmountable obstacle to customs union with Austria:

[56] For details as to methods of allocating customs revenues in customs unions, see T. E. Gregory, *Tariffs: A Study in Method* (London, 1921), pp. 16–18, and *Customs Unions, 1947*, pp. 17–19.

I regarded a customs union as an impracticable Utopia on account of the differences in the economic and administrative conditions of both parties. The commodities which formed the financial basis of the customs union in the north do not come into use at all in the greater part of Austro-Hungarian territory. The difficulties which the differences in habits of life and in consumption between North and South Germany brought about even now within the Zollverein, would be insurmountable, if both districts were to be included in the same customs boundary with the eastern provinces of Austria-Hungary. A fairer scale of distribution, or one more corresponding with the existing consumption of dutiable goods, could not be arrived at; every scale would be either unfair to the Zollverein, or unacceptable to public opinion in Austria-Hungary. There is no common measure of taxation for the Slovack or Galician with his few wants on the one side, and on the other for the inhabitant of the Rhenish provinces and of Lower Saxony.[57]

In the customs unions in which British Crown Colonies participated, as well as in some other customs unions, allocation was in general according to place of consumption. This formula would be difficult to apply either where imported raw materials were processed in one member territory for sale in another, or where wholesale distribution was concentrated in one territory. Two instances can be cited where the application of this formula gave rise either to difficulties of administration or to complaints of inequitable division of revenues.

When the Australian Commonwealth was established, the States were for a five-year period allotted shares in the customs revenue collections of the Commonwealth in proportion to consumption within the States of the imported commodities. Application of this formula involved elaborate bookkeeping, extremely burdensome administrative red tape, and extensive controversy.[58]

In the case of the customs union between Ruanda-Urundi, a territory under League of Nations mandate to Belgium, and the Belgian-Congo, duties collected on imports are credited to the territory of destination, which in application is taken to be the territory of last wholesale transaction. A member of the Mandates Commission, Mr. Merlin, in 1926 objected that the wholesale destination was often the

---

[57] *Bismarck the Man and the Statesman; Being the Reflections and Reminiscences of Otto Prince von Bismarck,* translated from the German under the supervision of A. J. Butler (London, 1898), I, 377–78.

[58] See Stephen Mills, *Taxation in Australia* (London, 1925), pp. 200–1.

Belgian Congo when the ultimate consumption was in Ruanda-Urundi. To this the Belgian representative before the Commission replied "that the situation explained by M. Merlin was the inevitable result of the Customs union the establishment of which was permitted by the mandate, and the consequences of which it was necessary to accept." [59]

In the various South African customs unions where allocation was according to consumption, the territory in which the import duties were actually collected was allowed a fraction of the receipts as compensation for administrative expense. In the Poland-Danzig Customs Union, which was established under League of Nations auspices in accordance with provisions in the Treaty of Peace with Germany following World War I, the allocation of customs revenues was to be by agreement between Poland and Danzig, but with consumption to be taken into account. Agreement was reached that division of total revenues was to be presumptively in accordance with per capita consumption, but that it was to be assumed that average consumption per head in Danzig was six times that in Poland; this arrangement was to be reconsidered at three-year intervals. [60]

In other customs unions receipts were divided according to agreed percentages (e.g., Austria-Modena, 1852; Austria-Liechtenstein, 1852), or a lump sum per annum allocation was made to a small member (e.g., Prussia-Schwarzburg, 1819; Italy-Albania, 1939), or special modifications were made in the allocation-by-consumption or allocation-by-collections formulas. In the Austro-Hungarian Customs Union, as in other cases where customs union was associated with political union, no provision was made for division of customs revenue. In the Austro-Hungarian case, not only did all the customs revenue go into the Dual Kingdom's treasury, but in addition "quotas" were assigned to the constituent states to meet the remainder of the needs of the central government.

[59] League of Nations, Permanent Mandate Commission, *Minutes of the Ninth Session*, Geneva, 1926, pp. 98–101.

[60] For the Danzig-Poland negotiations, and for general discussion of the problems arising out of the allocation of customs union revenues, see Martin Jos. Funk, *Die danzig-polnische Zollunion: Der bisherige und der künftige Zollverteilungschlüssel* (Jena, 1926).

An unusual provision was contained in the customs union agreements of 1930 of the Union of South Africa with Northern Rhodesia and with Southern Rhodesia. These agreements were really partial abrogations of the preexisting customs unions. As part of the movement toward tariff autonomy of the Rhodesias, it was provided in these agreements that each of the members of the respective unions was to pay the other specified percentages of the value of its manufactures exported to the other. These provisions seem to be instances where revenues lost as a result of effective protection of the industries of one member in the territory of the other had to be made up by the member profiting by the tariff protection, a type of provision which the Canadian Prairie Provinces, or Western Australia, would no doubt be happy to have applied to their relationships to the Dominion, or the Commonwealth, tariffs.

In the Report of the Second Joint Committee on Franco-Italian Customs Union there is no systematic discussion of the question of the mode of allocation of customs receipts, and the only comment suggests that allocation of receipts by ultimate destination of the imports is planned, and that the technical difficulties associated with this procedure are being seriously underestimated. When a common tariff is in operation—

the question of transfer of customs receipts will arise only in the case where an importer enters for customs in a territory of the union other than the territory of destination goods which will subsequently be sent on to this latter territory; it would seem that this question can be dealt with in a satisfactory manner, if each of the customs administrations sets up a special statistical service; the two governments could, to this effect, negotiate a special protocol.

[2]

The general theory of second best[1]

There is an important basic similarity underlying a number of recent works in apparently widely separated fields of economic theory. Upon examination, it would appear that the authors have been rediscovering, in some of the many guises given it by various specific problems, a single general theorem. This theorem forms the core of what may be called *the general theory of second best*. Although the main principles of the theory of second best have undoubtedly gained wide acceptance, no general statement of them seems to exist. Furthermore, the principles often seem to be forgotten in the context of specific problems and, when they are rediscovered and stated in the form pertinent to some problem, this seems to evoke expressions of surprise and doubt rather than of immediate agreement and satisfaction at the discovery of yet another application of the already accepted generalizations.

In this paper, an attempt is made to develop a *general* theory of second best. The first section gives, by way of introduction, a verbal statement of the theory's main general theorem, together with two important negative corollaries. The second section outlines the scope of the general theory of second best. Next, a brief survey is given of some of the recent literature on the subject. This survey brings together a number of cases in which the general theory has been applied to various problems in theoretical economics. The implications of the general theory of second best for piecemeal policy recommendations, especially in welfare economics, are next considered. This general discussion is followed by two sections giving examples of the application of the theory in specific models. These examples lead up to the general statement and rigorous proof of the central theorem. A brief consideration of the existence of second-best solutions is followed by a classificatory discussion of the nature of these solutions. This taxonomy serves to illustrate some of the important negative corollaries of the theorem. The paper is concluded with a brief discussion of the difficult problem of multiple-layer second-best optima.

A general theorem in the theory of second best

It is well known that the attainment of a Paretian optimum requires the simultaneous fulfilment of all the optimum conditions. The general theorem for the second-best optimum states that if there is introduced into a general equilibrium system a constraint which prevents the attainment of one of the Paretian conditions, the other Paretian conditions, although still attainable, are, in general, no longer desirable. In other words, given that one of the Paretian optimum conditions cannot be fulfilled, then an optimum situation can be achieved only by departing from all the other Paretian conditions. The optimum situation finally attained may be termed a second-best optimum because it is achieved subject to a constraint which, by definition, prevents the attainment of a Paretian optimum.

From this theorem there follows the important negative corollary that there is no *a priori* way to judge as between various situations in which some of the Paretian optimum conditions are fulfilled while others are not. Specifically, it is *not* true that a situation in which more, but not all, of the optimum conditions are fulfilled is necessarily, or is even likely to be, superior to a situation in which fewer are fulfilled. It follows, therefore, that in a situation in which there exist many constraints which prevent the fulfilment of the Paretian optimum conditions, the removal of any one constraint may affect welfare or efficiency either by raising it, by lowering it, or by leaving it unchanged.

The general theorem of the second best states that if one of the Paretian optimum conditions cannot be fulfilled a second-best optimum situation is achieved only by departing from all other optimum conditions. It is important to note that in general, nothing can be said about the direction or the magnitude of the secondary departures from optimum conditions made necessary by the original non-fulfilment of one condition. Consider, for example, a case in which the central authority levies a tax on the purchase of one commodity and returns the revenue to the purchasers in the form of a gift so that the sole effect of the tax is to distort relative prices. Then all that can be said in general is that given the existence and invariability of this tax, a second-best optimum can be achieved by levying some system of taxes and subsidies on all other commodities. The required tax on some commodities may exceed the given tax, on other commodities it may be less than the given tax, while on still others a subsidy, rather than a tax, may be required.

It follows from the above that there is no *a priori* way to judge as between various situations in which none of the Paretian optimum conditions are fulfilled. In particular, it is *not* true that a situation in which all departures from the optimum conditions are of the same direction and magnitude is necessarily superior to one in which the deviations vary in direction and magnitude. For example, there is no reason to believe that a situation in which there is the same degree of monopoly in all industries will necessarily be in any sense superior to a situation in which the degree of monopoly varies as between industries.

The scope of the theory of second best

Perhaps the best way to approach the problem of defining the scope of the theory of second best is to consider the role of constraints in economic theory. In the general economic problem of maximization a function is maximized subject to at least one constraint. For example, in the simplest welfare theory a welfare function is maximized subject to the constraint exercised by a transformation function. The theory of the Paretian optimum is concerned with the conditions that must be fulfilled in order to maximize some function subject to a set of constraints which are generally considered to be 'in the nature of things'. There are, of course, a whole host of possible constraints beyond those assumed to operate in the Paretian optimization problem. These further constraints vary from the 'nature-dictated' ones, such as indivisibilities and boundaries to production functions, to the obviously 'policy-created' ones such as taxes and subsidies. In general, there would seem to be no logical division between those constraints which occur in the Paretian optimum theory and those which occur only in the theory of second best. All that can be said is that, in the theory of the Paretian optimum, certain constraints are assumed to be operative and the conditions necessary for the maximization of some function subject to these constraints are examined. In the theory of second best there is admitted at least one constraint additional to the ones existing in Paretian optimum theory and it is in the nature of this constraint that it prevents the satisfaction of at least one of the Paretian optimum conditions. Consideration is then given to the nature of the conditions that must be satisfied in order to maximize some function subject to this new set of constraints.

It is important to note that even in a single general equilibrium system where there is only one Paretian optimum, there will be a multiplicity of second-best optimum positions. This is so because there are many possible combinations of constraints with a second-best solution for each combination. For this reason one may speak of the existence of *the* Paretian optimum but should, strictly speaking, refer to *a* second-best optimum.

It is possible to approach problems in the theory of second best from two quite different directions. On the one hand, the approach used in this paper is to assume the existence of one constraint additional to those in the Paretian optimum problem (e.g., one tax, one tariff, one subsidy, or one monopoly) and then to investigate the nature of the conditions that must be satisfied in order to achieve a second-best optimum and, where possible, to compare these conditions with those necessary for the attainment of a Paretian optimum. On the other hand, the approach used by Professor Meade is to assume the existence of a large number of taxes, tariffs, monopolies, and so on, and then to inquire into the effect of changing any one of them. Meade, therefore, deals with a system containing many constraints and investigates the optimum (second-best) level for one of them, assuming the invariability of all the others.[2] It would be futile to argue that one of these approaches was superior to the other. Meade's is probably the appropriate one when considering problems of actual policy in a world where many imperfections exist and only a few can be removed at any one time. On the other hand, the approach used in the present paper would seem to be the more appropriate one for a systematic study of the general principles of the theory of second best.

The theory of second best in the literature of economics

The theory of second best has been, in one form or another, a constantly recurring theme in the post-war literature on the discriminatory reduction of trade barriers. There can be no doubt that the theory of customs unions provides an important case study in the application of the general theory of second best. Until customs union theory was subjected to searching analysis, the 'free trader' often seemed ready to argue that any reduction in tariffs would necessarily lead to an improvement in world productive efficiency and welfare. In his path-breaking work on the theory of customs unions[3] Professor Viner has shown that the removal of tariffs from some imports may cause a decrease in the efficiency of world production.

One important reason for the shifts in the location of production which would follow the creation of a customs union was described by Viner as follows:

> There will be commodities which one of the members of the customs union will now newly import from the other, whereas before the customs union it imported them from a third country, because that was the cheapest possible source of supply even after payment of the duty. The shift in the locus of production is now not as between the two member countries but as between a low-cost third country and the other, high-cost, member country.

Viner used the term 'trade diversion' to describe production shifts of this sort and he took it as self-evident that they would reduce the efficiency of world production. Since it is quite possible to conceive of a customs union having only trade-diverting production effects, it follows, in Viner's analysis, that the discriminatory reduction of tariffs may reduce, rather than raise, the efficiency of world production.

Viner emphasized the production effects of customs unions,[4] directing his attention to changes in the location, and hence the cost, of world production. Recently Professor Meade has shown that a customs union has exactly parallel effects on the location, and hence the 'utility' of world consumption.[5] Meade isolates the 'consumption effects' of customs unions by considering an example in which world production is fixed. In this case Viner's problem of the effects of a union on the cost of world production cannot arise. Meade argues that, under these circumstances, a customs union will tend to raise welfare by encouraging trade between the member countries but that, at the same time, it will tend to lower welfare by discouraging the already hampered trade between the union area and the rest of the world. In the final analysis a customs union will raise welfare, lower it, or leave it unchanged, depending on the relative strength of these two opposing tendencies. The Viner–Meade conclusions provide an application of the general theorem's negative corollary that nothing can be said *a priori* about the welfare and efficiency effects of a change which permits the satisfaction of some but not all of the Paretian optimum conditions.

Another application of second-best theory to the theory of tariffs has been provided by S.A. Ozga who has shown that a non-preferential reduction of tariffs by a single country may lead 'away from the free trade position'.[6] In other words, the adoption of a free-trade policy by one country, in a multi-country tariff-ridden world, may actually lower the real income of that country and of the world. Ozga demonstrates the existence of this possibility by assuming that all commodities are, in consumption, rigidly complementary, so that their production either increases or decreases simultaneously. He then shows that in a three-country world with tariffs all around, one country may adopt a policy of free trade and, as a result, the world production of all commodities may decrease. This is one way of demonstrating a result which follows directly from the general theory of second best.

In the field of public finance, the problems of second best seem to have found a particularly perplexing guise in the long controversy on the relative merits of direct *versus* indirect taxation. It would be tedious to review all the literature on the subject at this time. In his 1951 article, I.M.D. Little[7] has shown that because of the existence of the 'commodity' leisure, the price of which cannot be directly taxed, both direct and indirect taxes must prevent the satisfaction of some of the conditions necessary for the attainment of a Paretian optimum. An indirect tax on one good disturbs rates of substitution between that good and all others while an income tax disturbs rates of substitution between leisure and all other goods. Little then argues that there is no *a priori* way to judge as between these two positions where some Paretian optimum conditions are satisfied while others are not. This is undoubtedly correct. However, Little might have gone on to suggest that there is an *a priori* case in favor of raising a given amount of revenue by some system of *unequal indirect taxes* rather than by either an income tax or an indirect tax on only one commodity. This interesting conclusion was first stated by W.J. Corlett and D.C. Hague.[8] These authors have demonstrated that the optimum way to raise any given amount of revenue is by a system of unequal indirect taxes in which commodities 'most complementary' to leisure have the highest tax rates while commodities 'most competitive' with leisure have the lowest rates. The reason for this general arrangement of tax rates should be intuitively obvious. When an equal *ad valorem* rate of tax is placed on all goods the consumption of leisure will be too high while the consumption of all other goods will be too low. The consumption of untaxed leisure may be discouraged by placing especially high rates of tax on commodities which are complementary in consumption to leisure and by placing especially low rates of tax on commodities which are competitive in consumption with leisure.

Professor Meade has recently given an alternative analysis of the same problem.[9] His conclusions, however, support those of Corlett and Hague. In theory at least, the tables have been completely turned and the indirect tax is proved to be superior to the income tax, provided that the optimum system of indirect taxes is levied. This conclusion is but another example of an application of the general theorem that if one of the Paretian optimum conditions cannot be fulfilled then a second-best optimum situation can be obtained by departing from all the other optimum conditions.

What is perhaps not so obvious is that the problem of direct versus indirect taxes and that of the 'consumption effects' of customs unions are analytically identical. The Little analysis deals with a problem in which some commodities can be taxed at various rates while others must be taxed at a fixed rate. (It is not necessary that the fixed rate of tax should be zero.) In the theory of customs unions one is concerned with the welfare and efficiency effects of varying some tariff rates while leaving others unchanged. In Little's analysis there are three commodities, X, Y and Z, commodity Z being leisure. By renaming Z home goods and X and Y imports from two different countries one passes immediately to the theory of customs unions. An income tax in Little's analysis becomes a system of non-discriminatory import duties while a single indirect tax becomes the discriminatory tariff introduced after the formation of a customs union with the producers of the now untaxed import. A model of this sort is considered later in the paper.

An application of the general theory of second best to yet another field of economic theory is provided by A. Smithies in his article, 'The Boundaries of the Production and Utility Function'.[10] Smithies considers the case of a multi-input firm seeking to maximize its profits. This will be done when for each factor the firm equates marginal cost with marginal revenue productivity. Smithies then suggests that there may exist boundaries to the production function. These boundaries would take the form of irreducible minimum amounts of certain inputs, it being possible to employ more but not less than these minimum amounts. It might happen, however, that profit maximization called for the employment of an amount of one factor less than the minimum technically possible amount. In this case production would take place 'on the boundary' and the minimum possible amount of the input would be used. However, in the case of this input, marginal cost would no longer be equated with marginal productivity, the boundary conditions forcing its employment beyond the optimum level. Smithies then shows that given the constraint, marginal cost does not equal marginal productivity for this input, profits will be maximized only by departing from the condition marginal cost equals marginal productivity for all other inputs. Furthermore, there is no *a priori* reason for thinking that the nature of the inequality will be the same for all factors. Profit maximization may require that some factors be employed only to a point where marginal productivity exceeds marginal cost while other factors are used up to a point where marginal productivity falls below marginal cost.

Problems of the 'mixed economy' provide an application of second-best theory frequently encountered in popular discussion. Consider, for example, a case where one section of an economy is rigidly controlled by the central authority while another section is virtually uncontrolled. It is generally agreed that the economy is not functioning efficiently but there is disagreement as to the appropriate remedy. One faction argues that more control over the uncontrolled sector is needed, while another faction pleads for a relaxation of the degree of control exercised in the public sector. The principles of the general theory of second best suggest that *both sides* in the controversy may be advocating a policy appropriate to the desired ends. Given the high degree of control in one sector and the almost complete absence of control in another, it is unlikely that anything like a second-best optimum position has been reached. If this is so, then it follows that efficiency would be increased either by increasing the degree of control exercised over the uncontrolled sector or by relaxing the control exercised over the controlled sector. Both of these policies will move the economy in the direction of some second-best optimum position.

Finally, mention may be made of the problem of 'degrees of monopoly'. It is not intended to review the voluminous literature on this controversy. It may be mentioned in passing that, in all but the simplest models, a Paretian optimum requires that marginal costs *equal* prices throughout the entire economy. If this equality is not established in one firm, then the second-best conditions require that the equality be departed from in all other firms. However, as is usual in second-best cases there is no presumption in favor of the same degree of inequality in all firms. In general, the second-best position may well be one in which prices greatly exceed marginal costs in some firms, only slightly exceed marginal costs in others, while, in still other firms, prices actually fall short of marginal costs.

A similar problem is considered by Lionel W. McKenzie in his article 'Ideal output and the interdependence of firms'.[11] He deals with the problem of increasing the money value of output in situations in which marginal costs do not equal prices in all firms. The analysis is not conducted in a general equilibrium setting and many simplifying assumptions are made such as the one that resources can be shifted between occupations as desired without affecting their supplies. McKenzie shows that even in this partial equilibrium setting if allowance is made for inter-firm sales of intermediate products, the condition that marginal costs should bear the same relation to prices in all firms does not provide a sufficient condition for an increase in the value of output. Given that the optimum conditions marginal cost equals price for each commodity cannot be achieved, a second-best optimum would require a complex set of relations in which the ratio of marginal cost to price would vary as between firms. Although the analysis is not of a full general equilibrium, the conclusions follow the now familiar pattern: (1) if a Paretian optimum cannot be achieved a second-best optimum requires a general departure from all the Paretian optimum conditions and (2) there are unlikely to be any simple sufficient conditions for an *increase* when a *maximum* cannot be obtained.

The theory of second best and 'piecemeal' policy recommendations
It should be obvious from the discussion in the preceding sections that the principles of the general theory of second best show the futility of 'piecemeal welfare economics'. To apply to only a small part of an economy welfare rules which would lead to a Paretian optimum if they were applied everywhere, may move the economy away from, not toward, a second-best optimum position. A nationalized industry conducting its price–output policy according to the Lerner–Lange 'Rule' in an imperfectly competitive economy may well diminish both the general productive efficiency of the economy and the welfare of its members.

The problem of sufficient conditions for an increase in welfare, as compared to necessary conditions for a welfare maximum, is obviously important if policy recommendations are to be made in the real world. Piecemeal welfare economics is often based on the belief that a study of the *necessary* conditions for a Paretian welfare optimum may lead to the discovery of *sufficient* conditions for an increase in welfare. In his *Critique of Welfare Economics*,[12] I.M.D. Little discusses the optimum conditions for exchange and production '... both as necessary conditions for a maximum, and as sufficient conditions for a desirable economic change'. Later on in his discussion Little says '... necessary conditions are not very interesting. It is *sufficient* conditions for improvements that we really want ....' But the theory of second best leads to the conclusion that there are in general no such sufficient conditions for an increase in welfare. There are necessary conditions for a Paretian optimum. In a simple situation there may exist a condition that is necessary and sufficient. But in a general equilibrium situation there will be no conditions which in general are sufficient for an increase in welfare without also being sufficient for a welfare maximum.

The preceding generalizations may be illustrated by considering the following optimum conditions for exchange: 'The marginal rate of substitution between any two "goods" must be the same for every individual who consumes them both.' Little concludes that this condition gives a sufficient condition for an increase in welfare provided only that when it is put into effect, '... the distribution of welfare is not thereby made worse'. However, the whole discussion of this optimum condition occurs only after Little has postulated '... a fixed stock of "goods" to be distributed between a number of "individuals"'. The optimum condition that all consumers should be faced with the same set of prices becomes in this case a sufficient condition for an increase in welfare, because the problem at hand is merely how to distribute efficiently a fixed stock of goods. But in this case the condition is a necessary and sufficient condition for a

Paretian optimum. As soon as variations in output are admitted, the condition is no longer sufficient for a welfare maximum and it is also no longer sufficient for an increase in welfare.

The above conclusion may be illustrated by a simple example. Consider a community of two individuals having different taste patterns. The 'government' of the community desires to raise a certain sum which it will give away to a foreign country. The community has made its value judgement about the distribution of income by deciding that each individual must contribute half of the required revenue. It has also been decided that the funds are to be raised by means of indirect taxes. It follows from the Corlett and Hague analysis that the best way to raise the revenue is by a system of *unequal* indirect taxes in which commodities 'most complementary' to leisure are taxed at the highest rates while commodities 'most substitutable' for leisure are taxed at the lowest rates. But the two individuals have different tastes so that commodity X is substitutable for leisure for individual I and complementary to leisure for individual II, while commodity Y and leisure are complementary for individual I and substitutes for II. The optimum way to raise the revenue, therefore, is to tax commodity X at a low rate when it is sold to individual I and at a high rate when it is sold to individual II, while Y is taxed at a high rate when sold to I but a low rate when sold to II. A second-best optimum thus requires that the two individuals be faced with different sets of relative prices.

Assume that the optimum tax rates are charged. The government then changes the tax system to make it non-discriminatory as between persons while adjusting the rates to keep revenue unchanged. Now the Paretian optimum exchange condition is fulfilled, but welfare has been decreased, for both individuals have been moved to lower indifference curves. Therefore, in the assumed circumstances, this Paretian optimum condition is a sufficient condition for a *decrease* in welfare.

A problem in the theory of tariffs

In this section the simple type of model used in the analysis of direct *versus* indirect taxes is applied to a problem in the theory of tariffs. In the Little–Meade–Corlett and Hague analysis it is assumed that the government raises a fixed amount of revenue which it spends in some specified manner. The optimum way of raising this revenue is then investigated. A somewhat different problem is created by changing this assumption about the disposition of the tax revenue. In the present analysis it is assumed that the government returns the tax revenue to the consumers in the form of a gift so that the only effect of the tax is to change relative prices.[13]

A simple three-commodity model is used, there being one domestic commodity and two imports. It is assumed that the domestic commodity is untaxed and that a fixed rate of tariff is levied on one of the imports. The optimum level for the tariff on the other import is then investigated. This is an obvious problem in the theory of second best. Also it is interesting to note that the conclusions reached have immediate applications to the theory of customs unions. In the second part of this section the conclusions of the first part are applied to the problem of the welfare effects of a customs union which causes neither trade creation nor trade diversion, but only the expansion and contraction of the volumes of already existing trade.

Second-best optimum tariff systems with fixed terms of trade
The conditions of the model are as follows: country A is a small country specializing in the production of one commodity (Z). Some of Z is consumed at home and the remainder is exported in return for two imports, X from country B and Y from country C. The prices of X and Y in terms of Z are unaffected by any taxes or tariffs levied in country A. It is further assumed that none of the tariffs actually levied by A are high enough to protect domestic industries producing either X or Y, that country B does not produce commodity Y and that country C does not produce commodity X. The welfare of country A is defined by a community welfare function which is of the same form as the welfare functions of the identical individuals who inhabit A.

It is assumed that A levies some fixed tariff on imports of commodity Y and that commodity Z is not taxed. It is then asked: what tariff ($\lessgtr 0$) on imports of commodity X will maximize welfare in country A? This tariff will be termed the optimum X tariff.

The model may be set out as follows: let there be three commodities, X, Y and Z. Let p_x and p_y be the prices of X and Y in terms of Z. Let the rate of *ad valorem* tariff charged on X and Y be $t_x - 1$ and $t_y - 1$.

$$u = u(x, y, z) \tag{1}$$

$$\frac{\partial u}{\partial x} = \frac{\partial u}{\partial z} p_x t_x \tag{2a}$$

$$\frac{\partial u}{\partial y} = \frac{\partial u}{\partial z} p_y t_y \tag{2b}$$

$$X p_x + Y p_y + Z = C \tag{3}$$

Equation (1) expresses country A's community welfare function. Equations (2a and b) are the demand equilibrium conditions. Equation (3) gives the condition that A's international payments be in balance.

These equations will yield a solution in general for any t_x and t_y, in X, Y and Z. Hence, for given p_x, p_y, C and whatever parameters enter into (1):

$$X = f(t_x, t_y) \tag{4a}$$
$$Y = g(t_x, t_y) \tag{4b}$$
$$Z = h(t_x, t_y) \tag{4c}$$

Attention is directed to the sign of the change in U when t_x changes with t_y > 1 kept constant. From equations (1) and (4):

$$\frac{\partial u}{\partial t_x} = \frac{\partial u}{\partial x} \cdot \frac{\partial x}{\partial t_x} + \frac{\partial u}{\partial y} \cdot \frac{\partial y}{\partial t_x} + \frac{\partial u}{\partial z} \cdot \frac{\partial z}{\partial t_x} \tag{5}$$

Substitute (2a and b) into (5):

$$\frac{\partial u}{\partial t_x} = p_x t_x \frac{\partial u}{\partial z} \cdot \frac{\partial x}{\partial t_x} + p_y t_y \frac{\partial u}{\partial z} \cdot \frac{\partial y}{\partial t_x} + \frac{\partial u}{\partial z} \cdot \frac{\partial z}{\partial t_x}$$

$$= \frac{\partial u}{\partial z} \left(p_x t_x \frac{\partial x}{\partial t_x} + p_y t_y \frac{\partial y}{\partial t_x} + \frac{\partial z}{\partial t_x} \right) \tag{6}$$

Next, take the partial derivative of (3) with respect to t_x.

$$p_x \frac{\partial x}{\partial t_x} + p_y \frac{\partial y}{\partial t_x} + \frac{\partial z}{\partial t_x} = 0$$

or

$$p_x \frac{\partial x}{\partial t_x} + p_y \frac{\partial y}{\partial t_x} = -\frac{\partial z}{\partial t_x} \tag{7}$$

Substitute (7) into (6):

$$\frac{\partial u}{\partial t_x} = \frac{\partial u}{\partial z} \left(p_x t_x \frac{\partial x}{\partial t_x} + p_y t_y \frac{\partial y}{\partial t_x} - p_x \frac{\partial x}{\partial t_x} - p_y \frac{\partial y}{\partial t_x} \right)$$

$$= \frac{\partial u}{\partial z} \left[p_x \frac{\partial x}{\partial t_x} (t_x - 1) + p_y \frac{\partial y}{\partial t_x} (t_y - 1) \right] \tag{8}$$

It is assumed, first, that some tariff is levied on Y but that X is imported duty free. Therefore, $t_x = 1$ and $t_y > 1$. Equation (8) reduces to:

$$\frac{\partial u}{\partial t_x} = \frac{\partial u}{\partial z}\left[P_y \frac{\partial y}{\partial t_x}(t_y - 1)\right] \tag{9}$$

In (9) $\partial u/\partial t_x$ takes the same sign as $\partial y/\partial t_x$. It follows that the introduction of a marginal tariff on X will raise welfare if it causes an increase in imports of commodity Y, will leave welfare unchanged if it causes no change in imports of Y and will lower welfare if it causes a decrease in imports of Y. Therefore, the optimum tariff on X is, in fact, a subsidy, if imports of Y fall when a tariff is placed on X, it is zero if the X tariff has no effect on imports of Y and it is positive if imports of Y rise when the tariff is placed on X.

It is now assumed that a uniform rate of tariff is charged on X and Y. Therefore, $t_x = t_y \equiv T$ and equation (8) becomes:

$$\frac{\partial u}{\partial t_x} = \frac{\partial u}{\partial z}(T-1)\left(P_x \frac{\partial x}{\partial T} + P_y \frac{\partial y}{\partial T}\right)$$

Substituting from (7):

$$\frac{\partial u}{\partial t_x} = -\left[\frac{\partial u}{\partial z} \cdot \frac{\partial z}{\partial t_x}(T-1)\right] \tag{10}$$

In (10) the sign of $\partial u/\partial t_x$ will be opposite to the sign of $\partial z/\partial t_x$. It follows that a marginal increase in the tariff on X will increase welfare if it causes a decrease in the consumption of Z, will leave welfare unchanged if it causes no change in the consumption of Z and will lower welfare if it causes an increase in the consumption of Z. It may be concluded, therefore, that the optimum tariff on X exceeds the given tariff on Y if an increase in the X tariff reduces the consumption of Z, that the optimum X tariff equals the given Y tariff if there is no relation between the X tariff and the consumption of Z and that the optimum X tariff is less than the given Y tariff if an increase in the X tariff causes an increase in consumption of Z.

In the case where an increase in the tariff on X causes an increase in the consumption of Y and of Z the optimum X tariff is greater than zero but less than the given tariff on Y.

Welfare effects of a customs union causing only trade expansion and trade contraction

It is assumed that country *A* initially charges a uniform *ad valorem* rate of tariff on imports of *X* and *Y*. *A* then forms a customs union with country *B*. Now *X* is imported duty-free while the pre-union tariff still applies to *Y*. What is the effect on *A*'s welfare of such a customs union? Some answers follow immediately from the previous analysis:

Case 1:   Any increase in the tariff on *X* causes a fall in the consumption of *Y*. The optimum tariff on *X* is, in fact, a subsidy. Therefore, the customs union must raise *A*'s welfare.

Case 2:   Variations in the tariff on *X* have no effect on consumption of *Y*. The optimum tariff on *X* is now zero. The customs union raises welfare in *A*. Furthermore, it raises it to a second-best optimum level (assuming that only the *X* tariff can be varied).

Case 3:   Variations in the tariff on *X* have no effect on the purchases of *Z*. The optimum tariff on *X* is equal to the *Y* tariff. The customs union lowers *A*'s welfare. Furthermore, the union disturbs an already achieved second-best optimum.

Case 4:   An increase in the tariff on *X* causes a fall in the consumption of *Z*. In this case the optimum tariff on *X* exceeds the given *Y* tariff. Therefore, the customs union lowers *A*'s welfare.

Case 5:   An increase in the tariff on *X* causes an increase in the consumption of both *Y* and *Z*. The optimum *X* tariff is greater than zero but less than the given *Y* tariff. The effect of the customs union on welfare is not known. Assume, however, that the *X* tariff is removed by a series of stages. It follows that the initial stages of tariff reduction must raise welfare and that the final stages must lower it. Although nothing can be said about the welfare effect of a complete removal of the *X* tariff, another important conclusion is suggested. A small reduction in tariffs must raise welfare. A large reduction may raise or lower it. It follows, therefore, that a partial preferential reduction of tariffs is more likely to raise welfare than is a complete preferential elimination of tariffs. Of course, this conclusion depends upon the specific assumptions made in the present model but it does provide an interesting and suggestive hypothesis for further investigation.

Nationalized industry in an economy with monopoly: A simple model

An interesting, and not unlikely, situation in which a 'second-best' type of policy may have to be pursued is that of a mixed economy which includes both nationalized industries and industries which are subject to monopoly control.

The monopoly is assumed to be one of the data: for one reason or another this monopoly cannot be removed, and the task of the nationalized industry is to determine that pricing policy which is most in 'the public interest'.

When there is full employment of resources then, if the monopoly is exercising its power, it will be producing less of the monopolized product than is required to give an optimum (in the Paretian sense) allocation of resources. Since there is less than the optimum production of the monopolized good, there will be more than the optimum production of the non-monopolized goods as a group.

Suppose that one of the non-monopolized industries is now nationalized. What should be its price–output policy? If it behaves competitively then it will tend to produce more of its product, relative to the monopolized good, than the Paretian optimum would require. If, on the other hand, it behaves monopolistically itself, then it will cut down the excess of its own production relative to that of the monopoly but will increase the excess of the remaining goods relative to both its own product and that of the monopolized industry. This is a typical 'second-best' situation: any policy will make some things worse and some better.

It is clear that no policy on the part of the nationalized industry can restore the Paretian optimum, for the existence of the monopoly prevents this. The nation-alized industry must aim at a second-best policy, designed to achieve the best that still remains open to the economy. In purely generally terms it is impossible to be more definite than this, as will be shown in a later section. Intuitively, however, one might expect that, in some situations at least, the best policy for the nationalized industry would be to behave something like the monopoly, but to a lesser extent. In the case of the simple model to be presented in this section, one's intuitions would be correct.

There are assumed to be, in the present model, three industries producing goods x, y, z. Labor is the only input, costs are constant, and the total supply of labor is fixed. These assumptions define a unique linear transformation function relating the quantities of the three goods:

$$ax + by + cz = L \tag{11}$$

The production functions from which this is derived are:

$$x = \frac{1}{a}l_x, \; y = \frac{1}{b}l_y, \; z = \frac{1}{c}l_z; \; l_x + l_y + l_z = L \tag{12}$$

The marginal costs are constant and proportional to a, b, c.

The 'public interest' is assumed to be defined by a community preference function, which is of the same form as the preference functions of the identical individuals who make up the society. For simplicity, this preference function is assumed to take the logarithmic form:

$$U = x^{\alpha} y^{\beta} z^{\gamma}, \; \alpha, \beta, \gamma > 0 \tag{13}$$

The partial derivatives of this are:

$$\frac{\partial U}{\partial x} = \alpha \frac{U}{x}, \frac{\partial U}{\partial y} = \beta \frac{U}{y}, \frac{\partial U}{\partial z} = \gamma \frac{U}{z}$$

so that the marginal utilities of x, y, z are proportional, respectively to α/x, β/y, γ/z. For a utility function of this type, all goods are substitutes in both the Edgeworth–Pareto and Hicksian senses.

If there were no constraints in the economy (other than the transformation function itself), the Paretian optimum would be that found by maximizing the expression $U - \lambda(ax + by + cz - L)$, where λ is the Lagrangian multiplier. This would lead to the three equations:

$$\left. \begin{array}{c} \dfrac{\partial U}{\partial x} - \lambda a = 0 \\[2mm] \dfrac{\partial U}{\partial y} - \lambda b = 0 \\[2mm] \dfrac{\partial U}{\partial z} - \lambda c = 0 \end{array} \right\} \tag{14}$$

which can be expressed in the proportional form:

$$\frac{a}{\alpha} x = \frac{b}{\beta} y = \frac{c}{\gamma} z \tag{15}$$

These conditions are of the familiar Paretian type, namely that the marginal utilities (or prices which, assuming the ordinary consumer behavior equations, are proportional to them) are proportional to the marginal costs. There being no monetary conditions, and the supply of labor being fixed, equality between prices and marginal costs is not necessarily implied.

Suppose now that the industry producing x is a monopoly. The monopoly will set the price of x higher (in terms of some numeraire, which will be taken to be z) in relation to marginal cost than in the conditions of the Paretian optimum. A numeraire is necessary since money, and money prices, are not being considered.

For the present purposes, the exact margin between marginal cost and price in the monopolized industry (relative to the numeraire) does not matter. It is necessary only for the problem that the monopolist set the prices of x higher, relative to the price of z, than the ratio of the marginal cost of producing x to the marginal cost of producing z.

In other words, the monopolist's behavior can be expressed by:

$$\frac{p_x}{p_z} > \frac{mc_x}{mc_z}$$

Substituting for $\dfrac{p_x}{p_z}\left(=\dfrac{\partial U}{\partial x}\bigg/\dfrac{\partial U}{\partial z}=\dfrac{\alpha z}{\gamma x}\right)$ and $\dfrac{mc_x}{mc_z}\left(=\dfrac{a}{c}\right)$, this gives:

$$\frac{\alpha z}{\gamma x} > \frac{a}{c}$$
$$c\alpha z > a\gamma x$$
$$= k a\gamma x \quad \text{where } k > 1 \tag{16}$$

The actual value of k (provided it is > 1) does not matter for the analysis. It is not necessary for the argument that k is constant as the monopolist faces the changes brought about by the policies of the nationalized industries, but it simplifies the algebra to assume this.

The behavior of the monopolist, assumed unalterable, becomes an additional constraint on the system. The best that can be done in the economy is to maximize U subject to two constraints, the transformation function (11) and the monopoly behavior condition (16). The conditions for attaining the second-best optimum (the Paretian optimum being no longer attainable) are found, therefore, as the conditions for the maximum of the function $U - \mu(c\alpha z - k a\gamma x) - \lambda'(ax + by + cz - L)$, where there are now two Lagrangian multipliers μ, λ'. Neither of these multipliers can be identified with the multiplier λ in the equations (14).

The conditions for attaining the second best are, therefore:

$$\alpha\frac{U}{x} + \mu k a\gamma - \lambda'a = 0 \tag{17}$$

$$\beta\frac{U}{y} - \lambda'b = 0 \tag{18}$$

$$\gamma\frac{U}{z} - \mu c\alpha - \lambda'c = 0 \tag{19}$$

To appreciate these conditions, it is necessary to compute the ratio p_y/p_z, compare it with the ratio mc_y/mc_z, and relate the result to both the Paretian optimum conditions and the mode of behavior of the monopolist.

Although there are three equations (17), (18), (19) above, these involve the two Lagrangian multipliers, so that there is actually only one degree of freedom. Hence, the policy of the nationalized industry (that which produces y) is sufficient for attaining the second best. If the nationalized industry sets its price, relative to its marginal cost, so as to satisfy the above conditions, it will have done all that is within its power to further the public interest.

To complete the solution it is necessary to determine μ and λ'. From (17)

$$\mu ka\gamma x = -\alpha U + \lambda' ax \qquad (20)$$

and from (19)

$$-\mu c\alpha z = \gamma U - \lambda' cz \qquad (21)$$

Hence

$$\mu(ka\gamma x - c\alpha z) = -(\alpha + \gamma)U + \lambda'(ax + cz)$$

but, from (16),

$$ka\gamma x - c\alpha z = 0$$

so that

$$(\alpha + \gamma)U - \lambda'(ax + cz) = 0$$

$$\lambda' = \frac{(\alpha + \gamma)U}{ax + cz} \qquad (22)$$

Substituting for λ' in (20)

$$\mu ka\gamma x = -\alpha U + \frac{(\alpha + \gamma)U}{ax + cz}$$
$$= \frac{\gamma ax - c\alpha x}{ax + cz} U$$

$$\mu = \frac{k-1}{k} \cdot \frac{-U}{ax + cz} \quad \left[c\alpha z = k\gamma ax, \text{ from } (16) \right] \qquad (23)$$

The correct pricing policy for the nationalized industry is given from the ratio p_y/p_z which is implicit in the equations (17), (18), (19).

$$
\begin{aligned}
\frac{p_y}{p_z} &= \frac{\dfrac{\partial U}{\partial y}}{\dfrac{\partial U}{\partial z}} \\[2ex]
&= \frac{\beta\dfrac{U}{y}}{\gamma\dfrac{U}{z}} \\[2ex]
&= \frac{\lambda'b}{\mu c\alpha + \lambda'c} \qquad\qquad \text{[From (18), (19)]} \\[2ex]
&= \frac{b}{c + \dfrac{\mu}{\lambda'}c\alpha}
\end{aligned}
$$

$$
= \frac{\dfrac{b}{c}}{1 - \dfrac{k-1}{k}\cdot\dfrac{\alpha}{\alpha+\gamma}} \qquad \text{(From (22), (23))} \qquad (24)
$$

Now $b/c = MC_y/MC_z$, from (12), so that:

$$
\frac{p_y}{p_z} = \frac{MC_y}{MC_z}\cdot\left(\frac{1}{1 - \dfrac{k-1}{k}\cdot\dfrac{\alpha}{\alpha+\gamma}}\right) \qquad\qquad (25)
$$

Consider the expression $((k-1)/k \cdot \alpha/(\alpha+\gamma))$. Since $k > 1$, $0 < (k-1)/k < 1$, and $\alpha/(\alpha+\gamma) < 1$ since $\gamma > 0$. Thus the bracketed expression on the right hand side of (25) is greater than unity.

In other words, $p_y/p_z > MC_y/MC_z$, so that, relative to the numeraire, the nationalized industry should set its price higher than its marginal cost and, to that extent, behave like the monopoly.

But now consider the relationship between the nationalized industry and the monopoly:

$$\frac{P_y}{px} = \frac{\beta\dfrac{U}{y}}{\alpha\dfrac{U}{x}}$$

$$= \frac{\dfrac{b}{a}}{\dfrac{\mu}{\lambda'}k\gamma+1}$$

$$= \frac{\dfrac{b}{a}}{-\dfrac{k-1}{\alpha+\gamma}\cdot\gamma+1}$$

$$= \frac{b}{a}\cdot\frac{\alpha+\gamma}{\alpha+k\gamma} \tag{26}$$

In this case, since $k > 1$, α, $\gamma > 0$, $(\alpha + \gamma)/(\alpha + k\gamma) < 1$. Since $b/a = MC_y/MC_x$, the nationalized industry should set its price less high, in relation to marginal cost, than the monopoly.

In short, in the particular model analyzed, the correct policy for the nationalized industry, with monopoly entrenched in one of the other industries, would be to take an intermediate path. On the one hand, it should set its price higher than marginal cost (relative to the numeraire) but, on the other hand, it should not set its price so far above marginal cost as is the case in the monopolized industry.

These conclusions refer, it should be emphasized, to the particular model which has been analyzed above. This model has many simplifying (and therefore special) features, including the existence of only one input, constant marginal costs and a special type of utility function. As is demonstrated later there can be no *a priori* expectations about the nature of a second-best solution in circumstances where a generalized utility function is all that can be specified.

A general theorem of the second best

Let there be some function $F(x_1 \dots x_n)$ of the n variables $x_1 \dots x_n$, which is to be maximized (minimized) subject to a constraint on the variables $\Phi(x_1 \dots x_n)$ $= 0$. This is a formalization of the typical choice situation in economic analysis.

Let the solution of this problem – the Paretian optimum – be the $n - 1$ conditions $\Omega^i(x_1 \dots x_n) = 0$, $i = 1 \dots n-1$. Then the following theorem, the theorem of the second best, can be given.

If there is an additional constraint imposed of the type $\Omega^i \neq 0$ for $i = j$, then the maximum (minimum) of F subject to both the constraint Φ and the constraint $\Omega^i \neq 0$ will, in general, be such that none of the still attainable Paretian conditions $\Omega^i = 0$, $i \neq j$, will be satisfied.

Proof
In the absence of the second constraint, the solution of the original maximum (minimum) problem is both simple and familiar. Using the Lagrange method, the Paretian conditions are given by the n equations:

$$F_i - \lambda \Phi_i = 0 \qquad i = 1 \ldots n \tag{27}$$

Eliminating the multiplier, these reduce to the $n - 1$ proportionality conditions:

$$\frac{F_i}{F_n} = \frac{\Phi_i}{\Phi_n} \qquad i = 1 \ldots n - 1 \tag{28}$$

where the nth commodity is chosen as numeraire.

The equations (28) are the first-order conditions for the attainment of the Paretian optimum. Now let there be a constraint imposed which prevents the attainment of one of the conditions (28). Such a constraint will be of the form (the numbering of the commodities is, of course, arbitrary):

$$\frac{F_1}{F_n} = k \frac{\Phi_1}{\Phi_n} \qquad k \neq 1 \tag{29}$$

It is not necessary that k be constant, but it is assumed to be so in the present analysis. There is now an additional constraint in the system so that, using the Lagrangean method, the function to be maximized (minimized) will be:

$$F - \lambda' \Phi - \mu \left(\frac{F_1}{F_n} - k \frac{\Phi_1}{\Phi_n} \right) \tag{30}$$

The multipliers λ', μ will both be different, in general, from the multiplier λ in (27).

The conditions that the expression (30) shall be at a maximum (minimum) are as follows:

$$F_i - \lambda'\Phi_i - \mu\left\{\frac{F_nF_{1i}-F_1F_{ni}}{F_n^2} - k\frac{\Phi_n\Phi_{1i}-\Phi_1\Phi_{ni}}{\Phi_n^2}\right\} = 0 \quad i=1...n \quad (31)$$

If the expression $(F_nF_{1i} - F_1F_{ni})/F_n^2$ is denoted by Q_i and the equivalent expression for the Φs by R_i, then the conditions (31) can be rewritten in the following form:

$$\frac{F_i}{F_n} = \frac{\Phi_i + \frac{\mu}{\lambda'}(Q_i - kR_t)}{\Phi_n + \frac{\mu}{\lambda'}(Q_n - kR_n)} \quad (32)$$

These are the conditions for the attainment of the second-best position, given the constraint (29), expressed in a form comparable with the Paretian conditions as set out in (28).

Clearly, any one of the conditions for the second best will be the same as the equivalent Paretian condition only if:

(i) $\mu = 0$
(ii) $\mu \neq 0$, but $Q_i - kR_i = Q_n - kR_n = 0$

The first of these cannot be true for, if it were, then, when $i = 1$, F_1/F_n would be equal to Φ_1/Φ_n, in contradiction with the constraint condition (29).

It is clear from the nature of the expressions Q_i, Q_n, R_i, R_n that nothing is known, in general, about their signs, let alone their magnitudes, and even the signs would not be sufficient to determine whether (ii) was satisfied or not.

Consider $Q_n = (F_nF_{1n} - F_1F_{nn})/F_n^2$. If F were a utility function then it would be known that F_1, F_n were positive and F_{nn} negative, but the sign of F_{1n} may be either positive or negative. Even if the sign of F_{1n} were known to be negative, the sign of Q_n would still be indeterminate, since it would depend on whether the negative or the positive term in the expression was numerically the greater. In the case of Q_i, where $i \neq n$, the indeterminacy is even greater, since there are two expressions F_{i1} and F_{ni} for which the signs may be either positive or negative.

The same considerations as apply for the Qs also apply for the Rs of course. In general, therefore, the conditions for the second-best optimum, given the constraint (29), will all differ from the corresponding conditions for the attainment of the Paretian optimum. Conversely, given the constraint (29), the application of these rules of behavior of the Paretian type which are still attainable will not lead, in general, to the best position in the circumstances.

The general conditions for the achievement of the second-best optimum in the type of case with which this analysis is concerned will be of the type $F_i/F_n = k_i(\Phi_i/\Phi_n)$, where $k_i \neq k_j \neq 1$, so that $F_i/F_j = \Phi_i/\Phi_j$, $F_i/F_j \neq F_k/F_j$, $\Phi_i/\Phi_j \neq \Phi_k/\Phi_j$, and the usual Paretian rules will be broken all round.

The existence of a second-best solution

The essential condition that a true second-best solution to a given constrained situation should exist is that, if there is a Paretian optimum in which F has a maximum (minimum) when the constraint is removed, then the expression (30) must also have a true maximum (minimum). There is no reason why this should, in general, be the case.

For one thing, whereas well-behaved functions F and Φ will always have a solution which satisfies the comparatively simple first-order conditions for a Paretian optimum, it is by no means certain that the much more complex first-order conditions (31) for a second-best solution will be satisfied, since these conditions involve second-order derivatives whose behavior (subject only to convexity–concavity conditions of the functions) is unknown.

If the first-order conditions for the existence of second-best solutions present difficulties, the difficulties are quite insurmountable in the case of the second-order conditions. Let it be supposed, for concreteness, that the nature of the case is such that F is to be maximized. Then the existence of a second-best solution requires that the first-order conditions (31) shall give a maximum, not a minimum or a turning point. This requires that the second differential of the expression (30) shall be negative. But the second differential of (30) involves the *third*-order derivatives of F and Φ. Absolutely nothing is known about these in the general case, and their properties cannot be derived from the second-order condition that the Paretian optimum represents a true maximum for F.

The nature of second-best solutions

The extraordinary difficulty of making *a priori* judgements about the types of policy likely to be required in situations where the Paretian optimum is unattainable, and the second best must be aimed at, is well illustrated by examining the conditions (32) in the light of possible knowledge about the signs of some of the expressions involved.

In order to simplify the problem, and to render it less abstract, the function F will be supposed to be a utility function and Φ, which will be supposed to be a transformation function, will be assumed to be linear. The second derivatives of Φ disappear, so that $R_i = 0$ for all i, and attention can be concentrated on the expressions Q.

With the problem in this form, the derivatives F_i are proportional to the prices p_i, and the derivatives Φ_i are proportional to the marginal costs MC_i. As an additional simplification which assists verbal discussion but which does not affect the essentials of the model, it will be supposed that price equals marginal cost for the nth commodity, which will be referred to as the numeraire.

From (32), with these additional assumptions, therefore:

$$\frac{F_i}{F_n} = p_i = \frac{MC_i + \theta Q_i}{1 + \theta Q_n}$$

where $\theta = \mu/\lambda'$ so that

$$p_i - MC_i = \theta(Q_i - p_i Q_n) \tag{33}$$

Thus, for the ith commodity, price is above, equal to, or below, marginal cost according as Q_i/p_i is greater than, equal to, or less than, Q_n.

Since $Q_i = (F_n F_{1i} - F_1 F_{ni})/F_n^2$, the most we can expect to know is the sign of Q_i, unless a specific social utility function is given. From signs only, we can deduce only the following:

(i) if $\theta > 0$, $P > 1$ if $Q_i > 0$, $Q_n < 0$
              $P < 1$ if $Q_i < 0$, $Q_n > 0$ (34)

(ii) if $\theta < 0$, $P > 1$ if $Q_i < 0$, $Q_n > 0$
              $P < 1$ if $Q_i > 0$, $Q_n < 0$

Nothing can be said about P if Q_i, Q_n are of the same signs.

Now consider Q_i. The denominator is always positive, and F_1, F_n are both positive, so that the determining factors are the signs of the mixed partial derivatives F_{1i} and F_{in}. It is assumed that goods are known to be substitutes ($F_{ij} < 0$) or complements ($F_{ij} > 0$) in the Edgeworth–Pareto sense. There are four possible cases:

(a) If $F_{1i} > 0$, $F_{ni} > 0$, then $Q_i \gtrless 0$

(b) If $F_{1i} < 0$, $F_{ni} < 0$, then $Q_i \gtrless 0$

(c) If $F_{1i} > 0$, $F_{ni} < 0$, then $Q_i > 0$

(d) If $F_{1i} < 0$, $F_{ni} > 0$, then $Q_i < 0$

In cases (c) and (d), but not in cases (a) and (b), therefore, the sign of Q_i is determinate.

To complete the picture the sign of θ is also needed. Where the sign of this can be found at all, it is found by putting $i = 1$ and substituting in the constraint condition (29). For concreteness, let k be > 1 (the first good will be referred to as the monopolized good). Then, since $(1 + \theta Q_1)/(1 + \theta Q_n) = k > 1$, it can be deduced that, if $Q_1 < 0$, $Q_n > 0$, then $\theta < 0$, and if $Q_1 > 0$, $Q_n < 0$, then $\theta < 0$. In all other cases the sign of θ is indeterminate.

For $Q_1 > Q_n$, it is known that F_{11}, $F_{nn} < 0$, and $F_{n1} = F_{1n}$ so that there are only two cases, $F_{n1} > 0$ and $F_{n1} < 0$. The information conveyed in each of the two cases is as follows:

I $F_{n1} > 0 : Q_1 < 0$, $Q_n > 0$, so that $\theta < 0$
II $F_{n1} < 0 : Q_1 \gtrless 0$, $Q_n \gtrless 0$, so that $\theta \gtrless 0$

The combination of cases I and II with the independently determined cases (a), (b), (c), (d) gives a total of eight cases. These are given in Table 12.1, showing the information which can be derived about the signs of Q_i, Q_n and θ, and the consequent information about P using the conditions (34).

Table 12.1   Determining relationship between price and marginal cost

Case		Sign of			Relationship of price
		Q_i	Q_n	θ	to marginal cost for x_i
I $F_{ni} > 0$	(a) F_{ij}, $F_{ni} > 0$	?	+	−	?
	(b) F_{ij}, $F_{ni} < 0$	?	+	−	?
	(c) $F_{1i} > 0$, $F_{ni} < 0$	+	+	−	?
	(d) $F_{1i} < 0$, $F_{ni} > 0$	−	+	−	Price exceeds marginal cost
II $F_{ni} < 0$	(a) F_{1i}, $F_{ni} > 0$	?	?	?	?
	(b) F_{1i}, $F_{ni} < 0$	?	?	?	?
	(c) $F_{1i} > 0$, $F_{ni} < 0$	+	?	?	?
	(d) $F_{1i} < 0$, $F_{ni} > 0$	−	?	?	?

Of the eight cases tabulated, the signs of Q_i, Q_n and θ are simultaneously determinate in only two, I(c) and I(d), and in only one of these two, I(d), does this lead to a determinate relationship between price and marginal cost. This sole case leads to the only a priori statement that can be made about the nature of second-best solutions on the basis of the signs of the mixed second-order partial derivatives of the utility function.

If the monopolized commodity is complementary (in Edgeworth–Pareto sense) to the numeraire, and the ith commodity is also complementary to the numeraire, but a substitute for the monopolized good, then, in order to attain a second-best solution, the price of the ith commodity must be set higher than its marginal cost.

Since knowledge of the sign alone of the derivatives F_{ij} reveals only one determinate case, it would seem worthwhile to examine the situation if more heroic assumptions can be made about the knowledge of the utility function. The additional information which is assumed is that two commodities may be known to be 'weakly related', that is, that the derivative F_{ij} is either zero or of the second-order relative to other quantities.

In the expression $Q_i = (F_n F_{1i} - F_1 F_{ni})/F_n^2$, for example, if the ith commodity and the numeraire are weakly related in this sense, then the term $F_1 F_{ni}$ can be neglected relative to the term $F_n F_{1i}$, and the sign of Q_i is wholly determined by the sign of F_{1i}.

If the monopolized good and the numeraire are weakly related, then $Q_1 < 0$ and $Q_n > 0$. This is similar to the case I, in which the two goods were complements, leading to the same conclusions. There are now, however, four additional cases to add to (a), (b), (c), (d), for various combinations of weak relatedness with substitution and complementarity as between the ith commodity and the monopolized good and the numeraire. All the cases which can be given in terms of the three relationships (weakly related, complements, substitutes) are shown in Table 12.2. There are now three determinate cases, which can be summarized as follows.

Table 12.2   Relationship between ith commodity, monopolized good and numeraire

Relationship between monopolized good and numeraire	Relationship of ith good to: Monopolized good	Numeraire	Signs of Q_i	Q_n	θ	Price of ith good relative to marginal cost
Complements, or	Complements	Complements	?	+	–	?
weak	Substitutes	Substitutes	?	+	–	?
	Complements	Substitutes	+	+	–	?
	Substitutes	Complements	–	+	–	Higher
	Complements	Weak	+	+	–	?
	Substitutes	Weak	–	+	–	Higher
	Weak	Complements	–	+	–	Higher
	Weak	Substitutes	+	+	–	?
Substitutes	Any	Any	$\left.\begin{array}{c}+\\-\\?\end{array}\right\}$?	?		?

If the monopolized good and the numeraire are either complements or only weakly related, then the second-best solution will certainly require the price of the ith good to be set above its marginal cost either if the good is a substitute for the monopolized good and either complementary or only weakly related to the numeraire, or if the good is weakly related to the monopolized good but complementary to the numeraire.

With any other combinations of relatedness among the goods, it cannot be determined, *a priori*, whether the second-best solution will require the price of any particular good to be above or below its marginal cost. In particular, if there is no complementarity between any pairs of goods, and the relationship between the monopolized commodity and the numeraire is not weak, then there are no determinate cases.

As a matter of interest it is possible to work out conditions that may be likely to bring about any particular result. For example, a possible case in which the price of a good might be set below its marginal cost would be that in which the monopolized good, the numeraire, and the other good were all substitutes, but the rate at which marginal utility diminished was small in the case of the monopolized good (so that Q_1, Q_n would both be positive, with Q_1 large compared with Q_n, giving a positive value for θ), and the relationship of the good under discussion was much stronger with the monopolized good than with the numeraire (so that Q_i might be negative). There can be few real cases, however, where such guesses about the magnitudes of the quantities involved could be made.

The problem of multiple-layer optima

In all the preceding analysis, the problems have been conceived in terms of a single-layer optimum. It has been assumed that the constraint which defined the Paretian optimum (the transformation function, for example) was a technically fixed datum, and was not, itself, the result of an optimization process at a lower level.

The characteristic of general economic systems is, however, that they usually involve several successive processes of optimization, of increasing generality. The transformation function, for example, may have been derived as the result of competitive firms maximizing their profits. Firms are assumed to have minimized their costs before proceeding to maximize their profits, and these costs are themselves derived from processes involving optimization by the owners of the various factors of production.

It is of the nature of the economic process, therefore, that optimization takes place at successive levels, and that the maximization of a welfare function subject to a transformation function is only the topmost of these. It is also of the nature of Paretian optima (due to the simple proportionality of the conditions) that the optimization at the different levels can be considered as independent problems.

In the case of a second-best solution, however, the neat proportionality of the Paretian conditions disappears: this immediately poses the question whether a second-best solution in the circumstances of a multiple-layer economic system will require a breaking of the Paretian conditions at lower levels of the system, as well as at the level at which the problem was initiated.

The present paper does not propose to examine the problem, for it is a subject that would seem to merit full-scale treatment of its own. There seems reason to suppose, however, that there may well be cases in which a breaking of the Paretian rules at lower levels of the process (moving off the transformation function, for example) may enable a higher level of welfare to be obtained than if the scope of policy is confined to one level only.

A two-dimensional geometric illustration that is suggestive, although not conclusive, is set out in Figure 12.1. *Ox*, *Oy* represent the quantities of two goods *x*, *y*. The line *AB* represents a transformation function (to be considered as a boundary condition) and *CD* a constraint condition. In the absence of the constraint *CD* the optimum position will be some point, such as *P*, lying on the transformation line at the point of its tangency with one of the contours of the welfare function.

If the constraint condition must be satisfied, only points along *CD* can be chosen, and the optimum point *P* is no longer attainable. A point on the transformation

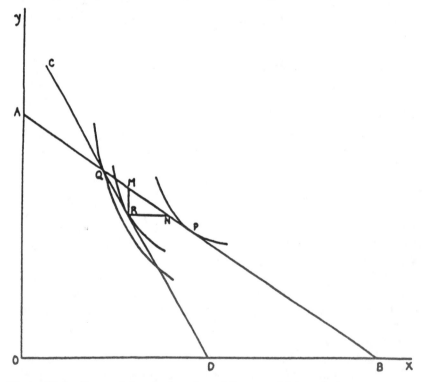

Figure 12.1   Determining the location of the second-best solution

line (Q) is still attainable. Will the second-best solution be at the point Q, or should the economy move off the transformation line? If the welfare contours and the constraint line are as shown in the diagram, then the second-best point will be at the point R, inside the transformation line.

It is obvious, of course, that the second best will never be at a point which is technically inefficient (has less of one commodity and no more of the other) relative to any attainable point. Although there are points (the segment MN) on the transformation line which are technically more efficient than R, these are not attainable. R is not technically inefficient relative to Q, even though R lies inside the transformation line.

If the line CD had a positive slope (as have the types of constraint which have been exemplified in the preceding analyses), the second best would always lie at its point of intersection with the transformation line, since all other points on CD would be technically inefficient relative to it.

Notes

1. Written with R.G. Lipsey and originally published in the *Review of Economic Studies*, 24 (1956), 11–32. At the suggestion of H.G. Johnson, then editor of the *Review*, independently written papers by the two authors, on the same topic but complementary in coverage, were combined into a single paper. The term 'second best' in this context was derived from Meade 1955b. In the original version, there was an algebraic error which affected two equations and a half page of text, but not the basic analysis, proof, or conclusions. A note was made of this when the paper was reprinted in Farrell, M.J. (ed.), *Readings in Welfare Economics*, London, Macmillan, 1973. Here the appropriate corrections have been made, affecting equations (32), (33) and some text.
2. Meade 1955b.
3. Viner 1950.
4. His neglect of the demand side allowed him to reach the erroneous conclusion that trade diversion necessarily led to a decrease in welfare. It is quite possible for an increase in welfare to follow from the formation of a customs union whose sole effect is to divert trade from lower- to higher-cost sources of supply. Furthermore this gain may be enjoyed by the country whose import trade is so diverted, by the customs union as an entity, and the world as a whole. See Lipsey 1957.
5. Meade 1955a.
6. Ozga 1955.
7. Little 1951.
8. Corlett and Hague 1953.
9. Meade 1955b, *Mathematica Appendix*.
10. Smithies 1936.
11. McKenzie 1951.
12. Little 1950.
13. If consumers have different utility functions then each consumer must receive from the government an amount equal to what he pays in taxes. However, if all consumers have identical homogeneous utility functions then all that is required is that all the tax revenue be returned to some consumer(s).
14. Obviously this is a problem in the theory of second best. The initial tariff on Y causes the consumption of Y to be too low relative to both X and Z. If the consumption of Y can be encouraged at the expense of X, welfare will be increased. However, if the consumption of Z is encouraged at the expense of X, welfare will be lowered. A tariff on X is likely to cause both sorts of consumption shift and the optimum X tariff will be one where, at the margin, the harmful effect of the shift from X to Z just balances the beneficial effect of the shift from X to Y.

[3]

Customs Union from a Single-Country Viewpoint*

In contrast to expressed governmental views, some academic economists have questioned whether customs unions always have a beneficial effect on countries joining them, and on world output. Among them, Professor Viner has argued that when a group of countries forms a union with a common tariff wall against outside countries, there are two possible consequences.[1] One is that higher-cost production within the union may displace lower-cost production in countries outside the union, with the result that world output is reduced and some countries within the union are made worse off. This occurs in the case of goods for which the union tariff is greater than the unit money-cost differences between the union and non-union sources. The other possible consequence of unions is the displacement of domestic production in one member-country by lower-cost imports from another member. In this case world output increases, and the union members benefit without any loss to outside countries. Since both displacement and diversion can occur simultaneously when many goods are traded, one must examine each case of union individually to determine the predominant effect on members, and on world output.[2]

This note will show that to examine customs unions in the light only of *production* effects, as Viner does, will give a biased judgment of their effect on countries joining them. It understates the gains to members in favorable cases, and it may lead to unfavorable conclusions where a union would in fact benefit the members. For, an additional element to consider is the response of consumers to the drop in import prices caused by the tariff removal. In order to examine such consumption effects, we shall consider how the position of a single country is affected by joining a union.

For the argument that follows we make a number of simplifying assumptions : (1) Country A initially carries on multilateral trade under a system of *ad valorem* tariffs, of uniform height against all imports from all countries. Other countries have the same system of tariffs. (2) There are only two goods, X and Y, both produced under constant costs and perfect competition, so that price equals average cost.[3] (3) A cannot influence the foreign price ratio of X and Y by varying the amount of either that it imports. In order to assure this we assume that one of the countries trading with A is producing X and Y simultaneously. Then any change in A's demand will merely cause a change in the proportion of resources devoted to X- and Y- production in the non-specialized country, without any change in their relative prices.[4] Moreover, this situation is assumed to exist for A both in the pre-union and post-union situations. (4) There is no foreign

* This note is the by-product of a paper on European integration written jointly with B. F. Johnston. I am indebted for criticism to Mr. Johnston, of the Food Research Institute, Stanford University, to E. Coen, of the University of Minnesota, and to E. McKinley of Indiana University.
    [1] Jacob Viner, *The Customs Union Issue* (1950 : New York), pp. 41-44.
    [2] Makower and Morton have given an ingenious elaboration of the Viner argument with examples involving numerous countries and commodities ; their conclusions are largely the same as those above although they are concerned mainly with world output effects. See H. Makower and G. Morton's, " A Contribution Towards a Theory of Customs Unions ", *Econ. Jour.*, LXIII, No. 249, March, 1953, pp. 33-49.
    [3] Incidentally, this assumption prevents us from considering certain additional gains which may result from customs union. These include economies of scale, and intensification of competition among producers. For a discussion of these, see F. Gehrels and B. F. Johnston, " The Economic Gains of European Integration ", *Journal of Political Economy*, August, 1955.
    [4] A clear geometrical demonstration of this proposition is given by J. E. Meade in *A Geometry of International Trade*, Chapter IV, especially p. 31 and figure XII.

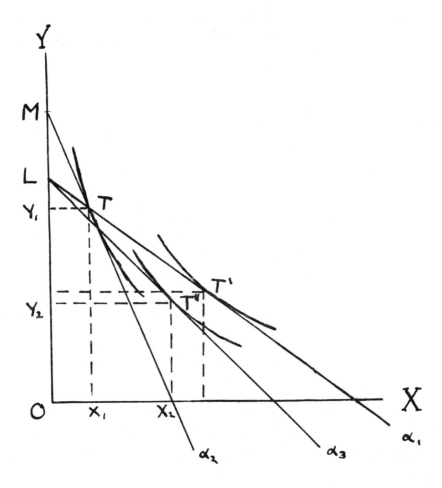

FIG. 1

lending or borrowing, and there are no costs of transportation. (5) The entire national income of A is spent on consumption, as the stock of capital is assumed constant and indestructible. (6) There being no governmental costs, the government levies tariffs only for regulatory purposes and distributes the proceeds in a way consistent with the desired pattern of income distribution. Thus disposable income exceeds factor income by the amount of tariffs reimbursed. (7) All individuals have identical and unchanging indifference maps, and the pattern of income distribution is held constant by means of appropriate taxes on and subsidies to personal income. This permits us to draw community indifference curves for both the pre- and post-union situation (by adding points with equal slope from curves of individuals) which are non-intersecting.[1]　(8) Consumers' levels of satisfaction are independent of the consumption of others.

We now consider what happens when A joins a customs union with a group of other countries, and they establish a common tariff wall against outside countries. We examine first the case where A's imports are diverted to a higher-cost source. Figure I depicts the pre-union and post-union situation for A.

A's national income at factor cost is measured in units of Y, the good in which it happens to specialize. National income is taken as the distance OL. The terms of trade it has before joining the union are given by α_1, which is also the cost ratio for X and Y in the non-specialized trading country. A's internal price ratio for X and Y is given by α_2. Its slope is steeper than that of α_1, by the amount of tariff per unit.

The disposable income of consumers in A is taken as the vertical distance OM, where LM is the transfer income received by consumers out of tariff reimbursements. In order to show the equilibrium position of consumers in A, we anchor α_2, the internal price line, at the point M and follow it to its point of tangency with an indifference curve. This is the point T, at which A exports LY_1 of Y for OX_1 of X, thus having OY_1 and OX_1 for its own consumption.[2] Since by assumption the foreign price ratio, given by the slope of α_1, is fixed, A could move to a point of tangency with a higher indifference curve, at point T', simply by removing its tariff.

However, here we wish to show that A can, by joining a customs union, move to a point somewhere between T and T', even with terms of trade less favorable than those given by α_1. The new terms of trade existing within the union are given by the price line α_3. α_3 is anchored at the point L (instead of M), because A no longer collects any tariff, all of its imported X now coming from within the union. Total consumer expenditures now equal factor income, which in turn is measured by OL. Moving along α_3, to a point of tangency with an indifference curve brings us to the point T'', in this case on a higher indifference curve than T. The volume of exports has increased from LY_1 to LY_2, and imports from OX_1 to OX_2. Thus despite worsened terms of trade, A has made itself better off by importing more from partners in the union than it did before from other partners ; and in this special case it has done so without any damage to its former trading partners.

But the point T'' need not lie on a higher indifference curve than T. Taking the shape of the indifference map as given two factors will determine whether T'' lies on a higher or lower indifference curve. These are : (*a*) How closely the cost of the imported good when purchased within the union (the slope of α_3) approaches the lowest cost obtainable by A (the slope of α_1). (*b*) How high is the tariff level, which was applied to all countries before union and now applies only to countries *outside* the union. It is the tariff level which determines the difference between slopes of α_1 and α_2. Thus for any given cost difference between union and non-union sources (the difference between slopes of α_1 and α_3), the *higher* the tariff the more likely is A to land on a higher indifference curve by joining the union.

Thus diversion of imports from a low to a higher-cost source of supply is not synonymous with a worsening of the importing country's position. A country may make itself either better off or worse off when its joining a customs union leads to such diversion.

---

[1] Assumption 7 means that we can permit relative income shares going to different occupations (functional distribution) to change, so long as the scale of distribution by income groups is held constant. This differs from Professor Meade's suggestion to hold functional distribution of income constant, on the ground that different occupational groups may have different taste patterns. See J. E. Meade, *Trade and Welfare* (Oxford : London, 1955) pp. 71-77.

[2] It may seem at first glance that the point T is not completely determined, because the amount of X imported (and Y exported) depends on the level of tariff revenues, while the level of tariff revenues in turn depends on the amount imported. However, it can easily be shown by algebraic substitutions that the amount of X imported depends only on factor income and the tariff rate, both of which are given.

However, world output will generally be reduced by diversion of trade, and countries outside the union may be damaged in the process.

The other situation mentioned at the outset, where joining a union leads to a displacement of domestic output by imports can be disposed of briefly. Here Country's A's position always improves for *two* reasons : (1) it is importing at lower cost what it was previously making at home ; (2) it is permitting imports to rise beyond this to the point where foreign and domestic price of the import are equal, as it should when foreign elasticity of supply at that price is infinite. Put differently, it is not only obtaining abroad at lower cost an amount of the good equal to the former domestic volume of production ; but it is importing and consuming a *greater* amount of that good because it is now relatively cheaper to consumers. The second action brings a gain which must be added to the first to give a true evaluation of A's improved position.

Bloomington, Indiana.   FRANZ GEHRELS.

Part II
Preliminaries

A
Tariff Changes and Welfare

TARIFFS AND TRADE IN GENERAL EQUILIBRIUM: COMMENT

By RONALD W. JONES*

A standard result in the theory of tariffs has been challenged by B. Södersten and Karl Vind in a recent issue of this *Review* [5]. After an explicit development of the general equilibrium model appropriate or this analysis, they conclude that the classic result on the possible effect of tariffs on domestic prices achieved in 1949 by Lloyd Metzler, [3] and [4], is incorrect. In the opinion of Södersten and Vind, a tariff levied on imports can never result in a lowering of the relative domestic price of the imported commodity.

This is a surprising conclusion, the more so as Metzler's result has gone unchallenged for almost twenty years. I propose to demonstrate that Södersten and Vind are themselves the guilty parties in this issue and that Metzler's result is indeed correct. In my opinion the general equilibrium analysis used by Södersten and Vind, essentially a model with eleven equations and eleven unknowns, is unnecessarily cumbersome for the purpose. Therefore in the first section of this paper I shall offer a simpler treatment of the same model to prove the important theorems in the standard theory of tariffs. In the concluding section, I shall point out where they have allowed errors to lead them to incorrect results. The reasons cited by Södersten and Vind for their departure from the standard

* The author is professor of economics at the University of Rochester.

Metzler result are irrelevant to the argument, for the real culprit lurks instead in a footnoted assumption about the behavior of consumption with a change in relative prices.

I. *The Analysis of Tariffs*

The setting for the analysis of tariffs is the same as that used by Södersten and Vind, although I shall employ a different terminology. Two countries, 1 and 2, are involved in trading two commodities, A and B, produced under conditions of increasing opportunity costs. Production is carried on under conditions of perfect competition, subject to tariffs levied on imports by both countries. Let (A_i, B_i) represent the consumption bundle, and (a_i, b_i) the production bundle, in country i. Country 1 is assumed to import commodity B, with M_1 equal to $B_1 - b_1$. Similarly country 2's imports are denoted by $M_2 \equiv A_2 - a_2$. Prices differ between countries because of tariffs. (p_a, p_b) represents domestic prices in country 1 while (π_a, π_b) represents prices in country 2. The ad valorem tariff of country i is t_i, and let T_i represent one plus the tariff rate. Thus p_b equals $T_1 \pi_b$ and π_a is given by $T_2 p_a$. As usual, in these models only relative prices count. Let commodity A serve as *numeraire* so that B's relative price ratio in country 1 is $p \equiv p_b/p_a$ and in country 2 is $\pi \equiv \pi_b/\pi_a$. Finally, consider the world terms of trade, the untaxed price of B in A units, β. Thus p equals $T_1 \beta$ and π equals β/T_2.

Tariff analysis is often portrayed by means of a diagram showing how a tariff serves to shift a country's offer curve, resulting in a new intersection with the other country's offer curve and a new equilibrium world terms of trade. In this spirit consider the representation shown by (1) and (2),

$$(1) \qquad M_1 = M_1(\beta; T_1)$$

$$(2) \qquad M_2 = M_2\left(\frac{1}{\beta}; T_2\right)$$

where each country's demand for imports is shown as a function of the *untaxed* relative price of those imports and of that country's tariff rate. Differentiate these expressions totally to obtain (3) and (4), where a caret

"^" over a variable denotes the relative change in that variable (e.g., $\hat{M}_1 \equiv dM_1/M_1$):

(3) $\hat{M}_1 = - \epsilon_1\hat{\beta} - \bar{\epsilon}_1\hat{T}_1$

(4) $\hat{M}_2 = \epsilon_2\hat{\beta} - \bar{\epsilon}_2\hat{T}_2$

where

$$\epsilon_1 \equiv - \frac{\beta}{M_1}\frac{\partial M_1}{\partial\beta}; \quad \epsilon_2 \equiv - \frac{\left(\dfrac{1}{\beta}\right)}{M_2}\frac{\partial M_2}{\partial\left(\dfrac{1}{\beta}\right)}$$

and

$$\bar{\epsilon}_i \equiv - \frac{T_i}{M_i}\frac{\partial M_i}{\partial T_i}$$

The ϵ_i are the traditional elasticities of demand for imports along the offer curves. These elasticities are defined so as to be positive. The $-\bar{\epsilon}_i$ define the change in each country's import demand as of constant world terms of trade. The reason I choose to label these $-\bar{\epsilon}_i$ will become apparent later.

Much of the complexity surrounding a general equilibrium analysis of tariffs arises from the necessity of breaking down the ϵ_i and $\bar{\epsilon}_i$ into more fundamental components. At a constant rate of tariff, a change in the world terms of trade induces a change in the consumption of importables. For there must also be a change in the domestic terms of trade and therefore substitution and income effects. In addition, production will generally alter along the production-possibility schedule. In terms of the fundamental determinants of a country's level of imports, the crucial variables are the domestic price ratio and real income.

Consider the analysis for country 1, whose demand for imports is shown functionally in equation (5).

(5) $M_1 = B_1(p, y_1) - b_1\left(a_1\left(\dfrac{1}{p}\right)\right)$

The term "y_1" denotes country 1's "real income" measured in units of A, the *numeraire*. It is only the change in real income that is of concern, and this can be defined

as the domestic price-weighted sum of the changes in consumption as in (6).[1]

(6) $dy_1 \equiv dA_1 + p\,dB_1$

The budget constraint for country 1, shown in (7), states that at domestic prices the value of consumption is limited by the value of production and the tariff

(7) $A_1 + pB_1 = a_1 + pb_1 + (T_1 - 1)\beta M_1$

revenue.[2] By differentiating this totally, and making use of the definition of the real income change shown in (6), it is possible (in (8)) to show the sources of any change in real income.

(8) $dy_1 = - M_1 dp + d\{(T_1 - 1)\beta M_1\}$

In deriving (8) use has been made of the general production relationship $\{da_1 + p\,db_1\} = 0$. If country 1 is incompletely specialized this reflects the tangency of the domestic price line and the transformation schedule. If country 1 is completely specialized to its export commodity and remains at the corner of its transformation schedule, da_i and db_i are each zero.

Although the expression for dy_1 in (8) is not yet in the form most useful for tariff analysis, it does reveal an interesting relationship between the optimum tariff and the tariff rate that would serve to maximize the tariff revenue. Assume that an increase in country 1's tariff rate would be protective in the sense of raising p.[3] In the neighborhood of a tariff that maximized tariff revenue (i.e., one for which $d\{(T_1-1)\beta M_1\}$ were zero) an increase in the tariff would lower real income. That is, a revenue maximizing tariff rate is higher than the optimum rate.

The domestic price of imports, p, equals

[1] Consider a utility function for country 1 of the form $U_1 = U_1(A_1, B_1)$. With differentiability, no satiation, and both commodities consumed, dU_1/U_{1A} equals $dA_1 + (U_{1B}/U_{1A})dB_1$. In a competitive world p equals the marginal rate of substitution, U_{1B}/U_{1A}. Now define dy_1 as dU_1/U_{1A}, which is free of cardinal utility connotations.

[2] Note that the tariff is levied on the world price, β.

[3] It can be shown that this must be the case in the neighborhood of the optimum tariff as ϵ_1 must exceed unity.

T_1 times the world price ratio, β. Differentiating this relationship and substituting into (8) yields expression (9)

(9) $dy_1 = - M_1 d\beta + (T_1 - 1)\beta dM_1$

as an alternative form for the change in country 1's real income. It illustrates the two basic means by which country 1's real income can be improved: first, by an improvement in 1's world terms of trade ($d\beta$ negative), which would serve to increase real income by an amount proportional to the original volume of imports, and second by any increase in imports in a situation in which the relative domestic valuation of the imported commodity, p, exceeds the relative cost of obtaining these imports on the world market, β. Note that $(T_1-1)\beta$ is precisely this price spread, $p-\beta$.[4]

With this expression for dy_1 at hand, it only remains to break down the separate price and income effects on the demand for imports. Differentiate (5) totally to obtain (10).

(10) $dM_1 = \dfrac{\partial B_1}{\partial p} dp + \dfrac{\partial B_1}{\partial y_1} dy_1$

$\qquad\qquad + \dfrac{db_1}{da_1} \dfrac{da_1}{d\left(\dfrac{1}{p}\right)} \dfrac{1}{p^2} dp$

Note that db_1/da_1, the slope of the transformation schedule, is given by $-1/p$.[5] Further simplification involves the definition of elasticities to capture: first, the substitution effect of a price change on the consumption of the imported commodity, $\bar{\eta}_1$; second, the marginal propensity to import, m_1; and third, the substitution effect as production changes along the transformation curve, e_1. Following the procedure used in Jones [1], define:

[4] For a discussion of the sources of a change in real income in a more complicated model involving capital mobility see Jones [2].

[5] If country 1 is specialized in producing commodity A, without there being a corner tangency, $db_1 = 0$ and the last term in (10) disappears.

$\bar{\eta}_1 \equiv - \dfrac{p}{M_1} \dfrac{\partial B_1}{\partial p} \geq 0$

$m_1 \equiv p \dfrac{\partial B_1}{\partial y_1} \geq 0 \qquad$ (by assuming no inferior goods)

$e_1 \equiv \dfrac{\left(\dfrac{1}{p}\right)}{(a_1 - A_1)} \dfrac{da_1}{d\left(\dfrac{1}{p}\right)} \geq 0$

These relationships can be substituted into (10). Finally, express dp in terms of $d\beta$ and dT_1 to obtain (11) as the expression for the relative

(11) $\hat{M}_1 =$

$$\dfrac{-\left[\bar{\eta}_1 + \dfrac{m_1}{T_1} + \dfrac{e_1}{T_1}\right]\hat{\beta} \; - \left[\bar{\eta}_1 + \dfrac{e_1}{T_1}\right]\hat{T}_1}{\left[1 - m_1 \dfrac{(T_1 - 1)}{T_1}\right]}$$

change in country 1's imports. Comparing this with the original breakdown of $\hat{M}_1$ in (3) it is possible to separate out the expressions for the elasticity of country 1's offer curve, ϵ_1, from the expression for the shift in its offer curve, given by $-\bar{\epsilon}_1$. Thus:

$$\epsilon_1 = \dfrac{\bar{\eta}_1 + \dfrac{m_1}{T_1} + \dfrac{e_1}{T_1}}{1 - m_1 \dfrac{(T_1 - 1)}{T_1}}$$

$$\bar{\epsilon}_1 = \dfrac{1}{\left\{1 - m_1 \dfrac{(T_1 - 1)}{T_1}\right\}} \left\{\bar{\eta}_1 + \dfrac{e_1}{T_1}\right\}$$

Several comments are in order. First, note that the expression in the denominator is reminiscent of a Keynesian type of multiplier phenomenon. If initially there is free trade, this multiplier effect disappears. If $T_1 > 1$, any increase in import spending increases tariff revenue. This increase in income is, in part, respent on imports, which serves further to increase tariff revenue in the next round. It is this phenomenon which makes it difficult to draw a tariff-ridden offer curve in a simple step-by-step fashion. Secondly, note that the numerator of ϵ_1 draws together two substitution terms ($\bar{\eta}_1$ in consumption and e_1/T_1 in production) which are positive, and a positive income effect. Finally, observe that the numerator of $\bar{\epsilon}_1$ consists only of the substitution terms. This is what moved me to call the shift expression $\bar{\epsilon}_1$, after using $\bar{\eta}_1$ to denote just the substitution effect in consumption. The reason why this contains only substitution terms is most readily seen in the case of initial free trade, when $\bar{\epsilon}_1$ is $(\bar{\eta}_1 + e_1)$. The term $-\bar{\epsilon}_1$ is the coefficient of $\hat{T}_1$. At initial free trade, real income can be affected by an increase in the tariff only if β, the world terms of trade, is affected and dy_1 would then equal $-M_1 d\beta$. Therefore, holding β constant (to capture the shift in the offer curve), one finds that an increase in T_1 reduces imports only by making commodity B at home more expensive and thus stimulating a reduction in consumption and an expansion in production (both substitution effects). If a tariff were initially in effect, real income would indeed be altered with β given, but as expression (9) shows, this real income change depends itself on a change in imports. It thus enters only via the multiplier phenomenon shown by the denominator in $\bar{\epsilon}_1$.

The expressions for the elasticity of country 2's offer curve, ϵ_2, and the shift in that offer curve induced by a change in T_2, $-\bar{\epsilon}_2$, being completely analogous, are not shown explicitly.

The analysis to this point has only involved changes in one country. Tariff theory is primarily concerned with the effects of tariff changes on world terms of trade, domestic prices, and real incomes. Answers to these questions can now easily be obtained by differentiating the market equilibrium condition shown in (12).

(12) $\beta M_1 = M_2$

At world prices the value of imports into each country must be equal. (Equilibrium is obtained at the intersection of the offer curves.) The relationship in terms of rates of change is shown by (13),

(13) $\hat{\beta} + \hat{M}_1 = \hat{M}_2$

and the solution for the change in the world terms of trade is found by substituting in (3) and (4) for the $\hat{M}_i$. This solution is exhibited in (14):

(14) $\hat{\beta} = \dfrac{1}{\Delta}\left\{\bar{\epsilon}_2 \hat{T}_2 - \bar{\epsilon}_1 \hat{T}_1\right\}$

$$\text{where } \Delta \equiv \epsilon_1 + \epsilon_2 - 1$$

The denominator, of course, is positive by the Marshall-Lerner conditions for stability. Once it has been established that the $\bar{\epsilon}_i$ are positive, it is easy to see that an increase in country i's import duty must serve to improve its world terms of trade (unless one of the ϵ_i is infinite). This is a standard result, not challenged by Södersten and Vind.

The crucial relationship that prompts this analysis concerns the impact of tariff changes on the relative domestic price of imports in country 1. Since $\hat{p}$ equals $\hat{\beta} + \hat{T}_1$, easy substitution into (14) yields this price change in (15).

(15) $\hat{p} = \dfrac{1}{\Delta}\left\{(\Delta - \bar{\epsilon}_1)\hat{T}_1 + \bar{\epsilon}_2 \hat{T}_2\right\}$

The question is whether, as Metzler maintained, an increase in T_1 can serve to lower p. To answer this question, it is necessary to make use of the breakdown of ϵ_1 (for it is contained in Δ) and $\bar{\epsilon}_1$ already provided. Thus a tariff can fail to be protective if the inequality shown by (16) is satisfied:

(16) $\epsilon_2 + \dfrac{m_1}{T_1\left\{1 - m_1 \dfrac{(T_1 - 1)}{T_1}\right\}} < 1$

Sufficiently small values for ϵ_2 allow this possibility.

Since this point has been challenged so strongly by Södersten and Vind, it is worthwhile to attempt a simple verbal explanation.

This is most easily done in the case of initial free trade, in which case a tariff levied by country 1 fails to be protective if $\epsilon_2 < 1 - m_1$. Consider the world market for 1's export commodity, A. In a stable market an increase in T_1 would raise A's domestic price in country 1 (and thus lower p) only if excess demand for A would be created at the initial

Otherwise, as (17) shows, an increase in the tariff rate by country 1 would, by reducing β, serve always to increase 1's real income. Although not necessary in deriving the formula for the optimum tariff, the solution for $\hat{\beta}$ in terms of the $\hat{T}_i$ shown by (14) can be substituted into (17) to obtain expression (19) for dy_1.

$$(19) \qquad dy_1 = \frac{\beta M_1}{\Delta} \left\{ \bar{\epsilon}_1[(T_1 - 1)(1 - \epsilon_2) + 1]\hat{T}_1 - \bar{\epsilon}_2[(T_1 - 1)\epsilon_1 + 1]\hat{T}_2 \right\}$$

value of the domestic price ratio, p. In country 1, the increase in T_1 would serve to lower β, i.e., improve 1's world terms of trade and therefore real income, at the initial domestic price ratio. Part of this increase in real income, $1 - m_1$, would spill over to increase 1's demand for its export commodity. This is the only source of change in demand and supply in country 1 at initial p since substitution terms do not operate. Opposed to this increased demand for A in country 1 is the reduction in net demand in country 2 as the decrease in β (at initial p) moves country 2 back along its offer curve for imports of A. (Note that 2's offer curve does not shift as, by assumption, it keeps T_2 constant at unity.) If the increase in demand for A by the home country, $1 - m_1$, exceeds the reduction in net demand abroad, given by ϵ_2, excess demand for A at initial p is created, forcing p down.

To conclude this section, consider the impact of tariff changes on country 1's real income. For this purpose, it is convenient to substitute $dM_2 - M_1 d\beta$, for the βdM_1 term found in (9). Then use (4) for dM_2 to obtain (17) as the expression for dy_1.

$$(17) \quad dy_1 = -\beta M_1 \left\{ [(T_1 - 1)(1 - \epsilon_2) + 1]\hat{\beta} + (T_1 - 1)\bar{\epsilon}_2 \hat{T}_2 \right\}$$

From this the formula for country 1's optimal tariff is obtained by noting that the rate must be such that the coefficient of $\hat{\beta}$ is zero. This immediately gives the optimal tariff formula shown in (18). Of course (18) presupposes that ϵ_2 exceeds unity.

$$(18) \qquad t_1^{opt} = \frac{1}{\epsilon_2 - 1}$$

The extra bit of information this yields is that any increase in 2's tariff rate must (by raising β) worsen country 1's real income.

II. *The Error in the Södersten-Vind Analysis*

The formal analysis presented by Södersten and Vind is not easy to follow and contains some minor errors that are not crucial.[6] The vital error is contained in the assumption made in [5], footnote 2 on p. 401. In my terminology, they are assuming that an increase in the relative domestic price of A in country i always raises i's consumption of B when income is constant in B-units. Most importantly, as I shall demonstrate below, this assumption is far from innocent, for it implies that for country 2, ϵ_2 must exceed

[6] As an example of the minor errors, according to my calculations, the coefficient of dt_1 in their equation (24), (p. 400) should read a_2 instead of a_1. Similarly, in equation (25) (p. 400) the last term in the coefficient of dt_1 should be $C_{12}(\partial C_{1m}/\partial Y_1)$ instead of $S_{12}(\partial C_{1m}/\partial Y_1)$, and the factor $(1+t_2)$ should be deleted from in front of the bracketed expression for β_2 in equation (19) (p. 399) and in between the two bracketed expressions in the coefficients for dt_2 in equation (25) (p. 400). Aside from the complexity inherent in treating this problem formally as an eleven equation model, their instructions how to proceed in their model are occasionally misleading. For example, equations (1a)–(11a) (p. 397) purport to represent differentials of equations (1)–(11) (pp. 396, 397). However, equations (6a) and (7a) merely restate equations (8) and (9). Similarly, equation (3a') (p. 398) follows not from equation (3a) (p. 397), but from (4a), with substitutions from equations (8a)–(11a) (p. 397). As a final example, equation (3a'') (p. 399) is not a rewritten form of (3a'). Rather, it follows from the balance of payments equilibrium condition with the aid of equations (1a), (2a), (6a), and (7a), (p. 397). As I say in the text, these errors are not crucial, but they do make it unnecessarily difficult to work through their model.

COMMUNICATIONS

unity. And, as we saw in condition (16), this is sufficient to rule out the Metzler effect.

Before proceeding to the proof, however, note that the model I have developed in the preceding section incorporates the same assumption about the distribution of the tariff proceeds as does the Södersten-Vind model: all proceeds are distributed to the private sector in lump-sum fashion. I stress this because Södersten and Vind claim that the difference between their results and the Metzler result derives from Metzler's assumption that the government spends the tariff proceeds according to its own arbitrary taste pattern. Furthermore, they suggest that Metzler's different result may in part be attributed to the fact that the foreign country was assumed not to levy a tariff.[7] On both counts the analysis presented in the preceding section, where Metzler's results are confirmed, adopts the same assumptions as Södersten and Vind.

The point I wish to make is perhaps best illustrated in Figure 1. To simplify, I assume that production in country 2 is represented by the endowment point, E, and is unresponsive to price changes.[8] Let the initial budget line be represented by the solid line QEN, and the initial consumption bundle by point ①. If π increases, the budget line rotates around E, becoming flatter. Suppose, instead, that at this new value for π income had been increased so that a new budget line, QV, preserves the same income in B units (OQ) as before the price change. The Södersten-Vind assumption is that the consumption bundle on budget line QV, point ②, must lie below ①. That is, the higher price for B must reduce 2's consumption of B. However, since the income effect (consume more B) runs counter to the substitution effect (consume less B) when π rises (and income in B-units remains at OQ), it would not be unusual for the consumption point to have been northeast of ①. In any case, the

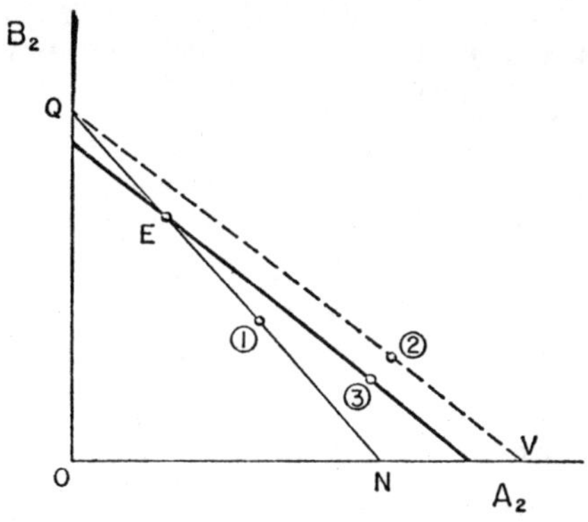

FIGURE 1

fact that the correct new budget line must pass through the production point, E, implies that if no goods are inferior the new consumption point, ③, involves an even lower consumption of B. Country 2's offer curve (not drawn) passes through E and points ① and ③ and therefore must be elastic. Södersten and Vind have implicitly assumed that $\epsilon_2 > 1$, and therefore by assumption have ruled out the possibility of Metzler's result.[9]

In conclusion consider the expression for the optimal tariff displayed by Södersten and Vind in their equation (34) [5, p. 406]. They claim that this is a new formula and, indeed, in the guise presented this appears to be the case. However, substitution reveals this to be the same expression, $1/(\epsilon_2 - 1)$ displayed in my (18) for the optimal tariff, and this is a standard result.

REFERENCES

1. R. W. JONES, "Stability Conditions in International Trade: A General Equilibrium Analysis," *Internat. Econ. Rev.*, May 1961, 2, 199–209.

2. ———, "International Capital Movements and the Theory of Tariffs and

---

[7] See [5], pp. 402–405.

[8] As the expression for ϵ_2 shows, the assumption I am making that $\epsilon_2 = 0$ serves to minimize the value of ϵ_2. I am demonstrating that this minimum value exceeds unity if the Södersten-Vind assumption that $\partial B_2/\partial(1/\pi)$ is positive is made.

[9] In equation (28) of [5], p. 401, the assertion is made that $(a_2\beta_1 - \Delta)$ is negative. This is not necessarily so if $\partial C_{2r}/\partial P$ is negative. In my terminology it can be shown that $\partial B_2/\partial(1/\pi)$ with income in B-units held constant equals $\beta M_1 \bar{\eta}_2 - A_2(1 - m_2)$. If this is assumed positive, substitution into the expression for ϵ_2 reveals that ϵ_2 must exceed unity.

Trade," *Quart. Journ. Econ.*, Feb, 1967, *81*, 399–431.

3. L. METZLER, "Tariffs, the Terms of Trade, and the Distribution of National Income," *Journ. Pol. Econ.*, Feb., 1949, 57, 1–29.

4. ———, "Tariffs, International Demand and Domestic Prices," *Journ. Pol. Econ.*, Aug., 1949, *57*, 345–51.

5. B. SÖDERSTEN AND K. VIND, "Tariffs and Trade in General Equilibrium," *Am. Econ. Rev.*, June, 1968, *58*, 394–408.

[5]

TRADE AND WELFARE IN GENERAL EQUILIBRIUM

TABLE OF CONTENTS

I. INTRODUCTION

In his 1939 article, Samuelson initiated the modern discussion of the gains from trade. Concerning himself with a small price-taking country and basing his cases on the compensation principle and the axiom of revealed preference, he established that the introduction of external trade could make all citizens better-off. His approach received a considerable amount of notice, but no further result came of it for some time. It was not until two decades later that Kemp (1962), along with Samuelson (1962), revived the subject by showing, under a more general condition, that the consumption possibility frontier of the post-trade situation lies uniformly outside that of the pre-trade situation.[1] Their findings, however, seem to call for further generalization.

Meanwhile, trade theorists have propagated the use of the "social indifference" map with the same properties as those of the "individual indifference" map. To substitute for the old tool of numerical example, Leontief (1933) provided a classic employment of this technique in his analysis of trade equilibrium. Scitovsky (1942) and Meade (1952), through their efforts to demonstrate the welfare implications of trade policies, made further contributions

---

[1] Kemp is concerned with the welfare properties of tariff-restricted trade equilibria (including as a limiting case free trade equilibria), providing a proof of the proposition for a general n-commodity case. In a separate companion paper, Samuelson illustrates the same point by the help of the famous "Baldwin" envelope (see Baldwin (1952)) for a special two-commodity case.

to the methodology, and thus stimulated a surge of similar analysis.   In the face of this development, Samuelson (1956) reexamined the conditions required to justify the fundamental concept of social indifference.   Today, many analysts are more critical than ever of this concept, but its use is still prevalent in the literature on trade and welfare.

Most of the theorists, while employing a social indifference map, assumed no allegiance to any *particular* map as a matter of course, and thus were, in reality, puristic in their conclusions.   The more policy-oriented economists, notably Meade (1955 a, b), often eschewed this nonchalant approach by invoking a specific social utility function.   Needless to say, the latter restrictive convention, though objectionable in many respects, makes it possible to evaluate the welfare of all situations without glossing over the underlying social value premises.   For instance, per capita real income as a measure of national welfare may be justified on the basis of a very special class of social utility functions.[2]

This paper is devoted to the study of trade and welfare in general equilibrium in which trade in intermediate goods and factor services, as well as the presence of non-tradeable commodities, is not excluded.[3]   For this purpose, we propose to employ a methodological device which captures the results of different approaches in one procedure.   In the following section the stage will be set for our analysis by considering a static competitive economy from a single country's viewpoint.   We shall define the basic concepts of this paper, such as, an economic situation, distribution, and competitive equilibrium.   In section III, there will be the introduction of a welfare criterion, which, with an appropriate reinterpretation, will imply each of the afore-mentioned prototypes.   In section IV, a general theorem of welfare comparison will be presented in the form of a simple formula derived from the definition of the country's excess demand, the aggregate budget constraint and the welfare criterion.   We shall then make extensive use of this theorem to analyze a number of important issues in trade and welfare.   Toward the end of the paper, we will also show that our single country's viewpoint is applicable to a group of countries and

---

[2] We refer here to the crude usage of this measure disregarding the problem of income distribution.   We shall have an occasion to discuss it again in Footnote 15.

[3] Most of the existing literature in this field still remains within the confines of the views of "trade-as-exchange-of consumer goods."   In a famous survey of trade literature Bhagwati (1964, p. 42) warns that a vast range of interesting problems applicable to economies using intermediate and produced goods, cannot get within the range of analysis until the theorists get away from the traditional picture of primary factors and integrated process of production. As he carefully notes, however, it does not follow that the present stock of knowledge will not survive the required change in the formulation of the models.   On the contrary, we should make it clear in advance that our investigation will confirm all the traditional welfare propositions in the presence of trade in non-consumer commodities.

the world as a whole under appropriate assumptions. Thus, this approach will enable us to generalize familiar theses, and, at the same time, simplify their derivations. It should be noted that, at several points, we will put forward somewhat novel propositions.

II. A TRADING ECONOMY: THE MODEL

Let us assume that there are n commodities in the world, some of which are primary factors and intermediate goods. Imagine the competitive economy of a single country engaging in trade with the rest of the world. There are three distinct classes of economic agents, namely producers, consumers, and the government. A producer is supposed to carry out a production plan which is a specification of the quantities of his inputs and outputs. Formally, let Y^j be the production set of the jth producer, which is closed in the n-dimensional commodity space and contains the origin. We assume thta it is possible for all producers together to dispose of all commodities. A consumers is supposed to carry out a consumption plan which is a specification of his consumption of commodities. A consumption plan is made subject to the constraint of the consumer's income composed of the value of his endowment of commodities, his share in producers' profits and his net transfer receipt. Let X^k be the kth consumer's consumption set, which is closed, convex and bounded below in the non-negative orthant of the n-dimensional commodity space. The set X^k is assumed to be completely pre-ordered by the kth consumer's preference relation (denoted by $\succsim^k$). No consumer is satiated in all commodities. We abstract from transportation costs and static external economies and diseconomies.

The role of the government, the third class of our economic agent, is manifold. First, it is assumed to tax and/or subsidize various economic activities, i.e., production, consumption and external trade. Secondly, it distributes income among consumers in a lump-sum fashion by changing the structure of individual shares in all income sources. For this purpose, the government is able to impose personal tax-subsidy schemes on incomes derived from the ownership of commodity endowment, the share in profits, and the net *private* transfer receipt. The government's net revenue (or cost) from all the taxes and subsidies is assumed to be disposed of by lump-sum transfers to consumers to help achieve the purpose of income redistribution.[4] Thirdly, the government carries out the production and consumption of commodities on its own. In this capacity, it is assumed to belong to the first two classes of economic

---

[4] The government's lump-sum taxes and subsidies are exempt from the distortion of price system since they effectuate nothing but the direct redistribution of income sources such as commodity endowment, profits and transfer receipt among individual consumers.

agents, i.e., producers and consumers. Together with the absence of externalities, this simplifies the problem of public production and consumption. We shall discuss this point briefly at the end of the paper.[5]

Let us now turn our eyes to the aggregate picture of our trading economy. We use the following basic notation:

x,   a non-negative n-vector of aggregate consumption.

y,   an n-vector of aggregate production; a positive (resp. negative) component denotes output (resp. input).

a,   a non-negative n-vector of aggregate endowment exogenously available to the country.

$e \equiv x - y - a$,   an n-vector of aggregate excess demand.

q,   a non-negative n-vector of world price.

p,   a non-negative n-vector of domestic price.

p_c,   a non-negative n-vector of domestic consumers' price.

p_r,   a non-negative n-vector of domestic producers' price.[6]

b,   a scalar denoting net aggregate transfer from abroad to consumers.

$Y \equiv \sum_j Y^j$,   the set of all possible y.

T,   an $n \times n$ diagonal matrix of *ad valorem* rates of tariffs (i.e., taxes or subsidies on imports and exports).

C,   an $n \times n$ diagonal matrix of *ad valorem* rates of taxes or subsidies on consumption.

R,   an $n \times n$ diagonal matrix of *ad valorem* rates of taxes or subsidies on production.

The model allows for the existence of non-tradeable commodities due to the international difference of tastes. If commodity i happens to be non-tradeable, then the ith component of vector e is identically zero. Similarly, if commodity i is *not* consumed at home, the ith component of x is identically zero, and if commodity i is not produced at home, the ith component of y is non-positive. Note also that we take into account the consumers' use of primary factors, especially in the form of leisure.[7]

It is important to understand the relationships between the four different price vectors, q, p, p_c, and p_r, pertaining to the economy under trade with the rest of the world. Needless to say, this difference arises in the presence of the governmental intervention in the private transactions via taxes and sub-

---

[5] For an alternative treatment of public production and consumption, see Diamond and Mirrlees (1971).

[6] We will consider x, y, a and e as column vectors, and p and q as row vectors in what follows.

[7] Thus, this model includes as a special case the classical setup in which primary factors, especially labor, is not tradeable.

sidies.[8] Let us denote by t_i the ith diagonal element of tariff matrix T, and by q_i and p_i the ith components of q and p respectively. We have then the arbitrage relationship

$$p_i = q_i(1 + t_i) .$$

If t_i is positive, it represents an import tax or an export subsidy depending on whether commodity i is imported or exported. If t_i is negative, it represents an export tax or an import subsidy. We can rewrite this relationship in matrix form as

(1) $$p = q(I + T)$$

where I is an identity matrix. Likewise, we have

(2) $$p_c = p(I + C)$$

(3) $$p_r = p(I + R)$$

which implicitly define the ith diagonal element c_i of matrix C and the ith diagonal element r_i of matrix R respectively. If c_i is positive (resp. negative), it indicates an tax (resp. a subsidy) on the consumption of commodity i. On the other hand, if r_i is positive (resp. negative), it represents a subsidy (resp. tax) on the production, or a tax (resp. subsidy) on the use in production, of commodity i depending on whether commodity i is an output or an input in the aggregate production process.

To delineate the posture of the economy completely, it is also necessary to take account of the external conditions with which the economy is faced. The net aggregate income transfer b stands for the country's net receipt of purchasing power from abroad available in the form of reparation, aid, personal remittance, and the like. In addition to this, we need to introduce here the concept of the "foreign environment" as a catchall terminology representing the state of technologies, tastes, commodity endowments, and the governmental policies in the rest of the world. In a limiting case in which the country is too small to affect the world market significantly, the foreign environment can be approximated by the prevailing world price of *tradeable* commodities. We refer to this special case as the state of a price-taking country without any monopoly power in world trade. In another limiting case in which the country keeps to itself in autarky, the specification of the foreign environment is still possible, but evidently irrelevant.

DEFINITION (economic situation): An economic situation (or simply situation) S is a specification of the followings.

---

[8] We assume that the unit of domestic currency is adjusted such that the exchange rate is always unity.

MICHIHIRO OHYAMA

(i)   the set of producers: Y^j for all j;
(ii) the set of consumers: $(X^k, \succsim^k)$ for all k;
(iii) the government's taxes and subsidies: (T, C, R);
(iv) the aggregate endowment and net income transfer: (a, b);
(v)   the foreign environment.

DEFINITION (distribution):   A distribution V is a specification of the percentage share of individual consumers in all income sources.[9]

Given an economic situations S and a distribution V, we assume the existence of a (usual) competitive equilibrium such that, under the prevailing prices, (a) each producer maximizes his profits over his production set; (b) each consumer maximizes his satisfaction over his budget set; and (c) all markets are cleared.[10]   To write out these conditions of an equilibrium, let a bar on top of a vector indicate its equilibrium value.   First of all, we write the equilibrium condition for producers as

$$\bar{p}_r \bar{y}^j \geq \bar{p}_r y^j \qquad \text{for all} \quad y^j \in Y^j$$

where y^j is the jth producer's production vector.   This implies the aggregate profit maximization condition

(4) $$\bar{p}_r \bar{y} \geq \bar{p}_r y \qquad \text{for all} \quad y \in Y.$$

Secondly, the equilibrium condition for cunsumers runs as

(5) $$\bar{x}^k \succsim^k x^k \qquad \text{for all} \quad x^k \in X^k \quad \text{such that} \quad \bar{p}_o \bar{x}^k \geq \bar{p}_o x^k$$

where x^k is the kth consumer's consumption vector.   Finally, in an autarkic situation, we have

(6) $$\bar{e} \leq 0 ; \qquad \bar{p}\bar{e} = 0$$

for any distribution.   In an open-economy situation, we simply have

(6') $$\bar{q}\bar{e} = b$$

for any distribution.   As a result of free-disposability and non-satiation, we may take all equilibrium vectors to be semi-positive.   Condition (6) shows the market clearance in an autarkic situation.   Some components of $\bar{e}$ in (6) may be negative as some commodities may be supplied in surplus.   On the

---

[9] Thus, if prices are given, a distribution V is a specification of the percentage share of individual consumers in the aggregate expenditure, and it can be represented by an interior point of the standard simplex.

[10] In particular, we have in mind an economy similar to the Arrow-Debreu model for the existence of competitive equilibria.   See, e.g. Debreu (1959) and Nikaidô (1968, Chapter 5). McKenzie (1959) allows for negative equilibrium prices, the possibility of which we exclude by assumption in this paper.   The demonstration of an existence theorem is, however, out of the scope of the present analysis.   The reader interested in this line of inquiry in the cotext of the present model is referred to Sontheimer (1971).

other hand, condition (6') represents the aggregate budget constraint of consumers in an open-economy situation.   A positive (resp. negative) component of $\bar{e}$ in (6') represents the import (resp. export) of a commodity.

III.   INTRODUCTION OF WELFARE CRITERION

The stage is now set to discuss the fundamentals of the present study.   To initiate the argument, consider two distinct situations, S' and S'', say.   Evidently, situation S' can be distinct from situation S'' in many different ways. We shall assume, however, that the set of consumers is given and invariant between the two situations.   This implies, among other things, that the set of consumers can be independent of the other elements of economic situation such as the government's taxes and subsidies, the foreign environment, etc.[11] With this assumption on hand, we wish to compare, from consumers' viewpoint, the welfare of the two situations S' and S''.   For this purpose, a brief detour is first necessary to pronounce on the criterion under which we plan to carry out the comparison.

Let us indicate the equilibrium vectors and other symbols relating to S' by single primes, and those relating to S'' by double primes, and, henceforth, omit bars on equilibrium vectors.   Let $E(S; V)$ be the set of tuples of equilibrium vectors $(p_o, x, \ldots)$ for a situation S and a distribution V.

DEFINITION (welfare criterion):   Situation S'' is said to be preferable to situation S' if condition $p_o'' x'' \geq p_o'' x'$ is satisfied for all tuples $(p_o', x', \ldots) \in E(S'; V')$, $(p_o'', x'', \ldots) \in E(S''; V'')$, and for all relevant distributions V' and V''.[12]

In a similar vein, the transition from situation S' to situation S'' will be occasionally said to be *beneficial*, and the reverse transition *harmful* under the same condition.   Thus, a policy change, say, is beneficial if it brings about an increase (or at worst non-decrease) in the aggregate real income in the so-called Paache backward index measure for all relevant distributions.

Caveats are in order concerning the scope of all *relevant* situations.   Needless to say, the relative desirability of a distribution for any situation can only be determined by the specification of one firm or another of social value judge-

---

[11] It should be understood that some trade in labor is in no way at variance with the given set of consumers.   At the present level of abstraction, we should be ready to account for the possibility that some kind of labor is traded internationally without affecting the set of consumers and the country's endowment of leisure.   For example, some laborers are able to offer their services for a foreign firm located inside the country.

[12] Note that the supply of primary factors is already taken care of in the expression $p_o'' x'' \geq p_o'' x'$ since individual consumption sets are defined over the exhaustive n-dimensional commodity space.

MICHIHIRO OHYAMA

ment involving the interpersonal comparison of utility. Thus, in the absence of such a specification, we must identify the set of relevant distributions with the set of all potentially feasible distributions. In this case, our definition is equivalent to the conventional Samuelson-Kennedy criterion.

LEMMA 1: *Let $p''_e x'' \geqq p''_e x'$ for all tuples $(p'_e, x', \ldots) \in E(S'; V')$, $(p''_e, x'', \ldots) \in E(S''; V'')$ and for all feasible distributions V' and V''. Then, given any distribution V' (resp. V''), there can be no distribution V'' (resp. V') such that some are strictly better-off, while others are not worse-off, in situation S' than they are in situation S''.* [13]

Proof: Consider a partition of the set of indices K of all consumers into two non-emply subsets K_1 and K_2 such that, for some distributions V' and V'',

$$x^{k_1'} \gtrsim^{k_1} x^{k_1'} \quad \text{for} \quad k_1 \in K_1$$

and

$$x^{k_2'} \succ^{k_2} x^{k_2'} \quad \text{for} \quad k_2 \in K_2,$$

where $x^{k'}$ (resp. $x^{k''}$) is an equilibrium consumption vector chosen by the kth consumer in situation S' (resp. S''). Then, from (5), we must have

$$p''_e x^{k_1'} \leqq p''_e x^{k_1'} \quad \text{for} \quad k_1 \in K_1,$$

and

$$p''_e x^{k_2'} < p''_e x^{k_2'} \quad \text{for} \quad h_2 \in K_2.$$

(Otherwise, the choice of $x^{k''}$ would be contradicted.) But this implies

$$\sum_{k \in K} p''_e x^{k''} < \sum_{k \in K} p''_e x^{k'},$$

or

$$p''_e x'' < p''_e x',$$

which contradicts the hypothesis. ||

The message is somewhat unsatisfactory in light of the compensation principle. Under the same condition, one may wish to establish the unambiguous proposition that, given any feasible distribution V', there exists a feasible distribution V'' such that none is worse-off in situation S'' than in situation S'. The latter proposition is certainly true in the special case in which all consumers have identical tastes and identical shares in all income sources as the only feasible distribution. In general, however, we cannot make this point without investigating the problem of the existence of competitive equilibrium which lies outside the scope of the present study. [14]

Alternatively, it is often assumed that there exists a certain social value judgement ordering the set of feasible distribution for each situation, and that the government redistributes income accordingly so as to achieve a best feasible

---

[13] This result is first observed by Samuelson (1950) and later generalized by Kennedy (1954). Kemp (1962) employs essentially the same reasoning in his discussion of gains from trade.

distribution. In this case, the set of relevant distribution reduces to the set of *best* feasible distributions. Thus, if the set of feasible distribution V'' contains the set of feasible distribution V', the condition given in our definition of welfare criterion evidently implies the non-deterioration of social welfare as a result of the transition from situation S' to situation S''. It is, however, only under some further assumptions that the use of a well-behaved social indifference map is known to be legitimate. Once we assume the existence of a social indifference map, we are able to abstract from individual consumers and concern ourselves only with the social consumption set X which is convex and completely pre-ordered by a social preference relation (denoted by $\gtrsim$). Relevant distribution V is then uniquely determined for each situation S, and the set of consumers is represented simply by the consumption set and preference relation, $(X; \gtrsim)$.[14] In this context, it is worthwhile to call attention to a possible property of preference relation $\gtrsim$ and its implications.

DEFINITION (convexity of preference relation): Preference relation $\gtrsim$ is said to be strongly convex if $x'' \gtrsim x'$ for distinct $x', x'' \in X$ implies $\lambda x'' + (1 - \lambda)x' > x'$ $(0 < \lambda < 1)$.[16]

LEMMA 2: *Suppose that preference relation $\gtrsim$ is strongly convex. Then, $p_c''x'' \geq p_c''x'$ implies $x'' > x'$, where x' (resp. x'') is an equilibrium aggregate consumption vector in situation S' (resp. S'').*

[14] One may, however, proceed in the desired direction as follows. Given $(p_o', x', \ldots) \in E(S'; V')$, show that it is possible to achieve a distribution V'' for situation S'' such that

$$p_o''x^{k''} = (p_o''x^{k'}/p_o''x')p_o''x''$$

where $(p_o'', x'', \ldots) \in E(S''; V'')$. Then, $p_o''x'' \geq p_o''x'$ implies

$$p_o''x^{k''} \geq (p_o''x^{k'}/p_o''x')p_o''x' = p_o''x^{k'} .$$

Thus, from (5), we obtain $x^{k''} \gtrsim^k x^{k'}$.

[15] See Samuelson (1956) and Negishi (1965). Chipman (1965) gives an extensive survey of the retated literature. Consider a limiting case where there is an additive social utility function with every consumer possessing an identical, linear homogeneous utility function. Write the social utility as

$$F(p_c) = \sum_{k \in K} u(x^k(p_c))$$

where u denotes the utility function common to all consumers and $x^k(p_c)$ the consumption vector chosen by the kth consumer at price p_o. Since u is linear-homogeneous, we obtain

$$F(p_c) = u(x(p_c)) \quad \text{where} \quad x(p_c) = \sum_{k \in K} x^k(p_c) .$$

At each price p_c, $u(p_c)$ is maximized over the set of the aggregate consumption vectors x such that $p_c x \leq p_c x(p_c)$. In this case, we have a social indifference map regardless of the state of distribution. In fact, all distributions are deemed equally good. Thus, our welfare criterion degenerates to the crude convention of measuring social welfare in terms of per capita real income with no reference to distribution.

[16] For a discussion of convex preference relation, see, for example, Debreu (1959), pp. 59–61.

Proof: To the contrary, suppose $x' \succsim x''$. Then, by the strong convexity of $\succsim$, we have $\lambda x' + (1 - \lambda)x'' \succ x''$ $(0 < \lambda < 1)$, where $\lambda x' + (1 - \lambda)x'' \in X$ by the convexity of X. But $p''_e x'' \geq p''_e x'$ implies $p''_e x'' \geq p''_e[\lambda x' + (1 - \lambda)x'']$ thereby contradicting the choice of x'' (see (5)). ||

Thus, if a social indifference map is assumed to exist with surfaces strictly convex toward the origin, our welfare criterion can be seen to give a sufficient (but by no means necessary) condition for a *strict* increase of social welfare from situation S' to situation S''. This conclusion may also be extended to the economy with non-consumable commodities provided that preference relation is strongly convex in the space of consumable commodities, and that there is no surplus in the supply of non-consumable commodities. In any case, it is vital to bear the above result in mind in interpreting the forthcoming propositions in proper relation to the traditional analyses of trade and welfare.

IV. A GENERAL THEOREM ON WELFARE COMPARISON

Leaving the discussion of welfare criterion, let us now turn to the central theme of this study. To avoid unnecessary repetition of similar reasoning, we wish to provide here a general theorem of welfare comparison focusing upon a basic formula comparing the welfare of two situations S' and S''. Simple as it is, the formula contains most of the important reculls in the area with which we are concerned, and will serve as a cornerstone of the subsequent analyses.

Suppose that S'' represents a situation under trade. Our strategy is to break down into several meaningful constituents the expression $p''_e(x'' - x')$, i.e., the change in the aggregate real income in the Paache sense involved in the transition from situation S' to situation S''. To carry this out, first recall the definition of excess demand:

(7) $$e = x - y - a .$$

Applying equations (1), (2), and (3) to situation S'', we get

(8) $$p''_e = q''(I + T'')(I + C'') ;$$

(9) $$p''_r = q''(I + T'')(I + R'') .$$

From (7) and (8), we are able to write

(10) $$p''_e(x'' - x') = q''(I + T'')(I + C'')\{(e'' + y'' + a'') - (e' + y' + a')\}$$
$$= q''(e'' - e') + q''T''(e'' - e') + q''(I + T'')C''(x'' - x')$$
$$+ q''(I + T''){(y'' - y') + (a'' - a')} .$$

In light of (1), (2), and (9), we find

(11) $$q''(I + T'') = p'' = p''_r - p''R'' .$$

Substituting (11) into (10), we obtain the desired decomposition as follows:

(12) $$p''_e(x'' - x') = q''(e'' - e') + q''T''(e'' - e') + p''C''(x'' - x')$$
$$+ p''R''(y' - y'') + p''_r(y'' - y') + p''(a'' - a')$$

THEOREM 1:   *If condition*

(13) $$q''(e'' - e') + q''T''(e'' - e') + p''C''(x'' - x')$$
$$+ p''R''(y' - y'') + p''_r(y'' - y') + p''(a'' - a') \geqq 0$$

is satisfied for all tuples $(p'_e, x', \ldots) \in E(S'; V')$, $(p''_e, x'', \ldots) \in E(S''; V'')$, and *for all relevant distributions* V' *and* V'', *situation* S'' *is preferable to situation* S'.

Proof: Straightforward from the definition of welfare criterion and equation (12). ||

Each term in condition (13) can be interpreted as a component of the real income change in the Paache sense.   Thus, the term $q''(e'' - e')$, if positive, shows the gain in the trade deficit from situation S' to situation S'' if world prices remain unchanged, or $q' = q''$.   Likewise, the terms $q''T''(e'' - e')$, $p''C''(x'' - x')$ and $p''R''(y' - y'')$ indicate in turn the gain in the government's net revenue arising from tariffs, taxes and subsidies on consumption, and taxes and subsidies on production on the assumption that $q' = q''$, $p' = p''$, $C' = C''$ and $R' = R''$.   The terms $p''_r(y'' - y')$ and $p''(a'' - a')$ show respectively the gain in producers' profits and the income from endowment if $p' = p''$ and $p'_r = p''_r$.

The lengthy expression of condition (13) may obscure its intrinsic usefulness for analytical purposes.   In what follows, however, we shall often (but not always) assume that the set of producers and the aggregate endowment are constant between situations S' and S''.[17]   This implies

$$a' = a'' ; \qquad Y' = Y'' .$$

Under this assumption, the profit maximization condition (4) implies

(14) $$p''_r(y'' - y') + p''(a'' - a') = p''_r(y'' - y') \geqq 0 .$$

Furthermore, we shall examine the effect of tariffs and other kinds of taxes and subsidies in isolation to focus upon its feature in sharp relief.   Therefore, it will be convenient to have the simplified version of the previous theorem on hand.

THEOREM 2:   *Assume that* $a' = a''$ *and* $Y' = Y''$.   (i) *Let* $C'' = R'' = 0$. *Then, if condition*

---

[17] Again, this should not be regarded as inconsistent with trade in primary factors.

MICHIHIRO OHYAMA

(15) $q''(e'' - e') + q''T''(e'' - e') \geqq 0$

is satisfied, situation S'' is preferable to situation S'.   (ii) *Let* $T'' = R'' = 0$.
Then, if condition

(16) $q''(e'' - e') + p''C''(x'' - x') \geqq 0$

is satisfied, situation S'' is preferable to situation S'.   (iii) *Let* $T'' = C'' = 0$.
Then, if condition

(17) $q''(e'' - e') + p''R''(y' - y'') \geqq 0$

is satisfied, situation S'' is preferable to situation S'.

Proof: Straightforward from Theorem 1 and (14). ||

Note that, in the statement of Theorem 2, we have tacitly avoided the complete enumeration of conditions as found in Theorem 1.   In order to alleviate scholastic wordiness, we shall follow this convention hereafter in the belief that no confusion is thereby incurred.

Now, suppose that S', as well as S'', represents an open-economy situation. By virtue of (6'), we can then write

(18) $q''(e'' - e') = (b'' - b') + (q' - q'')e'$

where the term $(b'' - b')$ indicates the gain in the net aggregate transfer from abroad, and the term $(q' - q'')e'$ the terms of trade improvement in the Laspeyres sense, from situation S' to situation S''.[18]   In this case, we are able to rewrite condition (13) accordingly.   In particular, conditions (15)–(17) become

(15') $(b'' - b') + (q' - q'')e' + q''T''(e'' - e') \geqq 0$;

(16') $(b'' - b') + (q' - q'')e' + p''C''(x'' - x') \geqq 0$;

(17') $(b'' - b') + (q' - q'')e' + p''R''(y' - y'') \geqq 0$.

We shall discuss in detail the more important economic implications of these results in the following pages.

V.   THE GAINS FROM TRADE REVISITED

Some trade is preferable to no trade.   Although this is one of the most familiar dicta in economics, one must be careful about the exact bearing of the adjective "some".   For instance, Bhagwati (1968 a) elucidates a distinction between trade restricted by tariffs and trade restricted by taxes and subsidies on domestic consumption and production.   Let us start out by restating the

[18] Note that if the price of an export (resp. import) commodity increases (resp. decreases) from situation S' to situation S'', the term $(q' - q'')e'$ will have to be, *ceteris paribus*, positive.

TRADE AND WELFARE IN GENERAL EQUILIBRIUM   49

celebrated theorem, originally formalized by Kemp (1962) and Samuelson (1962).   We use

DEFINITION (free trade):   Free trade is an open economy situation with neither tariffs nor *domestic* taxes and subsidies, i.e. $T = C = R = 0$.

With this in mind, we are able to state

PROPOSITION 1:   (i) *Free trade is preferable to no trade.*   (ii) *Trade restricted by taxes on imports and/or exports is preferable to no trade.*[19]

But we can in fact establish a more general proposition which applies to trade under tariffs comprising subsidies as well as taxes.   Let us introduce

DEFINITION (self-financing tariffs):   Tariffs are said to be self-financing if the net tariff revenue is non-negative.

Needless to say, there are self-financing tariffs when trade subsidies are virtually financed out of the proceeds from trade taxes.   To isolate the gains from trade, we assume that the net aggregate transfer is null.

PROPOSITION 2:   *Trade under self-financing tariffs is preferable to no trade.*

Proof: We identify no trade with situation S' and trade under self-financing tariffs with situation S'' in Theorem 2-(i).   As we assume $b'' = q''e'' = 0$, we can rewrite condition (15) as

$$q''T''e'' - p''e' \geq 0 .$$

Note that $q''T''e''$ is the net tariff revenue which is assumed to be non-negative. From (6), $e' \leq 0$.   Since $p'' \geq 0$, condition (15) is satisfied. ||

Proposition 1 follows at once as a corollary.   Clearly, the proof remains valid even if some commodities are free and some others are not available in the pre-trade situation.   Thus, proposition 2 covers trade arising from "vent for surplus" (see Myint (1958)) as well as trade based upon availabilities (see Kravis (1956)).   To our knowledge, this is the most comprehensive result ever obtained on the gains from trade.[20]

Let us turn to trade restricted by taxes and subsidies on consumption or production.   It differs from trade restricted by tariffs in that it creates a discrepancy between consumers' price and producers' price in the domestic market.   In the words of Bhagwati and Ramaswami (1963), trade restricted by *domestic* taxes and subsidies brings in perverse distortions along with trade, while trade restricted by tariffs simply opens up the country.   This generates a subtle, but definite dissimilarity between the two situations because of the

[19] By the same token, trade restricted by quotas is preferable to no trade.   See Kemp (1964), p. 166.

[20] Both Kemp and Samuelson avoid the discussion of trade with subsidies.

fact that consumers' price *counts* in the ultimate analysis of welfare economics as discussed above (Section III).

Now, let autarky correspond to situation S', and trade restricted by domestic taxes and subsidies to situation S'' in Theorem 2-(ii) or 2-(iii). We then obtain

PROPOSITION 3:   *If condition*

(19) $$p''C''(x'' - x') \geq 0$$

is satisfied, trade restricted by taxes and subsidies on consumption is preferable to no trade.

PROPOSITION 4:   *If condition*

(20) $$p''R''(y' - y'') \geq 0$$

is satisfied, trade restricted by taxes and subsidies on production is preferable to no trade.[21]

The proofs are straightforward from Theorem 2-(ii) or 2-(iii) and omitted here.   Concerning Proposition 3, we may presume

$$c_i'' \geq 0 \quad \text{if} \quad e_i'' > 0; \quad c_i'' \leq 0 \quad \text{if} \quad e_i'' < 0$$

since taxes and subsidies are supposed to restrict trade.   Thus, for instance, condition (19) will be satisfied if $x_i'' \geq x_i'$ for all i such that $e_i'' > 0$, and if $x_i'' \leq x_i'$ for all i such that $e_i'' < 0$.   An interesting special case is the situation in which taxes are levied only on the consumption of foreign luxuries unavailable in autarky.   Another less interesting special case is an exchange economy in which production has no role to play.   Generally speaking, however, the sign restriction on the matrix C'' is not sufficient to exclude the possibility that condition (19) fails to hold.   A similar conclusion will apply to Proposition 4.   To push this point further, Bhagwati (1968 a) constructs examples in which no trade is preferable to trade restricted by domestic tax-subsidy schemes.

Thus, it is not correct to presume that restricted trade is preferable to no trade regardless of the manner of restriction.   *A fortiori*, it is fallacious to say that *any* trade is preferable to no trade.   Consider for example a predatory trade which involves free transfer of national scarce resources.   We have ruled this out in this section by assuming the absence of (negative or positive) income transfer to consumers.   But we have not thereby eliminated situations not

---

[21] These two propositions correspond to the result of Kemp and Negishi (1970, theorems 3 and 4), which came to our notice after the completion of this study.   They interpret conditions (19) and (20) rather narrowly assuming that the same tax-subsidy scheme exists before and after trade.   As is clear from the derivation of these conditions, this assumption is not necessary.   We can freely identify situation S' with any autarkic situation in regard to the domestic taxes and subsidies.

quite dissimilar to a predatory trade.   Take for instance trade saddled with tariffs which are not self-financing.   It occurs only if the government finances the net tariff cost by lump-sum taxes, and therefore resembles a combination of trade and negative income transfer.   The autarkic situation may well be better than such trade.

VI.   THE TERMS OF TRADE IMPROVEMENT AND PRICE DIVERGENCE

It is a common presumption that the gains from trade will be greater, the more the external prices "diverge" from those of the autarkic state.   Samuelson (1939) muses over the problem, but quickly leaves it only asserting that his answer is in the affirmative.   Kemp (1964) suggests a useful concept of price divergence; Krueger and Sonnenschein (1967) adopt Kemp's concept to substantiate the price divergence conjecture to some extent; and yet Kemp (1969, p. 266) finally concludes that this speculation is false.   In this section, we shall generalize Kemp's definition of price divergence, and argue that the classical conjecture is not entirely unfounded.

We wish, however, first to clarify the welfare implication of the terms of trade improvement.   It will turn out to be fundamental to the price divergence thesis.   Let q' and q'' be the external price vectors found in two different trading situations, S' and S''.   Suppose that there are no tariffs and no domestic taxes and subsidies in both the situations, and that an autonomous improvement of the terms of trade in the Laspeyres sense takes place in the transition from S' to S'' with everything else being unchanged.   It is then immediate to reestablish the noted Krueger-Sonnenschen theorem in the present general context.

PROPOSITION 5:   *If free trade prevails, the terms of trade improvement in the Laspeyres sense is beneficial.*[22]

Proof: By hypothesis, Theorem 2 is applicable.   Let $T'' = C'' = R'' = 0$ and $b' = b''$.   Then, conditions (15')–(17') reduce to $(q' - q'')e' \geqq 0$.   As noted above, the terms of trade improvement from S' to S'' means $(q' - q'')e' > 0$, and the condition is satisfied with strict inequality. ||

To proceed to a rehabilitation of the price divergence thesis, we want to be able to compare alternative external prices in their relation to the autartic price in an appropriate manner.   For this purpose, we propose to normalize all price vectors such that their components add up to unity.   This procedure is necessary only for the rest of this section in which we continue to concern

[22] See Krueger and Sonnenschein (1967), pp. 123-124, and also Kemp (1969), pp. 262-265. Our theorem 2 gives a more general result regarding a trading situation with tariffs or other taxes and subsidies.

52   MICHIHIRO OHYAMA

ourselves with free trade situations *vis-a-vis* the autarkic situation.[23]   Let p^0 be
the autarkic price vector.   For any external price vector q, one can define a
diagonal matrix D such that

(21) $$q = p^0(I + D) .$$

Denoting by d_i the ith diagonal entry of D, we then have

$$d_i = (q_i - p_i^0)/p_i^0 .$$

In the following, we shall associate D (resp. d_i) consistently with q (resp. q_i).
For example, we shall write

$$q' = p^0(I + D') , \qquad q'' = p^0(I + D'') ;$$
$$d_i' = (q_i' - p_i^0)/p_i^0 , \qquad d_i'' = (q_i' - p_i^0)/p_i^0 , \quad \text{etc.}$$

Let us consider

DEFINITION (price divergence):   An external price vector q'' is said to diverge
more from the autarkic price vector p^0 than does q' if
   (i) $d_i'' \leq d_i'$ for all i such that $d_i' < 0$;
   (ii) $d_i'' \geq d_i'$ for all i such that $d_i' > 0$;
   (iii) $d_i'' = d_i'$ for all i such that $d_i' = 0$
with at least one strict inequality.

This definition seems intuitively natural as a characterization of the notion
of price divergence, and contains the concept of Kemp (1969, p. 266) as a
special case.   According to Kemp, q'' is said to diverge from p^0 by more than
does q' if q'' can be expressed as a convex combination of q'' and p^0, i.e.

$$q' = \lambda q'' + (1 - \lambda)p^0 \quad (0 < \lambda < 1) .$$

Obviously, this condition is satisfied if and only if $\lambda d_i'' = d_i'$ for all i in our
definition.

Given the autarkic price vector p^0, let us now define a binary relation "ν"
such that $q''\nu q'$ means "q'' is more divergent from p^0 than is q'."   One can
easily show that the relation "ν" satisfies transitivity.   Given a reference external price vector q^0 in addition, we may define a set of external prices

$$Q(p^0, q^0) = \{q \mid q^\nu q^0\} \cup \{q^0\} .$$

For $q \in Q(p^0, q^0)$, we introduce the hypothesis.

(H) $d_i < 0$ for all i with $e_i > 0$;
                     $d_i > 0$ for all i with $e_i < 0$

where e_i is the ith component of excess demand vector e associated in equilibrium with price vector q.   This means that the autarkic prices of importables

---

[23] The price normalization is permissible when we assume away all taxes and subsidies.

are higher and those of exportables are lower than the corresponding external prices.   It also implies

$$e_i \gtreqless 0 \quad \text{according as} \quad e_i^0 \gtreqless 0$$

where e_i^0 is the ith component of vector e^0 associated with the reference price vector q^0.   This means that the import-export pattern remains invariable for all $q \in Q(p^0, q^0)$.[24]   The price divergence conjecture may now be formalized as

PROPOSITION 6:   *Under hypothesis* (H), *for any* $q', q'' \in Q(p^0, q^0)$ *such that* $q''{}^\nu q'$, *free trade under price vector* q'' *is preferable to free trade under* q'.

Proof: Let S' represent free trade under q', and S'' free trade under q''. By hypothesis, we then have

$$d_i' - d_i'' \geqq 0 \quad \text{for all } i \text{ such that} \quad e_i' > 0 \, ;$$
$$d_i' - d_i'' \leqq 0 \quad \text{for all } i \text{ such that} \quad e_i' < 0 \, .$$

Hence, form (21)

$$(q' - q'')e' = p^0(D' - D'')e' > 0 \, .$$

That is, q'' represents a terms of trade improvement in relation to q', and the desired conclusion follows from Proposition 5. ||

Note that Proposition 6 is stated so as to capture "the greater, the more" property of the price divergence thesis.   In fact, we may suppose $q'{}^\nu q^0$ and conclude that free trade under q' is preferable to free trade under q^0, and that since $q''{}^\nu q'$, free trade under q'' is *more* preferable than free trade under q' to free trade under q^0.   In this case, we also note

$$(q^0 - q'')e^0 > (q^0 - q')e^0 > 0 \, .$$

In words, q'' means a greater terms of trade improvement over q^0 then does q'.   The converse of this relationship is, however, generally untenable as illustrated by Krueger and Sonnenschein (1967, p. 127).   But consider a subset $\bar{Q}$ of $Q(p^0, q^0)$ such that either $q''{}^\nu q''$ or $q''{}^\nu q'$ must hold for $q', q'' \in \bar{Q}$.   The set $\bar{Q}$ is not empty since, given p^0 and q^0, one can always find a pair of price vectors for which the specification is satisfied.   Now suppose $(q^0 - q'')e^0 > (q^0 - q')e^0$ and $q''{}^\nu q''$.   The former implies

$$(q' - q'')e^0 > 0 \, .$$

---

[24] These assumptions are not at all novel in the literature on the pattern of trade.   They reflect the doctrine of comparative advantage that a country's pattern of trade is determined by its autarkic cost structure *vis-a-vis* the external cost structure.   As Inada (1967) demonstrates, however, the possibility of locally unique multiple equilibria undermines their intuitive plausibility.

54   MICHIHIRO OHYAMA

But, under hypothesis (H), the latter implies $q'_i - q''_i \leq 0$ for $e^0_i > 0$ and $q'_i - q''_i \geq 0$ for $e^0_i < 0$ yielding a contradiction. Thus, we can generalize the trasitivity theorem entertained by Krueger and Sonnenschein as follows.

PROPOSITION 7: *Given p^0 and q^0, and under hypothesis* (H), *more of the terms of trade improvement is preferable to less of it if brought about by a shift within a subset $\bar{Q}$ of the price set $Q(p^0, q^0)$.*

To illustrate the purpose of this seemingly pedantic section, let us consider a small country who exports a few primary goods (e.g., tea and textiles), and imports a large number of intermediate goods and factor inputs (e.g., machines and oil) unavailable in the autarkic state. For such a country, the higher the world prices of tea and textiles, or lower those of machines and oil, the greater will be, *ceteris paribus*, the gains from free trade *unambiguously*. The country's technology and preference structure are such that it cannot change its obvious import-export pattern under all circumstances. The price divergence thesis is perhaps meant to convey this kind of message, and there is no reason to disregard the grain of truth it carries.

VII.   RANKING OF POLICIES UNDER TRADE

Tariffs and other forms of the government intervention in the economy have furnished one of the most exciting topics for economists. For example, using the two-by-two model of international trade, trade theorists have rigorously established that, under certain fundamental conditions, an increase in the level of tariffs will improve the country's terms of trade, but will diminish the volume of exports.[25] In the present study, however, we are not directly concerned with the result of comparative statics *per se*. Rather, the burden of this section is to derive, from our general theorem, some additional welfare statements regarding ranking of policies under trade.

We compare here two situations under trade which differ from each other only in the government's taxes and subsidies, (T, C, R). Thus, Theorem 2 is applicable with $b' = b''$, and conditions (15')–(17') simplify to

(15'') $(q' - q'')e' + q''T''(e'' - e') \geq 0 ;$

(16'') $(q' - q'')e' + p''C''(x'' - x') \geq 0 ;$

(17'') $(q' - q'')e' + p''R''(y' - y'') \geq 0 .$

To refresh memory, the first term on the left-hand side of each condition represents the terms of trade change occuring in the transition from S' to S''. The second term, on the other hand, expresses the complicated effect of the

[25] See, for example Mundell (1960), pp. 86–90, and Jones (1969).

change in the volume and composition of trade, consumption, or production. When the change in profits $p''_r(y'' - y')$ is of the second-order magnitude, conditions (15″)–(17″) correspond to the dichotomy of welfare change *a la* Meade (1955a).

It is conceivable and often likely that the two effects work in the opposite directions. First consider free trade as situation S'. The introduction of, say, some protective tariffs may contract the country's volume of trade, but improve the terms of trade. Consider the latter situation with tariffs as situation S'', and suppose that, in the presence of a well-behaved social indifference map, condition (15′) is satisfied. Then, in view of Theorem 2-(i), the tariffs will be said to be beneficial. Given such tariffs, one may proceed to examine the welfare effect of successive increases (or decreases) in the level of tariffs—each time applying Theorem 2-(i) as above—until condition (15′) is no longer tenable. This process of searching for the *optimal* level of tariffs underlies the reasonings of the MacDougal-Jasay cases for curtailing foreign investment, as well as the Bickerdike-Edgeworth argument for protective tariffs, envisioned in the simpler models of trade.[26] The same conjecture will also be applied to the restriction of trade by means of taxes and subsidies on domestic consumption or production.[27]

The country may, however, be too small to affect the terms of trade significantly via a change in the government's taxes and subsidies. For simplicity, suppose that the world price of tradeable commodities is completely independent of the country's imports and exports. On this assumption of a price-taking country, we shall investigate various policy problems for the rest of this section. To start with, consider Kemp's argument (1964) that the lower the level of tariffs, the greater will be the gains from trade in this special case. As Bhagwati (1968) points out, this conclusion is not generally supportable. From Theorem 2-(i), we can instead state

PROPOSITION 8: *If condition*

$$(22) \qquad\qquad q''T''(e'' - e') \geqq 0$$

is satisfied, a change in tariffs (and the abolition of domestic taxes and subsidies if any) from situation S' to situation S'' is beneficial for a price-taking country.

Proof: Since the world price of tradeable commodities is constant, we have $q'e' = q''e'$. Therefore, condition (15″) reduces further to (22). ‖

Consider, in particular, a uniformly proportionate variation of tariffs on the

---

[26] Jones (1967) presents a synthesis of the two cases in a capital-mobile, Heckscher-Ohlin model.

[27] Provided, of course, that there is a non-empty set of domestic tax-subsidy schemes preferable to free trade, not to mention the autarkic state.

MICHIHIRO OHYAMA

assumption that situation S' is possessed of some tariffs T'. In this case we have

$$T'' = \alpha T' \quad (\alpha > 0) .$$

Condition (22) can therefore be rewritten as

$$q''T''e'' \geq \alpha q'T'e' .$$

That is, the rate of increase (resp. decrease) in the net tariff revenue is not less (resp. greater) than the uniform rate of tariff increase (resp. decrease).

We can simplify conditions (16″) and (17″) in a similar fashion. If $T'' = C'' = R'' = 0$, these conditions are all satisfied by equality. Hence, we are able to state

PROPOSITION 9: *Free trade is preferable to any manner of restricted trade for a price-taking country.*

In practice, the government often pursues policies to achieve specific objectives of its own.[28] For instance, it may wish to raise a fixed amount of revenue by means other than lump-sum taxes.[29] The commodity tax structure which minimizes the harm to consumers in such a case is investigated by Dixit (1970). One of his results can be extended to the present model with considerable gains in generality as well as in interpretation.

PROPOSITION 10: *Given a fixed amount of government's revenue, trade with appropriate uniform-rate taxes on consumption is preferable, for a price-taking country, to a situation with tariffs and/or other domestic taxes and subsidies.*

Proof: Let S'' be the trading situation with uniform-rate taxes on consumption, and S' any other situation. Since a fixed amount of government's revenue is raised in both S' and S'', we have $b' = b'' = q''e'' = q'e'$. For a price-taking country, we observe

$$p''C''(x'' - x') = p''C''(e'' + y'' + a'' - e' - y' - a')$$
$$= c''q''(e'' - e') + c''p''(y'' - y')$$
$$= c''p''_r(y'' - y')$$

where c'' is the common rate of taxes on consumption such that $c''p''x'' = -b''$. Hence, from conditions (4) and (16″), follows the assertion. ||

This result shows that if the government is to raise a fixed amount of revenue, a uniform-rate consumption tax scheme is the appropriate policy optimal among all possible mixes of tariffs and domestic taxes and subsidies. Aside from its allowance for intermediate and non-tradeable commodities, Proposition 10 is, therefore, more comprehensive than the statement that a uniform consumption

[28] Bhagwati (1971) gives a detailed taxonomic account of some of such policies.
[29] Perhaps for the purpose of reparation payment or economic aid to the rest of the world.

tax structure is better than differentiated consumption tax structure as a means to provide the government with a given sum of purchasing power.[30]

On occasions the government may also wish to restrict the value of certain imports or exports, the value of certain consumptions, and the value of certain outputs or inputs at some fixed levels other than those of free trade. The policy problems which arise under such circumstances are discussed by Johnson (1964) and later elaborated by Ray (1971). Our method enables us again to give a thoroughgoing treatment of these issues.

PROPOSITION 11: *Given a fixed value of certain imports (resp. exports), trade with appropriate uniform-rate taxes or subsidies on those imports (resp. exports) is preferable, for a price-taking country, to a situation with other tariffs and/or domestic taxes and subsidies.*

Proof: Consider trade with appropriate uniformate tariffs as S'', and any other situation as S'. Let t'' be the common rate of tariffs applied to the group of imports or exports the value of which is to be restricted. Let $\hat{q}''$ be an n-vector obtained from q'' by merely replacing the prices of non-restricted commodities with zeros. By hypothesis, we then get

$$q''T''(e'' - e') = t''(\hat{q}''e'' - \hat{q}''e')$$

where $\hat{q}''e''$ and $\hat{q}'e'$ indicate the given value of imports or exports of the commodities under restriction. Since $\hat{q}'e' = \hat{q}''e'$ for a price-taking country, condition (22) is satisfied by equality. ||

Likewise, we can establish

PROPOSITION 12: *Given a fixed value of consumption of certain tradeable commodities, trade with appropriate uniform-rate taxes or subsidies on the consumption of those commodities is preferable, for a price-taking country, to a situation with tariffs and/or other domestic taxes and subsidies.*

PROPOSITION 13: *Given a fixed value of output (resp. input) of certain tradeable commodities, trade with appropriate uniform-rate taxes or subsidies on the output (resp. input) of those commodities is preferable, for a price-taking country, to a situation with tariffs and/or other domestic taxes and subsidies.*[31]

---

[30] Dixit considers this problem in the context of a closed economy on the assumption that all supply prices are constant and that there is a positive net transfer of purchasing power to consumers from somewhere like manna from the heaven. For a closed economy in which we have no terms of trade effect to worry about, Dixit's restrictive assumption is in fact unessential to the desired result.

[31] Note that these two propositions are concerned only with the case where the constrained variable is the value of consumption or production of *tradeable* commodities. The result does not extend to the case with restricted value of consumption or production of non-tradeable commodities.

Finally, it is most conceivable that tariffs and other forms of restrictive measures are invoked by the government to fix the volume of certain imports or exports, the volume of certain consumptions, and the volume of certain outputs or inputs at some assigned levels other than those of free trade.   Working with a two-commodity model, Johnson (1964) illustrates the principle that tariffs are superior to domestic taxes and subsidies for the purpose of restricting the volume of imports.   Similarly, Corden (1957) shows that a production subsidy is less costly than a tariff in achieving a given level of the import-competing production.   Bhagwati and Srinivasan (1969) study the case in which the use of a factor in production is restricted as well as the case in which the consumption of a commodity is the constrained variable.   It is an easy matter to generalize these diverse results and place them in the common analytical perspective of this paper.[32]

PROPOSITION 14:   *Given a fixed volume of certain imports (resp. exports), trade with appropriate tariffs on those imports (resp. exports) is preferable, for a price-taking country, to a situation with other tariffs and/or domestic taxes and subsidies.*

Proof: Let the trading situation with appropriate tariffs be represented by S'', and any other situation by S'.   Since the volume of restricted imports or exports is given and invariable for both S' and S'', we have $e_i' = e_i''$ for $t_i'' \neq 0$, implying that condition (22) is satisfied by equality. ||

Similarly, we can prove

PROPOSITION 15:   *Given a fixed volume of certain consumptions, trade with appropriate taxes or subsidies on those consumptions is preferable, for a price-taking country, to a situation with tariffs and/or other domestic taxes and subsidies.*

PROPOSITION 16:   *Given a fixed volume of certain outputs (resp. inputs), trade with appropriate taxes or subsidies on those outputs (resp. inputs) is preferable, for a price-taking country, to a situation with tariffs and/or other domestic taxes and subsidies.*

Propositions 11–16 confirm the point recognized by Bhagwati (1971) that when distortions have to be introduced into the economy in order to constrain the value of certain variables, the optimal (or least-cost) method of doing this is to choose that policy-intervention which creates the distortion affecting directly the constrained variable.   In a controversial article, Lipsey and Lancaster (1956–1957) claim that there is no *a priori* way to judge between sub-optimal situations.   Their claim is valid only if little is known *a priori*.   In fact, our

---

[32] Tan (1971) also extends these results to three special models which allow for inter-industry linkages, the use of intermediate goods, and non-tradeable commodities. Our method provides an alternative and more general treatment of the problem.

results suggest that policy makers should be able to survive by the help of their wisdom and expert knowledge.[33]

VIII. ECONOMIC GROWTH AND UNILATERAL TRANSFER

We have so far confined our attention to the economy with immutable technology and constant endowment. From the standpoint of this study, however, there is no special reason for us to adhere to this convention. After all, technology, as well as endowment, is just one of the structural determinants of the economy such as the foreign environment, the government taxes and subsidies, etc. Technological progress, along with endowment expansion, serves as a major factor in economic growth which is supposed to increase economic welfare under ordinary circumstances.[34] Nonetheless, they can be actually harmful to a country engaged in external trade. It is because of this ambiguity that we wish to discuss economic growth and also touch upon the comparable transfer problem.

Let us consider here trading situations with only tariffs since our method will apply readily to other cases. Suppose that an economic growth has changed situation S' into situation S''. The difference between the two is assumed to consist only of some technological progress and endowment expansion giving rise to the economic growth. Thus, we have to leave the hypothesis of Theorem 2 and instead postulate

$$a'' \geq a' \quad (a'' \neq a') ; \qquad Y'' \supset Y' \quad (Y'' \neq Y') .$$

From Theorem 1, we obtain

PROPOSITION 17: *If condition*

$$(23) \qquad (q' - q'')e' + q''T''(e'' - e') + p''\{(y'' - y') + (a'' - a')\} \geq 0$$

is satisfied, the economic growth is beneficial.

Proof: By assumption, we have $C'' = R'' = 0$, and therefore, $p''_r = p''$. Also, $b' = b''$ implies $q''(e'' - e') = (q' - q'')e'$. With these relationships, condition (13) simplifies to (23). ||

Note that the third term on the left-hand side of condition (23) contains the gain from the growth and is assumed to be positive. We cannot, however,

---

[33] Likewise, Bhagwati and Ramaswami (1963) asserts that a tariff is not necessarily superior to free trade in the presence of domestic distortions. But this assertion is also misleading. Using the same model, Ohyama (1972), along with Kemp and Negishi (1969), demonstrates the existence of a tariff superior to free trade.

[34] In this statement we consider endowment expansion as the phenomena such as the natural growth of cattle and timber woods. Naturally, we must except population growth which affects the set of consumers.

60   MICHIHIRO OHYAMA

be so sure of the sign of the first and second terms. Bhagwati (1958), for instance, argues that economic growth may lead to a sufficiently accute terms of trade deterioration imposing a loss of real income to override the primary gain from the growth itself. He aptly names this phenomenon "immiserizing growth".[35] Appropriately reinterpreting Theorem 1, we readily get

PROPOSITION 18: *If condition*

$$(24) \qquad (q'' - q')e'' + q'T'(e' - e'') - p'\{(y'' - y') + (a'' - a')\} \geq 0$$

is satisfied, the economic growth is harmful.

Now, the term $(q'' - q')e''$, if positive, measures the terms of trade deterioration in the Paache sense due to the economic growth. On the other hand, the term $p'\{(y'' - y') + (a'' - a')\}$ measures the gain in profits and endowment income in the Laspeyres sense. In the absence of tariffs, immiserizing growth will occur if

$$(q'' - q')e'' \geq p'\{(y'' - y') + (a'' - a')\}$$

that is, if the unfavorable terms of trade effect outweighs the growth effect. Thus, an export-biased expansion may not be felicitous when the world is not ready to absorb the additional output only with a moderate fall in price.

Consider now a small growth in a price-taking country which does not affect the world price of tradeable commodities. Under free trade there can be no dimunition of the growth gain. If there are tariffs, however, even a country without any monopoly power in world trade is not completely exempt from immiserizing growth. Since we assume $T' = T''$, sufficient condition for that eventuality is written as

$$q'T'e' - q''T''e'' \geq p'\{(y'' - y') + (a'' - a')\} \ .$$

The left hand-side of this condition, if positive, represents a reduction in the net tariff revenue brought about by the economic growth. Johnson (1967) shows that a technological progress in the domestic production of protected import-competing industry can actually hurt the country's economic welfare through a decrease in the tariff revenue.[36]

Receiving a unilateral transfer *in kind* from abroad resembles, at first sight, an autonomous expansion of the country's endowment. In fact, the condition for a beneficial transfer will take the same form as condition (23). This

---

[35] Earlier economists were as well aware of this possibility. For instance, Edgeworth (1894, p. 40) discussed the possible adverse consequence of a technological progress in the export industries attributing the paradox to John S. Mill.

[36] Bhagwati (1968 b) extends this possibility to the case of domestic distortions such as external economies and diseconomies and inter-industry factor reward differentials which we assume away in this paper. The underlying logic is, however, the same as in the case of tariffs.

TRADE AND WELFARE IN GENERAL EQUILIBRIUM   61

resemblance is, of course, rather superficial, and fades away as soon as one realizes that a transfer receipt in kind gives rise simultaneously to the contraction of endowment in the rest of the world. Its welfare effect will differ depending on the nature of the commodities that are transferred.[37] In case of a transfer in purchasing power, it is established in the context of a simpler model of trade that if certain fundamental assumptions are satisfied, "immiserizing" transfer receipt will never take place under free trade.[38] This, however, does not seem to be the case in the presence of tariffs.

Suppose that S' now corresponds to a situation with no foreign transfer and S'' to the same situation except for a transfer receipt b''. We may reinterpret Theorem 1 to obtain

PROPOSITION 19: *If condition*

$$(25) \qquad (q'' - q')e'' + q'T'(e' - e'') + p'(y' - y'') \geqq b''$$

is satisfied, the transfer receipt is harmful.

If world prices happen to be unchanged in the face of the transfer, condition (25) becomes

$$q'T'e' - q''T''e'' \geqq b''$$

meaning that the reduction in the tariff revenue be at least as large in value as the transfer receipt itself.[39] This condition may be fulfilled if some tariff-free tradeables are inferior in social consumption. From a practical point of view, however, it is more interesting to observe that a transfer receipt produces an additional welfare effect in the form of chainging tariff revenue on top of the obvious direct effect and the much discussed terms of trade effect. This point is hardly recognized in the literature on the transfer problem.[40]

We have so far assumed that tariffs are unchanged in the face of economic growth or unilateral transfer. But suppose that the sole objective of tariffs is to restrict the volume of imports or exports at some assigned level. Then, tariffs are to be modified so as to achieve this objective as economic growth or transfer receipt tends to affect the country's external trade. So far as this modification of tariffs is appropriately carried out, economic growth, as well as transfer receipt, is bound to be beneficial for a price-taking country. To see this point, note that the first two terms of condition (23) vanish to zero

---

[37] One must distinguish the transfer of tradeable commodities from that of non-tradeable commodities.

[38] See for example Mundell (1960), pp. 79–80.

[39] In this special case, the term $p'(y' - y'')$, as well as $(q'' - q')e''$, vanishes to zero. In fact, $p'y' \geqq p'y''$, but $p'y' = p''y' \leqq p''y'' = p'y''$.

[40] See Samuelson (1952, 1954), which investigate the terms of trade effect of a transfer payment. Ohyama (1970) provides a supplementing analysis pointing out the tertiary effect through a change in the volume and composition of trade under tariffs.

62   MICHIHIRO OHYAMA

under such a circumstance.   The same conclusion will also hold for a price-taking country with domestic taxes and subsidies designed to restrict the volume of certain consumptions, outputs, and inputs at some given level.

IX.   THE INFANT INDUSTRY ARGUMENT

We have already established that free trade is preferable to any other situation for a price-taing country.   Underlying this free-trade proposition, however, is the assumption that the productive capacity of the country is unaffected by the volume and composition of its foreign trade.   This assumption is at best questionable at times: it has indeed invited persistent challenges since the days of Hamilton and List.   These challenges have culminated in a legitimate case for protection.   The infant industry argument, as it is so-called, maintains that, in some industries, producers (or the firms) learn from the experience thereby adding to efficiency and expanding the basis of national productive capacity through time.   If free trade is expected to damage or extirpate such industries in their "infantile" stage through foreign competition, gains from trade must be weighed against the future benefit of the learning processes to be forgone.   The free-trade proposition is no longer tenable without qualifications.

Following Kemp (1960), let us digress to classify the relevant learning processes into two familiar categories.   A learning process is internal to the firm if it helps to remunerate only the firm which actually carries on production. In this case, we shall speak of dynamic internal economies.   Correspondingly, a process is external to the firm if the experience is non-appropriable, and necessarily benefits other firms inside (and perhaps also outside) the industry. We shall then speak of dynamic external economies.   Kemp asserts that, under certainty and perfect markets, the existence of dynamic *internal* economies can never be the pretext for protection.   But as Negishi (1968) and Ray (1970) point out,[41] Kemp's conclusion hinges crucially on his interpretation of Bastable's test for the legitimacy of infant industry protection.   According to his interpretation, Bastable's test requires that the future gain accruing to the matured industry be sufficient to compensate present cost falling on the infant industry during the learning period.   Kemp thus views Bastable's test only in terms of the producers' profitability in the long-run.   No wonder that the profit incentive is enough to carry out the venture which passes such a test.   It is, however, not the producers' profitability, but the consumers' welfare that counts in deciding upon the propriety of protection.   We wish to reconsider the infant industry argument as yet another application of our

[41] Negishi considers the infant industry argument from the viewpoint of the world.   We shall return to this problem later in Section XI to discuss the world gains from trade.

methodology supporting, in particular, the position taken by Negishi and Ray.

For simplicity, let us consider a two-period model of the economy. A commodity in the first (present) period and the same commodity in the second (future) period are, then, *different* economic objects. We have to reinterpret our vectors so that they now represent the quantities of the two periods:

$$x = ({}^1x, {}^2x)$$
$$y = ({}^1y, {}^2y)$$
$$p = ({}^1p, {}^2p) \quad \text{etc.}$$

where the left-hand superscripts indicate the period of the vectors. In a two-period equilibrium, the rate of interest is implicitly determined by the price vector, $p = ({}^1p, {}^2p)$. Assume that there exists a certain (positive) level of the infant industry output below which it cannot generate internal or external dynamic economies, and that the level is not achieved without protection in the first period. Since learning is a time-consuming process, dynamic economies are assumed to materialize only in the second period given the appropriate protection in the first. To sharpen the argumentative edge, let us further assume that there are no dynamic economies in the non-infant industries. As we have shown above, the desirable level of the infant industry outputs is best achieved by appropriate subsidies on those outputs.

Now suppose that situation S' stands for free trade without any protection, and S'' for the state with protection in the form of production subsides in the first period.

PROPOSITION 20:   *If condition*

(26) $$p_r''(y'' - y') + p''(a'' - a') \geq p''R''(y'' - y')$$

is satisfied, the infant industry protection by means of propoduction subsidies is beneficial for a price-taking country.

Proof: Let $T'' = C'' = 0$ and $q''(e'' - e') = 0$. Then, condition (13) in Theorem 1 reduces to (27). ||

According to Kemp's criterion, the protection is not to be recommended if there are only internal dynamic economies, for the desired level of infant industry outputs are assumed to be unprofitable. To discuss this point, let w and z be n-vectors of aggregate production of infant and non-infant industries. Thus

$$y = w + z$$

and we can rewrite condition (26) as

$$p_r''(z'' - z') + p''(a'' - a') \geq p''(w' - w'')$$

on the assumption that there are no taxes or subsidies on the production of non-infant industries.   In particular, if $w' = 0$, the right-hand side of this condition is positive since production w'' is unprofitable without protective subsidies, or $p''w'' < 0$.   On the other hand, the left-hand side may as well be positive in the presence of non-tradeable commodities because of the profit maximization condition for non-infant industries and the possible augmentation (in efficiency units) of factors of production *specific* to the firms of infant industries.   Despite the unprofitability assumption, condition (26) may be satisfied, and therefore protection justified even though the available learning processes are all internal to the firms.[42]   At any rate, condition (26) may or may not hold irrespective the nature of dynamic economies occuring in the infant industries.[43]

On the other hand, if there are neither dynamic external economies nor non-tradeable commodities, we obtain

$$p'(z' - z'') + p'(a' - a'') = 0 > p'w''$$

since, in this case, we must have $p' = p''$ and $a' = a''$.   It implies that the protection of unprofitable infant industries is harmful for a price-taking country.[44]   Kemp's argument is therefore valid in the special case in which all commodities are tradeable.

Finally, protection may take the form of import taxes in spite of the fact that they are more costly than production subsidies.   To consider this case, let S'' now represent the state with protective tariffs.   Proposition 20 is no longer relevant.   From Theorem 1, we instead get

PROPOSITION 21:   *If condition*

(27) $$p''\{(y'' - y') + (a'' - a')\} \geqq q''T''(e' - e'')$$

is satisfied, the infant industry protection by means of tariffs is beneficial for a price-taking country.

X.   THE CUSTOMS UNIONS ISSUE

Up to this point we have made no attempt to go beyond the viewpoint of a single country trading with the rest of the world.   This is of course due to

---

[42] At this point, it should be recalled that, under the convexity of social preference relation, condition (26) is merely sufficient (and not necessary) for the justification of infant industry protection.

[43] Haberler (1950) provided a diagramatic demonstration of the essential argument, which was somehow neglected in later controversies.

[44] If $w' = 0$, we have

$$p'(x' - x'') = p'(y' - y'') + p'(a' - a'')$$
$$= p'(z' - z'' - w'') + p'(a' - a'') .$$

the nature of our model described at the outset.   A little reflection, however, will reveal that we can at times reinterpret the single country's viewpoint so as to deal with the problem of many countries.   Our method remains indeed applicable whenever a group of several countries acts like a single country providing a common set of prices to measure and compare the sum of national consumption bundles of two situations.   The customs unions issue provides a shining example of such a circumstance, and certainly deserves a separate treatment on its own right.   Let us assume that (i) the customs unions abolish all tariffs among the member countries; (ii) it sets up common external tariffs; and (iii) it fully coordinates distributional policies inside the union.   Introducing picturesque concepts of trade creation and trade diversion, Viner (1950) aptly illustrates the generally ambiguous nature of the effect of the customs union.   In fact, like many other statements on trade and welfare, it is only conditional that the customs union will augment the welfare of any concerned party.

Suppose that there are v countries in the world, and that s $(< v)$ countries formed a customs union.   We indicate the countries by putting left-hand subscripts to all symbols.   Let S' and S'' represent the pre- and post-union situations wherein domestic taxes and subsidies are assumed to be non-existent.

PROPOSITION 22:   *If condition*

$$(28) \qquad (q' - q'') \sum_{h=1}^{s} {}_h e' + q'' T'' \left(\sum_{h=1}^{s} {}_h e'' - \sum_{h=1}^{s} {}_h e' \right) \geq 0$$

is satisfied, the post-union situation is preferable to the pre-union situation for the customs union as a whole.

Proof.   We may consider the members of the customs union as if they were a single country because of the distributional coordination available in the post-union situation.   Condition (15′) is then applicable with $b'' = \sum_{h=1}^{s} {}_h b'$, and may be rewritten as (28). ||

The first term on the left-hand side of condition (28) indicates the terms of trade effect, and the second term, the trade expansion (contraction) effect on the welfare of the customs union.   If the terms of trade effect is negligible, and free trade prevails in the rest of the world, we can discuss the gain from the formation of the union solely in terms of the trade expansion (contraction) effect along the line made popular by Meade (1955a).   For example, the expansion of the tariff-protected *net* imports will be, *ceteris paribus*, sufficient to suggest an increase of the world real income as well as the union's welfare. Note, however, that the much discussed trade creating effect does not appear explicitly in condition (28).   In fact it is buried in the omitted expression:

$$p'' \left(\sum_{h=1}^{s} {}_h y'' - \sum_{h=1}^{s} {}_h y' \right) \geq 0$$

and yet it certainly affects the condition indirectly through its expansive effect on external trade.   In general, condition (28), together with condition (15″), provides a complete set of references for testing the welfare effect on the union itself as well as on each country in the outside world.

Criticizing Viner's pioneering analysis, Meade (1955a), Gehrels (1956–57), and Lipsey (1957, 1960) demonstrate that the purely trade diverting union may just easily be beneficial in the presence of a convex social preference relation. To exclude trade creation and the terms of trade effect, they focus upon a customs unions of exchange economies with no monopoly power in world trade. Suppose as a limiting case that there is no trade diversion, either.   Then, condition (28) is satisfied by equality, and the members' welfare is shown to increase after the union (recall Lemma 3).   By continuity, we may conclude that the union remains beneficial even with some trade diversions.   In fact, their simple example relates to the case which fails to meet condition (28), and serves to remind us once again of the *sufficiency* nature of our welfare criterion under the convexity of consumers' preference relations.

More recently, Kemp (1964) and Vanek (1965) advocate an interesting scheme of the tariff-compensating customs union.   We may define it as the union which sets its common external tariffs so as to preserve the same volume and composition of net trade with the rest of the world as occured before it was formed.

PROPOSITION 23:   *A tariff-compensating customs union is bound to benefit itself.*

Proof: Refering back to Proposition 22, we find

$$\sum_{h=1}^{s} {}_h e' = \sum_{h=1}^{s} {}_h e''$$

for a tariff compensating customs union.   Hence,

$$(q' - q'') \sum_{h=1}^{s} {}_h e' = q' \sum_{h=1}^{s} {}_h e' - q'' \sum_{h=1}^{s} {}_h e'' = 0 \,.$$

Thus, both the first and the second terms in condition (28) vanish to zero. ‖

Clearly, a tariff-compensating union does not hurt the rest of the world. Therefore, it is also beneffcial for the world as a whole.[45]   As Vanek suggests, it may be useful to think of a customs union as adopting the compensating tariffs in the ffrst step, and then shifting to the final tariffs in the second. This amounts to a conceptual device of splitting up tiie welfare effect of the union conveniently into two parts to examine them separately.   The first step is necessarily beneficial.   The second step is analytically equivalent to a single

---

[45] In fact, the idea of a tariff-compensating customs union can be seen as a natural development of the Meade-Gehrels-Lipsey proposition.

country's act of tariff reform.[46]

XI. THE WORLD GAINS FROM TRADE

There seems to be little literature along the line of the present study which adequately deals with the world gains from trade. Since we have already set out to consider the situations explicitly involving several countries, we shall follow the logic to its end, and fill the void to some extent. The familiar free trade doctrine immediately follows from condition (28). Suppose that $s = v$. In other words, imagine that all the countries get together and form the world customs union. That is free trade. We may now rewrite (28) simply as

$$(q' - q'') \sum_{h=1}^{v} {}_h e' = -q'' \sum_{h=1}^{v} {}_h e' \geq 0 .$$

But this condition necessarily holds since $q'' \geq 0$ and $\sum_{h=1}^{v} {}_h e' \leq 0$. If the set of free commodities is identical for the two situations, the condition is to be satisfied by equality. Thus, free trade is preferable to any other situation for the world as a whole provided that there is a proper redistributional arrangement among nations.

In view of Proposition 1, we may also note that trade restricted by tariffs is preferable to no trade for all countries, i.e., for the world. Clearly, we cannot obtain the same unconditional statement for trade restricted by domestic taxes and subsidies.[47] To proceed further, let us assume the presence of a world government coordinating all the functions of national governments. First, we can apply Theorem 2-(ii) to obtain

PROPOSITION 24: *Let* $T'' = R'' = 0$. *Then, if condition*

(29) $$q''C'' \sum_{h=1}^{v} ({}_h x'' - {}_h x') \geq 0$$

is satisfied, situation S'' *is preferable to situation* S'.

Proof: Note that C'' represents the *common* taxes and subsides applied throughout the world in situation S''. Consequently, all consumers are supposed to face the same price, which makes Theorem 2-(ii) applicable to the world. It then suffices to rewrite condition (16) and note $(q' - q'') \sum_{h=1}^{v} {}_h e' \geq 0$. ||

---

[46] A single country's tariff reform, say a reduction of tariffs, however, will not be unambiguous in its effect on the welfare of the tariff-ridden world. See Meade (1955b, pp. 511–520) and also Ozga (1955).

[47] Similarly, trade may not be conducive to the world real income if non-self-financing tariffs are prevalent. This point generalizes Jones' observation (1961, pp. 173–174) about a Graham-esque, multi-country, multi-commodity model.

Similarly, from Theorem 2-(iii) we can derive

PROPOSITION 25:   *Let $T'' = C'' = 0$.   Then, if condition*

(30) $$q'' \sum_{h=1}^{v} {}_h R''({}_h y' - {}_h y'') \geq 0$$

is satisfied, situation S'' is preferable to situation S'.

In case there are only taxes and subsidies on production in situation S'', they can be different from country to country because of the fact that consumers' price is identical throughout the world.   In view of conditions (29) and (30), we find that there is a striking correspeondence between the world envisioned here and a price-taking country with no external tariffs.   In each case, we are able to disregard the cumbersome term $(q' - q'')e'$ reflecting the terms of trade effect.   Thus, a number of welfare propositions which are valid for a price-taking country are also applicable to the world.

First of all, proposition 9 corresponds to the free trade doctrine which we have just established.   Similarly, propositions 10, 15, 16 and 20 can be readily reformulated to fit in with the present context.   For example, we can state

PROPOSITION 26:   *Given a fixed volume of certain outputs (resp. inputs) in certain countries, trade with appropriate taxes or subsidies on those outputs (resp. inputs) is preferable, for the world as a whole, to a situation with tariffs and/or other taxes and subsidies.*

In correspondence to proposition 16, this result tells us that, from the viewpoint of the world, a national scheme of production taxes and subsidies is the optimal way of achieving a target level of any output or input in any country. We may then proceed to consider the infant industry protection by means of national production subsidies just as we considered it for a price-taking country.

PROPOSITION 27:   *If condition*

(31) $$\sum_{h=1}^{v} {}_h p_r''({}_h y'' - {}_h y') + q'' \left(\sum_{h=1}^{v} {}_h a'' - \sum_{h=1}^{v} {}_h a' \right) \geq q'' \sum_{h=1}^{v} {}_h R''({}_h y'' - {}_h y')$$

is satisfied, the infant industry protection by means of national production subsidies is beneficial for the world as a whole.

Generally speaking, if tariffs are non-existent, and if taxes and subsidies on consumption are common to all countries, we find a correspondence in the above sense between the world and a price-taking country.[48]   We may refer to this fact as a "correspondence principle" in trade and welfare.   It is speci-

---

[48] Strictly speaking, this correspondence fails to apply to the propositions on a price-taking country which depend not only on the absence of the terms of trade effect but also on the *constancy* of the price of each tradeable commodity.   Thus propositions 12 and 13 cannot be held valid for the world.

fically pertinent to the familiar notion of the "ideal" world economy where free trade prevails among countries except some national schemes of production subsidies designed to foster infant industries under the auspices of a world govrnment.[49]

XII. CONCLUDING REMARKS

We have derived numerous propositions from our basic theorem of welfare comparison thereby showing that most of the welfare propositions obtained in simple models of trade are viable in the presence of trade in intermediate goods and factor services as well as in the presence of any number of non-traded commodities. Some of our propositions may be considered to be worthwhile from a puristic viewpoint, while many of the conditional statements will only satisfy non-purists. But we wish to emphasize the simplicity and the methodological uniformity of our approach which compares two situations which may differ from each other in any manner and respect except in the set of consumers. If employed with enough caution, it may serve further useful purposes.

The lack of analysis of external economies and diseconomies may be pointed out as a major qualification of this study. When we consider the government as a producer or a consumer of *public goods*, this qualification may apper particularly restrictive: the external effect of public goods is often too obvious to escape one's eyes.[50] As is well-known, externalities among economic agents will give rise to interdependence among their behaviors and invalidate the equilibrium conditions for producers and consumers. To remedy such a situation, it would be necessary to set up a system of artificial markets for externalities so that both external economies and diseconomies are properly counted as commodities.[51] Note, however, that external *diseconomies* are comparable to the supply of labor, and their absence to the endowment of leisure.[52] In fact, external diseconomies are not themselves commodities, but

[49] An adept blueprint of such a world economy is found in Tinbergen (1962).

[50] As in the case of public goods which are not subject to the exclusion principle, the consumption, or production of some commodities by an economic agent may affect a number of other economic agents at the same time. In such an event, it would be necessary to establish an agreement among those affected on the individual shares in the price of the externalities. For closely related concepts, see Musgrave (1959).

[51] But for the governmental intervention in the economy as a law-enforced broker between potential sellers and buyers, the scheme would be largely impractical because of the thinness of many markets for externalities. In fact, it would be economically equivalent to an alternative remedy by means of domestic taxes and subsidies if both are administered properly.

[52] For example, consider a fisherman who suffers from a water-polluting factory only in business aspects. He is not in the position to *supply* his diseconomies beyond the degree of water pollution at which he goes out of business. Otherwise, he would supply an infinite amount of diseconomies at any positive price.

70   MICHIHIRO OHYAMA

rather losses of the commodities which, in their full endowment, represent perfect freedom from external diseconomies.   No one is, therefore, able to *supply* his external diseconomies beyond the tolerable degree of their irksomeness.   This point is indeed essential to the workability of artificial markets for externalities.   But as long as externalites are assumed to be internalized through such a scheme, the present model remains applicable without any formal modification.

ACKNOWLEDGMENTS

This paper was taken from my Ph. D. thesis submitted to the University of Rochester in February 1972.   I would like to thank Professors Lionel W. Mckenzie, Ronald W. Jones and Akira Takayama for their guidance and many helpful comments which led to improvements of my initial thoughts.   I am also indebted to Professors Murray C. Kemp, Henry Y. Wan, Leon L. Wegge, Masao Fukuoka, Kiyoshi Ikemoto, Yoko Sazanami, and my friends, Messrs. Alok Ray and Kunio Kawamata for their kind criticisms.   Finally, I would like to acknowledge my appreciation to Professors Noboru Yamamoto, Ichiro Ohkuma and Katsu Yanaihara of Keio University for their continued encouragement.

Keio University

REFERENCES

[1]   Baldwin, R. E., 1952, "The New Welfare Economics and Gains in International Trade" *Quarterly Journal of* Economics, Vol. 66 (February), 90–101.

[2]   Bhagwati, J., 1958, "Immiserizing Growth: A Geometrical Note," *Review of Economic Studies*, Vol. 25 (June), 201–205.

[3]   Bhagwati, J., 1964, "The Pure Theory of International Trade: a Survey," *Economic Journal*, Vol. 74 (March), 1–81.

[4]   Bhagwati, J., 1968 a, "The Gains from Trade Once Again."   *Oxford Economic Papers*, Vol. 20 (July), 137–148.

[5]   Bhagwati, J., 1968 b, "Distortions and Immiserizing Growth: a Generalization," *Review of Economic Studies*, Vol. 35 (October), 481–485.

[6]   Bhagwati, J., 1971, "The Generalized Theory of Distortions and Welfare," in J. Bhagwati *et al., Trade, Balance of Payments and Growth*, Papers in International Economics in Honor of Charles P. Kindleberger, Amsterdam: North-Holland.

[7]   Bhagwati, J. and V. K. Ramaswami, 1963, "Domestic Distortions, Tariffs, and the Theory of Optimum Subsidy," *Journal of Political Economy*, Vol. 71 (February), 44–50.

[8]   Bhagwati, J. N. and T. N. Srinivasan, 1969, "Optimal Intervention to Achieve Noneconomic Objectives," *Review of Economic Studies*, Vol. 36 (January), 27–38.

[9]   Chipman, J. S., 1965, "A Survey of International Trade: Part 2, the Neo-classical Theory," *Econometrica*, Vol. 33 (October), 685–760.

[10]   Corden, W. M., 1957, "Tariffs, Subsidies, and the Terms of Trade," *Economitrica*, Vol. 24 (August), 235–242.

[11]   Debreu, G., 1959, *Theory of Value*, New York: John Wiley and Sons.

[12]   Diamond, P. A., and J. A. Mirrlees, 1971, "Optimal Taxation and Public Production I: Production Efficiency" *American Economic Review*, Vol. 61 (March) 8–27.

[13] Diamond, P. A., and J. A. Mirrlees, 1971, "Optimal Taxation and Public Production II: Tax Rules," *American Economic Review*, Vol. 61 (June), 261–278.

[14] Dixit, A. K., 1970, "On the Optimal Structure of Commodity Taxes," *American Economic Review*, Vol. 60 (1970), 107–116.

[15] Edgeworth, F. Y., 1894, "The Theory of International Values," *Economic Journal*, Vol. 4 (March), 35–50.

[16] Gehrels, F., 1956–1957, "Customs Unions from a Single Country Viewpoint," *Review of Economic Studies*, Vol. 24 (1), 61–64.

[17] Haberler, G., 1950, "Some Problems in the Pure Theory of International Trade," *Economic Journal*, Vol. 60 (June), 223–40.

[18] Inada, K., 1967, "A Note on the Heckscher-Ohlin Theorem," *Economic Record*, Vol. 43 (March), 88–96.

[19] Johnson, H. G., 1960, "The Cost of Protection and the Scientific Tariff," *Journal of Political Economy*, Vol. 68 (August), 327–345.

[20] Johnson, H. G., 1964, "Tariffs and Economic Development: Some Theoretical Issues," *Journal of Development Studies*, Vol. 1 (October), 3–30.

[21] Johnson, H. G., 1967, "The Possibility of Income Losses from Increased Efficiency or Factor Accumulation in the Presence of Tariffs," *Economic Journal*, Vol. 77 (March), 151–154.

[22] Jones, R. W., 1961, "Comparative Advantage and the Theory of Tariffs: a Multi-Country, Multi-Commodity Model." *Review of Economic Studies*, Vol. 28 (June), 161–175.

[23] Jones, R. W., 1967, "International Capital Movements and the Theory of Tariffs and Trade," *Quarterly Journal of Economics*, Vol. 81 (February), 1–38.

[24] Jones, R. W., 1969, "Tariffs and Trade in General Equilibrium: Comment," *American Economic Review*, Vol. 59 (June), 418–424.

[25] Kemp, M. C., 1960, "The Mill-Bastable Infant Industry Dogma," *Journal of Political Economy*, Vol. 68 (February), 65–67.

[26] Kemp, M. C., 1962, "The Gains from International Trade," *Economic Journal*, Vol. 72 (December), 803–819.

[27] Kemp. M. C., 1964, *The Pure Theory of International Trade*, Englewood Cliffs, N.J.: Prentice-Hall.

[28] Kemp, M. C., 1968, "Some Issues in the Analysis of Trade Gains," *Oxford Economic Papers*, Vol. 20 (July), 194–161.

[29] Kemp, M. C., 1969, *The Pure Theory of International Trade and Investment*. Englewood Cliffs, N.J.: Prentice-Hall.

[30] Kemp, M. C. and T. Negishi, 1969, "Domestic Distortions, Tariffs, and the Theory of Optimum subsidy," *Journal of Political Economy*, Vol. 77 (Nov./Dec.), 1014–1016.

[31] Kemp, M. C. and T. Negishi, 1970, "Variable Returns to Scale, Commodity Taxes, Factor Market Distortions and their Implications for Trade Gains," *Swedish Journal of Economics*, No. 1 (January), 1–11.

[32] Kennedy, C., 1954, "An Alternative Proof of a Theorem in Welfare Economics," *Oxford Economic Papers*, Vol. 6 (February), 98–99.

[33] Kravis, I. B., 1956, "Availability and Other Influences on the Commodity Composition of Trade," *Journal of Political Economy*, Vol. 64 (April), 143–155.

[34] Krueger, A. O. and H. Sonnenschein, 1967, "The Terms of Trade, the Gains from Trade, and Price Divergence," *International Economic Review*, Vol. 8 (February), 121–127.

[35] Leontief, W. W., 1933, "The Use of Indifference Curves in the Analysis of Foreign Trade," *Quarterly Journal of Economics*, Vol. 47 (May), 493–503.

[36] Lipsey, R. G., 1957, "The Theory of Customs Unions: Trade Diversion and Welfare," *Economica*, Vol. 24 (February), 40–46.

72   MICHIHIRO OHYAMA

[37] Lipsey, R. G., 1960, "The Theory of Customs Unions: a General Survey," *Economic Journal*, Vol. 70 (September), 496–513.

[38] Lipsey, R. G. and Lancaster, K. J., 1956–1957, "The General Theory of Second Best." *Review of Economic Studies*, Vol. 24 (1), 11–32.

[39] McKenzie, L. W., 1959, "On the Existence of General Equilibrium for a Competitive Market," *Econometrica*, Vol. 27 (January), 54–71.

[40] Meade, J. E., 1952, *A Geometry of International Trade*, London: George Allen and Unwin.

[41] Meade, J. E., 1955a, *The Theory of Customs Unions*, Amsterdam: North Holland.

[42] Meade, J. E., 1955b, *Trade and Welfare* (The Theory of International Economic Policy, Vol. II), Oxford: Oxford University Press.

[43] Mundell, R. A., 1960, "The Pure Theory of International Trade," *American Economic Review*, Vol. 50 (March), 67–110.

[44] Musgrave, R. A., 1959, *The Theory of Public Finance*, New York: McGraw-Hill.

[45] Myint, H., 1958, "The Classical Theory of International Trade and the Underdeveloped Countries," *Economic Journal*, Vol. 68 (June), 317–337.

[46] Negishi, T., 1968, "Protection of the Infant Industry and Dynamic Internal Economies," *Economic Record*, Vol. 24 (March), 56–57.

[47] Negishi, T., 1963, "On Social Welfare Function," *Quarterly Journal of Economics*, Vol. 77 (February), 156–158.

[48] Nikaidô, H., 1968, *Convex Structures and Economic Theory*, New York: Academic Press.

[49] Ohyama, M., 1972, "Domestic Distortions, and the Theory of Tariffs," *Keio Economic Studies*, Vol. 9 (No. 1), 1–14.

[50] Ohyama, M., 1970, "Tariffs and the Transfer Problem," unpublished.

[51] Ozga, S. A., 1955, "An Essay in the Theory of Tariffs," *Journal of Political Economy*, Vol. 63 (December), 489–499.

[52] Ray, A., 1970, "On the Infant Industry Argument for Protection and its Policy Implications," unpublished.

[53] Ray, A., 1971, "A General Theorem on Uniform Versus Differentiated Tariff Structure," unpublished.

[54] Samuelson, P. A., 1939, "The Gains from International Trade," *Canadian Journal of Economics and Political Science*, Vol. 5 (May), 195–205.

[55] Samuelson, P. A., 1950, "Evaluation of Real National Income," *Oxford Economic Papers*, Vol. 2 (January), 1–29.

[56] Samuelson, P. A., 1952, "The Transfer Problem and Transport Costs: the Terms of Trade when Impediments are Absent," *Economic Journal*, Vol. 62 (June), 278–304.

[57] Samuelson, P. A., 1954, "The Transfer Problem and Transport Costs, II: Analysis of Effects of Trade Impediments," *Economic Journal*, Vol. 64 (June), 264–289.

[58] Samuelson, P. A., 1956, "Social Indifference Curves," *Quarterly Journal of Economics*, Vol. 70 (February), 1–22.

[59] Samuelson, P. A., 1962, "The Gains from International Trade Once Again," *Economic Journal*, Vol. 72 (December), 820–829.

[60] Scitovsky, T., 1942, "A Reconsideration of the Theory of Tariffs," *Review of Economic Studies*, Vol. 9 (Summer), 89–110.

[61] Sontheimer, K. V., 1971, "An Existence Theorem for the Second Best," *Journal of Economic Theory*, Vol. 3 (March), 1–22.

[62] Tan, A. H. H., 1971, "Optimal Trade Policies and Non-Economic Objectives in Models Involving Imported Materials, Inter-Industry Flows and Non-traded Goods," *Review of Economic Studies*, Vol. 38 (February), 105–111.

[63] Tinbergen, J., 1962, *Shaping the World Economy: Suggestions for an International Economic Policy*, New York: Twentieth Century Fund.

[64] Vanek, J., 1965, *General Equilibrium of International Discrimination: The Case of Customs Unions*, Cambridge, Mass.: Harvard University Press.

[65] Viner, J., 1950, *The Customs Union Issue*, New York: Carnegie Endowment for International Peace.

B
Optimum Tariffs and Retaliation

[6]

On Optimum Tariff Structures

This is an essay in welfare statics—in the strictest sense of the term. It seeks to apply to a classic problem in tariff theory a tool of considerable power and generality forged by Professor Paul A. Samuelson in his *Foundations of Economic Analysis*.[1] The tool to which I refer is a community's " possibility locus." Some of its salient properties are indicated in the first of the sections that follow. In the second I introduce a closely related concept, the community's " efficiency locus." The third is concerned with their application to the problem of determining optimum tariff structures, and discusses the argument—due essentially to Bickerdike[2] and Edgeworth,[3] writing at the turn of the century, but recently revived by a distinguished band of contemporary economists : Professor Lerner,[4] Mr. Kaldor,[5] Professor de Scitovszky,[6] Mrs. Robinson,[7] and Mr. Kahn[8]—that it is, in the absence of retaliation, *always* possible for a full-employment country to turn the terms of trade in its favour by imposing a " small " protective tariff on imports, and to benefit itself thereby. In the fourth section I examine rather critically Mr. Kahn's revival of Bickerdike's theory that the " small " tariff may, in fact, be quite a " large " one. A mathematical note concludes the paper. The treatment throughout differs essentially from that of Mr. Little's article on " Welfare and Tariffs "[9] in that the existence of no criterion is assumed on the basis of which interpersonal comparisons of well-being can be made.

I. THE POSSIBILITY LOCUS

Consider—for geometrical simplicity : the general case is treated in the mathematical note—a community consisting of but two citizens, Alpha and Beta. They are assumed to have definite preference scales, which can be represented by ordinal utility indexes, a and β. These indicate the disutility of effort as well as the utility of leisure and consumption. No special significance attaches to the particular indexes selected, but—once adopted—they must be adhered to without change. We shall maintain the convention that a rises whenever Alpha is able to satisfy his preferences more fully ; and we shall then say that his welfare has increased. A similar remark applies to β and Beta.

We do not assume the absence of external economies in consumption : when Alpha installs a telephone the utility of Beta's will probably grow.[10] Nor do we assume the absence of external diseconomies : when Beta buys ostentatious diamonds Alpha may well discard his in disgust.[11]

[1] P. A. Samuelson : *Foundations of Economic Analysis* (Cambridge, Mass. 1947), Chapter VIII.

[2] C. F. Bickerdike : " The Theory of Incipient Taxes," *Economic Journal*, December, 1906, pp. 529ff ; and his review of A. C. Pigou's *Protective and Preferential Import Duties*, *Economic Journal*, March, 1907, pp. 98ff.

[3] F. Y. Edgeworth : *Papers Relating to Political Economy*, Vol. II, pp. 340ff. (Reprinted from the 1908 *Economic Journal*.)

[4] A. P. Lerner : *The Economics of Control* (New York, 1944), pp. 382–5.

[5] N. Kaldor : " A Note on Tariffs and the Terms of Trade," *Economica*, November, 1940.

[6] T. de Scitovszky : " A Reconsideration of the Theory of Tariffs," REVIEW OF ECONOMIC STUDIES, IX (2), (1941–42), pp. 89–110. (Reprinted in *Readings in the Theory of International Trade*, Philadelphia, 1949.)

[7] Joan Robinson : " The Pure Theory of International Trade," REVIEW OF ECONOMIC STUDIES, XIV (2), (1946–47), pp. 107–8.

[8] R. F. Kahn : " Tariffs and the Terms of Trade," REVIEW OF ECONOMIC STUDIES, XV (1), (1947–48), pp. 14–19.

[9] I. M. D. Little : " Welfare and Tariffs," REVIEW OF ECONOMIC STUDIES, XVI (2), (1948–49).

[10] R. W. Souter : *Prolegomena to Relativity Economics* (New York, 1933), pp. 50ff.

[11] A. C. Pigou : " Some Remarks on Utility," *Economic Journal*, March, 1903, p. 62.

Now fix β at some arbitrary level, β_0, and make Alpha as well off as is possible under the circumstances. Just how great a value a will be able to attain will depend upon (i) the value β_0; (ii) the supply of goods and services available to the community; and (iii) the possibility of transforming goods and services of one kind into goods of another kind. This transformation can be performed in factories at home, or by trade with communities abroad. Its maximum extent cannot be unambiguously determined until we know how much provision is to be made for capital accumulation, and how much foreign indebtedness is to be incurred. It is not generally recognised that this knowledge can be obtained from nowhere but a *dynamic* welfare theory. Here, however, we are concerned solely with welfare statics. We must take the dynamic theory for granted, and derive our transformation possibilities from it.

A word of justification for this procedure might, however, be added. We are going to abide very firmly by the rule that interpersonal comparisons of well-being are inadmissible. We shall never say that the community's welfare has increased unless both Alpha and Beta are better off—or, more strictly, unless at least one is better off, the other being no worse off than before. But if we cannot make interpersonal comparisons among the living, still less can we make them among the unborn and the dead. That is why we confine ourselves to statics. In a dynamic world the composition of our community necessarily changes in the course of time. To be able to say something of its welfare, we must have a concept of welfare that is independent of the earthly existence of particular citizens. Into this problem it is inappropriate to enter at the moment. It is sufficient to note that we must have a dynamic theory before we can pursue our statics—perhaps this is an application to welfare theory of Professor Samuelson's well-known Correspondence Principle. But *any* dynamic theory will do—we do not have to have a particular one closely specified.

Once we have arrived at an unambiguous statement of the possibilities of transformation, the problem of making Alpha as well off as possible, subject to $\beta = \beta_0$, resolves itself into the problem of establishing the conditions for the Paretean General Optimum of Production and Exchange. The solution, involving the equality of marginal rates of transformation and substitution, is well known for a closed economy—in recent years it has penetrated to the level of the elementary texts. These, it is true, do not generally deal with external economies or diseconomies in consumption—but they too have been exhaustively handled.[1] Section III of this paper extends the analysis to open communities. For the moment it is sufficient to assume the solution, which will give us a particular value of a, say a_0, corresponding to β_0.

If we fix β at some other level (by means of a lump-sum tax or bounty, which is assumed to cost nothing to collect or distribute), we shall obtain another value of a.

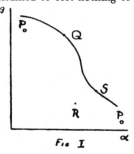

Fig. I

Proceeding in this way, we can map out a locus in the (a, β)-plane. This is Professor Samuelson's " possibility locus," and is illustrated by P_0P_0 in Fig. I. Its shape and position (for convenience, it has been drawn in the north-east quadrant) depend upon our particular choice of the indexes a and β. But the direction of slope is invariant.[2] It will normally slope downwards : Alpha can be made better off only at Beta's expense. In rare cases, however, it may slope upwards. Two examples deserve especial notice. The first is the one treated more fully in the mathematical note : external economies in consumption may be so marked and asymmetrical that

[1] G. Tintner : " A Note on Welfare Economics," *Econometrica*, January, 1946, pp. 69–78.
[2] Mathematical Note, equation (15).

a transfer of wealth from Alpha to Beta increases the welfare of each. One might expect this situation to be unstable, Alpha simply making Beta a gift. The second, and more important, example is where the community's productive power depends in an essential way on the distribution of wealth : where workers are underfed, a redistribution of wealth in their favour may so increase their efficiency that everybody benefits. It is an open question whether or not considerations of this kind belong to welfare statics or dynamics. I propose to interpret " statics " very strictly indeed, and to exclude these considerations from our analysis. Thus, in formal language, the transformation functions are assumed to be independent of the distribution of wealth.[1]

We are left then, with a downward-sloping possibility locus.[2] Some of its salient properties may conveniently be summarised at this stage. (This and the next paragraph lean very heavily indeed on Professor Samuelson's treatment) : Movements towards the locus are secured by establishing the conditions necessary for the Paretean General Optimum ; movements along the locus by lump-sum taxes and bounties— assumed to cost nothing to collect and distribute. No point to the north-east of it can be attained with the given state of technique, etc. To any point to the south-west of it there corresponds a better point on the locus itself—" better " because both Alpha and Beta are better off. Between points actually on the locus we cannot judge without a criterion for making interpersonal comparisons of well-being. We cannot say that a point on the locus, like Q, is better than a point off it, like R—for in Q Alpha is worse off than in R. But we can (and shall) say that Q is *potentially* better than R— for there necessarily exists a point S, in which both Alpha and Beta are better off than in R, and to which a mere redistribution of wealth can lead us. Whether or not such a redistribution should actually be made is, of course, another matter altogether, and cannot be decided without a criterion for interpersonal comparisons of well-being.[3]

Let us now confine ourselves to positions actually on the possibility locus—the more general situation is discussed in the next section—and consider a change such as might be caused by, for example, technological " progress." There are two distinct possi- bilities. On the one hand, the new locus may lie either wholly inside, or wholly outside, the old one. Such a movement we shall refer to as a *shift*. It is illustrated by $P_1 P_1$

[1] By " a distribution of wealth (or welfare) " is meant no more than " a point in the (α, β)-plane."
[2] It should perhaps be emphasised that, when we leave a two-person community, slightly stronger assumptions are required to insure that the possibility locus should slope downwards. For instance, in a three-person community it may slope upwards because of external *diseconomies* in consumption. Consider the community consisting of Alpha, Beta and Gamma. For simplicity, let us say that there is but one commodity, " riches," the supply of which is fixed. Assume that Alpha's utility is uninfluenced by the riches possessed by either Beta or Gamma, and that these in turn are uninfluenced by Alpha's possessions. But assume, too, that marked external diseconomies in consumption exist between Beta and Gamma. Then, if we are interested in the slope of the possibility locus in the (α, β)-plane, we must examine the rate of change of β when α is diminished slightly by a transfer of riches from Alpha to Beta, when γ (Gamma's index of utility) is kept constant. But the increase in Beta's riches makes Gamma worse off, so to keep γ constant it is necessary to transfer some riches to Gamma. This, however, makes Beta worse off on two scores : firstly, because the riches are taken from him ; and, secondly, because Gamma's possession of them increases. It is easy to construct examples along these lines in which the original small decrease in α causes β to decrease too, γ being kept constant, i.e. where the possibility locus slopes upwards in the (α, β)- plane. The marked external diseconomies we assumed to exist between Beta and Gamma can secure this result in spite of the fact that after the decrease in α both Beta and Gamma possess more riches than before. The matter is discussed more thoroughly in the mathematical note.
It should also be noted that when the possibility locus slopes upwards over a certain range there is not perfect symmetry between α and β in its definition—even in a two-person community. We get one result when we choose to hold β constant, and another when we hold α constant. The first will give α as a single-valued function of β ; the second β as a single-valued function of α. The complete locus is obtained by combining the two (i.e. by holding each constant in turn) to obtain what will in general be a multi- valued function of α, β, or both. The reader will have no difficulty in constructing a simple diagram to illustrate this, or in verifying that there is perfect symmetry between α and β when the locus slopes down- wards throughout the entire range.
[3] Cf. W. J. Baumol : " Community Indifference," and N. Kaldor : " A Comment," REVIEW OF ECONOMIC STUDIES, XIV (1), (1946–47), pp. 44–9.

Economic Integration and International Trade

in Fig. 2, which lies wholly outside $P_0'P_0''$. In this case a position on the new locus is clearly at least potentially superior to any position on the old one. Thus the technological " progress " can be said to be at least potentially beneficial. On the other

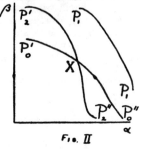

hand, the new locus may intersect the old one. This is represented by $P_2'P_2''$ in Fig. 2, where the intersection is in X. We shall refer to this as a *twist*. Now all that can be said is that the situations on $P_2'X$ are at least potentially superior to those on $P_0'X$; and that those on $P_0''X$ are at least potentially superior to those on $P_2''X$. We cannot say that the technological " progress " is even potentially beneficial unless we have some criterion on the basis of which we can judge between the situations on $P_2'X$ and those on $P_0''X$— some criterion for making interpersonal comparisons of well-being.

Fig. II

It might be thought that this indeterminacy, which arises whenever the loci cross, makes the whole possibility concept rather a clumsy one for welfare theory. To a certain extent this is true. But in a number of cases we can establish quite unambiguously that the locus shifts, and does not twist to intersect the old one. Thus we shall see that the erection of an optimum tariff structure can never twist the locus, but must always shift it outwards.

II. THE EFFICIENCY LOCUS

In any actual situation our community is unlikely to be on the possibility locus : it is likely to be well inside it. A redistribution of wealth by lump-sum taxes and bounties (which are assumed to cost nothing to collect and distribute) will normally move it to another position inside the locus. Any such redistribution will normally also affect the allocative efficiency of the system, increasing the degree of monopoly in some parts and diminishing it in others. The locus of all points in the (α, β)-plane traced out by redistributions of this kind we shall call the *efficiency locus*, because it indicates the allocative efficiency of the system for various distributions of welfare. Optimum allocative efficiency, for a particular distribution of welfare, is not attained unless the possibility and efficiency loci coincide in the point corresponding to that distribution. But optimum allocative efficiency is seldom achieved, and the efficiency locus will usually lie beneath the possibility locus.

Those steeped in the traditional surplus analysis may find it helpful to think of a point on the efficiency locus as indicating the total consumer's and producer's surplus enjoyed by each of Alpha and Beta in any actual situation. A point on the possibility locus, on the other hand, represents the maximum either could enjoy, given the amount enjoyed by the other, if the economic system were to be organised in an optimum manner—i.e. if the Paretean General Optimum were to obtain.

Technological progress, or a change of some other kind, is likely to affect both the possibility and the efficiency loci. It may shift one and twist the other, or affect both in the same way. There are, in fact, nine different combinations to consider : any one of the three different types of movement of the possibility locus can be associated with any one of the three different types of movement of the efficiency locus. For instance, an invention which shifts the possibility locus outwards may confer on the innovator monopoly power so great that the efficiency locus is given a twist, or even shifted inwards.

ON OPTIMUM TARIFF STRUCTURES   51

The question therefore arises : to which locus should we refer in judging the potential desirability of a particular change ? The answer, I think, depends upon the context. There is little point in bothering about possibility loci if there is no chance of the community ever attaining them. A change will lead us from a point on one efficiency locus to a point on another. Its potential desirability should normally be judged on this basis. Then we can consider the further question of improving the allocative efficiency of the system so as to make the efficiency locus approach closer to its possibility boundary. Such an improvement is always at least potentially beneficial. But it cannot be taken for granted. Its achievement is a matter quite distinct from the potential desirability of the change. Thus an invention which shifts the efficiency locus inwards should normally be regarded as potentially harmful, even if it shifts the possibility locus outwards. But it may well be that the same invention *plus* a vigorous trust-busting campaign would shift the efficiency locus outwards. In that case the invention *plus* the trust-busting, as opposed to the invention alone, is to be judged at least potentially beneficial. This would be true even if the invention were to involve an inward shift of the possibility locus—although, in the latter eventuality, it might be thought that the trust-busting without the invention might be potentially even more beneficial. This would not necessarily be correct, however, for the success of a given trust-busting campaign might not be altogether independent of the invention.

The question to which the various exponents[1] of " compensation tests " in welfare theory have addressed themselves is essentially a part of the wider problem of determining just what a particular change will do to the efficiency locus. But even the most powerful of these tests—Professor de Scitovszky's well-known double one— cannot always detect a twist in the locus. This reader can verify by glancing at Fig. 3. There we consider a move from R on the first locus to S on the second. It benefits Alpha, but Beta suffers. Alpha can, how-ever, profitably bribe Beta into accepting the change (cf. Q), and Beta cannot profitably bribe Alpha into rejecting it. Yet the loci cross. Professor de Scitovszky's test is not quite strong enough for our purposes. (It is, of course, perfectly correct to say that Q represents a point of greater welfare than R, for both Alpha and Beta are better off in Q than in R. But this is not to say that the change is even potentially beneficial. For there is no reason what- soever why we should judge the old situation with reference to the single point R. Nor is there any reason for judging the new situation with reference to Q alone.)

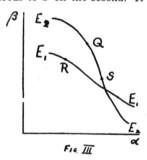

Fɪɢ. *III*

The problem of determining the behaviour of the efficiency locus in any actual situation is a very difficult one, and does not lend itself at all readily to theoretical treatment. In discussing optimum tariff structures in the next section, therefore, we shall concern ourselves chiefly with the possibility locus. But we should bear in mind that this is very much a second best, and that what we are really after is the efficiency locus.

[1] N. Kaldor : " Welfare Propositions and Interpersonal Comparisons of Utility," *Economic Journal*, 1939, pp. 549–52. J. R. Hicks : " The Foundations of Welfare Economics," *Economic Journal*, 1939, pp. 696–712 ; and " The Rehabilitation of Consumer's Surplus," REVIEW OF ECONOMIC STUDIES, VIII (1940–41), pp. 111–2. T. de Scitovszky : " A Note on Welfare Propositions in Economics," REVIEW OF ECONOMIC STUDIES, IX (1), (1941–42), pp. 77–88   and loc. cit. M. W. Reder : *Studies in the Theory of Welfare Economics* (New York, 1947).

4•

III. TARIFFS AND THE TERMS OF TRADE

In the first part of this section we shall simplify to the extent of considering a community where external economies and diseconomies are absent from both production and consumption. Let us adopt the following notation :—

π_i = the domestic price of the ith good.

p_i = the foreign price of the ith good.

z_i = the net import of the ith good into the country under consideration. (When z_i is negative it means that the ith good is exported.)

$F = \Sigma p_i z_i + K = 0$. We shall call F the *foreign trade transformation function*. It means that, correct provision being made for foreign lending (K)[1], trade must balance. Note that :

$$0 = dF = \sum_i \frac{\partial F}{\partial z_i} dz_i$$

$$= \sum_i \left\{ p_i + \sum_s \frac{\partial p_s}{\partial z_i} z_s \right\} dz_i$$

$$= \sum_i \left\{ p_i + a_i \right\} dz_i$$

So the *marginal rate of transformation through foreign trade* is :

$$- \frac{\partial F}{\partial z_i} \Big/ \frac{\partial F}{\partial z_j} = \frac{p_i + a_i}{p_j + a_j}$$

$a_i = \sum_s \frac{\partial p_s}{\partial z_i} z_s$. This indicates the total rate of change of world prices, weighted by quantities imported, as imports of the ith good are increased. Note that when " cross-elasticities " vanish identically, a_i/p_i reduces to the reciprocal of the ordinary elasticity ; and that, whether they vanish identically or not, $p_i (1 + a_i/p_i)$ represents the marginal cost to the country of importing the ith good (or, if it is an export, the marginal revenue derived from its sale).

It is well known that the establishment of the General Optimum in a closed economy requires that consumers' marginal rates of substitution between any two goods should equal the marginal rate of transformation of these goods into each other in home factories. It is usually suggested that this is to be effected through the price mechanism : consumers equate their marginal rates of substitution, and producers their marginal rates of transformation, to given domestic price ratios. In an open economy, however, the establishment of the General Optimum requires too that marginal rates of transformation in home factories should be equal to marginal rates of transformation through foreign trade. Therefore, these must also be equal to the domestic price ratios. That is to say :

$$\frac{p_i + a_i}{p_j + a_j} = \frac{\pi_i}{\pi_j} \qquad (i, j = 1, 2, \ldots, n) \quad \ldots\ldots\ldots\ldots\ldots\ldots\ldots (1)$$

The reader who doubts that the establishment of the General Optimum requires this equality of marginal rates of transformation is referred to equations (7) and (8) of the mathematical note ; but the matter is, after a little thought, rather obvious.

[1] For simplicity it is assumed that K is a constant, given independently of the level of prices. The details, but not the substance, of the argument is affected if this assumption is relaxed.

ON OPTIMUM TARIFF STRUCTURES 53

In the exceptional case where a_i/a_j is fortuitously proportional to p_i/p_j, equation (1) holds whenever domestic prices are proportional to foreign prices—as they always are under universal free trade, whatever the exchange rate. In this exceptional case, therefore, free trade establishes the General Optimum—i.e. lands us on the possibility locus.

In the more usual case, however, it will be necessary to adjust domestic prices (since foreign prices are not within our control) to secure the satisfaction of equation (1). The simplest method of adjustment is to put an *ad valorem* tax of a_i/p_i on the ith good whenever it crosses the frontier—the tax being calculated on the foreign price. Then we would have :

$$\frac{\pi_i}{\pi_j} = \frac{p_i \ (1 + a_i/p_i)}{p_j \ (1 + a_j/p_j)} \qquad\qquad (i, j = 1, 2, \ldots, n)$$

which is what is required. In the welfare terminology of previous sections, these taxes lead us to the possibility locus, and are therefore at least potentially beneficial : once they have been imposed wealth can be so redistributed that every citizen of our country is better off than he was under free trade. Stated in another way : compared with the free trade situation, the imposition of the optimum taxes shifts the possibility locus outwards.

This scheme of taxing both imports and exports is essentially the same as the one Professor Lerner suggests in *The Economics of Control*.[1] The only difference results from the fact that he implicitly assumes that all " cross-elasticities " of demand and supply vanish identically. It will readily be seen that whenever this procedure is legitimate our tax on imports reduces to the reciprocal of the foreign elasticity of supply, and our tax on exports to the reciprocal of the foreign elasticity of demand. This is Professor Lerner's elegant result. When the " cross-elasticities " cannot be neglected, however, it is likely to be a little misleading. For, in general, we cannot even say what the *signs* of the a_i will be ; and, as we shall see, cases can arise where the attainment of the General Optimum requires *subsidies* (or negative taxes) on both imports and exports. Yet this phenomenon is in no way related to changes in the signs of Professor Lerner's elasticities.

Our formula is also very closely related to the Bickerdike-Edgeworth-Kahn-Little formula for the optimum tariff. In fact, ours reduces to it in a world in which but two commodities are traded internationally[2], and where all the " cross-elasticities " vanish identically. We are then left with one export and one import. Denote them by e and m, respectively. Our General Optimum conditions (1) reduce to :

$$\frac{p_m + a_m}{p_e + a_e} = \frac{\pi_m}{\pi_e}$$

We have here but one international price ratio. To adjust the domestic import-export price ratio to it we need not tax both imports and exports : a single tax will do the trick. Thus if an *ad valorem* tariff, t, is imposed on imports (the tariff being reckoned on the foreign price), we must have :

$$\frac{p_m \ (1 + t)}{p_e} = \frac{p_m + a_m}{p_e + a_e}$$

or $t = \dfrac{a_m/p_m - a_e/p_e}{1 + a_e/p_e}$ .... (2)

[1] Loc. cit., pp. 382-5.

[2] Since we employ two prices in the argument that follows, we must have at least one domestic good (in addition to the two international ones) to play the role of *numéraire*. It is, therefore, not quite correct for Mr. Little to say that formula (3) gives the optimum tariff " for the two-good case ".

When all the " cross-elasticities " vanish identically, and we write η_d for the elasticity of foreign demand for exports (taken with a *minus* sign to make it positive) and η_s for the elasticity of the foreign supply of imports, (2) reduces still further to :

$$t = \frac{1/\eta_s + 1/\eta_d}{1 - 1/\eta_d} \quad \dots\dots\dots\dots\dots\dots\dots\dots\dots\dots\dots\dots\dots\dots\dots (3)$$

This is substantially the Kahn-Little formula. The assumptions which have to be made to derive it are rather restrictive. In particular, it is, of course, extremely unlikely that all " cross-elasticities " will ever vanish identically.[1] Even when all goods are independent in production (i.e. when all productive factors are completely specific), they still compete for the consumer's income. Indeed, only when all consumer demand schedules have unit elasticity is it possible for a change in the price of any one good to have no effect at all on the demand for one or more of the others. When there is some degree of substitutability in production, and demand schedules are not thus circumscribed, the " cross-elasticities " must be taken into account. To neglect them is to commit the unjustifiable act of carrying over into general equilibrium analysis assumptions appropriate to partial equilibrium analysis only.

The objection to the use of formula (3) rather than formula (2) is twofold. Firstly, it may give an exaggerated idea of the height of the optimum tariff. And, secondly, it obscures the interesting fact that the optimum " tariff " is sometimes a subsidy. This fact is interesting because it throws light on the usual discussion on Tariffs and the Terms of Trade, in which the possibility of a subsidy on imports being required to turn the terms of trade in one's favour is seldom considered.

Economists have been aware of the possibility of a country turning the terms of trade in its favour by protection ever since the time of John Stuart Mill[2]—if not Torrens and Ricardo.[3] But the actual effect of a tariff on the terms of trade is a rather complicated matter, and has seldom been analysed in detail. The fullest theoretical treatment available is probably that provided by Dr. Mosak, to whose monograph on *General Equilibrium Theory in International Trade*[4] the reader may find it helpful to refer. Briefly, the position is that if we make the simplifying assumption that the government spends the proceeds of the tariff on exports only, the terms of trade must, in a two-country, two-commodity model, move in favour of the protecting country—unless the imported good is markedly inferior, so that the demand for it increases as its price rises. In a multi-commodity world, on the other hand, it does not seem to be possible to generalise about the direction of the movement in the terms of trade—even when we abstract from the inevitable index number problem involved in saying what the terms of trade are when more than two commodities are traded internationally. The crucial factors turn out to be the relations of complementarity and substitution existing between the traded goods. They can turn the terms of trade in either direction.

The two-commodity case, however, is the one most theoretical economists have in mind when discussing problems of international trade. It is the easiest to handle geometrically ; and by talking of " two bales of commodities " rather than " two commodities " it can be invested with a fictitious air of generality. It is not altogether surprising, therefore, that they should have tended to ignore the rather odd case where imports are markedly inferior and the Giffen Paradox operates, and to have

[1] Mr. Kahn is aware of this when he warns that his elasticities are not true elasticities at all, but what might be called " elasticities in the Pigou sense." Cf. loc. cit., p. 17 and A. C. Pigou : *Public Finance*, third edition (London, 1947), pp. 199–200.
[2] *Essays on Some Unsettled Questions of Political Economy* (London, 1844), pp. 26–30, of L.S.E. reprint.
[3] Cf. J. Viner : *Studies in the Theory of International Trade* (New York, 1937), pp. 298–9 and 320.
[4] Bloomington (1944), especially pp. 65–8 and 103–5.

ON OPTIMUM TARIFF STRUCTURES   55

acquired the habit of stating, without qualification, that the terms of trade will move in favour of the protecting country. Marshall, it is interesting to recall, did not do this. In his *Memorandum on Fiscal Policy*[1] he suggested that the Giffen Paradox might operate in respect of imports of wheat into England, and pointed out that if it did the effect of a tariff on wheat would be to turn the terms of trade against her. But the Giffen Paradox is not an everyday market phenomenon ; and if it were it alone that could cause this perverse movement in the terms of trade, economists would be justified in dismissing the whole matter as a mere *curiosum*.

We do not live in a two-commodity world, however, and so it is not necessarily a *curiosum*. Our treatment has the advantage that it evades the difficult matter of what happens to the terms of trade and tackles the problem of the optimum taxes quite directly. It does seem, moreover, that when some of our optimum taxes turn out to be negative, those of us who are accustomed to think the matter through with reference to the terms of trade need not feel too suspicious. We need simply remind ourselves that in a multi-commodity world the terms of trade is a rather elusive concept, and that—however useful—it may occasionally play us tricks.

Leaving the matter of the terms of trade, we might—before concluding this section —pause for a moment to consider the modifications that would have to be introduced into our earlier analysis if we were to relax the assumption that external economies and diseconomies are absent from both production and consumption. If they are present in production, our formula for the optimum taxes remains the same, but domestic prices must be corrected by the imposition of proportionate taxes to bring marginal private rates of transformation in domestic factories into line with the marginal social rates—otherwise the General Optimum will not be attained, even in the closed economy. If they are present in consumption, our simple formula is no longer correct, but it remains true that free trade will land us on the possibility locus in quite exceptional (one might almost say " degenerate ") circumstances only. It is, therefore, in general, always possible to approach the locus more closely by imposing a suitable tariff structure. But the formula defining it is complicated, and little purpose would be served in deriving it here. It is worth noting, however, that it is still true that the attainment of the possibility locus requires that the marginal rates of transformation through foreign trade should equal the marginal social rates of transformation at home.[2]

Finally, it hardly requires emphasis that throughout the preceding analysis we have stuck rigidly to statics, and ignored completely such important dynamic considerations as the probability of retaliation and the chance of protection in an important country precipitating a world slump.

IV. TWO PROBLEMS OF CONSISTENCY

There remain for consideration two problems of consistency. Both are related to the matter of estimating the probable height of an optimum tariff. The first is concerned with the extent to which protection is consistent with the maintenance of a high degree of allocative efficiency in an economy. In the welfare jargon of earlier sections, the problem might be phrased : Granted that the imposition of an optimum tariff structure will shift the possibility locus outwards, may it not twist, or even shift inwards, the efficiency locus—for may not protection give birth to monopoly, and so disrupt the allocative efficiency of an economy ? This is one of those questions we cannot answer theoretically. But it does seem probable that considerations of this

[1] *Official Papers* (London, 1926), pp. 382–3.
[2] Cf. Mathematical Note, equation (7).

nature might require an appreciable *lowering* of the optimum taxes. They constitute an important qualification we should bear in mind when discussing the probable height of the taxes.

The point just made is closely akin to the classical distinction between revenue duties and protecting duties.[1] The burden of the former can be thrown on the foreigner, through the movement in the terms of trade ; whereas the latter " are purely mischievous," to use Mill's phrase. The distinction should not be pressed too far, however, for any actual duty cannot but be a compound of the two : it will affect the possibility and efficiency loci to different degrees.

The second problem of consistency is concerned with Mr. Kahn's revival of Bickerdike's argument that the optimum tariff is likely to be " large " rather than " small." Bickerdike, it will be recalled, maintained that " rather strong assumptions have to be made . . . if the rate of tax affording maximum advantage is to come below 10 per cent."[2] We are not here concerned with the fact that the formula on which this conclusion is based is itself dependent upon " rather strong assumptions " about " cross-elasticities " vanishing identically. The point is rather this : whatever the elasticities may be, there can be no escaping the fact that their magnitudes will depend upon the height of the tariff—they are functionally related. One relation which must exist between them at the optimum point has been produced, but there are undoubtedly others. Thus, consider the case where the foreign elasticity of demand is unity. This does not mean, as a simple substitution in Mr. Kahn's formula might seem to suggest, that the optimum tariff is infinitely high—for an infinite tariff is not consistent with a demand elasticity of unity. As the tariff grew one would expect the elasticity to change. Speaking very generally, there is perhaps a presumption that it will increase as the tariff grows ; and there is perhaps a further presumption that the foreign supply of imports will become more elastic too. Both these changes would tend to *reduce* the height of the optimum tariff. It is not quite legitimate, therefore, to make deductions about its probable height from so simple a formula as Mr. Kahn's—one can never be sure that the values one attributes to the elasticities are, in fact, consistent with the tariff the formula indicates.

Once it is recognised that the elasticities depend on the height of the tariff, it is natural to ask if it is possible to establish rather more precisely the nature of the dependence. Into this matter I do not propose to enter. But it is probably worth pointing out that one of the obvious factors influencing the final result is the way in which the tariff affects the prices of imports and exports. This in turn depends in part upon *domestic* elasticities of demand and supply, and so upon the domestic distribution of income.

We have here the resolution of two paradoxes. The first is Mr. Kahn's[3] : that the optimum tariff formula should depend upon the foreign elasticities only. The second is one which may have troubled the careful reader : We have been making no interpersonal comparisons of well-being ; we have merely been seeking a position on the possibility locus. There are an infinity of such positions, each corresponding to a different distribution of welfare. How is it that we have been able to derive a unique formula for the optimum tariff structure ? The answer is that, while the formula is unique, the actual tariff structure it indicates depends very intimately indeed upon the initial distribution of wealth—for this is one of the factors determining the consistency of the elements in the formula. *Thus we have an infinity of optimum tariff structures, each corresponding to a different initial distribution of wealth, but all deter-*

[1] Cf. Mill, loc. cit., pp. 26–8 ; and *Political Economy*, Book V, Chapter IV, 6.
[2] Loc. cit. (*Economic Journal*, 1907), p. 101.
[3] Loc. cit., p. 16, bottom.

ON OPTIMUM TARIFF STRUCTURES 57

mined by the same rule. We cannot judge between them without making interpersonal comparisons ; and their existence makes it rather difficult to attach significance to attempts at discovering the " probable height " of an optimum tariff.

The situation is precisely analogous to that encountered in a closed economy. There we can formulate a rule such as " equate marginal cost to price " which is quite general. But this rule will not tell us how high prices must be until we know something about the pattern of demand, and therefore the distribution of wealth. Without a criterion for judging between different distributions we cannot say at what level prices and marginal costs are to be equated ; and so we can say but little of the " probable height " of the prices.

This does not, of course, mean that we can never obtain any idea at all of the " probable height " of prices or tariffs, for it is at least conceivable that the infinity of possible heights will occasionally lie within a reasonably narrow range. But it does make the task of determining the range rather difficult. For this reason it may be thought that the preceding analysis has yielded few positive results. To a certain extent that is true. What has emerged very clearly, however, is that what I take to be Professor de Scitovszky's main conclusion is even more firmly based than his treatment might lead one to suspect. His conclusion, the reader will recall, was that it is, generally speaking, the *rational* thing for each country, acting separately, to try to turn the terms of trade in its favour by protection—that there is nothing *natural* about free trade, and that if we want it to obtain we must see that it is *imposed and enforced.*[1] The analysis of this paper has refined the argument somewhat. It has shown that its validity depends in no way upon the possibility of making interpersonal comparisons of well-being,[2] or upon the absence of external economies and diseconomies in production and consumption. It has unearthed the rather odd case where the optimum tariffs are, in fact, subsidies, and it has established that (whether tariffs or subsidies) their imposition is *always* at least potentially beneficial, unless it impairs the allocative efficiency of the economy.[3]

Thus the force of Professor de Scitovszky's conclusion is considerably strengthened. The moral to be drawn from it is too obvious to require emphasis.

V. MATHEMATICAL NOTE

Consider a community of N people. We adopt the convention that the services of productive factors are negative commodities, inputs negative outputs, and exports negative imports. Denote by $x_i{}^a$ the quantity of the ith commodity consumed by the ath citizen. Then the utility indexes take the form :

$$u^\theta = u^\theta\ (x) \qquad (\theta = 1,\ 2,\ .\ .\ .,\ N) \ \dots\dots\dots\dots\dots\dots\dots\dots\dots(1)$$

where x is the row vector of $x_i{}^a$ $(a = 1,\ 2,\ .\ .\ .,\ N\ ;\ i = 1,\ 2,\ .\ .\ .,\ n)$. In a community where external economies and diseconomies in consumption are unknown, we

---

[1] Loc. cit., especially pp. 100–101 and 109–10. Cf. also Kahn, loc. cit., pp. 18–19.

[2] Professor de Scitovszky's treatment does not make this quite clear, since he bases his welfare judgments upon but two of the infinity of possible distributions of wealth—viz. that obtaining in the free trade situation, and that obtaining once the tariff has been imposed.

[3] The reader familiar with Professor de Scitovszky's analysis of the optimum tariff problem will recall that he employs Marshallian offer curves super-imposed on a set of community indifference loci ; and that he is careful to distinguish cases where the community indifference loci intersect between the points representing free trade and the optimum degree of protection from those in which they do not intersect. In the former event we can, on his welfare criteria, make no statement about the desirability of the tariff ; in the latter event we can say that it is desirable. What our analysis (which runs along lines rather different from Professor de Scitovszky's) has shown is, in effect, that the community indifference loci can *never* intersect in the relevant range, unless the allocative efficiency of the system is impaired. I say " in effect " because it is rather difficult to translate our results into Professor de Scitovszky's language, because he considers an exchange- rather than a production-economy, and because I am by no means clear on just what his community indifference curves mean.

have u^θ independent of $x_i{}^a$ for $a \neq \theta$. For the moment, however, it is unnecessary to make this simplification.

We maintain the notation of Section III, and so have :

$$\sum_a x_i{}^a = X_i + z_i \quad\dots\dots\dots\dots\dots\dots (2)$$

where X_i is the home production, and z_i the net import, of the ith commodity. Our dynamic welfare theory is held to provide us with a domestic transformation function of the form :

$$T\ (X) = 0 \quad\dots\dots\dots\dots\dots\dots (3)$$

This tells us the maximum amount of any output we can obtain with given amounts of the other outputs, if our dynamic conditions are to be fulfilled—i.e. if correct provision is to be made for capital accumulation. Our dynamic welfare theory is also held to provide us with a foreign trade transformation function of the form :

$$F\ (z) = 0 \quad\dots\dots\dots\dots\dots\dots (4)$$

which tells us that, correct provision being made for foreign lending, trade must balance. The function F is specified more completely at the beginning of Section III.

Our problem is now to maximise, subject to (3) and (4), each in turn of the u^θ of (1), holding on each occasion all the other constant. The first order conditions can be written :

$$\sum_\theta \lambda^\theta \frac{\partial u^\theta}{\partial x_i{}^a} + \mu \frac{\partial T}{\partial X_i} = 0 \quad\dots\dots\dots\dots\dots(5)$$

$$\begin{array}{l}(a = 1, 2, \dots, N)\\(i = 1, 2, \dots, n)\end{array}$$

and : $$\sum_\theta \lambda^\theta \frac{\partial u^\theta}{\partial x_i{}^a} + \mu' \frac{\partial F}{\partial z_i} = 0 \quad\dots\dots\dots\dots\dots(6)$$

where μ, μ' and the λ^θ are Lagrange multipliers. It follows immediately that :

$$\frac{\partial T/\partial X_i}{\partial T/\partial X_j} = \frac{\partial F/\partial z_i}{\partial F/\partial z_j} \quad (i,\ j = 1, 2, \dots, n) \quad\dots\dots\dots\dots (7)$$

—i.e. that the marginal rates of transformation through foreign trade must equal those in domestic factories.

When there are no external economies or diseconomies in consumption, equations (5) and (6) reduce to :

$$\frac{\partial u^a/\partial x_i{}^a}{\partial u^a/\partial x_j{}^a} = \frac{\partial T/\partial X_i}{\partial T/\partial X_j} = \frac{\partial F/\partial z_i}{\partial F/\partial z_j} \quad \begin{array}{l}(a = 1, 2, \dots, N)\\(i,\ j = 1, 2, \dots, n)\end{array} \quad\dots\dots (8)$$

This is the situation primarily considered in the first part of Section III.

Our final problem is to derive an expression for the slope of the possibility locus. Multiplying equations (5) and (6) by $dx_i{}^a$, summing over the i and the a, and taking account of equations (2), (3), (4) and (7), we obtain without difficulty :

$$\sum_\theta \sum_a \sum_i \lambda^\theta \frac{du^\theta}{dx_i{}^a}\ dx_i{}^a = 0 \dots\dots\dots\dots\dots\dots\dots(9)$$

But, taking the total differentials of (1), we have :

$$du^\theta = \sum_a \sum_i \frac{\partial u^\theta}{\partial x_i{}^a}\ dx_i{}^a \quad (\theta = 1, 2, \dots, N) \quad\dots\dots\dots\dots(10)$$

ON OPTIMUM TARIFF STRUCTURES 59

Therefore, from (9) :

$$\sum_{\theta} \lambda^\theta \, du^\theta = 0 \dots\dots\dots\dots\dots\dots\dots\dots\dots\dots\dots\dots\dots\dots (11)$$

and so the slope of the possibility locus is given by :

$$\frac{\partial u^\alpha}{\partial u^\beta} = -\frac{\lambda^\beta}{\lambda^\alpha} \qquad (\alpha, \beta = 1, 2, \dots, N) \dots\dots\dots\dots\dots\dots\dots (12)$$

Now we have but to derive an expression for $\lambda^\beta/\lambda^\alpha$ $(\alpha, \beta = 1, 2, \dots, N)$. This may be done by selecting a subset of N of the $2Nn$ equations (5), (6), which are linear in the λ's. Thus, if we define the Nth order determinant, A_s, by :

$$A_s = \left| \frac{\partial u^\alpha}{\partial x_s\beta} \right| \qquad (s = 1, 2, \dots, n) \dots\dots\dots\dots\dots\dots\dots\dots (13)$$

(α indicating the columns, and β the rows), and denote by $A_s{}^\theta$ the determinant obtained by replacing each element in the θth column of A_s by unity, it is completely straightforward to show that :

$$\frac{\lambda^\beta}{\lambda^\alpha} = \frac{A_s\beta}{A_s\alpha} \qquad (\alpha, \beta = 1, 2, \dots, N) \dots\dots\dots\dots\dots\dots\dots (14)$$

Thus :

$$\frac{\partial u^\alpha}{\partial u^\beta} = -\frac{A_s\beta}{A_s\alpha} \qquad (s = 1, 2, \dots, n) \dots\dots\dots\dots\dots\dots\dots (15)$$

which is seen to be independent of the particular choice of s ; and the sign of which is invariant under any arbitrary transformations of the utility indexes of the form $\Phi(u)$, where $\Phi'(u) > 0$.

In a two-person community, (15) reduces to :

$$\frac{\partial u^\alpha}{\partial u^\beta} = -\frac{\dfrac{\partial u^\alpha}{\partial x_s\alpha} - \dfrac{\partial u^\alpha}{\partial x_s\beta}}{\dfrac{\partial u^\beta}{\partial x_s\beta} - \dfrac{\partial u^\beta}{\partial x_s\alpha}} \dots\dots\dots\dots\dots\dots\dots\dots\dots\dots\dots\dots\dots\dots\dots (16)$$

which shows that the possibility locus can slope upwards only when external economies in consumption are marked and asymmetrical. That is to say : in a two-person community, the absence of external economies in consumption is sufficient for a downward sloping locus.

In the general N-person community in which there are no external economies or diseconomies in consumption, all the off-diagonal elements of A_s vanish, and so the slope of the locus reduces to :

$$\frac{\partial u^\alpha}{\partial u^\beta} = -\frac{\partial u^\alpha/\partial x_s\alpha}{\partial u^\beta/\partial x_s\beta} \qquad (\alpha, \beta = 1, 2, \dots, N) \dots\dots\dots\dots (17)$$

which is necessarily negative. But when external economies and diseconomies are present the slope can be either positive or negative. Indeed, even when there are no external economies in consumption—i.e. when none of the off-diagonal elements of A_s are positive—the locus can acquire a positive slope in a community consisting of more than two people. On most definitions of social welfare, however, this would not correspond to positions of maximum welfare : when the possibility locus slopes positively we can make everybody better off.

Cambridge.   J. DE V. GRAAFF.

[7]

Optimum Tariffs and Retaliation

During recent years the proposition first advanced by Bickerdike, that a country can improve its welfare as compared with the free trade position by imposing a tariff on imports, has achieved general recognition in the literature of international trade theory. There is still, however, some confusion over what happens if other countries retaliate by imposing tariffs in their turn. Although Kaldor[1] in his classic revival of the Bickerdike proposition, referred explicitly to the possibility that a country might gain by imposing a tariff even if other countries retaliated—a possibility which is also indicated by considerations of general monopoly theory—the possibility is often overlooked : it being assumed, and argued against the " optimum tariff " theorem, that once retaliation occurs all parties are bound to lose as compared with the free trade position. The *locus classicus* of this error (and some others) is probably Professor Scitovszky's analysis of retaliation in his " Reconsideration of the Theory of Tariffs."[2]

The purpose of this article is to reassert the proposition that a country *may* gain by imposing a tariff, even if other countries retaliate ; and to determine the conditions under which it *will* gain in one special case. In the process, the theory of optimum tariff retaliation is restated. The argument is conducted throughout in terms of a two-country, two-commodity exchange model, in which country I exports commodity Y in exchange for imports of commodity II from country II. It is assumed—as is necessary for drawing any definite welfare conclusions from international trade theory— that each country pursues a definite social welfare policy (maximises a given social welfare function) so that its willingness to trade under various conditions can be summarised in a set of community indifference curves (community preference system) ; these curves are assumed to have the customary convexity and non-intersection properties. (The latter assumption, it may be noted, is not necessarily implied by the former.)

In the analysis itself, it is assumed that " retaliation " takes the form of the imposition of an optimum tariff, on the assumption that the other country's tariff will remain unchanged ;[3] and attention is confined to cases in which each country's demand for imports as a function of its terms of trade is elastic, so that the imposition of a tariff by either country reduces the total volume of imports it receives.[4]

The optimum tariff theory may be briefly summarised by reference to Fig. 1. In the diagram, U^I and U^{II} are the preference systems of countries I and II, $O.I$ and $O.II$ their respective offer curves, and P the free trade equilibrium point. Unless country II's offer curve is a straight line, country I can gain by imposing a tariff

[1] N. Kaldor, " A Note on Tariffs and the Terms of Trade," *Economica*, New Series, Vol. VII, November, 1940, pp. 377–80.

[2] T. de Scitovszky, " A Reconsideration of the Theory of Tariffs," REVIEW OF ECONOMIC STUDIES, IX (2), 1941–2, pp. 89–110. Reprinted in *Readings in the Theory of International Trade* (Philadelphia : Blakiston, 1949), No. 16, pp. 358–89.

[3] This assumption obviously begs the question of rationality if the world is really assumed to consist of only two countries ; following Scitovszky, the two-country analysis may be taken as representative of a monopolistically-competitive situation. The assumption that the interaction of trade policy proceeds by the successive imposition of optimum tariffs, rather than by slight changes in existing tariffs, is a simplification which would affect the result only if multiple trade-policy equilibria existed. Finally, while a country might " retaliate " by imposing a tariff other than the optimum, either from " good-neighbourliness " or from vindictiveness, such behaviour would imply that its welfare depended in part on the welfare (or illfare) of other nations as well as on its own consumption, and would therefore fall outside the strictly self-regarding assumptions of optimum tariff theory.

[4] This does not, however, restrict the validity of the conclusions to such cases.

which brings the trade equilibrium point anywhere within the range PQ on country II's offer curve, Q being the point on country II's offer curve which lies on the same country I indifference curve as P. Country I's optimum tariff is that which brings trade equilibrium at the point P' on the highest country I indifference curve touched by

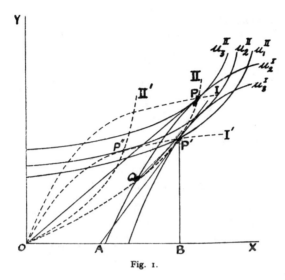

Fig. 1.

country II's offer curve. The rate of tariff which produces this result is $t_I = j - 1$, where j is the elasticity of country II's reciprocal demand curve $\left(\dfrac{EY}{EX}\right)$ at the point P' and is measured on the diagram by the ratio $\dfrac{OB}{AB}$.[1]

The imposition of the tariff t_I alters country I's offer curve to $O.I'$, which intersects $O.II$ at P'. It is worth noting that, in contrast to the procedure employed in general tariff theory, $O.I'$ is not found by shifting $O.I$ to the right[2] to an extent proportional to the tariff rate. This is because, in general tariff theory, the consumers are assumed to give up the tariff proceeds, which therefore do not affect their behaviour,[3] whereas in this case the tariff proceeds are assumed to be redistributed to the consumers (directly or indirectly) and so do influence their behaviour. Consequently, for any given amount of Y the corresponding amount of X on the new offer curve is not given by $(1 + t_I)$ times the corresponding amount of X on the old offer

[1] For the derivation of this and other formulæ, see H. G. Johnson, " Optimum Welfare and Maximum Revenue Tariffs," REVIEW OF ECONOMIC STUDIES, Vol. XIX (1), No. 48 (1950–51), pp. 28–35.

[2] To the right, because the theory assumes that tariff proceeds are spent on imports, either by the Government itself or by recipients of transfer payments from the Government, whichever is indicated as desirable by the social welfare function. This explicit statement is intended to dispel any confusion created by my failure to explain the point in my former article.

[3] L. A. Metzler, however (" Tariffs, the Terms of Trade, and the Distribution of the National Income," *Journal of Political Economy*, Vol. LVII, No. 1, February, 1949, pp. 1–29), assumes that the tariff proceeds are distributed to consumers and analyses the effects of the distribution on the location of the offer curve in terms of the marginal propensity to import ; and J. E. Meade, in his *A Geometry of International Trade* (London : Allen & Unwin, 1952) employs the same construction as that used here.

curve ; instead, it is given by the condition that at that point the marginal rate of substitution between X and Y should be equal to the ratio between their internal (i.e. tax-inclusive) prices. In terms of symbols,

$$\frac{dX}{dY} = -\frac{U'_y}{U'_x} = (1 + t_I)\frac{p_x}{p_y} ;$$

in terms of the diagram, at every point P' on $O.I'$ the tangent to the indifference curve through P' must intersect OX at A in such a way as to make the ratio $\frac{OB}{AB} = t_I + 1$. In one special case, however, which is analysed more fully later, the offer curves derived by the two methods are identical.[1, 2]

Faced by the new country I offer curve $O.I'$ and new equilibrium point P', country II will gain by imposing a tariff unless $O.I'$ is a straight line, since by definition country II's indifference curve through P' is tangent to OP'. The optimum tariff rate for country II is $t_{II} = k - 1$, where k is the elasticity of country I's new reciprocal demand curve $\left(\frac{EX}{EY}\right)$ at the point P''.

P'' may or may not be a position of final (commercial-policy) equilibrium, since the new country II offer curve through that point may or may not make it advantageous for country I to revise its tariff rate. To pursue the matter further, let us turn to Fig. 2, which concentrates on the situation at P''. In the diagram, AA' has been drawn tangent to the country I indifference curve through P'', and II_a', II_b', and II_c' have been drawn to represent possible positions of $O.II'$.

From Fig. 2, it is obvious that if $O.II'$ intersects AA' from the north-west (II_a') country I will gain by increasing its tariff rate ; if it intersects AA' from the north-east (II_b') country I will gain by lowering its tariff ; if $O.II'$ is tangent to AA' (II_c') country I cannot gain by changing its tariff. Since the slope of $O.II'$ at P'' is an indicator of the elasticity of country II's new (post-retaliation) reciprocal demand curve at that point, and the slope of AP'' reflects the elasticity of country II's original reciprocal demand curve at the point P', it follows that country I will raise its tariff if the elasticity of $O.II'$ at P'' is greater than the elasticity of $O.II$ at P' ; lower its tariff if the elasticity of $O.II'$ at P'' is less than the elasticity of $O.II$ at P' ; and leave it unchanged if the elasticities of $O.II'$ at P'' and $O.II$ at P' are the same. This conclusion, of course, may be arrived at directly from the formula for the optimum tariff.

The conclusion just stated contradicts that arrived at by Mr. Scitovszky, who concludes that at P'' country I either cannot gain by altering its tariff, or finds it

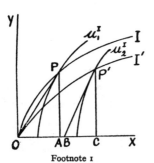

Footnote 1

[1] In the accompanying diagram, P and P' are points on the free-trade and optimum-tariff offer curves. OC, the amount of X now demanded in exchange for a given amount of Y, is only equal to $(1 + t_I)$ times OA (the amount of X formerly demanded) if $OA = BC$, since $\frac{OC}{BC} = j = 1 + t_I$. $AO = BC$ requires that OP be parallel to BP', which implies that the marginal rate of substitution between X and Y be independent of the quantity of X received and be dependent only on the quantity of Y given up.

[2] It follows from the assumed convexity of the community indifference curves that the reciprocal demand curve traced out by a higher tariff rate will always lie inside the curve traced out by a lower tariff rate, whether the latter is inelastic or not. Consequently, the imposition of a tariff cannot, on our assumptions, turn a country's terms of trade against it.

advantageous to raise its tariff still higher. His conclusion, which seems to derive from an uncritical extension of the argument for the situation at P' to that at P'', implicitly assumes that the elasticity of country II's tariff-ridden reciprocal demand curve at P'' is always higher than the elasticity of its free-trade reciprocal demand curve at P', an assumption for which there is no justification in the nature of the problem.[1]

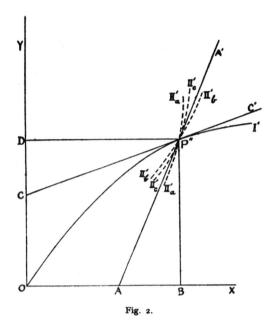

Fig. 2.

This point is easily understood when translated into more general terms. The imposition of the original tariff gave country I the benefit of an improvement in its terms of trade, secured at the cost of some reduction in the volume of trade. The imposition of a retaliatory tariff by country II both worsens country I's terms of trade and further restricts the volume of international trade. In the new situation, three courses are open to country I : it can raise its tariff, improving its terms of

---

[1] This assumption seems to be related to the argument developed by Scitovszky in connection with his welfare criterion, that as restriction increases trade is confined to goods for which the demand is less elastic (on the usual definition of elasticity), so that the possibility of exploiting the foreigner increases with restriction. However, both Scitovszky's analysis and ours assume that at some price-ratio country II would cease to gain from trade ; and at this price-ratio the elasticity of its demand for country I's goods must be infinite (i.e., unity on the definition of elasticity employed here). Consequently, the elasticity of country II's demand for imports cannot be presumed always to decrease as trade is restricted, and the argument referred to would not be sufficient to establish the validity of the conclusion disputed in the text.

This argument—that the more trade is restricted, the more inelastic the foreigner's demand becomes and the more he can be exploited—has been applied to the parallel case of import restriction by J. R Hicks (" Free Trade and Modern Economics," a paper read to the Manchester Statistical Society on March 14th, 1951), who deduces from it a successive tightening of import restrictions. His argument seems to overlook the consideration that by the same reasoning domestic demand for imports becomes less elastic as trade is restricted, so that the sacrifice of imports entailed in exploiting the foreigner further becomes more burdensome.

E

trade at the expense of a further restriction of trade volume ; it can lower its tariff, increasing the volume of trade at the cost of a further worsening of its terms of trade ; or it can leave the tariff and the volume of trade unchanged. Depending on the circumstances, any one of the three may be the most advantageous.

If P'' is not a position of commercial policy equilibrium, further successive adjustments of the tariffs of the two countries will take place. Before the possible outcomes of the adjustment process are considered in detail, two general points about it may be noted. First, the outcome will be unique, in the sense that, given that country I has made the first move, each succeeding step in the adjustment process is uniquely determined.[1] Second, each of the trade equilibrium points reached in the adjustment process must involve a volume of trade which is positive but less[2] than the trade volume under free trade conditions. That the adjustment process will never end in the elimination of trade is a logical consequence of the classical proposition that some trade is always better than no trade[3] ; that the volume of trade will be less than it would be under free trade may be inferred from the argument presented above.

Both of these points are denied by Mr. Scitovszky, who asserts that the outcome is not necessarily unique, and that retaliation may end in the termination of trade. The former assertion is probably a verbal slip ;[4] the latter seems to involve a confusion of optimum tariff theory with pessimum tariff history, and of trade in particular commodities with trade in general.

The process of adjustment may be studied in detail by means of a reaction-curve technique which is presented in Figs. 3 (a) and (b).[5] In Fig. 3 (a) are plotted the offer curves of the two countries at various levels of tariffs, as determined by the procedure outlined earlier ; $O.I_0$ and $O.II_0$ represent the offer curves under free trade (zero tariff) conditions. The tangency points of one country's indifference curves with the other's offer curves trace out *loci* of optimum-tariff equilibrium points (welfare-reaction curves) for the respective countries. Thus OR_I shows the optimum point for country I for each tariff that might be imposed by country II, the tariff required to bring country I to that point being given by the index of the $O.I$ curve through that point. The curve OR_I must pass through the origin, lie inside $O.I_0$ (except in the neighbourhood of the origin, where it coincides with $O.I_0$), move steadily to the right (i.e. Y must be a single-valued function of X), and meet $O.II_0$ below P ; otherwise it may

---

[1] Though the other country's reciprocal demand curve might be so shaped that it is touched more than once by the same indifference curve of the tariff-imposing country, it is reasonable to assume that one tangency point is consistently chosen in preference to the others. Problems of discontinuity of choice implied by this possibility are ignored in what follows.

[2] If the demand for imports as a function of the terms of trade were inelastic for one or both countries, trade in one commodity might be greater than under free trade.

[3] Except in a limiting case excluded by the definition of the present problem.

[4] It is difficult to be certain, since Mr. Scitovszky does not define the term, though he uses it in the same context as the present writer. Also, while his diagrammatic treatment proceeds on the same assumption as that adopted here—that adjustment is effected by the imposition of optimum tariffs—his verbal argument allows the possibility that he is assuming adjustment by small tariff changes ; this alternative assumption might allow a variety of paths to be followed from the same starting-point.

[5] Although the problem is formally one in bilateral monopoly, the technique of analysis employed below bears a strong family resemblance to the Cournot solution of the duopoly problem. Relaxation of the Scitovszky assumption that each country ignores the reactions of the other could lead to a Stackelberg type of analysis in terms of a policy-leader and a policy-follower. Thus, if country I proceeds on the assumption that country II will impose whatever tariff is optimum given the tariff imposed by country I, the tariffs imposed by the two countries will be determined by the tangency of a country I indifference curve with the country II welfare-reaction curve depicted in Fig. 3 (a). Country I might in this case be worse off than it would be if it could use its leadership to maintain free trade ; but, by reasoning analogous to that presented below, this result is by no means inevitable. A more interesting " leadership " model might be constructed on the assumption that country I's tariff-rate sets a maximum to the tariff-rate which country II can impose ; this assumption would define a locus of potential trade-equilibrium points, of which country I would choose the one which maximised its welfare.

This footnote was suggested by comments from Mr. Solomon Adler and Dr. Robert Solow.

OPTIMUM TARIFFS AND RETALIATION 147

take any shape. Similar conditions apply to OR_{II}. Each country is better off the farther along its welfare-reaction curve it is from the origin.

The welfare-reaction curves show the optimum trade-equilibrium points for each country, for all possible tariffs imposed by the other. A movement away from the origin on such a curve may imply either an increase or a decrease in the country's

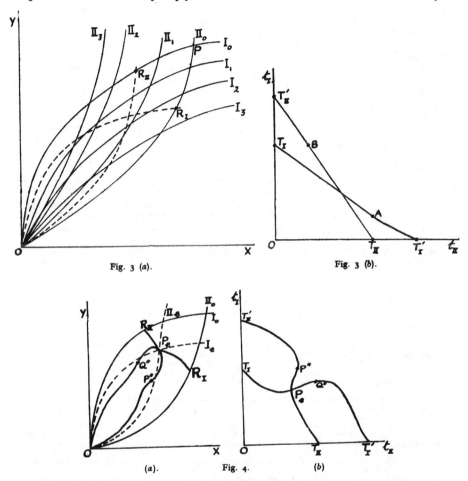

Fig. 3 (a).   Fig. 3 (b).

(a).   Fig. 4.   (b)

(optimum) tariff,[1] and it is convenient to supplement these curves with reaction curves showing the tariff required to maximise a country's welfare, given the tariff imposed by the other. These are presented in Fig. 3 (b). In the figure, $T_I . T'_I$ shows the optimum rate of tariff for country I for each actual tariff imposed by country II, and $T_{II} . T'_{II}$

---

[1] As Fig. 3 (a) is drawn, higher welfare for either country is associated with the imposition of a higher tariff.

gives the corresponding information for country II. T_I, the starting point of $T_I \cdot T'_I$, must be positive ; $T_I \cdot T'_I$ must move continually to the right (i.e., t_I must be a single-valued function of t_{II}) ; it must pass through some point A vertically above T_{II} ; it must meet the $O.t_{II}$ axis somewhere beyond T_{II}, at the point corresponding to the tariff-rate which would eliminate trade[1] ; and T_I must always be less than the latter-rate. But $T_I.T'_I$, and similarly $T_{II}.T'_{II}$, may take any shape which fulfils these conditions. Country I is worse off the farther along $T_I.T'_I$ it is from T_I, and country II is worse off the farther along $T_{II}.T'_{II}$ it is from T_{II}.

With the aid of this apparatus it can easily be seen that, starting from an interruption of free trade by the imposition of an optimum tariff by country I, the adjustment process may lead to either one of two possible outcomes. First, it may lead to a position of policy equilibrium, characterised by the tangency of one of each country's indifference curves with the other country's tariff-inclusive offer curve. Such a position would be represented by the intersection of the two countries' reaction curves (OR_I with $O.R_{II}$ in Fig. 3 (*a*), $T_I.T'_I$ with $T'_{II}.T_{II}$ in Fig. 3 (*b*)). In equilibrium, the tariff of either country may be either higher or lower than it was at the first stage of retaliation (P'' in Figs. 1 and 2) when country I had imposed an optimum tariff and country II had retaliated. The possibility that the tariff rates finally arrived at may be lower for both countries is illustrated in Fig. 4.[2]

The second possible outcome of the adjustment process is that policy equilibrium will never be reached ;[3] instead, the adjustment process may converge on a " tariff cycle,"[4] with (for example) an increase in country I's tariff leading to an increase in country II's tariff, which in turn provokes a decrease in country I's tariff which leads to a decrease in country II's tariff which leads country I to raise its tariff again. Such a " tariff cycle " is illustrated in Fig. 5.[5] In the diagrams, an increase in country I's tariff from $t_I \cdot _1$ to $t_I \cdot _2$ leads country II to raise its tariff from $t_{II} \cdot _1$ to $t_{II} \cdot _2$; country I retaliates by lowering its tariff to $t_I \cdot _1$; country II follows by lowering its tariff to $t_{II} \cdot _1$; country I raises its tariff again to $T_I \cdot _2$ and the cycle repeats itself.

To summarise, there are two possibilities ; the adjustment process may converge on a policy equilibrium point, or it may converge on a tariff cycle. The analysis thus far has assumed that the adjustment process begins with the interruption of free

---

[1] The tariff-rate which would eliminate trade is the same, whichever country imposes it, and is equal to one less than the ratio of the slope of the country I indifference curve through the origin to the slope of the country II indifference curve through the origin, both slopes being taken relative to the X-axis. More simply, it is the proportional excess of the price of X in country I over its price in country II, in the absence of trade. I am grateful to Dr. R. M. Goodwin for clarification of the restrictions on the shape of the tariff-reaction curve.

[2] The figure is drawn so that the same result follows whether country I or country II makes the first break from free trade. P'' and Q'' represent the first stage of retaliation in the two cases ; P_e, I_e and II_e the equilibrium point and equilibrium tariffs.

[3] I am indebted to a discussion with Mr. M. J. Farrell for elucidation of this possibility.

[4] Such a tariff cycle will ensue if the shapes of the tariff-reaction curves make it possible to draw about their intersection a rectangle with sides parallel to the axes and corners on the two reaction curves, such that :

    (*a*) the product of the slopes of the country I curve at the corners through which it passes is less than the product of the slopes of the country II curve at the corners through which it passes, both slopes being taken relative to the t_I axis ; and

    (*b*) T_I does not lie within the segment of the t_I axis cut off by the projection of the sides of the rectangle.

In the limiting case the " rectangle " may be the intersection point itself (as in Fig. 5 (*b*)) ; then condition (*a*) becomes the usual slope condition for an explosive cobweb cycle, and condition (*b*) excludes the possibility of unstable policy equilibrium.

[5] Since the cycle depends on an increase in one country's tariff making it advantageous for the other to lower its tariff, it could not arise if it were always advantageous for one country to respond to an increase in the other's tariff by an increase in its own. Thus the Scitovszky assumption excludes the possibility of tariff cycles. It may be remarked that a continued tariff cycle would eventually demonstrate the irrationality of the model's assumptions.

OPTIMUM TARIFFS AND RETALIATION   149

trade by the imposition of an optimum tariff by country I. Free trade may equally well be interrupted by the imposition of a tariff by country II ; and the outcome—whether a tariff cycle or policy equilibrium—may be different from the outcome when the process begins with a move by country I.[1] In short, the outcome of tariff retaliation may depend on which country first imposes a tariff.

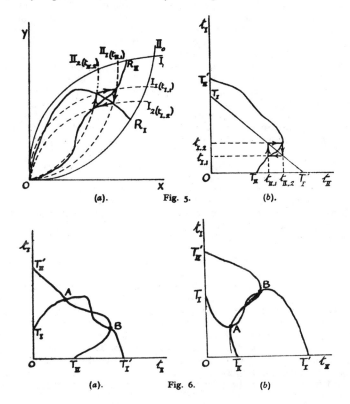

(a).   Fig. 5.   (b).

(a).   Fig. 6.   (b)

This does not, however, as assumed by Scitovszky and others, imply that a country necessarily winds up in a better position if it is the first to impose a tariff than if the other country begins the erection of tariff barriers. In those cases in which a position of policy equilibrium is reached,[2] it is also possible for a country to end up better off if the other country imposes the first tariff than if it makes the first move itself ; or for *both* countries to be worse off if one of them starts the tariff-erection process than if the other does. The first of these possibilities is illustrated in Fig. 6 (a),

---

[1] It may be remarked that in cases in which policy equilibrium is not achieved in the first two steps, and the Scitovoszky assumption that adjustment *always* involves tariff increase or no change holds good, the same position will be reached whichever country imposes the first tariff.

[2] The argument can be extended, with appropriate modifications, to cases in which the outcome is a " tariff cycle " rather than a policy equilibrium, by considering the least favourable position on the tariff cycle.

and the second in Fig. 6 (*b*). In each diagram, policy equilibrium is reached at *A* if country *II* imposes the first tariff and at *B* if country *I* imposes the first tariff. In Fig. 6 (*a*) each country ends up closer to the starting point of its reaction curve, and therefore better off, if the other country rather than itself imposes the first tariff. In Fig. 6 (*b*), both countries end up better off if country *II* imposes the first tariff than if country *I* does. Both of these cases involve reaction curves with ranges in which an increase in one country's tariff makes an increase in the other country's tariff advantageous ; if an increase in one country's tariff always prompted a decrease in the other's (the opposite of the Scitovszky assumption) a country would always be better off if it were the first to impose a tariff.

The foregoing argument has been devoted to a restatement of the theory of retaliation ; our central concern, however, is with the question of whether, as Mr. Scitovszky and others assert, both countries are necessarily worse off when retaliation is allowed for than they would be under free trade. In considering this problem, we shall for simplicity confine the argument to cases in which a policy equilibrium is attained.[1] Let us assume that P'' in Figs. 1 and 2 represents such an equilibrium. Then from Fig. 1 it is apparent that country *I* would be better off after both countries have imposed (consistent) optimum tariffs if the indifference curve through P'' passed to the right of *P*, the free-trade equilibrium point ; similarly country *II* would gain as compared with the free-trade situation if the country *II* indifference curve through P'' passed to the left of *P*. Whatever the final equilibrium point, one country *must* lose under tariffs as compared with free trade, since gain depends on obtaining an improvement in the terms of trade sufficient to outweigh the loss of trade volume, and this is impossible for both countries simultaneously ; and both countries *may* lose, as is in fact the case in Fig. 1 ; but it is not necessarily true that both *will* lose.

The same point emerges from Fig. 2, which represents the commercial-policy equilibrium point, but does not show the free-trade equilibrium point. All that is known about the latter is that it must lie to the north-east of P'' : if it lies to the left of AA', country *I* must, by the usual index-number logic, be better off than it would be under free trade[2] ; if it lies to the right of CC', country *II* must, by the same argument, be better off than it would be under free trade ; if it lies between AA' and CC', either country may be better off or both may be worse off than under free trade, depending on the location of *P* and the shapes of the indifference curves through P''.[3]

Unfortunately, while it is easy to demonstrate the possibility of one country being better off under (optimum) tariffs than under free trade, the conditions under which it will be so involve the relationship between the preference systems of the

---

[1] See previous footnote.
[2] By a simple geometrical argument it can be shown that a country's welfare is necessarily improved if the total proceeds of the tariff exceed the difference between the values of the free-trade quantity of imports at the new and the free-trade internal prices. Specifically, country *I* must be better off with tariffs if

$$\frac{t_1}{t_1+1} \, II_x \quad X_1 > (II_x - p_x) \, X_0$$

where X_0 and X_1 are the quantities imported under free trade and in tariff equilibrium, p_x and II_x are the internal price of *X* in terms of *Y* before and after the tariff, and t_1 is the tariff rate.
[3] Alternatively, the conclusion could be established by finding the rate of tariff for the other country which would leave the country in question exactly as well off, after it had retaliated, as it would be if both countries practised free trade, and marking the corresponding point on its welfare-reaction curve (Fig. 3 (*a*)) or tariff-reaction curve (Fig. 3 (*b*)). The country's welfare would be greater under tariffs than under free trade if the policy equilibrium point lay farther from the origin than that point on the former curve, or closer to the origin than that point on the latter curve.

OPTIMUM TARIFFS AND RETALIATION 151

two countries,[1] and are too complex to express in terms of simple and objectively assessable concepts. Mr. Kaldor's statement,[2] for example, that :

" if the elasticity of the country's own demand for foreign products is markedly higher than the elasticity of foreign demand for its own products—an unusual case—this policy may be advantageous even if the ' optimum degree of retaliation ' of foreign countries is allowed for."

is imprecise and almost meaningless, since, as has been seen above, the elasticities involved in the analysis lie on different and not closely related curves—of which they may not be parameters—and in any case the answer depends on the preference systems lying behind the curves.

Parenthetically, this is a general problem in the application of the optimum tariff theory, since the elasticities incorporated in the various optimum tariff formulæ (besides being " total " and not " partial " concepts) are likely to vary along the reciprocal demand curve, so that empirical observations on these elasticities may yield no useful guide to policy conclusions, except perhaps as to the desirable direction of change.[3]

There is, however, one special case in which the required conditions can be fairly readily established—that in which the reciprocal demand curves of the two countries have constant elasticities throughout their length. In this case, the implied community preference system of each country is such as to generate offer curves of the same elasticity, whatever the tariff the country imposes on its imports ; consequently, each country's optimum tariff is independent of the other's, and the same commercial policy equilibrium point is reached in only two steps from the free-trade position, whichever country first erects a tariff.[4] Finally, the conditions under which one country is better off under tariffs than under free trade can be stated in terms of the relation between the two elasticities of reciprocal demand—so that Mr. Kaldor's conclusion becomes meaningful and can be quantified.

Let the reciprocal demand curve of country I be $X = AY^k$, with constant elasticity k, and that of country II be $Y = BX^j$, with constant elasticity j. These demand equations imply utility functions $U^I = f^I (kX - AY^k)$ and $U^{II} = f^{II} (jY - BX^j)$, where the f's are any monotonically-increasing functions of the expressions in brackets, and for simplicity are henceforth omitted.[5]

Under free trade conditions, the equilibrium quantities of commodities exchanged will be :

$$X_0 = A^{\frac{1}{1 - jk}} B^{\frac{k}{1 - jh}}$$

$$Y_0 = A^{\frac{j}{1 - jh}} B^{\frac{1}{1 - kj}}$$

[1] There are also the difficulties discussed above that the outcome may be a tariff cycle instead of a policy equilibrium point and that the answer may depend on which country first imposes a tariff.

[2] Loc. cit., p. 380.

[3] Cf. Dr. Graaff's strictures on Professor Kahn's attempt to prove that the optimum tariff is likely to be high (J. de V. Graaff, " On Optimum Tariff Structures," THE REVIEW OF ECONOMIC STUDIES, Vol. XVII (1), No. 42 (1949-50), pp. 47-59).

[4] If one country only has a reciprocal demand curve of constant elasticity, equilibrium would still be the same, whichever country started tariff-erection, and would be reached in either two or three steps, depending on whether the other or that country imposed the first tariff.

[5] These utility functions do not necessarily imply a constant marginal utility of the imported good, since this depends on the (unspecified) sign of f'' ; but they do imply that the marginal rate of substitution between imports and exports depends only on the quantity of exports—which is why the effect of a tariff on the offer curve is a proportional displacement.

and the utility indices will be :

$$UI_0 = (k - 1)\ X_0$$
$$UII_0 = (j - 1)\ Y_0$$

Now assume that country I imposes a tariff t. The country's new offer curve is defined by the condition :

$$- \frac{UI_x}{UI_y} = A^{-1}\ Y^{1-k} = \frac{dY}{dX} = (1 + t)\ \frac{Y}{X}$$

(equality of the marginal rate of substitution with the internal (tariff-inclusive) price ratio) and its equation is $X = (1 + t)\ A Y^k$; thus the tariff merely displaces country I's reciprocal demand curve to the right (Fig. 1) and does not alter its elasticity.

When both countries impose their optimum tariffs the equations of reciprocal demand become $X = jAY^k$ and $Y = kBX^j$; the equilibrium quantities of goods exchanged become :

$$X_1 = j^{\frac{1}{1 - jk}}\ k^{\frac{k}{1 - jk}}\ A^{\frac{1}{1 - jk}}\ B^{\frac{k}{1 - jk}}$$

$$Y_1 = j^{\frac{j}{1 - jk}}\ k^{\frac{1}{1 - jk}}\ A^{\frac{j}{1 - jk}}\ B^{\frac{1}{1 - jk}}$$

and the utility indices become :

$$UI_1 = \frac{\left(k - \frac{1}{j}\right)\ j^{\frac{1}{1 - jk}}\ k^{\frac{k}{1 - jk}}}{k - 1}\ . (UI_0)$$

$$UII_1 = \frac{\left(j - \frac{1}{k}\right)\ j^{\frac{j}{1 - jk}}\ k^{\frac{1}{1 - jk}}}{j - 1}\ . (UII_0)$$

Hence country I is better or worse off under optimum tariffs than under free trade according as the multiplier of UI_0 in the expression above is greater or less than unity; the condition for country II to be better or worse off is, of course, symmetrical.

These conditions unfortunately cannot be reduced to the form of a more simple general relation between j and k ; however, it is possible to obtain a general idea of them by calculation of numerical examples. This has been done for values of j and k corresponding to elasticities of international demand as more usually conceived (elasticity of quantity demanded with respect to relative price, determined by the relations

$\eta_I = \frac{k}{k - 1}$, $\eta_{II} = \frac{j}{j - 1}$) ranging by tenths from 1.1 to 3.0 and by quarters from 3.0 to 5.0. The results are presented in Chart I. The shaded areas show elasticity combinations yielding individual gain or mutual loss, the unshaded " V "—shaped area represents untested intervals.[1] As an example, if the elasticity of country I's demand for imports were 2.0, country I would be better off under tariffs than under free trade if the elasticity of country II's demand were 1.5 or less ; both countries would be worse off if the elasticity of country II's demand lay between 1.6 and 2.8 inclusive ; while country II would be better off under tariffs than under free trade if (country I's elasticity remaining at 2.0) its elasticity of demand for imports were 2.9 or greater.

[1] The dividing lines between the areas obtained by graphical approximation on the chart are :
$$\eta_I = 1.75\ \eta_{II} - .65 \text{ and } \eta_{II} = 1.75\ \eta_I - .65.$$
Hence, approximately, a country is better off under (optimum) tariffs than under free trade if its elasticity of demand for imports is greater than one and three-quarter times the other country's elasticity of demand for imports less two-thirds.

OPTIMUM TARIFFS AND RETALIATION 153

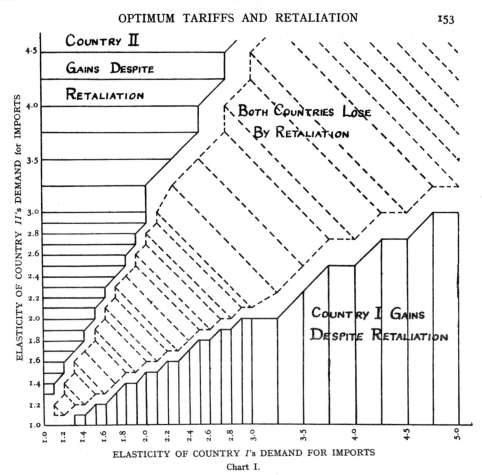

ELASTICITY OF COUNTRY *I*'s DEMAND FOR IMPORTS

Chart I.

To summarise, it has been shown in this article that, contrary to a widely held opinion,[1] a country *may* gain by imposing an optimum tariff even if other countries retaliate by following the same policy ; and the conditions under which it *will* gain have been investigated for a special case. The implication,[2] as in many other problems in the theory of international economic policy, is that the answer depends on the circumstances of the particular case ; and that anyone who asserts that one conclusion is universally valid is making an implicit assumption about the facts which ought to be explicitly defended—if it can be.

Cambridge.   HARRY G. JOHNSON.

[1] See, e.g., S. Enke and V. Salera, *International Economics*, second edition (New York : Prentice-Hall, 1951), pp. 272–3, and C. P. Kindleberger, *International Economics* (Homewood : Irwin, 1953), p. 195.
    D. B. Marsh, in *World Trade and Investment* (New York : Harcourt Brace, 1951), pp. 320 and 322, states the main point correctly, but his exposition is defective in other respects.
[2] A further implication of the general theory of optimum tariff retaliation presented here, and one which is too obvious to deserve elaboration, is that the optimum tariff theory is not a very useful approach to the explanation of tariff history. Contrast Scitovszky, loc. cit.

F

[8]

INTERNATIONAL ECONOMIC REVIEW
Vol. 31, No. 1, February 1990

THE OPTIMAL TARIFF STRUCTURE IN HIGHER DIMENSIONS

By Eric W. Bond[1]

This paper generalizes to higher dimensions the two good result that the optimal trade policy for a large country is an import tariff. A weak form of the optimal tariff, requiring that an import (export) good be most (least) protected holds under gross substitutability. Sufficient conditions are obtained for a strong form of the optimal tariff (which requires that all imports be more protected than any export), and also for the trade tax revenue to be nonnegative in the optimal policy.

1. INTRODUCTION

The traditional optimal tariff argument in a two good model with both goods produced competitively indicates that an active country can improve its welfare by restricting the level of trade through an import tariff, assuming that the other country remains passive. This result stands in contrast to models in which export industries are not competitive, where export subsidies may be welfare enhancing (for example, Brander and Spencer 1985). Recently, however, a number of papers have shown that when there are more than two goods, subsidies to some trade flows may be welfare enhancing even when all industries are competitive. Feenstra (1986) using a model with three goods, and Itoh and Kiyono (1987), using a model with a continuum of goods, have identified conditions under which export subsidies will be welfare enhancing.[2] Similar results involving the desirability of subsidies to traded factors have been obtained in models in which goods and factors are mobile.[3] In each case, interactions between the various goods may lead to the use of trade instruments that would not be used in the two good case.

The purpose of this paper is to examine what elements of the two good optimal tariff argument generalize to the n good case. This exercise is useful because it will yield a better understanding of the types of observed trade interventions that would be inconsistent with the standard optimal tariff argument, and therefore must be explained by other models of trade policy. We follow the constructive approach discussed by Ethier (1984) of deriving conditions which hold for some goods or will hold "on average" when extending the two good results to higher dimensions. The

---

[1] I thank Alan Deardorff, Tim Fries, Ron Jones, Murray Kemp, Carsten Kowalczyk, Peter Lloyd, Peter Neary, William Thomson, and anonymous referees for helpful comments on an earlier draft.

[2] Graaf (1949–50) first observed that in the many good case, the optimal tariff vector might contain trade subsidies. However, his analysis did not indicate the conditions under which negative elements would occur.

[3] For example, see Jones (1967) for the case of two goods and one mobile factor and Jones et al. (1986), Kuhn and Wooton (1987), and Bond (1989) for the case of one good and two mobile factors. The model of this paper deals only with the case of goods trade, but could easily be extended to consider the case of both goods trade and factor trade using techniques as in Neary (1985).

first problem that must be confronted in the many good case is that the pattern of trade taxation will be sensitive to the particular good that is chosen as numeraire (the untaxed commodity). In the *n* good case, the Lerner symmetry result says that there will be *n* possible patterns of trade taxation depending on the *n* different choices of numeraire. This is particularly destructive to discussions of taxation versus subsidization in higher dimensions because the sign of trade taxes will not be invariant to the choice of numeraire. The approach in Section 2 of the paper is to focus on the chain of protection, which is the ranking of goods by the ratio of the domestic price to the world price under the optimal policy. This ranking must be invariant to the choice of numeraire. Only the extreme goods in the chain will have trade taxes whose signs do not change with the choice of numeraire.

This suggests two questions to be asked when using the chain to generalize the optimal tariff argument. The first (weak) form of the optimal tariff argument is whether the extreme goods in the chain must be an import good that bears a tariff and an export good that bears a tax, and the second (strong) form is whether there is some choice of numeraire for which all exports and imports are taxed. It is shown that the assumption of gross substitutability is sufficient for the weak form of the optimal tariff to be satisfied but not for the strong form. A condition requiring goods to be better substitutes within trade groups than between trade groups is shown to be sufficient for the strong form of the optimal tariff.[4]

The results of Section 2 indicate that an assumption of gross substitutability is necessary in order to be able to say much about the placement of goods in the chain of protection. Therefore, Section 3 examines how paradoxical results may be in the absence of gross substitutability. Sufficient conditions are derived which ensure that the optimum cannot occur at a point where all goods are subsidized, and that the optimum cannot occur at a point where the net tariff revenue will be negative. The consideration of tariff revenue in generalizing the optimal tariff argument was suggested by Kemp (1967). Since the presence of nonnegative tariff revenue indicates an average sense in which the imports must have tariffs and exports must have taxes in the optimal policy, this generalization is in the spirit of the work of Deardorff (1980) and Dixit and Norman (1980) on the principle of comparative advantage.

2. THE OPTIMAL TARIFF STRUCTURE WITH *N* GOODS

In this section we analyze the optimal trade policy of an active home country facing a passive foreign country in a model in which there are *n* traded goods. We concentrate on developing a ranking of tariff rates that will hold regardless of the choice of numeraire, and on indicating the results that can be obtained on the order of the goods in this ranking.

---

[4] The concept which I refer to as the strong form of the optimal tariff has also been examined by Horwell and Pearce (1970), who derive sufficient conditions for there to be a choice of numeraire such that all imports have tariffs. This paper derives an alternative condition, which emphasizes the relationship between substitutability and the placement of goods in the chain of protection. To the best of my knowledge, the concept of the weak form of the optimal tariff is new.

Home country preferences are assumed to be represented by a strictly quasi-concave Meade utility function $U = U(m)$, where m is the n element column vector of home country net imports.[5] The home country's budget constraint requires that $p^{*T}m = 0$, where p^* is the vector of world prices and a T superscript indicates the transpose of a vector. Totally differentiating the home country utility function and using the first order conditions from the home country's constrained maximization problem yields $dy = p^T dm$, where $dy = dU/\lambda$ is the change in home real income and λ is the Lagrange multiplier from the home budget constraint. Totally differentiating the home budget constraint and combining with the expression for dy yields the Jones decomposition

(1) $$dy = -m^T dp^* + (p - p^*)^T dm.$$

The first term in (1) is the terms of trade effect and the second term is the trade volume effect. We define $t = (p - p^*)$ to be the vector of trade taxes. Note that $t_i > 0$ (<0) is a tariff (subsidy) for an import good and a subsidy (tax) for an export good.

Foreign excess demand functions are assumed to be continuous, homogeneous of degree zero in prices, and to satisfy the trade balance constraint $p^{*T}m^* = 0$.[6] Let M^* denote the $n \times n$ matrix of substitution effects $m_{ij}^* = (\partial m_i^*/\partial p_j^*)$, where i indicates the row and j the column of the matrix. We will assume the foreign excess demand functions are differentiable, so that M^* will be well defined for all price vectors. We then have:

(2a) $$p^{*T}M^* = -m^{*T}$$

(2b) $$M^*p^* = 0.$$

Condition (2a) follows from total differentiation of the budget constraint and (2b) follows from Euler's condition for homogeneous functions.

The objective of the home country is to maximize $U(m)$ subject to the constraint that $m = -m^*(p^*)$. The first order conditions for a maximum are obtained by setting $dy = 0$ from (1) with $dm = -dm^* = -M^*dp^*$.

(3) $$(p - p^*)^T M^* = m^{*T}.$$

Equivalently, (2a) can be used to express this system as

(4) $$p^T M^* = 0.$$

---

[5] Such a trade utility function can be derived using methods employed by Dixit and Norman (1980) and Woodland (1980) from the assumption that home country preferences over consumption bundles can be represented by a strictly quasi-concave function, and that the production technology is strictly convex and bounded above.

[6] These properties of the foreign excess demand functions are the properties of the individual excess demand functions (from agents maximizing strictly quasi-concave utility functions subject to a budget constraint) that are preserved under aggregation. Other properties of individual excess demands, such as the weak axiom of revealed preference, may not be preserved under aggregation. Therefore, we start with the more general case. The case in which the foreign country excess demand can be treated as that of a representative agent will be considered below.

Expression (4) expresses the requirement that the home country indifference curves be tangent to the foreign country offer surface at the optimum.

Since M^* is singular, the system in (3) or (4) must be solved by imposing a price normalization and then solving the remaining $n - 1$ equations for the system of trade taxes given the normalization. Let good i be the numeraire, and choose the numbering of products such that the ratio of domestic price to world price in the solution to (3) is increasing in the index of the product. This yields the "chain of protection"

$$(5) \qquad (p_1/p_1^*) < \cdots < (p_i/p_i^*) < \cdots < (p_n/p_n^*).$$

We assume throughout the rest of the paper that this chain is satisfied with strict inequalities, although statements of the propositions can be modified in obvious ways to allow for "ties" in the chain. We then have that with good i as numeraire, $t_j > 0 \ (<0)$ when $j > i \ (j < i)$.

The virtue of using the chain of protection to deal with the optimal pattern of trade taxes is that this ranking of relative prices is independent of choice of numeraire, whereas the sign of the trade taxes t_j will not be independent of which commodity is untaxed. This can be seen by observing that the relative prices of goods in both countries must be independent of the choice of numeraire, due to the homogeneity of the demand functions. It then follows that for goods 2, 3, ... , $n - 1$ there will be at least one choice of numeraire for which $t_j > 0$ and at least one for which $t_j < 0$. The only goods for which the signs of the trade taxes are unambiguous are the extreme goods, 1 and n.

Two approaches to generalizing the optimal tariff argument using the chain of protection will be considered:

DEFINITION 1.   *The chain of protection* (5) *satisfies the weak form of the optimal tariff (condition W) if good* 1 *is an export and good n is an import good. The strong form (condition S) is satisfied if good* 1, 2, ... , *k are exported goods and goods k* + 1, ... , *n are imports.*

Note that condition S is equivalent to the requirement that there be a choice of numeraire such that all imports have tariffs and all exports are taxed. Also, note that these two conditions are equivalent for $n \leq 3$.

2.1.   *Ranking Goods in the Chain of Protection.*   In this section we examine conditions on the matrix M^* under which the weak and strong forms of the optimal tariff will be satisfied. The role played by the substitution effects between goods can be seen by considering the jth necessary condition from (3)

$$(6) \qquad m_j^* - t_j m_{jj}^* - \sum_{i \neq j} t_i m_{ij}^* = 0.$$

The first term in (6) is the terms of trade effect of an increase in the price of good j, which will be negative if good j is a home country import good ($m_j^* < 0$). At the optimum, this unfavorable terms of trade effect must be matched by a favorable trade volume effect.[7]

Choosing an arbitrary export good k as untaxed, we investigate the condition under which good j lies to the right of k in the chain of protection ($t_j > 0$). With $m^*_{jj} < 0$, an increase in the price of import good j raises the quantity supplied by the foreign country, which is favorable when $t_j > 0$. In the two good case, this is the only trade volume effect so that t_j must be positive in order for (6) to be satisfied. In the many good case, (6) may be satisfied with an import subsidy if the interactions with other goods are such that $\Sigma_{i \neq j} t_i m^*_{ij}$ is sufficiently negative. The third term in (6) is more likely to be negative in cases where good j is a strong substitute for goods with $t_i < 0$ and/or a complement for goods with $t_i > 0$.

The above discussion of the necessary conditions indicates that in order to place goods in the chain of protection, it will be necessary to impose restrictions on the $t_i m^*_{ij}$ for $i \neq j$. This is simplest for the extreme goods in the chain, for which an untaxed commodity can be chosen such that the t_i all have the same sign. Consider (6) for $j = n$ and choose $t_n = 0$, so that $t_i < 0$ for $i \neq n$. If all other goods are gross substitutes for good n, the last term in (6) must be negative and the second term will equal zero. In order for (6) to be satisfied, good n must be an import of the home country. A similar argument establishes that good 1 must be an export. This establishes that gross substitutability is sufficient for the weak form of the optimal tariff.

The following example with four goods indicates that gross substitutability is not sufficient to ensure satisfaction of the strong form of the optimal tariff argument. Suppose that the substitution matrix with weak gross substitutability has the following elements at the optimum:

$$(7) \qquad M^* = \begin{bmatrix} -6 & 0 & 5 & 1 \\ 0 & -2 & 0 & 2 \\ 0 & 0 & -3 & 3 \\ 1 & 1 & 0 & -2 \end{bmatrix}$$

with $p^{*T} = (1, 1, 1, 1)$ and $m^{*T} = (5, 1, -2, -4)$. It is easily verified that this example satisfies (2). Choosing good 3 to be the numeraire, the optimal home country price vector can be calculated from (4) to be $p^T = (.6, 1.8, 1, 3.6)$. The chain of protection has the form export < import < export < import, violating conditions S. This example uses weak gross substitutability, but clearly extends to gross substitutability by replacing the 0's by ε small.

In order to develop a sufficient condition for the strong form of the optimal tariff, choose the export good that is the most protected good under the optimal policy to

---

[7] Note that this problem is similar to the literature on optimal commodity taxation (Diamond and Mirrlees 1971) and the literature on tax reform (Dixit 1975, Hatta 1977, and Hatta and Haltiwanger 1986). The tax reform literature examines the types of changes in tax rates that will improve welfare, starting from an exogenously given system of taxes. In the present context we are concerned with characterizing tax rates at the optimum, as in the optimal tax literature. However, the optimal tax literature is generally not concerned with the relationship between the ranking of tax rates in the optimal policy and the direction of trade, as we examine here. See also Woodland (1982) for a summary of results on tariff reform.

be untaxed. Denoting this commodity by k and letting X denote the index set of export goods, we have $t_i \leq 0$ for all $i \in X$ when good k is untaxed. We now decompose the first order conditions for an import good j by separating substitution effects within the import good category from those between imports and exports

$$(8) \qquad m_j^* - \sum_{i \in X} t_i m_{ij}^* - \sum_{\substack{i \in I \\ i \neq j}} t_i m_{ij}^* - t_j m_{jj}^* = 0,$$

where I is the index set of import goods. In order to show that $t_j > 0$ for any $j \in I$ under gross substitutability, it must be the case that the sum of the first three terms is negative. The first term in (8) is negative by choice of j as a home import, but the signs of the second two terms will conflict since $t_i > 0$ for $i \in I$ and $t_i < 0$ for $i \in X$. This suggests that a sufficient condition for the strong form may be found by restricting the substitution effects within the imported trade group (third term in (8)) to be larger than that between trade groups (second term).

The following condition on substitution effects has the desired property.

DEFINITION 2. *Let all goods be gross substitutes and define* $X = \{i | m_i^* > 0\}$ *and* $I = \{i | m_i^* < 0\}$. *We say that goods are stronger substitutes within trade groups than between trade groups if*

(a) for all $i, j \in I (i \neq j)$ *and for all* $k \in X$, *we have* $p_j^* m_{ij}^* \geq p_k^* m_{ik}^*$
(b) for all $i, k \in X$ $(i \neq k)$ *and* $j \in I$, *we have* $p_j^* m_{ij}^* \leq p_k^* m_{ik}^*$.

It is shown in the Appendix that if these conditions are both satisfied, then the strong form of the optimal tariff will hold.[8] Note that the example in (7) in which the strong form does not hold violates this condition because of the strong effect of the prices of import goods 3 and 4 on the export goods.

The results of this section can now be summarized in the following proposition:

PROPOSITION 1. *Under the optimal trade tax policy, the chain of protection (5) has the properties:*

(a) If all goods are gross substitutes in the foreign country, then condition W holds.

(b) If all goods are gross substitutes and the matrix M^* *satisfies the condition that goods be better substitutes within trade categories than between trade categories, then conditions S holds.*

Proposition 1 can also be interpreted in terms of the pattern of trade taxes that can be observed for a given choice of numeraire, i. For $i \neq n$, (a) indicates that there will be at least one import good that bears a tariff. For $i \neq 1$ there will be at least one

---

[8] Horwell and Pearce (1970) derive a sufficient condition for there to be a choice of numeraire for which all imports have tariffs. Their condition is on the matrix H^T, where $h_{ij} = s_{ij}^*/m_j^*$ and s_{ij}^* is the pure substitution effect (see equation (10)). The condition in Definition 2 has the advantage of being derived from the comparison of the relative substitution effects with the placement of goods in the chain of protection, and is therefore more easily interpreted in terms of two good comparisons.

export good that bears a tax. Equivalently, any optimal policy that includes import (export) subsidies must also include export (import) taxes under gross substitutability. Although subsidies may occur under gross substitutability, there is a limit to how prevalent these subsidies can be.

The results of this section have been derived assuming that all goods are gross substitutes. It should be noted that this does not require that they be gross substitutes everywhere, but only at the optimum. For example, the two good case with a backward-bending foreign offer curve does not exhibit substitutability for all world price vectors, but any home country optimum must occur in the region of the foreign offer curve that exhibits gross substitutability.

2.2. *Single Foreign Consumer.* In the case in which the foreign country excess demand functions can be treated as being derived from the maximization of utility by a representative foreign consumer, further results can be obtained by decomposing M^* into income and substitution effects. In this section we assume that the foreign demand functions can be written as real income constant demand functions $m^* = m^*(p^*, y^*)$, where y^* is foreign real income.

The change in foreign real income from a change in prices will be $dy^* = -m^{*T}dp^*$, using a derivation similar to that for (1). The matrix of substitution effects can be written as $M^* = S^* - \alpha^* m^{*T}$, where S^* denotes the matrix of pure substitution effects in consumption and production and α^* is the vector of income effects $(\partial m_i^*/\partial y^*)$. It is well known that these matrices have the following properties:

(9a) S^* is symmetric and negative semi-definite

(9b) $p^{*T}S^* = 0$

(9c) $p^{*T}\alpha^* = 1.$

Substituting this decomposition of the substitution matrix in (5) and making use of (3), (9b), and (9c) yields

(10) $t^T S^* = \beta m^{*T}$ where $\beta = p^T \alpha^*.$

Comparing (10) with (3), it can be seen that if $\beta > 0$, then the arguments used to derive Proposition 1 for the case of gross substitutability can be used to yield similar conclusions under the assumption that goods are substitutes in the compensated sense ($s_{ij}^* > 0$ for $i \neq j$) in the foreign country. A sufficient condition for $\beta > 0$ is that all goods be normal goods in the foreign country. If some goods are inferior, then β could be negative if the inferior goods are heavily protected in the home country.

3.   RELAXING SUBSTITUTABILITY ASSUMPTIONS

In this section, we examine what can be said about the optimal trade policy when the assumption of gross substitutability is relaxed. First, it should be noted that even in the two good case, it is possible to find examples in which the first order conditions for a maximum (3) are satisfied at a point where imports are subsidized. Two such examples, suggested by Kemp (1967), are illustrated in Figure 1. In each

110   ERIC W. BOND

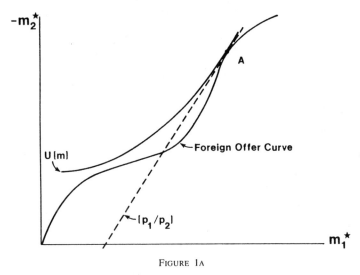

FIGURE 1A

GLOBAL OPTIMUM WITH SUBSIDIZED TRADE

case, a tangency between a home country indifference curve and the foreign offer curve occurs at a point where the home country offer curve is steeper than a ray from the origin. The domestic price of imports will then be lower than the foreign country price at the tangency, indicating an import subsidy. In Figure 1a, we have a case in which the foreign offer curve is not single valued. The tangency between the home offer curve and the foreign offer curve at point A is a global optimum for the home country along this offer curve. In Figure 1b, the home country offer curve is single valued, but there is a range (between points B and D) over which the foreign country import is a Giffen good. A tangency occurs at point C, although it can be seen that this point is a local maximum, but not a global maximum.

Although each of these cases requires extreme assumptions about the behavior of foreign excess demand functions, they indicate that it will not be possible to rule out subsidies to all goods in the many good case. Therefore, in this section we will examine what (local) conditions on the foreign offer curves will be sufficient to rule out the types of subsidized trade illustrated in Figure 1. In the many good case, it is possible to generalize the notion of subsidized trade in two ways. First, we consider the possibility that there is a choice of numeraire for which trade in all goods is subsidized. Second, we consider the possibility that there are both subsidies and taxes in the optimal policy, but the overall revenue collected from trade taxes is a subsidy.

3.1. *Subsidies to All Goods.* If the chain of protection is such that the first K goods in the chain are imports and the remaining $N - K$ are exports, then there will be a choice of numeraire for which all goods are subsidized. The following result

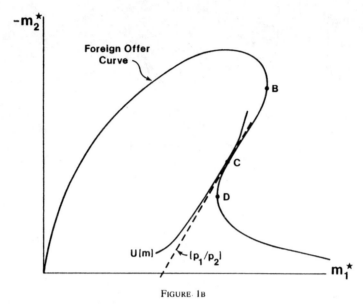

FIGURE 1B

LOCAL OPTIMUM WITH SUBSIZED TRADE

establishes a sufficient condition to rule out the possibility that all goods are subsidized.

PROPOSITION 2.   *Let M_i^* denote the $(n - 1) \times (n - 1)$ matrix obtained by deleting the ith row and column from M^*. If M_i^* is an NP matrix for all i, there cannot exist a choice of numeraire for which all goods are subsidized in the optimal policy.*

PROOF.   Good j is subsidized under the optimal policy if t_j and m_j^* have the same sign (both negative for imports, positive for exports). From (3), this occurs if and only if the jth element of t and the jth element of the vector $t^T M_i^*$ have the same sign. An *NP* matrix is a matrix whose principal minors alternate in sign, with those of odd order negative and those of even order positive. A theorem of Nikaido (1968, theorem 20.2) establishes that if M_i^* is an *NP* matrix, then there is no vector $z \neq 0$ such that the jth element of z and the jth element of $z^T M_i^*$ have the same sign for all j.   □

The condition that M_i^* is an *NP* matrix requires that all own price effects be negative, as in the case of gross substitutability. It generalizes gross substitutability by allowing for some complementarity between goods, as long as the complementarity effects are sufficiently small (in the sense defined by the principal minor condition). The univalence theorem of Nikaido (1968) indicates that if the condition of the theorem is satisfied, it will not be possible to find a numeraire i and price vectors p and q such that $p^* \geq q^*$ ($p^* \neq q^*$) and $m_j^*(p^*) > m_j^*(q^*)$ for $j \neq i$. This represents a sense in which demand is decreasing in price: increases in the prices of all goods relative to the numeraire cannot lead to increases in excess demands for all nonnumeraire goods.

3.2. *Negative Tariff Revenue.* A second approach to generalizing the example of subsidized trade in Figure 1 to the many good case is to consider the possibility that tariff revenue will be negative in the optimal policy. From (3) and the definition of t, the expression for tariff revenue can be written as $-t^T m^* = -p^T m^*$. Since altering the choice of numeraire results in multiplying p by a positive scalar, the sign of tariff revenue will not depend on which good is untaxed. It therefore represents an average sense in which trade is taxed or subsidized.

In order to establish the result on tariff revenue, we introduce the concept of a monotone offer curve.

DEFINITION 3. *The foreign offer curve is monotone with respect to numeraire i if $[p^* - q^*]^T [m^*(p^*) - m^*(q^*)] < 0$ for any prices p^* and q^* such that $p_i^* = q_i^* = 1$ and $p^* \neq q^*$.*

This definition can be interpreted as saying that the foreign offer curve is monotone when an increase in price reduces foreign import demand on average. The following result relates the concept of monotonicity to the tariff revenue at the optimum:

PROPOSITION 3. *Each of the following two conditions on the foreign offer curve are sufficient to ensure that the optimal policy involves nonnegative tariff revenue for the home country:*

(a) m^* is monotone for some choice of numeraire.
(b) foreign excess demands can be derived from those of a representative agent and all goods are normal.

PROOF. Substituting from the first order conditions for the optimal trade taxes (3), the level of tariff revenue can be written as[9]

(11) $$-t^T m^* = -t^T M^* t.$$

Mas-Collel (1985, Proposition 5.7.3) proves that if m^* is monotone for numeraire i, then the matrix M_i^* is negative quasi-semidefinite ($u M_i^* u \leq 0$ for any $n - 1$ element vector u). This ensures $t^T m^* \geq 0$.

To prove part (b), substitute (10) into the expression for tariff revenue to yield

(12) $$-t^T m^* = -(1/\beta) t^T S^* t.$$

Since S is negative semidefinite, tariff revenue will be nonnegative if $\beta \geq 0$. As noted above, a sufficient condition for $\beta > 0$ is that all goods be normal in the foreign country. □

---

[9] Feenstra (1986) derives this expression, and points out that in the absence of income effects this expression must be nonnegative from the negative semidefiniteness of the substitution matrix.

It should be noted that neither condition in Proposition 3 implies the other. It is straightforward to construct examples in which all goods are normal but the matrix M_i^* is not negative quasi-semidefinite. At least three goods are required for such examples. Similarly, monotone offer curves can be constructed in the two good case when one good is inferior. These conditions can also be related to the examples in Figure 1. The offer curve in 1a fails monotonicity because it is not single valued. The foreign offer curve in Figure 1b is not monotone with respect to either choice of numeraire, since the demand for imports is increasing in price over the region BD, and the supply of exports has a range over which it is decreasing in price. An offer curve that was backward bending, but did not have a section where import demand was increasing in price, would satisfy monotonicity when the import good is chosen as numeraire.

The offer curve in Figure 1b also fails condition b that all goods be normal, since the foreign import is inferior as noted above. The offer curve in Figure 1a fails condition b because it cannot be derived from the utility-maximizing behavior of a representative foreign agent with a strictly quasi-concave utility function, since it is not single valued.

One remaining question is the relationship of the NP matrix and monotonocity conditions that have been used to derive Propositions 2 and 3. The weak axiom of revealed preference guarantees that monotonocity must be satisfied if we compare any trade bundle with the autarky trade bundle. The weak axiom states that if $p^{*T}m^*(q^*) < p^{*T}m^*(p^*)$, then $q^{*T}m^*(p^*) > q^{*T}m^*(q^*)$. If q^* is chosen to be the autarky price vector, it immediately follows that $(p^* - q^*)^T(m^*(p^*) - m^*(q^*)) = (p^* - q^*)^T m^*(p^*) < 0$. However, monotonocity may be violated with respect to some other choice of q and p, and still have the weak axiom of revealed preference satisfied (as in Figure 1b). In the absence of income effects, when the substitution matrix is symmetric, the NP and monotonocity conditions will be equivalent because the M^* matrix is symmetric and negative semidefinite. With income effects, monotonicity is more restrictive than the NP matrix condition, as would be expected by comparison of Propositions 2 and 3. Monotonicity implies $u^T M_i^* u \leq 0$ for all $(n-1)$ vectors u. NP requires that there be no vector x for which every element of x has the same sign as the corresponding element of the vector $M_i^* x$. Failure of the NP condition implies failure of the monotonicity condition.

The cases in which the conditions of Propositions 2 and 3 are violated tend to be associated with perverse responses of foreign excess demands to changes in the world price. This suggests that it might be possible to rule out some of these optima because they would not be consistent with stability in world markets. However, such an analysis will not be able to eliminate all the perverse outcomes, since stability depends on both the home and foreign excess demand functions. The first order conditions for an optimum depend on the price responses of foreign excess demand functions, but say nothing about the price responsiveness of the home country excess demand functions. It should then be possible to construct home country indifference curves that are sufficiently price responsive locally to ensure market stability even when the foreign excess demand functions fail the monotonicity and NP matrix conditions.

4. CONCLUSIONS

This paper has examined the optimal trade tax structure in the presence of competitive industries, with the emphasis being on how the results of the two good case generalize to the case with an arbitrary number of goods. One approach was to concentrate on what can be said about the chain of protection that results under the optimal trade bundle. It was shown the assumption that all goods be substitutes, either gross substitutes or compensated substitutes (in the case of a single foreign consumer) is sufficient to establish a weak form of the optimal tariff that requires the most protected good to be an import and the least protected good to be an export can be obtained. However, stronger assumptions than gross substitutability are required to rank the interior goods in the chain of protection, so that gross substitutability is not sufficient to ensure that all imports are more protected than all imports at the optimum.

If the gross substitutability assumption is dropped, it was shown that as long as there is not too much inferiority in the foreign demand for goods or the foreign offer curve satisfies a monotonocity condition, then the optimal policy must involve nonnegative tariff revenue. Ohyama (1972) showed that if a system of trade taxes and subsidies results in positive revenue, then the trade bundle will be preferred to autarky. This leaves open the possibility that some configurations of trade taxes that involve a net subsidy to trade raise welfare over autarky. The results of this paper indicate that if the conditions of Proposition 3 are satisfied, then the optimum cannot occur in this region where trade is subsidized. Ohyama's results were derived using the weak axiom of revealed preference, which is not as strict as the assumption of monotonocity. Therefore, the possibility is still open for foreign offer curves that obey the weak axiom of revealed preference (but fail the monotonocity condition) to satisfy the first order conditions with a net subsidy to trade as indicated in Figure 1b. My paper (Bond 1987) examines the question of whether it is possible for these points to be global optima (as in Figure 1a), or whether they must be local optimal (as in Figure 1b).

Pennsylvania State University, U.S.A.

APPENDIX

In this appendix, we establish that satisfaction of Definition 2 ensures that condition *S* is satisfied (Proposition 1(b)).

PROOF. Let good k be the home country export that is most protected under the optimal policy, in the sense that $(p_k/p_k^*) > (p_i/p_i^*)$ for all $i \in X$. With good k as numeraire, we then have $t_i < 0$ for all $i \in X$. The result is proven by showing that for all $j \in I$, we must have $t_j > 0$.

For any import good j, the first order condition (8) must hold at the optimum. Multiplying (8) by p_j^* and subtracting the first order condition for the untaxed commodity k from that for the import j yields

(A.1) $$e_{jj}t_j + \sum_{\substack{i \in I \\ i \neq j}} t_i e_{ji} = c_j$$

THE OPTIMAL TARIFF   115

where $e_{ji} = (p_j^* m_{ij}^* - m_{ik}^*)$ for $i, j \in I$ and $c_j = (p_j^* m_j^* - m_k^*) - \Sigma_{i \in X} t_i (p_j^* m_{ij}^* - m_{ik}^*)$. The choice of j as a home import ensures that $(p_j^* m_j^* - m_k^*) < 0$, and part (b) of Definition 2 gives $(p_j^* m_{ij}^* - m_{ik}^*) \leq 0$, for $i \in X$. Since k has been chosen as the most protected export, we have $c_j < 0$. Part (a) of Definition 2 yields $e_{ji} \geq 0$ for $i \in I$, $i \neq j$.

Since (A.1) must hold for all import goods, then solutions for the t_i for $i \in I$ can be written in the form

(A.2) $$Et_I = c$$

t_I is the K element vector of taxes on import goods, where K is the number of imports. The matrix E is the $K \times K$ matrix of coefficients on the t_i from the left hand side of (A.1). By the arguments used for (A.1), the matrix E will have negative diagonal elements and positive off-diagonal elements. Similarly, c is the K vector of terms from the right hand side of (A.1), so $c < 0$ by the above arguments. If it can be shown that the matrix E has a quasi-dominant diagonal, then it follows that a system of equations of the form (A.2) with $c \leq 0$ has a solution $t_I \geq 0$ (Takayama 1985, Theorem 4.C.3).

We show that the matrix E has a dominant diagonal by showing that the column sums of the matrix must all be negative. The column sum of the jth column of E will be

(A.3) $$\sum_{i \in I} e_{ij} = \sum_{i \in I} (p_i^* m_{ji}^* - m_{jk}^*).$$

By condition (2b), $\Sigma_{i=1}^n p_i^* m_{ji}^* = 0$. Since all goods are gross substitutes and $j \in I$, it follows that $\Sigma_{i \in I} p_i^* m_{ji}^* < 0$. Since all goods are gross substitutes and $k \notin I$ (by choice of good k as a home export), $m_{jk}^* > 0$. Therefore, $\Sigma_{i \in I} e_{ij} < 0$ must hold for any column j, so the column sums of the matrix E must be negative.

This establishes that the matrix E has dominant diagonal, and therefore that the solution to (A.2) must have $t_I \geq 0$. Since we have chosen the numeraire such that $t_i < 0$ for all $i \in X$, it follows that the chosen numeraire k is the desired one for which all imports and exports are taxed. This is equivalent to condition S, which establishes part b of Proposition 1.

REFERENCES

BOND, ERIC W., "Can the Optimal Trade Tax Structure Involve a Subsidy to Trade," working paper, Department of Economics, Pennsylvania State University, September 1987.

———, "Optimal Policy Towards International Factor Movements with a Country-Specific Factor," *European Economic Review* 33 (September 1989), 1329–1344.

BRANDER, JAMES A. AND BARBARA J. SPENCER, "Export Subsidies and International Market Share Rivalry," *Journal of International Economics* 18 (February, 1985), 83–100.

DEARDORFF, ALAN V., "The General Validity of the Law of Comparative Advantage," *Journal of Political Economy* 88 (October 1980), 941–957.

DIAMOND, PETER AND JAMES MIRRLEES, "Optimal Taxation and Public Production," *American Economic Review* 61 (March/June 1971), 8–27, 261–278.

DIXIT, AVINASH, "Welfare Effects of Tax and Price Changes," *Journal of Public Economics* 4 (February 1975), 103–123.

116   ERIC W. BOND

—— and Victor Norman, *The Theory of International Trade* (Cambridge: Cambridge University Press, 1980).

Ethier, Wilfred J., "Higher Dimensional Issues in Trade Theory," in Ronald W. Jones and Peter B. Kenen, eds., *Handbook of International Economics* (Amsterdam: North Holland, 1984).

Feenstra, Robert, "Trade Policy with Several Goods and 'Market Linkages'," *Journal of International Economics* 20 (May 1986), 249–67.

Graaf, J., "On Optimal Tariff Structures," *Review of Economic Studies* 17 (1949–50), 47–59.

Hatta, Tatsuo, "A Theory of Piecemeal Policy Recommendations," *Review of Economic Studies* 64 (February 1977) 1–21.

—— and John Haltiwanger, "Tax Reform and Strong Substitutes," *International Economic Review* 27 (June 1986), 303–315.

Horwell, David J. and Ivor F. Pearce, "A Look at the Structure of Optimal Tariff Rates," *International Economic Review* 11 (February 1970), 147–161.

Itoh, Motoshige and Kazuharu Kiyono, "Welfare-Enhancing Export Subsidies," *Journal of Political Economy* 95 (February 1987), 115–137.

Jones, Ronald W., "International Capital Movements and the Theory of Tariffs and Trade," *Quarterly Journal of Economics* 81 (February 1967), 1–38.

——, Isaias Coelho, and Stephen Easton, "The Basic Model of International Factor Flows," *Journal of International Economics* 20 (May 1986), 313–327.

Kemp, Murray C., "Notes on the Theory of Optimal Tariffs," *Economic Record* 43 (September 1967), 395–403.

Kuhn, Peter and Ian Wooton, "International Factor Movements in the Presence of a Fixed Factor," *Journal of International Economics* 22 (February 1987), 123–140.

Mas-Collel, Andrew, *The Theory of General Economic Equilibrium: A Differentiable Approach* (Cambridge: Cambridge University Press, 1985).

Neary, Peter, "International Factor Mobility, Minimum Wage Rates, and Factor-Price Equilization: A Synthesis," *Quarterly Journal of Economics* 100 (August 1985), 551–570.

Nikaido, Hukukane, *Convex Structures and Economic Theory* (New York: Academic Press, 1968).

Ohyama, Michihiro, "Trade and Welfare in General Equilibrium," *Keio Economic Studies* 9 (1972) 37–73.

Takayama, Akira, *Mathematical Economics* (Cambridge: Cambridge University Press, 1985).

Woodland, A. D., "Direct and Indirect Trade Utility Functions," *Review of Economic Studies* 67 (October 1980), 907–26.

——, *International Trade and Resource Allocation* (Amsterdam: North Holland, 1982).

[9]

Journal of International Economics 23 (1987) 357–367. North-Holland

A NOTE ON THE OPTIMAL TARIFF, RETALIATION AND THE WELFARE LOSS FROM TARIFF WARS IN A FRAMEWORK WITH INTRA-INDUSTRY TRADE

Daniel GROS*

Université Catholique de Louvain, IRES, 1348 Louvain-La-Neuve, Belgium

Received December 1985, revised version received March 1987

This paper uses Krugman's (1980) model of trade with product differentiation and monopolistic competition to examine the effects of a uniform ad valorem tariff. The main results are: there exists an optimal tariff, even for a small economy, and the optimal tariff rate is an increasing function of the size of the economy and the degree of production differentiation.

Under reasonable parameter assumptions a tariff war between two countries of equal size in which each country retaliates by imposing its own optimal tariff causes a welfare loss equivalent to a drop in income of about 4 percent.

1. Introduction

This paper uses Krugman's (1980) model of trade with product differentiation and monopolistic competition to calculate the optimal tariff rate (with and without retaliation) in terms of the parameters of the model. Since models of trade with monopolistic competition and product differentiation have been developed mainly to explain intra-industry trade the contribution of this paper lies in examining the determinants of the optimal tariff and its effects on welfare under conditions of intra-industry trade. Indeed the main result of the paper is that even a small country has an optimal tariff. The rationale for this result is that under conditions of intra-industry trade each producer has some monopoly power, and it is in the interest of the home country that producers exercise this monopoly power abroad but not at home. The optimal tariff (in this case it can be thought of as an export tariff) achieves this by forcing producers to price discriminate between foreign and domestic sales. The optimal tariff rate for a small country is therefore equal to the proportional mark-up used by monopolistically competitive producers. Moreover, since in this model the monopolistically competitive equilibrium is Pareto optimal, the optimal tariff does not correct a domestic distortion.

*I wish to thank M. Mussa, P. Krugman, and C. Adams for helpful comments and discussions. D. Nieburg, G. Hinds, and K. Hannah were very helpful in typing this draft and providing the simulations.

The specific structure of the model used here has the advantage that it is possible to calculate the exact welfare consequences of the optimal tariff and tariff wars. Under reasonable assumptions about the mark-up of mono-polistic producers a tariff war between two countries of equal size would lower the welfare level of each country by almost 4 percent compared to the free trade equilibrium.

Section 2 reviews the basic features of Krugman's (1980) model. Section 3 derives an expression for the optimal tariff rate without retaliation, whereas section 4 analyzes the equilibrium that is obtained under retaliation. The tariff rates resulting from a tariff war are lower than the optimal tariff rates without retaliation. Section 5 calculates the welfare loss resulting from a tariff war. Section 6 contains some concluding remarks and differentiates the results of this paper from those of other discussions of trade policy under imperfect competition.

2. The model

To focus on the issue of the optimal tariff in the situation of intra-industry trade it is convenient to consider a generalized one-sector version of Krugman's (1980) model where there is only one industry producing a differentiated good with increasing returns to scale. The utility functions of consumers is given by

$$U = \left[\sum_{i=1}^{m} (c_i)^\theta \right]^{1/\theta}, \quad 0 < \theta < 1, \tag{1}$$

where c_i is consumption of good i of this industry;[1] m is the number of potential products, which will be assumed to be larger than the number of products actually produced. The production function for each good is given by $x_i = f(l_i)$, where l_i represents labor used to produce x_i; the function $f(\cdot)$ is assumed to be the same for all goods. The subscript i can therefore be supressed.

Assuming monopolistic competition it can be shown that output, of each firm, is equal to a constant, $\bar{x} = f(\bar{l})$, which is determined by the condition that in the monopolistically competitive equilibrium the degree of economies of scale, $f'(l)l/f(l)$, is equal to the degree of monopoly power, which in this case is equal to $1/\theta$.[2] It is important to note that the market equilibrium represents the social optimum so that the optimal tariff does not correct a domestic distortion.[3]

The equilibrium number of firms is determined by the labor market

[1]See Krugman (1981, 1982) for two and multisector extensions.
[2]For a more detailed description of the equilibrium, see Krugman (1980, 1981).
[3]For a proof of this proposition, see the appendix, eqs. (A.1)–(A.3).

equilibrium condition $n = L/\bar{l}$, where L represents the given economy wide labour supply. If this economy opens to trade with another economy of the same type all trade will be intra-industry trade. The equilibrium level of the number of varieties available to consumers with trade will be equal to the sum of the number of domestic and foreign varieties, as Krugman (1979, 1980) explains this increases welfare.

With free trade the terms of trade are equal to one and balanced trade requires that

$$nc_h^* = n(\bar{x} - c_h) = n^* c_f = n^*(\bar{x} - c_f^*),\tag{2}$$

where a^* refers to a foreign variable. The subscripts h and f refer to the origin of the good, e.g. $c_h(c_f)$ is the amount consumed at home of a typical good produced domestically (abroad) and $c_h^*(c_f^*)$ is the amount of this good consumed abroad, equal to $\bar{x} - c_h(\bar{x} - c_f)$.

3. The optimal tariff

A uniform ad valorem tariff does not change the elasticity of demand, because it just increases the price perceived by consumers proportionally. This implies that foreign and domestic firms will continue to produce the same output, which is determined only by the elasticity of demand and the cost function, both of which are not affected by the tariff. If output per firm is unchanged, the labor market equilibrium implies that the number of firms abroad and at home is also unaffected by the tariff.

However, the tariff does not affect the relative amounts of each foreign and domestic specification consumed at home since home consumers equate the marginal rate of substitution to the relative price they face in the market. Denoting the tariff rate by t, it follows that

$$\left(\frac{c_h^*}{c_f^*}\right)^{\theta-1} = \frac{p_h}{p_f(1+t)} = \frac{1}{q(1+t)},\tag{3}$$

where c_h indicates the consumption level of a typical home good and c_f indicates the level of consumption of a typical imported good and where p_h is the price of domestic goods and $q = p_f/p_h$ represents the (inverse of) terms of trade. A similar requirement for foreign consumers implies

$$\left(\frac{c_h^*}{c_f^*}\right)^{\theta-1} = \left(\frac{\bar{x} - c_h}{\bar{x} - c_f}\right)^{\theta-1} = \frac{(1+s)}{q},\tag{4}$$

where c_h^* is set equal to $\bar{x} - c_h$ and c_f^* is set equal to $\bar{x} - c_f$, on the assumption that the government (in both countries) rebates the tariff proceeds lump sum to consumers; s denotes the tariff (rate) imposed by the foreign country. Equilibrium of the balance of trade then requires that

$$qc_f n^* = nc_h^* = n(\bar{x} - c_h). \tag{5}$$

Since a tariff does not change the number of products available to consumers worldwide or relative prices inside the groups of domestically and foreign produced goods, consumers can be thought of as consuming two composite goods and utility of a consumer in the home country is given by

$$U = [n(c_h)^\theta + n^*(c_f)^\theta]^{1/\theta}. \tag{6}$$

In general, the optimal tariff maximizes the utility of the representative home country consumer. The optimal tariff rate, T, in terms of the parameters of the model can then be calculated by setting $d(U)/d(t)$ equal to zero. The values of dc_h/dt and dc_f/dt are obtained from the system (3)–(5) and by assuming that the foreign country does not retaliate, i.e. $ds \equiv 0$. The resulting expression for the optimal tariff rate can be simplified to[4]

$$1 + T = \frac{1}{\theta} + \frac{1-\theta}{\theta} N(1+s)^{1/(\theta-1)} q^{-\theta/(\theta-1)}, \tag{7}$$

where $N \equiv n/n^*$ indicates the relative size of the home economy. The result of (7) implies that even a small country, $N = 0$, will have a finite positive optimal tariff given by $T = (1/\theta) - 1 = (1-\theta)/\theta$.

The intuition behind this result becomes clearer if one considers that in this economy the only relevant price is that of imports in terms of domestic goods. The optimum tariff forces the market price to be equal to the social marginal cost ratio. The social marginal cost of domestic goods is given by the marginal cost of production, since the mark-up of domestic producers is just a transfer. However, the social marginal cost of imports is given by their price (for the small country that cannot affect the international price). The price charged by foreign producers is equal to $(1/\theta)$ times the marginal cost of production. Since marginal costs are the same across countries, it follows that the ratio of the social marginal cost of imports to that of domestic goods is equal to $1/\theta$ (always for the small country case). With the optimum tariff consumers see a market price of $p_f(1+T)/p_h = 1 + T$. From eq. (7), for $N = 0$, it is clear that $1 + T = 1/\theta$, i.e. a tariff of this rate forces the market price to be equal to the social marginal cost ratio.

For a country that is not small there is another externality which gives rise

---

[4]See the appendix, eqs. (A.4)–(A.11).

to the second term $[(1-\theta)/\theta]N(1+s)^{1/(\theta-1)}q^{-\theta/(1-\theta)}$ in the expression for the optimum tariff. This externality derives from the fact that domestic firms individually perceive an elasticity of demand for their products of $1/(1-\theta)$ since they take the actions of all other firms as given. However, all domestic firms, acting together, would face a lower elasticity of demand and therefore should charge a higher price (abroad). The optimal tariff forces them to do just that.

From eq. (7) it is apparent that, holding θ and q constant, the optimal tariff should be an increasing function of N. It can be proved that this is true even if account is taken of the effect of N on q.

Intuition also suggests that the optimal tariff should be an increasing function of the degree of product differentiation as measured by the degree of monopoly power, $1/\theta$, firms have. This implies that $dT/d\theta$ should be negative. For the small country case this is obvious from (7). It can also be proved that this continues to hold for the big country case, where one has to take into account the influence of θ on q.[5]

4. Retaliation

The expression for the optimal tariff (7) indicates that the home country will take any foreign tariff into account when choosing its own optimal tariff rate. Since it can be assumed that the foreign country does likewise, commercial policy in this context becomes a two-player game. This section considers a particular solution to this game. It is assumed that each country takes the tariff of the other country as given when choosing its own optimal tariff rate. A Nash equilibrium obtains when no country has an incentive to further adjust its own tariff rate.[6] In the present model, a tariff war leads to an equilibrium, since eq. (7) implies that the optimal tariff for the home country is a declining function of the tariff rate imposed by the foreign country.[7]

Denoting the tariff rates that represent the outcome of a tariff war by $\bar{s}$ and $\bar{t}$ the home country has no incentive to further adjust its tariff rate when (7) holds with $\bar{s}$ and $\bar{t}$ in place of s and T. Since the expression that gives the optimal tariff for the foreign country is symmetric to (7), an expression for the 'equilibrium' tariff rate for the home country can be obtained by substituting the foreign country equivalent of (7) into (7) which yields

[5]For a proof of these results, see Gros (1986).

[6]The process by which such a Nash equilibrium is reached is assumed to be the following. Starting from a free trade equilibrium, the home country imposes its own optimal tariff, the foreign country retaliates by imposing the tariff that is optimal given the initial tariff imposed by the home country. The home country in turn retaliates by adjusting the tariff it imposed in the first place and so on.

[7]For a proof, see Gros (1986).

$$(1+\bar{t})=\frac{1}{\theta}+\frac{1-\theta}{\theta}Nq^{-\theta/(\theta-1)}\left[\frac{1}{\theta}+\frac{1-\theta}{\theta}N^{-1}q^{\theta/(\theta-1)}(1+\bar{t})^{1/(\theta-1)}\right]^{1/(\theta-1)}$$

(8)

An equivalent expression determines the equilibrium tariff rate for the foreign country, $\bar{s}$. Since $dT/ds<0$, this tariff rate is lower than the rate the home country would impose in the absence of retaliation, i.e. if $s\equiv0$. It can be shown from (8) that the 'equilibrium' tariff rate for the home country, t, is an increasing function of the size of the home country, N.[8] Eq. (8) also implies that the 'equilibrium' tariff rate for the small country is given by $(1+t)=1/\theta$, i.e. the same tariff the small country would impose in the absence of retaliation. In a world with many small countries a generalized tariff war would thus lead to the same tariff rate, equal to $\bar{t}=(1-\theta)/\theta$, in all countries.

5. The welfare consequences of tariff wars

To calculate the consequences for the welfare of a representative consumer in the home country, it is necessary to compare the utility levels achieved with free trade and with a tariff war. The free trade utility level of a representative consumer can be calculated by using in eq. (6) the demand function (3) and eq. (A.11) from the appendix. The welfare levels under free trade (i.e. $s=t=0$) and with a tariff war (i.e. $s=\bar{s},t=\bar{t}$) can be calculated by inserting the appropriate values of t, s, and q in the resulting expression. The home country gains from starting a tariff war if $U_{s=\bar{s},t=\bar{t}}\geq U_{s=0,t=0}$ or if:

$$(N+[q(1+\bar{t})]^{\theta/(\theta-1)})(N+q[q(1+\bar{t})]^{1/(\theta-1)})^{-\theta}\geq(1+N)^{1-\theta}.$$

(9)

If eq. (9) holds with equality it can be interpreted as giving the critical value of N for which the home country is just indifferent between the free trade equilibrium and the outcome of a tariff war. This critical value of N depends on θ and is an increasing function of the degree of monopoly power, $1/\theta$. Panel B in table 1 lists the critical values of N as a function of $1/\theta$.[9] It is apparent that this critical value of N is an increasing function of $1/\theta$, the minimum appears to be equal to 2.6 as $1/\theta$ goes towards one.[10] This implies that only a country that is almost three times as big as the rest of the world can gain from a tariff war.[11]

[8]The proof is available from the author upon request.
[9]To calculate the critical value of N for which $U_{s=\bar{s},t=\bar{t}}=U_{s=0,t=0}$ it is necessary to use a system of equations consisting of eqs. (8) and (9) (with equality sign), eq. (A.12), and the foreign country equivalent to eq. (8).
[10]Using values of $1/\theta$ closer and closer to one in the simulations produced values of N that approached 2.6.
[11]Johnson (1955) discusses the conditions under which a country might gain from a tariff war. However, his numerical example is limited to the case of constant elasticity offer curves which implies that the optional tariff of each country is independent of the tariff of the other country.

Table 1

Panel A: The welfare loss from a tariff war[a]						
(θ)	$1/\theta$	N 2	1	0.5	0.1	0.01
(0.9)	1.11	−0.4	−1.8	−4.1	−12.0	−25.1
(0.8)	1.25	−0.8	−3.8	−8.5	−23.6	−45.4
(0.7)	1.43	−1.5	−6.2	−13.4	−34.7	−61.4
(0.6)	1.67	−2.3	−9.0	−18.8	−45.4	−73.6
Panel B: The critical value of N^b						
N	2.68	2.77	2.90	3.06		
$1/\theta$	1.11	1.25	1.43	1.67		

[a]Indicates the *percentage* differences between the utility level (of a typical consumer in the home country) under free trade and after a tariff war.

[b]The value 2.77 (for $1/\theta = 1.25$) means that only a country that is at least 2.77 times as large as the rest of the world can gain from a tariff war.

Panel A in table 1 also shows the welfare loss from a tariff war for countries that are smaller than the critical size of N calculated above (a negative value of G signifies a welfare loss). It appears that, at least for countries that are not as big as the rest of the world, $N < 1$, the potential loss from a tariff war is large – in the order of several percentage points of free trade welfare.

Since $(1/\theta) - 1$ is equal to the proportional mark-up of producers the values of θ used in table 1 were chosen as to give reasonable values for this mark-up. For $\theta = 0.8$ the mark-up is 25 percent, taking this as a reasonable approximation of reality, panel A then suggests that in a trade war between two countries of equal size ($N = 1$) the welfare of consumers in each country would drop by about 3.8 percent compared to the welfare level they could achieve under free trade.

6. Concluding remarks

In the traditional Heckscher–Ohlin analysis the rationale for an optimal tariff is that domestic producers fail to exercise their joint monopoly power on the world market. In the context of models of monopolistic competition, this rationale continues to exist because each individual producer uses only his individual monopoly power optimally and does not take into account that domestic producers have more monopoly power acting jointly than acting independently. The optimal tariff forces domestic producers to exploit this additional monopoly power on the world market. This rationale for a welfare increasing tariff relies on the ability of the home country to affect its terms of trade, it therefore depends on the relative size of the home economy.

However, under conditions of product differentiation and economies of scale there is another rationale for an optimal tariff since monopolistic competitors will charge a price that exceeds marginal cost. This implies that the social marginal cost of home goods (equal to marginal cost of production) will be below their market price, whereas the social marginal cost of imports is given by their international price (for a small country). The optimal tariff forces consumers to see the true social cost ratio (of home goods to imports) which is a function of the degree of monopoly power firms have. In this model, the degree of monopoly power is a constant, $1/\theta$, which alone determines the optimal tariff for a small economy. This does not imply that the optimal tariff corrects a domestic distortion because the closed economy equilibrium represents a social optimum in this model.

This effect depends on the existence of two-way trade in differentiated products. If the home country imported only a homogeneous good produced under perfect competition abroad the optimal tariff would be zero for the small country. The results of this paper differ therefore in two important respects from those contained in Venables (1982): in Venables (1982), the monopolistically competitive equilibrium is not Pareto optimal and the tariff is therefore a second-best policy to correct a domestic distortion. Moreover, this paper examines the optimal tariff under conditions of intraindustry trade; whereas Venables analyses the case of a (small) country that imports differentiated products, but exports only a homogeneous good.

The results of this paper also differ from other discussions of the effects of tariffs that are based on two way trade in homogeneous products, such as Venables (1985) and Brander and Spencer (1981, 1984).[12] In these models, a tariff is welfare increasing because it shifts rents from foreign firms to domestic firms or the government. In contrast, in this framework potential entry implies that firms always earn zero profits and a tariff does not affect output or profits of either domestic or foreign firms.

This paper has shown that it is possible to obtain explicit results for the effects of trade policy in this specific framework for intra-industry trade with differentiated products. From Lancaster (1984) it appears that it is not possible to obtain similar results in the framework proposed by Lancaster (1980). The quite restrictive assumptions about the structure of preferences embodied in this framework thus yield a pay-off because they allow one to calculate the welfare consequences of tariff wars and the optimal tariff rates as a function of country size and the degree of product differentiation.

Appendix

To show that the closed economy market equilibrium represents a social optimum, it is convenient to use the production function and the labor

---

[12]In order to have more than one firm producing the homogeneous product, in spite of the presence of internal economies of scale, these authors have to assume the existence of market imperfections. See Helpman and Krugman (1985, pp. 67–71) on the equilibrium with homogeneous products and internal economies of scale in the presence of contestable markets.

market equilibrium directly in the utility function. Using $c = f(l)$ and $L = nl$ yields the social planner's problem:

$$\max U^\theta = [L/l][f(l)]^\theta. \tag{A.1}$$

The first-order condition for this problem is

$$0 = L[-l^{-2}[f(l)]^\theta + l^{-1}\theta f'(l)[f(l)]^{\theta-1}]. \tag{A.2}$$

The second-order condition is always satisfied [see Gros (1986)]; eq. (A.2) can be transformed to yield:

$$\frac{lf'(l)}{f(l)} = \frac{1}{\theta}, \tag{A.3}$$

which is identical to the condition that determines output in the market equilibrium. This shows that the monopolistically competitive equilibrium is the social optimum. It implies that there is no effective domestic distortion that should be corrected by any tax.

A.1. Calculations for the optimum tariff

The system of eqs. (3)–(5) can be reduced to the following two-equation system in two variables, c_h and c_f:

$$(c_f/c_h)^{\theta-1} - (1+t)N(x-c_h)/c_f = 0, \tag{A.4}$$

$$(1+s)c_f[(\bar{x}-c_f)/(\bar{x}-c_h)]^{\theta-1} - N(\bar{x}-c_h) = 0. \tag{A.5}$$

Multiplying (A.4) by c_f and (A.5) by $(x-c_h)^{-1}$, the total differential of the system can be written as:

$$\begin{vmatrix} (1+t)N + (1-\theta)[q(1+t)]^{\theta/\theta-1} & \theta q(1+t) \\ N\theta & q\left[1 - \frac{(\theta-1)c_f}{(\bar{x}-c_f)}\right] \end{vmatrix} \begin{vmatrix} dc_h \\ dc_f \end{vmatrix} = \begin{vmatrix} c_f q\,dt \\ -\dfrac{c_f q}{1+s}\,ds \end{vmatrix}, \tag{A.6}$$

where the q comes from using (3) again after the differentiation.

The optimal tariff requires setting $d(U)/dt$ equal to zero, or

$$d(U^\theta)/dt = \theta[N(c_h)^{\theta-1}(dc_h/dt) + (c_f)^{\theta-1}(dc_f/dt)], \tag{A.7}$$

$$d(U^\theta)/dt = 0 = N\,dc_h/dt + q(1+t)\,dc_f/dt, \tag{A.8}$$

where dc_h/dt and dc_f/dt can be calculated from (A.6), with $ds=0$; using Cramer's rule [det denotes the determinant of (A.6)] this yields:

$$0 = \det^{-1} \left\{ q(1+t) \left[(Nq \left[1 - \frac{(\theta-1)c_f}{(\bar{x}-c_f)} \right] - N\theta q(1+t) \right] \right\}. \qquad (A.9)$$

Denoting the optimal tariff with T this can be simplified to

$$1 + T = \frac{1}{\theta} - \frac{(\theta-1)}{\theta} \frac{c_f}{(\bar{x}-c_f)}. \qquad (A.10)$$

This can be transformed into (7) in the text by using (A.11), which can be derived from the balance of trade equilibrium condition which implies $q = N(\bar{x}-c_h)/c_f$. Multiplying and dividing this expression by $(\bar{x}-c_f)$ and using (4) to solve out for q and $(\bar{x}-c_h)/(\bar{x}-c_f)$ yields:

$$\frac{\bar{x}-c_f}{c_f} = q^{1+1/(\theta-1)}(1+s)^{-1/(\theta-1)}N^{-1}. \qquad (A.11)$$

Substituting (A.11) into (A.10) yields (7). The optimal tariff rate as a function of N and θ is computed in Gros (1986). The results are available upon request from the author. The interested reader can himself calculate the sign of the derivatives dT/dN, $dT/d\theta$ and dT/dS by using an implicit function of q in terms of t, S, θ, and N which can be obtained by substituting out N in (5) and (3) and using (A.11) in the resulting equation:

$$H \equiv q^{\theta/(\theta-1)}(1+s)^{-1/\theta-1)} - q + N[q(1+t)]^{-1/\theta-1)} = 0. \qquad (A.12)$$

References

Brander, James A and B.J. Spencer, 1981, Tariff protection and imperfect competition, in H. Kierkowski, ed., Monopolistic competition and international trade (Clarendon Press, Oxford) 194–205.

Brander, James A. and B.J. Spencer, 1984, Tariffs and the extraction of foreign monopoly rents under potential entry, Canadian Journal of Economics 24, Aug., 371–389.

Gros, Daniel, 1986, Tariffs, quotas, retaliation and the welfare loss from protectionism in a framework with intra-industry trade, unpublished manuscript, DM/86/55, Aug. (International Monetary Fund, Washington).

Helpman, E., 1984, International trade in the presence of product differentiation, economies of scale, and monopolistic competition, Journal of International Economics 11, Aug. 305–340.

Helpman, E. and Paul R. Krugman, 1985, Market structure and foreign trade (MIT Press, Cambridge, MA).

Johnson, Harry, 1955, Optimum tariffs and retaliation, Review of Economic Studies XX, (2), 142–153.

Krugman, P., 1979, Increasing returns, monopolistic competition and international trade, Journal of International Economics 9, 469–479.

Krugman, P., 1980, Scale economies, product differentiation and the pattern of trade, American Economic Review 70, Dec., 950–959.

Krugman, P., 1981, Intraindustry specialization and the gains from trade, Journal of Political Economy 89, 959–973.

Krugman, P., 1982, Trade in differentiated products and the political economy of trade liberalization, in: J. Bhagwati, Import competition and response (University of Chicago Press, Chicago) 180–193.

Lancaster, K., 1980, Intra-industry trade under perfect monopolistic competition, Journal of International Economics 10, 151–175.

Lancaster, K., 1984, Protection and product differentiation, in: H. Kierzkowski, ed., Monopolistic competition and international trade (Clarendon Press, Oxford) 137–157.

Venables, A., 1982, Optimal tariffs for trade in monopolistically competitive commodities, Journal of International Economics 11, 225–241.

Venables, A., 1985, Trade and trade policy with imperfect competition: The case of identical products and free entry, Journal of International Economics 19, 1–19.

C
Tariff Reform

[10]

A Theory of Piecemeal Policy Recommendations

TATSUO HATTA

Saitama University and University of Kentucky

1. INTRODUCTION

The theory of the second best, first formally presented by Lipsey and Lancaster [16], maintains that the abolition of an arbitrarily chosen distortion in an economy with multiple distortions may reduce the welfare of the economy.

The main objective of the present paper is to formulate some piecemeal policy recommendations which would definitely result in a move towards efficiency. In particular, we will prove the following: (*a*) a policy which reduces all price distortions uniformly will improve the welfare of the economy, if it is stable in the Marshallian sense. (*b*) a policy which brings the highest distortion to the level of the next highest will improve the welfare of the economy, if the good with the highest distortion is substitutable for all the other goods and if the economy is stable in the Marshallian sense.

Our results integrate the characterization of the second best solution by Green [9], the analysis of the uniform reduction of tariff and excise tax by Foster and Sonnenschein [8] and Bruno [4], and the demonstration by Kemp [15] that the welfare effect of the tariff reduction in the two commodity world is related to the stability of the economy. In the present paper, an extensive use of the compensated demand function enables us to reveal the underlying relationship among these seemingly unrelated works.[1]

In Section 2, we will define the compensated demand function, and will present its properties used in this paper. The model will be presented in Section 3. In Section 4 we will establish that in an economy with constant-cost technology a uniform reduction in excise tax rates improves welfare provided that the aggregate of income terms weighted by marginal costs (AIM) is positive. We will also show that a reduction of the highest tax rate to the level of the next highest rate improves the welfare if the AIM is positive and if the good with the highest tax rate is substitutable for all other goods. In Section 5 the main theorems will be proved by establishing that the positivity of AIM in the propositions of Section 4 can be replaced by another condition if the economy is stable under the Marshallian adjustment mechanism (which is defined in the text). Section 6 will re-evaluate the theory of the second best from our framework. (This section can be read independently of Section 5.)

Throughout this paper, a matrix will be denoted by an upper-case letter; a lower-case bold-faced letter will represent a column vector; its transpose will be shown by a prime; and the ith element of the vector is denoted by the same letter with subscript i, unless stated otherwise.

2. THE COMPENSATED DEMAND FUNCTION

Consider a consumer who consumes n goods. Let his consumption vector c be in R^n_+, where R^n_+ denotes the non-negative orthant of the n-dimensional Euclidian space R^n. Let the function v from R^n_+ to R represent his utility function; namely $u = v(c)$, where u denotes the utility level. The range of v is denoted by U. The utility function v is said to be *well behaved* if it is (i) increasing in each argument on R^n_+, (ii) strictly quasi-concave on R^n_+, and (iii) twice continuously differentiable on the interior of R^n_+.

When the utility function v is well behaved, the commodity bundle that minimizes the expenditure $c'q$ under the given price vector q among the bundles that attain the given utility level u is uniquely determined, and we will denote this bundle by $f(q, u)$, and its ith element by $f_i(q, u)$. The function f from $R^n_+ \times U$ to R^n_+ may be called the *compensated demand function*.[2] The function f is continuously differentiable from the implicit function theorem, since the utility function v is assumed to be twice continuously differentiable.

Let

$$\lambda = \text{the marginal utility of income,}$$

$$f_{ij} = \partial f_i / \partial q_j,$$

$$f_{iu} = \partial f_i / \partial u,$$

$$F = \begin{bmatrix} f_{11} & \cdots & f_{1n} \\ \cdots\cdots\cdots \\ f_{n1} & \cdots & f_{nn} \end{bmatrix}, \quad \text{and} \quad f_u = \begin{pmatrix} f_{1u} \\ \vdots \\ f_{nu} \end{pmatrix}.$$

It is readily seen that f_{ij} and λf_{iu} are respectively the substitution and income terms of the pertinent Slutsky equation.[3] A pair of goods (i, j) is said to be *substitutable* (*complementary*) *in consumption* if f_{ij} is positive (negative). Good i is said to be *superior* (*inferior*) if f_{iu} is positive (negative). The following well-known properties of the substitution terms and income terms will be used later[4]:

Symmetry Condition of F.
$$F = F'$$

Homogeneity Condition of F.
$$Fq = 0.$$

Non-positive Definiteness Condition of F.

$$y'Fy \begin{cases} = 0 \text{ if } y = kq \text{ for some scalar } k. \\ <0 \text{ otherwise.} \end{cases}$$

Consistency Condition of f_u.

$$q'f_u = 1/\lambda.$$

We say the consumer has a *well-behaved compensated demand* function when the consumer has a well-behaved utility function and is maximizing his utility level regarding the price vector as given. Thus, a well-behaved compensated demand function satisfies all the three conditions of f stated above.

3. THE MODEL OF THE C-ECONOMY AND THE BASIC EQUATION

A. *The Model of the C-economy*

We assume that our economy satisfies the following conditions.

1. *There is only one consumer in the economy. He is a price taker and has a well-behaved utility function.*

Let the utility function be $u = v(c)$, and its corresponding compensated demand function be

$$c = f(q, u). \qquad \qquad \text{...(1)}$$

The function f is well behaved.

2. *The production possibility frontier is of the constant cost type.*

The frontier is represented by

$$a'x = b, \qquad \qquad ...(2)$$

where a' and b are constants, and x is the output vector. We can interpret b as the total amount of the single resource existing in the economy. Then a_i is the amount of the resource needed to produce one more unit of output of good i. Namely, a_i is the marginal cost in terms of the physical unit of the resource.

3. *Excise taxes and subsidies are the only causes that make producers prices diverge from consumers prices.*

In the following, we regard a subsidy as a tax whose tax rate is negative. The after-tax revenue that a producer receives by selling one unit of good i may be called the producer's price of good i and will be denoted by p_i. Let t_i be the excise tax rate of good i specified in terms of the producer's price. The following equation relates q_i, p_i, and t_i:

$$q_i = (1+t_i)p_i \quad i = 1, ..., n.$$

In matrix notation we have

$$q = \begin{bmatrix} 1+t_1 & 0 \\ & \ddots & \\ 0 & & 1+t_n \end{bmatrix} p. \qquad \qquad ...(3)$$

4. *Producers maximize their profit regarding producer's prices as given.*

Hence, an economy is always on the production frontier. Also, if one good being produced is less profitable than the other in any pair of goods, the resources will be re-allocated from the former industry to the latter. This process will continue until either the output level of the less profitable industry reaches zero, or the profitability of every industry becomes the same; then there will be no incentives for producers to shift the production bundle any more.

5. *All commodities are produced.*

Thus, we have $x > 0$. In view of the above remark, the present assumption implies that at an equilibrium, profitability of every industry is the same. Hence

$$p = ka \qquad \qquad ...(4)$$

for some constant k.

6. *The poll tax is imposed on the economy in such a way that the total revenue from both excise and poll taxes is zero.*

7. *Demand and supply are equal.*

Since there is no demand from the public sector by assumption 6, the only source of total demand is the private sector. Thus the present assumption implies that

$$c = x. \qquad \qquad ...(5)$$

The economy described above will be called the C-economy (reminiscent of constant cost). When equations (1)-(5) are satisfied, we say that *the C-economy is in full equilibrium*. Since the above system is homogeneous of degree zero with respect to k, q and p, we can normalize it with no loss of generality. Thus, we assume

$$a_1 = p_1. \qquad \qquad ...(6)$$

This implies $k = 1$ in (4), and we have

$$p = a. \qquad \qquad ...(4')$$

From (1), (2) and (5) we obtain

$$a' \cdot f(q, u) = b. \qquad \qquad ...(7)$$

It follows from (3) and (4') that

$$q = \begin{bmatrix} 1+t_1 & & 0 \\ & \ddots & \\ 0 & & 1+t_n \end{bmatrix} a. \qquad \qquad ...(8)$$

Equivalently,

$$q = A(1+t), \text{ where } A = \begin{bmatrix} a_1 & & 0 \\ & \ddots & \\ 0 & & a_n \end{bmatrix} \text{ and } t = \begin{bmatrix} t_1 \\ \vdots \\ t_n \end{bmatrix}. \qquad ...(8')$$

Substituting (8') for q in (7), we obtain

$$a'f(A(1+t), u) = b. \qquad \qquad ...(9)$$

This equation, whose only variables are t and u, implicitly determine equilibrium level(s) of utility for the given tax rates in the C-economy.

B. *The Basic Equation*

Let the correspondence h from R^n to R be defined by

$$h(t) = \{u : a'f(A(1+t), u) = b\}.$$

When $u \in h(t)$, it is the utility level of a full equilibrium associated with the tax vector t. The correspondence h is not in general a function.[5] However, if the appropriate Jacobian does not vanish at an equilibrium, then h is a continuously differentiable function in the neighbourhood of a full equilibrium by the implicit function theorem, and we can state

$$u = h(t).$$

The following lemma shows the effect of the change in t on u.

Lemma 1 (Basic Equation).   *At a full equilibrium of the C-economy the following holds if $a'f_u \neq 0$:*

$$\left(\frac{du}{dt}\right)' = -\frac{1}{a'f_u} a'FA. \qquad \qquad ...(10)$$

Proof. The total derivative of (9) gives

$$a'FA dt + a'f_u du = 0. \qquad \qquad ...(11)$$

This, together with the assumption $a'f_u \neq 0$, proves the lemma. ‖

Equation (10) will be called the Basic Equation, since it will play the key role in formulating policy proposals in the present paper. The jth element in (10), which represents the utility effect of the change in t_j alone, can be expressed as follows:

$$\frac{\partial u}{\partial t_j} = \frac{a'f_j}{a'f_u} \cdot a_j. \qquad \qquad ...(10')$$

This shows that the sign of $\partial u/\partial t_j$ is determined by the signs of the two expressions $a'f_u$ and $a'f_j$. The former expression is the aggregate of income terms weighted by the corresponding marginal costs, and will be called AIM. The latter is the aggregate of all the substitution terms of the jth good weighted by the corresponding marginal costs, and will be called ASM(j).

If all the goods in the economy are normal (i.e. $f_u \geq 0$), then AIM is positive. Even if some goods are strongly inferior, however, AIM is still positive when all the prices are equal to the corresponding marginal costs.[6] Of course, we are now concerned with the very situation where prices are different from the marginal costs. Even then AIM can be negative only when the degree of inferiority of some goods is so strong that in the expression of AIM the negative income terms of these goods outweigh the positive terms of all the superior goods. Thus without sacrificing much realism we will assume that AIM is positive in the present section.

What about the sign of ASM (j)? Unlike AIM, it is difficult to tell the most likely sign of ASM(j). Among the elements of vector f_j, the own substitution term f_{jj} is negative, while there is at least one positive cross-substitution term from the Hicksian demand theory. Thus, at least one positive term and one negative term appear simultaneously in an ASM(j). Also note that if all the marginal costs happen to be equal to the corresponding prices, ASM(j) is zero due to the Homogeneity Condition. This implies that ASM(j) could take either sign depending upon the way the marginal costs are different from the prices. Indeed, we can determine the sign of ASM(j) only when we make some additional assumptions. The theorems in this paper will be obtained by making assumptions of this kind.

Since we will analyse the welfare effect of simultaneous change in several tax rates in the following sections, it is convenient to express tax rates as a function of a parameter. Let t be a differentiable function of a scalar parameter s, namely

$$t_i = w_i(s) \quad i, ..., n$$

or

$$t = w(s).$$

The function w represents the reform programme of the excise tax structure, and the parameter s shows the stage of the reform. When h is a function, we have

$$u = h(w(s))$$

and u is a function of the parameter s. Since

$$\frac{du}{ds} = \frac{du}{dt}\frac{dt}{ds},$$

we obtain the following from Lemma 1,

$$\frac{du}{ds} = -\frac{1}{a'f_u} a'FA \frac{dt}{ds}, \qquad \qquad ...(12)$$

provided $a'f_u \neq 0$. Equation (12) shows the change in the level of utility as the stage of the tax reform programme progresses. In proving the subsequent theorems, we will use equation (12) under various assumptions on w.

The following lemma gives a useful alternative expression of the vector $a'F$ in (12).

Lemma 2. *For any number τ we have*

$$Fa(1+\tau) = FA(\tau-t), \qquad \qquad ...(13)$$

where $\tau' = (\tau, ..., \tau)$.

Proof. From the definition of A we have

$$Fa(1+\tau) = FA(1+\tau). \qquad \qquad ...(14)$$

On the other hand, the homogeneity condition and (8′) yield

$$FA(1+t) = 0. \quad \|$$

4. THE STATIC THEORY OF PIECEMEAL POLICY RECOMMENDATIONS

We are now in a position to derive policy implications of the basic equation.

A. *Selected Distortion Reduction*

The following theorem suggests a piecemeal policy recommendation applicable when the government can alter the tax rates of some, but not all, goods.

Theorem 1. *Suppose that at an equilibrium of the C-economy the goods on which the highest tax rate is imposed are substitutable for all the other goods and AIM is positive (negative). Then the reduction of the highest tax rate will continue to improve (decrease) the level of utility until the rate reaches the level of the next highest rate.*

Suppose that at an equilibrium of the C-economy the goods on which the lowest tax rate is imposed are substitutable for all the other goods and AIM is positive (negative). Then the increase of the lowest tax rate will continue to improve (decrease) the level of utility until the rate reaches the level of the next lowest rate.

Proof. We will only consider the case of reducing the highest tax rate when AIM is positive, since the proof procedure for the other cases is similar. Assume that $(n-m)$ commodities share the highest tax rate, and index commodities as follows,[7]

$$t_1 \leqq \ldots \leqq t_m < t_{m+1} = \ldots = t_n. \qquad \ldots(15)$$

By assumption, we uniformly reduce the tax rates of goods $m+1, \ldots, n$. Let the function w be such that

$$\frac{\partial t_i}{\partial s} - \frac{\partial w_i(s)}{\partial s} = \begin{cases} 0 & \text{for } i \leqq m \\ -1 & \text{for } i > m. \end{cases} \qquad \ldots(16)$$

The theorem will be proved if we can show that $du/ds > 0$ holds under assumptions of (15), (16), $a'f_u > 0$, and $F_{12} > 0$, where

$$F_{12} = \begin{bmatrix} f_{1,m+1} & \cdots & f_{1n} \\ \cdots & \cdots & \cdots \\ f_{m,m+1} & \cdots & f_{mn} \end{bmatrix}. \qquad \ldots(17)$$

From (13) we have

$$a'F = \frac{1}{1+\tau}(\tau'-t')AF.$$

By letting $\tau = t_n$ and applying (16) we obtain

$$a'FA \frac{dt}{ds} = \frac{1}{1+t_n}(t_n - t_1, \ldots, t_n - t_m, 0, \ldots, 0)AFA \begin{pmatrix} 0 \\ \vdots \\ 0 \\ -1 \\ \vdots \\ -1 \end{pmatrix}$$

$$= \frac{-1}{1+t_n}(a_1(t_n - t_1), \ldots, a_m(t_n - t_m))F_{12} \begin{pmatrix} a_{m+1} \\ \vdots \\ a_n \end{pmatrix}$$

$$< 0, \qquad \ldots(18)$$

where the last inequality follows from (15) and $F_{12} > 0$.

Thus, in view of (12) and assumption (i), we obtain $du/ds > 0$. ‖

Consider the situation when all the tax rates are different. Suppose that $t_1 < \ldots < t_n$ and AIM is positive. First lower t_n until $t_{n-1} = t_n$. Then reduce both t_{n-1} and t_n until $t_{n-2} = t_{n-1} = t_n$. Proceed in this manner, lowering the tax rates successively. The theorem indicates that this policy will improve the utility level at each step, as long as the relevant income and substitution terms behave properly. If the government pursues this policy until all the t_i's become equal, it will attain a Pareto optimum while monotonically improving the utility level in the process.

The assumption in the theorem that the good with the highest tax rate is substitutable for all the other goods is a natural one. If the good with the highest tax rate is a complement of another good, then these two goods together can be regarded as a composite good.

Thus, the reduction in the highest tax rate in this situation entails in decreasing the (average) tax rate of the composite good, which may not be the highest of all any more. (Note that here the term "composite good" is used in a different sense from Hicks'.)

Vanek [25] and Bhagwati [4] showed that in the two-commodity economy a reduction of the higher tax can reduce the level of utility if strong inferiority exists. Green [9], on the other hand, established that when $t_1 < t_2 < ... < t_{n-1}$ and the nth good is substitutable for all the other goods, the internal second best solution for t_n, if it exists at all, must be between t_1 and t_{n-1}. Our Theorem 1 clearly integrates these results in a unified framework. Detailed discussions on the relationship among these works will be given in Sections 4C, 4D and 6C.

Meade [21, pp. 120-121], Meade [20, pp. 14-33], Section 5 of Lipsey and Lancaster [16], and Bertrand and Vanek [2] showed that if the reduction of the highest tax rate increases the consumption of that good and lowers the consumption of all the other goods at the new equilibrium, then the utility level is increased. Despite the seeming similarity between their results and our Theorem 1, there is a difference. Their criteria for evaluating the welfare effect of the tax reduction are specified in terms of the direction of the uncompensated change in the equilibrium bundle of goods, while ours is specified in terms of compensated change along the indifference surface as in Green's. The advantages and disadvantages of the two approaches from the viewpoint of policy application are discussed in the last section of Hatta [13].

Although the dual specification of the model in terms of the compensated demand function simplifies the derivations of the results of Green, this approach is unsuitable for proving the aforementioned theorems of Meade, Lipsey and Lancaster, and Bertrand and Vanek. They employed the primary (as opposed to dual) approach in terms of the utility function, and that seems the best proof method for their results.

B. *Uniform Distortion Reduction*

We now consider a piecemeal policy applicable to the situation where the government is entitled to alter all the excise tax rates to some extent, even though their complete elimination is not allowed.

Suppose that in our economy not all the tax rates $t_1, ..., t_n$ are equal. We say the *distortions are reduced uniformly*,[8] if all the tax rates $t_1, ..., t_n$ are made proportionally closer to any given number τ. The proportionate reduction of tax rates is a special case of the uniform reduction of distortions where $\tau = 0$. The following theorem shows the welfare effect of the uniform reduction of distortions.

Theorem 2. *If AIM is positive (negative), a uniform reduction of distortions always improves (decreases) the utility level in the C-economy.*

Proof. We will only prove the positive AIM case, since the proof procedure for the negative AIM case is similar. Let function w be such that

$$\frac{dt}{ds} = \frac{dw(s)}{ds} = -(t-\tau). \qquad \qquad ...(19)$$

Then as a is increased $t_1, ..., t_n$ will approach τ proportionally. The theorem will be proved if we can show that $du/ds > 0$ when (19) holds for w and $a'f_u > 0$. From (13) and (19) we get

$$a'FA\frac{dt}{ds} = -a'FA(t-\tau)$$

$$= a'Fa(1+\tau).$$

Since not all t_i's are equal, we have from (8), $q \neq ka$ for all scalar k. Thus, from the nonpositive definiteness condition, the last expression is negative, and the theorem is proved in view of (12). ‖

8   REVIEW OF ECONOMIC STUDIES

Foster and Sonnenschein [8] obtained essential part of this result by using Brower's theorem on the invariance of domain.   Bruno [3] showed that the assumption of no inferiority goods in Foster and Sonnenschein can be substituted by a much weaker condition of positive AIM.   Our simple proof method in terms of the Basic Equation reveals the underlying relationship between their works and Green's.

C. *Geometric Interpretations of the Roles of AIM and ASM(j) in the Proofs of Theorems* 1 *and* 2

In the two-good economy, both Theorems 1 and 2 yield the following:

The reduction of the higher tax rate to the level of the other will improve (decrease) the utility if AIM is positive (negative).

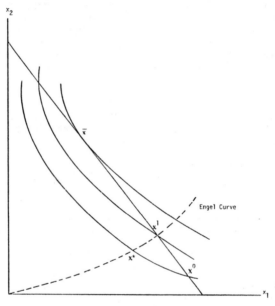

FIGURE 1

This proposition is included in Theorem 1, since the good with the higher tax rate can not be complementary with the other good in the two-commodity world.   The fact this is a special case of Theorem 2 immediately follows from the definition of the uniform reduction of tax.

Diagrams can illustrate this proposition.   Suppose that the economy of Figure 1 or Figure 2 is in equilibrium at x^0.   If the higher tax rate t_2 is reduced in Figure 1 (Figure 2), the equilibrium will move to a point like x^1, thus increasing (decreasing) the utility level. (The phenomenon that the reduction of the higher tax rate can decrease the utility level as is depicted in Figure 2 is often referred to as the Vanek-Bhagwati Paradox.)

We have seen that the sign of AIM is an important factor in determining the welfare effect of a tax change.   The definition of AIM straightforwardly yields the geometric interpretation of its sign.   If AIM is positive (negative) at an equilibrium, then the Engel curve passes through that point from the inside to the outside (from the outside to the inside) of the production possibility set Π as the utility level is increased. Point x^1 in Figure 1 (Figure 2) illustrates the positive (negative) AIM situation for the two-good economy. Theorems 1 and 2 are thus confirmed for the case of the two-good economy.

This graphical analysis can be generalized into the n-good economy. Assume that a change in the tax structure in an n-good economy brings the equilibrium point from x^0 to x^1. Let x^* be the point where the Engel curve passing through x^1 intersects the indifference surface passing through x^0. Then the change from x^0 to x^1 can be decomposed into two parts: the one from x^0 to x^* along an indifference curve and the other from x^*

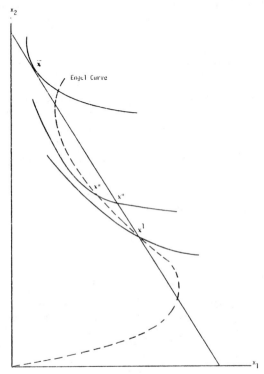

FIGURE 2

to x^1 along the Engel curve. Since x^* and x^0 are on the same indifference curve, we can compare the utilities of x^* and x^1 instead of those of x^0 and x^1. Suppose x^* is inside of Π, and the Engel curve passes x^1 from inside of Π as the utility level is increased. Then the utility level must be higher at x^1 than at x^*, and hence we get $v(x^1) > v(x^0)$.

Let the function y be defined by $y(s, u) = a'f(A(w(s)+1), u)$. Then we have

$$\frac{\partial y}{\partial s} = a'FA\frac{dt}{ds}.$$

This implies that x^* is contained in Π if and only if $a'FA(dt/ds)$ is negative. On the other hand, we already know that the Engel curve crosses Π from its inside if the AIM is positive. This explains geometrically why the basic equation indicates that the tax change increases utility level when the sign of $a'FA(dt/ds)$ is positive and that of $a'f_u$ is negative.[9]

In view of equation (11), we have

$$a'FA \frac{dt}{ds} ds + a'f_u du = 0.$$

The first term of the LHS of this equation shows the change in the level of the resource when we move from x^0 to x^* along the indifference surface, and the second term represents the change in the level of the resource as we move from x^* to x^1 along an Engel curve. When the levels of $a'FA(dt/ds)$ and $a'f_u$ are known, the above equality shows how much u has to be changed for a given increase in s so as to make the total amount of the resource requirement the same as before.

D. Multiple Equilibria and the Sign of AIM

So far we have only considered an equilibrium where AIM is not zero. In the neighbourhood of such an equilibrium the correspondence h (defined in Section 3B) is a function from the implicit function theorem. Globally, however, the correspondence h is not necessarily a function. For a given t, multiple equilibria may exist, and hence different levels of u may be consistent with the given t. Suppose, for example, the economy is in equilibrium at x^1 in Figure 2. It is readily seen that a point somewhere between $\bar{x}$ and x^0, the economy can be in equilibrium for the same tax rates as at x^1.

Let $\rho(x_1, x_2)$ denote the marginal rate of substitution at (x_1, x_2) in the two commodity world. If we only consider the points on the production possibility line, the marginal rate of substitution is determined for a given x_1, and we can define the function r by

$$r(x_1) = \rho(x_1, (b - a_1 x_1)/a_2).$$

In the two-commodity world, (8) implies that

$$\frac{(1+t_1)a_1}{(1+t_2)a_2} = \frac{q_1}{q_2} = r(x_1), \qquad \qquad \text{...(20)}$$

which yields

$$t_2 = (1+t_1)a_1/a_2 r(x_1) - 1. \qquad \qquad \text{...(21)}$$

Let $\tau_2(x_1; t_1)$ denote the RHS of this equation. (The symbol τ_2 has nothing to do with the τ in (13).) The value $\tau_2(x_1; t_1)$ is the rate of the excise tax on the second good that would make the point $(x_1, (b - a_1 x_1)/a_2)$ on the production possibility curve an equilibrium for the given t_1. We call $\tau_2(x_1; t_1)$ the *associated tax rate for the second good at* $(x_1; t_1)$. Rewriting (21) as

$$t_2 = \tau_2(x_1; t_1), \qquad \qquad \text{...(21')}$$

we can interpret (21) to imply that for a given point $(x_1, (b - a_1 x_1)/a_2)$ to be an equilibrium for a given t_1, the actual tax rate t_2 must be equal to the associated tax rate $\tau_2(x_1; t_1)$. Figure 4 is the graph of $\tau_2(x_1; t_1)$ for a fixed t_1 for the economy of Figure 2. Figure 3 duplicates Figure 2 with the labels used in Figure 4. We find from Figure 4 that when the actual tax rate t_2 is equal to α, equation (21') holds at B, D, and F. Thus any one of points B, D, and F in Figure 3 can be an equilibrium; they share the same level of the marginal rate of substitution, and a single Engel curve passes through these points. At point B, which is the closest equilibrium point to the Pareto Optimum point A, the Engel curve passes through the production frontier from the inside to the outside, and hence AIM is positive at B. As we move from B to the south-east, the sign of AIM alternates at each equilibrium unless one of the AIM's is zero; it is negative at D, and positive at F. This reveals that a negative AIM can occur only if multiple equilibria exist for the given structure of tax rates.

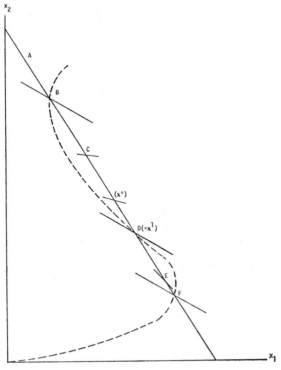

FIGURE 3

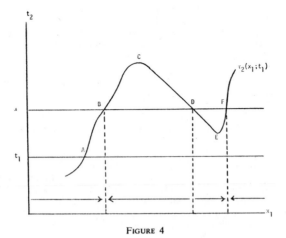

FIGURE 4

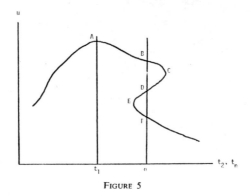

FIGURE 5

Figure 5 depicts the relationship between the utility level and t_2 of the economy portrayed in Figures 3 and 4. This shows that when $t_2 = \alpha$, a reduction in t_2, the higher tax rate, causes an increase in u at points B and F, and a decrease in u at point D. Since AIM is negative at D as we have just observed, this confirms our analysis in 4C.

Figure 4 shows that AIM is negative between equilibria C and E in Figure 3. Thus, the segment CE in Figure 5 corresponds to the equilibria with negative AIM, and a reduction in t_2 decreases the level of utility along this segment.

5. THE DYNAMIC THEORY OF PIECEMEAL POLICY RECOMMENDATIONS

In this section we will establish that the assumption of positive AIM in Theorems 1 and 2 can be replaced by a stability condition of the Marshallian adjustment mechanism. We will present this result after defining the adjustment mechanism. Readers not interested in dynamics can skip this section.

So far, we have analysed the situation in which the profitability of every industry is already made the same, as implied by equation (4). We now consider a more general situation where uniform profitability is not always attained due to frictions existing in factor mobility. Then, equation (4) may not be always satisfied. Let us still assume, however, that when profitability is unequal among the different industries, resources will be reallocated from the less profitable industries to the more profitable ones. The structure of this economy may be summarized as follows:

(i) The production bundle x at an arbitrary moment is located somewhere on the production frontier represented by (2). The exact position of the bundle is determined historically.

(ii) The consumer's price vector q is determined through an instantaneous bidding process in such a way as to clear the market for the historically determined production bundle.

(iii) Once the consumer's prices are determined by the market, the producer's prices are found by its definition, since tax rates are given exogenously.

(iv) For any pair of goods, producers compare its price ratio and the transformation ratio. If they are different, that is, if (4) does not hold, producers produce more of the profitable goods by reducing the production of the less profitable goods. For the new commodity bundle thus produced, the steps of (i), (ii), (iii) and (iv) will be repeated. This process will continue until (4) is reached.

Producers find the relative profitability of a pair of goods by comparing the producer's price ratio and the transformation ratio. Specifically, we assume the following:

" If $p_j/p_i > a_j/a_i$, resources will be shifted from the ith to the jth industry."

In the two-commodity world, we have from (3), (20), and the definition of $\tau_2(x_1; t_1)$ that

$$p_1/p_2 \gtreqless a_1/a_2 \text{ according as } t_2 \gtreqless \tau_2(x_1; t_1).$$

Thus, under the adjustment mechanism assumed above x_1 will increase if $t_2 > \tau_2(x_1; t_1)$, and x_1 will decrease if $t_2 < \tau_2(x_1; t_1)$. By definition, $\tau_2(x_1; t_1)$ implies the tax rate on the second good that equates the profitability of the two goods at $(x_1, (b-a_1 x_1)/a_2)$ when the tax rate on the first good is t_1. Thus, when $t_2 > \tau_2(x_1; t_1)$, the first good is more profitable than the second, and an increase in the output of the first good will incur a profit. When $t_2 < \tau_2(x_1; t_1)$, the production of x_1 will be reduced for the same reason.

Suppose that $t_2 = \alpha$ in Figure 4, but the economy is now producing and consuming the commodity bundle of A. Then $t_2 > \tau_2(x_1; t_1)$ holds and the economy is, of course, in disequilibrium. Thus, x_1 must increase. This process will continue as long as $\alpha > \tau_2(x_1; t_1)$, and stops when the economy reaches B, an equilibrium where $\alpha = \tau_2(x_1; t_1)$. On the other hand, if the economy is initially at C when $t_2 = \alpha$, we have $t_2 < \tau_2(x_1; t_1)$, and the production and the commodity bundle will move to B. The arrows along the x_1 axis shows the direction of the movement of the economy when $t_2 = \alpha$.

These arrows show that the equilibria B and F are stable and the equilibrium D is unstable. In view of Figures 3 and 5, this implies that when the economy is at a stable equilibrium, AIM is positive, and hence a decrease in the higher tax rate improves the utility level in the two commodity economy. The aim of the present section is to generalize this observation to the n-commodity economy.

Let z_i^j denote the difference between the producer's price ratio and the transformation ratio, for a pair of goods j and i:

$$z_i^j = p_j/p_i - a_j/a_i. \qquad ...(22)$$

Then the above adjustment mechanism may be formally expressed as[10]

$$\dot{x}_i = a^i(z_i^1, ..., {}^\nabla z_i^i, ..., z_i^n) \quad i = 1, ..., n, \qquad ...(23)$$

where

$$\dot{x}_i = 0 \qquad \text{if } z_i^j = 0 \text{ for all } j; \text{ and}$$

$$\partial a^i/\partial z_i^j < 0 \qquad \text{if } j \neq i.$$

This process of resource reallocation may be called the *Marshallian Adjustment Mechanism*. Thus, the dynamic adjustment model of this section consists of equations (1), (2), (3), (5), (6), and (23).

Under the assumption of this mechanism the following holds.

Theorem 3. *If the system (23) is locally stable at a full equilibrium, then*

$$a'f_u \geqq 0.$$

Before proving this theorem, we have to reduce (23) to an equivalent system of equations which contain x_i's as their arguments. Among the n equations of (23), one can be eliminated with no loss of information, for we have from (2)

$$a_1 \dot{x}_1 + ... + a_n \dot{x}_n = 0.$$

Hence, we may consider the following system instead of (23):

$$\dot{x}_i = a^i(z_i^1, ..., {}^\nabla z_i^i, ..., z_i^n) \quad i = 2, ..., n. \qquad ...(24)$$

Substituting (6) and (22) into (24), we can express $\dot{x}_i$ as a function of $p_2, ..., p_n$; formally

$$\dot{x}_i = b^i(p_2, ..., p_n) \quad i = 2, ..., n. \qquad ...(25)$$

On the other hand, p_i is a function of $x_1, ..., x_n$;

$$p_i = w^i(x_1, ..., x_n)$$
$$= w^i((b - \Sigma_2^n a_i x_i)/a_1, x_2, ..., x_n)$$
$$= g^i(x_2, ..., x_n) \quad i = 2, ..., n. \qquad \qquad ...(26)$$

Substituting (26) into (25), $\dot{x}_i$ is finally expressed as a function of $x_2, ..., x_n$:

$$\dot{x}_i = c_i(x_2, ..., x_n) \quad i = 2, ..., n. \qquad \qquad ...(27)$$

Thus, we may consider the stability of system (27) instead of (23).
    Let

$$a_{ij} = \frac{\partial a^i}{\partial z_j^i}, \quad b_{ij} = \frac{\partial b^i}{\partial p_j}, \quad c_{ij} = \frac{\partial c}{\partial x_j}, \quad g_{ij} = \frac{\partial g^i}{\partial x_j},$$

$$B = \begin{bmatrix} b_{22} & \cdots & b_{2n} \\ \cdots & \cdots & \cdots \\ b_{n2} & \cdots & b_{nn} \end{bmatrix}, \quad C = \begin{bmatrix} c_{22} & \cdots & c_{2n} \\ \cdots & \cdots & \cdots \\ c_{n2} & \cdots & c_{nn} \end{bmatrix} \quad \text{and} \quad G = \begin{bmatrix} g_{22} & \cdots & g_{2n} \\ \cdots & \cdots & \cdots \\ g_{n2} & \cdots & g_{nn} \end{bmatrix}.$$

Then the local stability condition for the system of differential equations (27) requires that all characteristic roots of C have non-positive real parts.[11] Thus, we obtain

$$(-1)^{n-1} | C | \geqq 0. \qquad \qquad ...(28)$$

By applying the chain rule to (25), (26) and (27), we get

$$C = BG.$$

Substituting this into inequality (28) yields

$$(-1)^{n-1} | B | | G | \geqq 0. \qquad \qquad ...(29)$$

We will later establish that inequality (29) leads to the non-negativity of AIM, namely $a' f_u \geqq 0$. The following lemma is necessary for its proof.

Lemma 3. *Let an $n \times (n-1)$ matrix F^* be defined by*

$$F^* = \begin{bmatrix} f_{12} & \cdots & f_{1n} \\ \cdots & \cdots & \cdots \\ f_{n2} & \cdots & f_{nn} \end{bmatrix}.$$

Then $(-1)^{n-1} |[f_u \mid F^*]| \geqq 0$.

    Proof. Let $v_i = \partial v / \partial c_i$, $v_{ij} = \partial^2 v / \partial c_i \partial c_j$, and

$$V = \begin{bmatrix} 0 & v_1 & \cdots & v_n \\ v_1 & v_{11} & \cdots & v_{1n} \\ \vdots & \vdots & & \vdots \\ v_n & v_{n1} & \cdots & v_{nn} \end{bmatrix}.$$

Since λf_u is the vector of the income terms and F is the matrix of the substitution terms we have[12]

$$V = \begin{bmatrix} \omega & \vdots & f_u' \\ --- & \vdots & ---- \\ f_u & \vdots & \frac{1}{\lambda} F \end{bmatrix}^{-1},$$

where ω is the co-factor of the element 0 in matrix V divided by $|V|$. Thus, the element of the second row and the first column of matrix V may be expressed as

$$v_1 = -|[f_u \,|\, (1/\lambda)F^*]| \times |V|.$$

Noting that $(-1)^n |V| \geq 0$ from the second-order condition for a maximum utility, we obtain $(-1)^{n-1} |[f_u \,|\, F^*]| \geq 0$. ‖

Proof of Theorem 3. In view of (22) and (23), we have

$$b_{ij} = \begin{cases} \dfrac{1}{p_i} a_{ij} & \text{if } i \neq j \\[2ex] -\dfrac{1}{p_i^2} \sum_{r \neq i}^{n} a_{ir} p_r & \text{if } i = j. \end{cases}$$

By letting $e_{ij} = a_{ij} p_j / p_i$,

$$B \begin{bmatrix} p_2 & & 0 \\ & \ddots & \\ 0 & & p_n \end{bmatrix} = \begin{bmatrix} -\sum\limits_{r \neq 2}^{n} e_{2r} & e_{23} & \cdots\cdots & e_{2n} \\[2ex] e_{32} & -\sum\limits_{r \neq 3}^{n} e_{3r}\cdots\cdots & & e_{3n} \\[1ex] \vdots & \vdots & \ddots & \vdots \\[1ex] e_{n2} & e_{n3} & \cdots\cdots & -\sum\limits_{r \neq n}^{n} e_{nr} \end{bmatrix}.$$

Since the matrix in the RHS of this equation has dominant diagonal elements, B is a quasi-dominant diagonal matrix. Thus, every characteristic root of B has a positive real part,[13] and we have $|B| > 0$. Thus, in view of (29), we get

$$(-1)^{n-1} |G| \geq 0. \qquad\qquad ...(30)$$

From (3) and (26), $(q_2, ..., q_n)$ is a function of $(x_2, ..., x_n)$. Let the matrix M be defined by

$$\begin{bmatrix} dq_2 \\ \vdots \\ dq_n \end{bmatrix} = M \begin{bmatrix} dx_2 \\ \vdots \\ dx_n \end{bmatrix}.$$

Then (30) yields

$$(-1)^{n-1} |M| \geq 0, \qquad\qquad ...(31)$$

since the signs of $|G|$ and $|M|$ are the same from (3) and the definition of G. By differentiating (1), we get

$$\begin{bmatrix} f_u^1 & | & f_{12}\cdots f_{1n} \\ \vdots & | & \vdots \quad\; \vdots \\ f_u^n & | & f_{n2}\cdots f_{nn} \end{bmatrix} \begin{pmatrix} du \\ dq_2 \\ \vdots \\ dq_n \end{pmatrix} = \begin{pmatrix} dx_1 \\ \vdots \\ dx_n \end{pmatrix}.$$

This, together with (2), gives

$$\begin{pmatrix} dq_2 \\ \vdots \\ dq_n \end{pmatrix} = \begin{bmatrix} 0 & 1 & & 0 \\ \vdots & & \ddots & \\ 0 & 0 & & 1 \end{bmatrix} \begin{bmatrix} f_u^1 & | & f_{12}\cdots f_{1n} \\ \vdots & | & \vdots \quad\; \vdots \\ f_u^n & | & f_{n2}\cdots f_{nn} \end{bmatrix}^{-1} \begin{bmatrix} -\dfrac{a_2}{a_1} \cdots -\dfrac{a_n}{a_1} \\ \hline 1 \quad 0 \\ \ddots \\ 0 \quad 1 \end{bmatrix} \begin{Bmatrix} dx_2 \\ \vdots \\ dx_n \end{Bmatrix}.$$

Thus, M is the product of the three matrices at the RHS. By letting $a'_* = (-a_2/a_1, ...,$ $-a_n/a_1)$, we have[14]

$$|M||f_u|F^*| = \begin{vmatrix} 0 & 0 & -I \\ a'_* & f_u & F^* \\ I & & \end{vmatrix}$$

$$= \begin{vmatrix} & a'_* \\ f_u & I \end{vmatrix}$$

$$= \frac{1}{a_1} a'f_u. \qquad\qquad ...(32)$$

By the way Lemma 3 and (31) yield

$$|M||f_u|F^*| \geq 0.$$

Thus, the last expression of (32) is non-negative. ∥

Theorems 1, 2 and 3 yield the following two theorems.

Theorem 4. *Suppose the following:*

(i) *The C-economy is at a stable full equilibrium in the Marshallian sense, and AIM is not zero.*

(ii) *The goods on which the highest (lowest) tax rate is imposed are substitutable for all the other goods.*

Then the reduction of the highest (the increase of the lowest) tax rate up to the level of the next highest (lowest) rate will improve the level of utility.

Theorem 5. *If the C-economy is at a stable full equilibrium in the Marshallian sense and AIM is not zero, then a uniform reduction of distortions will improve the level of utility.*

Theorems 4 and 5 are clearly extensions of the stability analysis of Kemp [15] for the two commodity economy.

In Theorem 3 the postulate that the economy is stable was used as a part of the sufficient conditions in obtaining results of comparative statics. This clearly serves as an example of the *correspondence principle*, and may be contrasted to the " current trend in comparative statics " described in the following remarks by Arrow and Hahn:[15]

" He [Samuelson] proposed a general correspondence principle that all meaningful theorems in comparative statics derive either from the second-order conditions on maximization of profits by firms or of utility by consumers or from the assumption that the observed equilibrium was stable. In fact, very few useful propositions are derivable from this principle.

The current trend in comparative statics and stability dates from the work of Mosak [1944] and Metzler [1945]. The emphasis has tended to be a little different from Samuelson's correspondence principle; rather, the tendency has been to formulate hypotheses about the excess-demand functions that imply both stability and certain results in comparative statics."

Note that in the proof of Theorem 3 a quasi-dominant diagonal matrix was naturally derived from the properties of the adjustment mechanism, rather than exogenously imposed through assumptions such as gross substitutability.[16] Our approach appears much closer to Samuelson's original conception of the correspondence principle than the " current trend ".

6. THE THEORY OF THE SECOND BEST REVISITED

Our analysis in terms of the Basic Equation sheds some light on the policy implications of the theory of the second best.

A. *The Theorem of the Second Best*

Let t_i represent the deviation of price from marginal cost for the ith good as before. Assume that the vector $(t_1, ..., t_s)$ is fixed and that there is at least one pair (i, j) such that $t_i \neq t_j$ and $i, j \leq s$. What is the vector $(t_{s+1}, ..., t_n)$ that maximizes u in the C-economy? This is the *problem of the second best* as applied to the C-economy. Its solution $(t^*_{s+1}, ..., t^*_n)$ is called the *second best solution*. Note that the above assumption, $t_i \neq t_j$ for some $i, j \leq s$, implies that a fixed distortion exists between the substitution and the transformation ratio of good i for good j, and the Paretian condition is violated, since (3) gives

$$\frac{q_i}{q_j} = \frac{(1+t_j)p_i}{(1+t_i)p_j}.$$

The theorem of the second best gives a characterization of this solution.

Theorem 6 (The Theorem of the Second Best). *In the second best problem the following does not necessarily hold:* $(t^*_{s+1}, ..., t^*_n) = t_k(1, ..., 1)$ *for some* $k \leq s$.

Proof. Consider a C-economy with three goods. Assume that AIM is positive and all the goods are substitutable for each other. Suppose that t_1 and t_2 are fixed and $t_1 < t_2$. Then Theorem 1 implies that the second best solution for t_3 must satisfy $t_1 < t_3 < t_2$. ∥

This theorem says that the policy which equates all the controllable tax rates to the kth rate, one of the fixed rates, does not generally yield the second best solution.[17] In other words, such a policy may actually reduce the utility level since the original rate structure before the policy enactment might be the second best solution.

This theorem may be restated using the concept of " distortion " to later facilitate our analysis. By letting $r_i \equiv t_i + 1$, we have from (3)

$$\frac{q_i}{q_j} = \frac{r_j}{r_i} \frac{p_i}{p_j}.$$

This implies that the Paretian condition is violated between goods i and j when $r_j/r_i - 1 \neq 0$. Hence, the quantity $(r_j/r_i - 1)$ will be called the *distortion* in pair (i, j). We say that *a distortion exists in* (i, j) if $r_j/r_i - 1 \neq 0$.

If all the controllable tax rates are made equal to some fixed rate t_k, then it will eliminate the distortions between the kth good and any goods whose rates are controllable. Hence, an interpretation of the theorem is that in the situation where certain distortions are controllable while at least one distortion is not, the elimination of some controllable distortions does not necessarily increase the utility level.[18]

B. *Its Negative Policy Implications*

We now turn to a discussion of the relationship between the theory of the second best and the reduction of distortions. We say *the distortion in* (i, j) *is reduced* if $| r_j/r_i - 1 |$ is reduced without changing the sign of $(r_j/r_i - 1)$. As the previous discussion showed the theorem of the second best is concerned with the elimination of some controllable distortions when certain other distortions are fixed. Hence, the theorem is *not* applicable to the situation where all the distortions are reduced without keeping any one fixed. For example, second best theory says nothing about the effect of a reduction in distortion in the two-good economy, where once one distortion is changed there is no other distortion to fix. As we have already seen, however, even in the two-good economy, an arbitrary reduction of

B—44/1

distortion can lower the utility level, when the Vanek-Bhagwati Paradox occurs. Moreover, the uniform reduction in tax distortions lowers the level of utility when AIM is negative. Thus, the essential element of the negative implication of the second best theorem stands even in the economy where fixed distortions do not exist. Accordingly, each of these cases where a reduction in distortion lowers the welfare may be regarded as a part of a more general phenomenon which may be called the Piecemeal Policy Perversity:

> A partial reduction in distortion, falling short of entire elimination, can reduce the utility level, whether or not a fixed distortion exists.

Our Basic Equation reveals that strong complementarity and inferiority cause the Piecemeal Policy Perversity, and that the assumption of fixed distortions is irrelevant.

C. *Its Positive Policy Implications*

In order to overcome the pessimism of the implication of the theorem of the second best, several attempts were made to derive necessary conditions for second best solutions. This approach, however, does not seem to yield much in the way of useful policy implications. The necessary condition of the second best solution derived by Green [9] may illustrate this. Consider a C-economy where only one tax rate, say t_n, is controllable and all the other rates are fixed. Define h as the correspondence from R to R representing the set of utility levels for each t_n in this economy. When h is single-valued, we can write

$$u = h(t_n).$$

Green proved that the first-order condition for the internal second best solution for t_n in $h(t_n)$ is

$$t_n = \frac{\Sigma_i t_i a_i f_{ni}}{\Sigma_i a_i f_{ni}} \quad i = 1, \dots, n-1. \tag{33}$$

Thus, he established that if the nth good is complementary with all the other goods, the second best solution for t_n must satisfy $t_{min} < t_n < t_{max}$, where t_{min} and t_{max} respectively represent the minimum and maximum elements in $(t_1, \dots, t_{n-1})$.

From this, however, we cannot (as Green did not) immediately recommend a policy of reducing t_n to the level of t_{max} even when $t_n > t_{max}$ holds initially. There are three reasons for this. First, the correspondence h may not have an internal maximum as illustrated in Figure 6. Second, even if h has an internal maximum, still it may have multiple extrema, as is depicted in Figure 7. Third, even when h has only one internal maximum and no other internal extremum, still our policy of reducing the highest tax rate may not work if h is not a function as Figure 5 illustrates. This is the case where multiple equilibria exist for

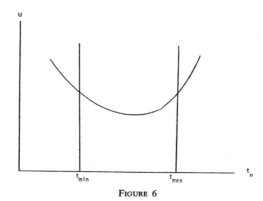

FIGURE 6

HATTA   PIECEMEAL POLICY RECOMMENDATIONS   19

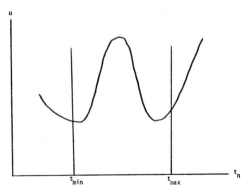

FIGURE 7

the given t_n. The reduction in t_2 from α will decrease the level of utility if the equilibrium is at D. Thus, direct characterization of the second best solution itself does not necessarily yield useful policy implications. On the other hand, our Basic Equation, indicating the slope of the graph of the correspondence h, enables us to tell the direction of the change in utility level caused by an immediate movement of t_n.[19] This approach seems more suitable for obtaining policy recommendations.

D. *A Concluding Remark on the Second Best Theorem*

There is no doubt that second best theory has played a very important role in reminding us, in a systematic manner, of the difficulties associated with piecemeal policies. Beyond this , however, the policy implications we can obtain from the analytical framework of the second best theory appear very limited. Specifically, the above discussion showed the following:

First, the essential aspect of the negative implication of the second best theory has nothing to do with the existence of a fixed distortion. It is a special case of the Piecemeal Policy Perversity.

Second, characterizing the second best solution is not so useful for policy formation as it first appears. A more useful approach is to study directly the sufficient conditions under which a particular change in policy variables improves the utility level.

First version received February 1975; *final version accepted August* 1975 (*Eds.*).

This paper is taken from the author's Ph.D. Dissertation, Hatta [10]. He is indebted to Professors Peter Newman and Carl Christ for innumerable and provoking comments. Discussions with Professors Trent Bertrand and Martin J. Bailey were also helpful. Professor Peter Diamond suggested the use of indirect utility function in his comment to a draft of the thesis. This suggestion was instrumental to the final proofs of major theorems in the dissertation and the present paper which utilize compensated demand functions. The author gratefully acknowledges the Brookings Institution for providing the Brookings Research Fellowship during 1971-72 for the present study. The author alone is responsible for the remaining errors.

NOTES

1. Although the present paper analyses the closed economy with constant cost technology, the compensated demand function is powerful in the study of other situations as well. Dixit [7] uses the compensated demand function in the analysis of welfare effects of distortion reductions in the closed economy with strictly convex technology. Hatta [13] (Chapter 8 of Hatta [10]) generalizes our Theorem 1 to the open economy with strictly convex technology. When the technology is strictly convex, the conditions imposed in the welfare propositions become complex, and neither author extends our Theorems 3, 4, and 5 to that situation.

2. See equation (43) of Samuelson [24, p. 103] and Arrow and Hahn [1, p. 104].

3. See Arrow and Hahn [1, p. 105].

4. The first two properties are proved in Hicks [14, pp. 310-311] and Samuelson [24, pp. 113-115]. For the non-positive definiteness condition, see Hatta [11]. The consistency conditions of f_u can be readily proved from the expression of $\partial x_j / \partial I$ in (35) in Samuelson [24, p. 102]. The expression $q' f_u$ represents the amount of increase in expenditure caused by a unit increase in the level of utility. Obviously, this is the inverse of the marginal utility of money λ.

5. A perverse welfare effect of a tax reduction when h is not a function is discussed in Sections 4D and 6C.

6. This is because $q' f_u = 1/\lambda > 0$ by the Consistency Condition.

7. If we consider the situation where $t_1 < \ldots < t_n$, the theorem immediately follows from (10′): The Homogeneity Condition and (8) gives $((1 + t_1)a_1, \ldots, (1 + t_n)a_n) f_n = p' f_n = 0$. Hence,

$$a' f_n = (1/(1 + t_n))((t_n - t_1)a_1, \ldots, (t_n - t_{n-1})a_{n-1}, 0) f_n > 0.$$

Equation (10′) shows that $a' f_n > 0$ and $a' f_u > 0$ yield $\partial u / \partial t_n < 0$.

8. The reason why we do not say that *taxes* are reduced uniformly is obvious—all *taxes* may be raised when distortions are reduced uniformly. This concept is equivalent to Foster and Sonnenschein's concept of *radial distortion reduction*. Although they claim that their concept is dependent upon the choice of the numeraire, it is not. See Hatta [12].

9. In the proofs of Theorems 1 and 2, the expression $a' FA(dt/dS)$ was shown to be negative under the given conditions. Geometrically, we were proving there that x^* is contained in Π. In the two good economy, the noncomplementarity assumption of Theorem 1 is automatically satisfied, and x^* is always contained in Π when the higher tax rate is lowered, as is illustrated in Figures 1 and 2. Thus, the reduction of the higher tax rate lowers the utility level only when the Engel curve passes the equilibrium from the outside of Π, namely when the Vanek Bhagwati Paradox occurs.

10. The symbol ∇ in equation (3) is an elimination mark. Namely

$$(z_i^1, \ldots, \nabla z_i^t, \ldots, z_i^n) = (z_i^1, \ldots, z^{t-1}, z^{t+1}, \ldots, z_i^n).$$

Note that the symbol a^t represents a function, while the symbol a_t denotes a marginal cost. It may be observed that each of the differential equations (23) that describes the Marshallian mechanism contains $(n-1)$ arguments; while each differential equation in the commonly assumed Walrasian mechanism has only one variable, the excess demand for the corresponding good. A lucid explanation of the original Marshallian mechanism will be found in Newman [22, pp. 106-108].

11. See Theorem 19 on p. 208 and the remarks on p. 213 in Pontryagin [23].

12. See Samuelson [25, p. 15].

13. Theorem 2 of McKenzie [18, p. 49].

14. Here we twice use the following property of determinants. If A, D and E are square matrices and E is partitioned as $E = \begin{bmatrix} A & B \\ C & D \end{bmatrix}$, then $|E| = |A - BD^{-1}C| \cdot |D|$, provided $|D| \neq 0$. See Dhrymes [6, p. 570] for the proof.

15. See Arrow and Hahn [1, p. 12].

16. Foster and Sonnenschein [8] contains a stability analysis of the latter type, and does not establish the exact relationship between non-negativity of AIM and the stability condition.

17. If the model is interpreted as a model of imperfect competition, it is to the price of the kth commodity that "the monopolist's reactions are geared" (Lipsey and Lancaster [17, p. 226]). See also McManus [19, pp. 209-213].

18. In the words of Lipsey and Lancaster, "The general theorem for the second best optimum states that if there is introduced into a general equilibrium system a constraint which prevents the attainment of one of the Paretian conditions, the other Paretian conditions, although still attainable, are, in general, no longer desirable " [16, p. 11], and " piecemeal application of single Paretian welfare conditions in a situation in which not all such conditions could be satisfied might well decrease, rather than increase, welfare " [17, p. 226].

19. Besides equation (33) can be easily obtained from the Basic Equation. Assuming the AIM is not zero, $\partial u / \partial t_n = 0$ implies $a' f_n = 0$ from (10′). This, together with the Homogeneity Condition $q' f_n = 0$ and (8), yields (33).

REFERENCES

[1]   Arrow, K. and Hahn, F. *General Competitive Analysis* (San Francisco: Holden Day, 1971).

[2]   Bertrand, T. and Vanek, J. " The Theory of Tariffs, Taxes and Subsidies: Some Aspects of the Second Best ", *American Economic Review*, 61, No. 5 (December 1971), pp. 925-931.

[3]   Bruno, Michael. " Market Distortions and Gradual Reform ", *Review of Economic Studies*, 39, No. 4 (July 1972), pp. 373-383.

[4]   Bhagwati, J. " The Gains from Trade Once Again ", *Oxford Economic Papers*, 20, No. 2 (July 1968), pp. 137-148.

[5]   Corlett, W. J. and Hague, D. C. "Complementarity and the Excess Burden of Taxation", *Review of Economic Studies*, 21 (1953), pp. 21-30.

[6]   Dhrymes, P. J. *Econometrics: Statistical Foundations and Applications* (New York: Harper and Row, 1970).

[7]   Dixit, A. " Welfare Effects of Tax and Price Changes ", *Journal of Public Economics*, **4** (1975), pp. 103-123.

[8]   Foster, E. and Sonnenschein, H. " Price Distortion and Economic Welfare ", *Econometrica*, **38**, No. 2 (March 1970), pp. 281-297.

[9]   Green, J. " The Social Optimum in the Presence of Monopoly and Taxation ", *Review of Economic Studies*, **29**, No. 1 (October 1961), pp. 66-77.

[10] Hatta, T. *A Theory of Piecemeal Policy Recommendations*, Ph.D. Dissertation (The Johns Hopkins University, 1973).

[11] Hatta, T. " A Note on a Theorem in ' Value & Capital ' ", *Western Economic Journal*, **11**, No. 2 (June 1973), pp. 164-166.

[12] Hatta, T. " Radial Change in Distortion and Choice of Numeraire ", *Econometrica* (May 1975), pp 519-520.

[13] Hatta, T. " A Recommendation for a Better Tariff Structure ", *Econometrica*, **45**, (November 1977).

[14] Hicks, J. R. *Value and Capital*, 2nd ed. (London: Oxford University Press, 1946).

[15] Kemp, M. " Some Issues in the Analysis of Trade Gains ", *Oxford Economic Papers*, **20**, No. 2 (July 1968), pp. 149-161.

[16] Lipsey, R. and Lancaster, K. " The General Theory of Second Best ", *Review of Economic Studies*, **24**, No. 1 (October 1956), pp. 11-32.

[17] Lipsey, R. G. and Lancaster, K. " McManus on Second Best ", *Review of Economic Studies*, **26**, No. 3 (June 1959), pp. 225-226.

[18] McKenzie, L. " Matrices with Dominant Diagonals and Economic Theory ", Chapter 4 of Arrow, Karlin, and Suppes (eds.), *Mathematical Methods in the Social Sciences*, 1959 (Stanford: Stanford University Press, 1960).

[19] McManus, M. " Comments on the General Theory of Second Best ", *Review of Economic Studies*, **26**, No. 3 (June 1959), pp. 209-224.

[20] Meade, J. E. *Trade and Welfare: Mathematical Supplement* (Oxford: Oxford University Press, 1955).

[21] Meade, J. E. *The Theory of Customs Unions* (North Holland Publishing Co., 1955).

[22] Newman, P. *Theory of Exchange* (Englewood Cliffs, New Jersey: Prentice Hall, 1965).

[23] Pontryagin, L. S. *Ordinary Differential Equations* (Reading, Massachusetts: Addison Wesley, 1962).

[24] Samuelson, P. A. *Foundations of Economic Analysis* (Cambridge, Massachusetts: Harvard University Press, 1947).

[25] Samuelson, P. A. " Prices of Factors and Goods in General Equilibrium ", *Review of Economic Studies*, **23**, (1953-54), pp. 1-20.

[26] Vanek, J. *General Equilibrium of International Discrimination: The Case of Customs Unions* (Cambridge, Massachusetts: Harvard University Press, 1965).

Part III
Results on Integration and Welfare

A
Integration and National Welfare

[11]

Inter-commodity substitution with constant real prices

2 The Graham demand case

This chapter is devoted to further study of the welfare effects of inter-commodity substitution in the case in which imports from a country's union partner (Y) are substitutes for both the domestically produced goods (X) and imports from the rest of the world (Z), *in the sense that a fall in the price of Y leads to a decrease in the quantities purchased of both X and Z*. The model of the last chapter is amended by adding a specific assumption about the nature of the demand for X, Y, and Z in country A. Study of this model sheds light on relationships which influence the welfare effects of customs unions, and also helps to illustrate some of the very general arguments of the last chapter.

The model case 2
All assumptions in Case 1 of the model continue to apply. Instead, however, of dealing with a completely general welfare function, $U = f(X,Y,Z)$, the function $U = X^{\alpha} Y^{\beta} Z^{\gamma}$ is introduced. In this case, a constant proportion of income is devoted to the purchase of each product irrespective of the structure of relative prices.[1] The fraction of total expenditure devoted to the purchase of X is $\dfrac{\alpha}{\alpha + \beta + \gamma}$, to Y is $\dfrac{\beta}{\alpha + \beta + \gamma}$, and to Z is $\dfrac{\gamma}{\alpha + \beta + \gamma}$. Thus all three products are substitutes for each other, and the demand for each may be expressed by a Marshallian demand curve of unit elasticity. This is the demand assumption made by F.D. Graham in his book *The Theory of International Values*[2] and it is referred to here as the Graham demand case. Use of this particular demand assumption gives two important advantages. First, the case is algebraically extremely simple to handle. The

45   *Inter-commodity substitution with constant real prices*

demand equilibrium conditions can be expressed in a set of simple
linear equations: $X = Y.p_y = Z.p_z$, where X, Y, and Z are quantities
consumed and p_y and p_z are the prices of Y and Z in terms of X.
Second, it provides an interesting case because the proportion of income
devoted to the purchase of the various commodities does not change as
relative prices change. It is thus the case appropriate to the study of
the relation between the proportion of income spent on different commodities and the welfare effects of customs unions.

In the first part of this chapter, it is assumed that income is divided
equally between the three products. The study of a single specific
example makes it possible to derive and graph actual relations which can
possibly be better understood in general by first being pictured in a
particular case. The case in which income is divided equally between the
three commodities also turns out to be an important special case. The
second part of the chapter is devoted to a study of the general Graham
demand case in which the division of income between the various commodities is a parameter to be varied at will.

The model case 2.a
Income is divided equally between the three commodities. The general
Graham welfare function is $U = X^\alpha Y^\beta Z^\gamma$, but in this case $\alpha = \beta = \gamma$
and, for convenience, the three indices are given a value of 1 so that the
welfare function becomes $U = XYZ$. The model may now be set out in
four equations:

$$U = XYZ , \qquad\qquad\qquad\text{(i)}$$

$$X = iYp_y , \qquad\qquad\qquad\text{(ii)}$$

$$X = jZp_z , \qquad\qquad\qquad\text{(iii)}$$

$$A - X = Yp_y + Zp_z, \qquad\text{(iv)}$$

where X, Y, and Z are quantities consumed, p_y and p_z are the prices of
Y and Z in terms of X, A is the fixed production of X in country A,
$i-l$ and $j-l$ are the rates of *ad valorem* tarriff on Y and Z respectively, and
U is an index function of welfare in country A.[3] Equation (i) shows
A's welfare as depending on the quantities of X, Y, and Z consumed.
Equations (ii) and (iii) give the demand equilibrium conditions that
domestic expenditure be divided equally between the three commodities. Equation (iv) gives the condition for A's international payments to

46   *Inter-commodity substitution with constant real prices*

be in balance.

If X is substituted from equation (ii), Z from equation (iii) and Y from equation (iv), equation (i) remains and expresses A's welfare as a function of her *output* of X, the prices of her two imports, and the rates of tariff on these imports.[4] This new equation is given below:

$$U = \frac{A^3 j^2 i^2}{p_y p_z \,(ji + j + i)^3} \, . \tag{1}$$

This is the basic equation which will be used for all subsequent lines of analysis.

It was argued in the last chapter that, for any given tariff on Z, there would be some tariff on Y which would maximise welfare. This second-best optimum tariff on Y may now be determined. The first step is to evaluate the partial derivative of U with respect to i in equation (1):

$$\frac{\partial U}{\partial i} = \Big[p_y p_z \,(ji + j + i)^3 \; 2A^3 \, j^2 \, i - A^3 \, j^2 \, i \, p_y p_z \,(3j^3 \, i^3 + 6j^3 i + 3j^3$$

$$+ \, 9j^2 \, i^2 + 12j^2 i + 3j^2 + 9ji^3 + 6ji + 3i^2\,)\Big]/[p_y p_z \,(ji + j + i)^3\,]^2.$$

This expression shows the way in which welfare changes as the tariff on imports of Y is varied, the tariff on Z being held constant. In order to maximise U, the expression is set equal to zero, the denominator disappears and, after dividing through by $A^3 j^2 i p_y p_z$, the following expression remains:

$$2j^3 \, i^3 + 6j^3 i^2 + 6j^3 i + 6j^2 i^3 + 12j^2 i^2 + 6j^2 i + 6ji^3 + 6ji^2 + 2j^3 + 2i^3 =$$

$$3j^3 i^3 + 6j^3 i^2 + 3j^3 i + 9j^2 i^3 + 12j^2 i^2 + 3j^2 i + 9ji^3 + 6ji^2 + 3i^3 \, .$$

Collecting terms, this reduces to:

$$i^3 \,(j^3 + 3j^2 + 3j + 1) - 3i \,(j^3 + j^2) - 2j^3 = 0. \tag{2}$$

It is now possible to substitute into equation (2) values for the tariff on Z $(j-1)$, and to obtain values for the tariff on $Y(i-1)$, which will maximise welfare. As would be expected when $j = 1, i = 1$, indicating that when no tariff is levied on imports of Z, welfare is maximised by

47   *Inter-commodity substitution with constant real prices*

leaving Y duty free. When $j > 1$, i is also greater than 1 but less than j. This result accords with the more general proof given in the mathematical appendix to Chapter 5 that, if Y is a substitute for both X and Z, the optimum Y tariff will exceed zero but be less than the given Z tariff. In the present example, as j approaches infinity, i approaches a

Figure 4   Source: Optimum Y Tariff equation 2 page 47
Critical Y Tariff equation 6 page 47

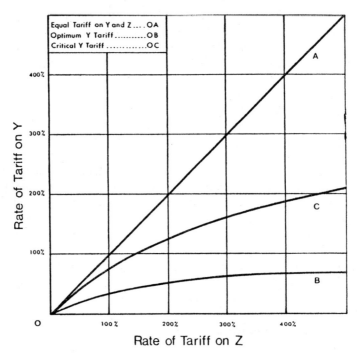

OPTIMUM AND CRITICAL TARIFFS
ON Y FOR GIVEN TARIFFS ON Z

48   *Inter-commodity substitution with constant real prices*

value of 2. Thus, no matter how high is the tariff on Z, the optimum tariff on Y does not exceed 100 per cent.

The relation between i and j is shown in Figure 4. The line $0A$ is drawn with a slope of $45°$ and thus indicates a uniform tariff on the two imports. The line OB is obtained by solving equation (2) for various values of j, and shows the optimum Y tariff for all levels of tariff on Z. Figure 4 also illustrates the conclusion drawn in the last chapter that, if originally a uniform tariff is levied on Y and Z and the tariff on Y is then removed by a series of small stages, welfare must rise at first but necessarily fall during the latter stages of tariff reduction. If, for example, the original uniform rate of tariff is 100 per cent, welfare will rise as the Y tariff is lowered to 33 per cent but will fall as the tariff is lowered from that figure to zero.

The question now arises: can the welfare reductions suffered in the latter stages of tariff reduction ever outweigh the welfare gains of the first stages, so that a complete removal of the Y tariff would lower rather than raise welfare? This question is answered by again considering equation (1):

$$U = \frac{A^3 j^2 i^2}{p_y p_z \left(ji + j + ij\right)^3} .\qquad (1)$$

If initially a uniform tariff is levied on both Y and Z, $i = j$ and equation (1) becomes:

$$U = \frac{A^3 j^4}{p_y p_z \left(j^2 + 2j\right)^3} .\qquad (3)$$

If the tariff on Y is removed, $i = 1$ and equation (1) becomes:

$$U = \frac{A^3 j^2}{p_y p_z \left(2j + 1\right)^3} .\qquad (4)$$

If expression (4) is greater than expression (3), the elimination of the Y tariff will raise welfare. The relation between the two expressions may be determined by writing: expression (4) = K.expression (3).[5] If $K > 1$, (4) is greater than (3).

49   *Inter-commodity substitution with constant real prices*

$$\frac{A^3 j^2}{p_y p_z \, (8j^3 \; + \; 12j^2 \; + \; 6j \; + \; 1)} = K. \; \frac{A^2 j}{p_y p_z \, (j^3 \; + \; 6j^2 \; + \; 12j \; + \; 8)} \, .$$

Cross-multiplying and dividing through by $A^3 j p_x p_y$:

$$K \; = \; \frac{j^4 \; + \; 6j^3 \; + \; 12j^2 \; + \; 8j}{8j^3 \; + \; 12j^2 \; + \; 6j \; + \; 1} \, . \qquad\qquad (5)$$

In equation (5) when $j = 1$, $K = 1$. This corresponds to the trivial solution that, when the initial uniform tariff is zero, the 'reduction' of the tariff on Y to zero will leave welfare unchanged. For all values of j greater than 1 however, K also exceeds 1. Therefore, in this case, welfare is always increased by the complete removal of the tariff on Y when initially a uniform tariff is charged on both imports; the losses cannot outweigh the gains.

If the tariff on Y is originally equal to the tariff on Z, the removal of the Y tariff necessarily raises welfare. If, however, the Y tariff is originally at its optimum level (which is less than the given tariff on Z), its removal must lower welfare. From this it follows that there must be some original level for the tariff on Y, greater than the optimum Y tariff but less than the given Z tariff, such that its removal leaves welfare unchanged. This tariff on Y may be termed the critical Y tariff. The complete removal of the Y tariff raises or lowers welfare according as the original Y tariff exceeds or falls short of the critical level.

The critical Y tariff may now be determined from equations (1) and (4). Equation (1) gives an index of welfare for any initial tariff situation. If the tariff on Y is removed, $i = 1$ and the index of welfare is given by equation (4). To determine the critical Y tariff, equations (1) and (4) are merely set equal to each other. This ensures that the level of welfare in the original position will be the same as the level obtained after the Y tariff is removed. Setting (1) equal to (4), cross-multiplying, and dividing through by $A^3 j^2 p_y p_z$, produces the following equation:

$$i^2 \, (2j + 1)^3 \; = \; (ji + j + i)^3,$$

which expands to:

$$i^3 \, (j^3 + 3j^2 + 3j + 1) - i^2 \, (5j^3 + 6j^2 + 3j + 1) + i \, (3j^3 + 3j^2) + j^3 = 0. \, (6)$$

50   *Inter-commodity substitution with constant real prices*

Equation (6) is a cubic equation, and for every value of j there will be three solutions for i. One of these three roots is 1 for all values of j. This corresponds to the trivial solution that, if the initial Y tariff is zero, a 'reduction' of the Y tariff to zero will leave welfare unchanged. The second root is always negative. This implies a negative price which has no economic meaning in this model. The third root, however, is always positive and, when j exceeds 1, it is also greater than 1 but less than j. The values for the critical Y tariff are shown in Figure 4 by the line OC. Consider, for example, a case in which the tariff on Z is 100 per cent. The optimum Y tariff is only 33 per cent, while the critical tariff is 79 per cent. To take another example, if the tariff on Z is 50 per cent, the optimum Y tariff is 20 per cent but the critical tariff is 47 per cent. This shows that, if the original Y tariff is even slightly less than the Z tariff, the complete removal of the tariff on Y may lower welfare. For example, if the pre-union rates of tariff are 50 per cent on Z and 45 per cent on Y, the customs union lowers A's welfare.

This completes the analysis of the special case in which expenditure s divided equally between the three commodities. The conclusions reached are summarised below.

1   For any given tariff on Z there is some optimum tariff on Y. This tariff, which maximises welfare subject to the given Z tariff, is always greater than zero but less than the tariff on Z.

2   For any given tariff on Z, there will be some critical Y tariff such that its removal leaves welfare unchanged. This critical Y tariff exceeds the optimum tariff but is less than the tariff on Z. It follows that, if originally a uniform tariff is levied on both imports, the tariff on Y must exceed its critical level and its removal necessarily raises welfare.

The model case 2.b
This model is identical to model 2.a with the single exception that the welfare function $U = X^\alpha Y^\beta Z^\gamma$ is dealt with in general (i.e., the assumption that $\alpha = \beta = \gamma$ is dropped). It is now possible to study the influence of variations in the division of total expenditure between the three commodities on the welfare effects of customs unions. The analysis is similar to that of the first part of this chapter, but the mathematics

51   *Inter-commodity substitution with constant real prices*

become rather cumbersome and are relegated to the mathematical appendix to this chapter. In the text an attempt is made to give only an intuitive understanding of the reasons for the conclusions that are demonstrated rigorously in the appendix. Throughout the rest of this chapter, the term *customs union* will be taken to mean a customs union of country A with country B which results in the *complete removal* of the tariff on imports of Y, when originally Y and Z had been taxed at a uniform *ad valorem* rate.

The conclusion that, for any given tariff on Z, the optimum tariff on Y is greater than zero but less than the Z tariff, has already been proven in general for all cases in which a fall in the price of Y leads to a decrease in purchases of both X and Z. It has also been shown to hold in the special case studied in the first part of this chapter, and the proof need not be repeated here. It may be recalled, however, that, as a consequence of this relation, the removal of a tariff on Y by a series of small steps from a position of equal Y and Z tariff necessarily raises welfare at first and eventually lowers it when the tariff is further reduced.

The conclusion reached for the model studied in the first part of this chapter, that a customs union necessarily raises welfare, does not hold in the general Graham case. The welfare consequences of a customs union depend on two different circumstances which must be considered separately. The first circumstance, which may be termed the *expenditure relation,* is the division of expenditure between the three products, X, Y, and Z. It will be recalled from the discussion of Chapter 5 that a customs union with country B eliminates the divergence between the market and real-price ratios of commodities X and Y while creating a divergence between the market- and real-price ratios for Y and Z.[6] *Ceteris paribus,* the former change tends to raise welfare and the latter change tends to lower it. The condition that the expenditure relation should be favourable to an increase in welfare, is quite simply that domestic expenditure on commodities whose domestic- and real-price ratios are restored to equality with each other should exceed expenditure on commodities whose domestic- and real-price ratios are moved away from equality. In other words, expenditure on domestic goods (X) and imports from union partners (Y) should exceed expenditure on total imports $(Y + Z)$. But the expenditure on Y appears in both sides of this relation (the customs union restores equality between the domestic- and real-price ratios of X and Y, but moves the domestic- and real-price ratios of Z and Y away from a position of equality), so that the expenditure relation reduces to one between expenditure on domestic goods and imports from non-union sources. If expenditure on domestic goods exceeds that on non-union imports, the expenditure effect is favourable to an increase in welfare, while if the reverse relation holds, welfare will tend to be lowered by the union.

This expenditure relation suggests two conclusions. First, a customs union is more likely to raise welfare the larger is the proportion of total expenditure allocated to domestic purchases and the less important is foreign trade to the country concerned. In the Graham demand case, if more than one half of total expenditure is allocated to the purchase of domestic goods, a customs union necessarily raises welfare. Second, *given the total volume of foreign trade,* a customs union is more likely to raise welfare the larger is the proportion of total foreign trade done with a country's union partners (the lower is the proportion done with the outside world). It must be remembered, however, that the important relation is between domestic expenditure and expenditure on imports from non-union sources. An increase in trade with union partners at the expense of domestic purchases would tend to *reduce* the chances of a customs union raising welfare, while an increase in trade with union partners at the expense of trade with the outside world would tend to *increase* the chances of a customs union raising welfare.

The second circumstance on which the gains from customs unions depend in this model is the height of the *initial* uniform *ad valorem* tariff. The higher is the pre-union *uniform* tariff, the more likely is it that a customs union will raise welfare. Indeed, if the pre-union tariff is large enough, any customs union will raise welfare no matter what is the relation between expenditure on the three products.[8] The general relation between the height of the pre-union tariff and the gains from customs unions can be seen by examining the special case studied in the first part of this chapter, in which expenditure is divided equally between the three commodities. In this case, expenditure on X and Z is equal. The expenditure relation may be said to be 'neutral', because expenditure on those products for which domestic and international price ratios are restored to equality (X and Y) is the same as expenditure on those products for which domestic and international price ratios are moved away from equality with each other (Y and Z). If there were no other influences, welfare would be unchanged by any customs union. This case is illustrated by curve III in Figure 5. This figure shows the percentage change in the index of welfare caused by a removal of the tariff on Y when originally both Y and Z were taxed at the same rate.[9]

53 *Inter-commodity substitution with constant real prices*

Figure 5 Relation between the values of the index of welfare before and after a customs union (Y axis) and the height of the pre-union non-discriminatory tariff or subsidy (X axis) for various divisions of expenditure between the three commodities X, Y and Z.

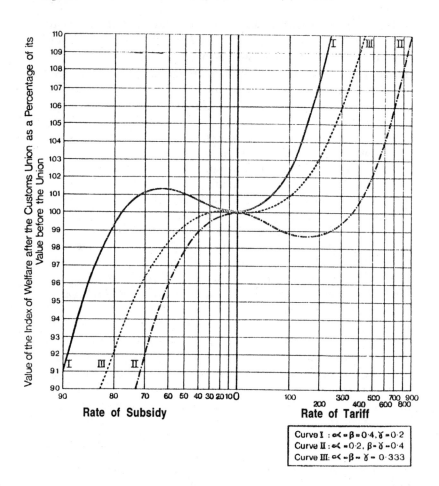

Curve I : $\alpha = \beta = 0.4, \gamma = 0.2$
Curve II : $\alpha = 0.2, \beta = \gamma = 0.4$
Curve III: $\alpha = \beta = \gamma = 0.333$

54   *Inter-commodity substitution with constant real prices*

For an infinitesimal initial tariff the customs union leaves welfare unchanged, but for any finite tariff a customs union raises welfare.
Furthermore, the larger is the initial tariff, the greater is the increase in
the index of welfare that results from removal of the tariff on *Y*.

Thus there are two factors influencing the gains or losses from
customs unions in this model. The first is the expenditure relation.
Ceteris paribus, the larger is the expenditure on *X* in relation to that on
Z, the more likely is it that the customs union will raise welfare; and, if
expenditure on *X* exceeds that on *Z*, the customs union *necessarily*
raises welfare. The second factor is the height of the pre-union tariff.
Ceteris paribus, the higher is the level of the pre-union tariff, the more
likely is it that the union will raise welfare. For any expenditure relation there is *necessarily* some finite level of tariff, such that the customs
union raises welfare if that tariff level is exceeded prior to the union
being formed. Whether or not any particular union will raise welfare
depends, therefore, on the severity of the *uniform* pre-union tariff and
on the division of expenditure between domestic products and imports
from non-union sources.

The relations discussed above may be illustrated by examining three
numerical examples. It is also necessary to allow for negative tariffs
(i.e., subsidies). Table 2 gives the numerical values selected.

Table 2. Proportion of income spent on commodities

	X	Y	Z
Case 1	40%	40%	20%
Case 2	20%	40%	40%
Case 3	33·3%	33·3%	33·3%

Figure 5 shows, for each of these examples, the percentage change in
the index of welfare resulting from the removal of the tariff or subsidy
from *Y* for various levels of uniform pre-union tariff or subsidy on *Y*
or *Z*.[10] Curve 1 illustrates the general relation when expenditure on
domestic goods *(X)* exceeds expenditure on imports from non-union
sources *(Z)*. The removal of the tariff from *Y* raises welfare whatever the
pre-union uniform rate of tariff on *Y* and *Z*. The removal of a subsidy
from *Y* raises welfare for small pre-union uniform subsidies on *Y* and
Z but lowers welfare if the pre-union subsidy rate is large enough.
Curve II illustrates the general relation when expenditure on *X* is less

than expenditure on Z. The removal of a subsidy on Y lowers welfare whatever was the level of the pre-union uniform subsidy on Y and Z. The removal of the tariff from Y lowers welfare if the pre-union uniform tariff on Y and Z was small but raises welfare if the pre-union tariff was large enough. The larger is the expenditure on Z in relation to that on X, the higher must be the pre-union uniform rate of tariff on Y and Z before the removal of the Y tariff will raise welfare. Finally, curve III shows the relation when expenditure on X is equal to expenditure on Z. The removal of a subsidy from Y lowers welfare whatever the initial uniform subsidy rate on Y and Z, while the removal of a tariff on Y raises welfare whatever the pre-union rate of uniform tariff on Y and Z.

The gains and losses from unions that reduce subsidies seem at first sight to show some curious divergences from the gains and losses from unions that reduce tariffs (see Figure 5). The shapes of the three curves in the range of subsidies must be accounted for. The curves show the change in the index of welfare resulting from the removal of the subsidy on Y, when originally both X and Y were subject to the same *ad valorem* rate of subsidy. A uniform subsidy on Y and Z leaves the ratio of their market prices equal to the ratio of their real prices but makes both goods appear cheaper relative to X. A uniform subsidy on the two imports is thus analytically equivalent to a single tax on the domestic goods X. The removal of the subsidy on Y restores the ratio of the market prices of X and Y to equality with the ratio of their real prices, and is thus analytically equivalent to placing an *ad valorem* tax on Y equal to the rate of tax on X. It follows that removing a subsidy from imports of Y is analytically equivalent to moving from a position where only one product is taxed (X) to one where two products are taxed (X and Y). It has already been shown in the case of customs unions which removed tariffs that the movement from a position where two commodities are taxed to a position where only one is taxed (i.e., forming a customs union), necessarily *raises* welfare if the rate of tariff is large enough. It follows, therefore, that in this model the removal of a subsidy from one product while leaving the subsidy at its original level on the other, necessarily *lowers* welfare if the rate of original subsidy on both products is high enough. In this sense, the effect of removing a subsidy is *the opposite* of the effect of removing a tax. The situation is complicated, however, by the fact that the expenditure relation is *the same* for subsidies as for tariffs. The removal of a subsidy from Y restores equality between market- and real-price ratios for X and Y,

56   *Inter-commodity substitution with constant real prices*

and disturbs an existing equality of market- and real-price ratios for Y and Z, the expenditure effect will be favourable to an increase in welfare (total expenditure on commodities for which price ratios are made equal exceeds total expenditure on commodities whose price ratios are moved away from equality). It will be remembered that the condition that expenditure on X exceed expenditure on Z was also the condition for the expenditure relation to be favourable when a tariff was removed from Y. Thus, when the expenditure relation is favourable, the removal of small subsidies does raise welfare (curve I), but for high rates of initial uniform subsidies the removal of the Y subsidy (the equivalent of taxing Y when X is already taxed) lowers welfare. If expenditure on X is less than that on Z (curve III), the removal of the subsidy from Y lowers welfare whatever the initial rate of subsidy.

This concludes the analysis of the Graham demand case, and the conclusions reached may be summarised briefly.

1   A customs union is more likely to increase welfare the larger is the proportion of total expenditure devoted to the purchase of domestic products and the smaller is the proportion of total expenditure devoted to imports in general.

2   A customs union is more likely to raise welfare, *given the total volume of imports of the country,* the larger is the proportion of these imports obtained from the country's union partners and the less is the proportion devoted to imports from the outside world.

3   In the Graham demand case at least, the higher is the general level of pre-union tariffs the more likely is it that a customs union will raise welfare. (This conclusion is not to be confused with the conclusion in Chapter 5 which states that a customs union is more likely to raise welfare the higher is the level of tariff charged on union imports *given the rate of tariff levied against the products of non-union countries.)*

4   The removal of a subsidy from some imports is more likely to raise welfare in the following circumstances:

(a) the larger is the expenditure on domestic products,

57   *Inter-commodity substitution with constant real prices*

(b) the smaller is the expenditure on imports from which subsidies are not removed,

(c) the higher are the subsidies removed in relation to those that
are not removed,

(d) the smaller is the reduction in the subsidy (if it is not completely removed), and

(e) the lower is the general level of all subsidies.

Mathematical appendix to chapter 6

1 Development of the welfare function
(a)   *The individual consumer*
Assume that an individual consumer devotes a constant proportion of
his total expenditure to each product irrespective of relative prices. The
demand conditions for n products can be expressed either by n Marshallian demand curves each of unit price elasticity, or by an indifference map composed of a set of n dimensional rectangular hyperboloids.
In the present model there are three commodities, X, Y, and Z, so that
the indifference map of the individual consumer is composed of a set
of indifference surfaces described by the formula $(X^{\alpha})(Y^{\beta})(Z^{\gamma}) = C$.
The larger is the constant C, the further is the particular indifference
surface from the origin. If C is replaced by U, a welfare function is
obtained in which U is an *index function of welfare.*
     We must first show that the function $U = X^{\alpha} Y^{\beta} Z^{\gamma}$ does in fact
imply a constant proportion of expenditure on each product. It is
simpler to state the equilibrium conditions in the form that marginal
utilities be proportional to prices, than in the form that marginal rates
of substitution between commodities be equal to their relative prices;
the two formulations, of course, give identical results.[1] The conditions
that marginal utilities be proportional to relative prices may be rewritten by simple cross-multiplication in the following form:

$$p_y \cdot \frac{\partial U}{\partial X} = p_x \cdot \frac{\partial U}{\partial Y} , \qquad\qquad (1)$$

E

58   *Inter-commodity substitution with constant real prices*

$$p_z \cdot \frac{\partial U}{\partial X} = p_x \cdot \frac{\partial U}{\partial Z} , \qquad (2)$$

where p_x, p_y, and p_z are the money prices of X, Y, and Z. Evaluating the partial derivatives of U with respect to X, Y, and Z from the welfare function, and substituting into equations (1) and (2), we obtain:

$$p_y \alpha X^{\alpha-1} \ Y^\beta Z^\gamma = p_x \beta \ X^\alpha Y^{\beta-1} \ Z^\gamma, \qquad (1)$$

$$p_z \alpha X^{\alpha-1} \ Y^\beta Z^\gamma = p_x \ X^\alpha Y^\beta Z^{\gamma-1} . \qquad (2)$$

Dividing (1) by $X^{\alpha-1} \ Y^{\beta-1} Z^\gamma$ and (2) by $X^{\alpha-1} \ Y^\beta Z^{\gamma-1}$ gives:

$$p_y \alpha Y = p_x \beta X , \qquad (1)$$

$$p_z \alpha Z = p_x \gamma X , \qquad (2)$$

or

$$p_x X = \frac{\alpha}{\beta} p_y Y , \qquad (1)$$

$$p_x X = \frac{\alpha}{\gamma} p_z Z , \qquad (2)$$

Therefore expenditure on X is a constant proportion $(\frac{\alpha}{\beta})$ of expenditure on Y and a constant proportion $(\frac{\alpha}{\gamma})$ of expenditure on Z. Now we may write:

$$p_x X = \frac{\alpha}{\alpha} p_x X ,$$

$$p_y Y = \frac{\beta}{\alpha} p_x X ,$$

$$p_z Z = \frac{\gamma}{\alpha} p_x X .$$

59   *Inter-commodity substitution with constant real prices*

The proportion of total expenditure devoted to X is

$$\frac{p_x X}{p_x X + p_y Y + p_z Z} = \frac{\frac{\alpha}{\alpha} p_x X}{\frac{\alpha}{\alpha} p_x X + \frac{\beta}{\alpha} p_x X + \frac{\gamma}{\alpha} p_x X} =$$

$$\frac{1}{\frac{\alpha}{\alpha} + \frac{\beta}{\alpha} + \frac{\gamma}{\alpha}} = \frac{\alpha}{\alpha + \beta + \gamma} \; .$$

Similarly, the proportion of total expenditure devoted to Y is
$\frac{\beta}{\alpha + \beta + \gamma}$, and to Z is $\frac{\gamma}{\alpha + \beta + \gamma}$. If $\alpha + \beta + \gamma = 1$, then α, β and γ
express directly the fractions of total expenditure devoted to the three
products.

It will be noted that, in the welfare function $U = X^\alpha Y^\beta Z^\gamma$, the
value of U is determined beyond a linear transformation and that it
thus satisfies the criterion of a *cardinal* index of welfare.[2] But U is
nothing more than the numerical value of the constant attached to a
particular indifference curve. The only thing that we are prepared to
assert is that if U increases, welfare also increases to some (unspecified)
extent. Therefore, we may write:

$$S = f(U)$$

where S is 'real' welfare, satisfaction, or utility. The only limitation
placed on this function is that S is a monotonic increasing function of
U. The value of S is therefore *not* determined up to a monotonic linear
transformation, and U is therefore only an *ordinal* index of 'real'
welfare.

(b) *The community welfare function*
The community is composed of r individuals each with the same
demand pattern, so that tastes are specified as follows:

$$U_i = X^\alpha Y^\beta Z^\gamma, \qquad\qquad (i = 1, \ldots, r).$$

These welfare functions are homogeneous of the degree $\alpha + \beta + \gamma$. It is
well known that, when all individuals have identical homogenous

60   *Inter-commodity substitution with constant real prices*

welfare functions (so that the relative quantities demanded depend only on relative prices, and not on incomes), the usual construction of community indifference curves gives rise to a unique set of non-crossing community indifference curves which are of the same form as those for the individuals composing the community.[3] Thus, the community indifference map is composed of a set of rectangular hyperboloids described by the formula $X^\alpha Y^\beta Z^\gamma = C$. Replacing C by U we obtain:

$$U = X^\alpha Y^\beta Z^\gamma$$

where U is an *index function of community welfare.*

(c) *The community welfare function used in the first part of the text*
In some cases it is convenient to define α, β, and γ as positive integers rather than as fractions. This is done by expressing the three fractions in terms of a common denominator so that: $\alpha = a/e$, $\beta = b/e$, and $\gamma = c/e$. Then

$$U = \sqrt[e]{X^a Y^b Z^c},$$

or $U^e = X^a Y^b Z^c.$

Since U is only an *index* of welfare we may write:

$$U_1 = U^e,$$

and we obtain the welfare function $U_1 = X^a Y^b Z^c$, where a, b, and c are positive integers. When $a = b = c = 1$, we may write:

$$U = XYZ,$$

which is the form of the welfare function used in the first part of the text of Chapter 6.

The argument in the first part of the text is self-contained, all of the mathematics being given in the text. The remainder of this appendix is concerned with the general Graham demand case. The propositions discussed, but not demonstrated, in the second part of Chapter 6 are here given formal proof. The first part of Chapter 6 is, of course, concerned with a special case of the Graham demand conditions. At various points in the general treatment of this appendix it is noted that, if the values $\alpha = \beta = \gamma = 1$ are substituted into the general equations, they reduce to those developed independently in the text.

2 Development of the fundamental equation

Model 2.b[4] may be expressed in four equations:

$$U \quad = \quad X^{\alpha} \, Y^{\beta} \, Z^{\gamma}, \tag{i}$$

$$\beta X \quad = \quad \alpha g i Y \,, \tag{ii}$$

$$\gamma X \quad = \quad \alpha h j Z \,, \tag{iii}$$

$$A - X = \quad g Y + h Z. \tag{iv}$$

The symbols used are as follows:

Production of X in country A	A
Consumption of X in A	X
Imports of Y into A	Y
Imports of Z into A	Z
Price of Y in terms of X	g
Price of Z in terms of X	h
Tariff on imports of Y	$i - 1$
Tariff on imports of Z	$j - 1$
Index of welfare in country A	U

The symbols g and h replace the symbols p_y and p_z used in the text for the prices of Y and Z in terms of X. This is done in order to avoid the use of subscripts in the manipulations that follow. Equation (i) is the welfare function. Equations (ii) and (iii) express the demand equilibrium conditions in the form that domestic expenditure (real prices plus tariffs) is divided in a constant proportion between the three products. Equation (iv) expresses the condition that A's international payments be in balance. X, Y, and Z may now be eliminated from the four equations above. Substitute X from equation (ii):

$$U \; = \; \left(\frac{\alpha g i Y}{\beta} \right)^{\alpha} Y^{\beta} \, Z^{\gamma}, \tag{i}$$

$$\gamma g i Y \; = \; \beta h j Z, \tag{iii}$$

62   *Inter-commodity substitution with constant real prices*

$$A - \frac{giY}{\beta} = gY + hZ. \qquad \text{(iv)}$$

Substitute Z from equation (iii):

$$U = \left(\frac{\alpha giY}{\beta}\right)^{\alpha} Y^{\beta} \left(\frac{\gamma giY}{\beta hj}\right)^{\gamma}, \qquad \text{(i)}$$

$$A - \frac{giY}{\beta} = gY + \frac{\gamma giY}{\beta j}, \qquad \text{(iv)}$$

or $\quad Y = \dfrac{A\beta j}{g(\alpha j i + \beta j + \gamma i)}. \qquad \text{(iv)}$

Substitute Y from (iv):

$$U = \left[\frac{A\alpha j i}{(\alpha j i + \beta j + \gamma i)}\right]^{\alpha} \left[\frac{A\beta j}{g(\alpha j i + \beta j + \gamma i)}\right]^{\beta} \left[\frac{A\gamma i}{h(\alpha j i + \beta j + \gamma i)}\right]^{\gamma}. \qquad (1)$$

This fundamental equation expresses A's welfare as a function of her domestic production of X, the prices of her two imports, and the tariffs levied on them. When $\alpha = \beta = \gamma = 1$, this equation reduces to:

$$U = \frac{A^3 j^2 i^2}{hj(ji + j + i)^3}$$

which is equation (1) in the text of Chapter 6.

3 A comparison of welfare before and after a customs union
We now wish to compare two situations: (1) a uniform *ad valorem* tariff is levied on imports of both Y and Z; and (2) a customs union is formed with the supplier of Y (country B) so that Y now enters A duty free. Z is still imported from country C and, therefore, remains subject to the original tariff. (Real prices, i.e., g and h, are by assumption unaffected by variations in A's tariffs.)

In the initial situation, a uniform tariff is levied on both Y and Z. Therefore, $i = j$ and equation (1) becomes:

$$U \text{ (pre-union)} = \left[\frac{A\alpha j^2}{(\alpha j^2 + \beta j + \gamma i)}\right]^{\alpha} \left[\frac{A\beta j}{g(\alpha j^2 + \beta j + \gamma j)}\right]^{\beta} \left[\frac{A\gamma j}{h(\alpha j^2 + \beta j + \gamma j)}\right]^{\gamma}.$$

63 *Inter-commodity substitution with constant real prices*

After the union the tariff on Y is removed. Therefore, $i = 1$ and equation (1) becomes:

$$U\text{(post-union)} = \left[\frac{A\alpha j}{(\alpha j + \beta j + \gamma)}\right]^{\alpha} \left[\frac{A\beta j}{g(\alpha j + \beta j + \gamma)}\right]^{\beta}$$

$$\left[\frac{A\gamma}{h(\alpha j + \beta j + \gamma)}\right]^{\gamma} . \tag{3}$$

We now define K: $K = \dfrac{index\ of\ post\text{-}union\ welfare}{index\ of\ pre\text{-}union\ welfare} = \dfrac{expression\ (3)}{expression\ (2)}$

$$K = \frac{A^{\alpha+\beta+\gamma}\ j^{\alpha+\beta}\ \alpha^{\alpha}\ \beta^{\beta}\ \gamma^{\gamma}}{g^{\beta}h^{\gamma}\ (\alpha j + \beta j + \gamma)^{\alpha+\beta+\gamma}} \quad \cdot \quad \frac{g^{\beta}h^{\gamma}\ (\alpha j^2 + \beta j + \gamma j)^{\alpha+\beta+\gamma}}{A^{\alpha+\beta+\gamma}\ j^{2\alpha+\beta+\gamma}\ \alpha^{\alpha}\ \beta^{\beta}\ \gamma^{\gamma}}$$

$$= \frac{(\alpha j^2 + \beta j + \gamma j)^{\alpha+\beta+\gamma}}{j^{\alpha+\gamma}(\alpha j + \beta j + \gamma)^{\alpha+\beta+\gamma}} \quad = \quad \frac{j^{\alpha+\beta+\gamma}(\alpha j + \beta + \gamma)^{\alpha+\beta+\gamma}}{j^{\alpha+\beta}(\alpha j + \beta j + \gamma)^{\alpha+\beta+\gamma}}$$

$$= \frac{j^{\beta}(\alpha j + \beta + \gamma)^{\alpha+\beta+\gamma}}{(\alpha j + \beta j + \gamma)^{\alpha+\beta+\gamma}} . \tag{4}$$

If $\alpha = \beta = \gamma = 1$, the equation reduces to:

$$K = \frac{j(j+2)^3}{(2j+1)^3}$$

which is equation (5) in the text of Chapter 6.

Now consider equation (4). When $j = 1$, $K = 1$. This corresponds to the trivial solution that, when the initial tariff is zero, a 'reduction' of the tariff on Y to zero will leave welfare unchanged. When $j > 1$, $K > 1$ for some values of α, β, and γ. Examples of this have already been given in the first part of Chapter 6 in which $\alpha = \beta = \gamma = 1$ *and* $K > 1$ for any $j > 1$. However, for some other values of α, β, γ, and j, $K < 1$.[5] This demonstrates that, under the assumed conditions, there will be some values of α, β, γ, and j (i.e., some divisions of expenditure between the three commodities together with some levels of initial tariff) for which a customs union will *lower welfare*.

4 The relation between α, β, γ, and K
We now wish to isolate the circumstances under which K will be less

64   *Inter-commodity substitution with constant real prices*

than 1 when j exceeds 1. It is now convenient to define α, β, and γ as positive fractions such that $\gamma + \beta + \alpha = 1$. Equation (4) now reduces to:

$$K = \frac{j^\beta (\alpha j + \beta + \gamma)}{\alpha j + \beta j + \gamma}. \qquad (5)$$

Now evaluate the partial derivitive of K with respect to j from equation (5):

$$\frac{\partial K}{\partial j} = \frac{(\alpha j + \beta j + \gamma)(\alpha j^\beta + \beta j^{\beta-1} [\alpha j + \beta + \gamma]) - (j^\beta [\alpha j + \beta + \gamma] [\alpha + \beta])}{(\alpha j + \beta j + \gamma)^2}$$

Expanding and collecting terms this expression becomes:

$$\frac{\partial K}{\partial j} = \frac{\alpha^2 j^2 + \alpha\beta j + \alpha\gamma j + \alpha\beta j^2 + \beta^2 j + \beta\gamma j + \alpha\gamma j + \beta\gamma + \gamma - j(\alpha + \beta + \gamma)}{\frac{j^{1-\beta}}{\beta}(\alpha j + \beta j + \gamma)^2}.$$

But $\alpha + \beta + \gamma = 1$ and, therefore, $\alpha = 1 - \beta - \gamma$. Substituting for α into the above expression and collecting terms we obtain:

$$\frac{\partial K}{\partial j} = \frac{j^2 (1 - \beta - 2\gamma + \beta\gamma + \gamma^2) + j(\beta - 2\beta\gamma + 2\gamma - 2\gamma^2 - 1) + \beta\gamma + \gamma^2}{\frac{j^{1-\beta}}{\beta}(j - \gamma j + \gamma)^2}. \qquad (6)$$

Substituting $j = 1$ into equation (6), we find that $\frac{\partial K}{\partial j} = 0$ for any α, β, and γ. Thus $K = 1$ and is at a minimum, a maximum, or an inflectional point when $j = 1$. In order to determine which of these three possibilities is the case, we evaluate the second-order partial derivitive of K with respect to j (Remembering that $\frac{1}{\frac{(j^{1-\beta})}{(\beta)}} = \beta j^{\beta-1}$.)

65   *Inter-commodity substitution with constant real prices*

$$\frac{\partial^2 K}{\partial j^2} = \Big[(j^2 - 2\gamma j^2 + 2\gamma j + \gamma^2 j^2 - 2\gamma^2 j + \gamma^2)(\beta j^{\beta-1})(2j - 2\beta j - 4\gamma j$$

$$+ 2\beta\gamma j + 2\gamma^2 j + \beta - 2\beta\gamma + 2\gamma - 2\gamma^2 - 1) + (j^2 - \beta j^2 - 2\gamma j^2$$

$$+ \beta\gamma j^2 + \gamma^2 j^2 + \beta j - 2\beta\gamma j + 2\gamma j - 2\gamma^2 j + \beta\gamma + \gamma^2 - j)(\beta j^{\beta-2})$$

$$(\beta - 1) - [\beta j^{\beta-1}(j^2 - \beta j^2 - 2\gamma j^2 + \beta\gamma j^2 + \gamma^2 j^2 + \beta j - 2\beta\gamma j$$

$$\frac{+ 2\gamma j - 2\gamma^2 j + \beta\gamma + \gamma^2 - j)(2j - 4\gamma j + 2\gamma + 2\gamma^2 j - 2\gamma^2)]}{(j - \gamma j + \gamma)^4}$$

when $j = 1$, this cumbersome expression reduces to:

$$\frac{\partial^2 K}{\partial j^2} = 1 - \beta - 2\gamma.$$

Therefore $\dfrac{\partial^2 K}{\partial j^2} > 0$ when $\beta + 2\gamma < 1$, $\dfrac{\partial^2 K}{\partial j^2} < 0$ when $\beta + 2\gamma > 1$, and $\dfrac{\partial^2 K}{\partial j^2} = 0$ when $\beta + 2\gamma = 1$. Thus, if $\beta + 2\gamma < 1$, K is at a minimum value of 1 when $j = 1$; if $\beta + 2\gamma > 1$, K is at a maximum value of 1 when $j = 1$; and, finally, if $\beta + 2\gamma = 1$, K is at a point of inflection (with tangent gradient parallel to the X axis) at a value of 1 when $j = 1$. From this it follows that, at least for small j's > 1, a customs union raises welfare if $\beta + 2\gamma < 1$ and lowers it if $\beta + 2\gamma > 1$.

The important relation in the above analysis is given by the expression $\beta + 2\gamma \gtrless 1$. This expression may be re-written:

$$\beta + \gamma \gtrless 1 - \gamma.$$

But $\gamma = 1 - \alpha - \beta.$

Substituting for γ in the right-hand side of the above expression gives:

$$\beta + \gamma \gtrless 1 - (1 - \alpha - \beta),$$

or $\beta + \gamma \gtrless \beta + \alpha.$

$\beta + \gamma$ is the proportion of total expenditure devoted to all imports and, thus, the expenditure for which apparent- and real-price ratios are

66   *Inter-commodity substitution with constant real prices*

moved away from equality with each other by the customs union. $\beta + \alpha$ is the proportion of total expenditure devoted to purchases within the union (to the purchase of domestic products plus imports from the union partner) and, thus, the expenditure for which the ratios of domestic and international prices are restored to equality by the union.

Finally it will be noted that β cancels out of the above expression, leaving the very simple relation $\gamma \gtreqless \alpha$. Thus, if expenditure on domestic goods exceeds expenditure on imports from non-union countries, the customs unions raises welfare at least for small j's > 1, while if expenditure on non-union imports exceeds that on domestic products, the union lowers welfare, at least for small j's > 1.

5 The relation between j and K
So far we have considered what happens to K as j passes through 1, and have found that K passes through a minimum value of 1 as j increases through 1 if $\alpha > \gamma$, and that K passes through a maximum value of 1 as j increases through 1 if $\alpha < \gamma$. We shall now consider the effect on K of increasing the value of j. In order to do this we return to the first-order partial derivitive of K with respect to j:

$$\frac{\partial K}{\partial j} = \frac{j^2 (1 - \beta - 2\gamma + \beta\gamma + \gamma^2) + j(\beta - 2\beta\gamma + 2\gamma - 2\gamma^2 - 1) + \beta\gamma + \gamma^2}{\frac{j^{1-\beta}}{\beta}(j - \gamma j + \gamma)^2} \qquad (6)$$

The numerator of this expression is of the general form $aj^2 + bj + c$. Consider now the sign of the three constants. The constant associated with j^2 is:

$$1 - \beta - 2\gamma + \beta\gamma + \gamma^2. \qquad (a)$$

But $\beta = 1 - \gamma - \alpha$. Substituting for β into expression (a) we obtain $\alpha(1 - \gamma)$ which expression is positive. Therefore, the constant associated with j^2 is positive for any values of α, β and γ.

The constant associated with j is:

$$\beta - 2\beta\gamma + 2\gamma - 2\gamma^2 - 1. \qquad (b)$$

Substituting $\beta = 1 - \gamma - \alpha$ into (b) we obtain:

$$2\gamma\alpha - \gamma - \alpha$$

67   *Inter-commodity substitution with constant real prices*

or $\propto (2\gamma - 1) - \gamma.$

Since $\gamma < 1$, $2\gamma - 1 < \gamma$.
Therefore this term is negative for all values of $\propto$, β, and γ. Finally we note that $\beta\gamma + \gamma^2 > 0$ for all values of $\propto$, β, and γ. It follows, therefore, that the numerator of the expression for $\frac{\partial K}{\partial j}$ is of the form: $aj^2 - bj + c$.
Now, for any finite positive values of these three constants the expression will become positive if j is made large enough. Therefore, $\frac{\partial K}{\partial j}$ necessarily becomes positive for large enough j's, whatever the values of $\propto$, β and γ. Furthermore, if the expression is positive for any particular j, it must be positive for all larger j's.

    We may now draw a number of conclusions from this analysis. If $\propto > \gamma$, a customs union raises welfare for small j's greater than 1. We now know that in this case $\frac{\partial K}{\partial j} > 0$ for all j's greater than 1, so that the customs union must raise welfare for all positive levels of pre-union tariff. If, on the other hand, $\propto < \gamma$, the customs unions lowers welfare for small j's greater than 1. We now know, however, that, whatever the relation between $\propto$ and γ, if j increases through large enough values, the ratio $\frac{index\ of\ post\text{-}union\ welfare}{index\ of\ pre\text{-}union\ welfare}$ must eventually increase. The final question now arises: although K must eventually increase as j is made large enough, whatever the relation between $\propto$ and γ, must it necessarily exceed 1 as j is increased, or will there be some values for $\propto$ and γ for which K will always be less than 1 whatever the (finite) value of j? This question is answered by inspecting the original expression for K:

$$K = \frac{j^\beta (\propto j + \beta + \gamma)}{\propto j + \beta j + \gamma}. \qquad (5)$$

K will exceed 1 if $\propto j^{\beta+1} + \beta j^\beta + \gamma j^\beta > \propto j + \beta j + \gamma$. Since, when $j > 1$, $\gamma j^\beta > \gamma$, K will definitely exceed 1 if: $\propto j^{\beta+1} + \beta j^\beta > \propto j + \beta j$. Since $\beta j^\beta > 0$, K will definitely exceed 1 if

$$\propto j^{\beta+1} > j(\propto + \beta),$$

or $\propto j^\beta > \propto + \beta,$

68   *Inter-commodity substitution with constant real prices*

or $j^\beta > \dfrac{\alpha + \beta}{\alpha}$.

But j^β approaches infinity as j approaches infinity. Therefore, by making j large enough, j^β can be made to exceed any value of $\dfrac{\alpha + \beta}{\alpha}$. Also, for any given values of α, β, and γ, the larger is j the more likely is it that $j^\beta > \dfrac{\alpha + \beta}{\alpha}$ and, therefore, the more likely is it that K will exceed 1.

It follows, therefore, that whatever the division of expenditure between the three products, if the initial tariff is large enough the customs union will raise welfare. Furthermore, for any given division of expenditure, the higher is the initial level of tariff, the more likely is it that a customs union will raise welfare.

Chapter 6

1   See the mathematical appendix to this chapter

2   F.D. Graham, *The Theory of International Values,* Princeton, N.J., Princeton University Press, 1948

3   If it is assumed that all individuals have identical welfare functions, the community welfare function can be derived from them in the

usual way. The functions will be homogeneous and all expansion paths linear (i.e., the ratios in which goods are consumed depends only on relative prices and not on incomes), so that the community welfare function will be of the same form and provide a unique ordering of all consumption-possibility positions (i.e., community indifference curves will not cross). See appendix to this chapter

4   The steps in obtaining equation (1) from equations (i), (ii), (iii) and (iv) are given in detail in the mathematical appendix to this chapter

5   The relation is expressed in this way rather than in the simpler form: expression (3) − expression (4) in order to make the algebra of the text similar to that of the mathematical appendix, in which K plays an important part.

6   See Chapter 5, inequality sets II and III, pp. 33-34

7   The terms 'more likely to raise welfare' and 'increase or decrease the chance of raising welfare' are used in the technical sense defined in the mathematical appendix. It may be well to state the generalisation here. Let $\propto$ be the proportion of total expenditure devoted to the purchase of X, and γ the proportion devoted to purchase of Z. For any level of pre-union tariff on Y and Z, welfare will be increased by the removal of the Y tariff if $\propto / \gamma$ exceeds a stated value (this value varies with the level of initial tariff on Y and Z). Thus, the larger is $\propto$ and the smaller is γ, the more likely is it that $\propto / \gamma$ will exceed the necessary value

8   I am unable to offer an intuitive explanation of why this should be true. In the mathematical appendix it is demonstrated that, for *any* division of expenditure between the three products, there will *necessarily* be some level of pre-union tariff which, if exceeded, will give a lower welfare level than that attained when the tariff is completely removed from Y. Undoubtedly, this is only necessary if there is no finite price at which demand for any product is zero (in the present example all demand curves are asymtotic to the quantity axes), so that welfare is lowered by any increase in tariffs. If the demand curve cuts the X axis,

welfare will be lowered by the imposition of tariffs only until
demand falls to zero, and further tariff increases on that product
will leave welfare unchanged. But it still might be true that the
higher was the level of tariffs, the greater was the chance of gain
when a customs union was formed. If this relation held in
general, it would be an important theorem in the general theory
of second best. It would mean that the piecemeal removal of
some taxes, tariffs, subsidies, was more likely to raise welfare
or efficiency the higher was the general level of all taxes, tariffs,
subsidies. In the absence of an intuitive explanation which
would provide an hypothesis to be either proved or disproved,
the only way to investigate this problem would seem to be to
select widely differing demand assumptions and see in which of
these the relation held. If it did not hold in some cases,
differences between the cases in which it held and those in which
it did not might suggest reasons for the relation. This study,
although interesting, would constitute a major task in itself, and
cannot be pursued as part of the present investigation of the
theory of customs unions.

9   The graph is obtained by solving equation (4) in the mathematical
        appendix for various values of j when $\alpha = \beta = \gamma = \frac{1}{3}$. $K-1$ is then
        the increase in the index of welfare, and $j-1$ the initial propor-
        tional uniform tariff

10   Figure 5 is obtained by substituting the values for each numerical
        example into equation (4) in the mathematical appendix to this
        chapter, and solving the equation for various values of j. A semi-
        logarithmic scale is used to plot the relation, because the range
        of variation of the subsidy is only from 100 per cent (a zero
        price) to zero, while that of the tariff is from zero to infinity
        (an infinite price)

Mathematical appendix to chapter 6

1   See J. R. Hicks. *Value and Capital,* Oxford, Clarendon Press, 1939, pp. 14ff.

2   See A.A. Alchian, 'The Meaning of Utility Measurement', *American Economic Review,* XLII, March 1953, pp. 26-50, for a general explanation of this problem

3   See, for example, Mishan, op. cit.

4   See Chapter 1, pp. 6-7

5   Since this may not be readily apparent, a numerical example may be given. Consider the values $j = 2$, $\alpha = 0.1$, $\beta = 0.1$, and $\gamma = 0.8$. Then

$$K = \frac{2^{1/10}\,(.2 + .1 + .8)}{.2 + .2 + .8} = 2^{1/10}\,\frac{(1.1)}{(1.2)} = .983$$

[12]

Journal of International Economics 9 (19) 341–354. © North-Holland Publishing Company

A 3×3 MODEL OF CUSTOMS UNIONS

Raymond RIEZMAN*

The University of Iowa, Iowa City, IA 52242, USA

Received January 1979, revised version received April 1979

In this paper we develop a three-country–three-good model of customs unions. The main result is that a sufficient condition for two countries to benefit from forming a customs union is that they are similar in the sense that their mutual trade is small. This result is obtained by analyzing the terms of trade effects rather than the more traditional emphasis on trade creation–trade diversion effects.

1. Introduction

The customs union theory literature has concentrated on analyzing the trade creation–trade diversion effects of customs unions [see Viner (1950), Meade (1955), Lipsey (1960), Bhagwati (1971)]. While this approach lends insight into the question of how customs unions affect world welfare, it has not produced answers to questions such as the following. Under what circumstances will two countries decide to form a customs union? Will customs unions lead to free trade?

Vanek (1965) and Kemp (1969) were the first to systematically study the terms of trade effects of customs unions. Vanek concentrated on determining the effect of customs unions on world welfare. Kemp directed his attention to individual country's welfare but, rather than determining when two countries would choose to form a customs union, he simply listed the possible outcomes that followed if two countries decided to form a union.

The purpose of this paper is to determine when two countries could benefit from and, thus, would choose to form, a customs union. We follow Kemp in that we focus on the terms of trade effects. Rather than using Kemp's three-country–two-good geometric model, we will analyze the problem in the context of a three-country–three-good mathematical model. The three-country–three-good model has the advantage that there is not the asymmetry that exists in the three-country–two-good case. We assume that, initially, no tariff discrimination is allowed and, in addition, we rule out international transfers.

*This paper is based on a chapter of my Ph.D. dissertation submitted to the University of Minnesota. I wish to thank my adviser, John S. Chipman, for his helpful comments and advice. An anonymous referee also provided helpful comments.

Our main result is that two countries can benefit from a customs union provided that their mutual trade is initially small and does not increase too much as a result of the agreement. Some other conditions must also hold, but they are essentially regularity conditions. The main result has an intuitive explanation. The effect of the customs union is to reduce the prices of the goods imported by the customs union countries relative to their export goods. Therefore, their terms of trade with respect to the rest of the world (the third country in this case) improve. However, in general, the change in intracustoms union trading will benefit one member at the expense of the other. Thus, if intra-union trade is small, any loss *vis-à-vis* a member country would be outweighed by the gain *vis-à-vis* the rest of the world.

This result says that a sufficient condition for two countries to benefit from forming a customs union is that their mutual trade be small. It does not say that countries whose mutual trade is large cannot benefit from a customs union. To determine if a country gains from a customs union for any specific case, one needs to weigh the gain from improvement in a country's terms of trade *vis-à-vis* the nonmember countries against the possible loss due to a deterioration in the terms of trade *vis-à-vis* other member countries. It seems that this theory lends itself easily to empirical tests and could be useful in empirical investigations of related questions.

The basic model is explained in section 2. Sections 3 and 4 contain the main results for the case in which there is a small reduction in tariffs. Section 5 extends these results to the full customs union case. In section 6 we interpret and summarize our results, and briefly relate them to the issue of transfer payments.

2. Notation and assumptions

We use the following notation:

X_j^i = consumption of good j in country i,

Y_j^i = production of good j in country i,

$Z_j^i \equiv X_j^i - Y_j^i$ net imports if positive (exports if negative) of good j in country i,

$Z_j = Z_j^1 + Z_j^2 + Z_j^3$,

P_j^i = price of good j in country i,

$p^i = (p_1^i, p_2^i, p_3^i)$,

$p = (p^1, p^2, p^3)$,

t_{jk} = tariff charged by country j on imports from country k,

$t = (t_{12}, t_{13}, t_{21}, t_{23}, t_{31}, t_{32})$,

I^i = is the national income of country i.

Our model consists of three countries numbered 1, 2 and 3, and three goods also numbered 1, 2, and 3. For convenience we assume that country 1 imports good 1 and exports goods 2 and 3. Similarly, country 2 imports good 2 and exports 1 and 3 and country 3 imports 3 and exports 1 and 2. Clearly, other trading patterns are possible; however, this one has the advantage that it is symmetrical. The question we wish to answer is: given that initially we have a symmetric situation, under what conditions will it pay two of the countries to form a customs union? A customs union agreement is one in which two or more countries agree to eliminate tariffs between themselves. Hence, in the context of our model, we want to determine when countries 1 and 2 could benefit from eliminating tariffs on their trade with each other.

In each country we assume that all production functions are continuously differentiable, homogeneous of degree one, and strictly convex to the origin. It follows that the supply of good j in country i, Y^i_j, is a single valued function $Y^i_j(p^i_1, p^i_2, p^i_3)$. Assume this function is continuously differentiable.

Aggregate demand for good j in country i, X^i_j, is assumed to be a continuously differentiable function $h^i_j(p^i_1, p^i_2, p^i_3, I^i)$ of domestic prices and national income. This demand function is generated by a Samuelson type social utility function $U^i(X^i_1, X^i_2, X^i_3)$.[1] Aggregate income I^i consists of income from production plus tariff proceeds:

$$I^i = p^i_1 Y^i_1(p^i) + p^i_2 Y^i_2(p^i) + p^i_3 Y^i_3(p^i) + \{\alpha^i(p^j_i t_{ij}) + (1 - \alpha^i)p^k_i t_{ik}\}Z^i_i,$$

$$i = 1, 2, 3, \qquad j = i + 1 \,(\text{mod } 3), \qquad k = i + 2 \,(\text{mod } 3) \tag{1}$$

(where α^i is the fraction of imports i receives from country j). From this formulation it is apparent that the demand for good i in country i, X^i_i, depends on I^i which in turn depends on X^i_i. Because of this circularity, we have to prove that the variable X^i_i can be expressed as a function of prices, tariffs, and alphas. We wish to show that there exists a function

$$\hat{X}^i_i(p^i, p^j_i, p^k_i, t_{ij}, t_{ik}, \alpha^i) = h^i_i[p^i, p^i_1 Y^i_1(p^i) + p^i_2 Y^i_2(p^i) + p^i_3 Y^i_3(p^i)$$

$$+ \{\alpha^i p^j_i t_{ij} + (1 - \alpha^i)p^k_i t_{ik}\}$$

$$\times \{\hat{X}^i_i(p^i, p^j_i, p^k_i, t_{ij}, t_{ik}, \alpha^i) - Y^i_i(p^i)\}], \tag{2}$$

$$i, l = 1, 2, 3, \qquad j = i + 1 \,(\text{mod } 3), \qquad k = i + 2 \,(\text{mod } 3).$$

We define the marginal propensity to consume good j in country i, m^i_j, by

$$m^i_j = p^i_j \frac{\partial X^i_j}{\partial I^i}. \tag{3}$$

---

[1]It is assumed that income is optimally distributed by the government to maximize this function, or that all individuals in each country have identical, homothetic utility functions.

$\hat{X}_i^i(p^i, p_i^j, p_i^k, t_{ij}, t_{ik}, \alpha^i)$ (for the case $i=l$) exists and is unique if there exists a μ such that

$$0 < m_i^i < \mu < p_i^i/(\alpha^i p_i^j t_{ij} + (1 - \alpha^i) p_i^k t_{ik})$$

and if $I^i > 0$ implies that $h_i^i(p^i, I^i) > 0.$[2]

We now define excess demand functions:

$$\hat{Z}_i^i(p^i, p_i^j, p_i^k, t_{ij}, t_{ik}, \alpha^i) = \hat{X}_i^i(p^i, p_i^j, p_i^k, t_{ij}, t_{ik}, \alpha^i) - Y_i^i(p^i),$$

$$i, l = 1, 2, 3, \qquad j = i + 1 \,(\text{mod } 3), \qquad k = i + 2 \,(\text{mod } 3). \tag{4}$$

We can write income as follows:

$$\hat{I}^i(p^i, p_i^j, p_i^k, t_{ij}, t_{ik}, \alpha^i) = p_1^i \, Y_1^i(p^i) + p_2^i \, Y_2^i(p^i) + p_3^i \, Y_3^i(p^i)$$

$$+ \{\alpha^i p_i^j t_{ij} + (1 - \alpha^i) p_i^k t_{ik}\}$$

$$\times \hat{Z}_i^i(p^i, p_i^j, p_i^k, t_{ij}, t_{ik}, \alpha^i), \tag{4a}$$

$$i, l = 1, 2, 3, \qquad j = i + 1 \,(\text{mod } 3), \qquad k = i + 2 \,(\text{mod } 3).$$

Next we assume that all demand and supply functions respond normally to price

$$\frac{\partial \hat{X}_j^i}{\partial p_k^i} \begin{cases} > 0, & \text{if } j \neq k, \\ < 0, & \text{if } j = k. \end{cases} \tag{5}$$

$$\frac{\partial Y_j^i}{\partial p_k^i} \begin{cases} > 0, & \text{if } j = k, \\ < 0, & \text{if } j \neq k, \quad i, j, k = 1, 2, 3. \end{cases} \tag{6}$$

(Note: For the case $i = j = k$ this is not an assumption. It follows from the convexity of the production-possibility set.)

Eqs. (5) and (6) imply

$$\frac{\partial \hat{Z}_j^i}{\partial p_k^i} \begin{cases} > 0, & \text{if } j \neq k, \\ < 0, & \text{if } j = k, \quad i, j, k = 1, 2, 3. \end{cases} \tag{7}$$

---

[2]Two things should be pointed out. First, the proof of this statement can be found in Riezman (1977b). Secondly, in equilibrium

$$p_i^i/(\alpha^i p_i^j t_{ij} + (1 - \alpha^i) p_i^k t_{ik}) = (1 + t_{ij})/t_{ij},$$

hence the first part of the condition becomes $0 < m_i^i < \mu < (1 + t_{ij})/t_{ij}.$

R. Riezman, *Customs unions* 345

Given the trading pattern, if each country trades every commodity we have the following equalities:

$$p_1^1 = p_1^2(1 + t_{12}),$$
$$p_1^1 = p_1^3(1 + t_{13}),$$
$$p_2^2 = p_2^1(1 + t_{21}),$$
$$p_2^2 = p_2^3(1 + t_{23}),$$
$$p_3^3 = p_3^1(1 + t_{31}),$$
$$p_3^3 = p_3^2(1 + t_{32}).$$

$$(8)$$

Using (8) and the condition of material balance, we can write excess demand Z_j^i as a function of $p' = (p_1^1, p_2^2, 1)$ (we assume p_3^3 is the numeraire) and all tariffs, t, i.e., $Z_j^i(p', t)$, $i, j = 1, 2, 3$. The equilibrium conditions are given by

$$F^1(p', t) = Z_1^1(p', t) + Z_1^2(p', t) + Z_1^3(p', t) = 0,$$

$$(9)$$

$$F^2(p', t) = Z_2^1(p', t) + Z_2^2(p', t) + Z_2^3(p', t) = 0.$$

$$(10)$$

Hence (9) and (10) define a function $F = (F^1, F^2)$ which maps a vector (p', t) into $0 \in R^2$. Thus, $F(p', t) = 0$. We assume that there exists an equilibrium set of non-negative prices and tariffs.[3] Mathematically, we assume there exists a $\bar{p}' > 0$ and $\bar{t} > 0$ such that $F(\bar{p}', \bar{t}) = 0$. We now use F to determine what happens to p_1^1 and p_2^2 when t_{12} and t_{21} are reduced.

3. The analysis of prices

In this section we establish sufficient conditions for p_1^1 and p_2^2 to fall when t_{12} and t_{21} are reduced. Simple application of the implicit function theorem gives this result.

Let F_x be the matrix with elements $(F_x)_{ij}$ where

$$(F_x)_{ij} = \frac{\partial F^i}{\partial p_j^j}, \qquad i, j = 1, 2.$$

$$(11)$$

Call the determinant of F_x, D. We wish to determine sufficient conditions for $D > 0$. Let

$$\eta_{jk}^i = \frac{\partial Z_j^i}{\partial p_k^k} \frac{p_k^k}{Z_j^i}, \qquad i, j = 1, 2, 3, \qquad k = 1, 2.$$

$$(12)$$

---

[3] The issue of existence of equilibrium is discussed by Shoven (1974) and Sontheimer (1971).

Consider the following condition:

I. $\lambda_{ij}\eta^i_{jj} > -\lambda_{ij}\eta^i_{jk}\left[\dfrac{p^j_j}{p^k_k}\right],$ (13)

where

$$\lambda_{ij} = \begin{cases} -1, & \text{if } i=j, \\ 1, & \text{if } i\neq j, \end{cases}$$

and $i = 1, 2, 3$, $j = 2$ and $k = 1$, or $j = 1$ and $k = 2$. (Condition I is actually six similar conditions on elasticities of excess demands.)

Lemma 3.1. If condition I holds then $D > 0$.

Proof. Directly calculating,

$$D = \frac{\partial F^1}{\partial p^1_1}\frac{\partial F^2}{\partial p^2_2} - \frac{\partial F^1}{\partial p^2_2}\frac{\partial F^2}{\partial p^1_1} > 0.$$ (14)

Hence $D > 0$ if

$$\frac{\partial F^1}{\partial p^1_1}\frac{\partial F^2}{\partial p^2_2} - \frac{F^1}{\partial p^2_2}\frac{\partial F^2}{\partial p^1_1} > 0.$$

This becomes

$$\left[\frac{\partial Z^1_1}{\partial p^1_1} + \frac{\partial Z^2_1}{\partial p^1_1} + \frac{\partial Z^3_1}{\partial p^1_1}\right]\left[\frac{\partial Z^1_2}{\partial p^2_2} + \frac{\partial Z^2_2}{\partial p^2_2} + \frac{\partial Z^3_2}{\partial p^2_2}\right]$$

$$> \left[\frac{\partial Z^1_1}{\partial p^2_2} + \frac{\partial Z^2_1}{\partial p^2_2} + \frac{\partial Z^3_1}{\partial p^2_2}\right]\left[\frac{\partial Z^1_2}{\partial p^1_1} + \frac{\partial Z^2_2}{\partial p^1_1} + \frac{\partial Z^3_2}{\partial p^1_1}\right].$$ (15)

Condition I says that the first term on the left-hand side is larger than the first term on the right-hand size in absolute value, the second term on the left-hand side is larger than the second term on the right-hand side, etc. Hence, condition I is sufficient to ensure that inequality (15) holds, therefore $D > 0$.

By our previous assumptions, given condition I, $F(p',t)$ is continuously differentiable. Applying the Implicit Function Theorem, if there exists a $(\bar{p}',\bar{t})$ such that $F(\bar{p}',\bar{t}) = 0$, then there exists a neighbourhood $N(\bar{t})$ around $\bar{t}$ in which a function ϕ can be defined such that for all $t \in N(\bar{t})$, $F(\phi(t),t) = 0$.

Also, we know that at any point $t \in N(\bar{t})$,

$$\phi_t = -F_x^{-1} \cdot F_t. \tag{16}$$

ϕ_t is a matrix with elements $(\phi_t)_{ij}$ where

$$(\phi_t)_{ij} = \frac{\partial p_i^i}{\partial t_j}, \qquad i = 1, 2, \qquad j = 1, \ldots, 6 \tag{17}$$

$(t_1 = t_{12}, \ t_2 = t_{13}, \ t_3 = t_{21}, \ t_4 = t_{23}, \ t_5 = t_{31}, \ t_6 = t_{32})$. F_t is a matrix with elements $(F_t)_{ij}$ where

$$(F_t)_{ij} = \frac{\partial F^i}{\partial t_j}, \qquad i = 1, 2, \qquad j = 1, \ldots, 6. \tag{18}$$

Let D_{ij} be the cofactor of the ijth element of F_x. Writing out (16) in matrix notation we obtain

$$\begin{bmatrix} \dfrac{\partial p_1^1}{\partial t_{12}} & \dfrac{\partial p_1^1}{\partial t_{13}} & \dfrac{\partial p_1^1}{\partial t_{21}} & \dfrac{\partial p_1^1}{\partial t_{23}} & \dfrac{\partial p_1^1}{\partial t_{31}} & \dfrac{\partial p_1^1}{\partial t_{32}} \\ \dfrac{\partial p_2^2}{\partial t_{12}} & \cdots & & & & \dfrac{\partial p_2^2}{\partial t_{32}} \end{bmatrix}$$

$$= -\frac{1}{D}\begin{bmatrix} D_{11} & D_{21} \\ D_{12} & D_{22} \end{bmatrix}\begin{bmatrix} \dfrac{\partial F^1}{\partial t_{12}} & \dfrac{\partial F^1}{\partial t_{13}} & \dfrac{\partial F^1}{\partial t_{21}} & \dfrac{\partial F^1}{\partial t_{23}} & \dfrac{\partial F^1}{\partial t_{31}} & \dfrac{\partial F^1}{\partial t_{32}} \\ \dfrac{\partial F^2}{\partial t_{12}} & \cdots & & & & \dfrac{\partial F^2}{\partial t_{32}} \end{bmatrix}. \tag{19}$$

Since we wish to determine how p_1^1 and p_2^2 change when both t_{12} and t_{21} are reduced, we need to find the signs of $dp_1^1/d\tau$ and $dp_2^2/d\tau$, where τ is a parameter[4] and

$$\frac{dp_1^1}{d\tau} = \frac{\partial p_1^1}{\partial t_{12}}\frac{dt_{12}}{d\tau} + \frac{\partial p_1^1}{\partial t_{21}}\frac{dt_{21}}{d\tau},$$

$$\frac{dp_2^2}{d\tau} = \frac{\partial p_2^2}{\partial t_{12}}\frac{dt_{12}}{d\tau} + \frac{\partial p_2^2}{\partial t_{21}}\frac{dt_{21}}{d\tau}.$$

One could make many different assumptions about $dt_{12}/d\tau$ and $dt_{21}/d\tau$, but for simplicity we assume $dt_{12}/d\tau = \xi t_{12}$ and $dt_{21}/d\tau = \beta t_{21}$. This means that

[4]For a more complete discussion of this matter see Riezman (1977b).

we consider constant percentage reductions for both tariff rates, although the rates may be different. From (19) we see that

$$\frac{dp_1^1}{d\tau} = \frac{-1}{D}\left[D_{11}\frac{dF^1}{d\tau} + D_{21}\frac{dF^2}{d\tau}\right],$$

$$\frac{dp_2^2}{d\tau} = \frac{-1}{D}\left[D_{12}\frac{dF^1}{d\tau} + D_{22}\frac{dF^2}{d\tau}\right], \tag{20}$$

where

$$\frac{dF^i}{d\tau} = \frac{\partial F^i}{\partial t_{12}}\xi t_{12} + \frac{\partial F^i}{\partial t_{21}}\beta t_{21}.$$

We can now state our first theorem.

Theorem 1.   Given condition I,

II. $$\hat{\eta}_{11}^2 \xi t_{12} > -\hat{\eta}_{12}^1\left(\frac{(1+t_{12})Z_1^1}{(1+t_{21})Z_1^2}\right)\beta t_{21},$$

and

III. $$\hat{\eta}_{22}^1 \beta t_{21} > -\hat{\eta}_{21}^2\left(\frac{(1+t_{21})Z_2^2}{(1+t_{12})Z_2^1}\right)\xi t_{12},$$

and given also that income effects are small, then $dp_1^1/d\tau > 0$ *and* $dp_2^2/d\tau > 0$

$$\left(\hat{\eta}_{jk}^i \equiv \frac{\partial \hat{Z}_j^i}{\partial p_k^i}\frac{p_k^i}{Z_j^i}, \quad i,j,k=1,2,3\right).$$

Proof.   The details of the proof are left to an appendix.

Remark.   Theorem 1 tells us that when conditions I–III hold, member countries 1 and 2 experience a fall in the domestic price of their imported good (i.e. p_1^1 and p_2^2 fall). p_3^1, p_3^2, and p_3^3 are all constant because p_3^3 was assumed to be the numeraire and t_{31} and t_{32} do not change in our analysis. Hence, for each member country, the price of its import good will fall relative to the price of the good which it exports to the nonmember. In this sense we can say that the member country's terms of trade improve relative to the nonmember country. We cannot determine from our analysis what happens to p_2^1 and p_1^2. Therefore, the change in the terms of trade between member countries is indeterminate.

Remark. Conditions I–III can be viewed as regularity conditions. They essentially require that own price elasticities of excess demand dominate the cross price elasticities.

4. Utility analysis

We have shown that, given some mild restrictions, when two countries mutually reduce tariffs the price of their imported good falls, the price of one exported good is constant, and the price of the other exported good is indeterminate. We show in this section that these price changes will imply an increase in utility for the participating countries, provided that their trade with each other is relatively small.

Theorem 2. Given that countries 1 and 2 mutually reduce tariffs, conditions I–III hold, income effects are small, and countries 1 and 2 initially trade relatively little with each other (i.e. for a sufficiently small $-Z_2^1$ and $-Z_1^2$), then utility will increase for both countries 1 and 2.

Proof. We will sketch the proof. [For a complete proof see Riezman (1977b).] Country 1 maximizes a social utility function,

$$U^1(X_1^1, X_2^1, X_3^1) = U^1[\bar{X}_1^1(p'(t(\tau)), t_{12}(\tau), t_{13}(\tau), t_{21}(\tau), t_{31}(\tau), \alpha^1(t(\tau)),$$
$$\bar{X}_2^1(\cdot), \bar{X}_3^1(\cdot)]$$
$$= U^1[\bar{X}_1^1(\tau), \bar{X}_2^1(\tau), \bar{X}_3^1(\tau)].$$

We wish to show that

$$\frac{dU^1[\bar{X}_1^1(\tau), \bar{X}_2^1(\tau), \bar{X}_3^1(\tau)]}{d\tau} < 0. \tag{21}$$

Expression (21) becomes

$$U_1^1 \frac{d\bar{X}_1^1(\tau)}{d\tau} + U_2^1 \frac{d\bar{X}_2^1(\tau)}{d\tau} + U_3^1 \frac{d\bar{X}_3^1(\tau)}{d\tau} < 0. \tag{22}$$

Using the first-order conditions for utility maximization, (22) becomes

$$p_1^1 \frac{d\bar{X}_1^1(\tau)}{d\tau} + \frac{p_2^2}{1+t_{21}} \frac{d\bar{X}_2^1(\tau)}{d\tau} + \frac{1}{1+t_{31}} \frac{d\bar{X}_3^1(\tau)}{d\tau} < 0. \tag{23}$$

Using the balance of payments condition and results from the previous section, it can be shown that for sufficiently small $-Z_2^1$ and $-Z_1^2$, given conditions I–III, and given also that income effects are small, (23) will hold, thus utility increases for country 1. The proof for country 2 is similar. Hence, we have shown that two countries can gain from mutually reducing tariffs provided that their mutual trade is small. This result is somewhat unexpected but can be explained intuitively. We showed in section 3 that the countries entering into the agreement to reduce tariffs both find that their trading position *vis-à-vis* the third country improves. However, their position with respect to each other may improve or deteriorate. Hence, if we require that initially the trade between members is small, any deterioration in their trading position *vis-à-vis* the other member will be outweighed by the improvement with respect to the rest of the world. Therefore, their trading position will improve overall.

This completes our results for small reductions in tariffs. In the next section we extend our results to a full customs union case.

5. The customs union case

We have shown that two countries can gain by mutually reducing their tariffs, provided that their trade with each other is not too large and that certain regularity conditions hold. In this section we show that this result is easily extended to the case of a full customs union. We do this by showing that a path exists along which tariffs are reduced to zero for the participating countries and along which utility is always increasing for both countries. Consider the path along which both member countries reduce tariffs by the same constant percentage amount. In terms of our model this implies that $\xi = \eta$. This path will approach the point $t_{12} = t_{21} = 0$, i.e. the customs union point. We now need to show that utility increases at every point along the path.

We first examine conditions I–III. Condition I does not have any terms containing t_{12} or t_{21}. Since it is essentially a regularity condition, there is no reason to believe condition I would not hold as t_{12} and t_{21} are reduced to zero. The counterpart of I in the customs union case is

$$I'. \quad \lambda_{ij}\eta^i_{jj} > -\lambda_{ij}\eta^i_{jk}\left(\frac{p^j_j}{p^k_k}\right), \qquad i=1,2,3, \quad j=2 \text{ and } k=1,$$

$$\lambda_{ij} = \begin{cases} -1, & \text{if } i=j, \\ 1, & \text{if } i\neq j, \end{cases} \quad \text{or } j=1 \text{ and } k=2,$$

at every point along the path as t_{12} and $t_{21} \to 0$.

Conditions II and III, which require that own price elasticities dominate cross price elasticities, contain terms with t_{12} and t_{21}. Thus, as t_{12} and t_{21}

are reduced to zero, conditions II and III will become $0 > 0$, which cannot hold in the limit. However, there is no reason to believe II and III will not hold as the tariffs are reduced. The fact that they cannot hold in the limit simply means that when $t_{12} = t_{21} = 0$, then $dp_1^1/d\tau = dp_2^2/d\tau = 0$. Conditions II and III become

II'. $\hat{\eta}_{11}^2 t_{12} > -\hat{\eta}_{12}^1 \left(\dfrac{(1 + t_{12}) Z_1^1}{(1 + t_{21}) Z_1^2} \right) t_{21},$

III'. $\hat{\eta}_{22}^1 t_{21} > \hat{\eta}_{21}^2 \left(\dfrac{(1 + t_{21}) Z_2^2}{(1 + t_{12}) Z_2^1} \right) t_{12},$

at each point along the path as t_{12} and $t_{21} \to 0$.

We can now state our customs union theorem.

Theorem 3.   Given that conditions I', II', and III' hold, and given also that income effects are small, countries 1 and 2 will gain from forming a customs union provided their trade with each other does not increase too much (i.e. for a sufficiently small $-Z_2^1$ and $-Z_1^2$).

Proof.   The proof is simple. If all the conditions hold, then theorem 2 holds at each point along the path of tariff reductions. As a result, utility is increasing at each point on the path. Therefore, both countries are better off at the end point of the path, which is a customs union.

Remark.   The Latin American Free Trade Association (LAFTA) appears to be an example of a customs union which meets the conditions of theorem 3. In particular, the member countries trade primarily with Europe, Japan and the United States. Viewed in this way LAFTA is a device which essentially improves the member countries' terms of trade (i.e. raises the relative price of the member countries' exportables). Obviously, there are other facets to customs unions, but empirical work done by Petith (1977) on the EEC suggests that the terms of trade effects are important.

6. Summary and interpretation

Theorem 3 says that to guarantee that both countries 1 and 2 can benefit from a customs union, their mutual trade cannot be too large. To see how this applies in practice we need to consider the intuitive explanation for this result. After formation of the union, both member countries gain from an improvement in their terms of trade with country 3. However, it may be that country 1's terms of trade with respect to country 2 deteriorate. Hence, country 2 is unambiguously better off as a result of the union. But again, country 1 has both a source of gain and of loss. Therefore, country 1 gains from the union if the gain due to the improvement in terms of trade with country 3 outweighs the loss incurred *vis-à-vis* country 2. This will be the case if countries 1 and 2 trade little with each other.

As a result, one interpretation of this theory is that, to determine if two countries can gain from forming a customs union, one needs to compare the gains *vis-à-vis* the rest of the world with the possible loss *vis-à-vis* the other member countries. This hypothesis seems readily testable by looking at price changes weighted by the volumes of the respective goods flows.[5] This approach should prove useful in explaining the size and composition of existing customs unions. In addition, one could predict what customs unions might be formed in the future.

Theorem 3 can also be used to shed some light on the issue of transfer payments. Another interpretation of theorem 3 is that, in the absence of transfer payments, countries which trade mainly with each other may not find customs unions mutually advantageous. Kemp and Wan (1976), on the other hand, show that if transfer payments are allowed, then any customs union is potentially advantageous for all countries. Therefore, theorem 3 combined with the Kemp and Wan result indicates that if countries trade largely (little) with each other a mutually beneficial customs union probably will (will not) require transfer payments. This result is consistent with the experience of the EEC. The EEC is a customs union consisting of countries whose mutual trade is large, and is characterized by significant transfer payments.

Consequently, the conclusion which emerges is that when members of a potential customs union trade largely with each other it is likely that transfer payments will be necessary to make the union advantageous for all member countries. If intra-union trade is small, transfer payments should be un-necessary. Hence, this model offers an explanation for and could be used to study the issue of transfer payments within a customs union.

Appendix

We wish to show that, if II and III hold and income effects are small, then

$$\frac{dp_1^1}{d\tau} > 0 \quad \text{and} \quad \frac{dp_2^2}{d\tau} > 0.$$

$$\frac{dp_1^1}{d\tau} = -\frac{1}{D}\left(D_{11}\frac{dF^1}{d\tau} + D_{21}\frac{dF^2}{d\tau}\right).$$

[5]Petith (1977) has investigated similar issues.

$$D_{11} = \frac{\partial Z_2^1}{\partial p_2^2} + \frac{\partial Z_2^2}{\partial p_2^2} + \frac{\partial Z_2^3}{\partial p_2^2} < 0,$$

$$D_{21} = -\left(\frac{\partial Z_1^1}{\partial p_2^2} + \frac{\partial Z_1^2}{\partial p_2^2} + \frac{\partial Z_1^3}{\partial p_2^2}\right) < 0.$$

Therefore, if

$$\frac{dF^1}{d\tau} > 0 \quad \text{and} \quad \frac{dF^2}{d\tau} > 0,$$

then

$$dp_1^1/d\tau > 0.$$

$$\frac{dF^1}{d\tau} = \frac{\partial F^1}{\partial t_{12}} \frac{dt_{12}}{d\tau} + \frac{\partial F^1}{\partial t_{21}} \frac{dt_{21}}{d\tau}$$

$$= \left(\frac{\partial Z_1^1}{\partial t_{12}} + \frac{\partial Z_1^2}{\partial t_{12}} + \frac{\partial Z_1^3}{\partial t_{12}}\right)\xi t_{12} + \left(\frac{\partial Z_1^1}{\partial t_{21}} + \frac{\partial Z_1^2}{\partial t_{21}} + \frac{\partial Z_1^3}{\partial t_{21}}\right)\eta t_{21}.$$

This can be written as

$$\frac{dF^1}{d\tau} = \left(\frac{\partial Z_1^2}{\partial t_{12}}\xi t_{12} + \frac{\partial Z_1^1}{\partial t_{21}}\eta t_{21}\right)$$

$$+ \left(\frac{\partial Z_1^1}{\partial t_{12}}\xi t_{12} + \frac{\partial Z_1^3}{\partial t_{12}}\xi t_{12} + \frac{\partial Z_1^2}{\partial t_{21}}\eta t_{21} + \frac{\partial Z_1^3}{\partial t_{21}}\eta t_{21}\right).$$

The last four terms are all income effects which are assumed to be small. The first two terms are positive if II holds, hence II implies that $dF^1/d\tau > 0$. In a similar manner it can be shown that III implies $dF^2/d\tau > 0$. Thus, II and III imply that $dp_1^1/d\tau > 0$. The proof for $dp_2^1/d\tau$ is similar.

References

Bhagwati, J., 1971, Trade diverting custom union and welfare improvement: A clarification, Economic Journal 81, 580–587.

Bhagwati, J., 1973, A reply to Professor Kirman, Economic Journal 83, 895–897.

Chipman, J.S., 1960, A survey of the theory of international trade, Econometrica 34, 18–76.

Chipman, J.S., 1972, The theory of exploitative trade and investment policies: A reformulation and synthesis, in: L.E. DeMarco, ed., International economics and development (Academic Press, New York).

Chipman, J.S. and J.C. Moore, 1972, Social utility and the gains from trade, Journal of International Economics 2(2), 157–172.

Kemp, M., 1969, A contribution to the general equilibrium theory of preferential trading (North-Holland, Amsterdam).

B

Kemp, M. and H.Y. Wan, 1976, An elementary proposition concerning the formation of customs unions, Journal of International Economics 6, 95–97.

Kirman, A.P., 1973, Trade diverting customs unions and welfare improvement: A comment, Economic Journal 83, 890–894.

Krauss, M.B., 1972, Recent developments in customs union theory: An interpretive survey, Journal of Economic Literature 10, 413–436.

Lipsey, R.G., 1960, The theory of customs unions: A general survey, Economic Journal 70(279), 496–513.

Meade, J.E., 1955, The theory of customs unions (North-Holland, Amsterdam).

Negishi, T., 1969, The customs union and the theory of second best, International Economic Review 10, 391–398.

Petith, H.C., 1977, European integration and the terms of trade, Economic Journal 87, 262–272.

Riezman, R., 1977a, A theory of customs unions: The three country–two good case, mimeo. Forthcoming in Weltwirtschaftliches Archiv.

Riezman, R., 1977b, A theory of preferential trading agreements (University of Iowa Working Paper no. 77–4A).

Samuelson, P.A., 1956, Social indifference curves, Quarterly Journal of Economics LXX, 1–22.

Shoven, J.B., 1974, A proof of the existence of a general equilibrium with ad valorem commodity taxes, Journal of Economic Theory 8, 1–25.

Sontheimer, K.C., 1971, The existence of international trade equilibrium with trade tax-subsidy distortions, Econometrica 39(6), 1015–1035.

Vanek, J., 1965, General equilibrium of international discrimination (Harvard University Press, Cambridge, Massachusetts).

Viner, J., 1950, The customs union issue (Carnegie Endowment for International Peace, New York).

[13]

Is Unilateral Tariff Reduction Preferable to a Customs Union? The Curious Case of the Missing Foreign Tariffs

By Paul Wonnacott and Ronald Wonnacott*

During the past decade and a half, an important part of the literature on customs unions has dealt with the question of whether a country might obtain the gains it would achieve from a customs union (*CU*) in an alternative way, by a unilateral tariff reduction (*UTR*). (*UTR* may involve a partial reduction in tariffs, or a reduction all the way to zero.) A widely accepted conclusion (see Eitan Berglas, p. 329; C. A. Cooper and B. F. Massell, 1965b, pp. 745–47; Roma Dauphin, ch. 2; Harry Johnson, p. 280; Melvyn Krauss, pp. 417–19; and Peter Robson)[1] is that *UTR* does indeed hold out the prospect for all the gains from a *CU*—without the disadvantages—if two important simplifying assumptions are made; namely, that we ignore economies of scale and the effects of a customs union on the terms of trade.[2] In the words of Berglas: "It is important to note that if a [preferential] trade agreement does not affect the terms of trade, then it does not allow for any mutually beneficial policy opportunities which are not open to each of the member countries separately [through *UTR*]" (p. 329).

If this conclusion is correct, it is very important, in that it undercuts the earlier literature on customs unions. The question asked by Jacob Viner in his pioneering work —whether a *CU* represents a net gain or a net loss in economic efficiency—becomes unimportant, except insofar as a customs union is based on terms-of-trade effects[3] or economies of scale,[4] since a *CU* can be summarily rejected in favor of *UTR*. The *UTR* case would mean that, for economists, the puzzle is not to identify the efficiency gains (or losses) from a *CU*, but rather to explain why countries form customs unions in the first place (Berglas, p. 329; Cooper and Massell, 1965b, p. 247; and Johnson, p. 270). Indeed, in his survey of *CU* theory, Krauss identifies the problem raised by Cooper and Massell—of *why* countries form customs unions—as "...the theoretical issue of the past decade [the 1960's] just as in the prior one the major issue, as explicitly defined by Jacob Viner (1950), was whether a customs union represented a movement towards freer trade or greater protection" (p. 413). The typical reply to the Cooper-Massell question is: Countries tend to form a *CU* for noneconomic reasons (Berglas, pp. 329–30).[5]

*University of Maryland and University of Western Ontario, respectively. We thank Christopher Clague, Mel Krauss, Clark Leith, Richard Lipsey, Arvind Panagariya, and John Williamson.

[1] The three primary articles are Berglas; Cooper and Massell, 1965b; and Johnson. The other works are surveys or elaborations of the primary articles.

[2] Johnson (pp. 274–82) discusses a third source of mutual benefit from a *CU*; namely, the existence of externalities in manufacturing.

[3] On terms of trade and customs unions, see Sven Arndt (1968, 1969); and Krauss (pp. 421–24).

[4] There has been a tendency in the *CU* literature, tracing back to Viner (p. 47), to dismiss economies of scale as unimportant (for example, see Krauss, p. 420). In our empirical work on North American free trade (1967), we concluded that economies of scale were much more important than the triangular welfare gains identified by traditional theory. In many cases, we question how enlightening it is to study a *CU* without considering economies of scale. Nevertheless, in this paper, we will stay within the traditional framework and ignore economies of scale, since we are studying a specific theoretical issue which has arisen in the literature. (On economies of scale and customs unions, see also W. M. Corden and John Williamson.)

[5] Johnson (pp. 258, 270, 279–81) explained why customs unions may be formed for a partly political reason. Specifically, he assumed that countries have a "...collective preference for industrial production..." (p. 258). Cooper and Massell (1965a) offer a similar rationale for the formation of customs unions among developing countries. Another argument for preferring a *CU* to *UTR* is that each member provides the other(s) with protection against third-country imports; this may

In this paper, our contention is that the *UTR* literature is not correct. (We believe that the earlier question raised by Viner—of the effects of a *CU* on efficiency—is the most important one, although the answers suggested by Viner were not completely satisfactory, as has been pointed out by such writers as Franz Gehrels; Richard Lipsey, 1957; and James Meade.) The *UTR* literature is fundamentally wrong, not in the sense of having made logical errors, but wrong in having begun from a series of assumptions— some explicit and some implicit—which in effect rule out the principal advantages of a *CU*. Suppose that we were to ask the average politician or business executive the $64 question raised by the *UTR* literature: "What economic advantage can there possibly be in forming a customs union?" The probable reply would be: "To get down the tariffs of our partners in the proposed customs union, and thus gain better access to their markets." It is therefore surprising that, in arguing the case for *UTR*, Cooper and Massell (1965b, p. 747) make only a concluding reference to market swapping, but conduct no analysis of the elimination of tariffs by the *CU* partner.[6] While this oversight is corrected elsewhere in the literature—most notably by Berglas— Berglas makes strong assumptions about Country *C* which mean that Country *A* cannot possibly gain from its newly acquired access to *B*'s markets. These include the implicit assumptions that Country *C* has no tariffs, and there are no transportation costs.[7] (We follow the standard terminology of two prospective *CU* partners, *A* and *B*, and an

outside Country *C*. The establishment of a *CU* involves the elimination of tariffs on trade between *A* and *B*, and the adoption by *A* and *B* of a common tariff on imports from *C*.)

Our major contention is that, in a world in which tariffs and other obstacles to trade exist, it is meaningless to analyze the effects of freeing trade between *CU* members if we assume that there are no impediments to trade with outsider *C*. It is misleading to analyze a *CU*, and in particular to compare a *CU* and *UTR*, unless all countries are recognized to have tariffs to begin with. Anything else is Hamlet without the prince. In more detail, we argue that:

1) In making the case for *UTR*, its proponents make either or both of the following assumptions (explicitly or implicitly): (a) That partner *B*'s tariffs can be ignored. (b) That outsider *C* has no tariffs, and there are no transportation costs in trade with *C*.

2) If we depart from both of these assumptions, a country can achieve gains from a customs union which are not possible with *UTR*.

3) This conclusion, that the dominance of *UTR* over a *CU* collapses if we reject assumptions 1a and 1b, holds even if we make the standard assumption that there are no gains in the terms of trade with outside Country *C*. Furthermore, it collapses even if we assume that the terms of trade among the members of the *CU* remain unchanged as a result of the formation of the *CU*. (In practice, there is very little chance that the terms of trade will remain constant. However, we shall examine this case because it occurs in parts of the literature,[8] and also because there is some confusion over intraunion terms of trade.)[9]

---

sustain the demand for labor and reduce short-run unemployment and other dislocation costs associated with a change in commercial policy.

[6] Cooper and Massell's conclusion is based on demand and supply curves for a single good, the import of Country *A*. No analysis is made of *A*'s exports to *B*.

[7] These implicit assumptions may be found in Figure 1 and Table 1 of the Berglas article. In his Figure 1, Berglas has outside Country *C* importing only one good (commodity 2). The price of that good in Country *C* is shown in his Table 1 to be identical to its price P_2 in exporting Country *A*. This can be so only if no tariffs or transportation costs are added to the price of commodity 2 as it goes from *A* to *C*. (More generally, his Table 1 involves the assumption that there are no transportation costs on any trade.)

[8] For example, Berglas makes such an assumption; or, more precisely, he assumes that a country is committed to compensate a partner for any adverse change in its bilateral terms of trade.

[9] Most notably, Krauss in his survey (p. 417) states that Cooper and Massell assume that the home Country *A* is unable to affect its terms of trade because the partner *B* and third Country *C* are large. This conclusion is incorrect; a *CU* is *especially* likely to lead to an improvement in the terms of trade if the partner is a big country. See our point 4 which will be explained later

4) When a *CU* is being established, the terms of trade is a slippery concept; we should be careful to state propositions about terms of trade precisely. For example, the assumption that *A* is very small, and is faced by a large *B* and a large *C*, does not mean that terms of trade can be ignored, since *B*'s agreement to cut tariffs will affect *A*'s terms of trade. Indeed, an important reason for *A* to want to get rid of *B*'s tariffs is to be able, for the first time, to trade at *B*'s domestic terms of trade.

5) The standard assumption, that *A* is very small compared to *C*, is not so reasonable as it seems at first glance; in particular, it is not nearly so reasonable in a many-good world as it seems in the common two- and three-good models of trade theory. In fact, no outside country or group of outside countries is likely to be predominant in the pricing of all goods.

One further preliminary point should be clarified. In attacking the case that *UTR* offers all the gains of a *CU* (except for terms of trade and economies of scale), we are not arguing that *UTR* never dominates a *CU*. That would obviously be going too far. (For example, many countries with high tariffs could improve efficiency by *UTR*; and for such a country it would be easy to imagine a heavily diverting potential *CU* that would reduce efficiency. Therefore, we should be able without difficulty to find examples of potential customs unions which are dominated by *UTR*.) What we do dispute is that a *general* case has been made that "...a more efficient allocation of resources could not be the reason why customs unions are formed..." (Krauss, p. 417).

I. A Preliminary Puzzle

Before we turn to our five main points, let us look at an example—quite different in its details and assumptions from the literature we criticize—which shows the implausibility of the argument that *UTR* will provide all the gains from a *CU*, provided economies of

scale and terms-of-trade effects are ignored. Consider a *CU* that would involve all the countries of the world except Nepal. Assume the special case where the *CU* would leave the terms of trade among members unchanged. For any member, such a *CU* would be essentially indistinguishable from worldwide free trade in the benefits it would provide. And any terms-of-trade effect with the third country (Nepal) would be trivial for the members of the *CU*. The *UTR* literature would have us believe that such a *CU* is no better than *UTR*. But surely there is something wrong here. For any member, this *CU* would offer essentially the same benefits as worldwide free trade, which in turn offers something that *UTR* doesn't: namely, the abolition of foreign tariffs. And the abolition of foreign tariffs is a clear and unambiguous advantage.[10] Somehow, somewhere, in coming to the wrong conclusion the *UTR* literature has made assumptions whose critical importance has gone unrecognized. Our task will be to explain the importance of these assumptions.

II. Reciprocal Gains from a Customs Union, with Terms of Trade Unchanged

In our example, with Nepal as outside Country *C*, we have eliminated the importance of terms-of-trade changes in a manner quite different from the *UTR* literature cited earlier. In order to bring our argument back toward the main body of *UTR* literature, we now make the more standard assumption: The *CU* partners live in a world in which outsider *C* is not small. Indeed, *C* is so large that its demand and supply functions appear

---

with Figure 4. (Actually, only Krauss, and not Cooper and Massell, made this error. Cooper and Massell assumed only that the third country is large, the partner is not.)

[10] Curiously, the comparison of *UTR* and *CU* led Johnson to argue that *multilateral* tariff reduction is no better than *UTR*. This argument of Johnson is considered in the final section of this paper. (On the face of it, Johnson's focus on the burden of the home tariff to the exclusion of foreign tariffs is puzzling. As Abba Lerner demonstrated, a 10 percent across-the-board import tariff is equivalent in equilibrium to an across-the-board export levy of the same height. But this in turn is equivalent to an across-the-board foreign levy on our exports, with one notable exception: the foreign government rather than the home government gets the revenue. Thus, there is a presumption that foreign tariffs create a greater burden than home tariffs of the same height.)

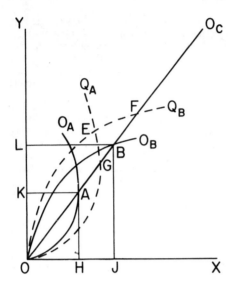

FIGURE 1. LARGE COUNTRY HAS NO TARIFFS
OR TRANSPORTATION COSTS

perfectly horizontal to CU members A and B. In a two-commodity general equilibrium framework, C's offer curve is a perfectly straight line.

In Figure 1, we derive the principal conclusion in the UTR literature (namely, that a CU offers nothing—apart from terms-of-trade improvements and economies of scale —that cannot be obtained through UTR).[11] We begin with the situation where C has no tariffs (although A and B do), and transportation costs between C and CU members are ignored. Not surprisingly, the offer curve of Country C, O_C has a dominant effect on international prices; A and B can trade any amount they like with C without affecting

[11] In this paper, we use offer curves to explain our case. In the UTR literature, the standard analytic tool has been single product demand and supply functions, with welfare triangles being the center of attention. Thus, there is some danger that, in using a different theoretical framework, we are writing at cross purposes to the other authors. To make clear how our points fit into the theoretical framework of the earlier articles, we elsewhere (1980) review the literature, explain in more detail how the authors fall into the traps we allege, and repeat our arguments with single product diagrams.

the relative prices given by the slope of C's offer curve. Prior to the establishment of the CU, the offer curves of A and B are O_A and O_B, respectively. Country A trades at point A, exporting OH of good X in exchange for OK of Y, and Country B trades at B, exporting OL of good Y in exchange for OJ of X.

Now suppose that a CU is formed between A and B, with a prohibitive common tariff on imports from C. Their offer curves, as seen by the CU partner, will move to the dashed curves Q_A and Q_B. With the prohibitive external tariff, no trade will take place with Country C, and equilibrium between A and B will occur at point E.

From the point of view of Country A, its move from A to E represents an improvement. Moreover, E is better than Country A can do by unilaterally eliminating its tariff and thus moving to G. But B could do better by a simple unilateral elimination of its tariffs, moving to point F. While Country A is better off at E (with a CU) than at G (with unilateral free trade), it has the problem (noted by Berglas) of persuading B to join the CU. If, in order to induce B to join, A has to compensate B for the amount by which E is inferior to F, then Country A would be better off to move unilaterally to reduce tariffs. (With standard assumptions, it can be shown that Country B's loss at E compared to F is greater than the amount by which Country A prefers E over G.) UTR dominates a CU. Indeed, within this framework, each partner should move all the way to unilateral free trade.[12]

(The country against which the terms of trade shift as a result of CU—Country B in our illustration—may be better or worse off as a result of a CU (at E) as compared to original point B, depending on the shapes and positions of the offer curves. But, in either case, it will be better off with a unilateral elimination of tariffs and a move to F than it would be with a customs union at E. Furthermore, in no case will Country A be able to "bribe" B to join a CU without itself ending at a position inferior to that obtainable through UTR.)

[12] Thus, this offer-curve framework, like Cooper and Massell's single product analysis (1965b, p. 747), leaves the puzzle of why countries have tariffs in the first place.

The main feature of this *UTR* argument is that *C* is freezing the world terms of trade at the slope of O_C: *C* will buy or sell unlimited quantities of *X* or *Y* at the relative price shown by its offer curve. Consequently, *A* and *B* have nothing to gain collectively by trading with each other rather than with *C*. Prior to the *CU*, it is a matter of indifference to Country *B* whether it conducts *OA* amount of trade with Country *A* and the remaining *AB* with Country *C*, or whether its total trade of *OB* is with Country *C*. And a *CU* is not collectively beneficial for *A* and *B*, compared to nondiscriminatory tariff removal and trade with *C*; while one country (*A*) will prefer a *CU*, the other (*B*) will even more strongly prefer trade with *C*. (In the special case where *E* falls on O_C, there is no difference between the outcome with a *CU* and that with unilateral moves to free trade by Countries *A* and *B*.)

The question is: In the real world, do prospective members of a *CU* have anything to offer one another that is not readily available from the outside world? The answer is yes. But what? Consider the United Kingdom and Germany. What can they gain from trade with one another that they can't gain from trade with the United States? A partial answer: they may *each* be in a position to offer the other a better price than the other could get by trading with the United States. How can that be? Because, in trading (for example) steel for coal with one another, they don't have to pay the costs of transportation to and from the United States, nor do they have to pay *U.S.* tariffs. In other words, by trading with each other, they can both benefit by sharing their net saving on transportation costs and *U.S.* tariffs.[13] A major problem, therefore, with the *UTR* literature is that it is based on the assumption that outsider *C* is not only large but it has no transportation costs nor tariffs. As a consequence, this literature has missed the important way in which a *CU* can provide mutual benefit to its members.

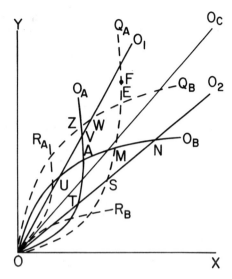

FIGURE 2. LARGE COUNTRY HAS TARIFFS
AND TRANSPORTATION COSTS

The case where *C* has transportation costs and tariffs is shown in Figure 2. With this figure, we illustrate the point at issue; that is, the possibility that a *CU* can provide gains not possible through *UTR*. With the introduction of *C*'s transportation costs and tariffs, Country *C* now presents not one, but rather two, offer curves. While the relative prices within *C* remain at the slope of O_C, the offer curve of *C* as seen by *A* and *B* will be either O_1 (if *A* or *B* purchase *X* by exporting *Y*) or O_2 (if *A* or *B* purchase *Y* by exporting *X*).

Thus, *C*'s transportation costs and tariffs drive a wedge between *C*'s offer curves (just as they drive a gap between the domestic and world prices in a simple demand/supply model). If this wedge—defined by the angle between O_1 and O_2—is wide enough, so that *A* and *B* trade within it both before (at *A*) and after the *CU* (at *E*),[14] it is as though

---

[13] *Net* saving on transportation costs; that is, the saving from transportation costs to the extent that they are lower between the U.K. and Germany than they are between Europe and America.

[14] The question may arise as to why, prior to the *CU*, Country *A* would be satisfied with point *A*, and not try to pick preferred point *V* by trading with Country *C*. The answer is that point *V* is not an option open to Country *A*. Point *V* is on the offer curve O_1 where

Country C did not exist. Its overwhelming dominance over A and B's trade disappears. With C "out of the picture," the question of whether the rest of the world (i.e., countries A and B) should form a CU reduces to the standard two-country free-trade question. Thus, in this case a CU can easily be shown to be beneficial under standard assumptions; both countries have a higher welfare at E than A. Moreover, for each country, a CU dominates unilateral free trade: A has higher welfare at E than M, while B is better off at E than W.[15]

(We ignore transportation costs between Countries A and B. Adding them unnecessarily complicates the analysis without altering the conclusions—so long as the CU is made up of geographically close members, with internal transportation costs less than those with third countries.)

This example resolves two puzzles. First, how can the contention of UTR writers—that UTR is always at least as good as a CU—be correct if C has prohibitive tariffs, so that trade with C is not even an option for A and B? The answer is that the UTR contention is incorrect; C's prohibitive tariffs open up a sufficiently wide wedge between O_1 and O_2 to drive C out of the picture, as in Figure 2, thus leaving a CU as the preferred policy. The second is the Nepal paradox. Nepal is so small that its offer curves are indistinguishable from the origin; curves O_1 and O_2 in such a diagram don't appear. Once again, in choosing between A and E, the two CU

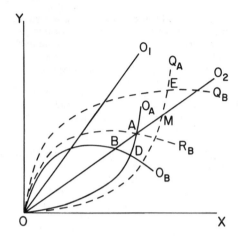

FIGURE 3. GAINS IN SPITE OF TRADE DIVERSION

members face the standard free-trade question.

A. *Gains with Trade Diversion*

Figure 2 presents an example of trade creation, where CU benefits are relatively easy to show. (An even simpler example would be the case where preunion tariffs of Countries A and B were high enough to completely prevent trade in these products, as shown by offer curves R_A and R_B.) However, our main point—that a CU may provide gains not possible through UTR—is valid also in the more complicated case of trade diversion (where diversion is defined simply as the shifting of the source of supply from outside Country C to partner B). This is shown with Figure 3.

Consider first the situation prior to a CU. Country A is such a large supplier of X that, if there were only bilateral trade with B, trade would take place at D. However, this price is lower than Country A can get from C; A therefore carries on some trade with C, at the after-transportation, after-tariff relative prices shown by the slope of O_2. Continuing our simplifying assumption that there are no transportation costs between countries A and B, we note that Country B chooses to trade with A at the relative set of

---

Country C exports X and imports Y. But Country A wants to export X and import Y. Because of tariffs and transportation costs, Country C is willing to import X and export Y only at a relatively high price for Y; that is, only at the relative prices given by offer curve O_2. Thus, in trading with C, Country A would end up at T, not V, and point A is clearly better for it than point T. Similarly, if Country B trades with C, it will end up at U, not N; and A is clearly preferred to U. Thus, Countries A and B choose trade with each other at point A, rather than trade with Country C at points T and U, respectively.

[15] If Country A unilaterally eliminates its tariffs, it still trades with Country B; its equilibrium with B (which still has tariffs) is at point M, and this is preferable to the point (S) that it could pick in trade with Country C. However, if Country B unilaterally removes tariffs, it will trade with C, since point W dominates Z.

prices which A offers in its trade with C; that is, the slope of O_2. Thus, prior to the CU, quantity OB of trade takes place between countries A and B, while BA takes place between countries A and C.

After the CU is established, trade takes place at point E. Countries A and B now trade only with one another; diversion of BA of trade has taken place.

The question is, how does each country compare the CU outcome with UTR? Consider first A's options. Unilaterally, A can improve its situation by eliminating tariffs, moving to point M. (The case here is the same as for unilateral free trade in Figure 1.) Clearly, for Country A, point E is better than UTR point M; a CU dominates UTR.

For Country B, unilateral gains are possible by a partial tariff cut which rotates its offer curve to R_B and increases its trade by BA.[16] Through negotiation of a CU and thereby reciprocal tariff elimination with Country A, Country B can achieve a further move from point A to E. We cannot be certain that E is superior to UTR point A from Country B's viewpoint: M is better than A, but E may be either superior or inferior to M, depending on the elasticity of Q_A. But our principal point holds: for Country B, point E *may* be superior to A (if Q_A is highly elastic and/or distance AM is large). Thus, for all members, a trade-diverting CU may represent a gain compared both to the original equilibrium, and to the options open under UTR.

Following the literature cited in our first paragraph, we have focused here on changes in welfare of the members of the CU. For these two countries, it does not matter whether the wedge between O_1 and O_2 is caused by tariffs or transportation costs. (More precisely, it does not matter provided that C's tariffs are fixed, and not open to negotiation.) However, if we consider world welfare, it does matter. A wedge caused by transportation costs involves the use of productive resources, and in this case a CU which improves the welfare of the member countries also improves world welfare. But insofar as the wedge reflects C's tariffs, a CU may mean a less efficient allocation of world resources, even though Countries A and B both gain. Specifically, the diversion of trade BA away from Country C in Figure 3 involves the loss of tariff revenues by C. In any worldwide welfare calculation, this loss must be weighed against the gains of the member countries.

Several loose ends remain to be tied up: the complications raised by the existence of more than one outside Country C; the existence of more than two goods; and ambiguities and confusions regarding the terms of trade.

III. Many Outside Countries

If A and B are trading with C, and C is a single large country, its tariffs are borne by A and B; the prices at which A or B can sell to C are reduced by the full amount of C's tariffs, and the full amount of C's tariffs (together with transportation costs) shows up in the gaps between O_C and O_1 and between O_C and O_2. In a more realistic case, where there are many outside countries, the situation is more complex, with the tariffs of outside countries falling partly on domestic consumers and partly on trading partners. In this case only part of an outside country's tariffs show up in the wedge in Figure 2. Indeed, it is conceivable that, if there are many outside countries operating in a highly competitive international marketplace, the tariffs of each of these countries will fall completely on their own consumers, and will have no effect on international prices at all. (This seems to be the implicit assumption of much of the literature.) But even in this case, there is a wedge because of transportation costs to and from outside countries; or, more precisely, because of higher transportation costs with outside countries than between members of the CU.

Our analysis of this wedge illustrates the obvious (but frequently ignored) reason why

---

[16]As we noted earlier in fn. 14, Country B can export good Y to Country C in exchange for X only at terms of trade O_1 because of C's tariffs and transportation costs. B can exchange at terms of trade O_2 only in trade with Country A. And, in the absence of reciprocal tariff cuts by Country A, the quantity of trade at such relative prices is limited to OA.

a *CU* usually includes geographically close countries, and excludes distant ones. Distance opens up the terms-of-trade wedge with outside countries, thus allowing mutually beneficial trade to take place between the members. Thus, this analysis raises doubts about the desirability from an efficiency viewpoint of geographically dispersed preferential systems such as the old British Commonwealth, where intermember transportation costs were generally no lower than transportation costs with third countries. (Of course, transportation costs are not the only thing to be considered when evaluating such an arrangement.)

IV. Many Goods

While offer curves provide a great advantage in drawing attention to general-equilibrium issues, they suffer from the severe limitation that only two goods can be considered. Logically, the offer curve analysis might be seen as involving N commodities in an N-dimensional space. But the problem is that a two-dimensional diagram like Figure 2 cannot be used to describe just two of the goods (X, Y) in an N-good world. In a two-good world, the exports of X will equal the imports of Y in equilibrium, but there is no presumption in an N-good world that the exports of any particular good, X, will equal any particular import, Y.

Faced with this problem, we depart from the formal model to offer some impressionistic conclusions regarding the plausibility, in a many-good world, of the common assumption that the terms of trade with the large third country are unaffected by A and B's tariffs. In a many-good world, even a huge country may not produce large amounts of every product. After all, even moderately sized single countries at present have substantial influence over the market of particular goods (Saudi Arabia in oil, Brazil in coffee, Canada in wheat). Thus, it seems implausible to see outside Country C as predominant in all commodities, and we must therefore question the rigid *UTR* assumption that C freezes the world terms of trade. For example, it is difficult to argue that the rest of the world could offer fixed terms of trade

to a South American *CU*. However, in order to directly address the *UTR* case on its own grounds, we have assumed in Figure 1 that C's offer curves do reflect fixed terms of trade, and we continue to make that assumption (together with the companion assumption that there are no economies of scale).

V. Further Terms of Trade Issues

We now consider how a *CU* may affect the terms of trade between members A and B. First, observe that we have drawn Figure 2 so that the terms of trade between the two members are the same at E as at point A. This illustrates our main contention: Each country (A and B) can obtain gains from a *CU* which it cannot achieve unilaterally, even if the *CU* does not change the terms of trade between members within the union, or between the union and outside Country C. Of course, as we noted earlier, there is little chance that the terms of trade between A and B will in fact remain exactly the same. But even where there is some deterioration in the terms of trade of one of the partners, that partner may achieve gains from a *CU* which are not available through *UTR*. This was just shown with Figure 3, in the comparison of points E and A from Country B's viewpoint. And it shows up even more strongly in Figure 2, if Q_B is redrawn to intersect Q_A at point F. Although the *CU* results in a deterioration in B's terms of trade as the equilibrium moves from A to F, it provides benefits not possible through unilateral free trade (for the same reason that E dominates W).

The second point is that, even if we assume that B is a large country, presenting Country A with an infinitely elastic offer curve, A can still have a terms of trade change and a gain from a *CU*. Indeed, A's gain will come precisely because its terms of trade improve as a result of B's tariff elimination, as illustrated in Figure 4.[17] The elimination of tariffs by B will cause its offer curve to rotate counterclockwise from O_B to Q_B, giving A better terms of trade and higher

---

[17]For more detail, see Lipsey (1970, pp. 88–89).

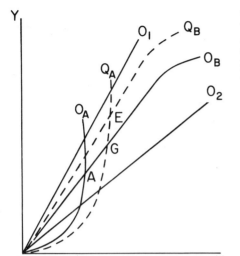

FIGURE 4. COUNTRY *B* MUCH LARGER THAN
COUNTRY *A*

real income at *CU* point *E* than at original point *A*. This equilibrium *E*—which represents a Pareto optimum (provided that Country *C*'s policy is taken as a given not subject to change) — is not achievable through unilateral tariff moves, since Country *B* has nothing to gain by removing its tariffs unilaterally. (They are borne by foreign rather than domestic consumers.) But it will be in the collective interest of countries *A* and *B* to get to point *E* by forming a *CU*; Country *A* will be able to compensate *B* for the establishment of a *CU* if *B* makes this a condition for agreement. Thus, optimum point *E* may be achievable through bilateral (customs union) bargaining.

Finally, we should be careful in fitting the terms of trade issue into the overall case for a *CU*. Returning to Figure 2, we note that, while the terms of trade do not change between the preunion point *A* and postunion point *E*, the terms of trade are not rigid; they can be changed by national action. For example, if, instead of forming a *CU*, Country *A* unilaterally eliminates its tariff, this will result in a deterioration in its terms of trade with the movement to point *M*. The

terms of trade gain for *A* when *B* also agrees to eliminate tariffs[18]—causing a move from *M* to *E*—will, in this special case, exactly offset the terms of trade loss from *A*'s initial move (and will leave each *CU* partner with a higher welfare than at initial point *A*).

The need for care in dealing with terms of trade issues becomes apparent if we consider a passage in which Johnson referred to the terms of trade in evaluating the relative merits of *UTR* and tariff bargaining:[19]

> ...the form and logic of bargaining for reciprocal tariff reductions [are] phenomena which are incomprehensible to the classical approach to tariff theory, according to which the source of gain is the replacement of domestic production by lower-cost imports, whereas *increased exports yield no gain* (*improved terms of trade apart*) to the exporting country, but a gain to the foreigner through the same replacement of domestic production by lower-cost im-

[18] Recognition of how a partner's tariff elimination may improve the terms of trade is important in disposing of another long-held belief—that when Country *A* diverts trade from outsider *C* to partner *B*, it necessarily incurs a terms-of-trade loss because it is no longer buying from the cheapest source *C*. (Lipsey and others have correctly pointed out that it will get a production and consumption gain, and the discussion has focused on how these two gains compare with the terms-of-trade loss.) However, there may not be a terms-of-trade loss at all; there may be a gain. Partner *B* may all along have been the cheapest free-trade source. But if this was the case, why wouldn't *A* have bought from *B* in the first place, before the *CU*? The answer is: *B*'s tariff may have prevented such trade. To illustrate, consider the following extreme case: Suppose *B* is the lowest-cost free-trade source, but *B* has imposed a prohibitive tariff that has precluded trade with all countries. Accordingly, *A* has been driven to trade with a less protectionist country, *C*. But if *A* and *B* form a *CU*, *A* will now trade with *B*, its lowest-cost free-trade source. (In less extreme cases, this same result may occur if *B*'s initial tariff is higher than *C*'s and sufficiently so to have choked off *A*'s natural initial trade with *B* and replaced it with trade with *C*.) In such circumstances, a failure to see beyond its own tariff could lead *A* erroneously to presume that *C* is its lowest-cost source. In this case, a *CU* is *A*'s means of diverting imports from a higher-cost source (outsider *C*) to its reciprocally cheapest source, *B*.

[19] Johnson applied this argument both to customs union bargaining and to multilateral, most-favored-nation bargaining.

ports. Since these gains are attainable by unilateral action, the classical approach provides no explanation of the necessity and nature of the bargaining process.   [p. 270, emphasis added]

A problem in interpreting this argument is an ambiguity in the passage we have italicized. If it is interpreted to mean that there can be no gain unless terms of trade change, then Johnson was wrong, as we have seen from our comparison of points A and E in Figure 2.

But there is a second possible interpretation of the italicized passage. Johnson may have been comparing points M and E in Figure 2 from Country A's viewpoint.[20] That is, he may have been saying that there is no gain to A from a reduction in B's tariff, if we ignore any change in the terms of trade associated with that reduction. But this interpretation makes Johnson's statement vacuous. *The* economic objective of A in negotiating foreign tariff cuts is to increase the demand for its exports. This involves a rotation in B's offer curve, and an improvement in A's terms of trade.[21] Johnson's argument that there is nothing, improved terms of trade apart, to be gained from foreign tariff cuts amounts to the proposition that there is nothing to be gained if the foreign offer curve is unaffected. But this means that the foreigners had no tariff to begin with. This is not a very enlightening line of argument. In brief, our plea for care in stating terms-of-trade issues is related to our plea that foreign tariffs not be implicitly assumed away in comparing *UTR* with a *CU*.

[20] This second interpretation is apparently what Johnson had in mind. See the later passage in Johnson where he argued that the case for a *CU* rather than *UTR* "...must rest on the possible terms-of-trade loss from unilateral tariff reduction and on the possible terms-of-trade gain for the union as a whole from discrimination against the outside world" (p. 280).

[21] There are two possible exceptions to the proposition that the rotation of B's offer curve will improve A's terms of trade: a) If there is a dominant third country, as explained with Figure 1. b) If Country A itself has a perfectly elastic offer curve. (In this instance, the *UTR* case is undercut, since A's tariffs fall on foreigners, not on domestic consumers.) The context of Johnson's passage makes it clear that he was not depending on either of these exceptions.

This paper demonstrates that *UTR* need not dominate a *CU* from an economic viewpoint. The proposition that *UTR* is dominant was based on an overemphasis on the cost-reducing effects of a country's own tariff reductions, and an underemphasis on the advantages in terms of the better access to foreign markets which follows the partner's tariff reductions. Once foreign tariffs are taken into account, there is no further reason for subscribing to the idea that *CU*s tend to be formed exclusively for noneconomic reasons. Such reasons may be present, and may be very important. But economists need not dismiss economic motives; in our view, the economic consequences of customs unions is a promising field for research.

REFERENCES

S. W. Arndt, "On Discriminatory vs. Non-preferential Tariff Policies," *Econ. J.*, Dec. 1968, *78*, 971–79.

———, "Customs Union and the Theory of Tariffs," *Amer. Econ. Rev.*, Mar. 1969, *59*, 108–18.

E. Berglas, "Preferential Trading Theory: The *n* Commodity Case," *J. Polit. Econ.*, Apr. 1979, *87*, 315–31.

C. A. Cooper and B. F. Massell, (1965a) "Towards a General Theory of Customs Unions for Developing Countries," *J. Polit. Econ.*, Oct. 1965, *73*, 461–76.

——— and ———, (1965b) "A New Look at Customs Union Theory," *Econ. J.*, Dec. 1965, *75*, 742–47.

W. M. Corden, "Economies of Scale and Customs Union Theory," *J. Polit. Econ.*, May 1972, *80*, 465–75.

Roma Dauphin, *The Impact of Free Trade in Canada*, Ottawa 1978.

F. Gehrels, "Customs Union from a Single-Country Viewpoint," *Rev. Econ. Stud.*, No. 1, 1956, *24*, 61–64.

H. G. Johnson, "An Economic Theory of Protectionism, Tariff Bargaining and the Formation of Customs Unions," *J. Polit. Econ.*, June 1965, *73*, 256–83.

M. B. Krauss, "Recent Developments in Customs Union Theory: An Interpretive Survey," *J. Econ. Lit.*, June 1972, *10*, 413–36.

A. P. Lerner, "The Symmetry between Import

and Export Taxes," *Economica*, Aug. 1936, 3, 306–13.

Richard G. Lipsey, "The Theory of Customs Unions: Trade Diversion and Welfare," *Economica*, Feb. 1957, *24*, 40–46.

_____, *The Theory of Customs Unions: A General Equilibrium Analysis*, London 1970.

James E. Meade, *The Theory of Customs Unions*, Amsterdam 1955.

Peter Robson, *The Economics of International Integration*, London 1980.

Jacob Viner, *The Customs Union Issue*, New York 1950.

John Williamson, "Trade and Economic Growth," in J. Pinder, ed., *The Economics of Europe*, London 1971.

Ronald J. Wonnacott and Paul Wonnacott, *Free Trade between the United States and Canada: The Potential Economic Effects*, Cambridge, Mass. 1967.

_____ and _____, "Is Unilateral Tariff Reduction Preferable to a Customs Union? The Curious Case of the Missing Foreign Tariffs; or, Beware of the Large Country Assumption," work. paper 80-37, Dept. of Econ. and Bur. Bus. Econ. Res., Univ. Maryland 1980.

[14]

Regional Science and Urban Economics 23 (1993) 355–367. North-Holland

Integration in goods and factors
The role of flows and revenue

Carsten Kowalczyk*

Department of Economics, Dartmouth College, Hanover, NH 03755, USA and National Bureau of Economic Research, Cambridge, MA 02138, USA

Received September 1992

This paper compares integration when trade and factor flows are impeded by revenue-generating policies to integration when trade impediments do not generate revenue. The paper argues that in the latter case large pre-integration trade and factor flows have an additional effect of promoting integration besides the conventional integration-impeding effect. The paper introduces the concepts of expanding and consolidating trading clubs, and it concludes by characterizing the optimal international integration strategy for a small country.

1. Introduction

The year 1992 will be remembered as a mixed year by those envisioning the European Economic Community (EEC) as one day becoming a United States of Europe. On the one hand, the year has been associated with the completion of the internal market – the much-heralded 'Europe 1992'. On the other hand, small Denmark said 'No' to the Maastricht agreement in a June referendum. With the self-imposed requirement by the EEC that the proposal to form a political union and establish a common currency would be void if any member rejected it, the EEC likely will go into 1993 with its process of political and monetary integration in disarray.

This paper addresses two theoretical issues motivated by the completion of the internal market, and by the case of a small country wielding political power. Comparing Europe 1992 with another recent integration effort between industrialized countries – the free trade agreement between Canada and the United States – the paper discusses the welfare calculus of integration when trade impediments raise tax revenue versus when they do not. The Danish referendum, on the other hand, raises the broader question

Correspondence to: Carsten Kowalczyk, Department of Economics, Dartmouth College, Hanover, NH 03755, USA.

*I am grateful to an anonymous referee for comments. Financial support from a Mellon Urban and Regional Studies Research Grant through the Nelson A. Rockefeller Center, and from the Haney and Rockefeller Funds to Dartmouth College is acknowledged with thanks.

of what a small country's aspirations should be in a world of preferential arrangements. This paper discusses which preferential policy strategy the small country should pursue when international trading clubs can be formed.

Hopes have been high that EC 1992 will bestow substantial welfare gains on the members, with estimates ranging from Cecchini's (1988) 2.5%–6.5% to Baldwin's (1989) more than 30%.[1] Expectations were never as high for the Canada–U.S. agreement where Hamilton and Whalley (1985) came in at the low end with an estimated 0.7% increase in Canadian income and Cox and Harris (1986) at the high end with 8.9%.[2] While the Canada–U.S. free trade agreement and Europe 1992 are similar in that pre-integration trade flows between the partners are large compared with trade with non-partners, the two integration efforts are dissimilar in one important respect: the Canada–U.S. agreement eliminates tariffs; Europe 1992, in an environment of no intra-EC tariffs, eliminates trade barriers which do not generate any revenue.

This paper demonstrates that the welfare calculus for the two situations, even abstracting from scale economies and imperfect competition, are quite different. In particular, the paper shows that the Canada–U.S. agreement took place in spite of their large mutual trade, while Europe 1992 takes place because of the members' large mutual trade. Defining as an *expanding* trading arrangement one where the hope for higher collective welfare for the participants lies in more intra-club trade, and as a *consolidating* arrangement one where larger collective gains can be derived from existing trade flows, the paper argues that the Canada–U.S. free trade agreement is expanding while Europe 1992 is consolidating.

The Danish rejection of Maastricht raises a host of questions, among which are, what constitutes an optimal currency area, and what is the price a nation is willing to pay to maintain a relatively large degree of political sovereignty? This paper considers a slightly different question which, however, has relevance even outside of the more narrow EC debate: In a world of preferential trading arrangements involving goods and factors of production, which aspirations can a small country hold when preferential trading arrangements with large partners are an option? In Kowalczyk (1990) it was argued that the small country's final optimal policy is an array of free trade agreements. This paper extends this analysis from an environment where trade was in goods only to one where factors are internationally mobile as well.

Section 2 derives the welfare expression for a country that trades goods

---

[1]The higher estimates take into account effects from trade liberalization to capital accumulation and thus growth. Rivera-Batiz and Romer (1991), and Rivera-Batiz and Xie (1992) are two recent works on integration and growth.

[2]Yet it has been proposed, most recently by Whalley (1992), that the Canada–U.S. agreement has been a disappointment for Canada. Canadian export growth to the United States has been low, and by leaving out key industries and permitting restrictive domestic content rules, the agreement is more one of trade than one of free trade, Whalley argues.

and factors internationally and which levies trade taxes on both goods and factor flows. Section 3 discusses how initial trade and factor mobility help determine which countries would find it mutually beneficial to establish a preferential relationship. Referring to an important result in the theory of customs unions by Riezman (1979), the section discusses how the prominence of integration efforts between countries with large mutual trade is a puzzle; it also considers different ways in which the puzzle might be resolved. Section 4 establishes the welfare calculus for a country whose trade-impeding policies do not generate any revenue. Policy now operates through an implicit terms-of-trade loss relative to nature, the size of which depends on the size of the initial trade and factor flows, and on the extent to which policies distort domestic prices away from the prices ruling outside the nation's borders. The section compares also the case where policies generate revenue to the one where they do not, and it introduces the concepts of *expanding* and *consolidating* preferential arrangements. Section 5 considers the policy problem of a small country that trades with large partners. It argues that the small country should seek preferential arrangements with each of its large partners where each agreement would cover a limited number of goods and factors. Section 6 offers concluding remarks.

2. The welfare effects from trade in goods and factors

Consider a world where N goods, indexed by n, are produced by F factors of production, indexed by f, in some, possibly all, of K countries, indexed by k, where n, f, and k are positive integers. Assuming that each good is produced in perfect competition by price-taking firms under constant returns to scale, the value of production in country k can be expressed by the revenue function $g(p^k, v^k)$, where p^k is the N-component column vector of domestic goods prices, and v^k is the F-component column vector of factor inputs used in country k. Denoting by p^e the N-dimensional column vector of tariff-exclusive prices at which the country trades its goods internationally and assuming that tariffs and subsidies are *specific*,[3] and are given by the N-component column vector t^k, the vector of domestic prices in country k is given by[4]

$$p^k = p^e + t^k. \tag{1}$$

---

[3]Kowalczyk (1989) demonstrates that even in a world of perfect competition the distinction between *ad valorem* and *specific* rates is important since identical reforms can yield quite different results in the two environments.

[4]More generally, if international price discrimination takes place, then country k would face $(K-1) \times N$ prices at which it could trade internationally. Country k could then even find itself importing from several countries at different tariff-exclusive prices if it were rationed in one or more of its markets. Section 6 of this paper discusses a situation where a small country trades exclusively with large ones and where the latter do not impose any rationing.

If there is international mobility of factors of production, then the vector of factor inputs in any given nation k, v^k, generally differs from its endowment of factors of production, denoted by the F-component column vector, v_0^k. The difference defines the F-dimensional column vector, z^k, where a positive value of a component, z_f^k, defines immigration of a factor f, while a negative entry corresponds to emigration of the factor,

$$v^k = v_0^k + z^k. \tag{2}$$

By analogy to the treatment of goods prices, the F-dimensional column vector, r^k, defines the domestic factor prices in country k, while r^e is a vector of the same dimension whose entries define the corresponding no-tax or no-subsidy returns. Any difference between these two vectors of factor prices is due to country k levying taxes or subsidies on earnings of foreign factors at work in country k or on earnings of domestic factors at work abroad. These taxes and subsidies are assumed to be *specific* and to be given by the F-component vector, q^k, where

$$r^k = r^e + q^k. \tag{3}$$

For a factor f, which migrates to country k, a positive value of q_f^k corresponds to a tax, while a negative value of q_f^k is a subsidy. On the other hand, for a factor f originating in country k but working abroad, a positive value of q_f^k is a subsidy to moving abroad, while a negative entry defines an emigration tax.

Defining $e^k(p^k, u^k)$ to be the expenditure function, where u^k is the level of utility of the representative consumer in country k, and defining m^k to be the N-dimensional column vector of country k's net imports, the budget constraint for country k can be written as

$$e^k(p^k, u^k) = g^k(p^k, v^k) - (r^k - q^k)z^k + t^k m^k. \tag{4}$$

Eq. (4) states that spending equals the value of domestic production, $g^k(p^k, v^k)$, minus net remittances to abroad, $r^k z^k$, plus net revenue from taxes on factors and goods given by the inner products $q^k z^k$ and $t^k m^k$, respectively. Differentiating (4), and denoting by e_u^k the inverse of the marginal utility from income, yields a first expression for the change in national welfare:

$$e_u^k du^k = -m^k dp^k + d(t^k m^k) - z^k dr^k + d(q^k z^k). \tag{5}$$

The first term states the change in *consumers'* and *producers' surplus* from a change in domestic goods prices, while the third term has the equivalent interpretation for a change in domestic factor prices. The second and fourth terms state that national welfare increases to the extent that *tariff and tax revenues* increase.

Let the change in welfare, $e_u^k \, du^k$, be denoted by $d\eta^k$. Further differentiation of (5) with respect to tax and tariff rates, and with respect to prices exclusive of taxes and tariffs, yields

$$d\eta^k = -m^k \, dp^e + (p^k - p^e) \, dm^k - z^k \, dr^e + (r^k - r^e) \, dz^k, \tag{6}$$

which gives the change in welfare as the sum of two *terms-of-trade* effects, expressed by the inner products $(-m^k \, dp^e)$ and $(-z^k \, dr^e)$, and two *volume-of-trade* effects, given by the inner products $(p^k - p^e) \, dm^k$ and $(r^k - r^e) \, dz^k$.

The expression reveals that improved terms of trade, whether with respect to goods or factors, will tend to benefit a nation. It states also that welfare increases to the extent that a country obtains more of a taxed good or factor.[5] When tariffs and taxes are arbitrary, however, there is room for apparently paradoxical welfare outcomes due to the interaction between terms. As discussed by, among others, Woodland (1982), a terms-of-trade improvement could induce a change in the volume of trade such that the net effect on welfare is negative. As the tariff-exclusive price of a low-tariff imported good falls, consumers might substitute away from other imports ridden with higher tariffs to such an extent that the net volume-of-trade effect would be negative and so large as to more than offset the welfare contribution from the positive terms-of-trade effect.[6,7]

3. Initial trade flows and preferential trade

Which countries would find a preferential arrangement mutually beneficial? Both the Canada–U.S. free trade agreement and the creation of a unified market in Europe between the members of the EEC suggest that the answer should be simple: countries that initially trade much with each other.

Canada is the United States' largest export market accounting for about 22% of total U.S. exports, and it is second only to Japan as a supplier to the United States by accounting for about 18% of U.S. imports.[8] From the Canadian side the situation is even more lopsided: a remarkable 74% of Canadian exports go to the United States, and 65% of its imports come from

---

[5]See, for example, Ohyama (1972), who derived the analogous expression for discrete policy changes. See also Wooton (1988).

[6]This mechanism resembles the one discussed by Gehrels (1956) and Lipsey (1957) when they pointed out that Viner's (1950) trade diversion effect had the potential to raise rather than lower welfare. In their example the welfare effect from the terms-of-trade loss from switching to a more expensive supplier of imports is more than offset by the positive welfare contribution from the larger volume of imports. See Kowalczyk (1990) for further discussion.

[7]In a slightly different vein, Grossman (1984) has shown, in a two-country model, that liberalization of factor flows can be harmful even for a nation that adjusts in optimal fashion its vector of trade taxes.

[8]See the United Nations (1991).

there.[9] EC 1992 likewise takes place between nations with large mutual trade. For example, about half of the U.K.'s, Germany's, and Denmark's exports and imports are with other members of the EEC, while about 60% of France's trade is within the EEC.

Somewhat surprisingly, the theory of customs unions does not predict that unions form between countries that trade much with each other. In particular, Riezman (1979) has stressed that if coalition partners do not engage in intra-union income transfers, then a large pre-club intra-club volume of trade could hinder rather than promote a preferential trade arrangement. From expression (6), the welfare expression for k involves, among other terms, $-m^{kj} dp^e$, where m^{kj} is the pre-club trade between two potential partners, k and j. The term captures the effect on k's welfare from any change in the tariff-exclusive prices at which it trades with j. Similarly, country j has, in its welfare expression, a term, $-m^{jk} dp^e$, which gives the contribution to its welfare from any price change in its trade with k. The two terms are of the same size but of opposite sign. Riezman's result follows, since the larger are the entries of m^{kj}, the more likely it is that the party suffering a loss through this term, say country k, will not be willing to join in a club with country j.[10]

A number of factors could counter this effect. If, for example, much of the trade between k and j is intra-industry, then there are likely large flows of similar goods going in both directions and even large changes in the tariff-exclusive prices might have only small effects on the countries' terms of trade as any country's import and export prices would change in the same direction. The terms-of-trade effect would be smaller the closer to being balanced is the partners' intra-industry trade.[11] Another, potentially off-setting effect, lies in the possibility that the preferential arrangement causes the members' extra-union terms of trade to improve.[12] The remaining possibilities for welfare improvement lie in the volume-of-trade effects, both intra- and extra-union. If initial tariffs are non-discriminatory the volume-of-

[9]With the proposal to expand the agreement to include Mexico it is interesting to consider Mexico's trade: Mexico is as biased towards the United States as is Canada with 70% of both exports and imports going to and coming from there; Mexico is also the United States' third largest trading partner: 6–7% of U.S. imports and exports are with Mexico, and migration is substantial. However, trade between Mexico and Canada is minuscule: less than 2% of both Mexico's imports and exports are with Canada, and less than 1% of Canada's trade in either direction is with Mexico. [Again, the year is 1989, and the source the United Nations (1991).]

[10]A number of already existing preferential arrangements are between countries with little mutual trade. See, for example, Fieleke (1992) and Foroutan (1992) for listings of existing arrangements.

[11]As discussed in Kowalczyk and Wonnacott (1992), integration efforts that are successful for reasons other than through obtaining better terms of trade relative to non-club countries will tend to raise rather than lower the club members' demand for extra-club products and thus bestow upon non-members a terms-of-trade improvement if the club is large in world markets.

[12]Such a union would, of course, have the unattractive feature of being harmful to non-union trading partners.

trade contribution to welfare will tend to be larger the larger are the initial tariffs and the larger are the increases in trade flows. If initial tariffs are discriminatory, however, then two cases need to be considered. If the integration leads to lower extra-club trade at the initial world market prices, then a low initial extra-union tariff and a low elasticity of response of extra-club trade is desirable. If, on the other hand, the integration leads to more extra-club trade at initial world market prices, then a high extra-union tariff and a high elasticity of response of extra-club trade is desirable.[13] (The welfare effect from increased intra-club trade would be larger in both cases, the higher are initial intra-club tariffs and the more elastic is the response in intra-club trade.)[14]

While similar results hold for factors when they are viewed in isolation, an additional consideration is raised by the interaction between factor and goods flows. As tariffs change, factors relocate. Terms-of-trade effects aside, both with respect to goods and factors, the preferential reduction in tariffs causes an outflow of the factor used intensively in import-competing production. This raises imports, thus bestowing an extra increase in welfare through the volume of trade in goods. The contribution will tend to be larger the more responsive is production and thus goods trade to the relocation of factors of production.

We can summarize these findings as follows:

Proposition 1. Two countries are more likely to form a preferential trading arrangement in goods and factors (i) *the smaller is their initial mutual trade in goods and factors,* (ii) *the larger are their initial tariffs and taxes,* (iii) *the more price-elastic is volume of trade in goods and factors, and* (iv) *the more responsive are goods flows to factor flows.*

We now return to the suggestion that the Canada–U.S. free trade agreement has had only little positive effect on Canada. The environment in which the agreement was negotiated and implemented can reasonably be characterized by (a) substantial initial trade between Canada and the United States, (b) small initial tariffs on this trade,[15] and (c) relatively insignificant non-tariff barriers. The low U.S. tariff implies that any Canadian terms-of-trade gains from being able to trade at the domestic U.S. prices would be

---

[13]Kowalczyk and Wonnacott (1992) refer to the former as a *substitute* club and to the latter as a *complement* club.

[14]An interesting political economy case can be built for further integration between countries that already trade much with each other. Suppose it takes time for trade flows to adjust to a new trade policy regime, and that the adjustment is faster if exporters already have a presence in foreign markets. Then policy-makers with relatively high discount rates due to a desire to be re-elected would prefer to sign agreements with countries with which they already trade much.

[15]Deardorff and Stern (1986), for example, propose that the average U.S. tariff on manufactured products was about 5%, and that the average Canadian tariff was less than 8%.

quite small. The low Canadian tariff implies that an extremely large increase in Canada's volume of trade relative to the United States would be required to generate a significant gain in Canadian welfare. In the absence of such an increase in Canada's trade flows, its best hope for a significant welfare improvement from the agreement would be increased factor flows. To some extent this did occur as foreign firms used Canada as the location from which to get access to the Canada–U.S. market: direct foreign investment into Canada from sources other than the United States more than doubled between 1985 and 1990. Over the same period, the flow of investments from the United States into Canada stayed relatively flat.[16]

4. Non-tariff barriers

EC 1992 is an array of about 300 directives spanning such diverse areas as safety and product regulation, competition policy, and customs treatment of intra-EC trade. For the purpose of the present analysis we focus on two features of this integration effort:
● the elimination of border controls on trade;
● the elimination of restrictions on intra-union factor flows.

In contrast to the situation in North America, the restrictions on intra-EC trade generate no tariff revenue. Rather, they take the form of delays at borders or they raise costs of transportation and production by requiring extensive customs procedures or through requirements and standards.[17] The fact that the trade impediments do not generate revenue, changes the welfare calculus of reform as compared with the tariff case. Specifically, the second and fourth terms in expression (5) vanish and the change in country k's welfare becomes

$$d\eta^k = -m^k(dp^e + dt^k) - z^k(dr^e + dq^k). \tag{7}$$

The variables t^k and q^k are no longer tariff and tax rates, but now are costs of transacting between home and abroad. Thus t^k represents the difference between domestic prices in country k and the prices charged by foreign exporters or paid by foreign importers. These differences could be due, for example, to costs of waiting or costs of hiring staff to do the customs work. The variable q^k represents the per-unit loss in similar activities when factors of production cross the border of country k. The reduction or elimination of either type of impediment will tend to raise welfare for country k where the terms $(-m^k dt^k - z^k dq^k)$ can be interpreted as terms-of-trade

---

[16]See Whalley (1992).
[17]It has been estimated by the EC Commission that customs formalities raise consumer prices by about 1%. See Cecchini (1988).

effects of country k relative to nature. The elimination of these barriers reverses an earlier self-inflicted terms-of-trade loss. It follows from (7) that:

Proposition 2. A country should eliminate its non-tariff barriers if the net effect on its terms of trade relative to other trading partners and relative to nature implies a terms of trade improvement.

A comparison of expressions (6) and (7) shows that the effect on welfare from trade and factor flows, and from their changes, differs greatly between a regime of revenue-creating tariffs and taxes and a regime where no revenue is generated. In particular, when trade is impeded by non-revenue barriers, the volume-of-trade source of welfare change is absent. Instead, the initial trade and factor flows now play dual roles: they remain potentially obstructing to integration due to the effect discussed by Riezman (1979), but they now also define the trade on which the loss from non-tariff barriers is incurred. For the latter of these effects, the larger is this base trade volume the larger are the income gains from eliminating trade restrictions.

Definition. A preferential trading arrangement is said to be *expanding* if, for given extra-club trade flows and terms of trade, higher collective welfare of the participants is due to larger intra-member trade and factor flows.

Definition. A preferential trading arrangement is said to be *consolidating* if, for given extra-club trade flows and terms of trade, higher collective welfare of the participants can be obtained on the basis of existing trade and factor flows.

Assume the existence of lump-sum income transfers between partner countries k and j. Abstracting from changes in extra-club trade flows and in extra-club terms of trade, the change in their collective welfare, $d\mu$, from a change in tariffs and factor taxes is obtained by adding their respective welfare expressions from (6), which gives

$$d\mu = (p^k - p^j)\, dm^{kj} + (r^k - r^j)\, dz^{kj}, \tag{8}$$

where dm^{kj} is the change in intra-club goods trade and dz^{kj} the change in intra-club factor trade between countries k and j. The expression reveals that intra-club terms-of-trade effects vanish and that any remaining effect on collective welfare relies on goods and factors to relocate to where their valuation is higher.[18]

---

[18]See Kowalczyk (1990) for a discussion of the case where extra-club goods flows and extra-club terms of trade are not assumed fixed.

When policies do not generate revenue, on the other hand, collective welfare for the club members is obtained by adding (7) for j and k, which gives the following welfare expression for their union (again maintaining, for the sake of simplicity, the assumption that extra-club trade and factor flows as well as extra-club terms of trade do not change):

$$d\mu = -m^{kj}(dt^k - dt^j) - z^{kj}(dq^k - dq^j). \tag{9}$$

Here the source of the welfare increase lies solely in the initial trade and factor flows. To the extent the partners' domestic prices approach each other, collective welfare increases. The increase is larger the larger are the initial trade and factor flows. In contrast to expression (8), where revenue was generated, there is no effect from changes in goods and factor flows when no revenue is generated. The size of the welfare gain relies entirely on the size of the initial flows and the size of the initial distortions, where the latter determine by how much the wedges can be reduced.

Certainly, some of the studies of the likely effects from the Canada–U.S. agreement have stressed the expectation that the integration of the two nations' markets would lead to improved economies of scale, and thus to more trade. However, to the extent that they could be characterized as being competitive economies, the nature of the integration effort between Canada and the United States, two large trading partners, appears different from the nature of the 1992 integration effort between the EC members as they rely on different features of their bilateral trade and factor flows. Thus, within the context of the present model, the arrangements can be characterized as follows:

Proposition 3. The Canada–U.S. free trade agreement is an expanding arrangement. EC 1992 is a consolidating arrangement.

5. The small country

In the context of this paper's analysis of integration of goods and factor markets the situation of small Denmark blocking the Maastricht process raises the broader question of which policy strategy a welfare-maximizing small country could reasonably pursue. In standard tariff theory, all nations are assumed to trade in world markets. A large country is defined as one that is able to affect the prices ruling in these markets and it can affect, therefore, its own terms of trade. A small country cannot affect these prices and, it is believed, must therefore take as given its own terms of trade. However, as argued in Kowalczyk (1990), the equivalence between world market prices and terms of trade breaks down for the small country in a world of preferential trade since the small country now has the option of seeking preferential access to trading partners' domestic markets. To the extent the partners' markets are protected and thus their domestic prices differ from world market prices, the small country experiences a terms-of-trade effect from joining a preferential trading arrangement.

Definition. A country is said to be small if it cannot affect world market prices of goods or factors.

What constitutes the optimal trade policy for a small country that trades only with large ones can be derived from expression (6). If the most attractive prices are not offered by the same trading partner, small country k would like to sign free trade agreements in goods with some trading partners and free trade agreements in factors with others, where each bilateral agreement covers only the good(s) and factor(s) that are particularly cheap (for k's imports) or expensive (for k's exports) in the country with which the agreement is obtained.[19]

Proposition 4. In a world where many countries trade many goods and factors, a small country's first-best trade policy is the array of bilateral free trade agreements in goods and factors that allows it to obtain each imported good and factor at the lowest possible price.

Due to the earlier discussed possibility that a terms-of-trade improvement can be welfare reducing when initial tariffs and taxes are arbitrary, the small country might not want to sign into this array immediately. Thus second-best considerations could imply that it should pursue a path of reform which would take the form of a sequence of preferential agreements where it is quite possible, if indeed not likely, that the preferred source nation of imports of a particular good or factor would differ from stage to stage. However, assuming that preferential clubs do not raise their external rate of protection, the small country, in the limit, would prefer the array that for each imported good or factor offers the lowest price. The reason is that, as its tariffs fall, any welfare effect from a smaller volume of imports of substitute goods would tend to become smaller and hence the beneficial terms-of-trade effects would eventually dominate.[20]

[19]Denmark, Norway and Sweden eliminated all impediments to mobility of labor between the three nations in 1954. This Free Nordic Labor Market has remained in place even after the Danish decision, in 1972, to join the EEC.

[20]As argued in Kowalczyk (1990), one situation where a large country would be willing to extend such a privilege to a small partner is if the small country's political support is required to implement some reform deemed desirable by the large country. The requirement of unanimity within the EEC on certain issues, or an expressed desire that the GATT be truly global, would be examples of situations where small countries would possess such political power.

6. Conclusion

This paper has discussed some aspects of the EC's completion of the internal market through a comparison with the recent Canada–U.S. free trade agreement. It has been argued that when policies generate revenue, a main contribution to welfare comes from larger trade and factor flows between the partners, whereas when policies do not generate revenue, it is the initial trade and factor flows that largely determine the size of the welfare improvement. The paper has also discussed the small country's aspirations in an environment where preferential trade in goods and factors is possible. It was argued that the hope of obtaining better terms of trade through preferential arrangements implies that the small country's club strategy is non-trivial. It is a corollary that unilateral free trade is not the small country's optimal policy.

Many intra-national impediments to trade do not generate revenue but are costs of transactions. This paper highlights the difference between incentives to integrate internationally versus regionally. In the former case, initial trade and factor flows affect the size of the intra-club terms-of-trade effect, a contentious variable. In the latter environment, initial trade and factor flows are less contentious for two reasons. Lump-sum transfers of income take place within nations, hence a region that loses due to an intra-regional terms-of-trade worsening is better able to obtain compensation than if the loss were on the region's international trade. Secondly, large initial trade and factor flows would imply large benefits from eliminating non-tariff distortions.

A nation that is constrained in its ability to undertake reform therefore faces the question of whether to integrate internationally or intra-nationally. This paper suggests that reform of international trade policy is the route to follow if tariffs are high, whether at home or abroad, while domestic, regional integration could be expected to yield large payoffs if the national economy is already strongly integrated but important non-tariff impediments to regional trade remain.

References

Baldwin, Richard, 1989, The growth effects of 1992, Economic Policy 4, 248–281.
Cecchini, Paolo, 1988, The European challenge 1992 (Gower, Aldershot).
Cox, David and Richard G. Harris, 1986, A quantitative assessment of the economic impact on Canada of sectoral free trade with the United States, Canadian Journal of Economics 19, 377–394.
Deardorff, Alan V. and Robert M. Stern, 1986, The Michigan model of world production and trade (The MIT Press, Cambridge, MA).
Fieleke, Norman S., 1992, One trading world, or many: The issue of regional trading blocs, New England Economic Review, May/June, 3–20.
Foroutan, Faezeh, 1992, Regional integration in sub-Saharan Africa: Past experience and future prospects, Mimeo. Presented at World Bank/CEPR Conference on New Dimensions in Regional Integration, Washington, DC.

Gehrels, Franz, 1956, Customs union from a single-country viewpoint, Review of Economic Studies 24, 61–64.

Grossman, Gene M., 1984, The gains from international factor movements, Journal of International Economics 17, 73–83.

Hamilton, Bob and John Whalley, 1985, Geographically discriminatory trade arrangements, Review of Economics and Statistics 67, 446–455.

Kowalczyk, Carsten, 1989, Trade negotiations and world welfare, American Economic Review 79, 552–559.

Kowalczyk, Carsten, 1990, Welfare and customs unions, NBER working paper no. 3476.

Kowalczyk, Carsten and Ronald Wonnacott, 1992, Hubs and spokes, and free trade in the Americas, NBER working paper no. 4198.

Lipsey, Richard G., 1957, The theory of customs unions: Trade diversion and welfare, Economica 24, 40–46.

Ohyama, Michihiro, 1972, Trade and welfare in general equilibrium, Keio Economic Studies 9, 37–73.

Riezman, Raymond, 1979, A 3 × 3 model of customs unions, Journal of International Economics 37, 47–61.

Rivera-Batiz, Luis A. and Paul M. Romer, 1991, Economic integration and endogenous growth, Quarterly Journal of Economics 106, 531–555.

Rivera-Batiz, Luis A. and Danyang Xie, 1992, GATT, trade, and growth, American Economic Review 82, 422–427.

United Nations, 1991, 1989 international trade statistics yearbook (United Nations, New York).

Viner, Jacob, 1950, The customs union issue (Carnegie Endowment for International Peace, New York).

Whalley, John, 1992, Regional trade arrangements in North America: CUSTA and NAFTA, Mimeo. Presented at World Bank/CEPR Conference on New Dimensions in Regional Integration, Washington, DC.

Woodland, Alan, 1982, International trade and resource allocation (North-Holland, Amsterdam).

Wooton, Ian, 1988, Towards a common market: Factor mobility in a customs union, Canadian Journal of Economics 21, 525–538.

B
Integration and Union Welfare

[15]

The Economic Journal, **91** *(September* 1981*)*, 697–703
Printed in Great Britain

WELFARE EFFECTS IN CUSTOMS UNIONS

The literature on preferential-trading arrangements lacks a clear statement of the conditions which ensure a country can gain by joining a customs union. Thus the question of why customs unions are formed is left open.

Much of the formal work on customs unions has been confined to the study of a two-commodity world.[1] In the two-commodity model the trade pattern is necessarily asymmetrical, with one member country being isolated from the rest of the world and trading only with its partner; moreover, relations of complementarity in demand can arise only in a model with at least three commodities. This paper examines welfare effects in the three-commodity customs-union model introduced by Meade (1955) and extended by Lipsey (1970) and Vanek (1965, Appendix). Necessary and sufficient conditions for a preferential-trading arrangement to be (second-best) rational from the point of view of each participating country are derived. The model is extended to the many-commodity, many-country case.

Following Meade, the expression 'customs union' is taken to encompass a small mutual reduction in tariffs and the complete mutual elimination of tariffs, as well as every possibility in between.

I. THE MEADE–VANEK–LIPSEY MODEL

The assumptions made are exactly those of Vanek (1965, pp. 189–91) and Lipsey (1970, pp. 32–3).[2] There are three countries, A, B and C. A and B have linear production-possibility frontiers such that A specialises in producing commodity X and B specialises in producing commodity Y.[3] Both A and B import commodity Z from country C. Countries A and B are small enough so that world prices P_x^w, P_y^w, P_z^w are never affected by their actions; world prices are determined by country C. Before union, country A imposes a uniform *ad valorem* tariff $t_z > 0$ on all imports. A and B now form a union, lowering or possibly abolishing tariffs on trade with each other but retaining tariffs on trade with C (the rest of the world). Thus A's tariff on commodity Z remains at t_z while its tariff on Y is reduced to t_y. Post-union domestic prices in country A are

$$P_x^a = P_x^w \tag{1}$$

$$P_y^a = (1 + t_y)P_y^w \tag{2}$$

$$P_z^a = (1 + t_z)P_z^w. \tag{3}$$

It is assumed that there is no transhipment of commodity Z within the union;

---

[1] On the two-commodity, three-country model, see Kemp (1969).

[2] Other 3 × 3 customs-union models, differing from the Meade–Vanek–Lipsey model in, among other ways, the assumed pattern of trade among countries, have been developed by Corden (1976), Berglas (1979), Collier (1979) and Riezman (1979). These 3 × 3 models have been synthesised and generalised by Lloyd (1980).

[3] It is further assumed that the production-possibility frontiers have slopes such that the tariff changes in question are never large enough to cause any country's pattern of specialisation to change.

this amounts to assuming A and B have a common tariff on commodity Z. Tariff proceeds are returned to consumers in lump-sum fashion.

Consumers' tastes are such that community indifference curves exist, represented by a strictly quasi-concave utility function $U(X, Y, Z)$, the arguments of which are aggregate consumption in country A of the three commodities. Country A's decision is to choose t_y (which, by equation (2), is the same as choosing P_y^a) so as to maximise its utility subject to the constraints (1) and (3) and subject to the balance of payments constraint

$$P_x^w X + P_y^w Y + P_z^w Z = P_x^w S, \qquad (4)$$

where S is A's total output of its exportable commodity, which is constant because of the assumptions of a linear production-possibility frontier and specialisation.

Note that the solution to this problem yields a not higher, and possibly much lower, level of utility than the solution to the problem of maximising utility subject solely to the constraint (4) (because the latter problem has fewer constraints). The solution to the latter problem would have $t_z = t_y = 0$; that is, free trade. The decision to keep t_z strictly positive must be made on non-economic (or at least non-welfare-maximising) grounds. The second-best problem to be investigated in the next section is, given country A's decision to retain the tariff on trade with country C, when is it rational to form a customs union with country B?

II. THE EXPENDITURE FUNCTION

Traditionally, welfare effects in customs union problems have been described by means of trade creation and trade diversion. This leads to inconclusive results, because trade creation is not a necessary condition for welfare gain and trade diversion is not sufficient for welfare loss. We avoid this approach, and instead describe welfare effects using the duality properties of the consumers' maximisation problem.

The expenditure function $E(P_x^a, P_y^a, P_z^a, u)$ shows the minimum expenditure necessary at domestic prices to achieve a given level of utility u. E is, with respect to prices, non-decreasing, concave and continuous. Assume E is twice differentiable and write E_x for $\partial E/\partial P_x^a$, E_{xy} for $\partial^2 E/(\partial P_x^a \partial P_y^a)$, E_{xu} for $\partial^2 E/(\partial P_x^a \partial u)$, etc. The partial derivatives of E with respect to P_x^a, P_y^a, and P_z^a are the compensated (Hicksian) demand functions for X, Y, and Z respectively. Thus the balance of payments constraint (4) can be rewritten

$$P_x^w E_x + P_y^w E_y + P_z^w E_z = P_x^w S. \qquad (5)$$

Differentiate (5) totally with respect to country A's control variable, P_y^a.

$$P_x^w E_{xy} + P_x^w E_{xu} (du/dP_y^a) + P_y^w E_{yy} + P_y^w E_{yu} (du/dP_y^a)$$
$$+ P_z^w E_{zy} + P_z^w E_{zu} (du/dP_y^a) = 0. \qquad (6)$$

Demand functions are homogeneous of degree zero in all prices; thus, by Euler's theorem,

$$P_x^a E_{xy} + P_y^a E_{yy} + P_z^a E_{zy} = 0. \qquad (7)$$

Rearranging (7), and using (1), (2) and (3),

$$P_z^w E_{zy} = -[P_x^w E_{xy} + (1+t_y)P_y^w E_{yy}]/(1+t_z). \tag{8}$$

Substituting (8) in (6), and rearranging

$$\frac{du}{dP_y^a} = \frac{-[t_z P_x^w E_{xy} + (t_z - t_y)P_y^w E_{yy}]}{(1+t_z)(P_x^w E_{xu} + P_y^w E_{yu} + P_z^w E_{zu})}. \tag{9}$$

Expression (9) allows us to evaluate the effects on country A's welfare of the customs union.

The terms in the second bracket of the denominator of (9) can be written as $\partial(P_x^w X + P_y^w Y + P_z^w Z)/\partial u$, which is the rate of increase with respect to u of the minimum expenditure at world prices to achieve the level of utility u; this must be strictly positive and so the denominator is always strictly positive.

Consider now the numerator of expression (9). The term E_{yy} is the derivative with respect to P_y^a of the compensated demand for good Y. Since the compensated demand curve is downward sloping, this term is negative. The term E_{xy} is the derivative with respect to P_y^a of the compensated demand for good X; it is positive, zero or negative as commodity X is respectively a net (Hicksian) substitute, independent, or a net complement for commodity Y. Thus whether or not the customs union is beneficial is determined by the Hicksian substitution relations between the commodities.[1]

III. WELFARE EFFECTS

When is a customs union involving only small tariff changes beneficial? (This was the question posed by Meade, 1955.) Before union country A has the same tariff rate on both Y and Z. Putting $t_y = t_z$ in (9),

$$\frac{du}{dP_y^a} \gtreqless 0 \quad \text{as} \quad E_{xy} \gtreqless 0. \tag{10}$$

That is, a small reduction in the tariff on good Y from the pre-union situation increases country A's welfare if and only if commodity X is a net substitute for commodity Y.

Realistically, customs unions involve significant, not marginal, reductions in tariffs. Condition (9) can be solved for what Lipsey (1970, p. 36) called the 'second-best optimum tariff' on commodity Y given the fixed tariff t_z on commodity Z. Putting $du/dP_y^a = 0$ and rearranging,

$$t_z - t_y = \frac{-t_z P_x^w E_{xy}}{P_y^w E_{yy}}. \tag{11}$$

Thus

$$t_z \gtreqless t_y \quad \text{as} \quad E_{xy} \gtreqless 0. \tag{12}$$

---

[1] This is consistent with a result of Lloyd (1974), who showed that the Hicksian substitution relations are enough to characterise second-best policies for an open economy. Dixit (1975) used the expenditure function to derive results on second-best policies.

The second-best optimum tariff on Y is less than the fixed tariff on Z if and only if commodity X is a net substitute for commodity Y.[1] The country gains from the lowering of tariffs consequent on the formation of the customs union if and only if the domestically produced commodity is a net substitute for the commodity imported from the partner country. Note that this result is independent of the nature of commodity Z and is independent of such variables as the size of the tariff with the rest of the world and the relative volumes of trade with the partner and with the rest of the world.

Equation (11) can be solved for the ideal tariff on trade within the union. Usually this will yield a non-zero value of t_y. Given the distortion of the fixed tariff on Z, free trade within the union will usually not maximise welfare; a partial customs union is usually preferable to a complete customs union. (This point was made by Meade, 1955, p. 110, and Lipsey, 1970, p. 38.)[2] A necessary and sufficient condition can be given, however, for free trade within the union to be optimal. Solving equation (11) for t_y and using (1) and (2),

$$t_y = \frac{t_z(P_x^a E_{xy} + P_y^a E_{yy})}{P_y^a E_{yy} - t_z P_x^a E_{xy}}. \tag{13}$$

If the customs union is beneficial, then $E_{xy} > 0$. Then, since $E_{yy} < 0$, the denominator cannot be zero. The numerator, by (7), is equal to $- t_z P_z^a E_{zy}$. Thus $t_y = 0$ if and only if $E_{zy} = 0$. Free trade within the union is optimal if and only if the commodity imported from the partner country is neither a net complement nor a net substitute for the commodity imported from the rest of the world.

Note also that (13) implies that if Y is a net substitute for X and Y is a net complement of Z, t_y is negative; that is, country A should subsidise intra-union trade. If Y is a net substitute for Z and X is a net substitute for Y, country A's tariff on trade with country B should be greater than zero but less than the tariff on trade with the rest of the world.

So far the problem has been considered only from the point of view of country A. Country B's actions have not entered the analysis. What has been described above as the formation of a customs union could be interpreted instead as a unilateral tariff reduction by country A. The analysis, however, is completely symmetrical. Elementary calculus says $E_{xy} = E_{yx}$; that is, X is a net substitute for Y if and only if Y is a net substitute for X. Assume the utility functions in country A and country B are identical (or at least similar enough to preserve the property of two goods' being net substitutes). Then the condition which ensures that country A gains from a small reduction in its tariff on commodity Y, namely that X is a net substitute for Y, is identical to the condition which ensures that country B gains from a small reduction in its tariff on commodity X, namely that Y is a net substitute for X. Country A gains from the formation of a customs union with country B if and only if B also gains from it.

[1] This result is consistent with, but generalises and simplifies, the taxonomy of special cases listed by Lipsey (1970, pp. 36–8). Note that Lipsey (1970, p. 156, n. 7) pointed out that his results, as they stand, cannot be expressed in terms of complementarity and substitutability.

[2] As Wonnacott and Wonnacott (1979) pointed out, this goes against GATT rules, which prohibit bilateral agreements partially to reduce tariffs but allow agreements to reduce tariffs to zero.

This result contrasts with results on welfare effects in the two-commodity customs union model. In the only pattern of trade possible in the two-good model, one country, say B, is isolated from the rest of the world and trades only with its partner, A. Then, as Kemp (1969, pp. 31, 72) showed, the customs union benefits only country B and makes country A worse off (though B's gains may be large enough that B has the potential to compensate A for its losses and itself remain better off). This asymmetry of gains reflects the asymmetry of the trade pattern in the two-good model.

IV. THE MANY-COMMODITY, MANY-COUNTRY CASE

Continue to assume that there are only three countries. The model can be extended to cover the case of many commodities by interpreting the three countries' commodities X, Y, and Z as composite commodities. (This is valid as long as there is no change in the relative prices of the basic commodities which make up the composite commodities; that means that if, for example, country A reduces its tariffs on imports from country B, the percentage reduction must be the same for all imports from country B.) Thus commodity X, for example, is composed of n basic commodities $X_1, ..., X_n$ (these basic commodities being defined by country of origin as well as physical characteristics), with world prices $P_{x_1}^w, ..., P_{x_n}^w$, respectively, such that

$$X = X_1 + (P_{x_2}^w/P_{x_1}^w)X_2 + ... + (P_{x_n}^w/P_{x_1}^w)X_n \tag{14}$$

and the price of X, P_x^w, is $P_{x_1}^w$. The Xs represent compensated demands. Differentiating partially with respect to the domestic price of composite commodity Y, and recalling that $X = E_x$,

$$E_{xy} = \frac{\partial X_1}{\partial P_y^a} + \frac{P_{x_2}^w}{P_{x_1}^w}\frac{\partial X_2}{\partial P_y^a} + ... + \frac{P_{x_n}^w}{P_{x_1}^w}\frac{\partial X_n}{\partial P_y^a}. \tag{15}$$

Thus E_{xy}, the sign of which determines whether or not the customs union is beneficial, is the price-weighted sum of individual substitution terms.

Now consider a world of m small countries, each specialised in the production of a particular (composite) commodity. Country C in the above analysis can be thought of as being made up of $m-2$ such countries and commodity Z is the aggregate of their output. Countries A and B are the remaining two countries. The composite commodities satisfy the standard assumptions of consumer theory. A well-known result from consumer theory says that every commodity has at least one net substitute. Thus for each country A there is another country B with which A can advantageously form a customs union. More can be said than that, however. A theorem due to Mosenson and Dror (1972) says that any good is connected by a chain of net substitutes to any other good. Start with each country imposing a uniform tariff on all its imports. Suppose A's and B's commodities are net substitutes and each lowers its tariff on the other's commodity. Among the countries making up the rest of the world, there will be another country D such that D's commodity is a net substitute for B's. Put A in with the rest of the world and consider the pair B and D. B's tariff on the composite good from the rest of the world is lower than its tariff on D's good (since B's tariff on the rest of the world is a weighted average of the tariff on A and that on all the other countries except D, and the tariff on A has been lowered). D's tariffs are still uniform. Thus condition (12) indicates that B and D can both gain by mutually lowering tariffs. Now consider another net substitute pairing D and E. A similar process occurs. Incentives exist for a sequence of bilateral agreements mutually to reduce tariffs, until every country has lowered tariffs on trade with at least one other country. Depending on the particular pattern of substitution relations, this process may or may not end up with free trade. A sufficient condition for such a sequence of (individually rational) bilateral tariff reductions to lead to free trade is that every commodity is a net substitute for every other commodity. (The presence of net complements can, however, prevent convergence of this process to free trade because then some second-best optimal tariffs are negative.) Kemp and Wan (1976) obtained, by a different argument and in a more general model, a related result, namely that there is an incentive for customs unions to enlarge until the world is one large customs union, that is, free trade prevails. Their result, however, unlike this one, required the transfer of lump-sum compensatory payments between union members.

V. CONCLUSION

The three-commodity, three-country model of customs unions due to Lipsey, Meade and Vanek was examined. A country gains from the lowering of tariffs following the formation of a customs union if and only if the domestically produced commodity and the commodity imported from the partner country are net substitutes (regardless of the nature of the commodity imported from the rest of the world). Moreover, in such circumstances, the partner country is also better off as a result of the union. There should be free trade within the customs union if and only if the commodity imported from the partner is neither a net substitute nor a net complement for the commodity imported from the rest of the world. If the two commodities imported by a member country are net complements, the country should subsidise intra-union trade. The model extends to the case of many commodities, via the composite-commodity theorem. In a many-country world there will be incentives for countries to make a sequence of bilateral agreements mutually to reduce tariffs, until each country has reduced its tariffs on trade with at least one other country. If each commodity is a net substitute for every other commodity, there are incentives for this process of piecemeal tariff reductions to continue until there is world-wide free trade.

Finally, note that this model ignores other ways in which a customs union could create welfare gains for its members, such as by exploiting economies of scale or terms-of-trade effects, or by countering domestic distortions.[1]

University of Western Ontario, Canada   JOHN McMILLAN

University of Canterbury, New Zealand   EWEN McCANN

Date of receipt of final typescript: November 1980

[1] On the first question, see Corden (1972); on the second, Melvin (1969) and Riezman (1979); and on the third, Whalley (1979).

REFERENCES

Berglas, E. (1979). 'Preferential trading theory: the *n* commodity case.' *Journal of Political Economy*, vol. 87 (April), pp. 315–32.

Collier, P. (1979). 'The welfare effects of customs union: an anatomy.' ECONOMIC JOURNAL, vol. 89 (March), pp. 84–95.

Corden, W. M. (1972). 'Economies of scale and customs union theory.' *Journal of Political Economy*, vol. 80 (May/June), pp. 465–75.

—— (1976). 'Customs union theory and the nonuniformity of tariffs,' *Journal of International Economics*, vol. 6 (February), pp. 99–106.

Dixit, A. (1975). 'Welfare effects of tax and price changes.' *Journal of Public Economics*, vol. 4 (February), pp. 103–23.

Kemp, M. C. (1969). *A Contribution to the General Equilibrium Theory of Preferential Trading*. Amsterdam: North-Holland.

—— and Wan, H. Y. (1976). 'An elementary proposition concerning the formation of customs unions.' *Journal of International Economics*, vol. 6 (February), pp. 95–8.

Lipsey, R. G. (1970). *The Theory of Customs Unions: A General Equilibrium Analysis*. London: Weidenfeld and Nicolson.

Lloyd, P. J. (1974). 'A more general theory of price distortions in open economies.' *Journal of International Economics*, vol. 40 (November), pp. 365–86.

—— (1980). '3 × 3 theory of customs unions.' Seminar Paper no. 144, Institute for International Economic Studies, University of Stockholm.

Meade, J. E. (1955). *The Theory of Customs Unions*. Amsterdam: North-Holland.

Melvin, J. R. (1969). 'Comments on the theory of customs unions.' *Manchester School*, vol. 36 (June), pp. 161–8.

Mosenson, R. and Dror, E. (1972). 'A solution to the qualitative substitution problem in demand theory.' *Review of Economic Studies*, vol. 39 (October), pp. 433–41.

Riezman, R. (1979). 'A 3 × 3 model of customs unions.' *Journal of International Economics*, vol. 9 (August), pp. 341–54.

Vanek, J. (1965). *General Equilibrium of International Discrimination: The Case of Customs Unions*. Cambridge, Mass.: Harvard University Press.

Whalley, J. (1979). 'Uniform domestic tax rates, trade distortions, and economic integration.' *Journal of Public Economics*, vol. 11 (April), pp. 213–21.

Wonnacott, P. and Wonnacott, R. (1979). 'Is unilateral tariff reduction preferable to a customs union? The curious case of missing foreign tariffs: or, beware of the large country assumption.' Working Paper 79–24, Department of Economics, University of Maryland.

[16]

Review of Economic Studies (1991) **58**, 391–397
© 1991 The Review of Economic Studies Limited

0034-6527/91/00240391$02.00

Delegation Games in Customs Unions

KONSTANTINE GATSIOS

University of Cambridge and Athens School of Economics and Business

and

LARRY KARP

University of Southampton and University of California, Berkeley

First version received August 1989; final version accepted August 1990 (Eds.)

We study a model in which a customs union trades with countries which behave strategically. Provided that the members of the customs union are similar but not identical, we show that both in the case in which intra-union transfers are allowed as well as in the one in which they are not, one country may want to delegate authority for making union policy to its partner. The delegation decision depends on whether the policies used by union and non-union countries are strategic substitutes or complements, and on which union member is more "aggressive".

INTRODUCTION

One of the distinguishing characteristics of customs unions is that member-states agree to bind themselves to common policies on their trade with the rest of the world (ROW). The main point this paper wishes to deliver, is that in a customs union it might be in one union member's best interests to delegate authority to set the external policy to the other member.[1] We therefore argue that the old question as to the level at which the common trade policy instrument should be set, must now be qualified by the determination of the optimal negotiating agent.

To demonstrate these points we construct a model with three strategic agents: two union members and ROW. We assume that the union members have the choice of delegating authority to set the common external policy to a policy-maker (PM). Since delegation of authority means that the PM chooses a common policy which *maximises its own welfare*, our delegation result seems counter-intuitive. It might, instead, seem more reasonable that, in the presence of intra-union transfers, the common policy should be chosen so that it maximises union welfare[2] (see, for instance, Lipsey (1970)). If, on the other hand, side-payments within the union are not possible, it might seem that the union members would vie to become PM (see, for instance, Riezman (1985)).

In neither case is the conjecture necessarily correct. The reason for this is simply that so long as the policy-setting agents behave strategically (so that ROW policy is not constant) we cannot simply look at the union's policy in isolation, but must take into account the strategic response of ROW. Put differently, the analysis must focus on the Nash equilibria of the policy game. These equilibria themselves depend on the delegation

---

1. So far as we know, such a possibility of delegation was first discussed in Gatsios (1987).
2. Henceafter, we refer to the supra-national agent as the one whose objective is to maximise the joint welfare of the union.

decision. This explains why a union member may be better-off delegating to its partner, rather than simply promising to use the policy that its partner would select in equilibrium. In the absence of delegation such a promise does not constitute an equilibrium to the game between the union and ROW: the delegating country cannot *credibly* commit to using the policies that its partner would use.

The assumption that ROW behaves strategically is clearly critical to our results. If one thinks of the model as representing a confrontation between the EEC and the U.S. or Japan, strategic behaviour is very likely. It is also important that the union is able to make the delegation decision before confronting ROW in a game. This is reasonable, since the union and ROW cannot engage in a game until the union has been formed; the manner in which union policy is decided (e.g. delegation) is a principal element of the structure of the union. For reasons of exposition, we assume that the union and ROW play a non-cooperative game, but qualitatively similar results would arise if they played a cooperative game in which the threat point was affected by the delegation decision.

In the next section we present the basic model, explain the logic of delegation and illustrate the chief point with a partial equilibrium example. In the conclusion we suggest possible extensions of our results and future direction of research.

2. THE DELEGATION RESULTS

2.1. *The basic model*

The basic ideas underlying the delegation results can be illustrated in the following way.

Suppose that t and t^* are the policies chosen by the customs union and ROW, respectively. For example these variables may represent import tariffs. The reduced-form welfare of union member i is $W_i(t, t^*)$ for $i = 1, 2$, and the welfare in ROW is $W^*(t, t^*)$. If country i is designated to be the PM it chooses t to maximize W_i, taking t^* as given; i's best-response function is $t_i(t^*)$. If the two member countries are similar but not identical, their best-response functions are close but not identical. The best response function of ROW is $t^*(t)$. Figure 1 graphs the best-response functions t_1, t_2 and t^*.

There are two stable equilibria to the non-cooperative game between the union and ROW, A and B, depending on whether country 1 or 2 is the PM. The curve W_1^0 graphs the set of points that give country 1 the same welfare level as it obtains at point A. ROW's best response function must intersect W_1^0; otherwise country 1 would be a Stackelberg leader in the game against ROW. Therefore there is an interval on ROW's best-response function over which country 1's welfare is higher than at A. This is the interval AC in Figure 1. If country 2 is more aggressive than country 1, so that it has a higher best-response tariff for any t^* than its less aggressive partner, and if country 2 is similar to country 1, so that its best-response function lies close to t_1, then country 1 wants to delegate to country 2. This is the case illustrated by Figure 1. Clearly country 2's welfare is higher at B than at A, so country 2 wants to assume authority: there is harmony of interests within the union. There is conflict of interest between the union and ROW, as regards the delegation decision. ROW's welfare is lower at B than at A. If the union countries are dissimilar, so that, for example, t_2 intersects t^* to the right of C, there would be disagreement within the union concerning delegation. This is the sense in which harmony of interests concerning delegation requires that the union countries be similar. If the countries were identical, nothing would be gained by delegation, but neither would there be any dispute about the policy.

The same line of reasoning can be applied to show that, in the presence of intra-union transfers, joint welfare may be higher if authority is delegated to the more aggressive

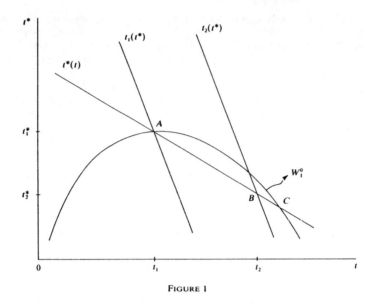

FIGURE 1

country than to a supra-national agent. This can occur because, for reasons which will become clear later, the best-reply function of the supra-national agent $\bar{t}(t^*)$ lies between t_1 and t_2. ·(It is not shown in order to avoid cluttering the figure.) The discussion above raises the central question of what determines the degree of aggression. The next section takes a step towards answering this question.

2.2. A partial equilibrium example

This section studies a simple partial equilibrium example, in which governments use trade policy to influence the behaviour of non-competitive firms. Our two objectives are to illustrate the techniques used to prove the possibility that delegation may be an equilibrium strategy and to demonstrate that the degree of aggression is negatively related to production costs so that the low cost producer will be chosen as PM.

We use the model studied by, amongst others, Brander and Spencer (1985), Dixit (1984) and Eaton and Grossman (1986). In both countries 1 and 2 there is a firm which produces for export to the third country, ROW. Firm i is the domestic firm in country i. Profits for firm i are

$$\pi_i(x_i, x_j; t, t^*) = [P(X) - (c_i + t + t^*)]x_i - F$$

where c_i is the constant unit cost in i, t is the export tax imposed by the union and t^* the import tariff imposed by ROW. By assumption the goods are perfect substitutes so price, $P(\cdot)$, depends only on aggregate supply, $X = x_1 + x_2$. The fixed cost, F, can be chosen to ensure that there is no entry into the industry.

We assume that firms play a non-cooperative quantity-setting game, taking t and t^* as given. The second-order condition for the maximization of firm i's profits is $\partial^2 \pi_i / \partial x_i^2 \equiv a_i = P''x_i + 2P' < 0$. We assume that $\partial^2 \pi / \partial x_i \partial x_j \equiv b_i = P''x_i + P' < 0$, so that the firms' best-response functions are downward sloping in the quantity space. Stability requires that

$\Delta \equiv a_1 a_2 - b_1 b_2 > 0$.[3] The comparative statics of the model imply $\partial x_i / \partial t = \partial x_i / \partial t^* = (a_j - b_i) / \Delta$. Although the sign of this is indeterminate, stability implies that aggregate production decreases with increases in t or t^*. Hereafter we shall assume that $\partial x_i / \partial t < 0$, $i = 1, 2$. This is certainly true in the case of linear demands and is used in order to simplify our exposition. It can be relaxed without altering the main results of the paper.

The solution to the game between firms provides the output levels chosen by them as functions of the export tax and import tariff, $\hat{x}_i = \hat{x}_i(t, t^*)$. These, in turn, induce the profit functions $\hat{\pi}_i(t, t^*)$, which are obtained by substituting the $\hat{x}$'s in the primitive profit functions.

Before the firms choose their output levels, governments choose their policies to maximize their welfare. The welfare (benefit) functions of the union countries and the country outside the union are given respectively by

$$W_i(t, t^*) = \pi_i(t, t^*) + t x_i, \qquad i = 1, 2 \qquad (1)$$

$$W^*(t, t^*) = u(X) - PX + t^* X \qquad (2)$$

where $u'(X) = P$ and the "$\hat{\ }$" over the variables is suppressed to simplify notation.

The importing country chooses its import tariff to solve $\partial W^* / \partial t^* = 0$. Its best reply function will then be given by

$$t^* = X(\partial P / \partial t^* - 1)(\partial X / \partial t^*)^{-1}. \qquad (3)$$

Obviously, $t^* > 0$ if $0 < \partial P / \partial t^* < 1$, that is, if the marginal increase in price is smaller than the marginal increase in the tariff itself. This is the "usual" case and we shall assume it henceforward.[4]

Turning to the union's policy we first consider the case where there are no intra-union transfers. If country i chooses the common union policy it sets t to solve $\partial W_i / \partial t = 0$. The best-reply function of the union will then be given by

$$t_i = -\frac{\left[\dfrac{\partial \pi_j}{\partial x_j} \dfrac{\partial x_j}{\partial t}\right]}{\dfrac{\partial x_i}{\partial t}} > 0. \qquad (3)$$

Suppose that firm 2 is the more cost-effective: $c_2 < c_1$. Under plausible conditions, the union's export tax is higher (for a given tariff) when country 2 chooses the policy.[5] That is $\partial W_2 / \partial t|_{t=t_1} > 0$ and $\partial W_1 / \partial t|_{t=t_2} < 0$. In this situation the best-response functions are as shown in Figure 1. Therefore the equilibrium when country 2 is the PM involves a higher export tax and a lower import tariff.

Finally, notice that along country i's best-reply function, its welfare is decreasing in the import tariff. This can be shown by evaluating $\partial W_i / \partial t^*$ on i's best-response function, using the envelope theorem, to obtain $\partial W_i / \partial t^*|_{t=t_i} = -x_i < 0$.

Figure 2 illustrates a case where country 1 would like to delegate to country 2. Notice that, according to our discussion in the previous paragraph, $W_1(t_1(t^*), t^*)$ is downward

3. Since $a_i = b_i + P'$, Δ can be rewritten as $P'(b_1 + b_2 + P')$ which is certainly positive if b_1 and b_2 are both negative. That is, the assumption that the best-response functions are downward sloping implies that the equilibrium is stable.

4. It holds true so long as demand is not "too convex" to the origin. For a more detailed discussion, see Brander and Spencer (1984).

5. Sufficient conditions for the low cost country to impose the largest export tax are $a_i < b_j$ for $i = 1, 2$, $j \neq i$ and demand is linear, concave or not very convex to the origin.

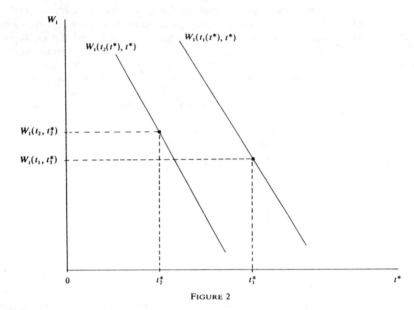

FIGURE 2

sloping. Furthermore for a given level of t^*, country 1 is better off if it is able to choose itself the export tax, as $W_1(t_1(t^*), t^*) > W_1(t_2(t^*), t^*)$ by the optimality of t_1. However, when the equilibrium response of ROW is considered, country 1 is better-off delegating to country 2, as $W_1(t_1, t_1^*) < W_1(t_2, t_2^*)$ where t_i and t_i^* are the equilibrium policies when country i is the PM. Similarly, country 2 will be always willing to act as the policy-maker; delegation to its partner would result in higher import tariffs (and lower export taxes) so that country 2 would be worse-off.

If there are intra-union side payments, and the supra-national agency chooses t to maximize joint welfare $W = W_1 + W_2$, the export tax $\bar{t}$ is given by

$$\bar{t} = -\frac{\left[\dfrac{\partial \pi_1}{\partial x_2}\dfrac{\partial x_2}{\partial t} + \dfrac{\partial \pi_2}{\partial x_1}\dfrac{\partial x_1}{\partial t}\right]}{\dfrac{\partial X}{\partial t}} > 0. \tag{4}$$

It is straightforward to show that $\bar{t}(t^*)$ lies between $t_1(t^*)$ and $t_2(t^*)$; this is because $\partial W/\partial t|_{t=t_1} = \partial W_2/\partial t|_{t=t_1} > 0$ since $\partial W_1/\partial t|_{t=t_1} = 0$ and, similarly, $\partial W/\partial t|_{t=t_2} < 0$. Furthermore, joint welfare is decreasing in the import tariff, along the best-reply function of the supra-national agency; in particular $\partial W/\partial t^*|_{t=\bar{t}} = -X < 0$, by using the envelope theorem. Therefore the fact that joint welfare may be higher if the more aggressive nation, rather than the supra-national agency, chooses t, follows from the same logic as above.[6]

3. CONCLUDING COMMENTS

Strategic behaviour by countries outside the union can strengthen the union for two reasons. The first and most obvious reason is that strategic behaviour by non-members

6. For a linear example illustrating these points, see our working paper, Gatsios and Karp (1989).

is likely to increase the cost of failing to form and maintain the union. Countries acting individually may be more vulnerable than when they coordinate their policies; this vulnerability is likely to be particularly serious if non-members act strategically.

The second, and more subtle reason, is that the ability to make credible commitments becomes particularly important when rivals behave strategically.[7] The formation of a customs union and delegation of authority to an aggressive member provide a method of making such a commitment. This observation is the basis of the paper.

Customs unions have generally involved nations which are similar but not identical. Our results suggest that a mild divergence of interest amongst union members may enhance the value of cooperation, rather than being a source of friction. This points to a previously unrecognised explanation for the coherence of groups of similar nations, such as the European Community and the partnership formed by the U.S.-Canada Free Trade Agreement.

An important insight we gain from our analysis is that the choice of the PM depends on whether the union and ROW policies are "strategic substitutes" or "complements"[8] (i.e. it depends on the effect of a unilateral change in one agent's policy on the optimal response of its rival). The policies are strategic substitutes if an increase in the level of one player's policy leads to a decrease in the other player's optimal response. This is what we have assumed in drawing the best-response functions as downward sloping in Figure 1. In such a case we observe that, if it is optimal to delegate, it is the more aggressive union member which is chosen as the PM. That is, the union wants to cultivate "the lean and hungry look".[9] In situations where both of the union members agree on the delegation decision, they are likely to find a supra-national agent (which maximizes the sum of their welfare) redundant. Their joint welfare is likely to be higher if one of the agents is chosen as the PM.

Recognition of the fact that nations may want to delegate authority is significant because it raises much deeper questions. Very little is known about how exogenous parameters, such as technology, endowments and tastes, are likely to affect a country's degree of aggression, and thus affect the delegation decision. The issue of informational asymmetries between the contracting parties in a union has also not been formally modelled; Gatsios and Seabright (1989) discuss the practical importance of this question.

We have shown that in a partial equilibrium model the country which is more cost-effective will be more aggressive, and consequently is likely to be chosen as the policy maker. Elsewhere (Gatsios and Karp (1989)), we have found that in a pure-exchange general equilibrium model with homothetic preferences the PM will be the country relatively better-endowed in the export good. These results provide only the beginning of a research programme aimed at improving our understanding of the decision-making process in customs unions.

Acknowledgement. This paper was presented in the Second European Research Workshop on International Trade, Bergen, Norway, 26–30 June 1989. Konstantine Gatsios would like to thank the participants in this workshop and, especially, Elhanan Helpman for very useful comments. We would also like to thank Hamid Sabourian and two anonymous referees for helpful remarks on a previous version of the paper. Of course, the usual exclusion holds.

7. Of course the ability to make credible commitments may also be important even if rivals behave competitively. Our point is simply that when rivals act strategically there are additional circumstances where commitment is important.

8. These terms are taken from Bulow, Geanakoplos and Klemperer (1985).

9. In a similar manner, if the policies are strategic complements, the union would rather appear as a "puppy dog" by delegating to the less aggressive union member. These descriptions are taken from Fudenberg and Tirole (1984).

REFERENCES

BRANDER, J. A. and SPENCER, B. J. (1984), "Trade Welfare: Tariffs and Cartels", *Journal of International Economics*, 16, 227-242.
BRANDER, J. A. and SPENCER, B. J. (1985), "Export Subsidies and International Market Share Rivalry", *Journal of International Economics*, 18, 83-100.
BULOW, J. I., GEANAKOPLOS, J. D. and KLEMPERER, P. D. (1985), "Multimarket Oligopoly: Strategic Substitutes and Complements", *Journal of Political Economy*, 93, 488-511.
DIXIT, A. (1984), "International Trade Policy for Oligopolistic Industries", *Economic Journal (Supplement)*, 94, 1-16.
EATON, J. and GROSSMAN, G. M. (1986), "Optimal Trade and Industrial Policy Under Oligopoly", *Quarterly Journal of Economics*, 101, 383-406.
FUDENBERG, D. and TIROLE, J. (1984), "The Fat-Cat Effect, the Puppy-Dog Ploy and the Lean and Hungry Look", *American Economic Review (Papers and Proceedings)*, 74, 361-366.
GATSIOS, K. (1987), "Customs Unions and the Core: A Reciprocal Dumping Model" (Economic Theory Discussion Paper Series, 119, University of Cambridge).
GATSIOS, K. and KARP, L. (1989), "Delegation Games in Customs Unions" (Economic Theory Discussion Paper Series, 140, University of Cambridge, and Centre for Economic Policy Research Discussion Paper Series, 337, London).
GATSIOS, K. and SEABRIGHT, P. (1989), "Regulation in the European Community", *Oxford Review of Economic Policy*, 5, 37-60.
LIPSEY, R. (1970) *The Theory of Customs Unions: A General Equilibrium Analysis* (I. S. E. Research Monograph, London).
RIEZMAN, R. (1985), "Customs Unions and the Core", *Journal of International Economics*, 19, 353-365.

C
Integration and World Welfare

[17]

Journal of International Economics 9 (1979) 503–511. © North-Holland Publishing Company

THE WELFARE EFFECT OF TARIFF RATE REDUCTIONS IN A MANY COUNTRY WORLD

Tatsuo HATTA*

The Johns Hopkins University, Baltimore, MD 21218, USA

Takashi FUKUSHIMA

Southern Methodist University, Dallas, TX 75222, USA

Received September 1978, revised version received April 1979

Consider a two-commodity *n*-country model without inferior goods where import tariffs are the only trade barriers. In this paper we establish that the world's welfare is improved if the country with the highest tariff rate unilaterally reduce its rate to the level of the second highest country or if all the countries of the world reduce tariff rates proportionally. The second rule serves as a theoretical justification of the Kennedy and Tokyo Round Tariff Reductions.

1. Introduction

When several countries are imposing tariffs on their imports, an arbitrary reduction of the tariff rates by some countries may *decrease* the welfare of the world as a whole. The celebrated 'theory of the second best' revealed such perverse welfare effects of a distortion reduction.

However, a tariff reduction can increase the welfare, if it is done under some rule rather than arbitrarily. In this paper we present two rules of tariff reduction that improve the welfare in a two-commodity *n*-country world, where each country has a strictly convex production possibility set and import tariffs are the only trade barriers. First, we establish that if there is no inferior good, a unilateral reduction of tariff rate by the country with the highest tariff rate to the level of the second highest country can improve the welfare of the world.[1] Secondly, we prove that if no inferior good exist, a proportional reduction of tariff rates by all the countries of the world improves the world welfare. This part serves as a theoretical justification of the Kennedy Round and the Tokyo Round Tariff Reductions.

Recently piecemeal policies in price-distorted economies have been extensively studied by Foster and Sonnenschein (1970), Bertrand and Vanek

---

*We are indebted to two anonymous referees of the Journal for their helpful comments and suggestions.

[1]For a three-country model with a *fixed output bundle* of the world, Vanek (1964) showed the effectiveness of this rule by a graphical method.

(1971), Kawamata (1974, 1977), Bruno (1972), Dixit (1975), Hatta (1977a, 1977b), and Fukushima (1979). An essential difference exists, however, between the models of this group and the present one. In the former models all consumers face the same price vector, and distortions exist between consumers' and producers' price vectors. In the present model, however, consumers of different countries face different price vectors due to tariffs; distortions exist among consumers' prices in different countries. In the former models the assumption of a representative consumer gives basic insight into the welfare effects of distortion changes. In the present model, it is impossible to make such an assumption because the type of distortions with which the present paper is concerned cannot exist under such an assumption. This forces us to employ the expansion of the world's utility possibility set as the criterion of welfare improvement.

2. The model

(1) *There are two goods x and y.*

(2) *There are n countries in the world.*

(3) *There is only one consumer in each country.*[2] *He is a price taker and has well behaved compensated demand functions for goods x and y.*

The compensated demand function of country i for good j may be written as

$$c_j^i = f_j^i(p_x^i, p_y^i, u^i), \qquad i = 1, \ldots, n; \quad j = x, y, \tag{1}$$

where

c_j^i = quantity demanded of good j by country i,
p_j^i = domestic price of good j in country i, and
u^i = utility level of country i.

(4) *The production possibility frontier of each country is smooth and concave to the origin.*

(5) *The producers in each country maximize their profits regarding prices as given.*

Let a_j^i be the output level of good j in country i. Then we have

$$a_j^i = h_j^i(p_x^i, p_y^i), \qquad i = 1, \ldots, n; \quad j = x, y, \tag{2}$$

---

[2]Alternatively, we can assume that there exist many consumers in each country and that their utility levels are represented by Scitovsky's community indifference curves. In this event, the utility levels of all but one consumer within a country are fixed by using lump sum income taxes and transfers.

where h_j^i is the compensated supply function of the jth good in the ith country.[3]

(6) *Both the consumers and producers in each country face the same prices.*

This assumption is implicitly used in eqs. (1) and (2). Let z_j^i denote the net import demand for the jth good in the ith country, i.e. $z_j^i \equiv c_j^i - a_j^i$. By virtue of eqs. (1) and (2), z_j^i is a function of p_x^i, p_y^i and u^i:

$$z_j^i = f_j^i(p_x^i, p_y^i, u^i) - h_j^i(p_x^i, p_y^i)$$
$$\equiv s_j^i(p_x^i, p_y^i, u^i). \tag{3}$$

We call s_j^i the net demand function. This is the compensated demand function for the system of trade indifference curves of Meade (1952). Note that s_j^i, like f_j^i and h_j^i, is positively homogeneous of degree zero with respect to p_x^i and p_y^i; for any positive number m, we have

$$s_j^i(p_x^i, p_y^i, u^i) = s_j^i(mp_x^i, mp_y^i, u^i). \tag{4}$$

(7) *Each country is small and takes the world prices p_x and p_y of the two goods as given.*[4]

(8) *No country imports or exports both goods.*

(9) *Each country imposes an ad valorem tariff for the imported good.*

Suppose country i imports good x and imposes the tariff rate τ_x^i on this good. Then the domestic prices are

$$p_x^i = (1 + \tau_x^i)p_x \quad \text{and} \quad p_y^i = p_y.$$

We assume that $\tau_j^i = 0$ if good j is exported by country i. Then we can write

$$p_j^i = t_j^i p_j, \qquad i = 1, \ldots, n; \quad j = x, y,$$

where

$$t_j^i = (1 + \tau_j^i).$$

Note that t_j^i is positive, and it is equal to or greater than one according as country i exports commodity j or imports commodity j. Thus, by virtue of eqs. (3) and (4) we can write

$$z_j^i = s_j^i(t_x^i, t_y^i p, u^i), \qquad i = 1, 2, \ldots, n, \tag{5}$$

---

[3]See Hatta (1977b, p. 1861) for the compensated supply function.

[4]This assumption differs from the well-known small country assumption employed by Viner's customs union model, which assumes a fixed world price level under tariff changes. In our model, the world price level is an endogenous variable.

where $p \equiv p_y/p_x$.

(10) *Total demand for x and y are equal to the total supply of goods x and y.*

Let z_j^i denote the net demand for the jth good in the ith country. The assumption implies that we have

$$\sum_{i=1}^{n} z_j^i = 0, \qquad j = x, y. \tag{6}$$

Substituting (5) into (6) we have

$$\sum_{i=1}^{n} s_j^i(t_x^i, t_y^i p, u^i) = 0, \qquad j = x, y. \tag{7}$$

This system of equations represents the equilibrium condition for the demand and supply of the world as a whole for goods x and y. The system involves two equations and $n+1$ variables, $u^1, \ldots, u^n$, and p; so the model is not quite complete.[5]

In order to complete the model we have to introduce a welfare criterion. In a multinational world, the efficiency can be said to have improved if the utility possibility set of the world expands in the new situation. In this paper we choose this criterion for the improvement of the world welfare; we show that when $u^1, \ldots, u^{n-1}$ are kept constant at the arbitrary original levels, u^n is increased in the new situation under certain change in the tariff structure. This criterion is, of course, originally due to Samuelson (1950).

Fixing $u^1, \ldots, u^{n-1}$ regarding only u^n as the variable leaves only two variables, p and u^n, in the two-equation system [eq. (7)]. This enables us to examine the effect of a change in the tax structure upon the utility level of country n when the utility levels of all the other countries are fixed.

(11) *Among the utility levels of all the countries, only that of country n is treated as a variable*

$$u^i = \bar{u}^i, \qquad i = 1, \ldots, n-1. \tag{8}$$

When u^n is increased while keeping other u^i's constant at arbitrary levels,

---

[5]If we were to construct a *positive* rather than a *normative* model of international trade, we would have to specify the budget condition in each country. Accordingly, the utility level of each country may be expressed as:

$$u^i = g^i(t_x^i, t_y^i, p), \qquad i = 1, \ldots, n.$$

We would then have $n+2$ equations and $n+1$ variables. These and Walras's law would complete the positive model.

we say the *welfare of the world is improved.*[6]

The system of eqs. (7) and (8) completes our normative model, and determines the equilibrium values of p and u^n for given values of t_x^i, t_y^i, and $\bar{u}^i$.

3. Basic lemma

Let a parameter r denote the stage of the reform program of the international tariff structure, and let the reform program itself be represented by the following system of equations:

$$\tau_j^i = w_j^i(r), \qquad i = 1, \ldots, n; \quad j = x, y.$$

Substituting this for τ_j^i in the definitional equation of t_j^i, we can express t_j^i as a function of r. For brevity, we write this function as

$$t_j^i = t_j^i(r), \qquad i = 1, \ldots, n; \quad j = x, y. \tag{9}$$

The lemma in this section gives the expression that represents the welfare effect of a change in r upon the level of u^n when u^i are kept constant for $i = 1, \ldots, n-1$.

In deriving this result, we use a few properties of the function s_j^i. Let $s_{jk}^i \equiv \partial s_j^i / \partial p_k^i$, $s_{ju}^i \equiv \partial s_j^i / \partial u^i$ and $\lambda^i \equiv$ marginal utility of income in the ith country. It is readily seen that $s_{jk}^i \equiv f_{jk}^i - h_{jk}^i$ and $s_{ju}^i \equiv f_{ju}^i$, and that f_{jk}^i, h_{jk}^i and $\lambda^i f_{ju}^i f_j$ are the Hicksian substitution and income terms, respectively.[7] Thus, the own net substitution term s_{jj}^i is negative and the following well-known properties hold.[8]

Homogeneity condition:

$$s_{xx}^i p_x^i + s_{xy}^i p_y^i = 0,$$
$$s_{yx}^i p_x^i + s_{yy}^i p_y^i = 0, \qquad i = 1, \ldots, n. \tag{10}$$

Symmetry condition:

$$s_{xy}^i = s_{yx}^i, \qquad i = 1, \ldots, n. \tag{11}$$

Lemma. At an equilibrium described by (7) and (8) the following holds:

$$\frac{\partial u^n}{\partial r} = \frac{\beta}{\alpha},$$

[6]Note that we do not lose generality by choosing the utility level of the nth country as the variable. After all, we can call any country the nth country by rearranging the indices.
[7]See Arrow and Hahn (1971, p. 105).
[8]See Hatta (1977b, pp. 1863–1864).

where

$$\alpha \equiv \sum s_{yy}^i t_y^i (s_{xu}^n + p s_{yu}^n t^i), \tag{12}$$

$$\beta \equiv -p^2 \sum_i^n \sum_j^n s_{yy}^i s_{yy}^j t_y^i (t^i - t^j)\left(t^i \frac{dt_x^i}{dr} - \frac{dt_y^i}{dr}\right), \tag{13}$$

and

$$t^i \equiv \frac{t_y^i}{t_x^i}.$$

Proof. Substitute (8) into (7) and differentiate it with respect to r. We have

$$\begin{bmatrix} s_{xu}^n & \sum s_{xy}^i t_y^i \\ s_{yu}^n & \sum s_{yy}^i t_y^i \end{bmatrix}\begin{pmatrix} \dfrac{\partial u^n}{\partial r} \\[2mm] \dfrac{\partial p}{\partial r} \end{pmatrix} = -\begin{pmatrix} \sum\left(s_{xx}^i \dfrac{dt_x^i}{dr} + p s_{xy}^i \dfrac{dt_y^i}{dr}\right) \\[2mm] \sum\left(s_{yx}^i \dfrac{dt_x^i}{dr} + p s_{yy}^i \dfrac{dt_y^i}{dr}\right) \end{pmatrix}.$$

From the definitions of p and t^i, we obtain

$$p_y^i/p_x^i = t^i p.$$

Taking this into account, the homogeneity condition (10) may be rewritten as follows:

$$s_{yx}^i = -p s_{yy}^i t^i,$$

and

$$s_{xx}^i = p^2 s_{yy}^i (t^i)^2, \qquad i = 1, \dots, n.$$

Applying these and noting the symmetry condition (11), we get

$$\begin{bmatrix} s_{xu}^n & -p\sum s_{yy}^i t_y^i t^i \\ s_{yu}^n & \sum s_{yy}^i t_y^i \end{bmatrix}\begin{pmatrix} \dfrac{\partial u^n}{\partial r} \\[2mm] \dfrac{\partial p}{\partial r} \end{pmatrix} = -\begin{pmatrix} p^2 \sum s_{yy}^i t^i\left(t^i \dfrac{dt_x^i}{dr} - \dfrac{dt_y^i}{dr}\right) \\[2mm] -p\sum s_{yy}^i\left(t^i \dfrac{dt_x^i}{dr} - \dfrac{dt_y^i}{dr}\right) \end{pmatrix}.$$

Thus, by the Cramer's rule we have

$$\frac{\partial u^n}{\partial r} = \frac{\beta}{\alpha},$$

where

$$\alpha = \begin{vmatrix} s^n_{xu} & -p\sum s^i_{yy}t^i_y t^i \\ s^n_{yu} & \sum s^i_{yy}t^i_y \end{vmatrix}$$

and

$$\beta = \begin{vmatrix} -p^2\sum_i^n s^i_{yy}t^i\left(t^i\dfrac{\mathrm{d}t^i_x}{\mathrm{d}r} - \dfrac{\mathrm{d}t^i_y}{\mathrm{d}r}\right) & -p\sum_j^n s^j_{yy}t^j_y t^j \\ p\sum_i^n s^i_{yy}\left(t^i\dfrac{\mathrm{d}t^i_x}{\mathrm{d}r} - \dfrac{\mathrm{d}t^i_y}{\mathrm{d}r}\right) & \sum_j^n s^j_{yy}t^j_y \end{vmatrix}.$$

This proves the lemma.   Q.E.D.

4. Unilateral tariff reduction

Now we are in a position to prove a welfare proposition concerning the unilateral tariff reduction.

Theorem 1.   Suppose neither x nor y is an inferior good in any country of the world. Then a unilateral reduction of the tariff rate by the country with the highest tariff rate to the level of the second highest country improves the welfare of the world.

Proof. Without loss of generality, we can assume that the first country imposes the highest tariff rate on x. Hence we have

$$t^1_x > t^i_x, \qquad i = 2, 3, \ldots, n.$$

This, together with the definition of t^i, implies

$$t^1 < t^i, \qquad i = 2, 3, \ldots, n. \tag{14}$$

The unilateral tariff reduction of the first country may be formally stated as

$$\mathrm{d}t^i_j/\mathrm{d}r = \begin{cases} -1, & \text{if } i=1 \text{ and } j=x, \\ 0, & \text{otherwise.} \end{cases} \tag{15}$$

This assumption implies that as r is increased, the first country reduces its tariff rate while other countries keep their rates fixed.

The theorem will be proved if we establish $\partial u^n/\partial r = \beta/\alpha > 0$ under assumptions (14) and (15). The negativity of α immediately follows from (12) since an own substitution term s_{yy}^i is always negative and s_{xu}^n and s_{yu}^n are non-negative owing to our noninferiority assumption.

Noting (15) we have

$$\beta = -p^2 \sum s_{yy}^1 s_{yy}^j t_y^j (t^1 - t^j) t^1 < 0,$$

where the last inequality follows from (14). Hence $\partial u^n / \partial r > 0$ follows.

Q.E.D.

5. The multilateral tariff reduction

We now analyze the welfare effect of a simultaneous reduction of tariff rates by all the countries of the world. As we indicated in the introduction, the arbitrary reduction of the tariff rates may lead us to a lower level of utility. The following theorem establishes, however, that a proportional reduction of all the tariffs, as intended by the Kennedy Round and the Tokyo Round Tariff Reductions, generally improves the welfare of the world.

Theorem 2. Suppose neither x nor y is an inferior good in any of the countries, then the proportional reduction of the tariff rates of all the countries improves the world welfare.

Proof. The proportional reduction of all the tariff rates may be formally stated as

$$dt_j^i / dr = 1 - t_j^i, \qquad i = 1, 2, \ldots, n; \quad j = x, y. \tag{16}$$

The theorem will be proved if we establish $\partial u^n / \partial r = \beta / \alpha > 0$ under assumptions $s_{xu}^i > 0$, $s_{yu}^i > 0$, and (16). From the proof of theorem 1, we already know that α is negative owing to the noninferiority assumption. In what follows we establish the negativity of β.

Without loss of generality, we can index the n countries in such a way that the following holds:

$$t_x^1 \geqq t_x^2 \geqq \ldots \geqq t_x^{k-1} > t_x^k = \ldots = t_x^n = 1$$

and

(17)

$$1 = t_y^1 = t_y^2 = \ldots = t_y^{k-1} < t_y^k \leqq \ldots \leqq t_y^n.$$

From the lemma and eq. (16) we get

$$\beta = -p^2 \sum_i \sum_j s_{yy}^i s_{yy}^j (t^i - t^j)(t_y^j t^i - t_y^j)$$

$$= -p^2 \sum_i \sum_{j<i} s_{yy}^i s_{yy}^j (t^i - t^j) \{ (t_y^j t^i - t_y^i t^j) + (t_y^i - t_y^j) \},$$

T. Hatta and T. Fukushima, *Tariff rate reductions*   511

where the last expression follows from the fact that

$$\sum_i \sum_j m_{ij} = \sum_i \sum_{j<i} (m_{ij} + m_{ji}), \quad \text{if } m_{ii} = 0 \text{ for } i = 1, \ldots, n.$$

Thus, we have

$$\beta = -p^2 \sum_i \sum_{j<i} \theta_{ij}, \tag{18}$$

where

$$\theta_{ij} \equiv s_{yy}^i s_{yy}^j (t^i - t^j) \{ t^i t^j (t_x^j - t_x^i) + (t_y^i - t_y^j) \}.$$

Inequalities (17) imply that $t_x^j \geq t_x^i$, $t_y^i \geq t_y^j$, and $t^i \geq t^j$ whenever $j < i$, where strict inequalities hold at least when $j \leq k - 1$ and $k \leq i$. Thus, we have

$$\theta_{ij} > 0, \quad \text{if } j < i.$$

This proves $\beta < 0$, and the theorem is proved.   Q.E.D.

References

Arrow, Kenneth and Frank Hahn, 1971, General competitive analysis (Holden Day, San Francisco).

Bertrand, Trent and Jaroslav Vanek, 1971, The theory of tariffs, taxes and subsidies: Some aspects of the second best, American Economic Review 61, no. 5, 925–931.

Bruno, Michael, 1972, Market distortions and gradual reform, Review of Economic Studies 39, no. 4, 373–383.

Dixit, Avinash, 1975, Welfare effects of tax and price changes, Journal of Public Economics 4, 103–123.

Foster, Edward and Hugo Sonnenschein, 1970, Price distortion and economic welfare, Econometrica 38, no. 2, 281–297.

Fukushima, Takashi, 1979, Tariff structure, nontraded goods and theory of piecemeal policy recommendations, International Economic Review 20, no. 2, 361–369.

Hatta, Tatsuo, 1977a, A theory of piecemeal policy recommendations, Review of Economic Studies 44, 1–21.

Hatta, Tatsuo, 1977b, A recommendation for a better tariff structure, Econometrica 45, 1859–1869.

Hicks, John R., 1946, Value and capital, 2nd edn. (Oxford University Press, London).

Kawamata, Kunio, 1974, Price distortion and potential welfare, Econometrica 42, 435–460.

Kawamata, Kunio, 1977, Price distortion and the second best optimum, Review of Economic Studies 44, 23–30.

Meade, James E., 1952, A geometry of international trade (George Allen and Unwin, London).

Samuelson, Paul A., 1950, Evaluation of real national income, Oxford Economic Papers (New Series) II, 1–29.

Vanek, Jaroslav, 1964, Unilateral trade liberation and global world income, Quarterly Journal of Economics 78, 139–147.

[18]

Open economies review **3**: 51—59, 1992.
© 1992 *Kluwer Academic Publishers. Printed in the Netherlands.*

Paradoxes in Integration Theory

CARSTEN KOWALCZYK
Dartmouth College and NBER, U.S.A.

Key words: integration, customs unions, tariff reform

Abstract

This paper presents a formal analysis of how global welfare is affected by changing tariff and subsidy rates. The discussion stresses three types of reform whereby, surprisingly, trade liberalization has the potential to reduce world welfare: a multilateral equi-proportionate reduction of tariffs and subsidies; a reduction of a tariff or subsidy rate which is not extreme; and the formation of a customs union.

At least since the publication in 1950 of Jacob Viner's *The Customs Union Issue*, it has been known that approaching the first-best situation from one that is initially distorted can be riddled with dangers. Specifically, and of immediate relevance for the debate surrounding the European Economic Community's intentions of becoming exactly that by the end of 1992, Viner demonstrated that the tariff reductions implied by a preferential trading agreement could reduce global welfare. Some of the mystique surrounding this result disappeared six years later when another of the giants of customs union theory, Richard Lipsey, in his seminal paper with Kelvin Lancaster on the theory of second best, demonstrated that when one margin is distorted it may no longer be optimal to leave all other margins undistorted.

Some concern for the welfare of outsiders has been raised under the headline "Fortress Europe," and in debates in several member countries, notably the smaller ones, doubt has been cast on whether the welfares of specific nations necessarily would be raised from integration. The former debate subsided, at least within the United States, after a European promise not to raise external trade barriers on transatlantic trade. The latter debate, on the other hand, has remained extensive and has sometimes even had emotional overtones, such as

52   CARSTEN KOWALCZYK

in 1972 when Britain, Denmark, and Ireland voted to join the European Community while Norway voted to remain outside. A replay can currently be observed in the remaining EFTA countries.

It may not be unreasonable to suggest that economists have tended to write off any objections to integration as being the mere gripes of special interest groups, and that they have treated, accordingly, the opponents with as much seriousness as does the doctor the hypochondriac. Although rarely explicitly stated, such a position must be based on a belief that either the likelihood or the size of any welfare loss is small and transitional, and that either is a price worth paying, if indeed not one that is necessary, to reach that bliss point of global free trade. It has thus been suggested that the process of liberalizing international trade is comparable to bicycling, and that stopping pedalling inflicts more pain than do the little bumps in the road. In the present context, it might perhaps be more precise to think of a group of bicyclists, and that the concern is that all riders, not only the strongest or those with most perseverance, arrive at the final destination. To facilitate the journey various support services should be in place, and the riders should be equipped with the most recent roadmaps which, ideally, can be read without stepping off the bike. It could be argued, of course, that any losses from misaligning prices are static, and are largely outweighed by dynamic gains due to scale economies and investment effects (suggesting that further down the road the bicycles can be traded in for motorcycles). This, however, is not inconsistent with the position that, *ceteris paribus*, easier travelling, even at the start of the tour, is desirable.

This paper presents a formal expression for the change in global welfare from changes in tariffs or subsidies, and it applies the expression to three types of reform: a multilateral equiproportionate reduction of tariffs and subsidies; a reduction of a tariff or subsidy rate which is not extreme; and the formation of a customs union. It is stressed how these reforms, in spite of apparently moving the world towards the first-best situation of global free trade, have the potential to reduce, in a paradoxical fashion, global welfare.

1. Three world welfare paradoxes

Assume a world of K countries, indexed by $k(k = 1, 2, \ldots, K)$, in which N goods, indexed by $i(i = 1, 2, \ldots, N)$, are traded. Each nation is inhabited by price-taking consumers and producers with convex preferences and constant returns to scale production technologies.

Tariff-exclusive world prices are denoted by the N-dimensional column vector p^e, while the domestic price vector in country k is given by the column vector p^k. The difference between these two vectors is due to tariffs or subsidies in country k. Assuming for the moment that all rates are *specific*, and that they are given by the N-dimensional column vector t^k, we thus have,

$$(k = 1, 2, \ldots, K) \quad p^k = p^e + t^k. \tag{1}$$

Let $e(p^k, u^k)$ denote the expenditure function in country k, where u^k is the level of utility of the representative consumer in that country. If, furthermore, v^κ is the vector of country k's factor endowments, then its gross-domestic-product function can be written as $r(p^k, v^k)$. When evaluated at domestic prices, and defining m^k to be the N-dimensional column vector of net imports into country k, the condition that nation k's trade is in balance implies that spending should equal total income. Total income is derived from two sources: factor payments and tariff revenue. As the latter is given by the inner product $t^k m^k$, the condition of balanced trade can be written as,

$$(k = 1, 2, \ldots, K) \quad e(p^k, u^k) = r(p^k, v^k) + t^k m^k. \tag{2}$$

In order to assess the effect on national income from changes in tariffs or subsidies, we differentiate this expression with respect to p^k and u^k. Utilizing the fact that the price derivative of the expenditure function, e_p^k, yields the vector of compensated demands while the price derivative of the gross-domestic-product function, r_p^k, yields the vector of supplies, we have that $m^k = e_p^k - r_p^k$. If e_u^k denotes the inverse of the marginal utility from income in country k, then the change in country k's national income, when measured in units of some arbitrarily chosen numeraire good, can be written as the sum of the change in *consumers'* and *producers' surplus*, which is given by the inner product $- m^k dp^k$, and the change in *tariff revenue*, which is given by the term $d(t^k m^k)$,

$$(k = 1, 2, \ldots, K) \quad e_u^k du^k = - m^k dp^k + d(t^k m^k). \tag{3}$$

Further differentiating this expression yields the change in national income as the sum of a *terms-of-trade* effect expressed by the inner product $- m^k dp^e$, and a *volume-of-trade* effect defined by the inner product $(p^k - p^e) dm^k$,

$$(k = 1, 2, \ldots, K) \quad e_u^k du^k = -m^k dp^e + (p^k - p^e) dm^k. \tag{4}$$

Assuming that international lump-sum transfers of income are feasible, the potential Pareto criterion becomes the relevant indicator of welfare for coalitions. In particular, setting all but one nation's, say country 1's, changes in national income equal to zero, and adding their expressions for income changes, yields the following criterion for a change in world welfare as measured in units of the numeraire good:

$$(k = 1, 2, \ldots, K) \quad dww = \sum_k (p^k - p^e) \, dm^k. \tag{5}$$

The insight, that world welfare increases if a reform of tariffs or subsidies causes goods to be reallocated towards their higher valuation, originates with James Meade (1955).

An even sharper intuition can be derived by solving for the change in world welfare from the market clearing conditions which, if 0 is an N-component column vector consisting of zeros, can be written as,

$$(k = 1, 2, \ldots, K) \quad \sum_k m^k = 0. \tag{6}$$

This expression constitutes N equations in the $(N - 1)$ relative commodity prices and in country 1's level of utility. Consider first the simplest case of two countries, that are denoted as Home and Foreign, and are indicated by superscripts H and F respectively, and which trade two goods, 1 and 2.[1] Differentiation of (6) with respect to u^H, the world market relative price of good 2 in terms of good 1, and both countries' tariff and subsidy rates, yields, after considerable manipulation, the change in world welfare as a function of the behavior of the wedge between the two countries' domestic relative prices. Specifically, and as discussed in the appendix of Kowalczyk (1989), the change in world welfare from one or both of the countries changing their tariffs or subsidies can be written as,

$$dww = B^*(p^H - p^F) \{dp^H - dp^F\}, \tag{7}$$

where

$$B^* = m_{22}^H \, m_{22}^F / [m_{1u}^H (m_{22}^H + m_{22}^F) + m_{2u}^H (p^H m_{22}^H + p^F m_{22}^F)]. \tag{8}$$

The compensated own-price elasticities of import demand, m_{22}^H and m_{22}^F, are negative, implying that a sufficient condition for B^* to be negative is that both goods are non-inferior in consumption, that is, that m_{1u}^H and m_{2u}^H are both positive. Given these assumptions, expression (7) states the very appealing proposition that world welfare is a monotonically decreasing function in the deviation of the price wedge from zero, where a zero wedge constitutes a Pareto optimal allocation. It is shown in Kowalczyk (1989) that no surprises loom in the case of *specific* rates: a reduction of the highest tariff rate or of the highest subsidy rate raises global welfare, as does an equi-proportionate reduction of both countries' rates whether both quote tariffs, both quote subsidies, or one quotes a tariff and the other a subsidy.[2]

Even though this is a world of perfect competition, it turns out that it can make a substantial difference for the world welfare consequences of reforms whether rates are quoted as *specific* or as *ad valorem*. Thus, suppose that τ_2^k is an *ad valorem* tariff or subsidy levied on good 2 in country k. If a circumflex denotes a relative change in a variable,[3] then the change in global welfare from changes in *ad valorem* rates can be written as,

$$dww = B(p^H - p^F)\{\hat{p}^H - \hat{p}^F\},\tag{9}$$

where B is given by

$$B = p^H m_{22}^H m_{22}^F / [m_{1u}^H(m_{22}^H(1 + \tau_2^H) + m_{22}^F(1 + \tau_2^F))$$
$$- m_{2u}^H(m_{12}^H(1 + \tau_2^H) + m_{12}^F(1 + \tau_2^F))].\tag{10}$$

As in the case of *specific* rates, world welfare is a monotonically decreasing function in the deviation of the price wedge from the value corresponding to undistorted trade, the value being zero for the absolute wedge, $p^H - p^F$, which is relevant when rates are *specific*, and one for the relative wedge p^H/p^F, which comes into play when rates are *ad valorem*. In the latter case, however, it becomes a possibility that approaching global free trade can reduce world welfare. Concretely, if one country quotes a tariff, and if at the same time the other country quotes a subsidy, then it is possible that an agreement to reduce both rates in the same proportion can pull the two countries' domestic prices apart rather than together, causing in turn a paradoxical reduction of world welfare.[4]

In order to investigate preferential trading arrangements, we introduce a third country, C, the "coalition partner." The market clearing conditions remain as given by (6), although for $k = H, C$, and F. If we assume, furthermore, that the three countries trade only two goods and that rates are *specific*, performing the very same steps that led from (6) to (7) yields as the relevant expression for a change in global welfare,[5]

$$dww = (1/A)[m_{22}^H \, m_{22}^C (p^H - p^C)\{dp^H - dp^C\}$$
$$+ \, m_{22}^H \, m_{22}^F (p^H - p^F)\{dp^H - dp^F\}$$
$$+ \, m_{22}^C \, m_{22}^F (p^C - p^F)\{dp^C - dp^F\}],\tag{11}$$

where A is defined by,

$$A = m_{1u}^H (m_{22}^H + m_{22}^C + m_{22}^F) + m_{2u}^H (p^H \, m_{22}^H + p^C \, m_{22}^C + p^F \, m_{22}^F)].\tag{12}$$

Suppose that in the initial equilibrium country H exports good 1 to both countries C and F, and suppose also that initial tariffs in the three countries are such that the domestic relative price of good 2 is lowest in country F and highest in country H, that is,

$$p^F < p^C < p^H.\tag{13}$$

Since A in expression (12) is negative if non-inferiority of both goods is assumed, and since the product of two nations' own-price derivatives of excess demand for good 2 is positive, reducing any or both of the two extreme tariff rates in the world raises global welfare. This result, which originates with Jaroslev Vanek (1964), follows from the fact that a lowering of the world's highest tariff rate on good 2 amounts to lowering p^H which raises global welfare since it brings the home country's domestic relative price closer to the domestic relative price of both of the two other countries.[6,7]

The potential for paradoxes reappears when a tariff rate, which is not extreme, is reduced. Thus consider a reduction of country C's import tariff on good 1. This raises country C's domestic relative price towards the relative price ruling in country H with an implied positive effect on world welfare; however, the gap relative to p^F is widened, which lowers global welfare. The net effect on world welfare is thus ambiguous, with a paradoxical worsening being more likely: (i) the larger is the initial price wedge between countries C and F; (ii) the smaller is the initial wedge between C and H; (iii) the larger is the compensated own-price elasticity of excess demand for good 2 in country F; and (iv) the smaller is the compensated own-price elasticity of excess demand for good 2 in country H. The possibility of this single rate paradox was originally proposed by Meade (1955) and S. A. Ozga (1955), and it was further discussed by Vanek (1964).

Were country C to go all the way and eliminate its tariff on trade

References

Fukushima, Takashi and Namdoo Kim (1989) "Welfare Improving Tariff Changes: A Case of Many Goods and Countries," *Journal of International Economics* 26, 383—388.

Hatta, Tatsuo and Takashi Fukushima (1979) "The Welfare Effect of Tariff Rate Reductions in a Many Country World," *Journal of International Economics* 9, 503—511.

Kowalczyk, Carsten (1989) "Trade Negotiations and World Welfare," *American Economic Review* 79, 552—559.

Kowalczyk, Carsten (1990) "Welfare and Customs Unions," NBER Working Paper No. 3476.

Lipsey, Richard G. and R. Kelvin Lancaster (1956) "The General Theory of Second Best," *Review of Economic Studies* 24, 11—32.

Meade, James (1955) *Trade and Welfare*. London: Oxford University Press.

Ozga, S. A. (1955) "An Essay in the Theory of Tariffs," *Journal of Political Economy* 63, 489—499.

Vanek, Jaroslev (1964) "Unilateral Trade Liberalization and Global World Income," *Quarterly Journal of Economics* 78, 139—147.

Viner, Jacob (1950) *The Customs Union Issue*, Carnegie Endowment for International Peace, New York.

[19]

Journal of International Economics 6 (1976) 95–97. © North-Holland Publishing Company

AN ELEMENTARY PROPOSITION CONCERNING THE FORMATION OF CUSTOMS UNIONS

Murray C. KEMP*

University of New South Wales, Sydney, Australia

Henry Y. WAN, Jr.

Cornell University, Ithaca, NY 14853, U.S.A.

1. Introduction

In the welter of inconclusive debate concerning the implications of customs unions, the following elementary yet basic proposition seems to have been almost lost to sight.[1]

Proposition.   Consider any competitive world trading equilibrium, with any number of countries and commodities, and with no restrictions whatever on the tariffs and other commodity taxes of individual countries, and with costs of transport fully recognized. Now let any subset of the countries form a customs union. Then there exists a common tariff vector and a system of lump-sum compensatory payments, involving only members of the union, such that there is an associated tariff-ridden competitive equilibrium in which each individual, whether a member of the union or not, is not worse off than before the formation of the union.[2]

A detailed list of assumptions, and a relatively formal proof, may be found in section 2. Here we merely note that there exists a common tariff vector which is consistent with pre-union world prices and, therefore, with pre-union trade patterns and pre-union levels of welfare for nonmembers.

The proposition is interesting in that it contains no qualifications whatever

---

*We acknowledge with gratitude the useful comments of Jagdish Bhagwati, John Chipman and two referees.

[1]A crude version of the proposition, together with an indication of the lines along which a proof may be constructed, can be found in Kemp (1964, p. 176). A geometric proof for the canonical three-countries, two-commodities case has been furnished by Vanek (1965, pp. 160–179). Negishi (1972, p. 187) has provided an algebraic treatment of the same canonical case.

[2]With the same common tariff vector and system of lump-sum payments there may be associated other competitive equilibria which are not Pareto-comparable to the pre-union equilibrium. For this reason, the assertion is worded with care.

[20]

The Move Toward Free Trade Zones

Paul Krugman

From World War II until about 1980, regional free trade agree-ments and global trade negotiations under the General Agreement on Tariffs and Trade (GATT) could reasonably be seen as comple-ments rather than substitutes—as two aspects of a broad march toward increasingly open international markets. Since then, how-ever, the two have moved in opposite directions. The 1980s were marked by stunning and unexpected success for regional trading blocs. In Europe, the European Community (EC) not only enlarged itself to include the new democracies of Southern Europe, but made a lunge for an even higher degree of economic unity with the cluster of market-integrating measures referred to as "1992." In North America, Canada ended a century of ambivalence about regional integration by signing a free trade agreement (which is also to an important extent an investment agreement) with the United States; even more startlingly, the reformist Salinas government in Mexico has sought, and appears likely to get, the same thing. And in East Asia, while formal moves toward regional free trade are absent, there was after 1985 a noticeable increase in Japanese investment in and imports from the region's new manufacturing exporters.

Meanwhile, however, the multilateral process that oversaw the great postwar growth in world trade seems to have run aground. The major multilateral trade negotiation of the decade, the Uruguay Round, was supposed to be concluded in late 1990. Instead, no agreement has yet been reached. And while some kind of face-saving document will probably be produced, in reality the Uruguay Round has clearly failed either to significantly liberalize trade or to generate good will that would help sustain further rounds of negotiation.

The contrast between the successes of regional free trade agreements and the failure of efforts to liberalize trade at the global level has raised disparate reactions. Official pronouncements, of course, call for renewed progress on all fronts. In practice, however, choices of emphasis must be made. Some politicians and economists despair of the multilateral process under the GATT, and would like to see further effort focused on regional or bilateral negotiations that seem more likely to get somewhere. Others, seeing the multilateral process as ultimately more important, fear that regional deals may undermine multilateralism. It is possible to find respected and influential voices taking fairly extreme positions on either side. For example, MIT's Rudiger Dornbusch has not only been a strong partisan of a U.S.-Mexico free trade pact, but has called for a U.S. turn to bilateral deals even with countries far from North America, such as South Korea. On the other side, Columbia's Jagdish Bhagwati, now a special adviser to the GATT, not only advocates remaining with the traditional process but has actually condemned the prospective U.S.-Mexico deal.

How can reasonable and well-informed people disagree so strongly? The answer lies, in part, in the inherent ambiguity of the welfare economics of preferential trading arrangements; it lies even more in the peculiarly contorted political economy of international trade negotiations.

Even in terms of straightforward welfare economics, the welfare effects of the creation of free trade areas are uncertain; indeed, it was precisely in the study of customs unions that the principle of the "second best," which says that half a loaf may be worse than none, was first formulated. A customs union, even if it only reduces trade barriers, may worsen trade distortions; moreover, consolidation of nations into trading blocs may lead even intelligent governments with the welfare of their citizens at heart to adopt more protectionist policies toward the outside world, potentially outweighing the gains from freer trade with their neighbors.

quickly survey some of the main results that seem to be relevant to the current problem of regionalism in world trade.

Trade creation vs. trade diversion

In a classic analysis, Jacob Viner (1950) pointed out that a move to free trade by two nations who continue to maintain tariffs against other countries could leave them worse rather than better off. Viner's insight remains fundamental to all analysis of preferential trading arrangements, and is worth restating.

The essential idea can be seen from a numerical example (Table 1).[1] Imagine that one country—which, not entirely innocently, we call Spain—can produce wheat for itself, import it from France, or import it from Canada. We suppose that the cost to Spain of producing a bushel of wheat for itself is 10, that the cost of a bushel of wheat bought from France is 8, and that the cost of a bushel bought from Canada is only 5.

Table 1
A Hypothetical Example of A Free Trade Area

	Tariff Rate		
	0	**4**	**6**
Cost of Wheat from:			
Spain	10	10	10
France, before customs union	8	12	14
France, after customs union	8	8	8
Canada	5	9	11

Suppose initially that Spain has a tariff that applies equally to all imported wheat. If it imports wheat in spite of the tariff, it will buy it from the cheapest source, namely Canada. This case is illustrated in the table by the column labeled "Tariff = 4." If the tariff is high enough, however—as in the case where it equals 6—Spain will grow its own wheat.

Now suppose that Spain enters a customs union with France, so that French wheat can enter free of tariff. Is this a good thing or a bad thing?

If the tariff was initially 6, the customs union is a good thing: Spain will replace its expensive domestic production with cheaper imported French wheat, freeing its own resources to do more useful things. If, however, the tariff was initially 4, the customs union will cause Spain to shift from Canadian wheat to more expensive French wheat, shifting from a low-cost to a high-cost source. In that case the customs union may well lower welfare.

As Viner pointed out, in the first, favorable case, the customs union causes Spain to replace high-cost domestic production with imports; it thus leads to an increase in trade. In the unfavorable case, by contrast, Spain shifts from a foreign source outside the free trade area to another source inside. Thus Viner suggested that "trade creating" customs unions, in which increased imports of trading bloc members from one another replace domestic production, are desirable; "trade diverting" customs unions, in which imports are diverted from sources outside the union to sources inside, are not. Loosely speaking, if the extra trade that takes place between members of a trading bloc represents an addition to world trade, the bloc has raised world efficiency; if the trade is not additional, but represents a shift away from trade with countries outside the bloc, world efficiency declines.

This simple criterion is extremely suggestive, and makes it easy to understand how regional trade liberalization can actually reduce rather than increase world efficiency. Perhaps the most obvious real-world example, as the illustration itself suggested, is the effect of EC enlargement on agricultural trade. The Southern European countries are induced, by their entry into the EC, to buy grain and other cold-climate products from costly European sources rather than the low-cost suppliers on the other side of the Atlantic. Meanwhile, the Northern European countries are now induced to buy Mediterranean products like wine and oil (and perhaps also labor-intensive manufactured goods) from Southern Europe rather than potentially cheaper suppliers elsewhere, for example, in North Africa. It is by no means implausible to suggest that because of these

can still be beneficial, through the normal gains from trade and specialization. Indeed, the idea that one could adjust tariffs so as to keep a customs union's trade with the outside world unchanged is the basis of a well-known demonstration that a customs union is always potentially beneficial to its members (Kemp and Wan 1976). But will a group of countries forming a trade area normally lower their external tariff sufficiently to avoid any trade diversion?

This depends on their motivations in forming the customs union in the first place. In practice, trading areas are formed for a variety of reasons, in which a careful assessment of costs and benefits is not usually high on the list. In the messy world of motivations discussed in the second part of this paper, it is possible either that a trading area might offer the rest of the world concessions in order to mollify it, or that the new bloc might have economically irrational autarkic tendencies as a way of emphasizing the political content of integration. For example, in the context of fairly amicable trade relations, one could imagine the EC cutting tariffs and subsidies in order to compensate the United States for any loss of markets due to increased European integration. In another context, one could imagine the emergence of a political context in which Fortress Europe shows a preference for self-sufficiency even beyond the beggar-thy-neighbor point.

Before we turn to political economy, however, let us at least ask what the economically rational action would be. And it is fairly obvious: not only would it not normally be in the interest of a trading bloc to throw away all of its terms of trade gain by reducing external tariffs, it would normally be in the bloc's interest to *raise* its external tariffs.

The reason is that a trading bloc will normally have more monopoly power in world trade than any of its members alone. The standard theory of the optimal tariff tells us that the optimal tariff for a country acting unilaterally to improve its terms of trade is higher, the lower the elasticity of world demand for its exports. So for a trading bloc attempting to maximize the welfare of its residents, the optimal tariff rate will normally be higher than the optimal tariff rates of its constituent countries acting individually.

This implies that the adjustment of external tariffs following formation of a regional trading bloc will not only not eliminate the beggar-thy-neighbor aspect, it will tend to worsen it.

Trading blocs and trade war

An individual trading bloc will tend to gain even in the face of trade diversion by improving its terms of trade at the rest of the world's expense. If one goes from envisioning a single bloc to imagining a world of trading blocs, however, the blocs may beggar each other. That is, formation of blocs can, in effect, set off a beggar-all trade war that leaves everyone worse off.

Imagine a world of *four* countries, A, B, C, and D. Imagine also that A and B enter negotiations to form a free trade area. They find that the area will primarily produce trade diversion rather than trade creation, but that it will still increase their welfare by improving their terms of trade at C and D's expense. Thus A and B will, correctly, form a free trade area; and this area will have an incentive to act as a trading bloc and raise its tariffs on imports from C and D. But suppose that C and D make the same calculation. Then both blocs will raise tariffs in an effort to exploit their market power. Obviously both cannot succeed; one bloc's terms of trade will actually deteriorate, while the other's will improve less than if it were acting on its own. Meanwhile, trade diversion will be taking its toll on world efficiency. The result of the tariff warfare may therefore be to leave all four countries worse off than they would have been had the trading blocs not been formed. And yet the members of each bloc are better off than they would have been if they had not joined their bloc, and thus left themselves at the mercy of the other bloc. So the game of free trade area formation itself may (though it need not) be a form of Prisoners' Dilemma, in which individually rational actions lead to a bad collective result.

This hypothetical example provides a simple justification for those who fear that the indirect costs of the move toward free trade areas will exceed the direct benefits. While it is an extremely stylized picture, it captures at least some of the concern of critics of regional trading arrangements, like Jagdish Bhagwati. The basic logic here

The importance of "natural" trading blocs

If transportation and communication costs lead to a strong tendency of countries to trade with their neighbors, and if free trade areas are to be formed among such good neighbors, then the likelihood that consolidation into a few large trading blocs will reduce world welfare is much less than suggested by the simple numerical example in Figure 3. The reason is straightforward: the gains from freeing intraregional trade will be larger, and the costs of reducing interregional trade, than the geography-free story suggests.

Imagine, for example, a world of six countries, which may potentially form into three trading blocs. If these countries are all symmetric, then three blocs is the number that minimizes world welfare, and hence this consolidation will be harmful. Suppose, however, that each pair of countries is on a different continent, and that intercontinental transport costs are sufficiently high that the bulk of trade would be between continental neighbors even in the absence of tariffs. Then the right way to think about the formation of continental free trade areas is not as a movement from 6 to 3, but as a movement of each continent from 2 to 1—which is beneficial, not harmful.

In practice, the sets of countries that are now engaging in free trade agreements are indeed "natural" trading partners, who would have done much of their trade with one another even in the absence of special arrangements. A crude but indicative measure of the extent to which countries are especially significant trading partners comes from comparison of their trade with what would have been predicted by a "gravity" equation, which assumes that trade between any two countries is a function of the product of their national incomes.

Even casual inspection of such gravity-type relations reveals the strong tendency of countries to focus their trade on nearby partners; that is, in spite of modern transportation and communications, trade is still largely a neighborhood affair.

The magnitude of the strength of natural trading blocs can be crudely calculated from a regression of the following form:

$$\ln(T_{ij}) = \alpha + \beta \ln(Y_i Y_j) + \sum_z \gamma^z D^z_{ij}$$

where T_{ij} represents the value of trade (exports plus imports) between some pair of countries i and j; and Y_i, Y_j represent the two countries' national incomes. We suppose that the countries belong to several groups that are or might become trading blocs, and we index these groups by z, with D^{zij} equal to 1 if the pair of countries i and j belong to group z, 0 otherwise. Then we would say that a potential trading bloc is natural to the extent that the estimated γ is strongly positive for that z.

The simplest regression of this kind that one can perform uses the G-7 countries (which after all account for most of world output in any case) and defines the two groupings as $z=1$: the United States and Canada, $z=2$: Europe. The results of that regression are shown in Table 2. To nobody's surprise, they point out very strongly the local bias of trade: the United States and Canada, according to the regression, do thirteen times as much trade as they would if they were not neighbors, while the four major European countries do seven times as much.

Table 2
A G-7 Gravity Regression

	Estimated Value	T-statistic
α	-8.4302	-6.894
β	0.7387	8.966
γ^1	2.6092	6.576
γ^2	1.9823	9.479

$R^2 = 0.7796$

Of course, these results are in part due to the fact that there are already special trading arrangements between the United States and Canada, on one side, and within the EC on the other. Yet the results are so strong that they make it overwhelmingly clear that distance still matters and still creates natural trading blocs.

Summary

The purely economic analysis of free trade areas suggests that, in principle, formation of such areas might hurt rather than help the world economy. Trade diversion could outweigh trade creation even with external protectionism unchanged; and the increased market power that countries gain by consolidating into trading blocs could lead optimizing but noncooperative governments to raise tariffs increasing the cost.

While some moves toward free trade surely do produce costly trade diversion, however, it seems unlikely that the net effect on world efficiency will be negative. The reason is geography: the possibly emergent trading blocs consist of more or less neighboring countries, who would be each others' main trading partners even without special arrangements. As a result, the potential losses from trade diversion are limited, and the potential gains from trade creation are large.

The main concern suggested by this economic analysis is distributional: inward-turning free trade areas, while doing little damage to themselves or each other, can easily inflict much more harm on economically smaller players that for one reason or another are not part of any of the big blocs.

The political economy of free trade areas

In a fundamental sense, the issue of the desirability of free trade areas is a question of political economy rather than of economics proper. While one could argue against the formation of free trade areas purely on the grounds that they might produce trade diversion, in practice (as argued above) the costs of trade diversion are unlikely to outweigh the gains from freer trade within regions. The real objection is a political judgment: fear that regional deals will undermine the delicate balance of interests that supports the GATT. Implicit in this concern is the idea that governments do not set tariffs to maximize national welfare, but that they are instead ruled by special interest politics disciplined and channeled by an international structure whose preservation is therefore a high priority.

To discuss the political economy of free trade areas, it is necessary to offer at least a rough outline of how trade policy actually works, and of why free trade areas rather than multilateral agreements seem to be the current trend. Only then can we ask whether such preferential agreements will help or hurt the overall prospects for trade.

GATT-think and trade negotiations

International trade policy has many horror stories. Examples of outrageous policy, like the sugar quota that for a time led U.S. producers to extract sucrose from imported pancake mix, are easy to come by. All microeconomic policy areas, however, offer similar stories of government actions that disregard efficiency and cater to organized interests. Indeed, one may argue that the surprising thing about trade policy is how good it is. Think of the way that the U.S. government handles water rights in the West, or tries to control pollution. These show a disregard for even the most elementary considerations of economic logic or social justice that make trade policy seem clean and efficient. Arguably trade policy is one of our best microeconomic policy areas—largely because it is disciplined by international treaties that have over time led to a progressive dismantling of many trade barriers.

One might be inclined to ascribe credit for this to the economists. After all, economists have for nearly two centuries preached the virtues of free trade. It seems natural to think of the GATT, and the relatively free trading system built around the GATT, as the result of the ideology of free trade.

Yet if one examines the reality of international trade negotiations, one discovers that the GATT is not built on a foundation laid by economic theory. That is not to say that there are no principles. On the contrary, one can make a great deal of sense of trade negotiations if one adopts a sort of working theory about the aims and interests of the participants, a theory that is built into the language of the GATT itself. The problem is that this underlying theory has nothing to do with what economists believe.

There is no generally accepted label for the theoretical underpin-

achieved the extraordinary dismantling of trade barriers accomplished by lawyers in the thirty years following World War II. If there are problems with the system now, they have more to do with perceptions that some countries are not playing by the rules than with a dissatisfaction of the political process with the rules themselves.

GATT-think, then, is very wrong, yet somehow turns out mostly right. Why?

The hidden logic of GATT-think

GATT-think is not, presumably, the product of a continuing mercantilist tradition, preserved by legislators and lawyers in defiance of economists—although it is probably true that a more or less mercantilist view of trade comes more naturally to the untutored than the economist's blanket endorsement of free trade. The reason why GATT-think works is, instead, that it captures some basic realities of the political process.

Trade policy is a policy of details. Only a tiny fraction of the U.S. electorate knows that we have a sugar import quota, let alone keeps track of such crucial issues (for a few firms) as the enamel-on-steel-cookware case. What Mancur Olson (1965) taught us is that in such circumstances, we should not expect government policy to reflect any reasonable definition of the public interest. Political pressure is a public good, and tends to be supplied on behalf of small, well-organized groups. In the case of trade policy, with few exceptions this means *producers*—producers of exported goods, producers of import-competing goods. The consumers who might have benefited from cheap imports, or the lower prices that would prevail if firms were not subsidized to provide goods to foreigners rather than themselves, count for very little.

This explains the first two principles of GATT-think: We need only append the words "for export producers" and "for import-competing producers," and one has statements with which economists can agree. Add that trade policy is set one industry at a time, so general equilibrium is disregarded, and that consumers are not at the table, and the mercantilist tone of trade negotiations is explained.

The third principle is more complicated. One would like to think that it reflects a residual concern with efficiency. Maybe it does. But it is also true that, on average, a dollar of exports adds more domestic value added than a dollar of imports subtracts, simply because not all imports compete directly with domestic goods. So perhaps the idea of gains from trade plays no role at all.

Yet the result of applying the principles of GATT-think has up to now been pretty good. The reason is the process of multilateral negotiation, which, in effect, sets each country's exporting interests as a counterweight to import-competing interests; as trade negotiators bargain for access to each others' markets, they move toward free trade despite their disregard for the gains from trade as economists understand them. (Notice also that in this context the GATT's harsh attitude toward export subsidies makes a great deal of sense: without such subsidies, export interests become a force for free trade; with free access to subsidies, they are not.)

During the 1980s, unfortunately, the effectiveness of the GATT process seemed to wane, with the focus shifting to regional free trade agreements. We must next ask why.

The erosion of the multilateral process

Everyone who thinks about it has his own list of problems with the GATT process. I would list four main factors that have eroded the effectiveness of the GATT mechanism at channeling special interests.

First is the decline of the U.S. leadership role. There is considerable disagreement among political scientists about the extent to which international policy coordination requires a hegemonic power. What is clear is that the dominant position of the United States in the early postwar period was helpful as a way of limiting free rider problems. The United States could and did both twist arms and offer system-sustaining concessions as a way of helping the GATT process work. With the United States accounting for a progressively smaller

its national influence best served by being part of a European whole. In the EC enlargement, as in the U.S. embrace of Mexico, politics played a large part: the wealthy EC nations wanted to reward and safeguard the Southern European transition to democracy.

Our second and third problems with the GATT—the complexities of dealing with modern trade and with modern trade barriers—are also, on the evidence, more easily dealt with at a regional level than at a global level. Europe's 1992 is not so much a trade agreement as an agreement to coordinate policies that have historically been regarded as domestic. That is, it is, in effect, a mutual sacrifice of national sovereignty. The Canada-U.S. FTA also involves significantly more than free trade: it is a pact over investment rules, and involves creation of dispute settlement mechanisms that limit the ability of the countries to act unilaterally.

Why can regional pacts do what global negotiations cannot? The answer appears to be that neighbors understand and trust one another to negotiate at a level of detail and mutual intrusiveness that parties to global negotiations cannot. One does not hear U.S. businessmen raising the arguments against free trade with Canada that they raise against Japan—nobody claims that Canada is so institutionally different from the United States, so conspiratorial a society, that negotiated agreements are worthless and ineffective. We think that we understand and can trust the Canadians; apparently the European nations have reached a similar point of mutual understanding and trust. North Americans and Europeans have not reached a comparable state with regard to one another, and both deeply distrust the Japanese.

And this is the final point. Whether or not Japan is really a radically different kind of player from other advanced nations,[7] the perception that it is has done a great deal to undermine the perceived effectiveness and legitimacy of the GATT in the United States and Europe. So the great advantage of regional pacts is that they can exclude Japan.

One could argue that the surge of interest in regional free trade agreements is actually a godsend to world trade. Given the loss of momentum in global trade negotiations, regional pacts offer a route through which trade can still increase. Of course this trade increase might, in principle, be diversion rather than creation, and hence make the world worse rather than better off. As argued in the first part of this paper, however, the importance of natural blocs is such that this is unlikely.

The real case against free trade agreements is that they may undermine the effort to deal with the problems of the multilateral system.

Free trade agreements and the international system

In the past two years there has been a schizophrenic mood in Washington regarding trade policy. On one side, the dismal prospects for the Uruguay Round, and the perceived lack of public spirit by the Europeans, have led to disillusionment with the prospects for the GATT—and, to at least some extent, a resigned acceptance of the likelihood of greater U.S. protectionism against Japan. On the other side, prospects for free trade with Mexico have brought out the traditional export sector support for liberalization with full force. It has been noted by a number of observers that the U.S. business community has put much more effort into supporting Mexican free trade than into any other trade area, even though Mexico remains a considerably smaller market than either the EC or Japan.

European enthusiasm over 1992 has similarly gone hand in hand with a rather sour attitude toward trade with non-European nations, and in particular, with a fairly notable failure to make any concessions on agriculture that would help make the Uruguay Round a success and thus help sustain the GATT's credibility.

Suppose that one could make the following two-part argument:

(1) By focusing on regional free trade, the United States and the EC have diverted political energies away from working on the problems of the GATT.

(2) Had they committed themselves to working within a multi-lateral framework, they could have achieved a solution to the GATT's difficulties that would have led to better results than the local solutions they have achieved instead.

If one believed this argument, one could then believe that the rise of free trade agreements has had an overall negative effect.

Part (1) of the argument clearly has some validity. Free trade agreements in Europe and North America have diverted some political, administrative, and intellectual capital away from the multilateral negotiating process. They have also reduced the sense of urgency about getting on with that process.

But would the GATT process really have done much better in the absence of moves toward regional free trade? This does not seem too plausible. The GATT's problems are deep-seated; it is hard to imagine achieving anything at the global level remotely approaching what the EC and the Canadian-U.S. pact have accomplished. And the problem of Japan seems extremely intractable.

It is understandable that economists and trade negotiators who have grown up in a world in which multilateral negotiations were the centerpiece of trade policy would be disturbed by a shift in emphasis toward regional agreements, especially if that shift seems to impair the effectiveness of the multilateral process—which it does. But while the move to free trade areas has surely done the multilateral process some harm, it is almost surely more a symptom than a cause of the decline of the GATT.

The impact of the move toward free trade zones

An unsophisticated view would see Europe 1992 and the move toward North American free trade as unadulterated good things. Global free trade would be better still, but these moves at least are in the right direction. And even if one is dismayed by the disappoint-ments of the Uruguay Round, one may still take comfort in the continuing integration of markets at a more local level.

A more sophisticated view sees both economic and political shadows. Free trade areas are not necessarily a good thing economically, because they may lead to trade diversion rather than trade creation. In the highly imperfect politics of international trade, regional free trade zones could upset the balance of forces that has allowed the creation of a fairly liberal world trading system.

The basic message of this paper is that the unsophisticated reaction is wrong in theory but right in practice. The prospects of trade diversion from free trade areas are limited, because the prospective trading blocs mostly fall along the lines of "natural" trading areas, countries that in any case do a disproportionate amount of their trade with one another. While regionalism does to some extent probably undermine the political force behind multilateral trade negotiations, the problems of the GATT are so deep-seated that it is unlikely that a world without regional free trade agreements would do much better.

The world may well be breaking up into three trading blocs; trade within those blocs will be quite free, while trade between the blocs will at best be no freer than it is now and may well be considerably less free. This is not what we might have hoped for. But the situation would not be better, and could easily have been worse, had the great free trade agreements of recent years never happened.

Appendix: Trading Blocs and World Welfare

This appendix lays out a simple model of the relationship between the number of trading blocs in the world economy and world welfare. It is based on Krugman (1991); as discussed in the text, it is intended as a guide to framing the issue rather than as a realistic tool for calculating the effects of free trade zones.

We imagine a world whose basic units are geographic units that we will refer to as "provinces." There are a large number N of such provinces in the world. A country in general consists of a large number of provinces. For the analysis here, however, we ignore the country level, focusing instead on "trading blocs" that contain a number of countries and hence a larger number of provinces. There will be assumed to be B<N trading blocs in the world. They are symmetric, each containing N/B provinces (with the problem of whole numbers ignored). In this simplified world, the issue of free trade zones reduces to the following: how does world welfare depend on B?

Each province produces a single good that is an imperfect substitute for the products of all other provinces. We choose units so that each province produces one unit of its own good, and assume that all provincial goods enter symmetrically into demand, with a constant elasticity of substitution between any pair of goods. Thus everyone in the world has tastes represented by the CES utility function

$$U = \left[\sum_{i=1}^{N} c_i^{\theta} \right]^{1/\theta},$$ (1)

where c_i is consumption of the good of province i, and the elasticity of substitution between any pair of products is

$$\sigma = \frac{1}{1-\theta}.$$ (2)

A trading bloc is a group of provinces with internal free trade and a common external ad valorem tariff. We ignore the realistic politics of trade policy, and simply assume that each bloc sets a tariff that maximizes welfare, taking the policies of other trading blocs as given. This is a standard problem in international economics: the optimal tariff for a bloc is

$$t^* = \frac{1}{\varepsilon - 1} \, ,$$
(3)

where ε is the elasticity of demand for the bloc's exports.

In a symmetric equilibrium in which all blocs charge the same tariff rate, it is possible to show that (see Krugman 1991)

$$\varepsilon = s + (1 - s) \, \sigma \, ,$$
(4)

where s is the share of each bloc in the rest of the world's income measured at world prices. The optimal tariff is therefore

$$t^* = \frac{1}{(1-s)(\sigma - 1)} \, .$$
(5)

It is apparent from (5) that the larger the share of each bloc's exports in the income of the world outside the bloc, the higher will be the level of tariffs on intra-bloc trade. This immediately suggests that a consolidation of the world into fewer, larger blocs will lead to higher barriers on inter-bloc trade.

One cannot quite stop here, however, because the share of each bloc in the rest of the world's spending depends both on the number of blocs and on the worldwide level of tariffs. Again after some algebra it is possible to show that this share equals

$$s = \frac{1}{(1+t)^\sigma + B - 1} \, ,$$
(6)

so that the share of each bloc's exports in the rest of the world's income is decreasing in both the tariff rate and the number of blocs.

Equations (5) and (6) simultaneously determine the tariff rate and the export share for a given number of blocs B. In Figure 1, the downward-sloping curve *SS* represents (6); it shows that the higher is the worldwide level of tariffs, the lower the share of each bloc in the spending of other blocs. The curve *TT* represents (5); it shows that the optimal tariff rate is higher, the smaller that export share. Equilibrium is at point *E*, where each bloc is levying the unilaterally optimal tariff.

Now suppose that there is a consolidation of the world into a smaller number of blocs. We see from (6) that for any given tariff rate, the effect of the reduction in B is increase *s*; thus *SS* shifts up to *S′ S′*. As a result, tariff rates rise, as equilibrium shifts from *E* to *E′*.

Clearly this change will reduce the volume of trade between any two provinces that are in different blocs. Even at an unchanged tariff, the removal of trade barriers between members of the expanded bloc would divert some trade that would otherwise have taken place between blocs. This trade diversion would be reinforced by the rise in the tariff rate.

Figure 1

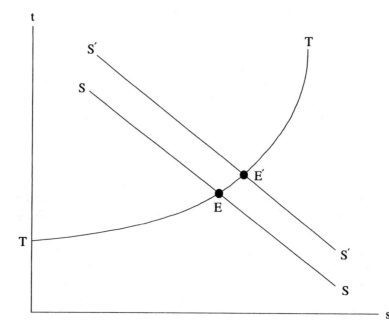

We now turn to welfare. Given the utility function (1), it is possible to calculate the welfare of a representative province as a function of the total number of provinces N, the number of blocs B, and the tariff rate t on inter-bloc trade. Since N plays no role in the analysis, we can simplify matters somewhat by normalizing N to equal 1. Again after considerable algebra, given in Krugman (1991), we find that the utility of a representative province is

$$U = \left[\frac{B}{(1+t)^\sigma + b - 1}\right]\left[(1-B^{-1}) + B^{-1}(1+t)^{\sigma\theta}\right]^{1/\theta}. \qquad (7)$$

If trade were free, this would imply a utility of 1. Since the tariff rate t is also a function of B, we can use (5), (6), and (7) together to determine how world welfare varies with the number of trading blocs.

The easiest way to proceed at this point is to solve the model numerically. This grossly over-simplified model has only two parameters, the number of trading blocs and the elasticity of substitution between any pair of provinces; it is therefore straightforward to solve first for tariffs as a function of B given several possible values of the elasticity, and then to calculate the implied effect on world welfare. Here the values of ε considered are 2, 4, and 10.

Figure 2 shows how world tariff rates vary with the number of blocs. Two points are worth noting. First, the relationship between tariff rates and the number of blocs is fairly flat. The reason is that when there are fewer blocs, trade diversion tends to reduce interbloc trade, and thus leads to less of a rise in each bloc's share of external markets than one might have expected. Second, except in the case of an implausibly high elasticity of demand, predicted tariff rates are much higher than one actually observes among advanced nations. This is not an artifact of the economic model: virtually all calculations suggest than unilateral optimum tariff rates are very high. What it tells us, therefore, is that actual trade relationships among advanced countries are far more cooperative than envisaged here.

Finally, we calculate welfare. Figure 3 shows the results. World welfare is, of course, maximized when there is only one bloc, in

Figure 2

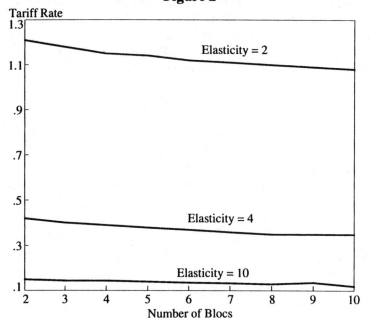

Figure 3

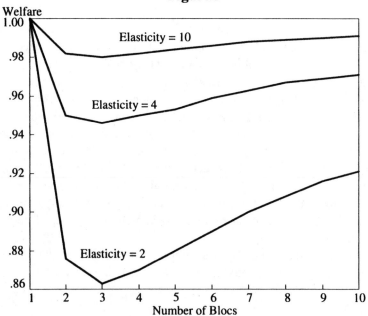

other words, global free trade. As suggested informally in the text, however, the relationship between welfare and the number of trading blocs is not monotonic but U-shaped. World welfare reaches a minimum when there are a few large blocs, and would be higher if there were more blocs, each with less market power.

The figure also shows a startling result: for the full range of elasticities considered, world welfare is minimized when there are three blocs.

As pointed out in the text, however, this result is an artifact of the assumption that under free trade any two provinces will trade as much as any other pair. That is, it ignores geography, which gives rise to natural trading blocs; as argued there, in practice, the strength of this natural linkage is strong enough to make it unlikely that consolidation of the world into regional blocs would actually reduce welfare.

Endnotes

[1]Indeed, this is one of those concepts that tends to get lost if one uses anything more high-powered than a numerical example.

[2]Hopes for large benefits from both the U.S.-Canada free trade agreement and Europe 1992 rest largely on increased competition and rationalization. In the North American case, the estimates of Harris and Cox (1984), which attempt to take account of competitive/industrial organization effects, suggest a gain for Canada from free trade that is about four times as large as those of standard models. In Europe, the widely cited, although controversial figure of a 7 percent gain due to 1992, presented in the Cecchini Report (Commission of the European Communities, 1988) rests primarily on estimates by Alasdair Smith and Anthony Venables of gains from increased competition and rationalization.

[3]Bhagwati and others have, of course, a much subtler view than this. They are not so much concerned with the fear that trading blocs will pursue optimal tariff policies as with the fear that regional trade negotiations will shift political resources away from the task of defending global trade against special interest politics. So this approach is only a rough metaphor for a real political story to be described in the paper's second part.

[4]This setup is clearly both too cynical and not cynical enough about the political economy of trade. The internal politics of trade are not nearly this benign. Governments do not simply (or ever) maximize the welfare of their citizens. At the same time, the external politics of trade show far more cooperation than this. An attempt at more realism follows later in the paper.

[5]The cost of an increase in protection here may seem surprisingly small. It is a familiar proposition to those who work with quantitative trade models, however, that the estimated costs of protection usually turn out to be embarrassingly small.

[6]It is surely also not irrelevant that with the collapse of the Soviet empire, the national security argument for fostering free trade among U.S. allies has suddenly lost its force.

[7]I believe that concerns that Japan is fundamentally different, and that negotiated trade liberalization is largely ineffective for Japan, are justified; but what is important here is not what is true but what is believed.

References

Commission of the European Communities. *The Economics of 1992, European Economy,* No. 35. Luxembourg: Commission of the European Communities, 1988.

Harris, R., and D. Cox. "Trade Liberalization and Industrial Organization: Some Estimates for Canada," *Journal of Political Economy,* 1985. pp. 115-145.

Kemp, M., and H. Wan. "An Elementary Proposition Concerning the Formation of Customs Unions," *International Economic Review,* 1976. pp. 95-97.

Krugman, P. "Is Bilateralism Bad?" in E. Helpman and A. Razin, eds., *International Trade and Trade Policy*, Cambridge: MIT Press, 1991.

Viner, J. *The Customs Union Issue.* New York: Carnegie Endowment for International Peace, 1950.

[21]

Multilateral Trade Negotiations and Preferential Trading Arrangements[*]

Alan V. Deardorff and Robert M. Stern

I. Introduction

For some years now, there has been a growing feeling in the United States and other major trading countries that their interests are not being well served by reliance on multilateral trade negotiations carried out under the auspices of the General Agreement on Tariffs and Trade (GATT). There has been considerable interest accordingly in seeking the benefits of freer trade by means of preferential bilateral/plurilateral trading arrangements of various kinds. The purpose of this chapter is to investigate these issues.

To put multilateralism and preferential arrangements in historical perspective, it is important to recall that bilateral and plurilateral deals and arrangements have always been an important part of the trade policy environment,[1] and have coexisted with multilateralism from the start. In this connection, we may note that, beginning in 1934, U.S. tariff authority was transferred from the Congress to the Executive Branch in

[*] The research underlying this paper was supported in part by a grant from the Ford Foundation to the Institute of Public Policy Studies at The University of Michigan for a program of research on trade policy. Helpful comments on earlier versions of the paper were received from members of the Research Seminar in International Economics at The University of Michigan, Jon D. Haveman, James A. Levinsohn, Ronald W. Jones, Gary R. Saxonhouse, Bernard M. Hoekman, Carsten Kowalczyk, and various conference participants. We wish to thank Judith Jackson and Tonia Short for typing and editorial assistance.

[1] The scope of bilateral arrangements is in fact much greater than implied here if account is taken of the many "friendship, commerce, and navigation" treaties and the bilateral investment treaties that have been negotiated over a long period of time. In addition, there are numerous sectoral agreements in existence.

accordance with the Reciprocal Trade Agreements Act (RTAA). As Winters 1990 p. 1289 has remarked, this was done in an effort to offset the detrimental effects of the Smoot–Hawley Act of 1930 that had increased U.S. tariff rates to historic highs and engendered foreign retaliatory actions against U.S. exports. The idea was that foreign markets for U.S. exports might be opened if the United States in turn was ready to make concessions to open its own market. Under the authority of the RTAA, the United States completed twenty bilateral trade agreements between 1934 and 1939. As Winters 1990 p. 1290 notes, the bilaterally negotiated tariff reductions were relatively small. But what was important here was that all the agreements provided for unconditional most-favored-nation (MFN) treatment. This was necessary to insure that an individual negotiating country would receive the benefits of whatever further tariff reductions might later be negotiated between the United States and other countries.

Bilateral reciprocity combined with MFN was subsequently adopted as the modus operandi of the GATT, and, as we will discuss below, there have been significant elements of bilateralism in all of the GATT negotiations from 1947 to the present. Thus, while we often think of the GATT as a system based on multilateralism, this may not give due recognition to the role that bilateralism has played in the system. A further manifestation of bilateralism in the GATT was the inclusion of Article XXIV relating to the formation of customs unions and free trade areas. We will note in our later discussion that a substantial number of preferential trading arrangements have in fact been set up within the GATT system, and that Article XXIV has been largely ineffective in overseeing and disciplining these arrangements. What all of this suggests then is that the current world trading system is best described as a coexistence of multilateralism and bilateral/plurilateral arrangements. It is apparent therefore that nations have not opted for a purely multilateral system. The question then is whether this mixture of trading arrangements may be conducive or detrimental to world economic welfare.

The chapter proceeds as follows. We begin in Section 2 with a discussion of the principles of GATT. In Section 3, we present a brief history of the main characteristics of the GATT negotiating rounds and an assessment of their accomplishments. Section 4 is devoted to how preferential trading arrangements are accommodated within Article XXIV of the GATT Articles of Agreement and to a discussion of the characteristics and consequences of existing preferential arrangements. In Section 5, we discuss more generally the advantages and limitations of multilateralism and preferential arrangements. In Section 6, we undertake a theoretical analysis of the welfare effects of the expansion of preferential trading blocs using a comparative advantage framework. We conclude in Section 7 with some implications for the design of trading blocs with the objective of enhancing world economic welfare.

II. The Principles of GATT[2]

The haphazard history of trade policy prior to World War II, including both unilateral protectionism and bilateral deals to undo that protectionism, led after the war to the formation of the GATT. A very strong case can be made that the GATT has had a profound and beneficial influence on the global trading system. Since World War II, the GATT has provided a consensual framework of rules and procedures for the efficient conduct of international trade. In addition, it has served as a negotiating forum in which major reductions in trade barriers have been agreed upon and carried out. The two main pillars or guiding principles of the GATT are well known: *nondiscrimination* and *reciprocity*.

The principle of nondiscrimination means essentially that a nation's trade policies are applied in a uniform and like manner to all of its trading partners. Individual nations or groups of nations are therefore not to be singled out for special preferential or punitive treatment as the case might be. For the principle of nondiscrimination to work effectively, nations must act cooperatively and seek to enhance world welfare. This would rule out aggressive or exploitative behavior that is designed to benefit individual nations or groups of nations at the expense of

---

[2] There are many excellent discussions of the principles and functioning of the GATT, including Baldwin 1987, Bhagwati 1990a,b, 1991, Finger 1979, Jackson 1989, Jackson and Davey 1986, Patterson 1989, Winters 1990, and Wolf 1987.

30   Issues in the Global Trading System

others. In the event of disputes between GATT signatories, the presumption is that there would be impartial adjudication. The interests of small nations especially would therefore be protected against the possibly detrimental actions of larger and more powerful nations.

The principle of reciprocity is more pragmatic in character and arises from the idea that trade liberalization should be viewed in a cooperative context in which countries will exchange concessions on a reciprocal basis. However, the principle of reciprocity does not necessarily rule out unilateral liberalization. Rather, as already noted, reciprocity stems in large measure from the efforts of the United States especially during the 1930s to use reductions in U.S. trade barriers as an inducement to get its trading partners to do likewise. Narrowly conceived, reciprocity implies that concessions will be balanced bilaterally, and this is in fact how trade liberalization was effected during the 1930s. Under the GATT, particularly prior to the Kennedy Round in 1963–67, negotiations were primarily bilateral. But what is crucially important is that the GATT embodies the Most-Favored-Nation (MFN) principle, so that any concessions that may be negotiated bilaterally are then automatically extended to all other GATT member nations. The GATT system can thus be viewed as a multilateral system in which there is nondiscrimination and reductions in trade barriers are made generally available to all countries that adhere to MFN.[3]

The GATT is intended to foster transparency of trade policy measures. This has been most evident in the legal binding of tariff rates by GATT member nations and efforts to reduce these bound rates by negotiation. Transparency has also been an objective with regard to the

---

[3] Krugman 1991b, 1992a asserts that the GATT is based on what he calls principles of "enlightened mercantilism." He refers to this as "GATT-think" whose basic principles are: (1) exports are good; (2) imports are bad; and (3) other things equal, an equal increase in imports and exports is good. He concludes nonetheless that the trading system has been well served by the principles of GATT-think. The reason is that GATT-think captures important political realities in terms of the way in which the interests of exporting firms are played off as a counterweight against the interests of import-competing firms. Seen in this light, reciprocity and MFN become the "hidden logic" in the GATT system as the prime vehicles for achieving the dismantling of trade restrictions and thus promoting the benefits of freer trade.

use of nontariff measures of various kinds. Greater transparency will thus facilitate international transactions by consumers and business firms.

The GATT focus on the reduction and removal of trade barriers and fostering transparency can be achieved most effectively in what Bhagwati 1990b has called a "fix rule trading regime." This means a regime in which trade is guided by a set of rules governing access to markets, that is, rules that permit markets to operate in such a way that the actions of private transactors will serve to enhance economic efficiency and welfare. This is to be distinguished from a "fix quantity rule trading regime," in which trade is managed more directly by government authority establishing quantitative targets for exports and imports without regard necessarily to the effects that managed trade may have on efficiency and welfare.

III. A Brief History of GATT Negotiating Rounds[4]

As indicated in Table 2.1, there have been eight rounds of GATT negotiations since 1947. In the first GATT round (Geneva 1947), there were 23 participating countries and $10 billion of trade affected by tariff concessions. For the United States in particular, concessions covered 56 percent of total dutiable imports, and, as Finger 1979 p. 423 notes, tariff reductions plus tariff bindings covered 78 percent of total imports. The next two negotiating rounds (Annecy 1949 and Torquay 1951) mainly involved newly acceding countries to the GATT, and in this sense these rounds can be considered as a completion of the first round. Once tariff bindings were effected, the Geneva (1956), Dillon (1960–61), and Kennedy (1963–67) Rounds then focused almost entirely on tariff reductions. There were 48 countries involved in the Kennedy Round and $40 billion of trade covered by tariff concessions. While tariff reductions also figured importantly in the Tokyo Round (1973–79), the primary focus by then was on nontariff measures. The Uruguay Round (1986–?) is the eighth negotiating round and at the time of writing (July

---

[4] The discussion here draws especially on Finger 1979 and Winters 1990.

TABLE 2.1. GATT Negotiating Rounds

GATT Round	Countries Participating	Trade Affected (Billions of $)	Average Depth of Cut[a]	U.S. Tariff Reductions Import Coverage[b]	Internalization Ratio Bilateral[c]	Internalization Ratio Multilateral[d]
1. Geneva, 1947	23	$10.0	35%	56%	n.a. %	84%
2. Annecy, 1949	33	n.a.	37	6	35	39
3. Torquay, 1951	34	n.a.	26	15	58	64
4. Geneva, 1956	22	2.5	15	20	74	89
5. Dillon, 1960–61	45	4.9	20	19	69	96
6. Kennedy, 1964–67	48	40.0	44	64	n.a.	91
7. Tokyo, 1973–79	99	155.0	34[e]	n.a.	n.a.	n.a.
8. Uruguay, 1986–?	100	n.a.	n.a.	n.a.	n.a.	n.a.

[a]Weighted by dutiable imports.
[b]Imports subject to tariff reductions as a percentage of total dutiable imports.
[c]Share of imports subject to a tariff reduction coming from the individual country receiving that concession.
[d]Share of imports subject to a tariff reduction coming from all countries participating in the negotiating round.
[e]Weighted by total imports.

Source: Adapted from Finger 1979 pp. 424–25, Jackson and Davey 1986 pp. 324–25, Deardorff and Stern 1986 p. 49, and Winters 1990 p. 1291.

1993) is still in progress. It involves some 100 participating countries and has a large agenda, including negotiations on: trade barriers; sectoral liberalization (e.g., agriculture and textiles and apparel); GATT rules, procedures, and the functioning of the GATT system; and "new" issues (intellectual property rights, trade-related investment measures, and services).

All of these multilateral rounds might suggest that the world shifted abruptly after World War II from bilateral deals to a system of purely multilateral cooperation. Such was not the case, however. As Winters 1990 notes, the negotiations themselves were completely bilateral in the early GATT rounds, and their multilateral implication arose solely from the requirement of MFN. In an effort to deal with problems of free riding, the negotiated concessions were lumped into a single package and were provisional until the overall agreement was completed and signed. This was intended to provide a means of assessing the reciprocity of concessions. In addition, efforts were made to maximize the benefits of the liberalization for the negotiating parties. Finger 1979 refers to this as *internalization*, and it is measured as the imports subject to tariff reductions as a percentage of all dutiable imports on either a bilateral or multilateral basis. In order to maximize the degree of internalization, countries negotiated on a product-by-product, *principal supplier* basis, meaning that concessions were to be exchanged bilaterally on goods for which the two countries were each other's major suppliers. The importance of internalization can be seen in Table 2.1, where it apparently became increasingly difficult to select goods for negotiating purposes in the successive rounds. That is, the import coverage of U.S. tariff reductions decreased from 56 percent in the Geneva Round (1947) to 19 percent in the Dillon Round (1960–61). At the same time, the bilateral internalization ratio in the Dillon Round grew to 69 percent and the multilateral ratio to 96 percent.

Given the obvious limitations of the product-by-product, principal-supplier approach in the Dillon Round, it was decided in the Kennedy Round to adopt an across-the-board form of tariff negotiation whereby tariff rates were to be reduced by a fixed percentage according to an agreed formula, with exemptions to be negotiated for industries that were deemed too sensitive to liberalize. It is evident from Table 2.1 that the import coverage of U.S. tariff reductions in the Kennedy Round was increased substantially as compared to the Dillon Round, and that the degree of multilateral internalization remained relatively high. This is noteworthy in view of the fact, as Winters 1990 points out, that the tariff negotiations still had a pronounced bilateral orientation. In addition to its tariff negotiations, the Kennedy Round agenda was intended to include negotiations on NTBs and agriculture and to give special attention to developing country exports. It was also decided to forego reciprocal concessions on the part of developing countries. As Winters 1990 and others have noted, the Kennedy Round did not succeed to any important extent in reducing existing NTBs, and the agricultural negotiations failed. It also appeared that the only developing countries to gain significantly in the Kennedy Round were those that did make reciprocal concessions, so that the"special and differential treatment" of developing countries was of questionable value to them.

The principle of across-the-board linear reductions of tariff rates with exemptions was continued in the Tokyo Round, again involving a significant element of bilateralism. But the Tokyo Round dealt primarily with the rules of the GATT system, including technical standards, customs valuation, import licensing and quantitative restrictions, safeguards, subsidies and countervailing duties, antidumping, government procurement, and civil aviation. The Tokyo Round constituted therefore a marked departure from earlier rounds in view of its focus on GATT rules and procedures. Since these are "constitutional" matters, they clearly do not lend themselves to quantitative assessment and to bilateral quid pro quo concessions. It also means that it is difficult to achieve consensus on the design and scope of the specific negotiating items, and, accordingly, that the negotiations may be protracted and nettlesome if there are significant disagreements among the major participants.

The United States led an effort to launch the eighth round of GATT negotiations at the GATT Ministerial Meeting in 1982, but this meeting was apparently badly timed in view of the ongoing world recession, and there were important disagreements about the agenda that was tabled. As already noted, the Uruguay Round was subsequently initiated in 1986. It is unquestionably the most far reaching of all the GATT rounds to date. The Uruguay Round has fourteen individual negotiating groups dealing with trade barriers, sectoral issues, GATT rules and procedures, and new issues. As Winters 1990 notes, it has an even stronger orientation towards "constitutional" matters than was the case in the Tokyo Round. It also seeks to address the difficult issues of agricultural subsidy programs, reaffirms the continuation of the special and differential treatment for most developing countries, and leaves the questions of the choice of formulae for reductions in tariffs and NTBs to be decided in the course of the negotiations.

The Uruguay Round was scheduled for completion in December 1990, but the negotiations were suspended because the United States and the Cairns Group of other major agricultural exporting countries considered the offer by the European Community (EC) to reduce its agricultural subsidies to be unacceptably small. The Uruguay Round negotiations have since been resumed, but their completion is still contingent on whether the EC will make agricultural concessions that the major agricultural exporters are willing to accept. This means that the rest of the Uruguay Round negotiating agenda is being held in abeyance.

The experience of the GATT negotiating rounds is instructive with regard to the successes achieved and also the problems that have been encountered. First, it is clear that the tariff rates of the major industrialized countries have been reduced to relatively low levels, and, as a consequence, that tariffs on the whole no longer constitute major barriers to trade for these countries. Even though there has been a distinct bilateral orientation in the tariff negotiations, the degree of multilateralization of the tariff concessions has been substantial. Second, it is also clear that NTBs have not been reduced to any significant extent, although some reductions may be possible if the Uruguay Round can be concluded on a positive note. Third, the Uruguay Round is the first time that issues of agricultural subsidies have been squarely faced on an international level. It comes as no surprise that the depth of domestic opposition to reductions in these subsidies is profound, given that the subsidies have been in place for decades and that agricultural incomes depend heavily on them. It is perhaps regrettable that there are many other important issues being held hostage to the agricultural negotiations, but it is arguable that the stakes in agricultural liberalization may be potentially greater as compared to these other issues. Finally, beginning with the Tokyo Round and continuing in the Uruguay Round, there has been a pronounced shift towards negotiations covering the rules and procedures of the GATT system. Many aspects of these rules and procedures touch directly on domestic policies in the major trading countries/blocs, so that there are bound to be important differences in the design and implementation of these policies and in the role that interest groups may play when it comes to making changes in policies.

The combination of the impasse in the agricultural negotiations and the pronounced shift towards negotiations on"constitutional" issues may be interpreted as testimony to the difficulties associated with multilateralism as efforts are being made to bring about changes in longstanding domestic policies in the major countries/blocs. It is in this light that the prospects for negotiating preferential arrangements seem appealing. In order to be able to evaluate the case to be made for preferential arrangements, it will first be useful to examine how these arrangements are handled within the GATT and to examine the characteristics and consequences of the important arrangements that have been implemented since World War II.

IV. Preferential Trading Arrangements and the GATT

GATT Article XXIV

In drafting the Articles of Agreement of the GATT, some allowance had to be made for preferential arrangements. The presumption was that such arrangements might be welfare enhancing provided certain criteria were met.[5] The details are set out in Article XXIV of the GATT, which is entitled "Territorial Application—Frontier Traffic—Customs Unions and Free Trade Areas." This Article is reproduced in the Appendix below.

---

[5] Bhagwati 1992a suggests a three-fold rationale for inclusion of Article XXIV in the GATT: (1) full integration of trade among a subset of countries would give the bloc a quasi national status that would be consistent with the single-nation MFN obligation towards other GATT members; (2) removal of all barriers would preclude special and more limited preferential arrangements; and (3) the formation of a trading bloc might further the achievement of freer trade on a global basis.

Article XXIV:4 states that:

"The contracting parties recognize the desirability of increasing freedom of trade by the development, through voluntary agreements, of closer integration between the economies of the countries parties to such agreements. They also recognize that the purpose of a customs union or of a free-trade area should be to facilitate trade between the constituent territories and not to raise barriers to the trade of other contracting parties with such territories."

It is further stated in Article XXIV:5(a),(b),(c) that"...the duties and other regulations of commerce...shall not be higher or more restrictive than...prior to the formation..." of the customs union or free-trade area (FTA) and that the arrangement is to be concluded "within a reasonable length of time." The GATT is to be provided (Article XXIV:7(a)) with information pertaining to the arrangement in order that reports and recommendations can be made as deemed appropriate, and compensatory adjustments may be sought if rates of duty are increased (Article XXIV:6). Finally, Article XXIV:8(a)(b) states that "...the duties and other restrictive regulations of commerce...are [to be] eliminated on substantially all the trade between the constituent territories in products originating in such territories."[6]

An indication of the major preferential arrangements that have been implemented between 1947 and 1991 is given in Table 2.2, which is adapted from Whalley 1991. A more detailed list of the 69 preferential agreements of various kinds and subsequent amendments thereto notified to the GATT between 1947 and 1988 is given in Schott 1989, who notes (pp. 24–25) that only four agreements were explicitly deemed to be compatible with Article XXIV and that no agreement was found to be incompatible.[7] This is not to say that criticisms of preferential arrangements have been absent in GATT deliberations. But it appears nonetheless that the GATT member countries have sidestepped whatever

---

[6] See Jackson and Davey 1986 p. 457 for a list of some of the problems of legal interpretation arising from the language of Article XXIV.

[7] See also the listings of regional and preferential trading arrangements in de la Torre and Kelly 1992 pp. 8, 9, 11, and 12 and Fieleke 1992 pp. 4-5.

Table 2.2. Major Preferential Trading Arrangements, 1947–91

1947   Article XXIV included in GATT. Allows formation of customs unions and free trade areas under certain conditions.

1957   Treaty of Rome established the European Economic Community. A customs union involving Belgium, Luxembourg, France, the Netherlands, Germany, and Italy. Treaty went into force 1 January 1958.

1959   Stockholm Convention established the European Free Trade Association (EFTA) to go into effect 1 July 1960. Members included Austria, Denmark, Norway, Portugal, Sweden, Switzerland, and the United Kingdom.

1960   Montevideo Treaty established the Latin American Free Trade Association (LAFTA) comprising Argentina, Brazil, Chile, Colombia, Ecuador, Mexico, Paraguay, Peru, and Uruguay.

1960   Central American Common Market (CACM) formed. Included Costa Rica, El Salvador, Guatemala, Honduras, and Nicaragua.

1963   Yaoundé Convention between the EEC and former French, Belgian, and Italian colonies in Africa. Gives these countries preferential access to the EC and set up the European Development Fund.

1965   Australia and New Zealand formed a free trade area.

1965   Canada and the United States sign Automobile Products Trade Agreement (Auto Pact).

1967   East African Community formed. Included Kenya, Tanzania, and Uganda.

1967   ASEAN formed. Included Brunei, Indonesia, Malaysia, Philippines, Singapore, and Thailand.

1969   Andean Pact formed. Included Bolivia, Chile, Colombia, Ecuador, Peru, and Venezuela.

1969   Yaoundé Convention extended.

1973   European Community enlarged to include Britain, Ireland, and Denmark.

1975   Yaoundé Convention superseded by Lomé Convention. Extended preferential arrangements to include former colonies of Britain and widened to include countries in the Caribbean and Pacific.

1983   Australia and New Zealand formed Closer Economic Relationship to provide for a free trade agreement.

1984   United States implements Caribbean Basic Economic Recovery Act to extend duty-free treatment to 21 beneficiary countries in the region for 12 years.

1985   United States-Israel Free Trade Area Agreement enters into force. Over a 10-year period, all tariffs between the two countries to be eliminated.

1986   Portugal and Spain join the European Community. Single European Act signed to provide for full European integration in 1992.

1989   Canada-U.S. Free Trade Agreement enters into force. Under agreement all items should be traded duty-free between the two countries by 1998.

1990   EC and EFTA undertake discussions on a European Economic Area which would provide for freer movement of goods, services, capital, and people between the two associations.

1990   United States announces "Enterprise for the Americas" initiative to explore a hemisphere-wide free trade zone involving countries of North, Central, and South America.

1991   United States, Mexico, and Canada enter discussions on a North American free trade area.

Source: Adapted from Whalley 1991.

40   Issues in the Global Trading System

discipline might have been justified with respect to particular arrangements that did not meet the criteria of Article XXIV.[8]

Having described the GATT provisions for preferential arrangements and the lack of any effective surveillance of them, it is of interest to consider some characteristics and consequences of some of the most noteworthy existing arrangements.

Characteristics and Consequences of Preferential Arrangements

A great deal of analytical attention has been devoted over the years to the economic issues posed by preferential arrangements, but it would take us too far afield to review these issues in detail. For our purposes here, a convenient summary of the issues is provided in Wonnacott and Lutz 1989 pp. 69–70, who identify several considerations that relate in particular to the likelihood of trade creation or trade diversion and therefore to whether world economic welfare may be increased or lowered as the result of a preferential arrangement.[9] They note that the ratio of trade creation to trade diversion will depend on whether:

1. The tariffs of outside countries are high and the initial tariffs of member countries are also high. In this case, the formation of a preferential arrangement is not likely to be trade diverting since there

---

[8] According to Patterson 1989 p. 361: "The effective destruction of Article XXIV as a serious restraint on FTA and customs unions began in earnest when the European Community was examined and subjected to very extensive debate under these provisions in 1957–58. No agreement was reached as to the legal question of whether the EC satisfied the requirements of Article XXIV. Apart from political considerations, which dictated a tolerant attitude on the part of some, including the United States, the participants in these discussions concluded that the EC was going to go forward as set out in the Treaty of Rome, and if it were formally found to be 'illegal,' the GATT as an institution would be mortally wounded." See also the discussion of the role of GATT in influencing regional arrangements in Bhagwati 1992a and Finger 1992.

[9] See de Melo, Panagariya, and Rodrik 1992 for a review and extension of the pertinent literature dealing with: (1) the welfare effects of trading blocs; (2) the role of economies of scale, factor mobility, and tariff revenues; and (3) institutional considerations. See also de la Torre and Kelly 1992 pp. 3–6 and Saxonhouse 1992.

Table 2.3. Trade Patterns of Preferential Trading Blocs (Percentage of Combined GDP of Member Nations)

Association and time period[a]	Internal trade			External trade			Total trade		
	Base	Later	Change	Base	Later	Change	Base	Later	Change
Readily apparent increases in internal trade									
Central American Common Market (CACM)[b] 1957–60 1966–70	1.8	10.0	8.2	33.4	33.2	-0.2	35.2	43.2	8.0
European Community (EC6)[c]									
1953–57/1963–67	8.1	13.1	5.0	20.0	17.9	-2.1	28.1	31.0	2.9
1953–57/1968–72	8.1	17.2	9.1	20.0	18.3	-1.7	28.1	35.5	7.4
European Community (EC9)[d] 1968–72/1978–82	17.6	24.3	6.7	17.9	24.0	6.1	35.5	48.3	12.8
European Free Trade Association (EFTA)[e] 1955–59/1965–69	6.9	8.7	1.8	30.1	27.4	-2.7	37.0	36.1	-0.9
Andean Pact[f] 1964–68/1974–78	0.9	2.4	1.5	30.5	38.2	7.7	31.4	40.6	9.2
No obvious effect on internal trade									
Association of Southeast Asian Nations (ASEAN)[g] 1967–71/1972–76	7.0	7.8	0.8	37.5	49.9	12.4	44.5	57.7	13.2
New Zealand-Australia FTA 1961–65/1971–75	1.7	1.8	0.1	28.6	24.8	-3.8	30.3	26.6	-3.7
Latin American Free Trade Area (LAFTA)[h]	1.6	1.6	0.0	19.0	13.1	-5.9	20.6	14.7	-5.9
East African Community (EAC)[i] 1968–72/1973–77	6.3	3.9	-2.4	35.6	34.5	-1.1	41.9	38.4	-3.5

[a]Except for EAC and ASEAN, the base period precedes establishment of the regional association. For EAC and ASEAN (both established in 1967), bilateral trade data from the period preceding establishment are not available.

[b]Members include: Costa Rica; El Salvador; Guatemala; Honduras; and Nicaragua.

[c]Members include: Belgium, France, W. Germany, Italy, Luxembourg, and the Netherlands.

[d]Members include: EC6 plus Denmark, Ireland, and United Kingdom.

[e]Members include: Austria, Denmark, Finland, Norway, Sweden, Switzerland, and United Kingdom.

[f]Members include: Bolivia, Chile, Colombia, Ecuador, Peru, and Venezuela.

[g]Members include: Brunei, Indonesia, Malaysia, the Philippines, Singapore, and United Kingdom.

[h]Members include: Argentina, Brazil, Chile, Colombia, Ecuador, Mexico, Paraguay, Peru, and Uruguay.

[i]Members include: Kenya, Tanzania, and Uganda. EAC effectively came to an end in 1977.

Source: Adapted from Wonnacott and Lutz 1989 p. 76 and based on IMF, *Direction of Trade*.

would not be a great deal of trade with outside countries. By the same token, the welfare effects of the preferential arrangement would be enhanced if the member-country tariffs on imports from outside countries were subsequently set at low rates.

2. The prospective member countries are already major trading partners and are close geographically.

3. There are important differences in comparative advantage among the member countries.

In addition they argue that a preferential arrangement is most likely to be viable if the member countries are at similar levels of development and the division of gains from the preferential arrangement can be achieved without major economic and political disagreement. In this connection, Schott 1991 pp. 2–3 emphasizes the importance of the sustainability of the trading relationships among the member countries and the compatibility of their laws and regulations governing trade flows among themselves and with third countries.

It is interesting in light of the foregoing considerations to examine Table 2.3, adapted from Wonnacott and Lutz 1989 p. 76, which lists the important preferential arrangements that have been established and the changes in trade patterns that have occurred. The eight arrangements are classified into two groups according to the changes in internal trade prior to and after the arrangement was put in place.[10] Wonnacott and Lutz draw a number of conclusions about the experiences of the preferential arrangements listed:

1. The preferential arrangements in the first group, in which internal trade increased, generally followed an across-the-board approach to the freeing of internal trade, whereas the second group followed primarily a product-by-product approach. In the latter case, except for the ASEAN, there was a decline in external trade. The substantial increases in internal trade and comparatively small declines in the

---

[10] It will be noted that Table 2.3 does not include the entry of Greece, Portugal, and Spain into the EC, the 1983 Closer Economic Relationship between Australia and New Zealand, and the 1985 U.S.–Israel and 1989 U.S.–Canada FTAs. Also, it does include arrangements that are no longer in force.

external trade of the European Community (EC) are especially note-worthy.

2. There is an apparently positive relationship between the expansion of internal trade and the similarity of development and economic structure, which is also suggestive of the fact that similar economies like those in Western Europe tend to be each other's best customers. Geographical proximity does not appear to be a controlling factor in all situations, as suggested particularly in the different experiences of the Central American Common Market and the East African Community.

The conclusions regarding the EC experience coincide with those of Schott 1991, who observes (pp. 4–5) that the "EC has substantially succeeded in promoting the integration of its member economies" and that "intra-EC trade has far outpaced the growth of exports to third markets." Further, he notes (p. 6) that the multilateral system has been able to accommodate the continuing integration of the European market and evolution of a strong regional trading bloc. Schott also examines the emerging North American trading bloc, which was not included in Table 2.3. As he notes, both Canada and Mexico conduct about two-thirds of their export and import trade with the United States as well as being large-scale recipients of U.S. foreign direct investment. While there are many similarities between the Canadian and U.S. economies in terms of their economic structure, level of development, and compatibility of their trade regimes, this is of course much less true in comparison to Mexico. But when account is taken of the far reaching unilateral economic reforms and liberalization achieved by Mexico in recent years and the commitment of the Mexican government to continue its policy reforms, the prospects for a successful North American trading bloc appear to be favorable despite the differences between Mexico and the United States and Canada.[11] Further, Schott judges that a North American Free Trade Area (NAFTA) is likely to be compatible with the multilateral trading system insofar as U.S. trade especially will continue to be directed very substantially to markets outside of North America and all

---

[11] For a computational analysis of a North American Free Trade Agreement, see Brown, Deardorff, and Stern 1992.

three NAFTA nations will look to the multilateral system to expand their trading opportunities and to provide a framework for governing their trade relations.

This brief review of existing preferential trading arrangements suggests that the most successful and durable arrangements have been those involving the already advanced industrialized regions in Western Europe and North America.[12] Preferential arrangements among developing countries have in contrast not been particularly successful and often not durable, especially because they have often been designed with import-substitution objectives in mind.[13] It is also noteworthy that Japan and the Asian newly industrializing countries (NICs) are not members of any *de jure* trading bloc. While it is conceivable that an Asian trading bloc might be formed in the future, it seems like a long way off, since, as Schott 1991 p. 14 notes, the countries in the Asia/Pacific region are very widely dispersed geographically, have rather different levels of development and different trade policies and regulatory regimes, and do not have a strong commitment to regionalism. This latter point is most compelling since a great deal of the international trade and investment of Japan and the other Asian countries relates to other parts of the world, especially the United States and Western Europe.

The conclusion that can be drawn from all of this is that the multilateral system has been able to accommodate a series of preferential arrangements over the past three decades, and it is arguable that the arrangements involving the advanced industrialized countries especially have been welfare enhancing on the whole both to the member countries and to the outside world. Further, it is especially noteworthy that there has been a continuing commitment to multilateralism on the part of the same countries that have participated in these preferential arrangements,

---

[12] This statement should apply as well to the Closer Economic Relationship between Australia and New Zealand.

[13] For more detailed and up-to-date empirical analyses of the experiences of developed and developing countries with preferential trading arrangements, see de Melo, Panagariya, and Rodrik 1992, de la Torre and Kelly 1992, Fieleke 1992, Irwin 1992, Nogués and Quintanilla 1992, Whalley 1992, and Winters 1992.

given that extra-bloc trade has usually remained important to them. This suggests that the powerful trading blocs and individually powerful trading nations have found it in their interest to adhere to an essentially cooperative form of international behavior rather than seeking to achieve benefits through exploiting their market power in trade.

V. The Advantages and Limitations of Multilateralism and Preferential Arrangements[14]

Having briefly examined the experiences of the GATT negotiating rounds and the characteristics and consequences of preferential arrangements within the GATT system, it is interesting next to juxtapose multilateralism and preferential arrangements and seek to identify their respective advantages and limitations. This discussion is not intended to answer which is necessarily better since, as already mentioned, the two are complementary in many respects. We nonetheless hope that our discussion may serve to identify the major elements of choice and compatibility between multilateralism and preferential arrangements and provide a basis for insuring that the international trading system will function to enhance world welfare.

The Case for Multilateralism

Trade liberalization can be undertaken unilaterally, and there are many instances when unilateral liberalization has in fact been carried out. But governments may often feel constrained by domestic interest groups who are opposed to unilateral liberalization. A case can be made accordingly for multilateral liberalization, as Finger 1979 and others have pointed out, on an economy-wide and reciprocal basis. This permits a balancing of the interests of consumers and exporting firms and workers who will

---

[14] The discussion in this section is based especially on Baldwin 1987, Bhagwati 1990a,b, 1992a,b, Finger 1979, Hoekman 1991, Jackson 1989, Krugman 1991b, 1992a,b, Patterson 1989, Nogués 1990, Schott 1989, 1991, Whalley 1991, Winters 1990, Wolf 1987, and Yarbrough and Yarbrough 1986.

46   Issues in the Global Trading System

benefit from multilateral liberalization against the interests of import-competing firms and workers who may experience displacement.[15] The presumption is that the benefits of liberalization will far outweigh the costs so that it should be possible, at least in principle, to devise a tax-subsidy arrangement or some other type of income redistribution so that in effect the gainers can compensate the losers.[16]

As already stated, the GATT system is premised on the desirability of cooperative behavior among nations. This is necessary so that the economic benefits derived from multilateral liberalization can be realized. If the system works effectively, there would be political benefits as well, insofar as nations would act in harmony and would avoid the introduction of exploitative trade policy measures and thus forestall possible retaliatory actions by aggrieved trading partners.

In a world of nation states, it is obvious that issues of national sovereignty and national interest will be of great importance. When trade disputes arise, it is inevitable that their reconciliation will require appropriate policy changes by governments. Since individual nations have agreed to certain obligations and have been guaranteed certain rights as a condition of their membership in the GATT, their acceptance of GATT dispute settlements will of necessity lead to overriding the opposition of domestic interest groups. In this way, national autonomy and sovereignty have to be superseded in order to enhance global welfare.

As already noted in our discussion, it is important to recognize that there is leeway in the existing multilateral trading system for nations to take actions or enter into agreements on a bilateral or plurilateral basis insofar as there are situations in which welfare enhancing mutual interests can be pursued on this more limited basis. In evaluating these

---

[15] This is the "hidden logic" that has made GATT successful according to Krugman 1991b, 1992a in spite of the seeming mercantilistic principles (GATT-think) that he identifies as underlying the GATT.

[16] Finger 1979 characterizes multilateral liberalization as a public good since it has the properties of being nonexclusive and nonrival. That is, because of MFN, access to markets is available to all foreign exporters (nonexclusion), and there is no limit on the amount of goods that any foreign supplier(s) or nation(s) can export (nonrivalness).

Multilateral Trade Negotiations 47

actions, what is important is whether or not they are detrimental to third countries. Indeed, as we have already noted, Article XXIV of the GATT permits preferential trading arrangements to be carried out, although subject to the qualification that such arrangements should not reduce world welfare. In this respect, the GATT system should be flexible enough to accommodate a variety of trading arrangements, but with the proviso mentioned that such arrangements not be detrimental to world welfare.

Role and Authority of the GATT in a Changing World Economy

Before discussing the litany of criticisms of multilateralism, it is important to realize that the world trading system is in continuous flux, being subjected to a variety of both long- and short-term economic and political influences. Some of these influences affect all nations in common while others will have differential impacts on particular nations and sectors. What this means is that the role and authority of an institution like the GATT must be able to cope with changing conditions.

Since the GATT is premised on a consensual framework, its ability to function and exercise authority is derived from the support that its members provide to it. The United States has played the central leadership role in the GATT since its inception, championing the cause of multilateralism and providing the initiative and momentum for the convening and completion of the successive GATT negotiating rounds. U.S. influence has waned in recent years, however, as the EC and Japan especially and some of the major developing countries have become economically more important and powerful in the global trading system. Some observers believe that a watershed in U.S. influence dates especially from the failed GATT Ministerial Meeting in 1982 when the U.S.-designed agenda for a new round of negotiations was rebuffed. In retrospect, the call for a new GATT round at a time when the world was experiencing the most severe recession since the 1930s may have been ill advised.

In any case, the rhetoric of U.S. trade policy has since been changed, with an expressed readiness to consider and actually carry to conclusion bilateral and plurilateral negotiating options at the same time that the multilateral option is also to be pursued. Indeed, there appears to be both a carrot and a stick at work here, insofar as the United States is saying that it will pursue the more limited negotiating options unless other major trading countries/blocs show a greater willingness to support multilateral liberalization. To date, neither the EC nor Japan has been willing to assume a leadership role in global negotiations, and the smaller industrialized countries are not important enough to make their influence felt. Some of the major developing countries have become more vocal and involved in the GATT, but these countries have been reluctant, at least formally, to give up whatever advantages they believe to have been derived from special and differential treatment in the past.[17]

The position of the United States in the global trading system during the 1980s was also markedly affected by the macroeconomic imbalance and associated deficits on trade and current account that occurred with dollar appreciation. Given the increased import penetration and problems with exporting that were experienced and the inability to achieve fiscal tightening, pressures in the U.S. Congress grew substantially for import protectionism to ward off allegedly "unfair trade" actions and for activism backed by threats of import restrictions designed to open foreign markets. Japan in particular has been singled out because of its substantial and enduring bilateral trade surplus with the United States. This has reinforced the notion that Japanese policies and domestic institutions are different than those in the other major countries and that Japan does not abide by the same rules and practices of its trading partners. Richardson 1991 has remarked that these interventionist pressures seem to have abated somewhat in the early 1990s, although it is possible that they could reemerge.

Our point is that the support for multilateralism and the GATT system was strongest when the United States played the dominant leadership role. This now seems to have changed, and other major

---

[17] This could be changing though, especially in the light of the often far reaching unilateral liberalization that has been carried out in many countries.

countries/blocs have thus far been slow to fill the void.[18]   Moreover, it appears to be especially difficult to effect multilateral trade liberalization at a time when major countries are experiencing significant macroeconomic imbalances.

Criticisms of Multilateralism and Advantages of Preferential Arrangements

Having discussed the case for multilateralism and the international economic environment in which the GATT must function, we can now consider a number of important criticisms that have been levied against multilateralism and the GATT. They include:

1.   The more countries that are involved in a multilateral negotiation, the more difficult and time consuming it will be to draw up a negotiating agenda and to conduct and conclude a negotiation.[19]   In view of the numerous parties involved in a GATT negotiation and the size and complexity of the negotiating agenda, individual countries/blocs may find themselves less able to focus on issues that concern them directly. It is possible furthermore that there may be foot dragging and a tendency for negotiating results to reflect the "lowest common denominator" of the countries participating in the negotiation. These difficulties can presumably be avoided in negotiating preferential arrangements in which fewer countries are involved and the negotiating agenda can be more readily agreed upon.

2. Because of MFN, concessions may be granted to individual countries without there being any quid pro quo. Free riding may thus occur, unless steps are taken to make concessions conditional as, for example, was done with certain Tokyo Round codes that apply only to signatory nations. The problem is all the more serious because special

---

[18] Of course, it may not be absolutely necessary to have a single country or regional bloc to serve a hegemonic role, but our reading of historical experience suggests that it can indeed make an important difference in the effectiveness of the trading system.

[19] See Table 2.1 for details on country participation and the length of time of the individual negotiating rounds.

50   Issues in the Global Trading System

and differential treatment was extended to developing countries beginning in the 1960s, with the consequence that these countries were exempted from making reciprocal concessions. Bilateral/plurilateral arrangements may therefore be appealing as a way of limiting free riding.

3. The GATT system of dispute settlement has not worked well, especially since an effective enforcement mechanism is lacking. Furthermore, the GATT rules are inadequate in important respects. For example, it has proven difficult to resist the introduction of nontariff restrictive measures of various kinds and to effectively constrain the use of domestic and export subsidies that impact directly on trade.

4. The GATT has also been too narrowly focused on trade in goods and has not dealt effectively with issues that lie outside the Articles of Agreement. Examples here include the "new" issues of services and trade related intellectual property rights and investment measures that were belatedly placed on the agenda of the Uruguay Round negotiations, and environmental issues that promise to become increasingly important. This suggests that bilateral or plurilateral negotiations can be more focused and tailored to specific circumstances.

5. Asymmetries exist with respect to the influence of large as compared to medium size and small countries. Large countries may believe that the GATT system ties their hands because of the nondiscrimination and MFN principles, and, accordingly, that their national economic and political interests would be better served in bilateral or plurilateral negotiations that are designed to protect their domestic firms and/or to open foreign markets to their exporters. Medium size and small countries, on the other hand, while recognizing the benefits of MFN, if their trade is predominantly with a single large trading country or bloc, may believe that they can get better and more assured access to its market by means of preferential trading arrangements rather than through multilateral negotiations.[20]

---

[20] We should note that a word of clarification is in order here, lest the foregoing remarks be interpreted to the effect that bilateral/plurilateral negotiations need be harmful particularly to nonmember countries. This will not be the case when bilateral/plurilateral negotiations succeed in achieving greater liberalization than would be possible in a multilateral negotiation and nonmembers are able to share in the benefits.

Multilateral Trade Negotiations 51

Criticisms of Preferential Trading Arrangements

Having articulated the various criticisms of multilateralism and arguments in support of preferential trading arrangements, we now call attention to a number of limitations of preferential arrangements, as follows:

1. Perhaps the chief concern over preferential trading arrangements is that they may be detrimental to world welfare because of the trade diverting effects that may result and because of the exploitative tariff behavior that the formation of large trading blocs may engender. However, as we have already indicated, there is no presumption that preferential arrangements need be welfare reducing. Indeed, we will show in our theoretical discussion below that the expansion of preferential arrangements may well constitute a move toward freer trade in some circumstances. Also, the formation of trading blocs need not in itself lead to exploitative behavior if there is a strong sense of commitment to international cooperation among governments in the design and implementation of trade policies and to the removal of trade barriers.[21] Of course, nothing can be guaranteed one way or the other. It will depend on the circumstances. Nonetheless, it might be argued that this agnostic conclusion is fraught with danger. That is, there is a case to be made that the world needs a strong multilateral system with effective rules and discipline to avoid the formation of welfare reducing trading blocs and to constrain their potentially exploitative behavior.

2. Critics of multilateralism have pointed to the slowness and cumbersomeness of GATT negotiations and thus to the greater comparative ease of bilateral/plurilateral negotiations. This favorable view of preferential arrangements has been questioned, however, by a number of proponents of multilateralism. For example, Schott 1989 argues that, while the GATT rounds typically last for several years, the serious and definitive negotiations are concentrated within a relatively short period

---

[21] Using a political economy framework, Krugman 1992b argues that a small number of large regional blocs may actually enhance global welfare by facilitating the bargaining process internationally, promoting greater liberalization within individual blocs, eliminating the need for a hegemon, and accommodating institutional differences. For criticism of Krugman's views, see especially Bergsten 1991 and Bhagwati 1992a.

of time. Also, most of the actual negotiations involve a limited number of the major trading countries/blocs. In contrast, Schott cites some specific drawbacks of preferential arrangements, including: (a) an inability or unwillingness to address NTBs and other problems more related to the multilateral system (e.g., subsidies); (b) difficulties in reconciling quid pro quo demands; (c) identifying which sectors are to be liberalized at a faster or slower pace than others or not all; (d) elaborating detailed and potentially costly rules of origin; and (e) the need in any event to cover in detail the same issues as in a multilateral negotiation and to reconcile possible divergences of rights and obligations between multilateral and preferential arrangements. Further, if existing preferential arrangements are to be extended to additional countries, a whole new set of negotiations may be required each time another member is to be admitted. A case can be made therefore that it is misleading and even false to believe that it may be relatively easy to negotiate preferential trading arrangements.

3. We mentioned above that the United States appears to have used the prospect of its entering into preferential arrangements as a means of inducing other major trading countries/blocs to pursue the multilateral option. It is not at all clear, however, whether this can be a successful strategy. The argument is especially problematic if the United States were in fact to enter into such preferential agreements. In that event, this could be interpreted by other countries as a signal that the United States was abandoning its unqualified support and preference for multilateral liberalization. Support for multilateralism might also be eroded in any case if a large part of the available negotiating effort and expertise were shifted to the preferential option. Furthermore, once a preferential arrangement is created, it may become dominated by vested interests who feel threatened by, and will thus oppose, multilateral liberalization. It is possible, finally, that the creation of a number of separate trading blocs could heighten international policy conflicts and frictions.

VI. Theoretical Analysis of the Welfare Effects of the Expansion of Trading Blocs

Having set out the advantages and limitations of both multilateralism and preferential arrangements, suppose now that the proliferation of preferential trading arrangements, in the form of FTAs or something similar, is inevitable. Is there anything that we can say theoretically about what this may portend for the welfare of the world?

There are many issues to be considered here, but we will confine our attention to only one: Is a world of a small number of trading blocs significantly inferior to a world of free trade? We say "significantly inferior" because it seems safe to assume that a world of perfectly free trade will never be reached by any mechanism. Experience suggests that multilateral negotiations can at best reduce trade barriers to low levels, but they cannot eliminate them. Since FTAs by definition reduce external barriers to zero within the included countries and do not presumably maintain or introduce intra-bloc barriers, it is potentially the case that a world of trading blocs, with each bloc forming an FTA, could raise world welfare closer to its free trade level than multilateral negotiations. In that case the world of blocs would not look altogether bad.

To illustrate this possibility in simple terms, imagine that we could measure welfare of a country or the world as a function of the size of trading blocs. Suppose, as we will discuss below, that world welfare rises rapidly as bloc size rises at first, then levels off and approaches the free trade level, W^F, as bloc size approaches the world as a whole, as drawn in Figure 2.1. Then if multilateral negotiations can only achieve a level of welfare somewhere short of the free trade level, as at W^M in Figure 2.1, there is a point beyond which blocs are large enough to yield a higher welfare than multilateral negotiations. Of course, it remains to

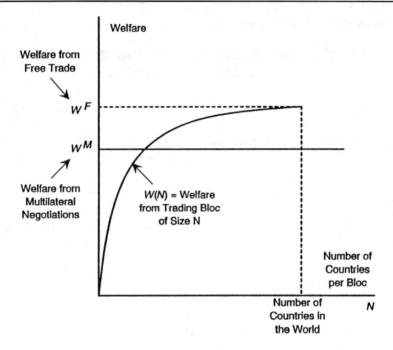

Figure 2.1 World Welfare with Trading Blocs
and Multilateral Negotiations

be seen whether the effect of bloc size on welfare shown in Figure 2.1 can be correct.[22]

The Krugman Argument

Krugman 1991a,b, 1992b has addressed this question directly.[23] He examines a model of a large number of countries, each of which produces a distinctive good and each of which initially levies its optimal tariff on all imports. He then computes world welfare as these countries are combined into various numbers of equal sized trading blocs, each with zero tariffs internally, and each revising their external tariffs to remain optimal against goods from outside the bloc. While no general result can be obtained from this model, Krugman finds computationally that world welfare declines as the number of blocs decreases (and countries are therefore combined into ever larger FTAs) until the number of blocs reaches three. World welfare then increases as the number of blocs is reduced still further to two, and it increases even more with the move to worldwide free trade in a single bloc. That is, world welfare is at a minimum when the number of blocs is three. Krugman therefore concludes in the context of his model that bilateralism is generally undesirable, since the formation of FTAs would reduce world welfare at almost every stage.

---

[22] The assumption in Figure 2.1 is that the time path of welfare is monotonic as trading blocs increase in size. Krugman 1991a and Bhagwati 1992a suggest that there could be other paths in which world welfare would not consistently rise.

[23] There is of course a large and venerable literature on the welfare effects of customs unions and free trade areas, including what determines whether particular combinations of countries forming trading blocs will raise or lower welfare. In addition to extensive discussions of trade creation and trade diversion, perhaps the most notable contribution is Kemp and Wan's 1976 demonstration that any grouping of countries into a customs union can be welfare improving, both for them and for the world as a whole, given a suitable selection of their common external tariff. None of this literature, however, seems to bear directly on the issue here of the welfare effects of the size of trading blocs. For a recent analytical survey of pertinent theory relating to the welfare effects of trading blocs, see especially de Melo, Panagariya, and Rodrik 1992. See also Kennan and Riezman 1990 and Kowalczyk 1989, 1990, 1992.

This is an ingenious argument. It is based, however, on a model that stacks the cards against bilateralism. In an alternative framework one might easily conclude that the formation of FTA trading blocs would be beneficial and that a world of a small number of blocs, even three, might be about as good as one could ask for.

A distinctive feature of Krugman's model is that the firms in each country are assumed to produce goods that are distinct from those produced by all other firms. This product differentiation allows him the simplicity of a single-sector monopolistic-competition model, and thus the kind of clean and simple theorizing that one has learned to expect from Krugman. However, the assumption also means that the countries of Krugman's model are subject to something very like the Armington assumption, which is that each country's products are imperfect substitutes for those of all other countries. This, we believe, is largely responsible for Krugman's results.

The Armington assumption has a long history in the construction of computable general equilibrium models of international trade.[24] However for some purposes, and especially for modeling the welfare effects of trade barriers, it has become increasingly recognized that the Armington assumption places an idiosyncratic stamp upon results.[25] In the context of FTAs and trading blocs, the Armington assumption seems especially likely to yield peculiar implications.

First, the Armington assumption makes it important for any country to import from every other country, since each has something unique to provide. This means that an extreme form of trading blocs in which blocs do not trade at all with each other would be welfare disasters. That is, depending on the functional form of the utility function, welfare would be either very low or infinitely low. This is not necessarily wrong, of course, but we find it rather implausible that each

---

[24] See, for example, Whalley 1985 and subsequent work based on Whalley's model by Harrison and Rustrom 1991 and Nguyen, Perroni, and Wigle 1991.

[25] Brown 1987 in particular has analyzed critically the implications of relying on the Armington assumption.

country's welfare should depend so sensitively on access to the products of each and every other country in the world.

Second, the Armington assumption increases the importance of trade diversion, as compared to trade creation, and therefore increases the likelihood that a preferential arrangement will be welfare reducing. Since this may be counter intuitive, the point requires some explanation.

As usually explained, trade diversion might seem to be impossible in a world of differentiated products. The classic description of trade diversion is the switch away from a low-cost external supplier of a good to a higher-cost supplier of the same good within an FTA. Since with differentiated products the same good is not available from different countries, this simple form of trade diversion is not possible. In addition, Krugman's model does not have differences in costs, and this too would seem to rule out trade diversion as usually described.

However, a more general definition of trade diversion would not involve identical products, and it would not require any particular differences in costs. Any time there is substitution away from one good in favor of another as a result of distorted price signals that incorrectly reflect costs, there will tend to be a welfare reduction.[26] If the two goods are both imported, then this substitution may usefully be labeled as trade diversion, for the welfare loss is from the same source as in the simpler, more familiar example.

Product differentiation in Krugman's model assures that any expansion of an FTA, short of subsuming the entire world, will involve such trade diversion. As long as any countries remain outside the union, there will be substitution away from their products when the FTA lowers the consumer prices of the products produced by new members of the FTA. Since the products of these two groups of countries previously faced the same tariffs, their relative prices within the FTA had been undistorted, and they become distorted by the FTA. Thus trade diversion necessarily occurs in Krugman's model, no matter how large the FTA becomes.

---

[26] Although this is not certain, just as trade diversion by the narrower definition is not necessarily welfare worsening. See Kowalczyk 1990 for a recapitulation of this argument.

There is trade creation too, of course, as substitution also occurs away from previously protected domestic goods and towards imports from new members of the FTA. However it is easy in Krugman's model for trade diversion to dominate trade creation.

To see why, suppose that the welfare effects depend only on the number of goods for which there is trade creation and trade diversion. In a world of many countries, when only two of these form an FTA, there is creation of trade for the goods produced by the partners, but diversion of trade away from all of the goods produced by all other countries. Since the number of the latter countries, and therefore goods, is much larger than the number of countries and goods in the FTA, it is not surprising that diversion outweighs creation. Then, as the FTA is made larger and larger, the number of countries inside the FTA—and hence the amount of trade creation—grows, while the number of countries still outside the FTA shrinks. But even when one enlarges the FTA to include one third of the world (the three-bloc case), there are still two thirds of the world's products from which trade is being diverted, and only one third for which trade is being created. Again, then, it is not surprising that each enlargement of the FTA up to this point lowers welfare and that the three-bloc case is the worst possible. Only when the goods and countries included in a bloc become as numerous as the goods and countries outside does trade creation finally have a reasonable chance of dominating trade diversion, and only then does the FTA raise welfare.

As this explanation is intended to suggest, then, the assumptions of complete product differentiation and the consequent exaggerated importance of each country and each country's goods for every other country's consumers may introduce a bias against the possibility that an FTA will be beneficial.

One other feature of the Krugman model should also be mentioned, since it may well contribute to his results even if it does not drive them. In his first paper on this subject, Krugman 1991a assumes that trading blocs maintain optimal tariffs against the rest of the world at all times. In part because of the high degree of product differentiation just discussed, these optimal tariffs tend to rise as bloc size increases, contributing to the welfare loss for the world as a whole. In a more recent analysis however, he questions the usefulness of this assumption and replaces it with a constant external tariff in his calculations. The conclusion that world welfare is minimized with either three or two blocs survives. Therefore, while the assumption of an optimal tariff may have exacerbated the welfare losses in the earlier analysis, it seems not to have caused them. The assumption of product differentiation instead seems to play the more important role.[27]

A Comparative Advantage Approach

As an alternative, suppose that trade among countries conforms more to the traditional model of comparative advantage. That is, all countries are capable of producing the same list of goods, but they differ in their abilities to do so either because of differences in technology or differences in factor endowments.[28] The effect of an FTA on world welfare then depends, we will argue first, on the differences among countries that join to form the FTA. Furthermore, as long as countries choose as partners others with whom enough differences in comparative advantage exist, they will tend to capture for themselves a significant portion of the gains from trade that would be available from a move to complete free trade by the world. In such cases it may well be that the majority of the gains from trade that would be possible with worldwide free trade can be captured by a group of trading blocs. The blocs would only need to be

---

[27] It is also noteworthy that Krugman 1991a,b, 1992b qualifies his analysis by noting that trade diversion may be lessened if the trading blocs consist of countries that are "natural" trading partners who would trade to a very large extent with each other in the absence of the formation of a trading bloc. While there may be some merit to this point, we have noted above that geographic proximity may not necessarily be a controlling factor. Bhagwati 1992a makes a similar point and also notes that relatively high substitution elasticities between nonmember and member country goods could prove detrimental to welfare.

[28] We abstract from considerations of imperfect competition and increasing returns to scale. More will be said on this below.

60   Issues in the Global Trading System

large enough and to include countries with a sufficiently divergent variety of comparative advantages.[29]

Unfortunately, we are not able to make these points with any great generality. However, we can illustrate them by means of simple examples, and that will be our approach.

A Four-Country Example

Consider first a four country version of the simple two-good Ricardian trade model that has been used for two centuries to illustrate the concept of comparative advantage.[30] Let the countries have identical preferences and labor endowments, and let unit labor requirements for producing the two goods, X and Y, be also the same in countries 1 and 2 and in countries 3 and 4, but differ between the two pairs of countries. That is, let countries 1 and 2 have a comparative advantage in good X relative to countries 3 and 4.

We will consider only the extremes of free trade and autarky to make our point. Suppose that prohibitive tariffs initially exist in all four countries, and that we now consider opening pairs of the four countries to free trade, thus forming trading blocs. It makes a great difference which pairs of countries we choose to form a bloc. If countries 1 and 2 were to form an FTA, they would not in fact trade with each other since their autarky prices are the same. They would gain nothing from trade. If countries 1 and 3 were to form an FTA, however, they would indeed trade and gain from trade exactly as in the traditional 2-country model. Thus it is only if countries with different comparative advantages join in an FTA that there can be trade creation, and only then are there gains from formation of the FTA.[31]

---

[29] The welfare gains would thus come mainly from an expansion of interindustry trade, and there would be presumably (transitional) costs of adjustment.

[30] The example works just as well with Heckscher–Ohlin assumptions.

[31] We assume here and in what follows that there are zero domestic barriers within any given country that would inhibit intra-bloc trade.

This example also illustrates our other point that worldwide free trade may not be necessary. In this example, with identical preferences and labor endowments and only two different sets of technologies, the worldwide free trade equilibrium is identical to the equilibrium that will be attained if any pair of countries with different technologies form an FTA, save only for size. That is, the equilibrium world price with free trade is also the equilibrium price within an FTA formed by, say, countries 1 and 3, and the quantities produced and consumed within each country are also the same. Only the total outputs are different, being twice for four countries what they are for two.

Thus, in this very special case, all of the gains from trade that can be achieved with worldwide free trade can also be achieved in two completely separate trading blocs, so long as each bloc includes countries with different technologies. This illustrates the point that trading blocs can in principle approximate (and in this case equal) the welfare levels of complete free trade.

In a more general model, one would not expect to find blocs equalling the welfare of free trade, but a tendency in this direction does seem likely. It seems plausible that blocs would in general achieve levels of welfare that are between autarky and free trade, being closer to the latter the larger are the blocs and the more diverse in terms of technologies represented. With only four countries we cannot capture much of this, but we can capture a part of it—and also foreshadow our next examples—by looking at blocs in terms of expected values.

Suppose in the four-country model that we are to form two blocs of two countries each, but that the composition of the blocs is to be decided randomly. What are the levels of welfare associated with two blocs in this sense, and how do they compare to autarky and complete free trade? The answer depends on what random mechanism is used for selecting blocs.

Let each possible pattern of blocs be equally likely. There are three such patterns: (1,2)(3,4), (1,3)(2,4), and (1,4)(2,3). Of these only the first has the countries staying at autarky levels of welfare, while the other two have the countries attaining free trade levels. Thus the formation of two random blocs yields an expected gain in welfare that is two-thirds that of free trade.

To be a bit more formal in preparation for the next example, assume there are two types of countries in this four-country case. Let countries 1 and 2 be type A and countries 3 and 4 be type B. Let the welfare attained by a country of type i when it trades in an FTA including countries of types $j,k,l,...$ be denoted $w^i_{jkl...}$. Thus w^A_A is the autarky welfare of a country of type A, w^A_{AB} is the welfare of a country of type A in an FTA with a country of type B, and so on.

Now let $W(I)$ be the level of expected world welfare associated with an equal number of blocs of size I. In the four-country example, the only possibilities are $I=1$ (autarky), 2 (two blocs) and 4 (free trade). Adding up over the four countries one can obtain world autarky welfare as

$$W(1) = 2w^A_A + 2w^B_B$$

and free trade welfare as

$$W^F = W(4) = 2w^A_{AB} + 2w^B_{BA}.$$

The world gains from free trade are then

$$G^F = G(4) = W(4) - W(1) = 2(w^A_{AB} - w^A_A) + 2(w^B_{BA} - w^B_B)$$

The expected welfare for a country of type A from two randomly chosen blocs is $(1/3)w^A_A + (2/3)w^A_{AB}$, and there is a similar expression for a country of type B. Therefore expected world welfare with two blocs is

$$W(2) = 2[(1/3)w^A_A + (2/3)w^A_{AB}] + 2[(1/3)w^B_B + (2/3)w^B_{BA}]$$

Comparing to $W(1)$, the expected gain in world welfare from two blocs is then

Multilateral Trade Negotiations 63

$$G(2) = W(2) - W(1)$$

$$= 2[(1/3)w_A^A + (2/3)w_{AB}^A] + 2[(1/3)w_B^B + (2/3)w_{BA}^B] - 2w_A^A - 2w_B^B$$

$$= (2/3) \, G^F$$

What this says is that the expected gain from forming two trading blocs, with the composition of the blocs randomly selected, is two-thirds of the gain that would arise from a single bloc, or free trade. That is, trading blocs do, on average, generate more than half of the gains from free trade.

A Six-Country Example

To allow for a slightly richer array of possibilities than the four-country model, now consider six. Again let there be just two goods and two technologies, so that the countries are of only two types, A and B, now with three of each. In addition to the extremes of autarky and free trade, there are now the possibilities of three blocs with two countries each, and of two blocs with three countries each. The two-country blocs have the same possibilities for welfare as before, but the three-country blocs do not: a country can join with zero, one, or two other countries of the same type as itself.

Levels of world welfare under autarky and free trade are the same as before, except that there are now six countries instead of three:

$$W(1) = 3w_A^A + 3w_B^B$$

$$W^F = W(6) = 3w_{AB}^A + 3w_{AB}^B$$

This gives a world gain from free trade of

$$G^F = G(6) = 3[w_{AB}^A + w_{AB}^B - w_A^A - w_B^B]$$

With blocs of two countries, there are fifteen ways that the six countries can be distributed across three blocs. In only six of these do all three blocs have one country of each type, so that they all attain the same welfare as under free trade. In the remaining nine, one bloc has two type-A countries, one has two type-B, and one has one of each. This leads to an expected world welfare of

$$W(2) = (2/5)[3w_{AB}^A + 3_{AB}^B] + (3/5)[2w_A^A + 2w_B^B + w_{AB}^A + w_{AB}^B]$$

and an expected gain from trade of

$$G(2) = (3/5)G^F$$

Thus with more countries, blocs of two countries still produce more than half the benefit of free trade, but the expected gain is somewhat smaller than in the four-country case.

      With two blocs of three countries there are ten ways that the six countries can be distributed across the blocs. One of those ways has all three type-A countries in one bloc and all three type-B in the other, leading to autarky levels of welfare in both. In the nine other ways that the two blocs can appear, each bloc has two countries from one type and one from the other. Expected welfare is therefore

$$W(3) = (1/10)[3w_A^A + 3_B^B] + (9/10)[2w_{AAB}^A + w_{AAB}^B + w_{ABB}^A + w_{ABB}^B]$$

Interpretation of this expression does not lead to anything as simple as the other cases, and we will not try to carry it further here. It seems likely, though we have not been able to prove it, that it involves higher expected welfare than $W(2)$.

      This example has one additional feature that would appear in a more general case but did not appear in the four-country case. It is quite possible for a country to achieve a level of welfare higher than world-wide free trade by joining an FTA. Consider a country of type A in an FTA with two other countries of type B, an "ABB" FTA in the notation used above. In a competitive model without increasing returns to scale, the free-trade equilibrium price in any group of countries is a weighted average of the autarky prices of the separate countries, the weights depending on the sizes of the countries. Thus the equilibrium price in an *ABB* FTA will be closer to the autarky price of the type *B* countries than will the equilibrium price under free trade where there are equal numbers of countries of the two types. Since the welfare of any country increases with the difference between the equilibrium price and its own autarky price, it follows that the type-*A* country is better off in the *ABB* FTA than it would be under free trade:

$$w_{ABB}^{A} > w_{AB}^{A}$$

A Many-Country Case

As our final example we consider a many-country case where comparative advantage is more generally defined in terms of relative autarky prices and may therefore reflect differences in technologies and/or factor endowments.

Suppose the world consists of $M + 1$ countries, numbered $i = 0, 1, ..., M$. Let these countries have, in general, different autarky prices but be otherwise identical in the following sense: each produces and consumes two goods, and their excess supplies of good one are

$$ES^{i}(p) = p - q^{i}$$

where p is the price of good one in terms of the numeraire good two, and q^{i} is the only parameter of this excess supply function that we allow to differ across countries. Since in autarky $ES^{i} = 0, q^{i}$ is the autarky price of good one in country i.[32]

---

[32] Note the assumption that price, p, appears in this function with a coefficient of one. What is important here is that each country have the same coefficient, indicating that behavior of both producers and consumers at the margin is identical across countries, and also that countries are in some sense equal in size (else a large country would have a much larger quantity response to a change in price than a small country). It is not important that the common coefficient happens to be one, which could always be assured

In addition to the autarky prices, one can also derive the world free-trade equilibrium price, p^F, from

$$\sum_{i=0}^{M} ES^i(p^F) = 0$$

as

$$p^F = \frac{1}{M+1} \sum_{i=0}^{M} q^i$$

which is simply the average of the autarky prices.[33]

Suppose that country O were to contemplate joining a trading bloc of some N other countries in addition to itself. If those N countries were $i = 1,...,N$, then the resulting equilibrium bloc price, $P^{O,N}$, would be

$$p^{O,N} = \frac{1}{N+1} \sum_{i=0}^{N} q^i = \frac{1}{N+1} q^O + \frac{N}{N+1} p^N \qquad (1)$$

where p^N is the equilibrium bloc price for countries $1,...,N$ (without country zero). That is, if country O joins the bloc it will face an equilibrium price that is a weighted average of its own autarky price and that of the bloc excluding itself, the weight on the latter being larger the more countries are in the bloc. But suppose that, instead of the participants in the bloc being known, country O will join a bloc with N

---

by appropriate choice of units. A somewhat more general formulation would permit a different coefficient on p for each country. This would add complexity, and would also invalidate the result to be derived, without some additional assumption. Such an additional assumption will be suggested in a footnote below.

[33] If countries have different coefficients on price in their excess supply functions, then this becomes a weighted average with those coefficients serving as weights.

other randomly selected countries. In that case its equilibrium bloc price will still be given by equation (1), but the equilibrium price of the N-bloc, p^N, will be random. Since (1) is linear, the expected equilibrium price for the bloc of $N + 1$ countries will be given in terms of the expected equilibrium price for the N-bloc:

$$Ep^{O,N} = \frac{1}{N+1} q^O + \frac{N}{N+1} Ep^N \qquad (2)$$

To calculate Ep^N, let $c(N)$ be the number of possible N country blocs that can be formed out of the M countries $1,...,M$. If each is equally likely, then

$$Ep^N = \frac{1}{c(N)} \sum_{j=1}^{c(N)} p^{Nj}$$

$$= \frac{1}{c(N)} \sum_{j=1}^{c(N)} \frac{1}{N} \sum_{i=1}^{N} q^{h^{ji}}$$

where p^{Nj} is the equilibrium bloc price for the jth possible bloc of size N, and h^{ji} is the index of the ith country in that j^{th} bloc. This is a simple average of all the autarky prices $q^1,...,q^M$, with each one repeated by the number of blocs in which it appears. Since each bloc is equally likely and all possible blocs are represented in this summation, each autarky price q^i for $i = 1,...,M$ must appear the same number of times in this summation, and thus have equal weight. Thus

$$Ep^N = \frac{1}{M} \sum_{i=1}^{M} q^i = p^M$$

which is just the equilibrium bloc price for the bloc of all M countries other than country zero. That is, the expected equilibrium price for a bloc of N countries chosen randomly from a larger group of M

countries is just the equilibrium price for the M countries themselves as a bloc.[34] Substituting this into equation (2), the result for a randomly selected bloc of size $N + 1$ including country zero is therefore

$$Ep^{O,N} = \frac{1}{N+1} q^O + \frac{N}{N+1} p^M \tag{3}$$

This result is illustrated in the top panel of Figure 2.2. The horizontal axis measures the number of countries in a bloc in addition to country zero, while the vertical axis measures various prices. The autarky price in country zero, q^O, is shown as lower than the equilibrium bloc price for all countries excluding zero, p^M. As the above equation indicates, the expected equilibrium bloc price for a bloc of country zero plus N other randomly selected countries rises to half way between q^O and p^M for $N = 1$ and continues thereafter to approach p^M. The graph stops at $N = M$, where the free trade price p^F is reached just short of p^M.

The bottom panel of Figure 2.2 gives information about the welfare of country zero in these various circumstances. The welfare of a country is given by its indirect utility function, which in this case takes the simple form[35]

$$V^i(p) = (p - q^i)^2$$

---

[34] This is the result we need, and it was in order to get it that we assumed the countries to be identical in such a strong way. If countries instead have different coefficients on price in their excess supply functions, it will not in general be true. (To see this, simply consider $N=1$ and $M=2$, with one country having a much larger coefficient and hence a large influence on the equilibrium price. The expected price in a one-country randomly chosen bloc is half way between their two autarky prices, while the equilibrium price for the two together is much closer to the autarky price of the high-coefficient country.) The result can nonetheless be salvaged if the coefficients are uncorrelated with the autarky prices.

[35] This is obtained by integrating the excess supply function above, and normalizing on a level of welfare of zero in autarky.

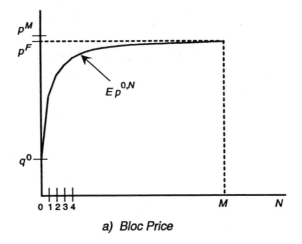

a) Bloc Price

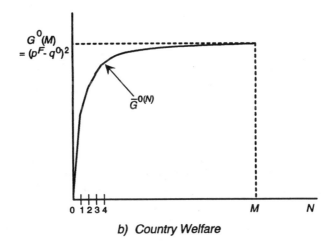

b) Country Welfare

Figure 2.2 Expected Bloc Price and Country
Welfare with Trading Blocs

Letting $G^O(N)$ be the expected gain in welfare of country zero from entering into a bloc with N other randomly selected countries,

$$G^O(N) = EV^O(p^{O,N}) \geq V^O(Ep^{O,N}) = (Ep^{O,N} - q^O)^2 \equiv \bar{G}^O(N) \quad (4)$$

using the convexity of $V(\cdot)$. Thus the bottom panel of Figure 2.2 graphs $\bar{G}^O(n) = V^O(Ep^{O,N})$ as a function of N, taking $Ep^{O,N}$ as given by (3) from the top panel. From the inequality in (4), this graph provides a lower bound on the gain to country zero from entering into blocs of various sizes. This graph illustrates the conclusion discussed throughout this section of the chapter: that much of the gains from free trade can be achieved, in this case for an individual country, by entering into FTA trading blocs of larger and larger size.

The curve $\bar{G}^O(N)$ in Figure 2.2 provides only a lower bound for the expected gains from entering into blocs of various sizes for a particular country. We are not able to place an upper bound on this gain, which could extend well above the curve and even above the level of welfare in free trade. Indeed, one can easily find cases where the expected welfare for a country from entering into a bloc that includes only part of the world will be higher than its welfare from free trade. Suppose in a world of many countries that one of them has an autarky price equal to the free-trade price. Then it has nothing to gain from free trade at all. But by entering into trading blocs with only part of the world, it is quite likely to meet a bloc price that differs from its autarky price, and therefore enjoy greater welfare. Thus for a particular country it is quite possible that trading blocs are better than free trade.

This cannot be the case for the world as a whole, however. We know from the literature on the gains from trade that world welfare cannot be larger with trade barriers than without, and will usually be smaller. Therefore the upper bound on world welfare is given by free trade. Since the lower bound can be obtained by adding together vertically curves like $\bar{G}^O(N)$ in Figure 2.2, the world expected gains from trading blocs of various sizes are indeed constrained to lie between

Multilateral Trade Negotiations   71

a curve like $W(N)$ in Figure 2.1 and the horizontal line shown for free trade, just as we surmised earlier.

Tariffs

Our discussion in this section has assumed that tariffs were always either prohibitive or zero. This may seem to be an important limitation in a world where actual tariffs are mostly neither of these. Furthermore, by excluding non-zero, non-prohibitive tariffs we have ruled out any possibility of trade diversion: with previously prohibitive tariffs there was no trade to be diverted by the formation of an FTA. Finally, this assumption has also made it unnecessary for us to consider the distinction between an FTA and a customs union: our FTAs continue to charge prohibitive tariffs against the rest of the world, and it therefore does not matter whether those tariffs are the same or not.

All of this seems to suggest that our analysis cannot be of much relevance. However, we would argue that our main result of the potential desirability of trading blocs can only be enhanced by now allowing for trade to occur over nonzero tariffs. As long as FTAs continue to involve zero tariffs internally, the presence of some trade externally can only raise welfare as compared to what it would have been in the prohibitive tariff case that we examined. Since we argued that expected welfare rises with the size of trading blocs and approaches the free-trade level as the blocs become large, the even higher welfare of blocs that do trade externally must have at least the second of these properties as well.[36]

---

[36] Haveman 1992 has developed a model of trading blocs that encompasses comparative advantage and positive (optimal) tariffs that apparently negates this conclusion and reinforces Krugman's conclusion that the formation of trading blocs will be detrimental to world welfare as the number of blocs increases to two rather than three as in Krugman's model. In Haveman's model, however, this result does depend on the assumption that external tariffs are levied optimally at each stage.

Extensions and Caveats

The analysis here has included only three very simple examples. There are many directions in which it would be desirable to go with this, and it is premature to suggest that we know what such extensions would yield. However, these results do seem sufficient to at least raise the possibility that trading blocs may be welfare improving, and even that they may approach the level of welfare that could have been attained by free trade.

However, the examples here are at the opposite extreme from the model of Krugman, in the sense that they stack the cards in favor of trading blocs just as his model stacks them against. This suggests that an important consideration is whether in fact most trade is driven by differences in comparative advantage, as in the examples here, or by other considerations such as the product differentiation that drives Krugman's model. In a world where comparative advantage dominates and countries act cooperatively rather than noncooperatively in their trade policies, trading blocs of diverse countries may not be so bad.

Similarly, the examples here have assumed constant returns to scale and perfect competition. If instead there are increasing returns to scale and/or imperfect competition of various sorts, the argument here would have to be modified and possibly weakened. As long as trading blocs are too small to permit minimum efficient scale in many industries, or too small to permit a reasonable amount of competition, enlarging the blocs will increase welfare more than in the case considered here for these additional reasons. If this process can be completed while the blocs still encompass only a fraction of the world, then these effects strengthen our argument, since welfare will rise with bloc size even more rapidly when blocs are still small. On the other hand, if the entire world market is needed to surpass minimum efficient scale in many industries, or to permit a satisfactory level of competition, then these effects could conceivably turn our concave function into a convex one. In that case, any division of the world into trading blocs could fall well short of free trade in terms of welfare.

Note, finally, that the conclusion of our theoretical discussion is that a group of trading blocs, if they are large enough, can approximate the level of welfare that may be feasibly attainable from a multilateral system. However, it is also clear that if such blocs are too small and if the trade between them is too limited, then the gains we have described will not be achieved. In terms of our Figure 2.1, blocs must be sufficiently large to bring us up the curve to the free trade level, or else barriers to trade will be detrimental to world welfare. Therefore, our analysis argues in favor of trading blocs only if they are sufficiently large and only if they collectively encompass the entire world.

It is quite possible that a multilateral system of controls would be needed to assure that blocs do achieve this size and comprehensiveness, as well as to prevent the blocs from increasing levels of protection among themselves. Thus, as we will elaborate further in the concluding section, we do not view this simple theoretical analysis as undermining the case for GATT or for multilateral oversight of trade policy. We would only suggest on the basis of this analysis that trading blocs might have a legitimate place in a multilateral system, and that their presence should not be taken as necessary evidence that the gains from multilateral trade are being foregone.

VII. Implications for the Design of Trading Blocs to Enhance World Welfare

From our institutional and historical discussion, it appears that preferential arrangements are an inevitable part of the world trading system. From our theoretical discussion, it appears that such arrangements are not necessarily the economic disasters that they have sometimes been supposed to be. It remains therefore to examine how the multilateral trading system should accommodate preferential arrangements, since it evidently must, in order to assure that their presence does not undermine other desirable features of the multilateral system and in order if possible to assure that they yield the greatest benefits and the fewest costs for the world as a whole. In this concluding section, therefore, we make several

74   Issues in the Global Trading System

suggestions for how the multilateral trading system should be structured to this end.[37]

    1. The GATT should recognize bilateral arrangements as an intrinsic part of any multilateral system, and not treat them as exceptions to the rule only to be tolerated. At present, in spite of Article XXIV, there is a tendency to regard new preferential arrangements as undermining the legitimacy of the GATT, and as long as they are treated that way they will indeed have that effect. Instead, much as the IMF came to accommodate the existence of flexible exchange rates in the 1970s, the GATT must accommodate preferential arrangements so that their presence will be seen as contributing to the system rather than tearing it apart.

    2. The requirement, already embodied in Article XXIV, that new preferential arrangements should not lead to an increase in the level of protection, must be strengthened and enforced. In fact, the evidence does not suggest that such arrangements have historically added significantly to the level of protection, so it should not be too difficult to enforce such a requirement. But, where cases can be brought to the GATT of violations of Article XXIV, they should be encouraged. That will not only serve in a minor way to restrain protectionism. But it will serve in a more major way to enhance the role of the GATT vis-a-vis such preferential arrangements and make it clear that the two can and should coexist.[38]

    3. Language should be added to the GATT encouraging the formation of preferential arrangements where they are most likely to be beneficial to the countries involved and to the world. On the basis of comparative advantage, the GATT should favor arrangements that combine countries with large, rather than small, differences in their

---

[37] See also Bhagwati 1992a,b and Whalley 1991 for related suggestions concerning the role and treatment of preferential arrangements within the multilateral system.

[38] It is essential here, as Bhagwati 1992a,b and others have stressed, that measures be taken to constrain the use of antidumping measures and voluntary export restraints. The limitation of these measures is of course desirable in its own right and is ostensibly being dealt with in the Uruguay Round negotiations. The improvements here would then presumably carry over to the enforcement of Article XXIV.

factor endowments and technologies. In particular, the GATT should encourage the inclusion of less developed countries within preferential arrangements, not involving only other developing countries like themselves, but involving also developed countries with whom they can benefit the most from trade.

4. Finally, and perhaps most importantly, the GATT should insist that preferential arrangements should have ways of accommodating new members, and that all countries (or at least all GATT members) should have access to joining some trading bloc, somewhere in the world. It will indeed be a disaster, politically as well as economically, if the formation of preferential trading arrangements leads not to an entire world of trading blocs, but rather to a world of blocs that include only the rich countries and a handful of their favored neighbors. Developments so far in Europe and America suggest a surprising and encouraging willingness to extend preferential treatment beyond the borders of the developed world. It remains to be seen whether this willingness will cease once the developed countries have acquired a comfortable buffer between themselves and the rest of the third world. The GATT could and should play an important role in preventing this from happening.

76   Issues in the Global Trading System

Appendix

General Agreement on Tariffs and Trade

Article XXIV

Territorial Application—Frontier Traffic—Customs Unions
and Free Trade Areas

1.   The provisions of this Agreement shall apply to the metropolitan customs territories of the contracting parties and to any other customs territories in respect of which this Agreement has been accepted under. Article XXVI or is being applied under Article XXXIII or pursuant to the Protocol of Provisional Application.   Each such customs territory shall,exclusively for the purposes of the territorial application of this Agreement, be treated as though it were a contracting party; *Provided* that the provisions of this paragraph shall not be construed to create any rights or obligations as between two or more customs territories in respect of which this Agreement has been accepted under Article XXVI or is being applied under Article XXXIII or pursuant to the Protocol of Provisional Application by a single contracting party.

2.   For the purposes of this Agreement a customs territory shall be understood to mean any territory with respect to which separate tariffs or other regulations of commerce are maintained for a substantial part of the trade of such territory with other territories.

3. The provisions of this Agreement shall not be construed to prevent:

(a) Advantages accorded by any contracting party to adjacent countries in order to facilitate frontier traffic;

(b) Advantages accorded to the trade with the Free Territory of Trieste by countries contiguous to that territory,provided that such advantages are not in conflict with the Treaties of Peace arising out of the Second World War.

Multilateral Trade Negotiations 77

4.   The contracting parties recognize the desirability of increasing freedom of trade by the development, through voluntary agreements, of closer integration between the economies of the countries parties to such agreements. They also recognize that the purpose of a customs union or of a free-trade area should be to facilitate trade between the constituent territories and not to raise barriers to the trade of other contracting parties with such territories.

5.   Accordingly, the provisions of this Agreement shall not prevent, as between the territories of contracting parties, the formation of a customs union or of a free-trade area or the adoption of an interim agreement necessary for the formation of a customs union or of a free-trade area; *Provided* that:

(*a*)   with respect to a customs union, or an interim agreement leading to the formation of a customs union, the duties and other regulations of commerce imposed at the institution of any such union or interim agreement in respect of trade with contracting parties not parties to such union or agreement shall not on the whole be higher or more restrictive than the general incidence of the duties and regulations of commerce applicable in the constituent territories prior to the formation of such union or the adoption of such interim agreement, as the case may be;

(*b*)   with respect to a free-trade area, or an interim agreement leading to the formation of a free-trade area, the duties and other regulations of commerce maintained in each of the constituent territories and applicable at the formation of such free-trade area or the adoption of such interim agreement to the trade of contracting parties not included in such area or not parties to such agreement shall not be higher or more restrictive than the corresponding duties and other regulations of commerce existing in the same constituent territories prior to the formation of the free-trade area, or interim agreement, as the case may be, and not to raise barriers to the trade of other contracting parties with such territories.

(*c*) any interim agreement referred to in sub-paragraphs (*a*) and (*b*) shall include a plan and schedule for the formation of such a customs union or of such a free-trade area within a reasonable length of time.

6. If, in fulfilling the requirements of sub-paragraph 5(*a*), a contracting party proposes to increase any rate of duty inconsistently with the provisions of Article II, the procedure set forth in Article XXVIII shall apply. In providing for compensatory adjustment, due account shall be taken of the compensation already afforded by the reductions brought about in the corresponding duty of the other constituents of the union.

7. (*a*) Any contracting party deciding to enter into a customs union or free-trade area, or an interim agreement leading to the formation of such a union or area, shall promptly notify the CONTRACTING PARTIES and shall make available to them such information regarding the proposed union or area as will enable them to make such reports and recommendations to contracting parties as they may deem appropriate.

(*b*) If, after having studied the plan and schedule included in an interim agreement referred to in paragraph 5 in consultation with the parties to that agreement and taking due account of the information made available in accordance with the provisions of sub-paragraph (*a*), the CONTRACTING PARTIES find that such agreement is not likely to result in the formation of a customs union or of a free-trade area within the period contemplated by the parties to the agreement or that such period is not a reasonable one, the CONTRACTING PARTIES shall make recommendations to the parties to the agreement. The parties shall not maintain or put into force, as the case may be, such agreement if they are not prepared to modify it in accordance with these recommendations.

(*c*) Any substantial change in the plan or schedule referred to in paragraph 5(*c*) shall be communicated to the CONTRACTING PAR-TIES, which may request the contracting parties concerned to consult with them if the change seems likely to jeopardize or delay unduly the formation of the customs union or of the free-trade area.

8. For the purposes of this Agreement:

(*a*) A customs union shall be understood to mean the substitution of a single customs territory for two or more customs territories, so that

(i) duties and other restrictive regulations of commerce (except, where necessary, those permitted under Articles XI, XII, XIII, XIV, XV and XX) are eliminated with respect to substantially all the trade between the constituent territories of the union or at least with respect to substantially all the trade in products originating in such territories, and,

(ii) subject to the provisions of paragraph 9, substantially the same duties and other regulations of commerce are applied by each of the members of the union to the trade of territories not included in the union;

(*b*) A free-trade area shall be understood to mean a group of two or more customs territories in which the duties and other restrictive regulations of commerce (except, where necessary, those permitted under Articles XI, XII, XIII, XIV, XV and XX) are eliminated on substantially all the trade between the constituent territories in products originating in such territories.

9. The preferences referred to in paragraph 2 of Article I shall not be affected by the formation of a customs union or of a free-trade area but may be eliminated or adjusted by means of negotiations with contracting parties affected. This procedure of negotiations with affected contracting parties shall, in particular, apply to the elimination of preferences required to conform with the provisions of paragraph 8(*a*)(i) and paragraph 8(*b*).

10. The CONTRACTING PARTIES may by a two-thirds majority approve proposals which do not fully comply with the requirements of paragraphs 5 to 9 inclusive, provided that such proposals lead to the

80   Issues in the Global Trading System

formation of a customs union or a free-trade area in the sense of this Article.

11. Taking into account the exceptional circumstances arising out of the establishment of India and Pakistan as independent States and recognizing the fact that they have long constituted an economic unit, the contracting parties agree that the provisions of this Agreement shall not prevent the two countries from entering into special arrangements with respect to the trade between them, pending the establishment of their mutual trade relations on a definitive basis.

12. Each contracting party shall take such reasonable measures as may be available to it to ensure observance of the provisions of this Agreement by the regional and local governments and authorities within its territory.

References

Baldwin, Robert E. 1987. "Multilateral Liberalization," in J. Michael Finger and Andrzej Olechowski (eds.), *A Handbook on the Multilateral Trade Negotiations*. Washington, D.C.: The World Bank.

Bergsten, C.F. 1991. "Commentary" on Paul Krugman, "The Move Toward Free Trade Zones," in Federal Reserve Bank of Kansas City, *Policy Implications of Trade and Currency Zones*. Kansas City: Federal Reserve Bank of Kansas City.

Bhagwati, Jagdish N. 1990a. "Departures from Multilateralism: Regionalism and Aggressive Unilateralism," in David Greenaway (ed.), "Policy Forum: Multilateralism and Bilateralism in Trade Policy: Editorial Note," *Economic Journal* 100:1304–1317.

Bhagwati, Jagdish N. 1990b. "Multilateralism at Risk: The GATT is Dead. Long Live the GATT," *The World Economy* 13:149–169.

Bhagwati, Jagdish. 1992a. "Regionalism and Multilateralism: An Overview," in Jaime de Melo and Arvind Panagariya (eds.), *New Dimensions in Regional Integration*. New York: Cambridge University Press, forthcoming.

Bhagwati, Jagdish N. 1992b. "The Threats to the World Trading System," in Robert M. Stern (ed.), "Symposium on Issues for the Global Economy in the 1990s," *The World Economy* 15:443–456.

Brown, Drusilla K. 1987. "Tariffs, the Terms of Trade and National Product Differentiation," *Journal of Policy Modeling* 9:503–526.

Brown, Drusilla K., Alan V. Deardorff, and Robert M.Stern. 1992. "A North American Free Trade Agreement: Analytical Issues and a Computational Assessment," *The World Economy* 15:11–29.

Deardorff, Alan V. and Robert M. Stern. 1986. *The Michigan Model of World Production and Trade: Theory and Applications*. Cambridge: MIT Press.

de la Torre, Augusto and Margaret R. Kelly. 1992. *Regional Trade Arrangements*, Occasional Paper 93. Washington, D.C.: International Monetary Fund.

de Melo, Jaime, Arvind Panagariya, and Dani Rodrik. 1992. "Regional Integration: An Analytical and Empirical Overview," in Jaime de Melo and Arvind Panagariya (eds.), *New Dimensions in Regional Integration*. New York: Cambridge University Press, forthcoming.

Fieleke, Norman S. 1992. "One Trading World, or Many: The Issue of Regional Trading Blocs," *New England Economic Review*, May/June:3–20.

Finger, C. Michael. 1992. "GATT's Influence on Regional Arrangements," in Jaime de Melo and Arvind Panagariya (eds.), *New Dimensions in Regional Integration*. New York: Cambridge University Press, forthcoming.

Finger, J.M. 1979. "Trade Liberalization: A Public Choice Perspective," in Ryan C. Amacher, Gottfried Haberler, and Thomas D. Willett (eds.), *Challenges to a Liberal Economic Order*. Washington, D.C.: American Enterprise Institute.

Harrison, Glenn W. and E.E. Rustrom. 1991. "Trade Wars, Trade Negotiations and Applied Game Theory," *Economic Journal* 101:420–435.

Haveman, Jon D. 1992. "Some Welfare Effects of Dynamic Customs Union Formation," in process.

Hoekman, Bernard M. 1991. "Multilateral Trade Negotiations and the Coordination of Commercial Policies," in Robert M. Stern (ed.), *The Multilateral Trading System: Analysis and Prospects for Negotiating Change*. Ann Arbor: University of Michigan Press, forthcoming.

Irwin, Douglas A. 1992. "Multilateral and Bilateral Trade Policies in the World Trading System: An Historical Perspective," in Jaime de Melo and Arvind Panagariya (eds.), *New Dimensions in Regional Integration*. New York: Cambridge University Press, forthcoming.

Jackson, John H. 1989. *The World Trading System: Law and Policy of International Economic Relations*. Cambridge: MIT Press.

Jackson, John H. and William J. Davey. 1986. *International Economic Relations*. Second Edition. St. Paul: West Publishing Co.

Kemp, Murray C. and Henry Wan, Jr. 1976. "An Elementary Proposition Concerning the Formation of Customs Unions," *Journal of International Economics* 6:95–97.

Kennan, John and Raymond Riezman. 1990. "Optimal Tariff Equilibria with Customs Unions," *Canadian Journal of Economics* 23:70–83.

Kowalczyk, Carsten. 1989. "Trade Negotiations and World Welfare," *American Economic Review* 79:552–559.

Kowalczyk, Carsten. 1992. "Paradoxes in Integration Theory," *Open Economies Review* 3:51–59.

Kowalczyk, Carsten. 1990. "Welfare and Customs Unions," National Bureau of Economic Research, Paper No. 3476. Cambridge: NBER.

Krugman, Paul R. 1991a. "Is Bilateralism Bad?" in Elhanan Helpman and Assaf Razin (eds.), *International Trade and Trade Policy*. Cambridge: MIT Press.

Krugman, Paul. 1991b. "The Movement Toward Free Trade Zones," in Federal Reserve Bank of Kansas City, *Policy Implications of Trade and Currency Zones*. Kansas City: Federal Reserve Bank of Kansas City.

Krugman, Paul. 1992a. "Does the New Trade Theory Require a New Trade Policy," in Robert M. Stern (ed.), "Symposium on Issues for the Global Economy in the 1990s," *The World Economy* 15:423–441.

Krugman, Paul. 1992b. "Regionalism vs. Multilateralism: Analytical Notes," in Jaime de Melo and Arvind Panagariya (eds.), *New Dimensions in Regional Integration*. New York: Cambridge University Press, forthcoming.

Ludema, Rodney D. 1991. "On the Value of Free-Trade Areas in Multilateral Negotiations," in process.

Nguyen, Trien T., Carlo Perroni, and Randall M. Wigle. 1991. "The Value of a Uruguay Round Success," *The World Economy* 14:359–374.

84   Issues in the Global Trading System

Nogués, Julio. 1990. "The Choice Between Unilateral and Multilateral Trade Liberalization Strategy," *The World Economy* 13:15–26.

Nogués, Julio and Rosalinda Quintanilla. 1992. "Latin America's Integration and the Multilateral Trading System," in Jaime de Melo and Arvind Panagariya (eds.), *New Dimensions in Regional Integration*. New York: Cambridge University Press, forthcoming.

Patterson, Gardner. 1989. "Implications for the GATT and the World Trading System," and "Comments" by John Whalley, in Jeffrey J. Schott (ed.), *Free Trade Areas and U.S. Trade Policy*. Washington, D.C.: Institute for International Economics.

Richardson, J. David. 1991. "U.S. Trade Policy in the 1980s: Turns—and Roads Not Taken," National Bureau of Economic Research, NBER Working Paper No. 3725 (June). Cambridge: NBER.

Saxonhouse, Gary. 1992. "Trading Blocs, Pacific Trade and the Pricing Strategies of East Asian Firms," in Jaime de Melo and Arvind Panagariya (eds.), *New Dimensions in Regional Integration*. New York: Cambridge University Press, forthcoming.

Schott, Jeffrey J. 1989. "More Free Trade Areas?" in Jeffrey J. Schott (ed.), *Free Trade Areas and U.S. Trade Policy*. Washington, D.C.: Institute for International Economics.

Schott, Jeffrey J. 1991. "Trading Blocs and the World Trading System," *The World Economy* 14:1–18.

Whalley, John. 1985. *Trade Liberalization Among World Trading Areas*. Cambridge: MIT Press.

Whalley, John. 1991. "Harnessing the New Regionalism," in process.

Whalley, John. 1992. "Regional Trade Arrangements in North America: CUSTA and NAFTA," in process.

Winters, L. Alan. 1990. "The Road to Uruguay," in David Greenaway (ed.), "Policy Forum: Multilateralism and Bilateralism in Trade Policy: Editorial Note," *Economic Journal* 100:1288–1303.

Winters, Alan. 1992. "The European Community: A Case of Successful Integration," in Jaime de Melo and Arvind Panagariya (eds.), *New Dimensions in Regional Integration*. New York: Cambridge University Press, forthcoming.

Wolf, Martin. 1987. "Why Trade Liberalization is a Good Idea," in J. Michael Finger and Andrzej Olechowski (eds.), *A Handbook on the Multilateral Trade Negotiations*. Washington, D.C.: The World Bank.

Wonnacott, Paul and Mark Lutz. 1989. "Is There a Case for Free Trade Areas?" and "Comments" by Isaiah Frank and Martin Wolf, in Jeffrey J. Schott (ed.), *Free Trade Areas and U.S. Trade Policy*. Washington, D.C.: Institute for International Economics.

Yarbrough, Beth V. and Robert M. Yarbrough. 1986. "Reciprocity, Bilateralism, and Economic 'Hostages': Self-enforcing Agreements in International Trade," *International Studies Quarterly* 30:7–21.

[22]

ELSEVIER

Journal of International Economics 40 (1996) 411–437

Journal of
INTERNATIONAL
ECONOMICS

The size of trading blocs
Market power and world welfare effects

Eric W. Bond*, Constantinos Syropoulos

Department of Economics, Pennsylvania State University, University Park, PA 16802, USA

Received 1 June 1993; revised 1 September 1995

Abstract

We construct an n-country n-commodity trade model to analyze the implications of bloc size for (Nash) equilibrium tariffs and welfare. The relationship between the absolute size of (symmetric) trading blocs and their market power is ambiguous, and we illustrate how this relationship varies with model parameters. In contrast, sufficiently large increases in the relative size of a bloc enhance its relative market power and cause the welfare of its country members to rise above the free trade level. We establish the existence of an optimal bloc size, and study the dependence of optimal size on the parameters of the model.

Key words: Regionalism; Trading blocs; Strategic interactions; Market power; Welfare

JEL classification: F02; F13; F15

1. Introduction

Much of the recent concern over the effects of the increase in the number of regional trading arrangements on the multilateral trading system has centered on the question of how the expansion of trading blocs will affect their external tariffs, and thus the level of world welfare.[1] One view, expressed in the concern over the

*Corresponding author: Tel. (814) 863-0315; Fax. (814) 863-4775; Email: ewb1@psuvm.psu.edu.
[1] Most of the existing work on preferential trading arrangements focuses on the effects of formation of customs unions, holding external tariffs constant. Since the work of Viner (1950) it has been known that a preferential reduction in tariffs generates ambiguous welfare effects, due to the second-best nature of the problem. Corden (1984) provides an excellent survey of the literature.

412   E.W. Bond, C. Syropoulos / Journal of International Economics 40 (1996) 411–437

formation of a 'Fortress Europe', is that blocs will increase their external barriers to trade to limit market access of non-member countries. Another view is that regional trading blocs will be stepping-stones to global free trade, in that they are likely to make tariff reductions with non-members easier to negotiate. Krugman (1991) has made an important contribution to this debate by constructing a formal model of regional trading arrangements in which the world consists of B equally sized trading blocs that allow free trade among member countries, but impose optimal tariffs on trade with the rest of the world. He examines the effect of an expansion in the size of trading blocs and shows that it raises their market power, in the sense that their external tariffs increase. This increase in tariffs reduces world welfare, and contributes to the conclusion that large blocs are 'bad' from the perspective of world welfare. In Krugman's model, world welfare is minimized when there are three trading blocs.

Our objective in this paper is to examine more fully the relationship between bloc size and the 'market power' of trading blocs when trading blocs levy a common external tariff.[2] Krugman's analysis is limited to the case in which all blocs increase in size symmetrically, which can be thought of as an increase in absolute bloc size, holding relative size constant. In one sense it seems surprising that an increase in absolute bloc size will necessarily increase the market power of trading blocs, since the size of other trading blocs increases as well. Therefore, one of our objectives is to examine the sensitivity of the relationship between absolute bloc size and tariff rates to generalizations in the endowment structure of the model considered by Krugman. Our second goal is to consider the case in which one trading bloc expands in size relative to other trading blocs, in order to identify the effects of changes in the relative size of trading blocs on tariffs and world welfare, and to compare these effects with those obtained in the symmetric case.

In Section 2 we present a simple endowment model of trade with a parameter that represents the degree of comparative advantage. We then use this model, of which Krugman's model is a limiting case, to analyze the effect of a symmetric expansion of trading blocs. We show that the effect of increases in the absolute size of trading blocs on Nash equilibrium tariffs is highly sensitive to the assumptions made regarding the pattern of endowments. When the share of importables in the endowment is zero (as in Krugman), equilibrium tariffs must increase with increases in absolute bloc size. In contrast, if the share of importables in the bundle is positive, there are elasticities of substitution sufficiently low for which the equilibrium tariffs must decrease with an increase in

---

[2]This work could also be extended to consider the impact of bloc expansion when countries form free trade areas (FTAs). Kennan and Riezman (1990) point out that the incentives for the choice of external tariffs differ between FTAs and customs unions, because FTA members do not internalize the effects of their tariffs on other members. Also, 'hub and spoke' systems (Kowalczyk and Wonnacott, 1992), in which a series of bilateral FTAs are formed involving a single 'hub' country could also be considered.

E.W. Bond, C. Syropoulos / Journal of International Economics 40 (1996) 411–437   413

bloc size. For intermediate values of the elasticity of substitution, tariffs increase in bloc size when blocs are small but decrease in bloc size when blocs are large. We use these equilibrium tariffs to characterize the number of trading blocs at which world welfare is minimized as a function of the pattern of endowments and the elasticity of substitution. We show that world welfare may be minimized when there are four or more blocs if the elasticity of substitution is low and the share of importables in the endowment bundle is small. If the share of importables in the bundle is sufficiently high, world welfare will be minimized when there are only two trading blocs.

Section 3 uses the endowment model to consider the effects of changes in relative bloc size. We examine a situation in which one bloc expands by drawing members symmetrically from the rest of the trading blocs. We show that the optimal tariff of the expanding bloc becomes arbitrarily large and its internal prices approach the free trade level as the fraction of countries included in the bloc increases. We also use these results to show that the expanding bloc can assure itself a welfare level that is above the free trade level by excluding some countries. This result is established by showing analytically that the welfare of the expanding bloc is decreasing in the size of its membership at the point where it includes all countries. We then use simulation analysis to illustrate the effects of bloc expansion on world welfare at intermediate sizes, and to show how the optimal size for the expanding bloc is affected by preferences and endowments.

Throughout our analysis, we concentrate on the determinants of market power of blocs in the case where inter-bloc tariffs are chosen to maximize national welfare in a one-period tariff-setting game. In doing so, we take the structure of trading blocs as exogenously given. However, these results can also yield insights regarding market power under other assumptions regarding the way in which blocs interact. For example, Dixit (1987) has suggested that the repeated interactions between countries allows them to sustain trade agreements that are Pareto-preferred to the Nash equilibrium of the one-period tariff game. Tacit cooperation can be obtained by using history-dependent strategies in which tariffs revert to those in the Nash equilibrium of the one-period tariff game, in the event that a country deviates from the trade agreement. The market power of trading blocs is one factor in determining which agreements can be supported in a repeated tariff game, since a bloc is more likely to deviate from an agreement the greater is its welfare level in the single-period Nash equilibrium.[3] A more general issue is the

---

[3] In Bond and Syropoulos (1995), we show how absolute and relative bloc size affect the range of agreements that can be supported, as well as the likelihood that a given agreement can be sustained by tacit cooperation, in repeated tariff-setting games between trading blocs. In related work, Bagwell and Staiger (1993a, Bagwell and Staiger, 1993b) study the dynamics of the trading bloc formation process, by considering how the formation of a free trade area or a customs union affects a country's trade relations with non-member countries, during the phase of negotiations over the formation of a trading bloc and after the bloc is formed. They also assume that tariffs between the member and non-member country are set in a repeated tariff-setting game.

414   E.W. Bond. C. Syropoulos / Journal of International Economics 40 (1996) 411–437

question of which trading blocs will actually be formed. Our results do give some insight on the forces that may be important in endogenous formation of blocs, since we show how welfare of members changes as a bloc adds members.[4]

2. The model with symmetric trading blocs

We consider a simple exchange model in which there are N countries and N goods.[5] Preferences over goods are assumed to be identical in all countries and are represented by a CES utility function, $U^i = \Sigma_j(c_j^i)^\theta)^{1/\theta}$, where U^i is the utility level of country i, and c_j^i is consumption of good j in country i. Letting p_k^i be the price of good k in country i, these preferences imply

$$\frac{c_j^i}{c_k i} = \left(\frac{p_j^i}{p_k^i}\right)^{-\sigma}, \tag{1}$$

where $\sigma \equiv 1/(1-\theta) \geq 1$ is the elasticity of substitution. Country i has an

---

[4]Full analysis of this problem would require the development of a non-cooperative model of coalition formation, which is beyond the scope of the current paper. One approach that has been taken towards formally analyzing the problem of stability is to define stable agreements to be those that are in the core. Riezman (1985) uses a three-country trade model in which there are no side payments between countries, and provides numerical examples in which the core may consist of an agreement including all three countries (i.e. a free trade agreement) or a customs union including only two of the countries. Kowalczyk and Sjostrom (1994) analyze a case where transfers are possible between countries, and show that free trade will be in the core in the model they consider. The core approach, however, does not involve a formal model of the bargaining process that leads to the formation of unions.

Utilizing a segmented markets oligopoly model, Yi (1993) investigates whether global free trade will arise under different rules regarding membership in blocs with endogenous formation of coalition structures. He finds that free trade is a stable outcome under the rule of 'open regionalism', where any country that applies must be accepted as a member. Under 'exclusive regionalism', on the other hand, free trade is typically not a stable outcome.

[5]Kennan and Riezman (1990) have used a three-country, three-good model with a similar endowment structure to compare the free trade welfare level with a customs union between two of the members. Throughout the analysis we maintain the assumption that the number of countries equals the number of goods. This assumption allows us to focus on issues related to bloc size, while abstracting from issues related to the composition of blocs, since in our setting the gains from bloc formation depend only on the size of blocs and not on the identity of their members. Deardorff and Stern (1994) consider the effect of relaxing the assumption that there are the same number of goods as countries. They argue that there are greater gains to be had from the formation of larger trading blocs in this case when blocs do not behave strategically in setting external tariffs. When tariffs are set optimally by blocs, composition becomes important because blocs may be formed to obtain monopoly power over a particular commodity. Haveman (1992) examines asymmetric trading blocs in a simulation model with three goods and ten countries. He considers the effect on world welfare of sequentially adding countries to the trading bloc, and compares the effects of combining the most different with the most similar. He finds that welfare decreases as the number of blocs is reduced.

E.W. Bond, C. Syropoulos / Journal of International Economics 40 (1996) 411–437   415

endowment $x+z$ of good i and an endowment of x of all other goods $j \neq i$, where $x,z > 0$. World supply of each good is thus $K = Nx + z$.

Choosing good 1 as the numéraire, i.e. $q_1 = 1$ where q_j is the world price of good j, the symmetry in the preference and endowment structures implies that the free trade price of each good will equal unity and every country will consume $x + z/N$ units of each good. Consequently, the volume of net imports of country i will be z/N for good $j \neq i$ and $(z/N) - z$ for good i. This endowment structure leads to a natural association of goods with countries, since each country has a comparative advantage in the good with the same index. For given K, the parameter z is positively related to the volume of trade in the free trade equilibrium. Thus, z serves as an index of the degree of comparative advantage.

2.1. Nash equilibrium tariffs

Now consider the effect of dividing the world into B identical trading blocs, with each bloc consisting of $n = N/B$ countries. We assume blocs are customs unions which levy no tariffs on intra-bloc trade and adopt a common external tariff. Blocs are assumed to behave non-cooperatively in setting external tariffs on imports from the rest of the world (ROW), with each bloc choosing its external tariffs to maximize the welfare of a representative member country given ROW tariffs.[6] In this section we derive the reaction function for a representative trading bloc, taking the number of trading blocs as exogenously given, and use this reaction function to solve for the Nash equilibrium tariff rates. Note that the symmetry in preferences and endowments ensures that the behavior of a trading bloc depends only on its size and not on the identity of its members. We can thus analyze the effect of absolute bloc size, the degree of comparative advantage, and the elasticity of substitution in consumption on Nash equilibrium tariffs by considering the effects of changes in B, z, and σ, respectively.

In light of the symmetric structure of the model, it is natural to conjecture the existence of a Nash equilibrium in which each bloc imposes the same tariff rate τ on its imports from all other blocs. We will proceed by assuming that each of the ROW blocs chooses the same tariff rates τ^{ROW} on its imports from all other blocs, and then show that the best response of the representative trading bloc, referred to as bloc 1, is a common tariff rate $\tau^1 = \phi(\tau^{ROW})$ on imports from blocs $2, \ldots, B$. It follows from the symmetry of the model that a fixed point of $\phi, \tau = \phi(\tau)$ will be a symmetric Nash equilibrium in which all blocs levy the same tariff.

---

[6] In light of the symmetry in size of members in each bloc, maximization of a representative country's welfare under a common external tariff structure is equivalent to maximization of the sum of individual members' welfare. If the members were allowed to choose export taxes for some of the goods exported by the bloc, there would be disagreement between them on the tax levels because one member country would export the good and the rest would import it. We assume that all exports are treated symmetrically, and therefore treat the representative export as the untaxed commodity.

416   E.W. Bond, C. Syropoulos / Journal of International Economics 40 (1996) 411–437

We first show that the behavior of ROW blocs can by analyzed by considering the behavior of a representative ROW bloc, designated as bloc 2. Under the assumptions made above regarding tariffs and the symmetry of endowments and preferences, the price of all goods exported by bloc 1 will be 1 (where the numbering of blocs is chosen so that country 1 is in bloc 1) and the price of exports of all ROW blocs will be q.[7] All goods imported into bloc 1 will have a common domestic price $q(1+\tau^1)$. Letting $c_j^{\ 1}$ denote consumption by a representative bloc 1 country of a good from bloc j, the common import price of non-bloc 1 goods implies $c_j^{\ 1}=c_2^1$ $(j\neq1)$. Similarly, the income levels of all ROW bloc countries will be equal, and imports from bloc 1 in ROW blocs will have a common domestic price $(1+\tau^{ROW})$. Letting c_1^i denote the consumption of a representative bloc 1 good in a representative bloc i country, it follows that $c_1^i=c_1^2$ $(i\neq1)$.

Since there is a single relative price to be determined in this case, the problem of choosing the optimal tariff for bloc 1 takes on a form very similar to that of the two-good optimal tariff problem. We now establish that the optimal tariff for bloc 1 is given by the traditional inverse elasticity formula, where the relevant elasticity is the price elasticity of the offer curve of a representative ROW bloc country, designated as 2.

Lemma 1. If blocs 2, . . . ,B impose a uniform tariff at rate τ^{ROW} on imports from all other blocs, then a best response for bloc 1 is a uniform tariff at rate

$$\tau^1 = \frac{1}{\epsilon_2 - 1},\tag{2}$$

where

$$\epsilon_2 \equiv \frac{\partial(c_1^2 - x)}{\partial q} \frac{q}{(c_1^2 - x)}.$$

Proof. Since there are n goods exported by each bloc, the utility of a bloc 1 country can be written as $U^1=N^{1/\theta}[\beta(c_1^1)^\theta+(1-\beta)(c_2^{1\theta})]^{1/\theta}$, where $\beta\equiv1/B$ is the fraction of countries contained in each bloc. The budget constraint of a bloc 1 country requires that the value of its consumption at world prices equal the value

---

[7]To see this, consider two goods j and k associated with the same trading bloc. The market-clearing $\Sigma_i c_j^i=K$. Using (1) and the assumption regarding tariffs, it follows that the market-clearing condition for good k can be written as $\Sigma_i c_k^i=(q_j/q_k)^\sigma(\Sigma_i c_j^i)=K$. Clearly, this requires $q_j=q_k$ for any goods from the same bloc. Thus, we can restrict attention to the $B-1$ prices associated with the respective trading blocs. Letting q_k denote the relative price of goods associated with bloc k, suppose that $q_2=q_3=\ldots=q_B$. It follows that $c_k^i=c_j^i$ for $i=1,\ldots,B$ and the market-clearing conditions will be identical for $k=2,\ldots,B$. It is then easy to show that there exists a q which solves this equation. Furthermore, since these preferences satisfy standard conditions for uniqueness of equilibrium, the solution with $q_2=\ldots=q_B$ will be the unique solution for the $B-1$ prices.

E.W. Bond, C. Syropoulos / Journal of International Economics 40 (1996) 411–437   417

of its endowments at world prices, i.e. $n[c_1^1 + q(B-1)c_2^1] = nx + z + nq(B-1)x$. It can be shown that trade balance for bloc 1 requires that the following condition hold between bloc 1 and each of the other blocs:

$$q(c_2^1 - x) = (c_1^2 - x). \tag{3}$$

This condition is derived by substituting the budget constraint for a ROW country into the market-clearing condition for a representative ROW good.[8] Market-clearing requires that overall trade between bloc 1 and the rest of the world be balanced. The symmetry of the model ensures that trade between bloc 1 and each of the other blocs will also be balanced.

The trade balance condition and the budget constraint of a representative bloc 1 country can now be substituted into the utility function to yield an expression for welfare of a representative bloc 1 country, i.e. $U^1 = N^{1/\theta}\{\beta[x + (z/n) - (B-1)(c_1^2(q) - x)]^\theta + (1-\beta)[(c_1^2(q) - x)/q + x]^\theta\}^{1/\theta}$, where $c_1^2(q) - x$ is the representative ROW country import demand function. Differentiating with respect to q yields the optimal tariff formula (2). It is shown in Appendix A that the assumption of a uniform tariff is not restrictive, in that welfare of bloc 1 cannot be improved by charging different tariff rates on imports from different blocs, which completes the proof of the lemma. $\square$

To obtain the elasticity of the foreign offer curve, we note that the budget constraint of a representative ROW bloc country requires that the value of consumption at world prices equal the value of production at world prices (denoted by Y_2^*), i.e.

$$n[c_1^2 + q(c_2^2 + (B-2)c_3^2)] = Y_2^* \equiv nx + q(nx(B-1) + z). \tag{4}$$

Substituting from (1) and using the fact that $p_1^2 = (1 + \tau^{ROW})$, $p_2^2 = q$, and $p_3^2 = q(1 + \tau^{ROW})$, we obtain

$$nc_1^2 = sY_2^*, \tag{5}$$

where $s = [1 + (B-2)q^{1-\sigma} + q^{1-\sigma}(1 + \tau^{ROW})^\sigma]^{-1}$ is the share of income of a ROW country spent on bloc 1 goods. The share parameter s is increasing in q (for $\sigma > 1$) and decreasing in τ^{ROW} and B. Using (5), the elasticity of demand of the ROW offer curve can be written as

---

[8]Market clearing for a representative ROW good, denoted good 2, requires that the value of bloc 1 imports of good 2 equal the value of exports by the rest of the world. Letting c_2^3 denote demand for good 2 by blocs $j \neq 1,2$, this equilibrium condition can be written as $nq(c_2^1 - x) = q[z - n((c_2^2 - x) + (B-2)(c_2^3 - x))] = q[z - n((c_2^2 - x) + (B-2)(c_3^2 - x))]$, where the second equality follows from symmetry of blocs $2, \ldots, B$. The budget constraint for country 2 at world prices requires that $n[c_1^2 + qc_2^2 + q(B-2)c_3^2] = n[x + q(B-1)x] + qz$. The trade balance condition (3) is obtained by substitution of this budget constraint into the expression for ROW exports in the market-clearing condition.

418   E.W. Bond, C. Syropoulos / Journal of International Economics 40 (1996) 411–437

$$\epsilon = [1 - \mu + (\sigma - 1)(1 - s)]\left(\frac{s}{s - \mu}\right),$$ (6)

where

$$\mu = \frac{nx}{nx + q[(B - 1)nx + z]}$$

is the share of ROW income that consists of bloc 1 goods.

Substituting (6) into the optimal tariff formula (2) yields

$$\frac{1}{\tau} = (1 - s)\left[\sigma - 1 + \frac{\mu\sigma}{s - \mu}\right].$$ (7)

From differentiation of (7) it can be established that the optimal tariff of bloc 1 is increasing in s and decreasing in μ. A greater share of income spent on bloc 1 goods lowers the elasticity of the ROW offer curve, and gives more market power to bloc 1. An increase in μ lowers the volume of ROW imports from bloc 1, and thus raises the elasticity of the ROW offer curve. This leads to a lower optimal tariff for bloc 1.

If the expression for s from (5) is substituted into (7), we obtain the reaction function for bloc 1, $\tau^1 = \phi(\tau^{ROW})$. The Nash equilibrium tariff is obtained by solving this expression for $\tau = \tau^1 = \tau^{ROW}$ and $q = 1$. In this case, $\mu = \beta/(1 + \alpha)$, where $\beta \equiv 1/B$ is the share of countries that are contained in each trading bloc, and $\alpha \equiv z/(Nx)$ is a measure of the degree of comparative advantage. Substituting these expressions into (6) and (7) yields an expression for the Nash equilibrium tariffs as a function of the three key parameters of the model, α, β, and σ:

$$\frac{1}{\tau} = (1 + \beta[(1 + \tau)^\sigma - 2])\left(\frac{\sigma - 1}{1 + \beta[(1 + \tau)^\sigma - 1]} + \frac{\sigma}{\alpha + \beta[1 - (1 + \tau)^\sigma]}\right).$$ (8)

The right-hand side of (8) is positive when evaluated at $\tau = 0$ and is increasing in τ. This ensures the existence of a unique Nash equilibrium tariff in which trade occurs. For the case in which countries have no endowments of importables ($x = 0$), $\alpha = \infty$ and the second term in parentheses goes to zero, yielding Krugman's result (obtained from his equations 10 and 16). As is standard in trade models of this type, there will also exist a continuum of autarkic Nash equilibria in which all blocs levy prohibitive tariffs.

Eq. (8) can be used to derive comparative statics results for the effects of changes in α, β, and σ on the Nash equilibrium tariffs. The right-hand side of (8) is decreasing in α, which means that the Nash equilibrium tariff is increasing in α. This result is due to the fact that a greater degree of comparative advantage results in a larger volume of trade, and a lower elasticity of offer curves. Similarly, it can be shown that the right-hand side of (8) is increasing in σ, so that a higher

E.W. Bond, C. Syropoulos / Journal of International Economics 40 (1996) 411–437   419

elasticity of substitution between commodities leads to lower tariffs in the Nash equilibrium.

For the limiting case of symmetric blocs of infinitesimal size ($\beta=0$), the optimal tariff satisfies $1/\tau=\sigma-1+\sigma/\alpha$. For finite σ, blocs maintain their market power in the limit because each bloc is the sole exporter of some good. There will in general be an ambiguous relationship between bloc size and the optimal tariff rate, which arises from two conflicting effects. One effect is that an increase in β will increase the share of income spent on bloc 1 goods by ROW blocs (i.e. s from (5)), which will increase the optimal tariff (from (7)). On the other hand, an increase in β will increase the share of bloc 1 goods in ROW endowments (i.e. μ from (6)), which will reduce the optimal tariff. Some insight regarding the relative magnitude of these effects can be obtained by considering several special cases. First, in the case considered by Krugman where each bloc is endowed only with its own goods (i.e. $\alpha=\infty$), the second term in parentheses in (8) is zero and the optimal tariff must be increasing in β. In this case increases in β have no effect on the share of bloc 1 goods in the ROW endowment ($\mu=0$) and the effect of β on the consumption share dominates. A second example is the case of Cobb–Douglas preferences with $\sigma=1$. In this case (8) simplifies to the equation $\beta\tau^2+\tau-\alpha=0$, and the Nash equilibrium is unambiguously decreasing in β. The effect of β on the endowment share dominates its effect on the consumption share in this case, so that equilibrium tariffs fall as blocs increase in absolute size.

These results indicate that the market power of blocs is increasing in β in cases when α is very large but decreasing in β when σ is at its lower bound. Fig. 1 illustrates the relationship between optimal tariffs and bloc size for intermediate values of σ and α. These three curves characterize the three different types of relationships observed between tariffs and bloc size in simulations over a wide range of assumptions regarding σ and α. The particular parameter values shown in Fig. 1 have been chosen such that they each yield $\tau=0.2$ for the case of $\beta=0$, since this facilitates comparison. For cases where σ and α are both large ($\sigma=6$ and $\alpha\to\infty$), tariffs are increasing in bloc size. If σ and α are relatively small ($\sigma=1$ and $\alpha=0.2$), the optimal tariff is decreasing in bloc size. For intermediate values ($\sigma=4$ and $\alpha=2$), tariffs initially increase and then decrease with increases in β.

The results of this section can be summarized as follows.

Proposition 1. The Nash equilibrium tariffs with symmetric trading blocs are (i) increasing in bloc size as $\alpha\to\infty$; (ii) decreasing in bloc size with $\sigma=1$. Also, $\lim_{\beta\to0}1/\tau=\sigma-1+\sigma/\alpha$.

2.2. World welfare and absolute bloc size

The equilibrium tariffs can now be utilized to capture the effects of an increase in the number of trading blocs on world welfare. The welfare level of a

420   E.W. Bond, C. Syropoulos / Journal of International Economics 40 (1996) 411–437

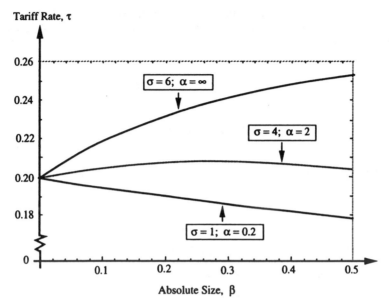

Fig. 1. Tariffs and the absolute size of trading blocs.

representative country in the Nash equilibrium is obtained by substituting the demand functions for a ROW bloc country given by (1) and (5) into the utility function and evaluating the resulting expression at the Nash equilibrium tariffs with $q = 1$. The equilibrium utility level will be

$$U = \frac{KN^{\frac{1}{\sigma-1}}[\beta(1+\tau)^{\sigma-1} + (1-\beta)]^{\frac{\sigma}{\sigma-1}}}{[\beta(1+\tau)^{\sigma} + (1-\beta)]}, \tag{9}$$

where τ satisfies (8) and the superscript for bloc 1 has been dropped because all countries will have the same welfare level. World welfare is at the free trade level $U = KN^{1/(\sigma-1)}$ when the world is a single trading bloc ($\beta = 1$). World welfare is at the free trade level when trading blocs are infinitesimal ($\beta = 0$). Even though blocs impose positive tariffs as $\beta \to 0$, the magnitude of the distortion created by these tariffs approaches zero.

The effect of changing the size of symmetric trading blocs on world welfare can be decomposed into two terms: the effect of an increase in the size of trading blocs at fixed tariff rates and the effect of the change in tariff rates as a result of bloc expansion. An increase in β at fixed tariffs has an ambiguous effect on world welfare, as is well known from the literature on customs union formation, because of the second best nature of a discriminatory tariff reduction. The increase in the size of trading blocs increases the volume of trade that is not subject to tariff distortions, which is a movement in the direction of global free trade. On the other hand, the expansion of trade diverts trade from non-member countries, which is welfare-reducing. Formally, we have

$$\frac{\partial U}{\partial \beta} = U\left[\left(\frac{\sigma}{\sigma - 1}\right)\frac{(1 + \tau)^{\sigma - 1} - 1}{1 - \beta + \beta(1 + \tau)^{\sigma - 1}} - \frac{(1 + \tau)^{\sigma} - 1}{1 - \beta + \beta(1 + \tau)^{\sigma}}\right]. \tag{10}$$

This expression is negative when evaluated at $\beta = 0$. Eq. (10) can be used to derive a closed form solution for the unique value of β at which $\partial U/\partial\beta = 0$. Since welfare is at the free trade level for $\beta = 0$ and $\beta = 1$, we have a U-shaped relationship between world welfare and the size of trading blocs as obtained by Krugman. The second effect of a change in β is the strategic effect, which is due to the change in optimal tariffs that results from a change in β. Differentiating (9) with respect to τ yields $\partial U/\partial\tau < 0$. Increases in the external tariffs of blocs reduce world welfare, since the consumption distortion is increased. The strategic effect of bloc expansion will decrease world welfare in cases where Nash equilibrium tariffs rise with the size of trading blocs.

Krugman (1991) provided simulation results showing that for a range of values of σ (assuming $\alpha = \infty$), bloc expansion reduced world welfare up until the point where $B = 3$. Since our results indicate that assumptions regarding the value of α and σ can have a significant effect on the Nash equilibrium tariffs, it is useful to examine how these parameters affect the bloc size at which world welfare is minimized. Fig. 2 illustrates the value of B at which world welfare is minimized as a function of the degree of substitutability in consumption and the degree of comparative advantage. Note that both the measure of substitutability ($\theta = (\sigma - 1)/\sigma$) and the measure of comparative advantage ($\alpha/(1 + \alpha)$) have been chosen such that they are restricted to the unit interval. The results indicate that when the degree of comparative advantage is relatively low, world welfare is minimized when there are two blocs. This result holds for all values of σ. For intermediate values of α, world welfare is minimized at $B = 3$. For high values of α, the minimum point of world welfare is decreasing in σ. In this case the minimum can occur with five or more blocs when the elasticity of substitution is close to one.

3. Asymmetric trading blocs

It is our view that if there are changes in market power when trading blocs form, such changes would be more likely if regional integration led to changes in relative size. Accordingly, in this section we analyze the effect of an increase in the size of bloc 1 from an initial symmetric Nash equilibrium, assuming that bloc 1 expands by drawing members symmetrically from the remaining $B - 1$ trading blocs. Letting n_1 be the number of countries in bloc 1, there will be $(N - n_1)/B$

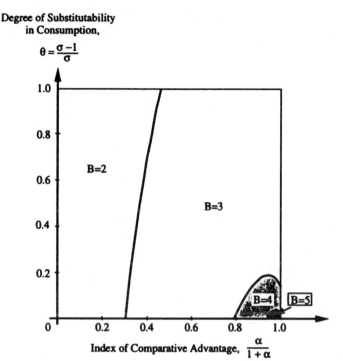

**Degree of Substitutability
in Consumption,**

$$\theta = \frac{\sigma - 1}{\sigma}$$

B=2

B=3

B=4   B=5

Index of Comparative Advantage, $\dfrac{\alpha}{1+\alpha}$

Fig. 2. The number of (symmetric) trading blocs at which world welfare is minimized.

countries in each of the remaining blocs. We let $\beta_i = n_i / N$ denote the fraction of countries in bloc i. This experiment allows us to examine the effects of an increase in the size of bloc 1, while holding the number of other trading blocs it interacts with constant.[9]

As in the previous section, we analyze the effects of the expansion of trading blocs on market power by considering how Nash equilibrium tariffs and utility levels change as β_1 increases. The analysis is more complex in the asymmetric case, because we must derive results for both bloc 1 and a representative small bloc. Due to the additional complexity of the asymmetric case, we cannot obtain analytic results for the general case. Therefore, we present two types of results to illustrate the market power effects of bloc expansion. The first is to derive unambiguous analytic results for the effects of increasing bloc size on tariffs,

[9]Our approach to introducing asymmetries between blocs is the simplest to deal with formally, because it results in there being only two types of blocs to analyze: the large bloc and a representative small bloc. An alternative approach would be to reduce the number of ROW blocs as bloc 1 expands. The results obtained under this alternative approach are similar to the ones reported below.

E.W. Bond, C. Syropoulos / Journal of International Economics 40 (1996) 411–437   423

world prices, and bloc welfare as $\beta_1 \to 1$, i.e. as bloc 1 becomes arbitrarily large relative to ROW blocs. We then supplement these analytic results with simulation analysis to illustrate the behavior of tariffs and bloc welfare for $\beta_1 \in [1/B, 1]$.

3.1. Nash equilibrium in the asymmetric case

In this section we derive reaction functions and characterize the Nash equilibrium tariffs for the asymmetric case. Our approach to modeling asymmetries allows us to maintain the two-country flavor of the derivation, since we can summarize behavior in terms of optimal tariffs for bloc 1 and a representative ROW bloc. In the symmetric case, we showed that increases in absolute bloc size had an ambiguous effect on the external tariffs of blocs, since increases in bloc size could be associated with either increases or decreases in external tariffs depending on the values of α and σ. The natural question to ask in the asymmetric case is whether increases in relative bloc size are associated with increases in external tariffs for the expanding bloc and decreases in external tariffs for the contracting (small) blocs. We will show that for all parameter values (α, σ, B), the external tariff of the expanding bloc becomes arbitrarily large as $\beta_1 \to 1$. This provides a sense in which bloc expansion must be associated with increased market power for sufficiently large trading blocs. In contrast, the tariffs of the small blocs will have a finite limit. However, a monotonic relationship between external tariffs and β_1 does not exist for all (α, σ, B).

We begin by showing that the Nash equilibrium in the asymmetric case can be characterized by three tariff rates: the external tariff of the large bloc, τ^1; the tariff of a representative small bloc (bloc 2) on trade with the large bloc, τ_1^2; and the tariff of a small bloc on imports from another small bloc, τ_3^2. The optimization problem for bloc 1 is to choose tariffs to maximize welfare of a representative member, given the tariffs imposed by the smaller blocs. If ROW blocs adopt the same tariff rates on their trade with bloc 1 (i.e. τ_1^i is the same for all $i = 2, \ldots, B$) and the same tariff rates on their trade with each other (τ_k^i is the same for $i, k = 2, \ldots, N$ and $i \neq k$), then it can be shown (using arguments similar to those in the lemma) that the best response of bloc 1 is a common ad valorem tariff, denoted τ^1. The optimal tariff problem for the small blocs, however, is more complicated because they are importing goods from a large bloc and from $(B-2)$ identical small blocs.

We make the following assumptions: (i) bloc 1 imposes a common tariff τ^1 on all imports from small blocs, and (ii) the other small blocs impose a common tariff on their trade with bloc 1 and a common tariff on their trade with other small blocs. Given these assumptions, it can be shown that the optimal policy for bloc 2 is a uniform tariff τ_1^2 on imports from bloc 1 and a uniform tariff τ_3^2 on imports from all other small blocs. Since all the small blocs are symmetric, the optimal tariffs chosen by every small bloc will be the same and the world prices of goods exported by all of the small blocs will also be the same, $q_2 = q_3$. In particular, this

424   E.W. Bond, C. Syropoulos / Journal of International Economics 40 (1996) 411–437

result ensures that the assumptions (i) and (ii) used to derive the optimal tariffs for bloc 2 are consistent with optimal tariffs chosen by other blocs. Thus, a Nash equilibrium can be characterized by the triple of tariffs $(\tau^1(\beta_1), \tau_1^2(\beta_1), \tau_3^2(\beta_1))$ that satisfy the respective optimal tariff formulae.

Consider the optimal tariff problem for bloc 1. Since the relative price of all ROW goods will be the same, the consumption levels of all ROW goods in bloc 1 will be equal to one another. We can thus express consumption of ROW goods using a representative ROW good, referred to as good 2. The utility function of a representative bloc 1 country can thus be written as $U^1 = N^{1/\theta}[\beta_1(c_2^1)^\theta + (1 - \beta_1)(c_2^1)^\theta]^{1/\theta} = N^{1/\theta}c[\beta_1((1+\tau^1)q)^{\theta\sigma} + (1-\beta_1)]^{1/\theta}$, where the second equality follows from (1). Arguments similar to those used in the proof of Lemma 1 can then be used to establish that the trade balance condition (3) between a representative bloc 1 country and a representative ROW bloc country holds, and that the optimal tariff formula for bloc 1 is given by (2).

In order to calculate the optimal tariff formula for bloc 1, we must derive the elasticity of the ROW offer curve. The budget constraint for a representative ROW bloc country will be $n_1c_1^2 + qn_2c_2^2 + q(B-2)n_2c_3^2 = n_1x + q[(N-n_1)x + z]$, where $n_2 \equiv (N-n_1)/(B-1)$ is the number of countries in a representative ROW bloc. Using the fact that $c_2^2/c_1^2 = [q/(1+\tau_1^2)]^{-\sigma}$ and $c_3^2/c_1^2 = [q(1+\tau_3^2)/(1+\tau_1^2)]^{-\sigma}$ from (1), the ROW demand for a representative bloc 1 good can be derived from the budget constraint to be

$$n_1c_1^2 = s_1^2Y_2^*, \tag{11}$$

where $s_1^2 \equiv \beta_1[\beta_1 + (1-\beta_1)q^{1-\sigma}\Delta]^{-1}$ and $\Delta \equiv (1+\tau_1^2)^\sigma((1+(B-2)(1+\tau_3^2)^{-\sigma})/(B-1))$.

Note that the only difference between (11) and the corresponding expression for the symmetric case, (5), is that the expenditure share must be adjusted to allow for the possibility that $\tau_3^2 \neq \tau_1^2$. (11) can be used to derive the elasticity of the ROW offer curve, which can be substituted into (2) to yield

$$\frac{1}{\tau^1} = [(1-\beta_1)q^{1-\sigma}\Delta]\left(\frac{\sigma-1}{\beta_1 + (1-\beta_1)\Delta q^{1-\sigma}}\right.$$
$$\left. + \frac{\sigma}{q(1-\beta_1 + \alpha) - (1-\beta_1)\Delta q^{1-\sigma}}\right). \tag{12}$$

In order to solve for the effect of changes in β_1 and Δ on bloc 1's optimal tariff, it remains to solve for the equilibrium price of ROW goods, q.

The equilibrium value of q can be obtained from the market-clearing condition (3). Since the demand for ROW goods by bloc 1 is given, it remains to derive the demand of a representative bloc 1 country for a representative ROW good, c_2^1. The budget constraint at world prices for a representative country in bloc 1 will be

E.W. Bond, C. Syropoulos / Journal of International Economics 40 (1996) 411–437   425

$n_1c_1^1 + q(N - n_1)c_2^1 = n_1x + z + q(N - n_1)x$. Utilizing (1) in the budget constraint yields bloc 1's demand function for ROW goods,

$$(N - n_1)c_2^1 = s_2^1 Y_1^* \tag{13}$$

where $s_2^1 \equiv q(1 - \beta_1)[q(1 - \beta_1) + \beta_1(q(1 + \tau^1))^\sigma]^{-1}$ is the share of ROW goods in the bloc 1 consumption bundle. Substituting (11) and (13) into the market-clearing condition yields

$$\frac{\alpha + \beta_1(1 - [q(1 + \tau^1)]^\sigma)}{(1 - \beta_1)q + \beta_1[q(1 + \tau^1)]^\sigma} = \frac{(1 - \beta_1 + \alpha) - (1 - \beta_1 \Delta q^{-\sigma})}{\beta_1 + (1 - \beta_1)\Delta q^{1-\sigma}}. \tag{14}$$

If trade takes place in equilibrium, bloc 1 must be an importer of ROW goods, i.e. $c_2^1 - x > 0$, and ROW blocs must import bloc 1 goods, $c_1^2 - x > 0$. The conditions $c_2^1 - x > 0$ and $c_1^2 - x > 0$ impose the following bounds on the world price,

$$\frac{\alpha + \beta_1}{\beta_1(1 + \tau^1)^\sigma} > q^\sigma > \frac{(1 - \beta_1)\Delta}{(1 - \beta_1 + \alpha)}, \tag{15}$$

where the left-hand side of (15) is the autarky price of bloc 1 and the right-hand side is the autarky price of the ROW blocs.

The market-clearing condition (14) and the optimal tariff formula (12) can now be used to solve for the optimal tariff of bloc 1 and the equilibrium price, given β_1 and Δ. The solution for the general case is quite complex. However, we can obtain a general result for the limiting behavior of the best responses $\tau^1(\beta_1, \Delta)$ and equilibrium prices $q(\beta_1, \Delta)$ as $\beta_1 \to 1$, if we impose the following restriction on the limiting behavior of Δ:

Condition A. ROW tariffs do not increase too rapidly as ROW blocs shrink in size: $\lim_{\beta_1 \to 1}(1 - \beta_1)\Delta = 0$.

Referring to the definition of Δ in (11), a sufficient condition for A to hold is that τ_1^2 have a finite limit. Note from the inequalities in (15) that this condition also implies that the limiting behavior of ROW tariffs does not prohibit trade with bloc 1. We show below that Condition A will be satisfied in the Nash equilibrium of the two bloc case where trade exists between bloc 1 and ROW blocs.

Proposition 2. If $\beta_1 \to 1$ and the tariffs of ROW blocs satisfy Condition A, then (a) $\lim_{\beta_1 \to 1} q(1 + \tau^1) = 1$; *(b)* $\lim_{\beta_1 \to 1} \tau^1 = \infty$.

Proof. From the right-hand inequality in (15), it follows that $(1 - \beta_1)\Delta q^{1-\sigma} < [(1 - \beta_1)\Delta]^{1/\sigma}(1 - \beta_1 + \alpha)^{(\sigma-1)/\sigma}$, which converges to zero as β_1 approaches one under the condition of the proposition. Similarly, $(1 - \beta_1)\Delta q^{-\sigma}$ converges to zero using the same argument. Using these two facts, the right-hand side of (14) converges to α. It follows that the values of $[q(1 + \tau^1)]^\sigma$ must be such that equality is

426   E.W. Bond, C. Syropoulos / Journal of International Economics 40 (1996) 411–437

maintained in (14) (i.e. the left-hand side must also converge to α). From the left-hand inequality in (15), $q < [(\alpha + \beta_1)/\beta_1]^{1/\sigma}$ for $\tau^1 \geq 0$, so $(1 - \beta_1)q$ must converge to zero. In order for the left-hand side of (14) to converge to α as $\beta_1 \rightarrow 1$, $[(1 + \tau^1)q]^{\sigma}$ must converge to one, which establishes part (a) of the proposition. To establish part (b), we take the limit of the right-hand side of (12). Since $(1 - \beta_1)\Delta q^{1-\sigma}$ converges to zero, the right-hand side of this expression must converge to zero as $\beta_1 \rightarrow 1$. $\square$

Proposition 2 shows that if the tariffs of ROW blocs are finite, the market power of the expanding bloc becomes arbitrarily large as β_1 approaches one and the prices of ROW bloc exports are driven to zero in the limit. The welfare of ROW blocs will be driven to the autarky level in the limit. Note however that this condition will not be satisfied in the autarkic Nash equilibrium in which all blocs levy prohibitive tariffs. A prohibitive ROW tariff would be one for which the right-hand side of (15) is no less than the left-hand side when evaluated at $\tau^1 = 0$, which requires $(1 - \beta)\Delta \geq (\alpha + \beta_1)(1 - \beta_1 + \alpha)/\beta_1$. Since the right-hand side of this expression is strictly positive for all $\beta_1 \in [0,1]$, the condition of Proposition 2 will not be satisfied for prohibitive tariffs.

We now turn to an analysis of the optimal tariff formulae for the ROW blocs. The simplest way to illustrate the impact of the expansion of bloc 1 on the market power of ROW blocs is to consider the case in which $B = 2$, so that we do not have to solve for the tariff rate τ_3^2. The optimal tariff for bloc 2 in this case will be $1/\tau_1^2 = -(\partial c_2^1/\partial q)(q/(c_2^1 - x)) - 1$. Substituting for the elasticity of demand in this case and using (13) yields

$$\frac{1}{\tau_1^2} = \frac{\sigma - 1}{1 + \dfrac{q(1 - \beta_1)}{\beta_1[q(1 + \tau^1)]^{\sigma}}} + \frac{\sigma}{\dfrac{\beta_1 + \alpha}{\beta_1[q(1 + \tau^1)]^{\sigma}} - 1}. \tag{16}$$

Given $\tau^1(\beta_1)$, we can solve for best responses $\tau_1^2(\beta_1, \tau^1(\beta_1))$ and equilibrium prices using (14) and (16). This yields the following result.

Proposition 3. *If $B = 2$ and bloc 1 tariffs $\tau^1(\beta_1)$ are not prohibitive, then* $\lim_{\beta_1 \rightarrow 1} \tau_1^2 < \infty$.

Proof. In order for τ_1^2 to approach infinity as $\beta_1 \rightarrow 1$, the denominators in the expressions on the right-hand side must both approach infinity. Since $\tau^1 \geq 0$, we must have $(1 - \beta_1)q^{1-\sigma} \rightarrow \infty$ for the first denominator to approach infinity. For $\sigma = 1$ this is clearly impossible. If $\sigma > 1$, the requirement of $(1 - \beta_1)q^{1-\sigma} \rightarrow \infty$ implies $q \rightarrow 0$ and hence $(1 - \beta_1)q^{-\sigma}\Delta \rightarrow \infty$. However, the latter condition is inconsistent with an equilibrium with trade, since it violates the right-hand inequality in (15). Therefore, the limit of the right-hand side of (16) must be strictly positive, which requires the optimal tariff of bloc 2 to be finite. $\square$

It can be shown that for given β_1, a Nash equilibrium exists in which there is trade.[10] The results of Proposition 3 guarantee that the limit of bloc 2 tariffs as $\beta_1 \to 1$ is finite in the interior Nash equilibria. It then follows that Condition A is satisfied, and the limits of the bloc 1 tariffs and world prices in the interior Nash equilibria are characterized by the results of Proposition 2. Utilizing the result that $q(1+\tau^1) \to 1$ as $\beta_1 \to 1$ in (16), we obtain $1/\tau_1^2 \to \sigma - 1 + \sigma/\alpha$. Note that this limiting tariff is identical to the tariff obtained for the symmetric bloc case as bloc size approached zero.

The formula for ROW blocs in the general case with $B > 2$ is slightly more complicated due to the fact that we must consider two relative prices, the relative price of the tariff-setting country's exportables (denoted q_2) and the price of its imports from other ROW blocs (q_3). Although q_2 will equal q_3 in equilibrium due to the symmetry of the blocs, each country has the ability to change the price of its own goods relative to that of imports from other ROW countries, and this market power must be taken into account in determining the optimal external tariffs. Due to the complexity of the solutions for the optimal tariff rates and world prices when $B > 3$, we illustrate the effect of bloc size on the tariff rates using simulation analysis. The effect of the expansion on tariffs for the case $B = 10$ is illustrated in Fig. 3. Fig. 3(a) illustrates the tariff imposed by bloc 1, τ^1, as its size expands. The simulations illustrate that $\tau^1 \to \infty$ as $\beta_1 \to 1$ as indicated by Proposition 2, but the dramatic increases in τ^1 occur only for values of β_1 that are very close to one. Simulations also indicate that the relationship between τ^1 and β_1 is not necessarily monotonic. For large B and α, the optimal tariff of the expanding bloc initially falls below the symmetric equilibrium level. For small B (e.g. $B = 3$), the tariff of the expanding bloc increases monotonically with increases in β_1.

Fig. 3(b) illustrates that the contracting blocs respond by initially decreasing their tariff against bloc 1 (τ_1^2). In general, their tariff on imports from all other blocs (τ_3^2) does not depend monotonically on β_1. Note also that the relative price of ROW bloc goods, q, falls monotonically as bloc 1 expands, which is illustrated in Fig. 3(c). The decline in relative price of small bloc goods results from rising tariffs against small bloc goods (by both the expanding blocs and the other small blocs). In addition to the decline in demand for small bloc goods resulting from these changes in tariffs, the change in composition of the trading blocs also

---

[10]The existence of a Nash equilibrium with trade in the two bloc case can be established using the following observations about the reaction functions $\phi_i(\tau_j)$ for bloc i ($i,j = 1,2$ and $j \neq i$) with CES preferences and $\beta_i \in [1/B, 1)$. First, if ROW tariffs are not prohibitive, there will be a unique non-prohibitive tariff that maximizes welfare of a representative bloc member for each bloc. The appropriate optimal tariff formula ((12) or (16)) and the market-clearing conditions imply continuous reaction functions for each of the blocs. Furthermore, these reaction functions must lie within the set of non-prohibitive tariffs described by (15). Second, reaction functions will have the property that each bloc's best response approaches zero as the other bloc's tariff approaches the prohibitive level. Letting $f' = (\phi')^{-1}$, the latter fact ensures that $\phi'(0) < f'(0)$. Therefore the reaction functions must intersect at some tariff pair that is not prohibitive.

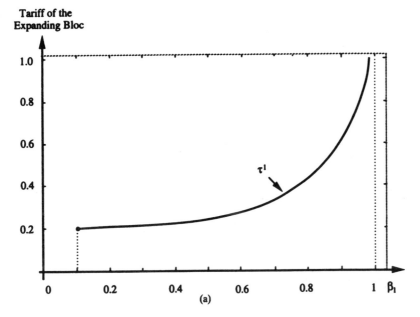

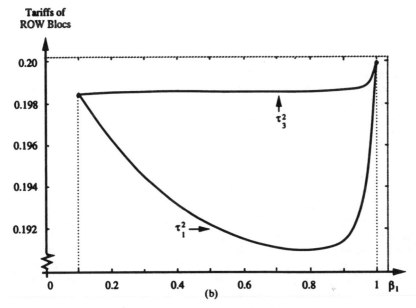

Fig. 3. Effects of relative bloc size on tariffs and the world price (parameter values: $B = 10$; $\alpha = 0.5$; $\sigma = 2$).

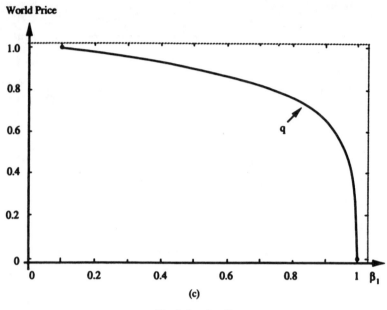

Fig. 3. (*continued*)

contributes to the decline in q. The movement of new countries behind bloc 1's external tariff results in a decline in the demand for ROW goods, since these countries were consuming some ROW goods duty-free when they were members of ROW blocs.

3.2. Bloc welfare in the asymmetric case

We now turn to an analysis of the effects of changes in relative bloc size on world welfare, using the results obtained for Nash equilibrium tariffs in the asymmetric case. The question we will examine first is whether the welfare of the expanding bloc rises monotonically from the Nash equilibrium level to the free trade level as it increases in size, or whether there is a bloc size for which welfare exceeds the free trade level. We will show that in the two bloc case, welfare does not rise monotonically, and there must be a bloc size for which welfare exceeds the free trade level. This indicates the existence of an optimal bloc size for bloc 1, at which the welfare of a representative member is maximized. We then use simulation analysis to illustrate the relationship between bloc size and bloc welfare for $B > 2$ and $\beta_1 \in (1/B, 1)$.

Utilizing (1) and (13), we can express the welfare of bloc 1 when it chooses its tariff optimally to be

$$V^1(\Delta,\beta_1) = \max_{\tau^1} U^1(\tau^1, q(\tau^1, \Delta, \beta_1), \beta_1)$$

$$= \frac{N^{\frac{\sigma}{\sigma-1}}(\beta_1[(1+\tau^1)q]^{\sigma-1} + (1-\beta_1))\frac{\sigma}{\sigma-1}(\beta_1 + \alpha + (1-\beta_1)q)x}{\beta_1[q(1+\tau^1)]^\sigma + (1-\beta_1)q},$$

$$(17)$$

where $q(\tau^1, \Delta, \beta_1)$ is the world price that solves the market clearing condition (14). The results of Section 2 indicated that the welfare level of a representative country in the symmetric Nash equilibrium will be below the free trade level when $0.5 \geq \beta > 0$. Since $q(1+\tau^1) \to 1$ and $q \to 0$ as $\beta_1 \to 1$ by Proposition 2, we obtain $V^1 \to U^F = N^{\sigma/(\sigma-1)}(1+\alpha)x$ from (17). Given any ROW tariffs $\Delta(\beta_1)$ satisfying Condition A, bloc 1 welfare will converge to the free trade level as its size expands to include all countries.

We now show that for any foreign tariffs $\Delta < \infty$, welfare of bloc 1 must exceed the free trade level in the neighborhood of $\beta_1 = 1$ in the two-bloc case. Since $V^1(\Delta, 1)$ equals the free trade level, we can establish this result by showing that $\partial V^1 / \partial \beta_1 < 0$ at $\beta_1 = 1$.

Proposition 4. If $B = 2$ and $\Delta < \infty$, then $\lim_{\beta_1 \to 1} \partial V^1 / \partial \beta_1 < 0$.

Proof. Using (17) and the envelope theorem yields

$$\frac{\partial V^1}{\partial \beta_1} = \frac{\partial U^1}{\partial \beta_1} + \frac{\partial U^1}{\partial q}\left(\frac{dq}{d\beta_1}\right). \tag{18}$$

The change in welfare of bloc 1 resulting from a relative expansion at constant ROW tariffs has two effects: the direct effect of expansion at fixed world prices, and the terms of trade effect resulting from bloc expansion. The first term in (18) is obtained from (17) to be

$$\left(\frac{\partial U^1}{\partial \beta_1}\right)\frac{1}{U^1} = \frac{1-q}{\beta_1 + \alpha + (1-\beta_1)q}$$

$$+ \frac{\sigma}{\sigma-1}\left(\frac{[q(1+\tau^1)]^{\sigma-1} - 1}{\beta_1[(q(1+\tau^1)]^{\sigma-1} + (1-\beta_1)}\right)$$

$$- \frac{[q(1+\tau^1)]^\sigma - q}{\beta_1[q(1+\tau^1)]^\sigma + (1-\beta_1)q}. \tag{19}$$

By Proposition 2(a), $q(1+\tau^1)$ converges to one as $\beta_1 \to 1$, so the second term in (19) converges to zero. Proposition 2 also ensures that $q \to 0$, which means that the first term converges to $1/(1+\alpha)$ and the last term converges to one. Therefore. (19) converges to $-\alpha/(1+\alpha)<0$.

The effect of the terms of trade on welfare of bloc 1 in (18) can be obtained from (17) as

$$
\left(\frac{\partial U^1}{\partial q}\right)\frac{q}{U^1} = \frac{(1-\beta_1)q}{\beta_1 + \alpha + (1-\beta_1)q} + \frac{\sigma\beta_1[q(1+\tau^1)]^{\sigma-1}}{\beta_1[q(1+\tau^1)]^{\sigma-1} + (1-\beta_1)}
$$

$$
-\frac{\sigma\beta_1[q(1+\tau^1)]^{\sigma} + (1-\beta_1)q}{\beta_1[q(1+\tau^1)]^{\sigma} + (1-\beta_1)q}.
\tag{20}
$$

Since $q(1+\tau^1)\to 1$ and $q\to 0$ as $\beta_1\to 1$, it follows that the first term in (20) converges to zero and the remaining terms each converge to σ. Therefore, (20) converges to zero. It is shown in Appendix A that this convergence is sufficiently fast that the product of (20) and $(\partial q/\partial\beta_1)(1/q)$ converges to zero. This establishes that $\partial V^1/\partial\beta_1 = \partial U^1/\partial\beta_1 < 0$. $\square$

The intuition underlying the proof of Proposition 4 is as follows. Proposition 2 indicates that the terms of trade continue to improve as bloc 1 expands, since the relative price, q, of ROW goods becomes arbitrarily low. At the same time, the range of goods that is being imported is shrinking, since more countries are being included within the bloc. The proof of Proposition 4 establishes that the range of goods is shrinking sufficiently fast that the terms of trade effects from bloc expansion become insignificant in the limit. Now let $\bar{\Delta}(\beta_1)$ denote the tariffs for bloc 2 in the interior Nash equilibrium. An argument similar to that of Proposition 3 establishes that these tariffs must be finite in the neighborhood of $\beta_1 = 1$. Therefore, by Proposition 4, welfare in an interior Nash equilibrium must exceed the free trade level in the neighborhood of $\beta_1 = 1$.

Note that the result of Proposition 4 is different from the one that would be obtained if we examined the case of a Nash equilibrium with prohibitive tariffs, where the assumption made regarding Δ is violated. With prohibitive tariffs, each bloc receives the autarky welfare, which is increasing in bloc size. Therefore, the welfare of bloc 1 would increase monotonically from the symmetric Nash equilibrium to the point where $\beta_1 = 1$.

In light of the complexity of the model for values of β_1 that are not in the neighborhood of one and for cases in which there are more than two blocs, simulation analysis was used to obtain insights about expansion of bloc 1 for $\beta_1 \in (1/B,1)$. Simulations involved substitution of calculated values of the equilibrium values of the optimal tariffs, $(\tau^1(\beta_1),\tau_1^2(\beta_1),\tau_3^2(\beta_1))$, and relative price of ROW goods, $q(\beta_1)$ into the utility function to obtain values for $U^1(\beta_1)$ and $U^2(\beta_1)$. World welfare was calculated as the weighted average of bloc 1 and ROW country welfare, $U^w = \beta_1 U^1 + (1-\beta_1)U^2$.

Fig. 4(a) illustrates the effect of bloc expansion on welfare when there are a

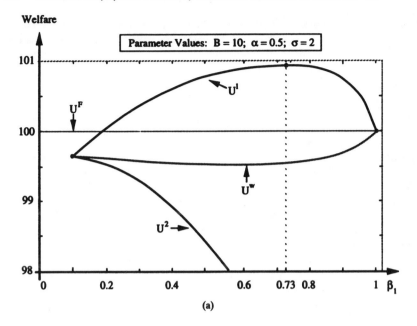

(a)

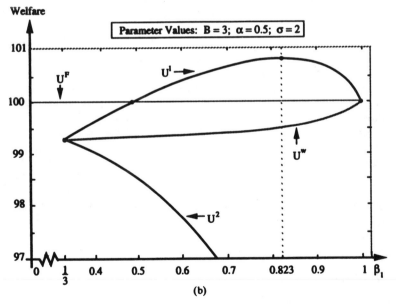

(b)

Fig. 4. Effects of relative bloc size on welfare.

large number of blocs ($B = 10$), with $\alpha = 0.5$ and $\sigma = 2$. The values of N and x (which represent scale parameters in the model and have no effect on any relative prices) were chosen so that the free trade utility level of a representative country, $U^F = N^{(\sigma/(\sigma-1))}(1 + \alpha)x$, was 100. Welfare in the symmetric Nash equilibrium in this case involves a loss of approximately 0.5% from the free trade equilibrium, with tariffs of 0.198. The results indicate that the welfare of a representative bloc 1 country increases as bloc 1 expands, reaching a maximum at $\beta_1 \approx 0.73$. The optimal bloc size involves a welfare gain of approximately 1% above the free trade level for the member countries. Welfare of non-member countries decreases monotonically as bloc 1 expands, and approaches the autarky utility level of 66.67 as $\beta_1 \to 1$. World welfare declines initially and then increases to the free trade level.

Fig. 4(b) illustrates a similar analysis for the case in which there are a smaller number of trading blocs ($B = 3$), but the same values of α and σ. The Nash equilibrium in this case involves lower symmetric Nash equilibrium welfare level and higher Nash equilibrium tariffs. Welfare of the expanding bloc is maximized at $\beta_1 = 0.823$. The primary difference between this case and the previous one is that world welfare increases monotonically from the symmetric Nash equilibrium to the free trade level. This appears to be due to the fact that the symmetric equilibrium with $B = 3$ involves a larger loss in world welfare than does the symmetric equilibrium with $B = 10$.

The results in Fig. 4 are representative of the pattern achieved in simulations over a range of values of α and σ. These simulations indicate that the welfare of bloc 1 in the optimally sized trading bloc increases as α increases, which suggests that a greater degree of comparative advantage allows the large bloc to extract more surplus from the smaller blocs. The value of β_1 at which bloc 1 welfare is maximized was decreasing in α and increasing in σ.

In summary, an increase in relative size is a means for a bloc to achieve a welfare level that is above that of the free trade equilibrium. This result suggests that it is an increase in relative size which increases a bloc's market power. Does this mean that the expansion of a bloc to a relatively large share of the world's countries should be discouraged? The simulations suggest that if the criterion for evaluating bloc expansion is world welfare, the answer depends on the number of trading blocs. Expansion of one bloc is desirable in situations where the symmetric Nash equilibrium results in a large welfare loss relative to the free trade equilibrium. However, it should also be noted that the fact that the large bloc has a welfare level above the free trade level might make it more difficult to negotiate a global free trade agreement.

4. Conclusions

This paper has explored the relationship between the size of trading blocs, the market power of trading blocs (as captured by the level of their optimal tariffs) and world welfare. We have shown that the relationship between absolute bloc size (holding relative size constant) and market power depends on assumptions regarding endowments and preferences. Since increasing market power is associated with lower world welfare in the resulting Nash equilibrium, our conclusions are less pessimistic about the effect of increases in absolute bloc size on world welfare than are those of Krugman (1991). We have shown analytically that there is an incentive for blocs to add members (and for countries to want to enter large blocs) in the sense that there is always a bloc size at which the expanding bloc can increase its welfare above the free trade level. We have used simulations to illustrate how optimal bloc size is affected by the parameters of the model. Interestingly, these expansions may either increase or decrease world welfare, depending on the level of tariffs in the initial (symmetric bloc) Nash equilibrium.

Our analysis has analyzed the market power of trading blocs assuming that countries use national welfare as their objective in setting tariff rates. However, we anticipate that these market power effects would carry over to political economy models in which policies are chosen to maximize a weighted national income. For example, Grossman and Helpman (1993) present a political economy model in which policy is chosen as if policymakers were maximizing weighted national income with the greater weight assigned to some groups, reflecting the ability of these groups to organize and influence policy through campaign contributions to politicians. They show that the optimal tariffs in the large country case will depend on the elasticity of the foreign offer curve and the weights placed on the various interest groups. Thus, the market power effects considered here, which are reflected in the elasticity of the offer curve of ROW blocs, will continue to play a role in political economy models of protection where terms of trade effects matter.

Acknowledgments

We thank Jim Anderson, Shannon Mitchell, Avinash Dixit, anonymous referees, and participants at seminars at Columbia, Florida, Iowa State, UC at Irvine, Michigan, Penn State, AEA meetings, CEA meetings, Summer Meetings of the Econometric Society and the Midwest International Trade meetings for helpful comments and suggestions. A previous version of this paper circulated under the title 'Optimality and stability of regional trading blocs'.

Appendix A

Proof of optimality of a uniform tariff in Lemma 1.

In the derivation of (3) in the text, it was assumed that bloc 1 imposes a uniform tariff. We now justify this assumption by showing that at the optimal uniform tariff, there are no welfare gains available by altering tariffs on imports from any

E.W. Bond, C. Syropoulos / Journal of International Economics 40 (1996) 411–437   435

subset of the ROW blocs. Let $dy^1 = dU^1/(\partial U^1/\partial c_1^1)$ be the change in national welfare measured in units of good 1. Following Bond (1990), this can be expressed as

$$dy^1 = -\sum_{i=2}^{B} n[(c_i^1 - x)dq_i - \tau_i^1 q_i dc_i^1]$$

$$= n\sum_{i=2}^{B}\left[-z + \left(\sum_{k=2}^{B}(c_i^k - x)\right) - \left(\sum_{k=2j=2}^{B}\sum_{j=2}^{B}\tau_j^1 q_j \frac{\partial c_j^k}{\partial q_i}\right)\right]dq_i.$$

(A.1)

The first equality follows from totally differentiating the bloc 1 budget constraint at world prices, and is the standard welfare decomposition of terms of trade effects and trade volume effects. The second equality follows from substitution for c_i^1 and dc_i^1 using the market-clearing condition for good i. (A.1) yields $(N-1)$ equations to be solved for the optimal tariffs τ_j^1. It is readily verified using (1) that with $\tau^1 = \tau_2^1 = \ldots = \tau_B^1$ and $q_2 = \ldots = q_B = q$, $\partial y^1/\partial q_i = \partial y^1/\partial q_j$ for $i,j = 2, \ldots, B$. Therefore, the optimal uniform tariff must satisfy $\partial y^1/\partial q_i = 0$ for all i. $\square$

Proof of Proposition 4.

In order to complete the proof of Proposition 4 in the text, it is necessary to show that

$$\left(\frac{\partial U^1}{\partial q}\frac{q}{U^1}\right)\left(\frac{\partial q}{\partial \beta_1}\frac{1}{q}\right) \to 0 \text{ as } \beta_1 \to 1.$$

(A.2)

It was shown in the text that the first term in parentheses approaches zero, so it remains to evaluate the second term in parentheses using the market equilibrium condition. Defining $m_i^k = (c_i^k/x) - 1$, the market clearing condition (3) can be written as $qm_2^1 = m_1^2$. From (11) and (13), we have

$$m_1^2 = \frac{q(1 - \beta_1 + \alpha) - (1 - \beta_1)q^{1-\sigma}\Delta}{\beta_1 + (1 - \beta_1)q^{1-\sigma}\Delta} \cdot m_2^1$$

$$= \frac{\alpha + \beta_1(1 - [q(1 + \tau^1)]^\sigma)}{\beta_1[q(1 + \tau^1)]^\sigma + (1 - \beta_1)q}.$$

(A.3)

Totally differentiating (A.3) the market-clearing condition yields

$$\left(\frac{\partial q}{\partial \beta_1}\frac{1}{q_1}\right) = \frac{\left[\left(\frac{\partial m_1^2}{\partial \beta_1}\right)\frac{1}{m_1^2} - \left(\frac{\partial m_2^1}{\partial \beta_1}\right)\frac{1}{m_2^1}\right]}{(1 - \epsilon_1 - \epsilon_2)},$$

(A.4)

where $\epsilon_1 \equiv -(\partial m_2^1/\partial q)(q/m_2^1)$ and $\epsilon_2 \equiv (\partial m_1^2/\partial q)(q/m_1^2)$ are the elasticities of the respective offer curves.

436   E.W. Bond, C. Syropoulos / Journal of International Economics 40 (1996) 411–437

To establish (A.2), we must evaluate $(\partial q/\partial\beta_1)(1/q)$ as $\beta_1 \to 1$. First, we note that ϵ_2 converges to one (from the result that $\tau^1 \to \infty$ in Proposition 2) and ϵ_1 converges to $\sigma(1+\alpha)/\alpha$ (from the argument following Eq. (16)) as $\beta_1 \to 1$. Therefore, the denominator of (A.4) must be finite. To evaluate the numerator, we differentiate (A.3):

$$\left(\frac{\partial m_1^2}{\partial\beta_1}\right)\left(\frac{1}{m_1^2}\right) = \left(\frac{1 - [q(1+\tau^1)]^\sigma}{\alpha + \beta_1(1 - [q(1+\tau^1)]^\sigma)}\right.$$
$$\left. - \frac{[q(1+\tau^1)]^\sigma - q}{\beta_1[q(1+\tau^1)]^\sigma + (1-\beta_1)q}\right), \tag{A.5a}$$

$$\left(\frac{\partial m_1^2}{\partial\beta_1}\right)\left(\frac{1}{m_1^2}\right) = \left(\frac{q^{-\sigma}\Delta - 1}{(\alpha + 1 - \beta_1) - (1-\beta_1)q^{-\sigma}\Delta} + \frac{q^{1-\sigma}\Delta - 1}{\beta_1 + (1-\beta_1)q^{1-\sigma}\Delta}\right). \tag{A.5b}$$

The following facts were established in the proof of Proposition 2: (i) $(1 - \beta_1)q^{-\sigma}\Delta \to 0$; (ii) $q(1+\tau^1)^\sigma \to 1$; (iii) $q \to 0$. (ii) and (iii) guarantee that (A.5a) converges to zero. The denominator of each of the terms in (A.5b) is finite from (i). The numerators will not have a finite limit, as a result of (iii). However, $(1-\beta_1)(\partial m_1^2/\partial q)(q/m_1^2)$ will converge to zero by (i), which, when combined with the fact that $(\epsilon_1 + \epsilon_2 - 1) > 0$, means that $(1-\beta_1)(\partial q/\partial\beta_1)q^{-1}$ will converge to zero. Therefore, the product $(\partial U^1/\partial q)(\partial q/\partial\beta_1)$ will converge to zero if $(\partial U^1/\partial q)(1-\beta_1)^{-1}$ has a finite limit as $\beta_1 \to 1$. Eq. (20) in the text can be rewritten as

$$\left(\frac{\partial U^1}{\partial q}\frac{q}{U^1}\right)\frac{1}{(1-\beta_1)} = \frac{\alpha + \beta_1(1 - [q(1+\tau_1)]^\sigma)}{(\beta_1 + \alpha + (1-\beta_1)q)(\beta_1[q(1+\tau^1)]^\sigma + (1-\beta_1)q)}$$
$$+ \frac{\sigma\beta_1[q(1+\tau^1)]^{\sigma-1}q - [q(1+\tau^1)]^\sigma}{(\beta_1[q(1+\tau^1)]^{\sigma-1} + (1-\beta_1)(\beta_1[q(1+\tau^1)]^\sigma + (1-\beta_1)q)}.$$

Using (ii) and (iii), it can be seen that the first term in brackets will have a limit of α and the second term will have a limit of zero. Therefore, $(\partial U^1/\partial q)(1-\beta_1)^{-1}$ has a finite limit, which establishes that (A.2) holds. □

References

Bagwell, K. and R. Staiger, 1993a, Multilateral tariff cooperation during the formation of regional free trade areas, Working Paper 4364 (NBER).

Bagwell, K. and R. Staiger, 1993b, Multilateral tariff cooperation during the formation of customs unions, Working Paper.

Bond, E.W., 1990, The optimal tariff structure in higher dimensions, International Economic Review 31, 103-116.

Bond, E.W. and C. Syropoulos, 1995, Trading blocs and the sustainability of inter-regional cooperation, in: M. Canzoneri, W. Ethier, and V. Grilli, eds., The new transatlantic economy (Cambridge University Press, Cambridge).

Corden, W.M., 1984, The normative theory of international trade, in: R.W. Jones and P.B. Kenen eds., Handbook of international economics (North-Holland, Amsterdam).

Deardorff, A. and R. Stern, 1994, Multilateral trade negotiations and preferential trading arrangements, in: A. Deardorff and R. Stern, eds., Analytical and negotiating issues in the global trading system (University of Michigan Press, Ann Arbor).

Dixit, A., 1987, Strategic aspects of trade policy, in: T. Bewley, ed., Advances in economic theory (Cambridge University Press, Cambridge).

Grossman, G. and E. Helpman, 1993, Trade wars and trade talks, Working Paper 4352 (NBER).

Haveman, J., 1992, On the consequences of recent changes in the global trading environment, Unpublished doctoral dissertation (University of Michigan).

Kennan, J. and R. Riezman, 1990, Optimal tariff equilibria with customs unions, Canadian Journal of Economics 23, 70-83.

Kowalczyk, C. and T. Sjostrom, 1994, Bringing GATT into the core, Economica 61, 301-318.

Kowalczyk, C. and R.J. Wonnacott, 1992, Hubs and spokes, and free trade in the Americas, Working Paper 4198 (NBER).

Krugman, P., 1991, Is bilateralism bad?, in: E. Helpman and A. Razin, eds., International trade and trade policy (MIT Press, Cambridge).

Riezman, R., 1985, Customs unions and the core, Journal of International Economics 19, 355-365.

Viner, J., 1950, The customs union issue (Carnegie Endowment for International Peace, New York).

Yi, S.S., 1993, Endogenous formation of trading blocs, Mimeo (Dartmouth College).

Part IV
Other Results

A
Customs Unions versus Free Trade Areas

[23]

Optimal tariff equilibria with customs unions

JOHN KENNAN and RAYMOND RIEZMAN
University of Iowa

Abstract. We construct a model of customs unions in which countries charge optimal tariffs. Customs unions internalize the externality that exists whenever two countries import the same good. Also, customs unions make several countries into one large unit with more market power. Big customs unions can improve their members' welfare relative to the free trade. Our model of customs unions separates the effects of tariff reduction from the effects of policy co-ordination. The movement from Nash equilibrium to a Free Trade Association improves global resource allocation. Moving from a Free Trade Association to a full customs union has ambiguous resource allocation effects.

Equilibres avec droits de douane optimaux quand il y a union douanière. Les auteurs construisent un modèle d'union douanière dans lequel les pays imposent des droits de douane optimaux. Les unions douanières internalisent l'externalité qui existe quand deux pays importent le même bien. De plus, les unions douanières créent une unité plus grande qui a un pouvoir de marché agrandi en agrégeant plusieurs pays. Les grandes unions douanières peuvent améliorer le bien-être de leurs membres par rapport à ce que procurerait le libre échange. Le modèle d'union douanière proposé sépare l'effet des réductions de droits de douane de l'effet de la coordination de politiques. Le déplacement d'un équilibre à la Nash vers une association de libre-échange améliore l'allocation globale des ressources. Un déplacement d'une association de libre-échange vers une union douanière complète a des effets ambigus sur l'allocation de ressources.

I. INTRODUCTION

Since Jacob Viner's pioneering work (1950), customs union research has focused on isolating characteristics of customs unions that affect worldwide economic efficiency. Customs unions are usually analysed by comparing a particular customs

We thank Forrest Nelson for valuable comments on earlier drafts. The final version of the paper was completed while Kennan was a visiting scholar at the Hoover Institution. Kennan acknowledges funding from the National Science Foundation, under grant SES-8607771.

Canadian Journal of Economics Revue canadienne d'Economique, XXIII, No. 1
February février 1990. Printed in Canada Imprimé au Canada

union equilibrium with some arbitrarily given tariff equilibrium (e.g., see Lloyd 1982). The choice of the customs union's common external tariff has been extensively discussed using what Corden (1984) calls the 'non-optimality assumption,' which allows customs unions (and also non-member countries) to set non-optimal tariffs. (See, e.g., Vanek 1965, Takayama 1972, Kemp and Wan 1976, and Grinols 1986.)

While this line of research has been useful, it ignores some interesting questions, such as: (1) What are the nationalistic motivations for customs union membership? (2) Will the process of customs union formation lead toward free trade? (3) What determines which countries choose to form a customs union? (4) How does a custom union choose the common external tariff?

In seeking to answer questions of this sort, the natural assumption is that self-interest dictates what tariffs countries choose and which customs unions they join. We view the process as a two-stage game. In the second stage, tariffs are chosen for a given coalition structure.[1] In the first stage, countries chose coalition partners. In this paper we analyse the second stage of this game, since it is logically prior to the first: to understand how coalitions form one must first understand the equilibrium that would result from any given coalition structure.[2]

We construct a model in which all countries charge optimal tariffs, given the coalition structure and the tariffs charged by other countries.[3] Members of a customs union have internal free trade and jointly set a common optimal external tariff. Customs union equilibria are compared with a Nash equilibrium in tariffs, and with free trade. This makes the non-member country's reaction to the customs union's tariff policy explicit.

An inevitable difficulty is that the analysis of optimal tariffs is very complicated, even when customs unions are not considered (see, e.g., Otani 1980). We simplify the problem by considering a pure exchange economy in which commodity demands in each country are generated by a linear expenditure system. This model delivers explicit formulae for the effects of alternative tariff patterns on world prices, trade volumes, and consumption levels, and optimal tariffs can then be calculated by numerical methods for any given specification of preferences and endowments. We use this framework to generate examples with three countries and three goods which illuminate some important strategic issues in customs union theory.

The first issue concerns the circumstances in which a customs union can improve the welfare of its members compared with free trade, even when the non-member country retaliates with its own optimal tariffs. To .investigate this we develop an

---

1 See Riezman (1985) for further discussion of the coalition formation game.
2 See Hamilton and Whalley (1983) and Markusen and Wigle (1987) for empirical studies of whether actual tariff rates are at the levels that optimal tariff theory would suggest.
3 Arndt (1968, 1969) presented a general discussion of customs union tariff policy, assuming that pre-union tariffs were optimal, but without solving explicitly for optimal post-union tariffs. Takayama (1972) obtained some results on optimal customs union tariffs: a zero tariff between members is optimal, and the standard optimal tariff formula applies to the union's tariff to the third country. This latter result depends crucially on his assumption that there are only two goods: in our 3×3 model, for example, if customs union members have asymmetric endowments, they will have different optimal external tariffs.

72   John Kennan and Raymond Riezman

example in which endowments are symmetric and all countries have the same preferences. We find that whenever each country's endowment of its export good is not too large, relative to the total world endowment, any pair of countries can benefit (compared with free trade) by forming a customs union. This stands in sharp contrast to the more familiar results for a symmetric two-country model, where both countries lose a tariff war (see Johnson 1958 and Kennan and Riezman 1988). In the three-country case this is still true, but only if countries cannot form customs unions.

This example has some interesting implications. In a symmetric world where any pair of countries can benefit from a customs union it is difficult to see how free trade could be an equilibrium, since each pair of countries has an incentive to defect. Thus the possibility of customs unions may be an additional barrier to free trade rather than a 'stepping stone' toward free trade.

In the symmetric example we can compute the set of endowments for which customs unions are beneficial, albeit for a special case. In this context we show that the size of a customs union relative to the excluded country is important in determining whether the customs union can improve its members' welfare. Thus, one motivation for customs union formation is to make the member countries into one larger country for the purposes of trade policy, so that they can compete more effectively with larger countries and with other customs unions.

Our examples also illustrate a pervasive externality associated with tariffs. When one country imposes tariffs on the goods it imports, the world prices of these goods fall, conferring an uncompensated benefit on all other countries that import the same goods. Customs unions internalize this externality by setting tariffs jointly: this provides another motivation for the formation of customs unions.

Finally, our examples illustrate the effects of customs union formation on prices, tariffs, and the volume of trade. Using these results we discuss the effect of trade agreements on global efficiency and the argument that customs unions are a 'stepping stone' to free trade.

II. A LINEAR EXPENDITURE SYSTEM WITH TARIFFS

We use a model in which n countries, indexed by the superscript i, trade m goods, indexed by the subscript j. Each country contains many consumers with identical utility function:

$$U^i = \sum_{j=1}^{m} \beta_j^i \log X_j^i, \quad \sum_{j=1}^{m} \beta_j^i = 1; \quad i = 1, 2 \ldots n. \tag{1}$$

where U^i is the utility of country i, with taste parameters β_j^i, and X_j^i is the aggregate consumption of good j in country i, which is divided equally over individuals within the country.

Define the total world endowment of each commodity as one unit. Country i's endowment of good j is ω_j^i, so that $\sum_i \omega_j^i = 1$, for each good j. The endowments are divided equally between consumers within countries. The volume of trade in each good is $Z_j^i \equiv X_j^i - \omega_j^i$, where a negative value of Z_j^i means that country i exports good j, and a positive value denotes an import. Country i charges a tariff at the rate t_j^i on imports of good j.[4] The world price of good j is denoted by P_j, so the domestic price in i is $(1 + t_j^i)P_j$.

Consumers in i maximize U^i subject to the budget constraint

$$\sum_{j=1}^{m} P_j(1 + t_j^i)X_j^i = I^i = \sum_{j=1}^{m} P_j(1 + t_j^i)\omega_j^i + P_j t_j^i Z_j^i, \qquad i = 1, 2 \ldots n. \tag{2}$$

Income I^i includes the value of endowments at domestic prices, plus the net revenue from tariffs,[5] which is divided equally over individuals.[6] We assume that individual consumers ignore the (small) effect of changes in Z_j^i on their share of tariff revenue. The logarithmic form of U^i leads to a linear expenditure system, in which consumers spend a fixed proportion of their income on each commodity. The demand functions are

$$(1 + t_j^i)P_j X_j^i = \beta_j^i I^i, \qquad i = 1, 2 \ldots n, j = 1, 2 \ldots m. \tag{3}$$

Expenditure $E_j^i = P_j X_j^i$ on good j, valued at world prices P_j, and aggregate expenditure E^i, can then be written as $E_j^i = \theta_j^i I^i$ and $E^i = \theta^i I^i$, where

$$\theta_j^i = \frac{\beta_j^i}{1 + t_j^i} \text{ and } \theta^i = \sum_{j=1}^{m} \theta_j^i. \tag{4}$$

Thus expenditure is allocated across goods in the proportions $E_j^i = b_j^i E^i$, where $b_j^i = \theta_j^i/\theta^i$. This has the interpretation that the tariffs charged by country i cause the consumers in i to act as if their loglinear utility function had weights b_j^i instead of β_j^i.

The budget constraint (2) implies that, regardless of tariffs, the aggregate expenditure in each country must equal the value of the endowment vector, at world prices:

$$E^i = \sum_{j=1}^{m} P_j X_j^i = \sum_{j=1}^{m} P_j \omega_j^i \tag{5}$$

The world supply of each good is one unit, so the world price of each good is equal to aggregate world expenditure on that good:

$$\sum_{i=1}^{n} E_j^i = P_j \sum_{i=1}^{n} X_j^i = P_j \sum_{i=1}^{n} \omega_j^i = P_j, \qquad j = 1, 2 \ldots. \tag{6}$$

4 We allow export subsidies (i.e., negative tariffs on exports).
5 In the case of a customs union, we assume that each member country retains the tariff revenue from its own external trade (i.e., the customs union does not pool tariff revenues).
6 It is possible that the tariff system yields negative revenue, in which case the deficit is covered by lump-sum taxation.

74   John Kennan and Raymond Riezman

Thus prices can be written in terms of the expenditure variables E^i_j, and these are proportional to the aggregate expenditures E^i. Then, from equation (5),

$$E^i = \sum_{j=1}^{m} \sum_{s=1}^{n} b^s_j E^s \omega^i_j. \tag{7}$$

Define

$$\alpha^i_s \equiv \sum_{j=1}^{m} b^s_j \omega^i_j \tag{8}$$

Then equation (7) can be rewritten as

$$E^i = \sum_{s=1}^{n} \alpha^i_s E^s, \qquad i = 1, 2 \ldots n. \tag{9}$$

This is a system of n equations in the n variables E^i, but these equations are linearly dependent, since the units of expenditure are arbitrary. We normalize by setting aggregate world expenditure to 1, so that equation (9) can be replaced by the matrix equation

$$
\begin{bmatrix}
\alpha^1_1 - 1 & \alpha^1_2 & \cdots & \alpha^1_{n-1} & \alpha^1_n \\
\alpha^2_1 & \alpha^2_2 - 1 & \cdots & \alpha^2_{n-1} & \alpha^2_n \\
\cdots & \cdots & \cdots & \cdots & \cdots \\
\cdots & \cdots & \cdots & \cdots & \cdots \\
\cdots & \cdots & \cdots & \cdots & \cdots \\
\alpha^{n-1}_1 & & \cdots & \alpha^{n-1}_{n-1} - 1 & \alpha^{n-1}_n \\
1 & 1 & \cdots & 1 & 1
\end{bmatrix}
\begin{bmatrix}
E^1 \\
E^2 \\
\cdots \\
\cdots \\
\cdots \\
E^{n-1} \\
E^n
\end{bmatrix}
=
\begin{bmatrix}
0 \\
0 \\
\cdots \\
\cdots \\
\cdots \\
0 \\
1
\end{bmatrix}
\tag{10}
$$

The equilibrium expenditure levels are determined by this equation, since the coefficient matrix depends only on preferences, endowments, and tariffs. The equilibrium price vector can then be found from (6), and substitution of the demand functions (3) in the utility function (1) gives the utility levels resulting from any tariff pattern.

Equation (10) illustrates the complications involved in optimal tariff calculations. We did not consider production, and we assumed a nice functional form for preferences, but the effect of tariff variations on equilibrium consumption and utility levels is still far from transparent. Optimal tariffs cannot be determined analytically, except in very special cases (as illustrated in Kennan and Riezman 1988). Equations (10), (6), (3), and (1) do, however, provide an analytical expression for utility as a function of tariffs, for any given preference and endowment pattern, so that optimal tariffs can be determined numerically.

III. SOME ILLUSTRATIVE EXAMPLES

We develop four examples using the model described above, with three countries and three goods. These examples were chosen to highlight the effect of variations in two features of the world economy: the degree of symmetry across countries, and the size of each country in its export market. In the symmetric examples (A and B) the three countries are identical up to a relabelling of the goods. In this set-up we can consider how a customs union can arise for purely strategic reasons, rather than as a response to special features of the economy. In example A each country dominates its export market (in the sense that it has more than half of the world endowment) whereas exporters are not dominant in example B (each has half of the world endowment). The asymmetric examples were chosen to compare a small customs union (example C) with a large one (example D). The endowments in all four examples are such that each country exports one good and imports the other two in all of the equilibria we consider.[7]

In each example the countries' preferences are assumed to be symmetric over goods, in the sense that $\beta_j^i = 1/3$ for all i and j. In examples A and B the endowment matrix $\Omega = (\omega_j^i)$ is also symmetric. In examples C and D the endowment matrix is symmetric with respect to countries 2 and 3 only, with 1 being dominant in example C, and 2 and 3 dominant in example D. For each example we compute utility, optimal tariffs, prices, and consumption at four alternative equilibria: free trade (FT), Nash equilibrium (NE), free trade association (FTA), and customs union (CU). Free trade means that the tariff matrix $T = (t_j^i)$ is zero. Nash equilibrium means that no country could gain by changing its tariffs, given the tariffs charged by the other countries. This equilibrium is characterized by a system of six equations in the six off-diagonal elements of T, which we solved by a cobweb algorithm. The first country uses the procedure outlined in section II to find its optimal tariffs, given the tariffs set by 2 and 3. Then the second country chooses t_1^2 and t_3^2, given the other elements of T, and so on, until T repeats itself, indicating that no country desires to make further tariff adjustments.

An FTA is an agreement between two countries to eliminate tariffs on their two export goods, without restricting the tariffs charged on the third good. Here, the equilibrium tariff matrix is computed as in NE, except that tariffs within the FTA are set to zero. For example, to compute an FTA between countries 2 and 3 we fix t_3^2 and t_2^3 at zero and proceed as in the NE case.

In a customs union there is internal free trade (as in the FTA), and in addition the members jointly set a common tariff on the third good. This poses two new problems. First, a tariff externality exists. Second, members of a customs union will not necessarily agree on what the external tariff should be.

The tariff externality arises whenever two large countries import the same good, because a tariff imposed by one country lowers the price paid by both. A CU differs from an FTA in that this externality is internalized by having the members set the

---

7 This is one of two possible symmetric trade patterns, the other being where each country exports two goods and imports the other one.

76   John Kennan and Raymond Riezman

external tariff jointly. Although this generally involves a conflict of interest between the member countries we avoid this conflict by considering only symmetric cases, so that members of a customs union always agree on what the external tariff should be.[8]

To compute the tariff equilibrium when countries 2 and 3 form a customs union, for example, we fix t_3^2 and t_2^3 at zero. Then we compute tariffs as in NE except that countries 2 and 3 jointly choose both t_1^2 and t_1^3, with the constraint that these must be equal.

For each example, table 1 lists the endowment matrix assumed, and the equilibrium values of utility, tariffs, world prices, and consumption. When a customs union or free trade association exists, the member countries are 2 and 3, and 1 is the non-member. The utility function used is

$$U = 200 + 100 \sum_{j=1}^{3} 1/3 \log X_j^i.$$

IV.   THE TARIFF EXTERNALITY

Member countries derive two distinct benefits from a customs union. In this section we discuss examples which illustrate the first of these, which comes from internalizing the tariff externality. In section VI we consider the benefit that comes from being part of a larger trading unit.

The only difference between the FTA and CU equilibria is that CU is computed by letting country 2 choose tariffs for both CU members. In example A, the effect of this is to increase the CU tariff from 42 per cent to 156 per cent. Country 1 responds by lowering its tariff to 134 per cent from 167 per cent. The increased CU tariff and lower non-member tariff are entirely attributable to internalizing the tariff externality. The other examples give similar results.

In all four examples the move from FTA to CU improves the terms of trade for CU members at the non-member's expense. Intra-customs union trade increases and trade between the customs union and the rest of the world decreases. Internalizing the tariff externality results in higher member country welfare and lower non-member welfare.

In examples A and C co-ordination of tariff policy fails to provide enough benefits for CU members to do better than they would at free trade. The co-ordination effect is large enough in examples B and D so that CU is better than FT for the member countries. These examples highlight the policy co-ordination role of customs unions. Next, we consider the effects customs unions have on efficiency.

V.   RESOURCE ALLOCATION EFFECTS

Do customs unions improve the allocation of resources, relative to a Nash equilibrium in tariffs? This is a second-best problem with no general answer. A common

---

8 The appendix contains an example with asymmetric endowments, where the CU members disagree on the optimal external tariff.

TABLE 1

Examples

Example A: Symmetric, big exporters

			Endowments	1	2	3			

$$\Omega = \begin{bmatrix} 0.8 & 0.1 & 0.1 \\ 0.1 & 0.8 & 0.1 \\ 0.1 & 0.1 & 0.8 \end{bmatrix}$$

Eq^m	Country	Utility	Tariffs			Prices	Consumption		
	1:	90.14	0	0	0	0.3333	0.3333	0.3333	0.3333
FT	2:	90.14	0	0	0	0.3333	0.3333	0.3333	0.3333
	3:	90.14	0	0	0	0.3333	0.3333	0.3333	0.3333
	1:	79.77	0	1.5414	1.5414	0.3333	0.5596	0.2202	0.2202
NE	2:	79.77	1.5414	0	1.5414	0.3333	0.2202	0.5596	0.2202
	3:	79.77	1.5414	1.5414	0	0.3333	0.2202	0.2202	0.5596
	1:	86.91	0	1.6672	1.6672	0.3726	0.5534	0.2465	0.2465
FTA	2:	84.95	0.4202	0	0	0.3137	0.2233	0.3767	0.3767
	3:	84.95	0.4202	0	0	0.3137	0.2233	0.3767	0.3767
	1:	68.80	0	1.3423	1.3423	0.2727	0.5754	0.1842	0.1842
CU	2:	88.56	1.5616	0	0	0.3636	0.2123	0.4079	0.4079
	3:	88.56	1.5616	0	0	0.3636	0.2123	0.4079	0.4079

Example B: Symmetric, small exporters

			Endowments	1	2	3			

$$\Omega = \begin{bmatrix} 0.5 & 0.25 & 0.25 \\ 0.25 & 0.5 & 0.25 \\ 0.25 & 0.25 & 0.5 \end{bmatrix}$$

Eq^m	Country	Utility	Tariffs			Prices	Consumption		
	1:	90.14	0	0	0	0.3333	0.3333	0.3333	0.3333
FT	2:	90.14	0	0	0	0.3333	0.3333	0.3333	0.3333
	3:	90.14	0	0	0	0.3333	0.3333	0.3333	0.3333
	1:	89.34	0	0.3028	0.3028	0.3333	0.3944	0.3028	0.3028
NE	2:	89.34	0.3028	0	0.3028	0.3333	0.3028	0.3944	0.3028
	3:	89.34	0.3028	0.3028	0	0.3333	0.3028	0.3028	0.3944
	1:	89.57	0	0.3099	0.3099	0.3368	0.3927	0.3045	0.3045
FTA	2:	89.85	0.1273	0	0	0.3316	0.3037	0.3477	0.3477
	3:	89.85	0.1273	0	0	0.3316	0.3037	0.3477	0.3477
	1:	87.48	0	0.2388	0.2388	0.3022	0.4121	0.2881	0.2881
CU	2:	90.33	0.3982	0	0	0.3489	0.2940	0.3560	0.3560
	3:	90.33	0.3982	0	0	0.3489	0.2940	0.3560	0.3560

78   John Kennan and Raymond Riezman

TABLE 1 (*concluded*)

Examples

Example C: Asymmetric, small customs union

$$\Omega = \begin{bmatrix} 0.8 & 0.25 & 0.25 \\ 0.1 & 0.5 & 0.25 \\ 0.1 & 0.25 & 0.5 \end{bmatrix}$$

Endowments: 1, 2, 3

Eq^m	Country	Utility	Tariffs			Prices	Consumption		
FT	1:	116.38	0	0	0	0.3333	0.4333	0.4333	0.4333
	2:	73.89	0	0	0	0.3333	0.2833	0.2833	0.2833
	3:	73.89	0	0	0	0.3333	0.2833	0.2833	0.2833
NE	1:	117.36	0	1.2358	1.2358	0.3971	0.6226	0.3669	0.3669
	2:	67.11	0.4453	0	0.3133	0.3014	0.1887	0.3594	0.2737
	3:	67.11	0.4453	0.3133	0	0.3014	0.1887	0.2737	0.3594
FTA	1:	117.71	0	1.2490	1.2490	0.4003	0.6216	0.3691	0.3691
	[2:	67.58	0.2486	0	0	0.2998	0.1892	0.3154	0.3154
	[3:	67.58	0.2486	0	0	0.2998	0.1892	0.3154	0.3154
CU	1:	112.63	0	1.0473	1.0473	0.3511	0.6383	0.3375	0.3375
	[2:	69.34	0.6920	0	0	0.3244	0.1808	0.3312	0.3312
	[3:	69.34	0.6920	0	0	0.3244	0.1808	0.3312	0.3312

Example D: Asymmetric, big customs union

$$\Omega = \begin{bmatrix} 0.5 & 0.1 & 0.1 \\ 0.25 & 0.8 & 0.1 \\ 0.25 & 0.1 & 0.8 \end{bmatrix}$$

Endowments: 1, 2, 3

Eq^m	Country	Utility	Tariffs			Prices	Consumption		
FT	1:	54.47	0	0	0	0.3333	0.2333	0.2333	0.2333
	2:	104.11	0	0	0	0.3333	0.3833	0.3833	0.3833
	3:	104.11	0	0	0	0.3333	0.3833	0.3833	0.3833
NE	1:	43.33	0	0.4665	0.4665	0.2766	0.3222	0.1680	0.1680
	2:	98.85	1.2857	0	1.4740	0.3616	0.3389	0.5925	0.2395
	3:	98.85	1.2857	1 4740	0	0.3616	0.3389	0.2395	0.5925
FTA	1:	49.79	0	0.5315	0.5315	0.3181	0.3098	0.1888	0.1888
	[2:	104.38	0.2592	0	0	0.3409	0.3451	0.4056	0.4056
	[3:	104.38	0.2592	0	0	0.3409	0.3451	0.4056	0.4056
CU	1:	36.61	0	0.3900	0.3900	0.2307	0.3417	0.1475	0.1475
	[2:	106.11	1.1583	0	0	0.3846	0.3291	0.4262	0.4262
	[3:	106.11	1.1583	0	0	0.3846	0.3291	0.4262	0.4262

procedure in analysing customs unions (see Lloyd 1982) is to compare some arbitrary initial tariff equilibrium with a customs union, assuming that the non-member is passive and that the formation of the customs union does not affect the tariffs that members charge to non-members. This procedure is natural in models that do not specify how the tariffs were set in the first place, or how a customs union chooses its tariffs. These decisions are the focus of our model, which requires that pre- and post-union tariffs are optimal given the other tariffs. This implies a comparison between Nash equilibrium and customs union equilibrium.

The comparison between Nash and customs union equilibria can usefully be made in two steps: eliminating tariffs on the two goods that the member countries export (NE to FTA), and co-ordinating the tariffs charged by the CU members on the non-member country's good (FTA to CU). In all four examples moving from NE to FTA decreases the tariffs charged by the FTA members, and increases the non-member's tariffs. The terms of trade shift in favour of the non-member, but everyone is better off at FTA than at NE and both inter- and intra-FTA trade increase. In example A the non-member country actually benefits more from the move to FTA from NE than the members; in example B the members benefit more.[9]

We next consider the second step in the CU process: moving from an FTA to CU. In all the examples this leads to an increase in the tariffs charged by the customs union members and a decrease in the non-member's tariffs. The terms of trade shift in favour of the customs union, and there is more intra-CU trade and less trade between the CU member countries and the non-member country. The members' utility rises, while the non-member's utility falls.[10] Thus, the resource allocation effect of the move from FTA to CU is ambiguous.

The two steps have opposing effects on tariffs and on the terms of trade. The net effect on tariffs is ambiguous, but the terms of trade always move in favour of the customs union. Overall, the customs union increases the welfare of its members, while the non-member gains in the first step (NE to FTA) and loses in the second (FTA to CU). In our examples, the non-member's gains in the first step are outweighed by its losses in the second, so that the customs union benefits its members (relative to NE) at the expense of the non-member country.

VI.   DO BIG CUSTOMS UNIONS WIN TARIFF WARS?

Even if endowments are symmetric and preferences are identical across countries, it may yet be true that each pair of countries has an incentive to defect from free trade and form a customs union. This was shown in example B. In this case it is difficult to see how free trade could be an equilibrium.

9 These results suggest that moving from NE to FTA is a 'stepping stone' towards freer trade, in that all countries gain from an improvement in the global allocation of resources. Recall, however, that our examples require that the FTA members have symmetric endowments. In the appendix we briefly discuss an example where this requirement is dropped, and we find that one FTA member is made worse off in the move from NE to FTA.

10 Although we do not specifically analyse unilateral tariff reductions (UTR), the external tariff coordination provided by a customs union is an additional reason why a customs union would be superior to UTR (see Wonnacott and Wonnacott 1981, 1984, and Berglas 1983).

80   John Kennan and Raymond Riezman

It can also happen, as was shown in example A, that each country is better off at free trade than it would be in any customs union. In this section we determine the set of symmetric endowments for which this result holds. We show that a customs union can improve welfare over free trade if the member countries are large enough.

When countries are symmetric the endowment matrix can be written as

$$\Omega(y) = \begin{bmatrix} y & 0.5(1-y) & 0.5(1-y) \\ 0.5(1-y) & y & 0.5(1-y) \\ 0.5(1-y) & 0.5(1-y) & y \end{bmatrix},$$

where y is each country's percentage share of the world endowment of their export good.

We let y vary from 0.98 to 0.36 and for each y we compute NE, CU, and FT, where the CU members are countries 2 and 3. The problem reduces to determining which values of y imply that customs unions improve members' welfare over free trade.[11] Since reporting the results for each y would be too cumbersome we report only a summary.

The critical value of y is (approximately) 0.66919. If each country's endowment of y (their export good) is less than 0.66919 then member countries do better at CU than at FT; otherwise they do worse. Of course, the non-member is worse off at CU no matter what the endowment.

This result may seem puzzling, since it means that customs unions are beneficial is y is small. We next show that y's being small is equivalent to the customs union's being large. This can be seen by collapsing the three-country model to two countries, treating the customs union as a single country. This can be done, since the customs union members (countries 2 and 3) decide their tariffs jointly and they are symmetric. In addition, since the relative price of goods 2 and 3 is always unity, these goods can be aggregated into a composite commodity. Note, however, that the customs union's preferences over good 1 and the composite good will not be symmetric.

We combine countries and aggregate goods and renormalize so that there is one unit of both good 1 and the composite good, with the resulting endowment matrix

$$\Omega_2(y) = \begin{bmatrix} y & 0.5(1-y) \\ 1-y & 0.5(1+y) \end{bmatrix}.$$

In a 2×2 version of this model with symmetric preferences Kennan and Riezman (1988) showed that a sufficient condition for a country to win a tariff war is that it be large in the sense that the sum of its endowments is greater than some critical number. It can also be shown that this condition remains approximately valid for a broad range of asymmetric preferences. In the present context this condition means

---

11 Following the discussion in section V above, note that the terms of trade move in favour of the customs union, for all values of y. In addition, the customs union members are always better off relative to NE, at the expense of the non-member.

that the customs union wins a tariff war if $(1 - y) + 0.5(1 + y) > 1.2$. This is equivalent to $y < 0.6$, which is close to the condition we derived in the 3×3 case. The difference is due to the fact that in the aggregated case the correct preferences would not be symmetric over goods. Hence, the condition that customs unions gain if $y < 0.66919$ means that customs unions that are big enough gain compared with free trade. In other words, customs unions can be regarded as a device to increase country size for the purposes of trade policy.

VII. CONCLUSION

The analysis of optimal tariff equilibria with customs unions presents a formidable theoretical puzzle, and general results in this area do not yet exist. As a first step, we have developed a prototype model which illustrates, by means of examples, some important pieces of the puzzle.

Two distinct motivations for customs union formation were demonstrated. First, a custom union enables its members to internalize the tariff externality that exists whenever two countries import the same good. Second, a customs union can make several countries into one larger one for the purpose of trade policy. If the customs union is big enough it can improve its members' welfare over free trade. One implication of this argument is that even if countries are initially symmetric, it may be difficult to sustain free trade as an equilibrium.

Our model was also used to separate the tariff reduction aspect of customs unions from the policy co-ordination aspect. The movement from a Nash equilibrium in tariffs to an equilibrium in which two of the countries form a Free Trade Association with zero internal tariffs improved global resource allocation. Moving from a Free Trade Association to a full customs union in which the member countries agree on a common external tariff had ambiguous resource allocation effects.

There are two obvious directions for further research. First, the robustness of the examples should be investigated, by extending the model to include production and by examining more general preferences. A particularly attractive prospect is that such a model could be used to analyse optimal tariff policies under imperfect competition. Perhaps the best way to do this is to embed our optimal tariff calculations within the computable general equilibrium models of Whalley (1985, 1986) or Harrison (1986). Second, the model can provide a base on which to build a practical framework for empirical applications. For example, it might be used to analyse how the initial formation and subsequent expansion of the European Community affected tariffs charged on U.S. exports to Europe, and tariffs charged by the United States on imports from Europe. The model could also be used to study the effect of the Canada-U.S. free trade agreement on their external tariff policies and the response of the EEC and Japan to these changes.

APPENDIX: AN ASYMMETRIC CUSTOMS UNION

Here we give an example (table A1) in which an FTA makes one of its members worse off, relative to Nash equilibrium. The endowments of countries 2 and 3 are not

82   John Kennan and Raymond Riezman

symmetric, so they do not set the same tariff on good 1 when they form an FTA: country 2 picks 17 per cent and 3 picks 37 per cent. Country 3 is made worse off in the move from NE to FTA. The reason for this is that country 3 is large and can use tariffs to turn the terms of trade in its favour. The FTA restricts this market power, and country 3's terms of trade substantially deteriorate.

The example also illustrates the conflict of interest between CU members when endowments are not symmetric. Two alternative equilibria are shown: in CU_2 country picks the common external tariff, and in CU_3 country 3 picks the tariff. Either version of the customs union makes the members better off relative to both free trade and Nash equilibrium.

TABLE A1

Endowments

$$\Omega = \begin{bmatrix} 0.5 & 0.15 & 0.05 \\ 0.25 & 0.7 & 0.05 \\ 0.25 & 0.15 & 0.9 \end{bmatrix}$$

Eq^m	Country	Utility	Tariffs			Prices	Consumption		
FT	1:	54.47	0	0	0	0.3333	0.2333	0.2333	0.2333
	2:	90.14	0	0	0	0.3333	0.3333	0.3333	0.3333
	3:	116.38	0	0	0	0.3333	0.4333	0.4333	0.4333
NE	1:	37.96	0	0.4203	0.5044	0.2580	0.3196	0.1984	0.1220
	2:	74.76	0.8142	0	1.0120	0.2925	0.3043	0.4868	0.1575
	3:	117.92	2.3359	2.5167	0	0.4493	0.3760	0.3146	0.7204
FTA	1:	49.53	0	0.4517	0.6072	0.3160	0.3104	0.1957	0.1802
	⎡2:	91.23	0.1658	0	0	0.3452	0.3206	0.3422	0.3488
	⎣3:	115.93	0.3678	0	0	0.3386	0.3689	0.4620	0.4709
CU_2	1:	42.54	0	0.3878	0.5268	0.2708	0.3242	0.1722	0.1590
	⎡2:	91.26	0.6617	0	0	0.3674	0.2929	0.3587	0.3645
	⎣3:	118.04	0.6617	0	0	0.3616	0.3828	0.4689	0.4764
CU_2	1:	33.63	0	0.2829	0.4145	0.2083	0.3543	0.1444	0.1328
	⎡2:	90.97	1.5341	0	0	0.3984	0.2773	0.3675	0.3725
	⎣3:	119.33	1.5341	0	0	0.3931	0.3682	0.4880	0.4946

REFERENCES

Arndt, Sven (1968) 'On discriminatroy vs. non-preferential tariff policies.' *Economic Journal* 78, 971–9
— (1969) 'Customs unions and the theory of tariffs.' *American Economic Review* 59, 108–18
Berglas, Eitan (1983) 'The case for unilateral tariff reductions: foreign tariffs rediscovered.' *American Economic Review* 73, 1141–2
Corden, Max (1984) 'The normative theory of international trade.' In R. Jones and P. Kenen, *Handbook of International Economics*, vol. 1 (Amsterdam: North-Holland)

Grinols, Earl (1986) 'Foreign investment and economic growth: characterization of a second best policy for welfare gains.' *Journal of International Economics* 21, 165–72

Hamilton, Bob and John Whalley (1985) 'Optimal tariff calculations in alternative trade models and some possible implications for current world trading arrangements.' *Journal of International Economics* 15, 323–48

Harrison, Glenn (1985) 'A general equilibrium evaluation of tariff reductions.' In Srinivasan and Whalley, eds, *General Equilibrium Trade Policy Modeling* (Cambridge, MA: MIT Press)

Johnson, Harry G. (1958) 'Optimum tariffs and retaliation.' *Review of Economic Studies* 21, 142–53; revised version in chap II of H.G. Johnson, *International Trade and Economic Growth* (Cambridge, MA: Harvard University Press)

Kemp, Murray and Henry Wan (1983) 'An elementary proposition concerning the formation of customs unions.' Reprinted in J. Bhagwati, ed., *International Trade: Selected Readings* (Cambridge, MA: MIT Press)

Kennan, John and Raymond Riezman (1988) 'Do big countries win tariff wars?' *International Economic Review* 29, 81–5

Lloyd, Peter J. (1982) '3 × 3 theory of customs unions.' *Journal of International Economics* 12, 41–64

Markusen, James and Randall Wigle (1987) 'Nash-equilibrium tariffs for the U.S. and Canada: the roles of country size, scale economies and capital mobility.' Paper presented at the Sixth Annual Conference on International Trade Theory, London, Ont., 11–12, April

Otani, Yoshihiko (1980) 'Strategic equilibrium of tariffs and general equilibrium.' *Econometrica* 48, 643–62

Riezman, Raymond (1985) 'Customs unions and the core.' *Journal of International Economics* 19, 355–66

Takayama, Akira (1972) *International Trade* (Holt, Rinehart & Winston)

Vanek, Jaroslav (1965) *General Equilibrium of International Discrimination* (Cambridge, MA: Harvard University Press)

Viner, Jacob (1950) *The Customs Union Issue* (New York: Carnegie Endowment for International Peach)

Whalley, John (1985) *Trade Liberalization Among Major World Trading Areas* (Cambridge, MA: MIT Press)

— (1985) 'Impacts of a 50% tariff reduction in an eight-region global trade model.' In Srinivasan and Whalley, eds, *General Equilibrium Trade Policy Modelling* (Cambridge, MA: MIT Press)

Wonnacott, Paul and Ronald Wonnacott (1981) 'Is unilateral tariff reduction preferable to a customs union? The curious case of the missing foreign tariffs.' *American Economic Review* 71, 704–14

— (1984) 'How general is the case for unilateral tariff reduction?' *American Economic Review* 74, 491

[24]

ELSEVIER   European Economic Review 39 (1995) 1429–1437

EUROPEAN
ECONOMIC
REVIEW

Tariff revenue competition in a free trade area

Martin Richardson

Department of Economics, University of Otago, P.O. Box 56, Dunedin, New Zealand

Received April 1992; final version received November 1994

Abstract

This note argues that important consequences for the analysis of free trade areas (FTAs) follow from the observation that, with no transport costs, producer prices must be equalised across member countries of a FTA, even if external tariffs differ. In particular, the well-known tariff externality of a FTA is exacerbated by *internal* trade deflection and competition for external tariff revenues. Consequently, a FTA will involve lower external tariffs than might otherwise be expected. We illustrate an extreme case of a FTA between identical partners wherein equilibrium, if it exists at all, is one of zero external tariffs.

Keywords: Tariff revenue competition; Free trade area; External tariff

JEL classification: F15

1. Introduction

A free trade area (FTA) is a form of preferential trading area which entails full free trade amongst members but in which each country chooses its own external tariffs. It has long been recognised in the literature that, if member countries have different tariffs against non-members on some homogeneous good, restrictions on re-exporting (Lambrinidis, 1965) will be required to maintain any differences in domestic prices that might otherwise be eroded through such trade deflection (Corden, 1984). Where rules-of-origin are effective in preventing such behaviour, however, the presumption in the literature has been that external tariff differences between members then imply differences in domestic prices, for both producers and consumers.

The central point of the present note stems from the observation that, even when trade deflection and consumer arbitrage are prevented, internal free trade

1430   M. Richardson / European Economic Review 39 (1995) 1429–1437

implies that prices at which *producers* can sell are equated across members of a FTA, regardless of external tariff differences. This is because all intra-FTA production of a good can be sold anywhere within the FTA duty-free. While this observation has not previously been made [1], certain important implications follow from it.

In particular, this producer price equalisation [2] leads to a new source of competition between member countries in the setting of external tariffs. Consider a FTA in which some good is imported by both partners. Assume that total intra-FTA production of the good is less than consumption in either country at all relevant prices. If one partner, say country A, were to levy a slightly higher tariff on the good than the other, country B, then, ignoring any transport costs [3], all of B's production would be sold in A at the higher price: the world price plus A's tariff. All of B's consumption would then be imported from outside of the FTA, raising tariff revenue for the government of B. If A were to reduce its tariff to slightly below that of B then the roles would reverse and the government in A would pick up tariff revenue on all consumption in A. Thus there is some conflict within a FTA over tariff revenues from trade with non-members. This competition implies lower external tariffs in the FTA than would otherwise prevail; indeed, we provide an example in which it leads to either zero tariffs or to the non-existence of equilibrium.

In the next section we show that producer prices can *not* differ within a FTA and, in a partial equilibrium setting, expose our main results. A third section interprets the results and discusses their robustness to extensions of the model.

2. A partial equilibrium analysis

2.1. Producer price equalisation in a FTA

Consider two countries, A and B, in a FTA excluding the rest of the world (country C.) We assume no transport costs at this point. By arbitrage and internal free trade, the only goods in which consumer prices in A and B can differ, in the absence of non-trade taxes, are those which both members either import from or

---

[1] While a referee suggests that it has long been known that this might raise problems regarding equilibrium, these problems have not been formally articulated. See Richardson (1994) and Grossman and Helpman (1994) for treatments of endogenous policy that *do* allow for this, both building on Richardson (1992).

[2] Henceforth we use the term 'producer price' in country A, for example, to refer to the price actually received by a producer in A: if she sells in country B then this is B's domestic price. A referee notes that this is *not* the common usage of this term but we maintain the present usage for ease of exposition.

[3] We discuss below the impact of introducing transport costs into the model.

export to the rest of the world – consumer prices may then differ to the extent that external tariffs differ. However, prices received by producers must be equalised.

To see this, consider some homogeneous good X which both A and B import from C, subject to different tariffs. Let specific tariffs, domestic prices, supplies and demands in country $i = $ A, B be denoted t^i, p^i, $X^i(p^i)$ and $D^i(p^i)$ respectively. Suppose, without loss of generality, that t^B exceeds t^A so that p^B exceeds p^A. Now, all of A's production of X can legitimately be sold in B, tariff-free, netting A's suppliers the higher price p^B, so long as $X^A(p^B) + X^B(p^B) < D^B(p^B)$. If this inequality does not hold then B will import no X from C and p^B will be driven down until one of the following occurs: either (a) $X^A(p^{B\prime}) + X^B(p^{B\prime}) = D^B(p^{B\prime})$ at some $p^{B\prime}$ weakly in excess of p^A, or (b) if $X^A(p^A) + X^B(p^A) > D^B(p^A)$, until p^B exactly equals p^A and producers in the FTA are indifferent about the destination of their sales. In every case producer prices within the FTA are equalised (as are consumer prices in the last case only.) This occurs not from *trade* deflection but rather from deflection of sales of *domestic* production from the low- to the high-tariff member so it cannot be stopped in a FTA. [4]

2.2. Tariff revenue competition and equilibrium

It has long been recognized that if FTA partners have external market power then there is a negative externality associated with independent tariff-setting: "if country A raises its tariff on imports from C... this improves not only its own terms of trade, but... will also improve B's terms of trade" for tariffs on goods imported by both partners (Corden, 1984, p. 122). We argue that a pure strategy Nash equilibrium in external tariffs in a FTA, if it exists, will in addition be characterised by competition over tariff revenues as described in the Introduction. So Nash equilibrium tariffs are even lower than the externality argument alone suggests. Indeed, we shall show that if a pure strategy equilibrium exists at all for identical FTA members in this context it is at zero external tariffs. Further,

---

[4] It should be stressed that consumer prices need not be equated in a FTA. We have argued that producer arbitrage will lead all intra-FTA production to be sold in only the higher-tariff country so any arbitrage to erode consumer price differentials must require internal cross-border movements of goods that originate *outside* the FTA. This, however, violates rules-of-origin and so contravenes both the principle and the operation of FTAs in practice. FTAs are increasingly common and the evolution into what would effectively be customs unions (CUs), with common external tariffs (CETs), that such consumer arbitrage would imply (as described in Vousden (1990, pp. 234–235)) is not apparent. In Canada, for example, proposals for greater integration with the U.S. (such as a CU) are roundly opposed. Second, trade deflection à la Corden *is* closely monitored and prevented in FTAs so that consumer price differences due to tariff differences are not eroded by re-exporting. Third, travellers within FTAs are restricted in the value of goods they can transship. All in all, the extent of arbitrage that consumers can undertake is highly limited and is unlikely to erode consumer price differences due to different external tariffs.

1432 *M. Richardson / European Economic Review 39 (1995) 1429–1437*

non-existence of a pure strategy equilibrium is possible as a result of this revenue competition.

Using the notation above, welfare in country A is the sum of consumer surplus, $CS(p^A)$, producer surplus, PS, and tariff revenues, $t^A M_C^A$, where M_C^A denotes imports into A from country C. Country C's inverse excess supply of X is given by an increasing function $p^* = p^*(M_C)$ where $M_C \equiv M_C^A + M_C^B$. An assumption maintained throughout this paper, for concreteness, is

Assumption 1. Aggregate intra-FTA supply of X is less than demand in either partner at any relevant prices: $X^i(p^j) + X^j(p^j) < D^j(p^j)$ for $i,j = A,B$, $i \neq j$, where $t^j \geqslant t^i$.

The ability to trade freely within the FTA renders A's welfare discontinuous in its own tariff. To see this, note that if $t^A < t^B$ then all of A's production will be sold in B at a price $p^B > p^A$ so producer surplus is $PS(p^B)$ (which is unaffected by a small change in t^A). Further, A will import its entire demand from country C in this case so earning tariff revenue of $t^A D^A(p^A)$. Thus $W^A = CS(p^A) + PS(p^B) + t^A D^A(p^A)$ if $t^A < t^B$. However, if $t^A = t^B$ then we have the usual case in which domestic production is sold at home and all imports come from country C so $W^A = CS(p^A) + PS(p^A) + t^A[D^A(p^A) - X^A(p^A)]$. Finally, in the case in which t^A strictly exceeds t^B then all of A *and* B's production will be sold in A so $W^A = CS(p^A) + PS(p^A) + t^A[D^A(p^A) - X^A(p^A) - X^B(p^A)]$. In sum,

$$W^A = \begin{cases} CS(p^A) + PS(p^B) + t^A D^A(p^A) & \text{if } t^A < t^B, \\ CS(p^A) + PS(p^A) + t^A[D^A(p^A) - X^A(p^A)] & \text{if } t^A = t^B, \\ CS(p^A) + PS(p^A) + t^A[D^A(p^A) - X^A(p^A) - X^B(p^A)] & \text{if } t^A > t^B. \end{cases}$$

For a given level of t^B, then, W^A is discontinuous in t^A at $t^A = t^B$: a small increase in t^A above t^B will induce a discrete fall in W^A as imports from C, subject to A's tariff, are displaced by duty-free imports from B. Conversely, a small cut in t^A when $t^A = t^B$ will induce a discrete increase in W^A as consumption previously met by domestic production is now met by imports from C which raise tariff revenues. Note that this production deflection has no effect on the FTA's aggregate position vis-à-vis the rest of the world: if $t^A = t^B$ and then t^A is cut slightly, for instance, then B's imports from C will fall by $X^A(p^B)$ but A's imports from C will rise by $X^A(p^A)$.

This discontinuity in a country's welfare function implies that there can be no Nash equilibrium in which $t^A = t^B > 0$. If tariffs are low enough there is a welfare loss associated with tariff reductions (as terms of trade with C worsen) but this effect can be made arbitrarily small by a sufficiently small tariff cut. The revenue shifting effect noted above is a discrete welfare improvement regardless of the size of the tariff reduction, so a small unilateral tariff cut away from a symmetric outcome will always increase a country's welfare given the partner's positive tariff.

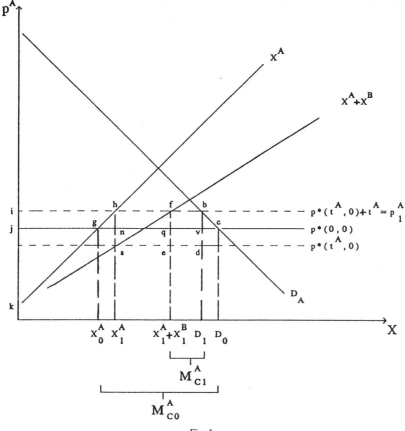

Fig. 1.

At $t^B = 0$, however, there are two possibilities to consider depending on whether or not the terms of trade gains to A from levying a positive tariff against C exceed the discrete losses from B's free-riding. Fig. 1 captures the issue here. The world price, p^*, depends on aggregate FTA imports which depend on the external tariffs chosen by A and B. Accordingly, we can write the world price as $p^*(t^A, t^B)$, a declining function of t^A and t^B. Fig. 1 shows A's demand curve for X, D^A, A's supply curve, X^A, the FTA's aggregate supply curve, $X^A + X^B$, and the world price when $t^A = t^B = 0$ ($p^*(0,0)$). In free trade A's consumption is D_0, its production is X_0^A and it imports $M_{C0}^A = D_0 - X_0^A$ all from country C. Welfare is simply consumer surplus (the area labelled acj beneath D^A but above $p^*(0, 0)$) plus producer surplus (area kgj). Suppose that, given $t^B = 0$ and given C's excess supply curve, A's optimal tariff is that shown as t^A in the figure and that,

1434 *M. Richardson / European Economic Review 39 (1995) 1429–1437*

consequently, the world price would be $p^*(t^A, 0)$. The domestic price in A would then rise to $p_1^A = p^*(t^A, 0) + t^A$ and, in the standard analysis ignoring the effects we have discussed above, consumption and imports would fall to D_1 and $D_1 - X_1^A$ respectively. Thus consumer surplus would fall by $bcji$ as the domestic price in A increases and producer surplus would rise by $hgji$. Non-discriminatory tariffs would yield increased tariff revenue of $bdsh$ for a net gain of $vdsn - hng - bcv$, the first term representing the usual terms of trade gain from an optimal tariff and the last two the tariff's production and consumption losses respectively.

However, this tariff would actually induce B to sell in A, duty-free, so revenue of only $bdef$ would be earned (on imports from C of $M_{C1}^A = D_1 - (X_1^A + X_1^B)$) for a net gain of $vdeq - ghfq - bcv$. This equals the gain in the non-discriminatory case less $hfes$ which, in turn, is $t^A X^B(p_1^A)$: the foregone tariff revenue on imports now coming from B. If the net gain from such a tariff is negative then A will choose $t^A = 0$ and full free trade is an equilibrium outcome. If the net gain is positive then A would levy this tariff and suffer B's free-riding. B then would not choose $t^B = 0$ (rather, $t^B = t^A - \epsilon$) and full free trade is not a pure strategy Nash equilibrium either.

We can state more exactly the conditions under which free trade can prevail as an equilibrium. For $t^B = 0$, any $t^A \geqslant 0$ puts us in the regime in which $t^A \geqslant t^B$. [5] Given the slopes of the demand and supply functions here, $\partial W^A / \partial t^A > 0$ at $t^A = t^B = 0$ is sufficient to establish that A's optimal tariff is positive. Differentiating W^A, holding $t^B = 0$,

$$dW^A = [-D^A + X^A] \, dp^A + t^A [dD^A - dX^A - dX^B]$$
$$+ [D^A - X^A - X^B] \, dt^A. \tag{1}$$

But $p^A = p^*(t^A, 0) + t^A$ so $dp^A = dp^* + dt^A$ and, where $dp^* = (\partial p^*(0, 0))/(\partial t^A) \, dt^A$,

$$dW^A|_{t^B = t^A = 0} = -(D^A - X^A) \, dp^* - X^B dt^A. \tag{2}$$

The two terms in this expression correspond to areas $+vdsn$ and $-hfes$ respectively in Fig. 1. Overall, this expression is more likely to be negative, and thus the free trade outcome more likely, ceteris paribus, the larger is the partner country's supply (X^B), the larger is domestic supply (X^A), the smaller is domestic demand (D^A) and the less responsive is the world price to a change in A's tariff ($\partial p^*(0,0)/\partial t^A$). The first three of these effects increase the losses to A from B's free-riding, the last decreases the terms of trade gain from a tariff against C. In all cases B's free-riding is more costly to A, relative to terms of trade gains against C, if $t^A > 0$ is chosen in response to $t^B = 0$. Thus a response of $t^A = 0$ is more likely in each case.

---

[5] Note that the only difference between W^A when $t^A = t^B$ and W^A when $t^A > t^B$ comes from differences in tariff revenues and thus they are equivalent at $t^A = 0$.

M. Richardson / European Economic Review 39 (1995) 1429–1437 1435

To summarise, under our maintained Assumption 1 we have argued that there is no pure strategy Nash equilibrium in FTA external tariff setting involving equal, positive tariffs in the two member countries. [6] Further, full free trade may or may not be a Nash equilibrium depending on whether (2) is negative or positive for a small increase in t^A which itself depends on a number of factors identified above.

An implication of this analysis is that where the two FTA members are *identical* (so that any equilibrium is symmetric) the only possible pure strategy Nash equilibrium is full free trade; alternatively there is no such equilibrium at all.

3. Interpretation and robustness

The zero-tariff equilibrium described above is similar to the 'Bertrand paradox' outcome but not exactly analogous. In the latter, two identical firms, producing a homogeneous good and competing in prices, price at marginal cost as each attempts to undercut the other and being undercut yields zero sales. In the FTA game, gains from undercutting are traded off against terms of trade gains against non-members; it may still pay to levy a tariff even if one is undercut so the zero-tariff outcome is a possibility only. [7]

In the case where no equilibrium exists, each country attempts to export its production to the other which contrasts with the pre-FTA case where no trade occurs between A and B. This is trade diversion but of an unusual sort, occurring between net importers of the *same* good, rather than between an exporter and importer.

We conclude with some discussion of the robustness of our results. While the exact results presented above are specific to the case of identical partners, zero transport costs and homogeneous goods, the broad implication that tariff revenue competition in a FTA leads to lower external tariffs than might otherwise be expected seems quite general. First, the partial equilibrium framework employed here is not critical – we have shown elsewhere (Richardson (1992), available on request) that our results also hold in a general equilibrium setting. Second, if domestic and foreign goods were only imperfect substitutes then a country would not serve the entire FTA market by marginally undercutting its partner and a

---

[6] If Assumption 1 does *not* hold then the incentive to undercut is lessened but still exists (unless total production exceeds total FTA consumption so the good is not an import in the first place). It is lessened because undercutting reduces the producer price in the high-tariff country rendering that tariff redundant and reducing producers' income for the free-rider. But it still exists because of the increased tariff revenue still associated with any intra-FTA production deflection.

[7] Were consumer arbitrage possible within the FTA this Bertrand-like equilibrium of full free trade would *always* prevail: when consumer prices are equalised the higher of the two tariffs is redundant but there are still gains from undercutting. Revenue competition then drives tariffs to zero and, as in Vousden (1990), internal arbitrage turns a FTA into a CU, but one with a zero CET!

Economic Integration and International Trade

symmetric equilibrium with positive tariffs could obtain. However, an incentive for some undercutting, relative to the tariffs that would prevail if the price equalisation were ignored, would still remain. Third, increasing the number of FTA members simply exacerbates the effects noted here: each country's pre-FTA Nash tariff is lower (as the tariff externality is worsened) but the gains from undercutting one's partners are unchanged.

Fourth, our exact results do depend on symmetry. If one partner is relatively large then an asymmetric equilibrium with positive tariffs is possible as this country may choose to bear the other's free-riding in order to reap external terms of trade gains. This has the empirical implication that a FTA is more tenable where one member country is large and, indeed, many actual FTAs have this structure.

Finally, the analysis would be affected by internal transport costs within the FTA, as the potential for the trade diversion we have identified is then lessened. If per-unit transport costs were constant at some rate τ, say, then country A's welfare function is still discontinuous in t^A but at $t^A = t^B - \tau$ rather than at t^B. To disturb the pre-FTA symmetric equilibrium by undercutting B, A must reduce its tariff by a discrete amount thereby incurring a discrete terms of trade loss vis-à-vis C (a loss which is increasing in the size of the tariff cut). So if τ is sufficiently high the pre-FTA equilibrium may remain in the FTA. But if τ is low enough that undercutting is attractive at that equilibrium, a new outcome may obtain in which $t^A = t^B > 0$. Thus, while the extreme nature of our earlier result with identical countries (zero tariffs if there is any pure strategy equilibrium at all) does not hold here, the general tendency for lower external tariffs still does. This is also the case if per-unit transport costs are increasing in the volume of trade and $\tau(0) = 0$. In this case the welfare discontinuity stressed earlier would disappear completely but a small tariff cut would still be attractive at the pre-FTA equilibrium as it would displace some domestic production with revenue-increasing imports. Accordingly, a symmetric equilibrium with positive tariffs can occur but again with lower tariffs than the usual analysis suggests.

Acknowledgment

I am grateful to Dominique Desruelle, Serge Moresi and, particularly, Marius Schwartz and two anonymous referees for very helpful comments on this paper. Any remaining errors are, of course, my own.

References

Corden, W.M., 1984, The normative theory of international trade, in: R.W. Jones and P.B. Kenen, eds., Handbook of International Economics, Vol. I (North-Holland, Amsterdam) 63–130.

Grossman, G. and E. Helpman, 1994, The politics of free trade agreements, American Economic Review, forthcoming.

Lambrinidis, J.S., 1965, The structure, function and law of a free trade area (Praeger, for The London Institute of World Affairs, New York).

Richardson, M., 1992, On equilibrium in a free trade area, Mimeo. (Georgetown University, Washington, DC).

Richardson, M., 1994, Why a free trade area? The tariff also rises, Economics and Politics 6, no. 1, 79–96.

Vousden, N., 1990, The economics of trade protection (Cambridge University Press, Cambridge).

B
Integration and Sidepayments

[25]

Journal of International Economics 11 (1981) 259–266. North-Holland Publishing Company

AN EXTENSION OF THE KEMP–WAN THEOREM
ON THE FORMATION OF CUSTOMS UNIONS

Earl L. GRINOLS*

Cornell University, Ithaca, NY 14853, USA

Received January 1980, revised version received October 1980

Kemp and Wan (1976) proved that nations forming a customs union can always compensate each other so that no nation will be worse off, relative to the pre-union equilibrium. Their proof, however, is existential, giving no clue how to construct such compensation schemes. This paper proposes a particular compensation scheme which is always feasible. Further, there are circumstances where this scheme is the only feasible one. At world prices the arrangement breaks even for each nation. At post-union internal prices, member compensations sum to the union's tariff receipts. The proof that such a scheme is feasible depends upon the Grandmont–McFadden theorem.

1. Introduction

In August of 1961, the British government applied for membership in the European Economic Community. After an initial rejection and further years of hard bargaining, Britain became a full member on January 1, 1973 in accordance with the treaty of accession signed the previous year. The entire process, therefore, took eleven years and five months from first negotiations to final entry.

The intriguing aspect of the British experience is that in spite of the supposed advantages to free trade, the negotiations were as difficult as they were and opposition to British entry came from within Britain as well as the Common Market. The question under what conditions a nation will benefit from the formation of a customs union, however, is not new. It dates back at least to the publication of Viner's *The Customs Union Issue* (1950). Further, in 1976 Kemp and Wan showed that as long as perfect competition prevails inside the union a compensation scheme between members can always be found whereby every individual is made better off or no worse off after the formation or enlargement of the customs union than he was before. The fact that the world does not freely trade, therefore, must be explained on other grounds. One obstacle, suggested by Kemp and Wan, which seems to be borne out by the British experience, is the difficulty of settling upon a compensation scheme. Either the venality and self-interest of the member

*I would like to thank Henry Wan and Murray Kemp for their insightful and helpful comments.

nations make it impossible to reach an early agreement, or the technical problems of calculating mutually beneficial terms have overwhelmed the various negotiators. We address the latter issue here.

We show that a simple compensation scheme yielding the Kemp–Wan result can always be defined in terms of observable trade flows and market prices. Moreover, there are circumstances in which the proposed scheme is the only feasible one. Using world prices for evaluation each and every country 'breaks even' under the proposed scheme, receiving a transfer which has zero value. Thus, from the point of view of world prices the transfer is financially neutral. Using post-union internal prices for valuation, member nations may have to pay or receive a net transfer. The sum of such transfers can be shown to equal the union's total tariff revenue from the rest of the world, thus providing a serendipitous revenue-sharing rule for the tariff yields.

Section 2 below provides an intuitive discussion of the compensating scheme and its existence proof, the formal derivation being relegated to the appendix. Section 3 describes the two properties of the scheme mentioned above and concluding remarks are contained in section 4.

2. The compensation scheme

At the micro-level, no individual will become worse off if he is offered the option of consuming exactly the same bundle that he consumed before the formation of the union. If there were no production this could be accomplished by redistributing existing endowments to every individual in the union as a subsidy-in-kind which is equal to the difference between his true endowment vector and the pre-union consumption vector. Summing over all consumers in each nation and canceling the intra-national trade, the scheme promises each member nation a subsidy equal to its pre-union trade vector. Summing over all member nations and canceling out the intra-union trade, the scheme promises the union a subsidy equal to the net trade vector with the rest of the world at the pre-union level according to pre-union world prices. If the resultant economy after redistribution has an equilibrium leaving world prices at their initial level with competitive equilibrium within the union we have succeeded in making all individuals no worse off than before. This is so since in a competitive equilibrium no consumer can be worse off than consuming his endowment, and the 'endowment' in our contrived equilibrium is the pre-union consumption vector. For the union as a whole the shortfall in needed endowments is obtained from the rest of the world through trade.

When production is present allowance needs to be made for the distribution of firm profits and the possibility that pre-union consumption of some goods may be greater than their availability in the post-union equilibrium. A simple redistribution of existing endowments and trade flows will no longer work. Instead each individual can be assured the ability to purchase his pre-union consumption bundle at the prices he faces in the post-union equilibrium.[1] The resources needed by each country to cover these commitments will exceed the value of its domestic production and endowments by no more than its pre-union trade flows evaluated at post-union prices.[2] Summing over all member nations and canceling out the intra-union trade, the union needs income above the value of its own production and endowments no greater than the value of its pre-union trade vector with the rest of the world. If after the various transfers are made to each consumer and production is chosen in each firm to maximize profits, the economy has a competitive equilibrium, then we have succeeded in making each individual no worse off than before for the same reasons given in the pure trade case.

In proving the existence of an equilibrium Kemp and Wan rely on the second fundamental theorem of welfare economics, which says that every Pareto optimum can be supported by a competitive equilibrium with appropriate redistributions including the possibility of redistribution across national borders. Their proof is 'existential' rather than 'constructive', however, and gives no clue about the compensation scheme which has to be employed. In our case we have specified the necessary distribution to each nation as its pre-union trade vector and need a theorem showing that any Pareto noninferior allocation can be supported as a competitive equilibrium without further redistributions across national borders.[3] We therefore appeal to the Grandmont–McFadden theorem, which satisfies these requirements, to obtain the following propositions.

Proposition 1. Consider a world trading equilibrium, with any number of countries and commodities and with no restrictions whatever on the tariffs and other commodity taxes of individual countries and with costs of transport fully recognized. Let the subset $1, \ldots, K$ of countries form a customs union with

---

[1]A precise description of such arrangements can be found in Grandmont and McFadden (1972). Following them, each individual is given an income function, $I^i = P^* c^i + \theta^i [I - \sum_i P^* c^i]$, where P^* is the vector of equilibrium prices, c^i is individual i's vector of pre-union consumption, θ^i are scalars between zero and one and summing to unity, and I is total income available at the national level for distribution. Individuals know their income for any set of prices in the same way that a Debreu consumer endowed with labor, for example, knows his income for any given price of labor. The plan is feasible if the government can assure in equilibrium that I^i is large enough to purchase c^i. This, of course, is equivalent to $I - \sum_i P^* c^i$ greater than or equal to zero.

[2]Since $c = y + e + x$, where c is consumption, y is production, e endowments and x is trade with the rest of the world all listed in vector terms, income needed to purchase c at the post union price vector P^* will be $P^* y + P^* e + P^* x$, where y^* is the profit maximizing production at prices P^*. Since $P^* y$ is at most equal to $P^* y^*$, $P^* (y^* + e)$ needs to be augmented by no more than $P^* x$.

[3]The usual proof is also based on Debreu (1959) which describes a private ownership economy, whereas the present paper describes an economy with government determination of incomes. The Debreu theorem would therefore require certain other minor modifications.

competitive free trade internally. Then there exists a common tariff barrier and well-defined distribution policy of lump-sum compensatory payments such that each individual, whether a member of the union or not, is not worse off than before the formation of the union. The compensatory payments across national borders have zero value when valued at world prices and add to union tariff revenues with the rest of the world when valued at internal post-union prices.

A description of the exact compensations referred to and the proof of proposition 1 is given in the appendix. Applied to the world as a whole, proposition 1 implies the following:

Proposition 2. Given the conditions of proposition 1, let countries $1,...,K$ represent the entire world. Let the world move to competitive free trade. Then there exists a well-defined distribution policy of lump-sum compensatory payments such that each individual is not worse off than before the move to free trade. Furthermore, compensatory payments across national borders have zero value when valued at pre-free-trade prices, and add to zero when valued at post-free-trade prices.[4]

The proof of proposition 2 is given in the appendix. We turn now to the implications of propositions 1 and 2 on a national level and a description of the implied financial arrangements.

3. Properties of the compensation scheme

We said in section 2 that the only compensations which are needed allow all households and firms the option of continuing their pre-union consumption and production plans if they so choose. In the post-union equilibrium, however, they will generally recontract to new positions representing different consumption and higher profits at the post-union prices.[5] The union countries keep world prices at their pre-union level by creating a common tariff to bridge the gap between world prices and the post-union equilibrium prices. The compensation to each country is given by its pre-union trade vector. Since trading is assumed to be balanced at world prices, the world-price valuation of such compensation must always be zero.

---

[4]This last property is added for completeness relative to the statement of proposition 1. It follows trivially from the fact that the 'union' represents the entire world and trade with the 'outside' is a null vector.

[5]The latter follows from profit maximization by firms at the new set of prices.

For the union as a whole the tariff revenues equal the difference between the union trade vector valued at domestic prices and at the world prices. Since the external trade vector of the union has zero value at world prices (trade being balanced) the magnitude of tariff receipts are equal to the value of the union's trade at domestic prices. But, the union's trade with the rest of the world is equal to its pre-union trade, thus the sum of compensations to member nations equals tariff receipts. The compensation scheme therefore yields as a by-product a revenue-sharing rule for the common tariff.

The proposed scheme is always feasible since by proposition 1 there exists an equilibrium when the necessary promises are made which is consistent with them being carried out. We now show that there are situations in which the proposed compensations are the only ones which will work. This follows since there are demand structures and production sets such that if the country got anything less it could not make everyone better off. For example, consider the one-person, two-good economy of country A in fig. 1,

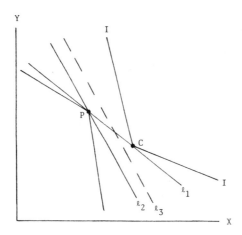

Fig. 1. Compensation in a one-person, two-good economy.

where P is the pre-union vector of production and C is the pre-union vector of consumption. Proposition 1 implies that country A is given income equal to the value of the vector $P-C$ at post-union prices corresponding to the line l_2. (Balanced trade implies $P-C$ has zero value at world prices corresponding to line l_1.) Anything less would leave it with a budget line such as the dotted l_3 which lies to the left of C. In other situations, of course, substitutability in production and consumption might imply each country could be able to get by with somewhat less. Verifying this would require knowledge of preferences, however, and would be difficult to check. In the absence of restrictions on production and consumption, the above arrangements are the only ones which will work in all cases.[6]

4. Conclusions

We have described compensation arrangements for uniform welfare improvement from the formation of customs unions which are always feasible and depend only on the information contained in prices and pre-union trade flows. As a final comment, we note that should there exist two sectors of a given region such as two geographic locations in the world, or two well defined sets of consumers and firms within a nation, that proposition 1 can be applied to those subsets as easily as to nations. What is required is the ability to transfer the net value of production to consumers inside the respective subsets. If a nation cannot eliminate all barriers to free trade, it may be able to make welfare gains by doing so in some sectors. This is possible without hurting any consumer.

Appendix

Let countries $1,\ldots,K$ be the countries considering forming a customs union. Consider next the fictitious economy where each nation's endowment consists of its usual endowment plus its share of the pre-union net excess supply of the rest of the world. Let Y_k denote the net production set of country K (production plus endowment). Following Grandmont and McFadden, suppose that:

(Y.1) Y_k is a closed subset of R^N,
(Y.2)   Inaction is possible: $0 \in Y_k$,
(Y.3) Y_k is convex,
(Y.4)   There is free disposal, $y \in Y_k$, $y' \leq y$ implies $y' \in Y_k$,
(Y.5)   The set of efficient points in Y_k is bounded.[7]

Assumption (Y.2), in the context of net production, implies that each nation is able to meet its pre-union trading commitments.

---

[6]Changes in member compensations can easily be related to profits if one desires. Let c_k, y_k, e_k, and x_k be the vectors of aggregate pre-union consumption, production, endowments, and trade for country k, respectively, and let y_k^*, P^* be the vectors of post-union production and prices. If y_k^* is known, country k's subsidy can be as little as $P^* \cdot x_k - P^*(y_k^* - y_k)$ and leave it enough income to fulfil its promises to be able to purchase pre-union consumption. This follows since $P^*(y_k^* + e_k) + P^* x_k \geq P^*(y_k^* + e_k) + [P^* x_k - P^*(y_k^* - y_k)] = P^*(y_k + e_k + x_k) = P^* c_k$. The first relation follows from the fact that $P^*(y_k^* - y_k) \geq 0$ by firm profit maximization. The second is cancellation of terms and the third follows from the definition of consumption. Thus $P^* x_k$ is a high enough subsidy in all cases while $P^* x_k - P^*(y_k^* - y_k)$ is the least that will work for commitments $P^* c_k$.

[7]See Grandmont and McFadden for a discussion of weaker conditions than (Y.5).

On the demand side, define the set of goods as N and the subset N_k as $\{n \in N \mid y_n > 0$ for some $y \in Y_k$, $y \geq 0\}$. Prices on N and N_k are $P = \{(p_1, \ldots, p_n) \mid 0 \leq p_n < +\infty$ for $n \in N\}$ and $P_k = \{(p_1, \ldots, p_n) \mid 0 \leq p_n < +\infty$ for $n \in N_k$, $p_n = +\infty$ for $n \notin N_k\}$. $\bar{P}_k$ will denote $P \cup P_k$. Suppose:

(D.1) Consumer i of nation k can subsist on goods in N_k, i.e. there is a vector x with $x_n = 0$ for $n \notin N_k$ upon which consumer i can subsist.

(D.2) Values of the demand function are non-empty for positive prices and incomes above subsistence level.

(D.3) Consumer i's demand correspondence is positively homogeneous of degree zero on prices and income, is a closed upper hemicontinuous correspondence for prices in P and incomes above subsistence, is a convex subset of individual i's budget set, and all income is spent.

(E.1) The pre-union allocation of goods in nation k is such that the value of each consumer's commodity vector exceeds his subsistence income at each non-zero price vector in P_k for which $p \cdot y_k$ is maximized. For each $p \in P_k$ with $\sum_{n \in N_k} P_n > 0$ national income exceeds the sum of minimum incomes needed for subsistence of its citizens.[8]

(E.2) There is at least one commodity which can be supplied in every nation, and at least one consumer in each nation who, when given an income above his subsistence level and a price vector with a zero price for that good, will demand an unbounded amount of some commodity.

Assumption (E.2) is an assumption of convenience to rule out the possibility of fragmented equilibria where subeconomies have no dealings with one another. (E.1) in turn, rules out the possibility of starvation for any individual.

Given the above definitions, the following theorem adapted from Grandmont and McFadden applies to the formation of customs union:

Theorem. Suppose that nations $1, \ldots, K$ with the fictitious endowments satisfy conditions (Y.1)–(Y.5), each consumer in nation k satisfies (D.1)–(D.3), (E.1) and (E.2) hold. Then there exists a free trade competitive equilibrium for the distribution policy whereby each nation gives income to each consumer equal to the value of his pre-union consumption at post-union prices and a non-negative fraction of the remaining national income. This equilibrium is Pareto non-inferior for the consumers of each nation $1, \ldots, K$ when compared to their initial allocation. Further, if the prices and initial allocations were not a competitive equilibrium and if every consumer is locally nonsatiated at the pre-

---

[8]A mild sufficient condition for (E.1) is that each consumer have an allocation on which he can survive which is strictly smaller than his given allocation in every component. See Grandmont and McFadden (1972, p. 119) for other conditions.

union allocation, then the allocation achieved under union is Pareto preferable for the union's consumers to their initial allocation.

This nearly completes the proof of proposition 1.

The required vector of common tariffs in proposition 1 may be computed as the vector of pre-union world prices less the vector of internal union prices. Proposition 2 follows from the application of the above theorem to every nation simultaneously. On a national level the income $p \cdot y_k$ is distributed for post-union equilibrium prices p. Since this differs from the value of domestically produced goods and services by the value of pre-union trade flows, each country must receive a portion of the union's tariff revenues equal to its pre-union trade flows valued at internal post-union prices.

References

Debreu, Gerard, 1959, Theory of value (Cowles Foundation for Research in Economics, New Haven, CT).

Kemp, M. and H.Y. Wan, 1976, An elementary proposition concerning the formation of customs unions, Journal of International Economics 6, 95–97.

Grandmont, J.M. and D. McFadden, 1972, A technical note on classical gains from trade, Journal of International Economics 2, 109–125.

Viner, Jacob, 1950, The customs union issue (Carnegie Endowment for International Peace, New York).

[26]

Economica (1994) 61, 301–17

Bringing GATT into the Core

By Carsten Kowalczyk* and Tomas Sjöström†

Tufts University and NBER; †Harvard University

Final version received 28 October 1993.

This paper analyses how international side-payments can be used to facilitate international trade negotiations. We present a model where many countries trade many goods, and we calculate, by use of the Shapley value, international income transfers which will induce nations to eliminate their distortionary trade policies.

Introduction

The preamble to the General Agreement on Tariffs and Trade expresses the belief that a liberal and non-discriminatory world trading system will raise welfare. Consequently GATT has, ever since its inception in 1947, played several roles in the pursuit of global free trade: it has helped design rules for the conduct of international commerce, and it has helped enforce these rules. It has also periodically revisited them through rounds of multilateral trade negotiations.

In spite of its noble goal and many activities, GATT has in recent years been subjected to increasing criticism. It has been accused of being irrelevant, and of being a 'General Agreement to Talk and Talk'. It has even been accused of being dead. Signs of its diminishing role are already visible as even traditional 'globalists', like the United States, are beginning to re-direct their political efforts towards 'regional' integration.[1] It could be argued that these are just signs that the institution has outlived itself, and that it should be allowed to fade away. Against that goes the fact that GATT remains a unique forum where nations can exchange trade policy concessions. The world remains ridden with policies aimed at distorting international trade, and threats of trade conflicts abound. It seems to us that trying to reform the institution holds far more promise for the world trading system.

One of GATT's problems is that much of the world's trade remains outside of its jurisdiction owing to waivers, as prominently exemplified by agriculture and textiles, or to a lack of rules, as exemplified by trade in services. A second difficulty is that GATT has shown itself unable to impose effective discipline on the use of non-tariff policies. In some cases, such as anti-dumping, GATT policy is too permissive, while in other cases countries disguise their trade policy as domestic intervention.[2] A third problem is that it appears to have become increasingly difficult to reform the system; in particular, it seems to have become harder to complete in timely and successful manner a trade negotiation round. The 1947 Geneva Round had 23 participants and lasted less than a year. The second-to-last round, the Tokyo Round, had 99 participants, took seven years to complete, and even that was not an entire success as it did not manage to get unanimous support for the important subsidies code.[3] The just completed

Uruguay Round, which was launched in 1986, had more than 100 participants.[4,5]

While these problems appear to be sufficiently dissimilar as to exclude any hope of simple and sweeping changes, we present in this paper an investigation of a policy instrument that we believe has the potential for being a part of a solution to them all. More concretely, we propose that GATT can become more effective in solidifying already obtained gains, and in further reforming the world trading system, if international side-payments become a part of the GATT system. This paper is a first step in investigating the nature of such payments—a step that eventually could lead to the recommendation that GATT adopts a financial mechanism as part of its institutional structure.

It is quite likely that the informal give and take that goes on during a multilateral trade negotiation round involves promises or threats of changes in, for example, foreign aid. However, there is no tradition in GATT for encouraging or for chanelling transfers of income in the context of a trade round. This stands in interesting contrast to recent practices in Europe, where both the EC and EFTA have used international income transfers in connection with adjustments of trade policy. Thus, the EC's budget serves, among other purposes, as a channel for income redistribution, while EFTA has used income transfers on several occasions to facilitate changes in trade policy.[6] Most recently, the same two parties have established, in their May 1992 Agreement on the European Economic Area, a financial mechanism to transfer about 145 million ECUs per year over a period of five years from members of EFTA to members of the EC (*European Community* 1992).[7] The existence and the apparent ease with which members of EFTA and members of the EC on several occasions have managed to negotiate major adjustments of trade policies suggest that the ability to use such payments could prove helpful in a negotiation.

There is a simple and compelling theoretical reason why income transfers would make a difference. In a two-country tariff game, Harry Johnson (1953) showed that a country might want to deviate from free trade even if its trade partner retaliates. As a result of Pareto optimality of unimpeded trade in that model, the losing country would be willing and able to pay an amount up to its loss relative to global free trade if, in return, the partner would agree to re-establish free trade. Both countries would gain relative to the tariff-ridden situation.

Theoretical work on tariff reform and customs unions routinely assumes, for the purpose of discussing coalition welfare, the possibility of international income transfers. Only two papers have, however, dealt explicitly with international transfers of income. In a standard many-country, many-good trade model with price-taking firms and consumers, Murray Kemp and Henry Wan (1976) demonstrate the existence of intra-club income transfers which raise the welfare of all members of a customs union that otherwise sets its common external tariff such as to leave non-members indifferent. Earl Grinols (1981) extends this by showing that, if each member of such a customs union receives a transfer equal to its pre-change intra-club trade, then no member will be hurt from the expansion of the union.

With few exceptions, it has been the principle in GATT to require unanimity both when reforming and when enforcing its rules. Thus a proposal, and its implied allocation, will fail to be passed if there exists one contracting party (or a group of them) that prefers an alternative feasible allocation (the status quo, for example). If such a situation occurs, then the proposal is said to be *blocked*. The *core* is the set of proposals (allocations) that are not blocked. In other words, if a proposal implies an allocation in the core, then there exists no country or group of countries that would object to its realization. Such a proposal would pass.

This paper is a first attempt at investigating the existence and character of a global financial mechanism that, when in conjunction with the recommendation to eliminate all distortionary trade practices, will be endorsed by all nations and all possible coalitions of nations—that is, will bring GATT into the core. In the theory of international economic integration, the core has been considered previously by Raymond Riezman (1985), who investigates when global free trade is not blocked by either a single nation or a customs union in a three-country exchange model. He rules out, however, international income transfers.

We present a many-country model of world trade where each country is inhabited by price-taking consumers and by a single firm that produces a good in which it has a world-wide monopoly. By allowing countries the opportunity to form preferential trading blocs, we prove that the core of the corresponding world economy is not empty. We then identify a particular payoff vector in the core (the one implied by the *Shapley value*), and derive the policy prescription that implements this vector. The policy prescription takes the form of requiring that countries form the grand coalition and that an international financial mechanism be put into place. The side-payments constituting the financial mechanism have the appealing feature of being expressed in terms of differences in countries' underlying taste and cost parameters. They also have the straightforward intuition that countries with much to gain from cooperation will tend to pay countries with little to gain from cooperation. In the process of establishing this result, we derive, under restrictive assumptions, two simple formulae for the Shapley value. Thus, the Shapley value can be expressed either as giving to a player (a country) what it can guarantee itself plus half of the total value created by it when cooperating with other players, or as giving to a player its payoff if the grand coalition forms plus half of the difference between what the player would gain from ceasing to cooperate and what its partners would gain from no longer cooperating with it (each of these gains can be negative and their sum will be). The first interpretation implies that the Shapley value shares the property displayed by many cooperative solutions of 'splitting the difference" (see also Shubik 1984, chapter 7). The second interpretation makes clear the role of side-payments as a missing instrument: if offering to cooperate is not enough to induce a player to cooperate, then raise the value of the offer by adding a payment.

These expressions for the side payments are due to two features of our model when a country joins a preferential trading club: first, that outsiders are not affected, which is necessary in order to allow us to use the characteristic function approach; and second, that the gains from cooperation between the new member and an initial member of the trading depend only on attributes of these two parties and are, in particular, independent of the number and attributes of the other initial members of the club. This second feature is not necessary for use of the cooperative approach. It is a property of the model that we would not expect to hold in richer environments.

In approaching the problem of restructuring GATT as a cooperative game, we are downplaying, at least at this stage of the research, some aspects of international cooperation that undoubtedly play an important role in the actual workings of the GATT system. We are not, for example, discussing how an actual process of GATT contracting parties submitting offers and counter-offers would or should work, and whether it would lead to the outcome that we propose here.[8] Rather, our approach can be interpreted as representing a situation where a GATT arbitrator has extensive information about the relevant parameters of the member countries, and can cut short any time-consuming bargaining process by presenting a proposal to adopt the Shapley value. Another issue of considerable importance for the actual design of international agreements is to design them such that they are self-enforcing, that is to ensure, for example through establishing a dispute settlement mechanism or a retaliation mechanism, that no country or group of countries has an incentive to cheat on the agreement or to leave it all together. This becomes particularly relevant in dynamic environments, where agreements are struck without knowing with certainty what future periods will offer.[9] The model that we consider in this paper is static, and one of full and perfect information. In particular, the setting of policies, the writing of checks for international income transfers and the international exchange of goods take place simultaneously. Were a country to renege on a payment to another country, for example, the latter country would immediately cancel its preferential trade agreement with the former while leaving its agreements with all other countries intact. The retaliation is credible and would be borne out, and the former country would lose compared with its not breaking the agreement. Thus, under the strict assumptions that we apply, enforceability is assured.

Section I presents the model. Section II introduces preferential trading clubs and derives some welfare properties from integration in this model. Section III derives a financial mechanism which brings about Pareto-optimal world trade. Section IV shows when international side-payments are needed for the global trading club to form. Section V concludes and stresses the limitations of the approach taken here. An Appendix derives expressions for consumer's surplus and profits as functions of underlying parameters.

I. THE MODEL

We consider a world of n countries. In each country i there is a representative consumer who chooses a consumption vector c^i to maximize the quasi-linear preferences,

$$(1) \qquad u^i(c^i) = c_0^i + \sum_{j=1}^{n} \frac{(c_j^i)^{\theta_j^i}}{\theta_j^i}, \qquad 0 < \theta_j^i < 1, \qquad i = 1, \ldots, n,$$

where c_0^i is the consumption in country i of good 0, c_j^i is the consumption in country i of good j, and θ_j^i is a taste parameter.[10]

Goods $1, \ldots, n$ are produced, and are traded internationally. The consumer in country i is endowed with $\bar{I}_0^i$ units of good zero. They can be consumed, sold as input to the domestic firm or used as a medium of international income transfer. If p_j^i denotes the domestic price of good j in country i, if good 0 is chosen as numeraire, and if I^i denotes full income of the representative consumer in country i, the budget constraint can be written as

$$(2) \qquad c_0^i + \sum_{j=1}^{n} p_j^i c_j^i = I^i, \qquad i = 1, \ldots, n.$$

Equations (1) and (2) imply that demand in country i for each traded good j is given by the function

$$(3) \qquad c_j^i = (p_j^i)^{1/(\theta_j^i - 1)}, \qquad i, j = 1, \ldots, n.$$

Given the assumed preferences, only the own price determines demand.[11] This feature is crucial since it will later enable us to introduce the characteristic function.

In each country i there is only one firm. It will sometimes be referred to as firm i, and it produces x^i units of good i with cost function

$$(4) \qquad l_0^i = \beta^i x^i, \qquad i = 1, \ldots, n,$$

where l_0^i is its demand for good 0 and $\beta^i > 0$ is a constant cost parameter.

Firm i sells x_j^i units in market j. We assume that it declares on each unit not only where the product is made, but also for which market, and that penalties for reselling goods across markets are sufficiently high to segment markets completely. The price charged by firm i in market j is denoted $(p^e)_i^j$, and its profits are given by

$$(5) \qquad \pi^i = \sum_{j=1}^{n} [(p^e)_i^j - \beta^i] x_j^i, \qquad i = 1, \ldots, n.$$

In the absence of any policy restrictions, $(p^e)_i^j$ will be the monopoly price, as determined by the mark-up rule,

$$(6) \qquad (p^e)_i^j = \frac{\beta^i}{\theta_i^j}, \qquad i, j = 1, \ldots, n,$$

where we have used that the price elasticity of demand implied by (3) is $1/(1 - \theta_j^i)$.

II. POLICY, PREFERENTIAL CLUBS AND WELFARE

For ease of exposition we cast the policy analysis in terms of price ceilings.[12] A welfare-maximizing government, say the one in country j, will always restrict its domestic firm to charge only marginal costs in its home market since this raises national welfare. Furthermore, and as shown in Figure 1, a ceiling on the export price by j to i reduces country j profits by area I, but raises country i consumer's surplus by area I + II raising global welfare by II. Thus, there exists a side-payment from country i to country j that would trigger such an export price ceiling.[13,14]

We define a *preferential trading club* to be an agreement between its members to price at costs in each other's markets. The *grand coalition* is then the agreement by all countries in the world to charge marginal costs in all markets. We define also an *increase in coalition welfare* to mean that, if side-payments within a coalition are possible, then the gaining members of the coalition can compensate the losing members of the same coalition and still be better off. An

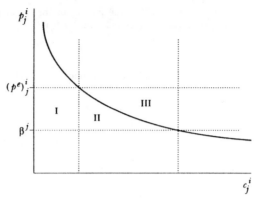

FIGURE 1

increase in world welfare is defined in analogous manner for the grand coalition.[15]

For all i and j, define δ_j^i to be the increase in consumer's surplus in country i from firm j reducing its price to marginal costs, and let π_i^j be the reduction in j's profits. We can then establish a number of welfare implications from trading clubs, including the grand coalition.

Proposition 1. A preferential trading club raises coalition welfare of its members by an amount equal to the dead weight losses from their monopoly pricing on each other.

Proof. Since δ_j^i equals area $I + II$ in Figure 1, and π_i^j equals area I, collective welfare increases by area II, which equals $(\delta_j^i - \pi_i^j)$. An analogous area equal to $(\delta_i^j - \pi_j^i)$ is gained from firm i reducing its price to marginal costs in market j, and the welfare increase for the pair is given by $[(\delta_j^i - \pi_i^j) + (\delta_i^j - \pi_j^i)]$. The increase in coalition welfare is finally found by adding these gains over all pairs of members of the coalition.   □

Proposition 2. The increase in coalition welfare is larger if country i joins K' than if it joins K, where all members of K are members of K', and i is not a member of either.

Proof. Let $\{K' - K\}$ be the set of countries that are members of K' but not of K. By Proposition 1, for each agreement country i signs with a member, h, of this set, coalition welfare increases by $[(\delta_h^i - \pi_i^h) + (\delta_i^h - \pi_h^i)]$, which is positive for all h. For given i, adding these gains over all h yields the result.   □

Kowalczyk and Wonnacott (1991) define a *substitute trading club* as one that leads to reduced import demand from the rest of the world, and as a *complement trading club* one leading to higher import demand from the rest of the world when evaluated at initial extra-club tariff-exclusive prices. We define here a trading club to be *neutral* if it does not affect its members' import demand from the rest of the world. For the present model, we then have the following result.

Proposition 3. Preferential trading clubs are neutral. They have no effect on non-members.

Proof. By the earlier definition of a preferential trading club, its members do not change their policy relative to non-member countries. Although income increases among the club members, equation (3) implies that their demand for imports from non-member countries does not change. Higher club income translates into higher consumption of non-traded good 0 by club members. There is no effect on costs of production, and export prices remain constant. This establishes that trade volumes and prices between club members and non-members stay constant. It follows that non-members' welfare stays constant.   □

It is an empirical question whether a trading club is substitute or complement (or neutral), and from that perspective it is not desirable that the model presented here allows only neutral clubs. However, from an analytical point of view it is essential that our model implies only neutral clubs. Indeed, the assumptions of quasi-linear preferences and constant costs were made with this very property in mind. The reason is that in order to calculate side-payments we need to introduce, in the next section, the *characteristic function*. This function measures the payoff that members of a coalition can guarantee among themselves. For the function to be defined it must, in particular, be the case that this payoff is independent of non-members' coalition choices. Neutral trading clubs guarantee that this requirement is satisfied.

Proposition 4. The grand coalition is Pareto-optimal

Proof. For any product, the grand coalition equalizes consumer prices across all countries and sets them equal to the costs of producing the good.   □

It is a question of long standing in the theory of customs unions whether the formation or expansion of a particular preferential trading club raises or lowers world welfare. The possibility that a trading club could reduce world welfare even in a competitive world economy was first demonstrated by Jacob Viner (1950). More than a quarter of a century later, Kemp and Wan (1976) managed to calm these fears when showing that, in a competitive world economy, members of a trading club can always adjust their external tariffs in such a way that non-members remain indifferent while the coalition welfare of the members increases. In recent work, however, Paul Krugman (1991) has revived Viner's concern by showing, in his model of monopolistic competition, that for reasonable assumptions on preferences world welfare is U-shaped in the number of trading clubs, with a minimum at three clubs.

A result similar to Krugman's does not hold in the present model. Rather, as shown in Figure 2, Propositions 2 and 4 imply that in our model world welfare increases monotonically—at an increasing rate, even—as preferential trading clubs are expanded and the grand coalition approached. We hasten to add that our model is even more stylized, if not unrealistic, than is Krugman's, and that the trade policy we investigate is not tariffs. Nevertheless, it does bear on the question, 'Is bilateralism bad?'[16]

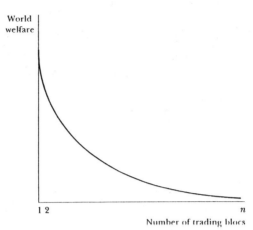

FIGURE 2

III. DIRECTION AND SIZE OF INTERNATIONAL SIDE-PAYMENTS

The agreement by all countries to charge marginal costs might not be incentive-compatible, since there may be countries that prefer to break away from such an arrangement and charge mark-up prices in some foreign markets. Assuming that GATT's objective is to implement the grand coalition of world-wide marginal cost pricing, we proceed by calculating the side-payments that will permit the world's trading nations to exploit fully the gains from trade. We do so by applying cooperative game theory to our model economy. This requires that countries can negotiate, coordinate policies and make binding commitments. It seems that these are all reasonable assumptions in the context of GATT negotiations.

We denote the set of all *players* (i.e. the world's trading nations) by $N = \{1, \ldots, n\}$. A *coalition*, i.e. a preferential trading club, is a subset $K \subseteq N$, which has $|K| = k$ members. The *payoff* that coalition K can assure itself is given by the *characteristic function* $v(K)$, which, in a world where side-payments are feasible, is a mapping from all permutations of the members in K (and non-members of K) into a real number; this number is also known as the *worth* of coalition K. The units of $v(K)$ are utils or, in our model, good 0. A game of this type is referred to as a *transferable utility game*.

The *core* of a transferable utility game is defined as the set of payoff vectors that will be blocked by no coalition of countries including coalitions containing only one country, where a vector of payoffs y is said to be *blocked* by some group of countries K if they can guarantee among themselves a higher payoff, i.e. if $\Sigma_{i \in K} y_i < v(K)$. In many games the core is empty. We show next that this is not the case here.

Define the *marginal contribution* of country i to coalition K by $[v(K) - v(K \backslash \{i\})]$, where $v(K \backslash \{i\})$ denotes the worth of coalition K when i is not a member.[17] A transferable utility game is said to be *convex* if, for $K \subseteq K'$, the marginal contribution from i joining the larger coalition K' exceeds the marginal contribution from joining the smaller coalition K, that is, if

(7) $\quad v(K') - v(K'\backslash\{i\}) \geq v(K) - v(K\backslash\{i\})$.

Proposition 2 in the previous section established that this property holds in the economy analysed here, and we can therefore rely on the following result, due to Lloyd Shapley (1971).

Theorem 1. In a convex transferable utility game the core is non-empty.

   Proof. See Shapley (1971).   □

Investigating which allocations lie in the core, and thus could be pursued by a consensus-seeking GATT, could quickly become a large undertaking. The calculations could be involved, and in case the core contains several payoff vectors, some criterion for selecting between them might be needed. Using a further result by Shapley (1971), we follow instead a more direct approach of identifying one particular payoff vector in the core, and we then assume that GATT strives to implement that vector. Admittedly, this does not model the problem of how to select between several core payoff vectors if such exist. However, we believe that this is relatively unimportant when compared with what we perceive as the immediate challenge faced by GATT: ridding the world of distortionary trade policies.

Theorem 2. The Shapley value is the central point in the core of a convex transferable utility game.

   Proof. See Shapley (1971).   □

The *Shapley value* for the transferable utility game (N, v) is the payoff vector $\Phi(N, v)$ that assigns to country i

(8) $\quad \Phi^i(N, v) = \sum_{K \subseteq N} \dfrac{(|K|-1)!(n-|K|)!}{n!}$

$$\times [v(K) - v(K\backslash\{i\})], \qquad i = 1, \ldots, n.$$

Calculating the Shapley value directly by use of this definition is, in general, quite involved.[18] However, we can establish the very helpful result for the class of economies where the gains from cooperating are a given constant that the Shapley value splits equally the gains from cooperation between two parties.

Lemma. Let (N, v) be a transferable utility game. If there exist fixed numbers g_j^i, for $i \in N$ and $j \in N$, such that, for all $K \subseteq N$ and all $i \notin K$, $v(K \cup \{i\}) = v(K) + v(i) + \sum_{j \in K} (g_i^j + g_j^i)$, then the Shapley value is

(9) $\quad \Phi^i(N, v) = v(i) + \frac{1}{2} \sum_{j \in N} (g_i^j + g_j^i)$

for all $i \in N$.

Proof. Let the marginal contribution of i to K be $v(i) + \sum_{j \in K} (g_i^j + g_j^i)$. Then (8) becomes

$$\Phi^i(N, v) = \sum_{\substack{K \subseteq N \\ i \in K}} \frac{(|K| - 1)!(n - |K|)!}{n!} [v(i) + \sum_{j \in K} (g_i^j + g_j^i)]$$

$$= v(i) + \sum_{j=1}^{n} (g_i^j + g_j^i) \sum_{\substack{K \subseteq N \\ i, j \in K}} \frac{(|K| - 1)!(n - |K|)!}{n!}.$$

Simplifying yields

$$\sum_{\substack{K \subseteq N \\ i, j \in K}} \frac{(|K| - 1)!(n - |K|)!}{n!} = \sum_{k=1}^{n} \sum_{\substack{i, j \in K \\ |K| = k}} \frac{(k - 1)!(n - k)!}{n!}$$

$$= \sum_{k=1}^{n} \frac{(k - 1)!(n - k)!}{n!} \frac{(n - 2)!}{(n - k)!(k - 2)!}$$

$$= \sum_{k=1}^{n} \frac{(k - 1)!(n - 2)!}{n!(k - 2)!}$$

$$= \sum_{k=1}^{n} \frac{(k - 1)}{n(n - 1)}$$

$$= \frac{1}{n(n - 1)} \sum_{k=1}^{n} (k - 1) = \tfrac{1}{2}. \qquad \square$$

Let S_j^i be consumer's surplus in country i if country j charges only marginal costs on its exports to i, and $(S_j^i - \delta_j^i)$ be consumer's surplus in i if j charges its monopoly price. We can then express the characteristic function for coalition K as

$$(10) \qquad v(K) = \sum_{i \in K} \left\{ \bar{l}_0^i + \sum_{j \in N} S_j^i - \sum_{j \notin K} \delta_j^i + \sum_{j \notin K} \pi_j^i \right\}.$$

The first term is the coalition members' aggregrate endowment of good 0. The second term is total consumer's surplus for all members of K if the grand coalition forms. The third term is the loss in coalition K consumer's surplus when some of the world's countries are not in preferential trading club K. (Thus the second and third terms together give actual consumer's surplus.) Finally, the last term is total profits earned by firms in trading club K when selling in markets outside of K. For the special case, where a coalition consists of a single-member h, (10) becomes

$$(11) \qquad v(h) = \bar{l}_0^h + \sum_{j \in N} S_j^h - \sum_{j \neq h} \delta_j^h + \sum_{j \neq h} \pi_j^h.$$

As argued in the proof of Proposition 1, if $h \notin K$, then

$$(12) \qquad v(K \cup \{h\}) = v(K) + v(h) + \sum_{j \in K} [(\delta_h^j - \pi_h^j) + (\delta_j^h - \pi_j^h)].$$

Setting $h = i$ in this equation, and defining $g_i^j = \delta_i^j - \pi_i^j$ and $g_j^i = \delta_j^i - \pi_j^i$, it follows that the lemma applies to the world economy analysed here. Substitution of

(11) into (9) thus yields,

$$\Phi^i(N, v) = \bar{I}_0^i + \sum_{j \in N} S_j^i - \sum_{j \neq i} \delta_j^i + \sum_{j \neq i} \pi_j^i$$

$$+ \tfrac{1}{2} \sum_{j \neq i} [(\delta_i^j - \pi_i^j) + (\delta_j^i - \pi_j^i)]$$

$$= \bar{I}_0^i + \sum_{j=1}^n S_j^i + \tfrac{1}{2} \sum_{j=1}^n [(\pi_j^i - \delta_j^i) - (\pi_i^j - \delta_i^j)].$$

The following result has hence been proved.

Theorem 3. In the preferential trading club game (N, v), the Shapley value is given by

$$(13) \qquad \Phi^i(N, v) = \bar{I}_0^i + \sum_{j=1}^n S_j^i + \tfrac{1}{2} \sum_{j=1}^n [(\pi_j^i - \delta_j^i) - (\pi_i^j - \delta_i^j)], \qquad i = 1, \ldots, n.$$

If the grand coalition forms but no side-payments take place, country i obtains

$$(14) \qquad \bar{I}_0^i + \sum_{j=1}^n S_j^i, \qquad i = 1, \ldots, n.$$

Together, (13) and (14) imply an alternative interpretation of the Shapley value in a model where the gains from cooperation are constant: it is the payoff vector that assigns to each country what it would receive if the grand coalition formed but no side-payments took place plus half of what the country would gain relative to its trading partners were the grand coalition to break up. Indeed, subtracting (14) from (13) yields the transfer scheme that implements the Shapley value. The analysis thus yields the following policy recommendation for the model under consideration.

Proposition 5. Forming the grand coalition, and implementing the vector of international side-payments $T(N, v)$ which assigns to country i the net transfer

$$(15) \qquad T^i = \tfrac{1}{2} \sum_{j=1}^n [(\pi_j^i - \delta_j^i) - (\pi_i^j - \delta_i^j)], \qquad i = 1, \ldots, n,$$

will bring GATT into the core.

For any country i, this formula determines its overall net transfer by comparing i's welfare gains from not trading at costs with each of its partners j, with the welfare gains of each j from not trading at costs with i. The overall net transfer to or from i is then found by adding these differences over all i's partners. Thus, $(\pi_j^i - \delta_j^i)$ is country i's net welfare gain form charging its mark-up price on country j and have j retaliate, while $(\pi_i^j - \delta_i^j)$ is j's net welfare gain from not trading preferentially with i.[19] For any bilateral comparison, equation (15) prescribes that the country with larger net gains from non-cooperation receives a transfer from the country with smaller net gains from non-cooperation. Alternatively, the country that gains more from cooperation pays a fee to the country gaining less from cooperation to induce a preferential trade arrangement. Country j gains more from cooperation with country i, (a) the less elastic is j's demand for good i, (b) the lower are i's costs, (c) the more elastic is i's demand for good j, and (d) the higher are j's costs. (We note for the sake of completeness that the mechanism is balanced: the sum of receipts equals the sum of payments.)

It is somewhat at odds with observed international income transfers, which show a tendency of going from richer to poorer countries, that the side-payments implied by (15) are independent of nations' relative income levels.[20] The reason is that in our model transfers have the very specific, and narrow, function of being the price for obtaining a preferential trading arrangement, while actual income transfers serve additional purposes, including foreign aid's objective of making incomes more equal across countries. The financial mechanism derived in this paper would co-exist with other transfer schemes, and it might not be of sufficient importance to raise substantially or reverse the direction of the transfers that we actually observe.[21]

The Appendix describes how consumer's surplus, profits, and income can be expressed as functions of the model's parameters. Drawing on these expressions, Table 1 presents some illustrative examples of the side-payments implied

TABLE 1

$\theta 1$	$\theta 2$	$\theta 3$	$\theta 4$		Y	T	$T/Y(\%)$	$T/(Y-1)(\%)$
0·3	0·5	0·7	0·9	for country 1	1018·78	18·03	1·77	95·98
$\beta 1$	$\beta 2$	$\beta 3$	$\beta 4$	for country 30	1037·57	−3·54	−0·34	−9·42
10	10	10	10	for country 60	1075·14	−7·20	−0·67	−9·59
$l1$	$l2$	$l3$	$l4$	for country 95	1056·35	−7·29	−0·69	−12·93
1000	1000	1000	1000					
$\theta 1$	$\theta 2$	$\theta 3$	$\theta 4$					
0·3	0·5	0·7	0·9	for country 1	1008·20	6·12	0·61	74·61
$\beta 1$	$\beta 2$	$\beta 3$	$\beta 4$	for country 30	1016·40	0·43	0·04	2·63
100	10	10	10	for country 60	1024·60	−3·23	−0·32	−13·14
$l1$	$l2$	$l3$	$l4$	for country 95	1032·81	−3·32	−0·32	−10·12
1000	1000	1000	1000					
$\theta 1$	$\theta 2$	$\theta 3$	$\theta 4$					
0·3	0·5	0·7	0·9	for country 1	5008·20	6·12	0·12	74·61
$\beta 1$	$\beta 2$	$\beta 3$	$\beta 4$	for country 30	1016·40	0·43	0·04	2·63
100	10	10	10	for country 60	1024·60	−3·23	−0·32	−13·14
$l1$	$l2$	$l3$	$l4$	for country 95	1032·81	−3·32	−0·32	−10·12
5000	1000	1000	1000					

by expression (15). We assume that a GATT negotiation round has 100 participants, and that they can be divided into four equal-sized groups where countries within a group are identical. We assume also that countries have identical, but not symmetric, preferences with demand for good 1 being relatively inelastic, demand for goods 2 and 3 more elastic, and demand for good 4 most elastic. The table contains three sets of calculations. In the first set, the four groups are identical with respect to costs and endowment of good 0, as given by l. The table shows that side-payments go from each of the three groups producing the goods in relatively elastic demand to group 1, which produces the relatively inelastically demanded good. The next set of calculations shows the effect of raising costs of production in group 1. The net transfer to countries in group 1 falls to about one-third of the transfer in the first calculation, and net payments by each of the other three groups fall; group 2 even becomes a net recipient. The final calculation illustrates how raising the endowment of good

0 in each of the countries in group 1 raises income Y in group 1 but has no effect on transfers.

In all three cases, and independent of whether countries receive or pay, are the transfers less than 2% of national income Y. As discussed in the Introduction, this is the same order of magnitude as Richard Baldwin's (1992) estimate of the EFTA countries' payments to the EC countries in connection with the European Economic Area. Table 1 reveals, furthermore, that the side-payments can be a substantial fraction of a country's gains from trade as measured by $(Y-I)$. In all three sets of calculations payments are about 10% of the gains from trade while receipts range from about 2% to a remarkable 96%. In fact, it is possible that a country receives transfers that exceed the size of its gains from trade.[22]

IV. WHEN ARE INTERNATIONAL SIDE-PAYMENTS NEEDED?

Under which conditions can the global trading system—as modelled in this paper—reach a first-best trading equilibrium without a financial mechanism? We stated in (14) that country i's surplus from the grand coalition equals $\bar{I}_0 + \sum_{j=1}^{n} S_j^i$ in the absence of international side-payments. When the grand coalition forms but no side-payments take place, the surplus to a group of countries K is

$$(16) \quad v(K) = \sum_{i \in K} \left\{ \bar{I}_0 + \sum_{j \in N} S_j^i \right\}.$$

The grand coalition without side-payments is in the core if and only if for all $K \subseteq N$ the surplus from the grand coalition exceeds the surplus from any other preferential trading arrangement, that is, if the following inequality holds

$$(17) \quad \sum_{i \in K} \left\{ \bar{I}_0 + \sum_{j \in N} S_j^i \right\} \geq \sum_{i \in K} \left\{ \bar{I}_0 + \sum_{j \in N} S_j^i - \sum_{j \in K} \delta_j^i + \sum_{j \in K} \pi_j^i \right\},$$

where the right-hand side of the inequality is the worth of coalition K as defined earlier by expression (10). Proposition 6 follows immediately.

Proposition 6. The grand coalition without side-payments is in the core if and only if

$$(18) \quad \sum_{i \in K} \sum_{j \in K} \delta_j^i \geq \sum_{i \in K} \sum_{j \in K} \pi_j^i.$$

This inequality will not necessarily hold since it is possible that, for some K, profits earned by members of K, which are given by the right-hand side of this expression, exceed the loss in consumer's surplus in K from retaliation, which is the left-hand side of the expression.

In the special case where all countries are identical with respect to tastes and costs, (18) reduces to

$$(19) \quad k(n-k)\delta \geq k(n-k)\pi$$

which is always satisfied since $\delta \geq \pi$. Hence when countries are identical or almost identical there is no need to use side-payments in a global trade negotiation.

These findings are consistent with earlier work. Raymond Riezman (1985) presents a three-country example where a single country blocks global free trade even though the other countries respond by forming a customs union which sets its optimal external tariff. He finds that global free trade is less likely to be upset if countries are similar. In an analysis of the role of country size in blocking global free trade, Kennan and Riezman (1988) argue that, in a two-country exchange economy, the larger country, because of its relatively more elastic offer curve, is the likely beneficiary from a tariff war (see also Jensen and Thursby 1980). They extend that analysis to three countries in Kennan and Riezman (1990), and present, among other examples, one where global free trade is upset by a pair of countries forming a customs union (or a free trade area).

V. CONCLUSION

This paper has calculated exact values of income transfers that will induce countries to cooperate and form the grand coalition in a world where a large number of countries produce and trade a similarly large number of goods. The formula for the transfers confirms the interpretation of the role of an international income transfer mechanism as one of reining in stronger nations: in order to establish a globally Pareto-optimal trading order, it may be necessary to tax those that have much to gain from it, and subsidize those that do not. While perhaps unappealing at first glance, such transfers have the attractive feature of inducing nations with large positive externalities on other countries to take part in the global process.

The model that we use to derive the international transfer schema is highly stylized. It has the unusual feature that global free trade is not Pareto-optimal. The model implies also that countries will not use tariffs; rather, the policy game between nations that is stressed in this paper—although not the only one implied by the model—is essentially one of regulation. These idiosyncrasies are a consequence of our forcing the problem of global policy coordination with international side-payments into a very simple model of international trade to which the characteristic function approach applies. We do not consider them appealing. However, they do render in return an explicit formula for international transfers in a world of many countries and many goods. Furthermore, situations where *laissez-faire* fails to be Pareto-optimal are becoming increasingly urgent: just witness the need for international cooperation on environmental issues which, we believe, is another area where our model transfer mechanism could be applicable. In conclusion, we consider this to be only a first step towards proposing a financial mechanism for GATT.

APPENDIX

From equation (3) in the text, the inverse demand function in country i for good j is

(A1) $p_j^i = (c_j^i)^{(\theta_j - 1)}, \qquad i, j = 1, \ldots, n,$

which implies that the area under the demand curve is given by

$$(A2) \quad \int_0^{c^*} p_j^i \, dc_j^i = \frac{1}{\theta_j^i} (c_j^i)^{\theta_j^i}, \quad i, j = 1, \ldots, n,$$

where c^* is a limit of integration. If good j is obtained at cost, then $p_j^i = \beta^j$, and $c_j^i = (\beta^j)^{1/(\theta_j^i - 1)}$. Substituting this demand into (A2) and subtracting from the resulting expression total spending by consumer i on good j, which equals

$$(A3) \quad p_j^i c_j^i = (\beta^j)^{\theta_j^i/(\theta_j^i - 1)}, \quad i, j = 1, \ldots, n,$$

yields consumer i's surplus when j is purchased at cost to be:

$$(A4) \quad S_j^i = [(1 - \theta_j^i)/\theta_j^i](\beta^j)^{\theta_j^i/(\theta_j^i - 1)}, \quad i, j = 1, \ldots, n.$$

If good j is purchased instead at the monopoly price $p_j^i = \beta^j/\theta_j^i$, then $c_j^i = (\beta^j/\theta_j^i)^{1/(\theta_j^i - 1)}$ and i's spending on good j equals

$$(A5) \quad p_j^i c_j^i = (\beta^j/\theta_j^i)^{\theta_j^i/(\theta_j^i - 1)}, \quad i, j = 1, \ldots, n.$$

Let $(S_j^i)'$ be consumer's surplus in i if j is purchased at the monopoly price. Substituting the corresponding demand into (A2), and subtracting (A5), then gives

$$(A6) \quad (S_j^i)' = [(1 - \theta_j^i)/\theta_j^i](\beta^j/\theta_j^i)^{\theta_j^i/(\theta_j^i - 1)}, \quad i, j = 1, \ldots, n.$$

Defining $\delta_j^i = S_j^i - (S_j^i)'$, and subtracting (A6) from (A4), gives the increase in consumer's surplus from reducing the price of j to marginal costs as

$$(A7) \quad \delta_j^i = [(1 - \theta_j^i)/\theta_j^i][1 - (\theta_j^i)^{\theta_j^i/(1 - \theta_j^i)}](\beta^j)^{\theta_j^i/(\theta_j^i - 1)}, \quad i, j = 1, \ldots, n.$$

Firm i's profits from sales to j are found by substituting equations (6) and (3) of the text (the latter properly relabelled) into equation (5) of the text:

$$(A8) \quad \pi_j^i = (1 - \theta_i^j)(\beta^i/\theta_i^j)^{\theta_i^j/(\theta_i^j - 1)}, \quad i, j = 1, \ldots, n.$$

Finally, income in country i, when the grand coalition forms, is given by

$$(A9) \quad Y^i = \bar{I}_0^i + \sum_{j=1}^n S_j^i, \quad i, j = 1, \ldots, n.$$

ACKNOWLEDGMENTS

We are grateful to Robert Baldwin and an anonymous referee for helpful comments. We have benefited also from comments at the 1992 NBER–CEPR Trade Policy Conference, the NBER Summer Institute, the North American Summer Meeting of the Econometric Society, the Midwest Meetings, and at seminars at Albany, Brigham Young, and Cornell. We thank, in particular, Pat Conway, Alan Deardorff, Konstantinos Gatsios and Sang-Seung Yi. Aly Jeddy provided helpful research assistance.

NOTES

1. It must be emphasized that both unilateral and plurilateral initiatives can promote rather than hinder a liberal trading order. Thus, a unilateral threat of tariffs by a large country can be used to pry open otherwise closed foreign markets, and preferential arrangements—of which regional ones constitute one example—certainly have the potential for being stepping stones to global free trade.
2. The Draft Final Act (also known as the Dunkel Draft) addresses both types of omissions. It attempts to bring agriculture and textiles under GATT discipline, and it contains proposals on both TRIPs and TRIMs. It creates also a new body entitled the Multilateral Trade Organization, whose members would accept not only the Dunkel Draft in its entirety but also the Tokyo Round Subsidies Code, a new Disputes Settlement Understanding and a Trade Policy Review Mechanism.
3. Ten years after its completion, only 24 countries had ratified the subsidies code. (See Jackson 1989.)
4. The Atlantic Council of the United States (1976) recommended in its GATT Plus proposal that assigning votes to contracting parties according to their role in world trade, instead of

the current system of one nation–one vote, would enable GATT to work faster and more effectively. Robert Baldwin (1993) has revisited the idea most recently.

5. An additional problem with GATT's current emphasis on unanimity has been pointed out in Kowalczyk (1990), who shows that, contrary to conventional wisdom, a small country prefers a preferential trading arrangement to unilateral free trade, and furthermore that it might prefer joining an exclusive customs union or free trade area to supporting a global effort at liberalizing trade.

6. The European Community (1993) contains the budget, while the European Free Trade Association (1987) has a brief survey of some EFTA income transfer programmes.

7. Richard Baldwin (1992) estimates that the annual costs to EFTA from it transfer to the EC are less than 1% of EFTA's income in 1992.

8. Faruk Gul (1989) presents a non-cooperative bargaining game that has the Shapley value as its solution.

9. Kyle Bagwell and Robert Staiger (1993) investigate how permitting the formation of free trade areas affects which most-favoured-nation tariffs can otherwise be supported as equilibrium rates.

10. As shown in Daniel Gros's (1987) analysis of tariffs in a Krugman-type model of monopolistic competition, linear preferences imply non-zero cross-price effects, and hence bystanders would tend to get affected from others integrating. We assume quasi-linear preferences as a simple way to avoid spill-overs on to outsiders (which is crucial for our later ability to define the characteristic function).

11. Demand for good 0 is found by substituting (3) into (2) for all traded goods, and then solving (2) for c_0^i.

12. All results of the paper, including the formulae for side-payments, would be unaltered had we investigated import subsidies instead. We note also that, because of the assumed preferences, positive import taxes would never be observed in the world economy specified here as they reduce both consumer's surplus in the importing country and profits in the exporting one.

13. The assumption that governments always make their domestic firms charge only marginal costs in their home markets has the additional effect of precluding dumping.

14. If, in this model, governments are allowed to restrict prices on imports, then there is no room for cooperation since some governments will always use an import price ceiling and others will have no reason not to retaliate. The only equilibrium will be the non-cooperative, but Pareto-optimal, one where all countries use import price ceilings. Since the objective of our analysis is to investigate how side-payments can play a role in inducing cooperation, we assume that countries cannot use import price ceilings. Only ceilings on export prices and on the prices charged in firms' domestic markets are available policy instruments.

15. We do not require that the compensatory payments are actually executed. Thus, the welfare criterion is that of a *potential* Pareto Improvement.

16. Alan Deardorff and Robert Stern (1994) present an example where members of preferential clubs are chosen by random device. They show that under certain conditions expected world welfare is monotonically increasing as the number of blocs falls.

17. The marginal contribution can alternatively be defined as $v(K \cup \{i\}) - v(K)$, in which case $v(K)$ is the worth of K when i is not a member.

18. For discussions of the Shapley value see, among others, Friedman (1977), Harsanyi (1977) and Shubik (1984). Hart and Mas-Colell (1989) have recently demonstrated the existence of, as well as characterized, a function, denoted the *potential function*, which facilitates obtaining the Shapley value.

19. Either of these net welfare gains can be positive, negative, or zero.

20. Intra-EC payments, for example, tend to run from richer to poorer member countries.

21. As an aside, if transfers according to (15) were applied within a sub-group of countries forming a preferential trading club, then no group of potential members would want to block the coalition consisting of all the members of that sub-group. This has interesting implications for current problems in the EC.

22. However, a country would never pay more than it gains if autarky is an option.

REFERENCES

ATLANTIC COUNCIL OF THE UNITED STATES (1976). *GATT Plus: A Proposal for Trade Reform.* New York: Praeger.

BAGWELL, K. and STAIGER, R. W. (1993). Multilateral tariff formation during the formation of regional free trade areas. National Bureau of Economic Research Working Paper no. 4364.

BALDWIN, R. (1992). The economic logic of EFTA countries joining the EEA and the EC. EFTA Occasional Paper no. 41.

BALDWIN, R. E. (1993). Adapting the GATT to a more regionalised world: a political economy perspective. In Kym Anderson and Richard Baldwin (eds.), *Regional Integration and the Global Trading System*. New York, Harvester Wheatsheaf.

DEARDORFF, A. V. and STERN, R. M. (1994). Multilateral trade negotiations and preferential trading arrangements. In Alan V. Deardorff and Robert M. Stern (eds.), *Analytical and Negotiating Issues in the Global Trading System*. Ann Arbor: The University of Michigan Press.

EUROPEAN COMMUNITY (1992). *Agreement on the European Economic Area*. Brussels: EC Council Secretariat.

—— (1993). *European Economy*, no. 54. Brussels: Directorate-General for Economic and Financial Affairs.

EUROPEAN FREE TRADE ASSOCIATION (1987). *Det Europeiske Frihandelsforbund*. Geneva: EFTA Secretariat.

FRIEDMAN, J. W. (1977). *Oligopoly and the Theory of Games*. Amsterdam: North-Holland.

GRINOLS, E. (1981). An extension of the Kemp–Wan theorem on the formation of customs unions. *Journal of International Economics*, **11**, 259–66.

GROS, D. (1987). A note on the optimal tariff, retaliation, and the welfare loss from tariff wars in a framework with intra-industry trade. *Journal of International Economics*, **23**, 357–67.

GUL, F. (1989). Bargaining foundations of Shapley value. *Econometrica*, **57**, 81–95.

HARSANYI, J. C. (1977). *Rational Behavior and Bargaining Equilibrium in Games and Social Situations*. Cambridge University Press.

HART, S. and MAS-COLELL, A. (1989). Potential, value and consistency. *Econometrica*, **57**, 589–614.

JACKSON, J. (1989). *The World Trading System*. Cambridge, Mass: MIT Press.

JENSEN, R. and THURSBY, M. (1980). Free trade: two non-cooperative equilibrium approaches. Ohio State University, Department of Economics Working Paper no. 58.

JOHNSON, H. G. (1953). Optimum tariffs and retaliation. *Review of Economic Studies*, **21**, 142–53.

KEMP, M. C. and WAN, H. Y. (1976). An elementary proposition concerning the formation of customs unions. *Journal of International Economics*, **6**, 95–7.

KENNAN, J. and RIEZMAN, R. (1988). Do big countries win tariff wars? *International Economic Review*, **29**, 81–5.

—— and —— (1990). Optimal tariff equilibria with customs unions. *Canadian Journal of Economics*, **23**, 70–83.

KOWALCZYK, C. (1990). Welfare and customs unions. NBER Working Paper no. 3476.

—— and WONNACOTT, R. (1991). Substitute and complement trading clubs. Dartmouth College, Department of Economics Working Paper no. 91-16.

KRUGMAN, P. R. (1991). Is bilateralism bad? In Elhanan Helpman and Assaf Razin (eds.), *International Trade and Trade Policy*. Cambridge, Mass.: MIT Press.

RIEZMAN, R. (1985). Customs unions and the core. *Journal of International Economics*, **19**, 355–65.

SHAPLEY, L. S. (1971). Cores of convex games. *International Journal of Game Theory*, **1**, 11–26.

SHUBIK, M. (1984). *Game Theory in the Social Sciences: Concepts and Solutions*. Cambridge, Mass.: MIT Press.

VINER, J. (1950). *The Customs Union Issue*. New York: Carnegie Endowment for International Peace.

C
Integration and Growth

[27]

Measurable Dynamic Gains from Trade

Richard E. Baldwin

Columbia University

Productive factors, such as human and physical capital, accumulate, and trade policy can affect their steady-state levels. Consequently, in addition to the usual static effects, trade liberalization has dynamic effects on output and welfare as the economy moves to its new steady state. The output impact of this dynamic effect is measurable and appears to be quite large. The welfare impact of this dynamic effect is also measurable. The size of this dynamic gain from trade depends on the wedge between social and private returns to capital. Rough numerical estimates of the output and welfare effects are provided.

Empirical researchers consistently find that trade liberalizations raise aggregate income by an amount that is negligible (0.1 percent [Deardorff and Stern 1986]) or small (8.6 percent [Harris and Cox 1984]). The oral tradition in international trade counters this "Harberger triangle problem" with the assertion that the most important gains from trade are dynamic, not static. Empirical studies of trade liberalizations ignore such factors since dynamic trade effects are poorly understood and supposedly impossible to measure. This paper exposits and measures one type of dynamic effect of trade liberalization. The results confirm the oral tradition by showing that dynamic output effects are large. The source of this particular dynamic effect is simple. If a liberalization raises the return to capital, it will induce

I gratefully acknowledge the comments and suggestions of Elhanan Helpman, Peter Svedberg, Victor Norman, Jim Markusen, and Torsten Persson. Avinash Dixit suggested the use of Laplace transforms in gauging welfare effects. I thank the Institute for International Economic Studies in Stockholm for providing a fertile environment for this work and the Centre for Economic Policy Research for financial support.

[*Journal of Political Economy*, 1992, vol. 100, no. 1]

capital formation and thereby raise output more than static effects alone would predict. Since capital accumulation takes time, the effect shows up as a medium-term rise in the growth rate. The welfare gain from this effect is also measurable and depends on the divergence between the social and private returns to capital.

Ricardo (1815) first emphasized the link between trade and steady-state factor supplies. In his model the steady-state growth rate is zero because of diminishing returns; however, trade postponed the arrival date of the steady state since "England's agriculture is stationary, but Manchester and Birmingham make her the workshop of the world which pays in food and primary products for the expanding output of the workshop" (Findlay 1984, p. 190). Stiglitz (1970), Findlay (1978), Srinivasan and Bhagwati (1980), Findlay and Kierzkowski (1983), Galor (1989), Manning and Markusen (1989), and others have explored the link more formally. Findlay (1984) and Smith (1984) survey the literature. None of these papers quantifies the output or welfare impact of induced capital formation, and most assume a constant savings rate. This effect is quite distinct from the Grossman-Helpman models of trade and growth.[1] Those models link long-run growth rates to trade policy. The current paper looks at the link between liberalization and the steady-state level of factors. Baldwin (1989) studies the impact of liberalization on growth but does not present a formal model and does not consider welfare implications.

Section I presents the basic model and a comparative steady-state analysis of liberalization. Section II examines the welfare consequences. Section III quantifies the output and welfare effects for an explicit model. Section IV presents concluding remarks.

I. Induced Capital Formation

By the Stolper-Samuelson theorem, trade liberalization may raise or lower the return to capital. Consequently, liberalization has effects similar to a subsidy (tax) on the steady-state capital stock. The resulting capital accumulation (decumulation) amplifies (mitigates) the standard output effects of the liberalization. Section III presents an explicit model that permits quantification; however, to emphasize their generality, the results are first derived in an implicit model. Assume that the world's real output, y, is well approximated by $f[k, \tau]$, where k is the world capital stock (other factors are suppressed for convenience), τ is an index of global trade barriers, $f_k > 0$, and $f_\tau < 0$ (subscripts denote partial derivatives). The real return on forgone

---

[1] The seminal papers are Grossman and Helpman (1990, 1991). Also see Krugman (1988) and Murphy, Shleifer, and Vishny (1988).

consumption, r, is assumed to be well approximated by $r[k, \tau]$, where $r_k < 0$ and r_τ may be positive or negative (according to the Stolper-Samuelson theorem). Furthermore, assume that investment is forgone consumption. If one ignores depreciation,

$$\dot{k} = y - c, \tag{1}$$

where c is real consumption. The representative, infinitely lived consumer maximizes

$$U = \frac{1}{1 - (1/\sigma)} \int_0^\infty e^{-\rho t} c(t)^{1 - (1/\sigma)} dt \tag{2}$$

subject to a lifetime budget constraint. Here ρ and σ are the constant discount rate and the intertemporal elasticity of substitution. The necessary conditions imply

$$\frac{\dot{c}}{c} = \sigma[r(t) - \rho]. \tag{3}$$

Denoting steady-state levels of c and k with a bar, we get

$$\bar{c} = f[\bar{k}, \tau], \quad r[\bar{k}, \tau] = \rho. \tag{4}$$

The eigenvalues of the Jacobian evaluated at $\bar{c}$ and $\bar{k}$ are $f_k \pm [(f_k^2 - 4\sigma r_k)^{1/2}/2]$. Since $r_k < 0$ and $f_k > 0$, the system is saddle path stable.

Liberalization has two effects on income in this model:

$$\frac{dy/y}{d\tau/\tau} = \left(\frac{\partial f/y}{\partial k/k}\right)\left(-\frac{\partial r/r}{\partial \tau/\tau}\Big/\frac{\partial r/r}{\partial k/k}\right) + \frac{\partial f/y}{\partial \tau/\tau}. \tag{5}$$

The second term captures the usual static efficiency effects. The first term reflects the induced capital formation effect. If liberalization raises (lowers) r, it induces capital accumulation (decumulation), thereby amplifying (mitigating) the output impact of the static effect. The welfare interpretation of this add-on effect is not as straightforward as the output effect. To the infinitely lived consumer, the rise in consumption due to induced capital accumulation is largely, or entirely, offset by the necessary forgone consumption.

II. Welfare: Dynamic Gains from Trade

The direct way to measure the welfare effects would be to solve for the adjustment path of c and evaluate it with the utility function. Since the system is nonlinear, this is not possible. Another approach would be to linearize the system around the steady state and work with the resulting linear system. Since my aim is to show that dynamic effects are large, an approach that is correct only for very small changes in c and y is unsatisfactory. Judd (1985, 1987) shows that welfare effects can be obtained without an analytic solution for the consumption path. To see this, note that the optimal consumption path is a function of time and τ. If we differentiate (2) (evaluated at $\bar{c}$) with respect to τ, $dU/d\tau$ is $\bar{c}^{-1/\sigma} \int_0^\infty e^{-\rho t} c_\tau(t)\,dt$. In other words, the welfare impact depends on the Laplace transform of the induced change in the consumption path. This comment is germane since Judd (1985) showed that it is easier to deal with the Laplace transforms of state variables' paths than with the paths themselves.

Consider a general perturbation of the time path of τ. Inserting $\tau[1 + \epsilon h(t)]$ in (1) and (3) in place of τ, where $h(t)$ is an arbitrary time path, differentiating with respect to ϵ, and evaluating the result at $\epsilon = 0$ yield

$$\begin{pmatrix} \dot{c}_\epsilon \\ \dot{k}_\epsilon \end{pmatrix} = \mathbf{J} \begin{pmatrix} c_\epsilon \\ k_\epsilon \end{pmatrix} + \begin{pmatrix} \tau\bar{c}\sigma h(t)\,r_\tau \\ \tau h(t) f_\tau \end{pmatrix}, \tag{6}$$

where

$$\mathbf{J} = \begin{pmatrix} 0 & \bar{c}\sigma r_k \\ -1 & f_k \end{pmatrix},$$

and the Jacobian is evaluated at $\bar{c}$ and $\bar{k}$. Next, multiply by $e^{-\omega t}$, integrate over time, and then integrate the left-hand side by parts to get

$$\begin{pmatrix} C_\epsilon(\omega) \\ K_\epsilon(\omega) \end{pmatrix} = (\omega\mathbf{I} - \mathbf{J})^{-1} \begin{pmatrix} \tau\bar{c}\sigma H(\omega)\,r_\tau + c_\epsilon(0) \\ \tau H(\omega) f_\tau \end{pmatrix}, \tag{7}$$

where $C_\epsilon(\omega)$, $K_\epsilon(\omega)$, and $H_\epsilon(\omega)$ are the Laplace transforms of c_ϵ, k_ϵ, and h_ϵ; for example, $C_\epsilon(\omega)$ is defined as $\int_0^\infty e^{-\omega t} c_\epsilon(t)\,dt$. Notice that integration by parts turns the differential equations into an algebraic system in Laplace transforms. Since capital does not jump, the only unknown in (7) is the size of the consumption jump at time 0, $c_\epsilon(0)$.

By the transversality condition, $K_\epsilon(\omega)$ must remain finite for all values of ω. Consider ω equal to the positive eigenvalue of $\mathbf{J}$ (call this μ). Since $\mu\mathbf{I} - \mathbf{J}$ is singular, it must be true that (see Judd [1985] for details)

$$\tau\bar{c}\sigma H(\mu)r_\tau + c_\epsilon(0) - \mu\tau H(\mu) f_\tau = 0. \tag{8}$$

This fact pins down $c_\epsilon(0)$, so the welfare impact is

$$\frac{dU/d\epsilon}{\bar{c}^{-1/\sigma}} = \tau\left(\left(\frac{\rho - f_k}{\Delta}\right)\{\bar{c}\sigma r_\tau[H(\rho) - H(\mu)] + H(\mu) f_\tau \mu\}\right.$$

$$\left. + \left(\frac{\bar{c}\sigma r_k}{\Delta}\right)[f_\tau H(\rho)]\right), \tag{9}$$

where Δ is the determinant of $\rho\mathbf{I} - \mathbf{J}$, and all partials are evaluated at $\bar{c}$ and $\bar{k}$. For many policy changes, $h(t)$, it is possible to obtain a closed-form solution for $H(\omega)$. For such $h(t)$, it is a straightforward exercise to evaluate (9). For example, in the case of a one-off change in τ,

$$
\frac{dU/\bar{U}}{d\tau/\tau} \Big/ \frac{dU/\bar{U}}{dc/c} = \left[\left(\frac{1}{\rho}\right)\left(\frac{\partial y/\bar{y}}{\partial\tau/\tau}\right) \right]
$$
$$
+ \left[\left(\frac{\rho - f_k}{\bar{c}\sigma r_k + \rho^2 - \rho f_k}\right)\sigma\rho\left(\frac{1}{\rho} - \frac{1}{\mu}\right)\left(\frac{\partial r/\bar{r}}{\partial\tau/\tau}\right) \right].
$$
(10)

This expression is easy to interpret. The first term is equal to the present discounted value of the static gain. The second term captures the welfare effect of the induced capital formation. If there are no external economies of scale in the employment of capital, then $r[\bar{k}, \tau]$ $= f_k[\bar{k}, \tau] = \rho$, so the dynamic gain from trade is zero. Although induced capital formation amplifies the output effect, it does not contribute to welfare (as predicted by the envelope theorem). The consumer is optimizing (taking τ as a parameter) between consumption today and savings that will yield consumption in the future. For small changes in τ, the change in the objective function is the same with and without reoptimizing on k.

If there are external economies of scale or other distortions such as taxes, the social return to capital may exceed the private rate, so there will be dynamic gains from trade due to induced capital formation. To see this, note that with external economies $r[\bar{k}, \tau]$ need not equal the social marginal product of capital, $f_k[\bar{k}, \tau]$. Consequently, ρ can be less than $f_k[\bar{k}, \tau]$. The determinant of $\rho\mathbf{I} - \mathbf{J}$ is negative and the positive eigenvalue of $\mathbf{J}$ is greater than $r[\bar{k}, \tau]$, so the second term in (10) has the same sign as $r_\tau[\bar{k}, \tau]$. Proposition 1 summarizes this discussion.

PROPOSITION 1. *Necessary condition for dynamic gains from trade.*—If the social and private returns to capital are identical, induced capital formation has no effect on welfare on the margin. If the social rate exceeds the private rate, then induced capital formation has a positive welfare effect on the margin *only if* the liberalization raises the return to capital. If the liberalization lowers the return to capital, the dynamic welfare effects tend to offset the static gains from trade.

The result that induced capital formation may lower welfare should be interpreted in the light of the theory of the second best. External economies drive a wedge between the private and social rates of return. In all such cases, many types of intervention may improve welfare. The best policy (if one ignores the efficiency cost of government revenue) is to subsidize capital formation directly *and* liberalize trade. Evaluating the exact impact of a large policy change would require the solution of nonlinear differential equations. Nevertheless, extension of the envelope theorem implies that even when the social and private returns to capital coincide, a large liberalization leads to dynamic gains from trade.

III. An Explicit Model

This section adopts an explicit model that enables quantification of the positive and welfare effects. As we shall see, the derived functional forms imply that r is everywhere decreasing in τ. Of course, one can construct models in which liberalization has the opposite effect on r.

Consider a two-country world in which each country produces N distinct goods. Preferences of the infinitely lived, representative consumer in each country are given by (2) taking c to be

$$2N \prod_{i=1}^{2N} c_i(t)^{1/2N},$$

where c_i is consumption of good i. Investment is forgone consumption; depreciation is ignored. Countries are endowed with $\overline{L}$ units of labor. Technology is identical for all goods, requiring each firm to incur a fixed cost of κ units of labor each period, after which capital, k_i, and labor, l_i, produce output according to $Ak_i^{\alpha} l_i^{1-\alpha}$ (A is total factor productivity). There are m firms producing each good and playing Cournot in the home and foreign markets, which are assumed segmented. Trade is subject to nontariff barriers that have the effect of "melting" τ percent of exports without giving rise to revenue.[2] The typical firm maximizes $p_i x_i + [p_i^* x_i^*/(1 + \tau)] - wl_i - rk_i - w\kappa$, subject to $x_i + x_i^* = Ak_i^{\alpha} l_i^{1-\alpha}$. In equilibrium, $p_i^* = p_i(1 + \tau)$, and the quantity of resources devoted to making good i for domestic and foreign consumption is unaffected by τ.

It can be shown that firms' first-order conditions for capital and labor together with the aggregate demand function imply

$$\left(\frac{\alpha}{K}\right) A\beta K^{\alpha} L^{1-\alpha} \left(1 - \frac{1}{m}\right) = \frac{r}{P(t)} \tag{11}$$

---

[2] Most trade barriers in the industrialized world do not give rise to revenue. For instance, the average tariff receipts are only 2.43 percent of imports for OECD countries (OECD 1985, p. 27). This prevalence of nonrevenue barriers is also evident in the fact that the vast majority of liberalization effects in the Uruguay Round talks do not involve revenue-producing trade barriers.

and

$$\left(\frac{1-\alpha}{L}\right) A\beta K^{\alpha} L^{1-\alpha}\left(1 - \frac{1}{m}\right) = \frac{w}{P(t)}, \tag{12}$$

where β is $(1 + \tau)^{-1/2}$, $L = \bar{L} - mN\kappa$, K is the national capital stock, and $P = \prod_{i=1}^{2N} (p_i)^{1/2N}$. Likewise, it can be shown that nominal gross domestic product is given exactly by the function

$$PY = PA\beta K^{\alpha} L^{1-\alpha}. \tag{13}$$

The true determinants of total factor productivity are not well understood. The neoclassical growth model assumes that it is driven by exogenous technological progress, whereas the new growth theory (see Romer 1983, 1986, 1987a, 1987b; Lucas 1988) endogenizes the advancement of primary factor productivity. The dynamic effect demonstrated here does not depend on the exact source of productivity growth, so rather than tie the model to a specific school of thought, assume that $A = e^{\eta t} K^{\theta} L^{\varphi}$, where η is the exogenous rate of technological progress and θ captures the external economies in the usage of capital. There are several possible interpretations of θ and φ. The most straightforward is standard external economies of scale. That is, the typical production function is $Y^{\psi} k_i^{\alpha} l_i^{1-\alpha}$, where ψ measures external scale economies. In this case, $\alpha + \theta = \alpha/(1 - \psi)$ and $1 - \alpha + \varphi = (1 - \alpha)/(1 - \psi)$. Alternatively, Romer (1987a) argues that external economies are entirely captured by $K^{\alpha+\theta}$, and η and φ are zero. In the Solow model, θ is zero and $\varphi = 1 - \alpha$. For convenience, take L equal to unity and η equal to zero. Allowing for exogenous technological progress is a straightforward exercise.

With these additional assumptions, the proportional rise in Y due to a liberalization is

$$\hat{Y} = \left(\frac{1}{\alpha + \theta} - 1\right)^{-1} \hat{\beta} + \hat{\beta}, \tag{14}$$

where a circumflex indicates percentage change and $\hat{\beta}$ is the static output effect of the liberalization considered (the increase in gross national product with no change in the capital stock). Measurement of the size of this output effect requires only two readily available estimates: the capital-output elasticity of the GNP function ($\alpha + \theta$) and an estimate of the size of the static gain ($\hat{\beta}$). To illustrate the measurability of this effect, let us take the European Community's 1992 program as an example.

The size of $\alpha + \theta$ is an unsettled empirical question. Prior to the new growth literature, it was widely assumed that $\alpha + \theta$ equaled capital's share of income (or one minus labor's share of income).

TABLE 1

ESTIMATES OF AGGREGATE CAPITAL-OUTPUT ELASTICITY ($\alpha + \theta$)

Source	France	Germany	Netherlands	United Kingdom	Belgium
Denison (1967) and Denison and Chung (1976)	.23	.263	.26	.222	
Maddison (1987)	.305	.3	.296	.255	
Kendrick (1981)	.382	.349		.348	
Christensen, Cummings, and Jorgenson (1980)	.403	.386	.446	.385	
Caballero and Lyons (1989a)	.366	.477		.339	.426
Minus one standard error	.288	.39		.195	.276
Plus one standard error	.444	.564		.483	.576

SOURCE.—First four rows from Maddison (1987), table 8. Fifth row from Caballero and Lyons (1989a), taking .3 as capital's share of income. The first four rows of figures come from the growth accounting calibration procedure and thus have no standard errors.

Table 1 reproduces a number of such estimates for France, Germany, the Netherlands, and the United Kingdom. The numbers range from .446 to .222. A recent survey (Maddison 1987) takes .3 as the consensus figure. Econometric estimation of the GNP function is problematic because of simultaneity between optimal factor choice and random productivity shocks. Hall (1988a) and Caballero and Lyons (1989a, 1989b) have pioneered new techniques to skirt this problem. Using these, Caballero and Lyons (1989a) estimate the sum of capital and labor output elasticities for France, Germany, Belgium, and the United Kingdom. To recover $\alpha + \theta$ from the Caballero-Lyons numbers, we must multiply their aggregate number by capital's cost share. Since the authors use panel data on capital's cost share, it is not possible to recover the exact $\alpha + \theta$. We get a rough approximation by multiplying the Caballero-Lyons aggregate numbers by Maddison's .3. To test the results for sensitivity to the estimates, the same calculation must be done for their point estimates plus and minus one standard error. Table 1 lists the resulting numbers.

Equation (14) shows that the induced capital formation effect can be thought of as a multiplier on the static effect. The size of this multiplier can by itself tell us how important the induced capital formation effect is. For instance, the low estimate of $\alpha + \theta$ for France yields a multiplier of 30 percent. In other words, when the endogeneity of capital is ignored, empirical estimates of the static effect alone underestimate the total output effect by at least 30 percent. Table 2 presents the multipliers that correspond to the high and low values of $\alpha + \theta$ from table 1 for each country. They range from 24 to 136 percent.

TABLE 2

UNDERESTIMATE OF GDP RISE BY IGNORING INDUCED CAPITAL FORMATION (%)

	France	Germany	Netherlands	United Kingdom	Belgium
Low	30	36	35	24	38
High	80	129	124	93	136

NOTE.—Figures were calculated by the author. The percentage underestimate is 100 times $(\alpha + \theta)/(1 - \alpha - \theta)$.

To get estimates of this dynamic effect of the 1992 program, multiply the various estimates of the multiplier by an estimate of the static output impact of 1992. Here we employ the Cecchini, Catinat, and Jacquemin (1988) estimate that 1992 will lead to a one-off increase in the European Community GDP of between 2.5 and 6.5 percent. Take the high and low estimates of the multiplier for each country from table 2 and multiply these by the high and low estimates of the static effect from Cecchini et al. The results are listed in table 3. The first and second rows in table 3 present 1992's effect on the European Community GDP (in percentage points) due solely to the indirect effect. Of course there would be no indirect effect without the static gain, so the total effect (the static range of 2.5–6.5 plus the high and low ranges from the first row) of 1992 on the European Community GDP is presented in the third and fourth rows of table 3. The most robust conclusion from table 3 is that the indirect effect is considerable in all cases. At the very least, it means that the endogenous rise in capital will boost the European Community GDP by an extra 0.6 percent.

TABLE 3

EVENTUAL INCREASE IN GDP DUE TO 1992

	France	Germany	Netherlands	United Kingdom	Belgium
Indirect Effect on GDP Due to Rise in Steady-State Capital Stock*					
Low	.8–2	.9–2.3	.9–2.3	.6–1.6	1–2.5
High	2–5.2	3.2–8.4	3.1–8.1	2.3–6	3.4–8.9
Total Effect (Static Plus Dynamic)†					
Low	3.3–8.5	3.4–8.8	3.4–8.8	3.1–8.1	3.5–9
High	4.5–11.7	5.7–14.9	5.6–14.2	5.8–12.5	5.9–15.4

NOTE.—Based on table 2 and the estimate of the static effect in Cecchini et al. (1988).
* Percentage points are to be added to the static range.
† The percentage rise in GDP due to 1992.

For our explicit model, the proportional changes of r and Y with respect to τ are identical, so

$$\frac{dU/\overline{U}}{d\epsilon} \bigg/ \frac{dU/\overline{U}}{dC/C} = \frac{1}{\rho}\frac{\partial Y/\overline{Y}}{\partial \tau/\tau} + \phi\frac{\partial Y/\overline{Y}}{\partial \tau/\tau}, \tag{15}$$

where

$$\phi \equiv \left[\frac{\theta}{1 - \alpha - \theta + (\theta/\sigma)}\right]\left(\frac{1}{\rho} - \frac{1}{\mu}\right),$$

and the positive eigenvalue of $\mathbf{J}$, μ, equals

$$\left(\frac{\rho}{2\alpha}\right)\{\alpha + \theta + [(\alpha + \theta)^2 + 4\alpha\sigma(1 - \alpha - \theta)]^{1/2}\}.$$

The term $(\partial Y/\overline{Y})/(\partial \tau/\tau)$ is what empirical studies of trade liberalizations measure. Consequently, it may be useful to think of ϕ as a welfare multiplier. That is, in addition to the well-known static gains from trade, the induced capital formation effect leads to a further welfare gain that is proportional to the static gain. Let us now turn to approximating its size.

Estimates of all the parameters in the multiplier are readily available in the literature. Table 4 presents the calculated values of the welfare multiplier for the Caballero-Lyons capital-output elasticities and these estimates plus one standard error. In all cases, the discount rate is equal to .05, the intertemporal elasticity of substitution is .1 (this is the average figure from Hall [1988b]), and α is equal to Maddison's .3.

The main point to emerge from table 4 is that this dynamic gain from trade is significant. For France, Germany, the United Kingdom,

TABLE 4

SIZE OF THE WELFARE MULTIPLIER

	France	Germany	United Kingdom	Belgium
	Caballero-Lyons Estimates of $\alpha + \theta$			
Multiplier	.29	.64	.17	.50
$\alpha + \theta$	.37	.48	.34	.43
	Cabellero-Lyons Estimates Plus One Standard Error			
Multiplier	.53	.83	.64	.87
$\alpha + \theta$	.44	.56	.48	.58

NOTE.—Figures were calculated by the author on the basis of rows 5 and 6 of table 1. The welfare multiplier is due to the dynamic effect. Numbers are to be multiplied by the static effect on GDP.

and Belgium the multiplier ranges from .17 to .87. That is, the induced capital formation effect accounts for an extra rise in welfare that is somewhere between 15 and 90 percent of the static output effect of the liberalization. However, the dynamic gain from trade is small relative to the static gain from trade. The welfare impact of the static effect is the percentage rise in output (with k held constant) multiplied by something like 20 (for $\rho = .05$). The welfare impact of the dynamic effect is the output effect multiplied by a number that is less than unity. Intuitively, this reflects the fact that the static gain is "for free" whereas the dynamic gain is largely offset by the forgone consumption necessary to build the capital stock.

IV. Conclusions

Productive factors such as human and physical capital are accumulated. Since the steady-state levels of such factors are determined endogenously, trade policy can affect these levels. A trade liberalization therefore has a dynamic effect on output and welfare as the economy moves to its new steady state. This paper shows that both the positive and normative impacts of this dynamic effect are measurable. The extra output change due to this dynamic effect appears to be quite large. The size of the welfare impact depends on the divergence between the social and private returns to capital. This dynamic effect is not dependent on the new growth models; it is present even in the Solow growth model.

References

Baldwin, Richard. "The Growth Effects of 1992." *Econ. Policy* 4, no. 9 (October 1989): 247–83.
Caballero, Ricardo J., and Lyons, Richard K. "Increasing Returns and Imperfect Competition in European Industry." Working paper. New York: Columbia Univ., 1989. (*a*)
———. "The Role of External Economies in U.S. Manufacturing." Working Paper no. 3033. Cambridge, Mass.: NBER, 1989. (*b*)
Cecchini, Paolo; Catinat, Michel; and Jacquemin, Alexis. *The European Challenge, 1992*. Brookfield, Vt.: Gower, 1988.
Christensen, Laurits R.; Cummings, Diane; and Jorgenson, Dale W. "Economic Growth, 1947–73: An International Comparison." In *New Developments in Productivity Measurement and Analysis*, edited by John W. Kendrick and Beatrice N. Vaccara. Chicago: Univ. Chicago Press (for NBER), 1980.
Deardorff, Alan V., and Stern, Robert M. *The Michigan Model of World Production and Trade: Theory and Applications*. Cambridge, Mass.: MIT Press, 1986.
Denison, Edward F. *Why Growth Rates Differ: Postwar Experience in Nine Western Countries*. Washington: Brookings Inst., 1967.
Denison, Edward F., and Chung, William K. *How Japan's Economy Grew So Fast: The Sources of Postwar Expansion*. Washington: Brookings Inst., 1976.

Findlay, Ronald W. "An 'Austrian' Model of International Trade and Interest Rate Equalization." *J.P.E.* 86 (December 1978): 989–1007.

———. "Growth and Development in Trade Models." In *Handbook of International Economics*, vol. 1, edited by Ronald W. Jones and Peter Kenen. New York: Elsevier, 1984.

Findlay, Ronald, and Kierzkowski, Henryk. "International Trade and Human Capital: A Simple General Equilibrium Model." *J.P.E.* 91 (December 1983): 957–78.

Galor, Oded. "Tariff, Income Redistribution and Welfare in a Small Overlapping-Generations Economy." Working paper. Providence, R.I.: Brown Univ., 1989.

Grossman, Gene M., and Helpman, Elhanan. "Comparative Advantage and Long-Run Growth." *A.E.R.* 80 (September 1990): 796–815.

———. "Endogenous Product Cycles." *Econ. J.* 101 (1991), in press.

Hall, Robert E. "Increasing Returns: Theory and Measurement with Industry Data." Working paper. Stanford, Calif.: Stanford Univ., 1988. (*a*)

———. "Intertemporal Substitution in Consumption." *J.P.E.* 96 (April 1988): 339–57. (*b*)

Harris, Richard G., and Cox, David. *Trade, Industrial Policy and Canadian Manufacturing.* Toronto: Ontario Econ. Council, 1984.

Judd, Kenneth L. "Short-Run Analysis of Fiscal Policy in a Simple Perfect Foresight Model." *J.P.E.* 93 (April 1985): 298–319.

———. "The Welfare Cost of Factor Taxation in a Perfect-Foresight Model." *J.P.E.* 95 (August 1987): 675–709.

Kendrick, John W. "International Comparisons of Recent Productivity Trends." In *Essays in Contemporary Economic Problems: Demand, Productivity, and Population,* edited by William Fellner. Washington: American Enterprise Inst., 1981.

Krugman, Paul R. "Endogenous Innovation, International Trade, and Growth." Paper presented at the conference on the Problem of Development, State Univ. New York, Buffalo, May 1988.

Lucas, Robert E., Jr. "On the Mechanics of Economic Development." *J. Monetary Econ.* 22 (July 1988): 3–42.

Maddison, Angus. "Growth and Slowdown in Advanced Capitalist Economies: Techniques of Quantitative Assessment." *J. Econ. Literature* 25 (June 1987): 649–98.

Manning, R., and Markusen, James. "National Product Functions in Comparative Steady-State Analysis." Working Paper no. 8808C. London: Univ. Western Ontario, 1989.

Murphy, Kevin M.; Shleifer, Andre; and Vishny, Robert W. "Income Distribution, Market Size and Industrialization." Working paper. Chicago: Univ. Chicago, 1988.

OECD. *Costs and Benefits of Protection.* Paris: OECD Publications, 1985.

Ricardo, David. "Essay on the Influence of a Low Price of Corn on the Profits of Stocks." 1815. Reprinted in *The Works and Correspondence of David Ricardo,* vol. 4, *Pamphlets and Papers, 1815–1823,* edited by Piero Sraffa. Cambridge: Cambridge Univ. Press (for Royal Econ. Soc.), 1951.

Romer, Paul M. "Dynamic Competitive Equilibria with Externalities, Increasing Returns and Unbounded Growth." Ph.D. dissertation, Univ. Chicago, 1983.

———. "Increasing Returns and Long-Run Growth." *J.P.E* 94 (October 1986): 1002–37.

————. "Crazy Explanations for the Productivity Slowdown." In *NBER Macroeconomics Annual,* vol. 2, edited by Stanley Fischer. Cambridge, Mass.: MIT Press (for NBER), 1987. (*a*)

————. "Growth Based on Increasing Returns Due to Specialization." *A.E.R. Papers and Proc.* 77 (May 1987): 56–62. (*b*)

Smith, Alasdair. "Capital Theory and Trade Theory." In *Handbook of International Economics,* vol. 1, edited by Ronald W. Jones and Peter Kenen. New York: Elsevier, 1984.

Srinivasan, T. N., and Bhagwati, Jagdish N. "Trade and Welfare in a Steady State." In *Flexible Exchange Rates and the Balance of Payments: Essays in Memory of Egon Sohmen,* edited by John S. Chipman and Charles P. Kindleberger. Amsterdam: North-Holland, 1980.

Stiglitz, Joseph E. "Factor Price Equalization in a Dynamic Economy." *J.P.E.* 78 (May/June 1970): 456–88.

[28]

Comment

Do Static Gains from Trade Lead to Medium-Run Growth?

Joy Mazumdar

Emory University

I. Introduction

The trade growth nexus has been a topic of active research for quite
some time. A number of mechanisms have been suggested to explain
how trade leads to growth. In the traditional trade theory framework,
trade leads to growth by increasing the relative price of the good that
is relatively capital intensive (see, e.g., Stiglitz 1970; Deardorff 1973,
1974; Smith 1984). In this framework, trade can lead to medium-run
growth only. In the new trade growth literature, trade leads to an
increase in the *long*-run growth rate by encouraging research and
development activity, which is the determinant of long-run growth
(see, e.g., Romer 1990; Grossman and Helpman 1991; Rivera-Batiz
and Romer 1991). Trade increases long-run growth by increasing
the availability of resources for R & D, increasing the availability of
specialized inputs, increasing the size of the market, and so forth.
One explanation of why trade might lead to growth, which has been
emphasized by Baldwin (1989, 1992), is the effect of static efficiency
gains from liberalization on medium-run capital accumulation and
growth.[1] The easiest way one can see this is to assume a constant
savings rate. According to traditional trade theory, which is static,
trade leads to an increase in real income due to static efficiency gains.
However, if the savings rate out of real income is a constant as in the

    I would like to thank Alan Deardorff for providing detailed and helpful comments
and encouragement. I am also grateful to Susanto Basu, Ron Cronovich, and E. Soma-
nathan for helpful comments and discussion. Any errors are entirely my own.
    [1] In Baldwin's framework, static efficiency gains might lead to long-run growth too
if there are constant or increasing returns to capital.

[*Journal of Political Economy*, 1996, vol. 104, no. 6]

Solow model, it would seem then that savings would increase as a result of trade, leading to greater capital accumulation and a movement to a new steady state with a higher level of per capita income. Thus if the economy starts out in the steady state initially, after trade liberalization it would experience medium-run growth, besides the usual increase in the *level* of income.

Baldwin asserts that empirical studies that focus only on static gains underestimate the gains from trade since they ignore the dynamic gains from trade, which can be substantial. The increase in efficiency resulting from trade, which leads to static gains in income, also leads to dynamic gains in the form of medium-run growth by increasing the savings that result from an increase in income. This paper critically examines Baldwin's claim that static gains lead to dynamic gains in the medium run.

Baldwin's mechanism is illustrated in figure 1, which is the usual Solow diagram. The per capita capital stock k is measured along the horizontal axis (in physical units). Savings and depreciation expenditure are measured along the vertical axis. The $sf(k)$ curves represent per capita savings (I have suppressed the per capita output curve to maintain clarity). The autarky savings curve is denoted by the subscript A, and the savings curve after trade is denoted by the subscript T. The δk curves represent depreciation expenditure needed to maintain different levels of capital stock. Ignore the dashed line δk_X for the moment. The autarky steady state is at the capital stock k^*. If the savings rate is a constant, then according to Baldwin the curve representing savings would shift up to $sf(k)_T$ as a result of trade, since real income would rise after trade. This would lead to positive capital accumulation, and the economy would move from A to T, the point of intersection of the new savings curve and δk. The new steady-state capital would be k^{**}. As the economy moves from the old steady state to the new, there will be positive medium-run growth that would not have occurred under autarky.

Baldwin's mechanism depends solely on the existence of static gains from trade and does not rely on the direction of trade. That is, trade will lead to growth, regardless of what kinds of goods are being imported or exported, as long as there are income gains from trade. In this paper I shall show that this is not correct. While trade liberalization always leads to an increase in the *level* of real income, whether or not it leads to *growth* will depend on the kind of good that is imported, that is, whether the import is a consumption good or a capital good. Specifically, trade will not lead to growth if the consumption good is the import and the capital good is the export. This result holds even though in the model presented in this paper the relative factor intensities are the same across sectors. This is unlike

Savings,
Depreciation

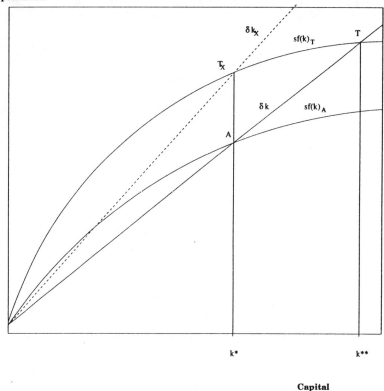

FIG. 1

the traditional trade growth literature in which it is the difference in relative factor intensities between sectors and not the nature of use (i.e., consumption vs. investment) of the goods being imported that determines the effect of trade on growth. The result in this paper that trade leads to growth only if the import is the capital good holds true for the case in which the savings rate is a constant, as in the Solow model, as well as for the case in which the savings rate is variable and optimal. Therefore, whether or not empirical studies on the gains from trade should take into account dynamic gains depends on the nature of goods being imported (and exported).

In this paper, I develop a simple model with two goods to show the results stated above. I have tried to keep my model as close to Baldwin's framework as possible to facilitate comparison. I have two goods instead of one (Baldwin's model has only one good) in order to show the origin of the static gains. Since Baldwin uses a single-good model, he shows the efficiency gains as an outward shift in the production possibility frontier without being able to show where these gains come from. He makes the crucial assumption that a single-good economy is a reasonable approximation for a multigood one and that this assumption does not make any difference to his basic result that trade leads to growth as long as trade increases real income. This assumption is incorrect and leads to his misleading conclusion. Therefore, I have to have more than one good in my model.

The remainder of this paper is divided into three sections. In Section II, I describe a small economy with two goods and two factors: capital and labor. I assume that the savings rate is a constant as in the Solow model. I describe what happens to the economy when it opens up to trade. In that section I show that trade does not lead to growth if the consumption good is imported and the capital good is exported. I discuss the case with the constant savings rate first because it is the more interesting case. In Section III, the savings rate is no longer a constant but is a result of the consumer's optimization decision. I show that again trade does not lead to growth if the consumption good is imported and the economy continues to be in the old steady state although at a higher level of real income. In Section IV, I present conclusions.

II. Constant Savings Rate

Consider a small country. In the economy, there are two goods, one consumption good and one capital good, and two factors, one primary factor (labor) and one produced factor (capital). Each consumer supplies one unit of labor inelastically. All goods and factors are perfectly mobile within the country, and there is perfect competition in both good and factor markets. In this model, there is a positive depreciation rate, no uncertainty, no technical progress, and no population growth.

Both sectors use Cobb-Douglas technology. The production functions of the two produced goods are as follows:

$$y_i = A_i l_i^\alpha k_i^{1-\alpha} \quad \text{for } i = 1, 2. \tag{1}$$

The subscript 1 denotes the consumption goods sector and the subscript 2 denotes the capital goods sector.

I assume that the capital-labor intensities are the same for the two sectors. This makes the analysis easier and also helps me to abstract from the Stolper-Samuelson effects of trade,[2] which do not play any role in Baldwin's analysis.

Since we have constant returns to scale, the production functions will be the same for both per capita and total quantities. Henceforth, all quantity variables (y, l, and k) should be interpreted as per capita quantities, that is, per consumer in the economy (and not per worker in the industry).

Since the capital-labor intensities are the same across industries and we have profit maximization behavior by firms and perfect competition, the capital-labor ratios will be the same for both industries. Therefore, the capital-labor ratios in each industry will equal the economywide capital-labor ratio, which is equal to k since each agent supplies one unit of labor inelastically and holds capital stock k. The relative price between the goods that is needed for both to be produced will not be influenced by the capital-labor ratios since they are the same, but it is determined solely by the technology parameter A. The relative prices in autarky will therefore be constant, being dependent solely on the technology, which is constant:

$$\frac{p_i}{p_j} = \frac{A_j}{A_i} \quad \text{for } i, j = 1, 2. \tag{2}$$

The better the level of technology in a sector relative to the other sector, the lower the relative price of the good produced in that sector.

I shall assume that the representative consumer saves a constant fraction s out of real income. Since there is only one consumption good, the constant savings rate, together with the production function, will determine uniquely how many investment goods and consumption goods are produced in the economy. I shall assume in this section that capital depreciates in this economy at a constant rate δ so that there is a steady state in this economy. In the steady state there is no net investment.

Suppose that the economy is in steady state under autarky; that is, savings equal depreciation. I shall also assume that there is no international lending since I want to focus solely on the effects of trade on growth. International capital flows do not play any special role in Baldwin's framework either. Let this economy start trading with a large foreign country. Since the capital-labor intensities are the same across sectors, differences in factor endowments will not be the basis of comparative advantage. In this model differences in

---

[2] The Stolper-Samuelson theorem says that trade will increase the return to the factor that is used more intensively in the exportable and decrease the return to the factor that is used more intensively in the importable.

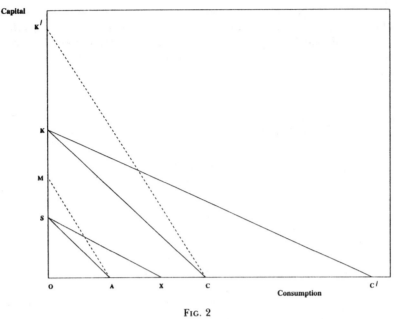

FIG. 2

technology will drive trade. Assume that this country has a comparative advantage in good 2, the capital good; that is, $A_1/A_2 < A_1^*/A_2^*$,
where the asterisks refer to the foreign country.

The effects of trade can be seen in figure 2. Given our assumption
of identical factor intensities across sectors, the production possibility
frontier (and the autarky consumption possibility frontier) is a
straight line shown as KC in the figure.[3] The vertical axis measures
units of the capital good and the horizontal axis measures units of the
consumption good. The distance OK is the value of national output in
terms of the capital good. The slope of KC is the autarky relative price
of the consumption good and equals A_2/A_1. Let OS be the amount of
capital goods produced in the economy under autarky. The constant
savings rate equals OS/OK (and also OA/OC). Since I have assumed the
economy to be in steady state, OS is just enough to cover depreciation.
Therefore, OS is also equal to depreciation expenditure. Savings (and
depreciation expenditure) in terms of the consumption good are
equal to OA on the horizontal axis, which is obtained by drawing a
line with slope equal to the relative price of the consumption good
(i.e., parallel to KC) through point S.

[3] The reason is that the opportunity cost of producing one more unit of any good
will equal the relative price of that good, which according to (2) will be a constant
throughout.

Trade will lead to growth only if it results in savings that exceed
OS, the depreciation expenditure on the existing capital stock. In that
case there will be capital accumulation and medium-run growth.
Since the economy has a comparative advantage in the capital good,
the relative price of the consumption good falls as a result of trade.
The economy specializes completely in the production of the capital
good so that an amount OK of the capital good is produced. The
consumption possibility frontier shifts to KC'. The slope of KC' is
equal to the relative price of the consumption good after trade. National income in terms of the capital good remains the same and
equals OK. Since the fraction of income saved does not change, the
same amount OS is saved and invested domestically. An amount KS
is exported in exchange for XC' of consumption goods. Since OS was
just enough to cover depreciation, there is no net capital accumulation after trade.

The income gains from trade can be seen in terms of the consumption good. Income in terms of the consumption good increases from
OC to OC' after trade. Also, depreciation expenditure (which is equal
to savings) in terms of the consumption good increases from OA to
OX at the new posttrade prices. That is, while income goes up, so
does depreciation expenditure. This can be seen in figure 1. If savings
and depreciation expenditure are being measured in terms of the
consumption good, then trade leads to a shifting up of both the savings curve and depreciation expenditure curve by the same proportion so that the steady state continues to be at the old steady state.
That is, while the savings curve shifts up to $sf(k)_T$, the depreciation
expenditure curve also shifts up to δk_X, leading to no change in the
steady-state level of capital. The economy would just move to the
point T_X. In Baldwin's analysis, the savings curve shifts up but the
curve representing depreciation expenditure does not. This would
be incorrect if liberalization led to the trade pattern assumed above.

Baldwin's analysis would be correct only if trade led to the import
of the capital good and the export of the consumption good accompa-
nied by an increase in the price of the consumption good instead of
the capital good. This scenario is shown by the dashed lines in figure
2. The economy will now specialize in the production of the consumption good and will therefore produce OC. In this case income and
savings in terms of the consumption good stay the same after trade.
However, income and savings in terms of the capital good increase
to OK' and OM, respectively. Since OM is greater than OS and only
an amount OS of capital was required to meet depreciation expenditure at the old steady-state capital, there will be capital accumulation
and growth.

III. Trade and Growth with an Optimal Savings Rate

The analysis in the previous section can be extended to the case in which the savings rate is no longer a constant but is derived from optimizing behavior of the consumer. I assume that consumers are infinitely lived and maximize utility over an infinite time horizon. As before, there is a consumption good and a capital good. The production functions are the same as before. I shall assume in this section that there is no depreciation, technical progress, or population growth.[4]

The representative consumer maximizes the following lifetime utility function:

$$\int_T^\infty e^{-\theta(t-T)} u(c_t)\, dt$$

subject to the constraint

$$p_2 k = w + r p_2 k - c.$$

I choose the consumption good to be the numeraire. The representative consumer starts out at time T and maximizes utility $u(c)$[5] over an infinite horizon subject to the constraint that savings each period are equal to income minus expenditure. The consumer derives utility from the consumption of good 1 denoted by c. The consumer discounts the utility from future consumption by the discount rate θ so that consumption today is more valuable than the same amount of consumption in the future. The consumer saves by accumulating capital.

I shall again assume that the economy is in steady state under autarky. The steady-state condition with optimizing consumers and no technical progress or depreciation is

$$r = \frac{A_1(1-\alpha)}{p_2 k^\alpha} = \theta, \tag{3}$$

where r is the rate of return to capital[6] and k is the capital stock per capita.

---

[4] This assumption does not make any difference to the basic results of the paper.

[5] Assume that the instantaneous utility function $u(c)$ exhibits constant intertemporal elasticity of substitution.

[6] The expression for r comes from the fact that r has to equal the marginal product of capital in each sector divided by the price of capital and from the fact that the capital-labor ratio in each sector equals the economywide capital-labor ratio. The rate of return, r, also equals $A_2(1-\alpha)/k^\alpha$. This can be obtained by substituting the expression for p_2 from (2) in eq. (3).

The intuition behind the steady-state condition is simple. The rate of return to capital, r, is the reward for saving and investing. The discount rate θ is a measure of the cost of saving or a measure of the utility forgone if one decides to curtail consumption this period. If the reward for saving r is greater than the cost of saving θ, then there is an incentive to save and there will be capital accumulation and hence growth. The greater the difference between r and θ, the greater the growth rate in consumption and output. In the steady state, $r = \theta$, the cost of saving exactly equals the return from saving, and there is no incentive to save or dissave. This means that there is zero net investment and hence zero growth in the steady state.

Trade will lead to growth in this model only if r increases as a result of trade so that it exceeds θ. As can be seen from (3), this will happen only if p_2 decreases since k will stay the same right at the point of trade liberalization. This can occur only if the country has a comparative advantage in the consumer good and it specializes in the production of the consumer good and imports the capital good. On the other hand, if the country exports the capital good, the economy specializes in the production of the capital good, and r remains equal to $A_2(1 - \alpha)/k^\alpha$. There is, therefore, no capital accumulation or growth. In the latter case, while the marginal product of capital *in terms of the consumption good* increases as a result of trade, so does the price of capital, which keeps r unchanged after trade. Note that this is similar to the scenario with a constant savings rate in which an increase in the relative price of capital increases both savings and depreciation expenditure (in terms of the consumption good) in the same proportion, keeping real savings unchanged.

Trade does not increase the return to capital in my model because of Stolper-Samuelson effects, which depend on different factor intensities across sectors, but because of an increase in the relative price of capital. Trade might increase the marginal product or the *rental price* of capital in terms of the consumption good, but if the price of the capital good also increases by the same proportion, the rate of return stays unchanged.[7]

Therefore, trade does not lead to growth in either the case of a constant savings rate or the case of an optimal savings rate when the capital good is the export. The reason is the same in both cases. The increase in the relative price of capital keeps unchanged real savings in the former case and the rate of return in the latter.

---

[7] The Stolper-Samuelson effects will matter of course if the factor intensities are different across sectors.

IV. Conclusion

Baldwin has recently emphasized the dynamic gains from trade and has asserted that empirical studies focusing only on static gains underestimate the gains from trade since they ignore the dynamic gains from trade, which can be substantial. The increase in efficiency resulting from trade, which leads to static gains in income, also leads to dynamic gains in the form of medium-run growth, either by increasing the return to capital (in the case of optimizing consumers) or by increasing savings that result from an increase in income (when the consumers save a constant fraction of their income). I have shown in this paper that the presence of static income gains from trade is not sufficient to generate growth. The pattern of trade is crucial in determining growth. Specifically, if the consumption good is the import and the capital good is the export, then trade will not lead to growth, although there might be substantial income gains. The reason is that the relative price of the investment good rises as a result of trade, thereby counteracting any effect trade might have had on savings or the rental price of capital. Therefore, while estimating the gains from trade, one need not take into account dynamic effects if trade liberalization does not lead to imports of capital goods.

References

Baldwin, Richard E. "The Growth Effects of 1992." *Econ. Policy,* no. 9 (October 1989), pp. 247–81.

———. "Measurable Dynamic Gains from Trade." *J.P.E.* 100 (February 1992): 162–74.

Deardorff, Alan V. "The Gains from Trade in and out of Steady-State Growth." *Oxford Econ. Papers* 25 (July 1973): 173–91.

———. "A Geometry of Growth and Trade." *Canadian J. Econ.* 7 (May 1974): 295–306.

Grossman, Gene M., and Helpman, Elhanan. *Innovation and Growth in the Global Economy.* Cambridge, Mass.: MIT Press, 1991.

Rivera-Batiz, Luis A., and Romer, Paul M. "Economic Integration and Endogenous Growth." *Q.J.E.* 106 (May 1991): 530–55.

Romer, Paul M. "Endogenous Technological Change." *J.P.E.* 98, no. 5, pt. 2 (October 1990): S71–S102.

Smith, Alasdair. "Capital Theory and Trade Theory." In *Handbook of International Economics,* vol. 1, edited by Ronald W. Jones and Peter Kenen. New York: Elsevier, 1984.

Stiglitz, Joseph E. "Factor Price Equalization in a Dynamic Economy." *J.P.E.* 78 (May/June 1970): 456–88.

[29]

Comparative Advantage and Long-Run Growth

By Gene M. Grossman and Elhanan Helpman*

We construct a dynamic, two-country model of trade and growth in which endogenous technological progress results from the profit-maximizing behavior of entrepreneurs. We study the role that the external trading environment and that trade and industrial policies play in the determination of long-run growth rates. Cross-country differences in efficiency at R&D versus manufacturing (i.e., comparative advantage) bear importantly on the growth effects of economic structure and commerical policies. (JEL 411, 111, 621)

What role do the external trading environment and commercial policy play in the determination of *long-run* economic performance? This central question of international economics has received surprisingly little attention in the theoretical literature over the years.

Previous research on trade and growth has adopted the neoclassical framework to focus on factor accumulation in the open economy. (See the surveys by Ronald Findlay, 1984, and Alasdair Smith, 1984.) This research largely neglects the effects of trade structure on rates of growth, however, addressing instead the reverse causation from growth and accumulation to the pattern of trade.[1] The direction that the research followed almost surely can be ascribed to the well-known property of the standard neoclassical growth model with diminishing returns to capital that (endogenous) growth in per capita income dissipates in the long run.

For this reason, the familiar models that incorporate investment only in capital equipment seem ill-suited for analysis of long-run growth.

The available evidence collected since the seminal work of Robert Solow (1957) also leads one to look beyond capital accumulation for an explanation of growth. Exercises in growth accounting for a variety of countries generally find that increases in the capital to labor ratio account for considerably less than half of the last century's growth in per capita incomes.[2] Although econometric efforts to explain the residual have been somewhat disappointing (see, for example, Zvi Griliches, 1979), professional opinion and common sense continue to impute much of this residual to improvements in technology.[3] We share the view, expressed by Paul Romer (1986, 1990), that a full understanding of growth in the long run requires appreciation of the economic determinants of the accumulation of knowledge.

In this paper we draw on the pioneering work by Romer to construct a model that highlights the roles of scale economies and technological progress in the growth process. As in Romer's work, our model im-

*Grossman: Woodrow Wilson School, Princeton University, Princeton, NJ 08544. Helpman: Department of Economics, Tel Aviv University, Ramat Aviv, Israel. We are grateful to Avinash Dixit, Carl Shapiro, and Lars Svensson for their comments on an earlier draft, and to the National Science Foundation and the Alfred P. Sloan Foundation for financial support. Grossman also thanks the World Bank and Helpman thanks the International Monetary Fund for providing support and a stimulating environment during part of our work on this project. These organizations are not responsible for the views expressed herein.

[1] An exception is Max Corden (1971), who studies how the opening up of trade affects the speed of transition to the steady state in a two-factor neoclassical growth model with fixed savings propensities.

[2] See Angus Maddison (1987) for a careful, recent exercise in growth accounting.

[3] The benefits of education and experience undoubtedly contribute part of the explanation for the growth residual. See, for example, Robert Lucas (1988) and Gary Becker and Kevin Murphy (1990) for growth models that highlight the role of human capital accumulation as a source of growth.

plies an endogenous rate of long-run growth in per capita income, and we study its economic determinants. Our primary contribution lies in casting the growth process in a two-country setting. We provide, for the first time, a rigorous analysis linking long-run growth rates to trade policies and other international economic conditions. Moreover, we show that recognition of cross-country differences in economic structure impinge upon conclusions about the long-run effects of domestic shocks and policies.

Our model incorporates the essential insights from Romer (1990), although we introduce some differences in detail. The building blocks are an R&D sector that produces designs or blueprints for new products using primary resources and previously accumulated knowledge, an intermediate-goods sector consisting of oligopolistic producers of differentiated products, and a consumer-goods sector in each country that produces a country-specific final output using labor and intermediate inputs. As in Wilfred Ethier (1982), total factor productivity in final production increases when the number of available varieties of differentiated inputs grows. Thus, resources devoted to R&D contribute over time to productivity in the production of final goods, as well as to the stock of scientific and engineering knowledge.

The new elements in our analysis stem from the assumed presence of cross-country differences in the effectiveness with which primary resources can perform different activities, that is, *comparative advantage.* For simplicity we specify a one-primary-factor model, and allow the productivity of this factor in the three activities to vary internationally. Similar results could be derived from a multifactor model with interindustry differences in factor intensities (see Grossman and Helpman, 1989d, and Grossman, 1989). In any event, we find that many comparative dynamic results hinge on a comparison across countries of parameters reflecting efficiency in R&D relative to efficiency in manufacturing the goods that make use of the knowledge generated by R&D. The effects of policy in a single country, of accumulation of primary resources in a single

country, and of a shift in world tastes toward the final output of one of the countries all depend upon the identity of the country in which the change originates in relation to the international pattern of comparative advantage.

We describe the economic setting in Section I below. Then, in Section II, we derive the dynamic equilibrium of the world economy and calculate two reduced-form equations that determine the steady-state growth rate. In Section III, we investigate the structural determinants of long-run growth. There, the implications for growth of variations in consumer preferences, primary-input coefficients in one or both countries, and stocks of available primary resources are considered. Section IV contains policy analysis. We study barriers and inducements to trade in consumer goods and subsidies to research and development. The analysis is extended in Section V to incorporate lags in the dissemination of knowledge and asymmetries in the speed of diffusion within and between countries. We use the extended model to reconsider the effects of trade policies on the steady-state rate of growth. Finally, Section VI provides a brief summary of our findings.

I. The Model

We study a world economy comprising two countries. Each country engages in three productive activities: the production of a final good, the production of a continuum of varieties of differentiated middle products (i.e., intermediate inputs), and research and development (R&D). A single primary factor is used in production, and is taken to be in fixed and constant supply in each country. Although we refer to this factor as "labor," we have in mind an aggregate of irreproducible resources that for any given level of technical know-how limits aggregate output.

At a point in time, output of final goods in country i is given by

$$Y_i = BA_i L_{Yi}^{1-\beta} \left[\int_0^n x_i(\omega)^\alpha \, d\omega \right]^{\beta/\alpha},$$

$$0 < \alpha, \beta < 1,$$

where L_{Yi} represents employment in the final-goods sector, $x_i(\omega)$ denotes the input of middle product ω, A_i is a country-specific productivity parameter, and n is (the measure of) the number of varieties of middle products available at that time.[4] This production function exhibits constant returns to scale for given n, but an increase in the measure of varieties of middle products raises total factor productivity. This specification, which we borrow from Ethier (1982), captures the notion that an increasing degree of *specialization* generates technical efficiency gains. The economy's potential for augmenting the degree of specialization by developing new middle products implies the existence of dynamic scale economies at the industry level that are external to the individual final-good-producing firms.

Competition in the final-goods sectors ensures marginal-cost pricing. Hence, by appropriate choice of the constant B, producer prices satisfy

$$(1) \quad p_{Yi} = \left(\frac{w_i}{A_i}\right)^{1-\beta}\left[\int_0^n p_X(\omega)^{1-\varepsilon}d\omega\right]^{\beta/(1-\varepsilon)},$$

$$\varepsilon = \frac{1}{1-\alpha} > 1,$$

where w_i is the wage in country i and $p_X(\omega)$ is the price of variety ω. Final-good producers worldwide pay the same prices for (freely traded) middle products.

At every moment in time, the existing producers of middle products engage in oligopolistic price competition. The producer of a variety ω in country i chooses $p_X(\omega)$ to maximize profits,

$$\pi_i(\omega) = \left[p_X(\omega) - w_i a_{LXi}\right]$$

$$\times \frac{p_X(\omega)^{-\varepsilon}}{\int_0^n p_X(\omega)^{1-\varepsilon}d\omega}\beta\Sigma_i p_{Yi}Y_i,$$

where a_{LXi} is the unit labor requirement for production of intermediates in country i. This expression for profits comprises the product of profits per unit (in square brackets) and derived demand for variety ω, where the latter incorporates the assumption that neither the prices of competing products nor the value of final production varies with $p_X(\omega)$. The first-order condition for a profit maximum implies the usual fixed-markup pricing rule,

$$(2) \quad \alpha p_X(\omega) = w_i a_{LXi}.$$

It is clear from (2) that varieties originating from the same country bear the same price. Letting p_{Xi} represent the price of a variety produced in country i and n_i be the number of intermediate inputs produced there, equations (1) and (2) imply

$$(3) \quad p_{Yi} = \left(\frac{w_i}{A_i}\right)^{1-\beta}\left(\sum_j n_j p_{Xj}^{1-\varepsilon}\right)^{\beta/(1-\varepsilon)},$$

$$(4) \quad \alpha p_{Xi} = w_i a_{LXi}.$$

With these prices, profits per firm can be expressed as

$$(5) \quad \pi_i = (1-\alpha)p_{Xi}X_i/n_i,$$

where X_i is aggregate output of intermediates in country i (n_i times per-firm output) and is given by

$$(6) \quad X_i = \frac{n_i p_{Xi}^{-\varepsilon}}{\sum_j n_j p_{Xj}^{1-\varepsilon}}\beta\left(\sum_j p_{Yj}Y_j\right).$$

As in our 1989c paper (see also Kenneth Judd, 1985), resources devoted to research generate "blueprints" that expand the measure of differentiated products. Research outlays are made by private, profit-maximizing entrepreneurs, who appropriate some of the benefits from a new technological innovation in the form of a stream of oligopoly profits. We assume that innovators receive indefinite patent protection, but that blueprints are not tradable, so that all profits must be derived from production in the country in which a middle product has been developed. Then, with free entry by entrepreneurs, if resources are devoted to R&D in country i at time t, the present value of future operating profits from producing there—discounted to time t—must equal the current cost of R&D. We denote R&D costs by $c_{ni}(t)$ and write the zero-profit condition as

$$\int_t^\infty e^{-[R(\tau)-R(t)]}\pi_i(\tau)\,d\tau = c_{ni}(t),$$

where $R(t)$ is the cumulative interest factor from time 0 to time t $(R(0)=1)$. Differentiating this condition with respect to t, we find

$$(7) \qquad \frac{\pi_i + \dot{c}_{ni}}{c_{ni}} = \dot{R}.$$

Equation (7) expresses a standard no-arbitrage condition. Recognizing that $c_{ni}(t)$ represents the value of an input-producing firm in country i at time t, (7) equates the instantaneous rate of return on shares in such a firm (the sum of dividends and capital gains) to the rate of interest.

We follow Romer (1990) in assuming that R&D generates a second output, which takes the form of a contribution to the stock of disembodied knowledge. Knowledge here includes all general scientific information, as well as some forms of engineering data with more widespread applicability, generated in the course of developing marketable products. Knowledge contributes to the productivity of further research efforts by reducing the amount of labor needed for an inventor to develop a new product. Due to the more general and non-patentable nature of this product of the R&D effort, appropriation of the resulting returns by the creator seems problematic. We assume to begin with that general knowledge disseminates immediately and costlessly throughout the world. This approximates a situation in which information spreads through technical journals, professional organizations, and interpersonal commercial contacts, and where literature, scientists, and business-

people move freely across international borders (see Luigi Pasinetti, 1981, ch. 11). We relax this assumption by introducing lags in the dissemination of knowledge in Section V.

With these knowledge spillovers in mind, we specify our R&D technology as follows. If L_{ni} units of labor engage in research in country i, they generate a flow of new products $\dot{n}_i$ given by

$$(8) \qquad \dot{n}_i = L_{ni}K / a_{Lni},$$

where K is the current stock of knowledge and a_{Lni} is a country-specific productivity parameter. We take the stock of knowledge to be proportional to cumulative experience in R&D; that is, there are no diminishing returns to research in adding to scientific understanding. By choosing units for K so that the factor of proportionality is unity, we have $K = n$ and

$$(9) \qquad \dot{K} = \sum_i L_{ni}K / a_{Lni}.$$

Since knowledge has been assumed to be a free input to each individual entrepreneur, the cost of product development in country i can be written as

$$(10) \qquad c_{ni} = w_i a_{Lni} / n.$$

We turn now to the demand side of the model. Consumers worldwide share identical, homothetic preferences. They view the final goods produced in the two countries as imperfect substitutes. We represent preferences by a time-separable intertemporal utility function

$$(11) \quad U_t = \int_t^\infty e^{-\rho(\tau-t)}$$
$$\times \log u[y_1(\tau), y_2(\tau)]\,d\tau,$$

where ρ is the subjective discount rate and $y_i(\tau)$ is consumption of final goods from country i in period τ. The instantaneous sub-utility function $u(\cdot)$ is nondecreasing, strictly quasi-concave, and positively linearly homogeneous.

800   *THE AMERICAN ECONOMIC REVIEW*   *SEPTEMBER 1990*

A typical consumer maximizes (11) subject to an intertemporal budget constraint. With $u(\cdot)$ linearly homogeneous, this optimization problem can be solved in two stages. First, the consumer maximizes static utility for a given level of expenditure at time τ, $E(\tau)$. The solution to this subproblem generates an indirect utility function, $v[p_{Y1}(\tau), p_{Y2}(\tau)]E(\tau)$, where p_{Yi} is the price of Y_i. In the absence of barriers to trade in final goods, these prices are common to consumers in the two countries. The second-stage problem involves choosing the time pattern of expenditures to maximize

$$(12) \quad V_t = \int_t^\infty e^{-\rho(\tau - t)}\{\log v[p_{Y1}(\tau), p_{Y2}(\tau)]$$

$$+ \log E(\tau)\}\, d\tau$$

subject to

$$(13) \quad \int_t^\infty e^{-[R(\tau) - R(t)]}E(\tau)$$

$$\leq \int_t^\infty e^{-[R(\tau) - R(t)]}w(\tau)\, L\, d\tau + Z(t),$$

where $w(t)$ is the consumer's wage rate at time t, L is his labor supply, and $Z(t)$ is the value of his time t asset holdings. The interest factor in (13) is common to all individuals as a result of trade on the integrated world capital market, but the wage rate varies by country.

From the first-order conditions to this problem, we find that the optimal path for expenditure obeys

$$(14) \quad \frac{\dot{E}}{E} = \dot{R} - \rho.$$

Savings are used to accumulate either ownership claims in input-producing firms or riskless bonds issued by these same firms. Arbitrage ensures that the rates of return on these two assets are equal, and in equilibrium consumers are indifferent as to the composition of their portfolios.

II. Equilibrium Dynamics

During the course of the development of our model in the previous section, we provided some of the equilibrium conditions. For example, we derived pricing equations for goods and a no-arbitrage condition relating equilibrium asset returns. In this section we complete the list of equilibrium requirements by adding conditions that stipulate market clearing in factor and final-goods markets. We then derive and discuss a reduced-form system that describes equilibrium dynamics.

Static equilibrium in the markets for the two final goods implies

$$(15) \quad p_{Yi}Y_i = s_i E,$$

where $s_i(p_{Y1}, p_{Y2})$ is the share of world spending allocated to Y_i and E is world spending on consumer goods. The share function is, of course, homogeneous of degree zero. We establish below that relative commodity prices are constant in the vicinity of a steady state with active R&D sectors in both countries. For this reason, we take s_i to be constant in our subsequent analysis, and omit its functional dependence on relative prices.

The labor-market clearing conditions equate labor supply and labor demand in each country. Using (3) and Shephard's lemma, we see that final-goods producers demand $(1 - \beta)p_{Yi}Y_i / w_i$ workers. The demand for labor by middle-products manufacturers is $a_{LXi}X_i$, while (8) and the fact that $K = n$ imply demand for labor by product developers of $(a_{Lni}/n)\dot{n}_i$. Hence,

$$(16) \quad (a_{Lni}/n)\dot{n}_i + a_{LXi}X_i$$

$$+ (1 - \beta)p_{Yi}Y_i / w_i = L_i,$$

where L_i is the labor force available in country i.

Since we neglect here the monetary determinants of the price level, we may choose freely a time pattern for one nominal variable. It proves convenient to specify the numeraire as follows:

(17a) $p_{X1} = n(a_{LX1}/a_{Ln1})^{1/\epsilon}$.

We show in Appendix A of our 1989a working paper that, with this normalization, a necessary condition for convergence to a steady state with positive R&D in both countries (i.e., nonspecialization) is

(17b) $p_{X2} = n(a_{LX2}/a_{Ln2})^{1/\epsilon}$.

Together, (17a) and (17b) imply that relative prices of middle products are constant along the convergent path, which further implies with (4) the constancy of relative wages, and with (3) the constancy of relative prices of final goods. This last fact justifies our treatment of expenditure shares as fixed.

Let $g(t)$ denote the rate of growth of the number of products and the stock of knowledge; that is, $g \equiv \dot{n}/n = \dot{K}/K$. Then from (17) and (4) we see that prices of intermediates and wages grow at rate g, while from (10), product development costs are constant. Equations (5)–(7), (10), (15), and (17) imply

(18) $X_i = \dfrac{n_i b_i^{1/\alpha}}{\Sigma_j n_j b_j} \dfrac{\beta E}{n}$

and

(19) $\dot{R} = \dfrac{1}{\epsilon - 1} \dfrac{\beta E}{\Sigma_j n_j b_j}$,

where $b_i \equiv (a_{Lni}/a_{LXi})^{\alpha}$. The coefficients b_i will serve as our measures of *comparative advantage*. Country 1 enjoys comparative advantage in conducting R&D if and only if $b_1 < b_2$.

Since wages grow at the same rate as n, it proves convenient to define $e \equiv E/n$. Letting $\sigma_i \equiv n_i/n$ be the share of products manufactured in country i and noting that $g = \Sigma_i \dot{n}_i/n$, (16), (15), (17), (4), and (18) imply

(20) $g = H - \dfrac{\beta e}{\sigma} - \dfrac{1-\beta}{\alpha} se$,

where we have defined $H \equiv \Sigma_i L_i/a_{Lni}$, the total *effective* labor force, $\sigma \equiv \Sigma_i \sigma_i b_i$, a weighted average of the comparative advantage parameters with product shares as weights, and $s \equiv \Sigma_i s_i/b_i$. Observe that the parameter σ, which provides a useful summary of the static intersectoral resource allocation, grows (shrinks) over time if and only if the growth rate of the number of differentiated middle products in the country with comparative *disadvantage* in R&D exceeds (falls short of) that of the other country.

We are now prepared to derive two equations that describe the dynamic evolution of the world economy. From the definition of e, we have $\dot{e}/e = \dot{E}/E - g$, or, substituting (14), (19), and (20),

(21) $\dfrac{\dot{e}}{e} = \dfrac{\beta e}{\alpha \sigma} + \dfrac{1-\beta}{\alpha} se - H - \rho$.

Hence, the rate of increase of spending per middle product is larger the greater is spending per product and the smaller is the share of the country with comparative disadvantage in R&D in the total number of varieties.

Now, from the definition of the product shares σ_i, their rates of change are given by $\dot{\sigma}_i/\sigma_i = \dot{n}_i/n_i - \dot{n}/n$. Using (16) together with (17), (4), (18), and (20), we obtain

(22) $\dot{\sigma}_i = h_i - \dfrac{s_i}{b_i} \dfrac{1-\beta}{\alpha} e$

$\qquad - \sigma_i \left(H - \dfrac{1-\beta}{\alpha} se \right)$,

where $h_i \equiv L_i/a_{Lni}$ is effective labor in country i, and $\Sigma_i h_i = H$. Since the evolution of the two product shares are related by $\Sigma_i \dot{\sigma}_i = 0$, we can replace (22) by a single differential equation in σ. Making use of the fact that $\dot{\sigma} = \Sigma_i \dot{\sigma}_i b_i$, we find

(23) $\dot{\sigma} = h - \dfrac{1-\beta}{\alpha} e - \sigma \left(H - \dfrac{1-\beta}{\alpha} se \right)$,

where $h \equiv \Sigma_i h_i b_i$.

802   THE AMERICAN ECONOMIC REVIEW   SEPTEMBER 1990

$h/H < 1/s$

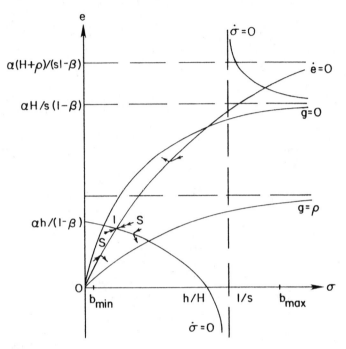

FIGURE 1

Equations (21) and (23) constitute an autonomous system of differential equations in e and σ. The solution to this system, together with (13), (20), and the definition of σ, provide a complete description of the evolution of spending and the number of products in each country. From these, the paths for outputs, employments and final-goods prices are easily derived. Thus, we shall use this two-equation system to analyze equilibrium dynamics.[5]

In Figures 1 and 2 we depict the stationary points for e. We draw the $\dot{e} = 0$ locus as increasing and concave (see (21)). To understand the positive slope of this curve, observe from (19) that the interest rate can be expressed as

$$(24) \qquad \dot{R} = \beta e / \sigma (\varepsilon - 1).$$

Thus, an increase in spending per product increases the interest rate and (from (20)) reduces the rate of growth of n (the former because the profitability of R&D rises with

---

[5]A restriction that we have not explicitly taken into account to this point is that product development must be nonnegative in each country. This condition certainly is satisfied in the neighborhood of a steady-state equilibrium with positive growth, but it need not hold all along the convergent path to such an equilibrium.

Thus, strictly speaking, the equilibrium dynamics that we describe below apply for sure only in the vicinity of a steady state.

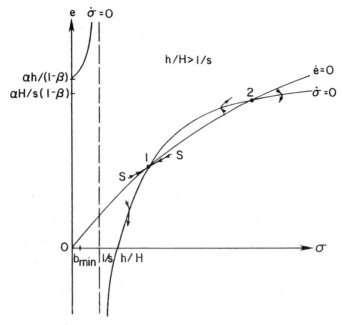

FIGURE 2

derived demand, the latter because more spending means less savings and hence less investment). Since an increase in the interest rate raises the rate of growth of nominal spending, and the rate of growth of e is just the difference between the rates of growth of E and n, it follows that an increase in e raises the growth rate of e. To compensate for this acceleration in spending per product, if e is to be stationary, σ must rise. An increase in σ lowers the interest rate and raises the rate of growth of n, thereby reducing the rate of growth of e.

Next, we distinguish two subcases depending on the relative sizes of h/H and $1/s$.[6] It can be shown that $h/H > 1/s$ if

and only if $(b_2 - b_1)(h_2 b_2 / s_2 - h_1 b_1 / s_1) > 0$. Therefore, the case $h/H > 1/s$, depicted in Figure 2, applies, for example, if the shares of the two countries' final outputs are in proportion to their relative *effective* labor forces; that is, $h_1 / s_1 = h_2 / s_2$. But a bias in size relative to budget share of final output can reverse the inequality and hence the relationship between h/H and $1/s$. This gives us the case $h/H < 1/s$, shown in Figure 1, with which we begin the discussion.

In general, both $1/s$ and h/H must lie between b_{min} and b_{max}. The $\dot{\sigma} = 0$ curve in Figure 1 is everywhere downward sloping, crosses the horizontal axis at h/H, and is discontinuous at $\sigma = 1/s$. The slope of the curve is understood as follows. For $\dot{\sigma} = 0$, we must have $\dot{\sigma}_1 = 0$, which requires that the resources available for R&D in each country be just sufficient to preserve the country's *share* in the world's number of

---

[6]A borderline case arises when $b_1 = b_2$; that is, when comparative advantage is absent. Then $h/H = 1/s$, and $\sigma = b$ always. Convergence to the steady-state level of e is immediate in this case; see Grossman and Helpman (1989a).

varieties. Consider country 1 and suppose for concreteness that this country has comparative advantage in R&D. Then an increase in σ lowers σ_1, thereby reducing the resources needed for production of middle products. The fall in σ_1 also reduces the amount of R&D country 1 must perform to preserve its share in the number of products. *Ceteris paribus*, σ_1 would tend to rise. An increase in e, on the other hand, diverts resources away from R&D to production of middle and final products in country 1. But it also causes the world's rate of product growth to fall, thereby diminishing the amount of R&D country 1 must undertake to maintain its share of middle products. The relative magnitudes of these two effects depend upon country 1's relative size, and on the share of its final product in aggregate spending. In the case under consideration, the second effect dominates, and so the $\dot{\sigma} = 0$ curve slopes downward.

In this case, there exists a unique steady state shown as point 1 in the figure. For initial values of σ not too different from that at point 1, a unique trajectory (saddlepath) converges to the steady state. This trajectory, labeled *SS*, fulfills all equilibrium requirements and satisfies the intertemporal budget constraint with equality. Along this trajectory (in the vicinity of the steady state), the interest rate and profit rate are declining (see (24)) and nominal expenditure E is rising. If the country with comparative advantage initially has a share of products that is smaller (larger) than its steady-state share, expenditure rises more slowly (rapidly) than the number of products.

The case depicted in Figure 2 arises when $h/H > 1/s$. Then the $\dot{\sigma} = 0$ schedule slopes upward. If the curve intersects the $\dot{e} = 0$ locus in the positive orthant at all, it must intersect it twice, as at points 1 and 2.[7] The

lower point (point 1) represents the steady state with the higher rate of growth (growth rates increase as we move down along the $\dot{e} = 0$ schedule, as we demonstrate below) and indeed the growth rate corresponding to point 2 may be negative. More importantly, as we show in Appendix B of our 1989a working paper, the equilibrium at point 1 exhibits saddle-path stability, whereas that at point 2 is locally unstable.[8] To the right of point 1, the saddle-path leading to that point remains trapped in the area bounded by the $\dot{e} = 0$ locus and the line segment joining points 1 and 2, and is everywhere upward sloping. Thus, the qualitative properties of the dynamic trajectory that leads to a stable, positive-growth equilibrium in Figure 2 mimic those of the stable saddle-path in Figure 1.

For the remainder of this paper we shall restrict our discussion to stable steady-state equilibria with positive rates of growth. That is, we focus our attention on equilibria such as those at the points labeled 1 in Figures 1 and 2. In the steady state there occurs intraindustry trade in middle products and interindustry trade in consumer goods, with the long-run pattern of trade determined by comparative advantage, productivities in the two final-goods industries, and consumer preferences.

III. Determinants of Long-Run Growth

Our model generates an endogenous rate of long-run growth. We now are prepared to explore how economic structure and economic policy affect this growth rate. In this section, we derive the implications of sec-

---

[7] The geometry supports this claim, once we recognize that the $\dot{\sigma} = 0$ curve asymptotes to the horizontal line at $\alpha H/s(1-\beta)$, whereas the $\dot{e} = 0$ curve asymptotes to the horizontal line at $\alpha(H+\rho)/s(1-\beta)$. The algebra provides confirmation, as simple manipulation reveals that the steady-state growth rate solves a quadratic equation.

[8] We strongly suspect, however, that whenever there exist two positive-growth, steady-state equilibria in the admissible range, there also exists a third (saddle-path stable) steady-state equilibrium with zero growth. We have established the existence of such an equilibrium for some parameter values, but so far have been unable to construct a general existence proof. Since the equilibrium at point 1 in Figure 2 can only be reached if the initial value of σ is less than that at point 2, we suspect that initial values of σ in excess of that at point 2 (and perhaps only these) imply convergence to a steady state with zero growth.

toral productivity levels, country sizes, and demand composition for the steady-state growth rate. The influence of trade policies and of subsidies to R&D are treated in the next section.

We derive the long-run values of e and σ by setting $\dot{e}$ and $\dot{\sigma}$ to zero in (21) and (23). The steady-state magnitudes, $\bar{e}$ and $\bar{\sigma}$, solve

$$(25) \qquad \frac{\beta\bar{e}}{\alpha\bar{\sigma}} + \frac{1-\beta}{\alpha}s\bar{e} = H + \rho;$$

$$(26) \qquad \frac{1-\beta}{\alpha}\bar{e}(1-\bar{\sigma}s) + \bar{\sigma}H = h.$$

Whenever $1/s > h/H$, these equations provide at most one solution for $(\bar{e},\bar{\sigma})$ consistent with $\bar{g} > 0$. When $1/s < h/H$, there may be two such solutions, in which case we select the stable equilibrium, that is, the one with the smaller values for $\bar{e}$ and $\bar{\sigma}$. Stability implies, in this latter case, that the $\dot{\sigma} = 0$ curve intersects the $\dot{e} = 0$ curve from below (see Appendix B of our 1989a working paper). We make use of this condition, namely,

$$(27) \qquad \frac{\beta\bar{e}}{(H+\rho)\bar{\sigma}^2} > \frac{\alpha H - (1-\beta)s\bar{e}}{\bar{\sigma}H - h}$$

$$\text{for} \quad 1/s < h/H,$$

in signing the comparative-dynamics derivatives that follow.

The growth rate of the number of varieties in the steady-state equilibrium can be derived from the solution to (25) and (26), together with (20). From this, we can easily calculate the growth rate of output. In the steady state, nominal expenditure grows at rate $\bar{g}$, while (3) implies that p_{Yi} grows at rate $[1-\beta/(1-\varepsilon)]\bar{g}$. From these facts and (15), we deduce that final output grows at rate $\beta\bar{g}/(1-\varepsilon)$.

It is worth noting at this point that the steady-state equations (25) and (26), as well as the equation for $\bar{g}$, do not rely on our assumption of perfect capital mobility. In

the absence of capital mobility, the steady state would be the same as long as consumers worldwide share identical preferences (and therefore common subjective discount rates).[9]

It is instructive to begin the discussion with the case in which neither country exhibits comparative advantage in conducting R&D; that is, $b_1 = b_2 = b$. This case has $h = bH$ and $s = 1/b$. Then (25) and (26) provide a unique solution for $\bar{e}$ and $\bar{\sigma}$, which upon substitution into (20) yields the long-run growth rate

$$(28) \qquad \bar{g} = \frac{\beta(H+\rho)}{\varepsilon} - \rho.$$

This equilibrium growth rate shares much in common with that derived by Romer (1990) for a closed economy. In particular, the growth rate rises with effective labor H and declines with the subjective discount rate. Our measure of effective labor adjusts raw labor for productivity in R&D (recall that $H = \Sigma_i L_i/a_{Lni}$), so greater effectiveness in research in either country, as well as a larger world labor force, necessarily means faster growth. Long-run growth does not, however, depend upon coefficients that determine absolute productivity in the intermediate or final goods sectors (such as A_i or a_{LXi}). Nor do properties of the instantaneous utility function $u(\cdot)$, including the product composition of final demand, play any role in the determination of $\bar{g}$. As we shall see presently, all these features (except for the absence of an effect of A_i on $\bar{g}$) are special to a world without any comparative advantage.

Consider next the case with $1/s > h/H$. The curves $\dot{e} = 0$ and $\dot{\sigma} = 0$ in Figure 3 describe the initial situation, with a unique initial steady state at point 1. Now suppose

[9]The cases of perfect and imperfect capital mobility differ in their implications for the steady-state share of each country in aggregate spending E. However, as should be clear from (25) and (26), the cross-country composition of E does not matter for the issues taken up in the present section.

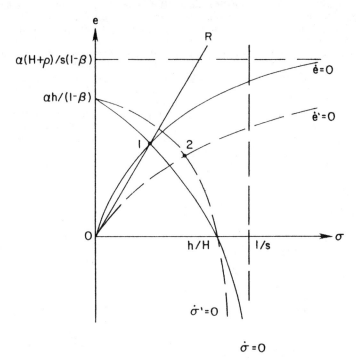

FIGURE 3

that preferences change so that s increases. This corresponds to a shift in tastes in favor of the final good produced by the country with comparative advantage in performing R&D. From (25), we see that the $\dot{e} = 0$ curve shifts down, say to $\dot{e}' = 0$ in the figure. Equation (26) implies that the $\dot{\sigma} = 0$ schedule shifts out (in the positive orthant) to $\dot{\sigma}' = 0$. The new steady state occurs at a point such as 2. But observe that all points on $\dot{e}' = 0$ to the right of its intersection with ray OR are characterized by slower steady-state growth than at point 1. This claim follows from (20) and (25), whence

$$(29) \qquad \bar{g} = \frac{\beta \bar{e}}{(\varepsilon - 1)\bar{\sigma}} - \rho.$$

Since the intersection of $\dot{\sigma}' = 0$ and $\dot{e}' = 0$ necessarily lies to the right of the intersection of the latter curve with OR, we have established that an increase in s reduces steady-state growth.

When tastes shift unexpectedly toward the final good of the country with comparative advantage in R&D, resources there must be reallocated to satisfy the relatively higher consumer demand. A process begins whereby labor there shifts out of R&D and the manufacture of middle products. Products accumulate more slowly in this country than in the other, and over time its share of middle products falls (i.e., σ rises). Output per middle product changes by the same proportion in both countries (see (18)). So, in the new steady state, the country with comparative disadvantage in R&D is responsible for a relatively larger share of the world's innovation, with adverse consequences for the common steady-state growth rate. Of course, the opposite conclusion applies when *s* falls. Moreover, the same results obtain at stable equilibrium points when $1/s < h/H$ (see our 1989a working paper). We have thus proven the following:

PROPOSITION 1: *Stronger relative demand for the final good of the country with comparative advantage in R&D lowers the long-run share of that country in the number of middle products and slows long-run growth of the world economy. In the absence of comparative advantage in R&D, the long-run growth rate is independent of the relative demand for final goods.*

Next we consider the dependence of growth on the sizes of the effective labor forces. Effective labor may grow without affecting cross-country comparative advantage either because the stock of irreproducible resources expands, or because the productivity of labor in all uses (or in R&D and intermediate-good production) rises equiproportionately. In the first experiment, suppose that both countries experience equiproportionate, once-and-for-all increases in the sizes of their effective labor forces. We have already seen that this change would augment world growth in the absence of comparative advantage. In our 1989a working paper we prove that the same result carries over to a world with intercountry differences in relative productivities at R&D and manufacturing. We establish the following there:

PROPOSITION 2: *An equiproportionate, once-and-for-all increase in the effective labor forces of both countries accelerates long-run growth.*

Greater resources generate faster growth in our model, as in Romer (1990), essentially because dynamic scale economies characterize long-run production.

We investigate next the effects of an increase in the effective labor force of a single

country. Conceptually, it proves convenient to decompose this change into two elements. First, we increase *h* and *H* by the same percentage amount. This percentage is chosen to equal the product of the share of the expanding country in the world's effective stock of labor times the percentage increase in effective labor force that the expanding country actually experiences. This accounts for the total percentage change in *H* when H_i changes. Then we must adjust *h* with *H* fixed to arrive at the appropriate change in *h*.

As an intermediate step, let us consider the effects of an increase in *h* alone. This corresponds to an increase in the effective labor of the country with comparative disadvantage in R&D, and a decrease in the effective labor of the other, so that the sum remains constant. This imaginary reshuffling of the world's resources shifts the $\dot{\sigma} = 0$ schedule upward when $1/s > h/H$, and downward otherwise. In either case, the $\dot{e} = 0$ curve is unaffected and the new steady-state point lies on this curve to the right of the original point. Noting (29), this proves the following:

LEMMA 1: *A reallocation of resources between countries that maintains a constant world stock of effective labor raises the long-run growth rate and increases the long-run product share of the relatively R&D efficient country if and only if the share of this country in effective labor increases.*

When the effective labor force of only country 1 (say) increases, *h* rises by proportionately more or less than *H*, according to whether country 1 has comparative disadvantage or advantage in R&D. If country 1 has comparative advantage in R&D, then both the uniform increase in *H* and *h* and the adjustment (lowering) of *h*, that together comprise the effect of an increase in H_1, serve to accelerate world growth. But if country 1 has comparative disadvantage in R&D, the two effects work in opposite directions. The increase in resources, by Proposition 2, speeds growth; but the reallocation of given resources, by Lemma 1, slows growth. The net effect is ambiguous, as the numerical examples that we present in Appendix D of our 1989a working paper serve to demonstrate. We have established the following:

PROPOSITION 3: *The long-run growth rate is higher the larger is the effective labor force of the country with comparative advantage in R&D. A larger effective labor force in the country with comparative disadvantage in R&D may be associated with faster or slower growth, depending upon the extent of productivity differences. In the absence of comparative advantage, long-run growth is faster the larger is the effective labor force of either country.*

These results emphasize the novel features of growth in a world with distinct countries and intercountry differences in relative productivities. They also suggest that findings reported by Paul Krugman (1990) may be somewhat special. A country need not enjoy faster growth by joining the integrated world economy, if the country enjoys substantial comparative advantage in R&D. Moreover, growth in resources or improvements in the productivity of existing resources do not guarantee faster long-run growth in a world equilibrium with free trade. If resources expand or become more efficient in the country with comparative disadvantage in R&D, then the resulting intersectoral reallocation of resources worldwide might slow innovation and growth everywhere.

IV. Economic Policy

In this section we discuss the effects of tariffs, export subsidies, and R&D subsidies on long-run growth. In order to do so, it is necessary for us to introduce the relevant policy parameters into the equations that describe instantaneous and steady-state equilibrium. To avoid repetition of the detailed arguments presented in Section I, we present here only the necessary modifications of the model and then explain their implications for the steady-state conditions. We restrict attention to small taxes and subsidies; this restriction facilitates exposi-

tion, as the channels through which economic policies affect long-run growth can be seen more clearly. We confine our analysis of trade policies to those that impede or encourage trade in final goods.

The introduction of taxes and subsidies to the model necessitates consideration of the government's budget. As usual, we assume that the government collects and redistributes net revenue by lump-sum taxes and subsidies. In a static framework, this specification suffices to determine completely the government's budgetary policy. But in a dynamic framework the budget need not balance period by period, so budgetary policy in general must specify the intertemporal pattern of lump-sum collections and transfers. However, with perfectly foresighted and infinitely lived agents, our model exhibits the Barro-Ricardo neutrality property. Hence, we need not concern ourselves with the intertemporal structure of budget deficits so long as the present value of the government's net cash flow equals zero.

The presence of the aforementioned policies modifies the decision problem for consumers in country 1 in two ways. First, we replace the price of good i in (12) by $T_i p_{Yi}$, where $T_1 = 1$. With this formulation, p_{Yi} remains the producer price of final good i, $T_2 > 1$ represents a tariff in country 1 on imports of consumer goods, and $T_2 < 1$ represents a subsidy by country 2 on exports of final output.[10] Second, we add the present value of net taxes to the right-hand side of (13) as a lump-sum addition to consumer wealth. The amount of this collection or redistribution will differ across countries according to their policies.

These modifications do not affect (14), which continues to describe the optimal intertemporal pattern of expenditures for consumers worldwide as a function of the pattern of equilibrium interest rates. In a steady state with $\dot{e} = 0$, (14) reduces to

$$(30) \qquad \dot{R} = \bar{g} + \rho.$$

---

[10]The effects of a country 2 import tariff and a country 1 export subsidy can be derived symmetrically, so we neglect these policies here and leave the maximand for consumers in country 2 as before.

Notice that (30) implies that in any steady state in which countries grow at the same rate, long-run equalization of interest rates obtains. This property of our model holds irrespective of the presence or absence of international capital mobility and the presence or absence of tariffs or export subsidies on final goods and subsidies to research and development.

Turning to the production side, our policies do not alter equations (3)–(8) describing pricing and output relationships in the intermediate and final-goods sectors and the technology for knowledge creation. However, R&D subsidies do change the private cost of R&D. We replace (10) by

$$(10')\qquad c_{ni} = w_i a_{Lni} / nS_i,$$

where $S_i > 1$ represents subsidization of research costs in country i. It proves convenient to redefine our numeraire to normalize for the effect of the R&D subsidy on the price of intermediate inputs in country 1. Our new normalization dictates a modified equation for the price of intermediates produced in country 2 as well. Together, these relationships, which replace (17a) and (17b), can be written as

$$(17')\qquad p_{Xi} = n(S_i a_{LXi} / a_{Lni})^{1/\varepsilon}$$

As for the market-clearing conditions, the factor-markets equation (16) is not affected, but we must replace (15) by

$$(15')\qquad p_{Yi} Y_i = \frac{s_{i1} E_1}{T_i} + s_{i2} E_2,$$

where E_i denotes aggregate spending by consumers in country i, and the shares of spending devoted to good i by residents of country 1 and country 2 are $s_{i1} = s_i(p_{Y1}, p_{Y2} T_2)$ and $s_{i2} = s_i(p_{Y1}, p_{Y2})$, respectively. Although import tariffs and export subsidies on final goods do not affect steady-state producer prices of final output in our model,[11] the direct response of

spending shares in country 1 to changes in trade policy must now be taken into account. Moreover, R&D subsidies, if introduced at different rates in the two countries, will affect the steady-state value of p_{Y1} / p_{Y2}, and may therefore influence the long-run spending shares in both countries.

This completes the necessary modifications of the equilibrium relationships. We can now use the extended model to derive the equations describing steady-state equilibrium in the presence of policy intervention. In a steady state, employment in the R&D sector is given by $a_{Lni} \dot{n}_i / n = a_{Lni} \bar{g} \bar{\sigma}_i$. Making use of (4), (5), (7), (30), (10'), and (17') (which together imply $\dot{c}_{ni} = 0$ in a steady state), we find employment in the manufacture of middle products equal to $a_{Lni} \bar{\sigma}_i (\bar{g} + \rho)(\varepsilon - 1)/S_i$. Substitution of these terms into (16) yields the steady-state labor market–clearing condition,

$$(31)\qquad \bar{g}\bar{\sigma}_i + \frac{(\varepsilon - 1)(\bar{g} + \rho)}{S_i}\bar{\sigma}_i$$

$$+ \frac{1-\beta}{\alpha b_i S_i^{1/\varepsilon}}\bar{q}_i = h_i,$$

where $q_i \equiv p_{Yi} Y_i / n$. Next, from (4)–(7), (30), and (17'), we obtain

$$(32)\qquad (\varepsilon - 1)(\bar{g} + \rho)\left(\sum_i \frac{\bar{\sigma}_i b_i}{S_i^\alpha}\right)$$

$$- \beta \sum_i \bar{q}_i = 0.$$

Naturally, we also require

$$(33)\qquad \sum_i \bar{\sigma}_i = 1.$$

Finally, (15') implies

$$(34)\qquad \bar{q}_i = \frac{\bar{s}_{i1}\bar{e}_1}{T_i} + \bar{s}_{i2}\bar{e}_2.$$

It is straightforward, now, to verify that (31)–(34) imply (25) and (26) when $T_i = S_i = 1$ for $i = 1, 2$ (with $\bar{e} = \Sigma_i \bar{e}_i$). This provides a

---

[11]This statement can be verified using equations (3), (4), and (17').

consistency check on the extended model, with policy instruments.

We consider trade policies first. From (34), the ratio $\bar{q}_1 / \bar{q}_2$ satisfies

$$(35) \qquad \frac{\bar{q}_1}{\bar{q}_2} = \frac{\bar{s}_{11}\bar{e}_1 + \bar{s}_{12}\bar{e}_2}{\bar{s}_{21}\bar{e}_1 / T_2 + \bar{s}_{22}\bar{e}_2}.$$

Now, for given expenditure levels $\bar{e}_i$, equations (31)–(33) and (35)—which constitute a system of five equations—provide a solution for $(\bar{g}, \bar{\sigma}_1, \bar{\sigma}_2, \bar{q}_1, \bar{q}_2)$. In this system, the trade policy parameters appear only in (35). Therefore, the long-run effects of trade policy depend only on their effects on $\bar{q}_1 / \bar{q}_2$, taking into account the induced adjustment in the spending levels $\bar{e}_1$ and $\bar{e}_2$. Moreover, for small trade policies (i.e, with an initial value of $T_2 = 1$), the spending shares are equal across countries ($\bar{s}_{i1} = \bar{s}_{i2}$), so the effect on $\bar{q}_1 / \bar{q}_2$ of changes in the cross-country composition of aggregate spending "washes out."

Further inspection of (35) reveals that an increase in T_2 starting from free trade with $T_2 = 1$ (i.e., a small import tariff in country 1) unambiguously raises $\bar{q}_1 / \bar{q}_2$.[12] A tariff shifts demand by residents of country 1 toward home consumer products, and since relative producer prices do not change in the long run, steady-state relative quantities must adjust. The effect of this change on the steady state is qualitatively the same as for an exogenous increase in world preference for final good 1, such as we studied in the previous section when we varied s_1.

---

[12] The easiest way to see this is to write the right-hand-side of (35) as

$$(\bar{p}_{Y1}, \bar{p}_{Y2})[\phi_1(\bar{p}_{Y1}, T_2\bar{p}_{Y2})\bar{e}_1 + \phi_1(\bar{p}_{Y1}, \bar{p}_{Y2})\bar{e}_2]/$$

$$[\phi_2(\bar{p}_{Y1}, T_2\bar{p}_{Y2})\bar{e}_1 + \phi_2(\bar{p}_{Y1}, \bar{p}_{Y2})\bar{e}_2],$$

where $\phi_i(\cdot)$ is minus the partial derivative of $r(\cdot)$ from (1) with respect to its ith argument divided by $r(\cdot)$. Then an increase in T_2 with $\bar{p}_{Y1} / \bar{p}_{Y2}$ constant clearly raises demand for final good 1 in country 1 (the first component of the bracketed term in the numerator increases) and lowers the demand there for final good 2 (the first component of the bracketed term in the denominator falls).

Similarly, a small export subsidy in country 2 (a reduction in T_2 to a value slightly below one) biases country 1 demand in favor of foreign final output. So we may apply directly our results from Proposition 1 to state the following:

PROPOSITION 4: *A small import tariff or export subsidy on final goods reduces a country's steady-state share in middle products and R&D. It increases the rate of long-run growth in the world economy if and only if the policy-active country has comparative disadvantage in R&D.*

Commercial policies *do* affect long-run growth rates. They do so by shifting resources in the policy-active country out of the growth-generating activity (R&D) and into production in the favored sector. At the same time, a resource shift of the opposite kind takes place abroad in the dynamic general equilibrium. The net effect on world growth hinges on the identity of the country that favors its consumer-good industry. If import protection or export promotion is undertaken by the country that is relatively less efficient in conducting R&D, then growth accelerates; otherwise, growth decelerates.

Next, we investigate the effects of small subsidies to R&D, introduced from an initial position of *laissez faire*. For these policy experiments, $T_2 = 1$ before and after the policy change, so the expenditure levels $\bar{e}_i$ cancel from (35). Suppose, first, that both countries apply subsidies at equal *ad valorem* rates; that is, $S_1 = S_2 = S$. In this case, relative prices of final output do not change across steady states. Therefore, the spending shares $\bar{s}_{ij}$ do not change. In Appendix C of our 1989a working paper, we totally differentiate (31)–(33) and (35) with respect to S to prove the following:

PROPOSITION 5: *A small R&D subsidy by both countries at a common rate increases the rate of long-run growth in the world economy.*

This proposition is not surprising, and corresponds to a similar result for the closed economy derived by Romer (1990). Since R&D represents the only source of gains in per capita income in our model, stimulation of this activity promotes growth.

What is more interesting, perhaps, is the effect of a small R&D subsidy in a single country. As for bilateral subsidies, a unilateral subsidy promotes growth by bringing more resources into product development in the policy-active country. But now, relative final-good prices change, so the spending shares in (35) must be allowed to vary unless the utility function has a Cobb-Douglas form. Depending on whether the elasticity of substitution between final products exceeds or falls short of one, this induced change in the pattern of spending can be conducive to or detrimental to growth. Moreover, an R&D subsidy in a single country will alter the relative shares of the two countries in product development. If the subsidy is introduced by the country that is relatively less efficient at performing R&D, this effect too can impede growth. In Appendix D of our 1989a working paper we show, by means of a numerical example using a Cobb-Douglas utility function, that an R&D subsidy introduced by the country with comparative disadvantage in R&D might (but need not) reduce the world's growth rate. We also prove in Appendix C that, for the case of constant spending shares, an R&D subsidy must encourage growth if it is undertaken by the country with comparative advantage in R&D. Thus we have the following:

PROPOSITION 6: *The provision of a subsidy to R&D in one country increases long-run growth if spending shares on the two final goods are constant and the policy is undertaken by the country with comparative advantage in R&D. Otherwise, the long-run growth rate may rise or fall.*

Our results here on the long-run growth effects of government policy have no immediate normative implications, both because we perform only steady-state comparisons and because the initial *level* of utility may differ along alternative growth paths. But in our 1989b paper we conduct a complete

welfare analysis for a small country with endogenous growth generated by technological progress as here. We find that the market determined rate of growth is suboptimally low due to the presence of the nonappropriable spillovers in the process of knowledge generation. An R&D subsidy that speeds growth improves welfare for the small country until some optimal growth rate is achieved. Further increases in the subsidy rate reduce welfare even as they accelerate growth. We show also that trade policy need not raise welfare, even if it successfully speeds growth. The explanation for this lies in the presence of a second distortion in our economy, one that stems from the pricing of middle products above marginal cost. The mark-up pricing practiced by intermediate producers gives rise to suboptimal use of middle products in the production of final goods. Trade policy that accelerates growth but reduces the output of middle products in the general equilibrium can be detrimental to welfare. Conversely, commercial policy that augments the output of middle products can improve welfare even if the growth implications of such policy are adverse.

These results do not carry over immediately to the current environment, though the considerations we found to be relevant in our 1989b paper are certainly applicable here as well. Normative analysis in the present two-country setting is complicated by the terms-of-trade effects that arise when policy alters the relative price of the final goods, changes the price of intermediates (if sectoral trade in middle products is not balanced), or varies the interest rate. Because of these various terms-of-trade effects we have been unable thus far to find simple conditions under which growth-enhancing policy by one government raises that country's welfare.

V. Lags in the Diffusion of Knowledge

We have assumed all along that research and development creates as a by-product an addition to the stock of knowledge that facilitates subsequent R&D. Moreover, we supposed that the knowledge so created becomes available immediately to scientists and engineers worldwide. We now relax the latter assumption, in recognition of the fact that privately created knowledge, even if nonappropriable, may enter the public domain via an uneven and time-consuming process. Also, since legal and cultural barriers may inhibit the free movement of people and ideas across national borders, we shall allow here for the possibility that information generated in one country disseminates more rapidly to researchers in the same country than it does to researchers in the trade partner country. After extending the model we will reconsider the effects of trade policies on the steady-state rate of growth.

In place of our earlier assumption that world knowledge accumulates exactly at the rate of product innovation (equation (9)), we suppose now that R&D expenditures contribute to country-specific stocks of knowledge according to

$$(9^\dagger) \quad K_i(t) = \lambda_h \int_{-\infty}^{t} e^{\lambda_h(\tau-t)} n_i(\tau)$$

$$+ \lambda_f \int_{-\infty}^{t} e^{\lambda_f(\tau-t)} n_j(\tau)\, d\tau,$$

where $K_i(t)$ is the stock of knowledge capital at time t in country i. With this specification, the contribution of a particular R&D project to general knowledge is spread over time. At the moment after completion of the project, none of its findings have percolated through the scientific and professional community. After an infinite amount of time has passed, the R&D project makes, as before, a unit contribution to knowledge. After finite time, the contribution lies between these extremes of zero and one, as given by the exponential lag structure in $(9^\dagger)$. The parameters λ_h and λ_f (with $\lambda_h \geq \lambda_f$) distinguish within-country and cross-country rates of diffusion.

The introduction of lags in the diffusion of knowledge alters two of the fundamental equations of the model. First, (8) becomes

$$(8^\dagger) \quad \dot{n}_i = L_{ni} K_i / a_{Lni}.$$

Second, we have in place of (10),

$$(10^\dagger) \quad c_{ni} = w_i a_{Lni} / K_i.$$

In a steady state with $\dot{n}_1 = \dot{n}_2 = g$, we have $n_i(\tau) = n_i(t) e^{g(\tau-t)}$, so that

$$(36) \quad K_i(t) = \frac{\lambda_h}{\lambda_h + \bar{g}} n_i(t) + \frac{\lambda_f}{\lambda_f + \bar{g}} n_j(t)$$

$$= \left[\frac{\lambda_h}{\lambda_h + \bar{g}} \bar{\sigma}_i + \frac{\lambda_f}{\lambda_f + \bar{g}} \bar{\sigma}_j \right] n(t)$$

$$\equiv \mu_i(\bar{\sigma}_1, \bar{\sigma}_2, \bar{g}) n(t).$$

So in the steady state, knowledge in each country is proportional once again to the total number of middle products. But the factor of proportionality has become country-specific and endogenous. This means that the steady-state labor-input coefficient for R&D in country i, a_{Lni}/μ_i, also is endogenous; that is, relative productivity in R&D depends now not only on relative natural abilities in performing this activity, but also on relative cumulative experience in research, as summarized by the σ_i's. This consideration leads us to draw a distinction henceforth between *natural* and *acquired* comparative advantage in R&D.

From (36) we see that when $\lambda_h = \lambda_f \to \infty$ (i.e., when diffusion lags are very short), $\mu_1 = \mu_2 \to 1$, and the extended model reverts to the earlier formulation. For $\lambda_h = \lambda_f$ finite, $\mu_1 = \mu_2$, so that the ratio of the natural-plus-acquired productivity parameters for each country is the same as for the natural productivity parameters alone. In this case, the pattern of comparative advantage cannot be reversed by endogenous learning, and all results from before continue to apply. We concentrate here on cases in which the rates of diffusion are *unequal* but the difference between them is small.[13]

---

[13]A large difference between the within-country and across-country rates of diffusion may imply that, in the steady-state equilibrium, all R&D is carried out by one country. Such specialization, which is common in mod-

We derive the long-run effects of trade policy in the extended model using equations (31)–(33) and (35), but with $S_1 = S_2 = 1$ (no R&D subsidies), with b_i replaced by b_i / μ_i^α (natural plus acquired comparative advantage in place of just natural comparative advantage), and with h_i replaced by $h_i \mu_i$ (natural plus acquired effective labor in place of natural effective labor). For clarity of exposition, we shall also assume for the remainder of this section that the spending shares s_i are constant. This assumption is valid when $u(\cdot)$ takes a Cobb-Douglas form.

The new elements that diffusion lags introduce to the analysis of policy stem from the effects of *relative size* and *demand-side bias*. Before considering these new aspects, let us suppose that labor forces are equal and demand for the two final goods is symmetric. By totally differentiating the system of steady-state equations (see Appendix E of our 1989a working paper), we establish the following:

PROPOSITION 7: *Suppose* $L_1 = L_2$, $s_1 = s_2$, $a_{LX1} = a_{LX2}$, *and* $\lambda_h - \lambda_f > 0$, *but small. Then a tariff on imports of final goods in country i raises the long-run growth rate if and only if* $a_{Lni} > a_{Lnj}$.

In this case, the effects of acquired comparative advantage necessarily *reinforce* those of natural comparative advantage. The country that is relatively more productive in creating new blueprints will attain, in the steady-state equilibrium prior to the introduction of policy, a majority share of the world's middle products. By its greater concentration in R&D, it will gain more experience in research and attain a higher steady-state stock of knowledge. Thus, the effects of learning will augment its initial comparative advantage in R&D. When policy is introduced in one country or the other,

the implications of the dynamic resource reallocation for the global efficiency of R&D will be all the more significant.

Now suppose that the two countries differ initially only in (effective) size, as measured by h_i. Recall that with equal rates of diffusion, a small tariff in either country does not affect the long-run rate of growth. Now, however, we find the following:

PROPOSITION 8: *Suppose* $b_1 = b_2$, $s_1 = s_2$ *and* $\lambda_h - \lambda_f > 0$, *but small. Then a small tariff on imports of final goods raises the long-run growth rate if and only if the policy is introduced by the country with the relatively smaller effective labor force.*

Here, the larger country will come to acquire comparative advantage in R&D, though it starts with none. The reason is as follows. With differential rates of diffusion, knowledge takes on the characteristics of a *local public good*. The larger country will have more (effective) scientists to benefit from this nonexcludable good as its share in world R&D exceeds one half. So it acquires over time a relatively larger knowledge base and hence a relatively more productive corps of researchers. Trade policy that serves to divert resources away from the R&D sector in the larger country once comparative advantage has been established must be detrimental to growth.

The effects of demand-size bias are similar. The country whose good is in relatively greater demand must devote relatively more of its resources to final-goods production. Thus, its R&D sector initially will be smaller. This country develops over time a comparative disadvantage in R&D, as its learning lags that in its trade partner country. Protection in this country will improve world efficiency of R&D and thereby speed growth.

Once we allow for lags in the diffusion of scientific knowledge and differential speeds of diffusion within versus between countries, we find a richer set of possibilities for the long-run effects of trade policy. Comparative advantage continues to play a critical role in determining whether policy in one country will speed or decelerate growth.

---

els with a national component to increasing returns to scale, necessarily occurs here if static preferences are Cobb-Douglas and $\lambda_f = 0$ (i.e., all spillovers are internal). Then the equations that we have developed to describe the steady-state equilibrium (which presume non-specialization in each country) would not be valid.

But comparative advantage now must be interpreted with care, because it reflects not only natural ability but also the (endogenous) benefits from cumulative experience.[14] Since steady-state productivity in R&D varies positively with the size of the R&D sector, all determinants of the equilibrium allocation of resources to this sector come to be important in the analysis of policy.

VI. Conclusions

In this paper, we have analyzed a dynamic, two-country model of trade and growth in which long-run productivity gains stem from the profit-maximizing behavior of entrepreneurs. We have studied the determinants of R&D, where research bears fruit in the form of designs for new intermediate products and in making further research less costly. New intermediate products permit greater specialization in the process of manufacturing consumer goods, thereby enhancing productivity in final production. In order to highlight the role of endogenous technological improvements as a source of growth we have abstracted entirely from factor accumulation. But Romer (1990) has shown that capital accumulation can be introduced into a model such as the one we have studied without affecting the analysis in any significant way.

The interesting features of our analysis arise because of the assumed presence of *cross-country differences* in efficiency at R&D and manufacturing. Considerations of comparative advantage in research versus manufacturing of intermediate goods bear importantly on the implications of economic structure and economic policy for long-run patterns of specialization and long-run rates of growth. We find, for example, that growth in world resources or improvements in R&D efficiency need not speed the rate of steady-state growth, if those changes occur predominantly in the country with comparative disadvantage in R&D.

Concerning policy, we find for the first time a link between trade intervention and long-run growth. Any (small) trade policy that switches spending toward the consumer good produced by the country with comparative advantage in R&D will cause long-run growth rates to decline. Subsidies to R&D will accelerate growth when applied at equal rates in both countries, but need not do so if introduced only in the country with comparative disadvantage in R&D. When knowledge spillovers occur with a time lag and diffusion is faster within the country of origin than across national borders, comparative advantage becomes endogenous. Once we recognize that comparative advantage can be *acquired* as well as natural, we find a role for country size and demand-size bias in determining the long-run effects of policy.

Our emphasis on comparative advantage in research and development highlights only one channel through which trade structure and commercial policy might affect long-run growth. In other contexts, the trade environment might influence the rate of accumulation of human capital or the rate at which a technologically lagging (less developed) country adopts for local use the existing off-the-shelf techniques of production. Investigation of the links between trade regime and these other sources of growth seems to us a worthy topic for future research.

---

[14] Endogenous comparative advantage also plays a central role in Krugman's (1987) analysis of commodity-specific learning-by-doing. There, as here, productivity increases with cumulative experience. But each good is produced in only one country in Krugman's model, so long-run comparative advantage is fully determined by the initial pattern of specialization.

REFERENCES

Becker, Gary S. and Murphy, Kevin M., "Economic Growth, Human Capital and Population Growth," *Journal of Political Economy*, forthcoming, 1990.

Corden, W. Max, "The Effects of Trade on the Rate of Growth," in J. Bhagwati et al., eds., *Trade, Balance of Payments, and Growth: Papers in Honour of Charles P. Kindleberger*, Amsterdam: North-Holland, 1971.

Ethier, Wilfred J., "National and International Returns to Scale in the Modern Theory of International Trade," *American Economic Review*, June 1982, *72*, 389–405.

Findlay, Ronald, "Growth and Development in Trade Models," in R. Jones and P. Kenen, eds., *Handbook of International Economics*, Amsterdam: North-Holland, 1984.

Griliches, Zvi, "Issues in Assessing the Contribution of Research and Development in Productivity Growth," *Bell Journal of Economics*, Summer 1979, *10*, 92–116.

Grossman, Gene M., "Explaining Japan's Innovation and Trade: A Model of Quality Competition and Dynamic Comparative Advantage," National Bureau of Economic Research Working Paper No. 3194, December 1989.

_____ and Helpman, Elhanan, (1989a) "Comparative Advantage and Long-Run Growth," National Bureau of Economic Research Working Paper No. 2809, January 1989.

_____ and _____, (1989b) "Growth and Welfare in a Small, Open Economy," Woodrow Wilson School Discussion Paper in Economics No. 145, June 1989.

_____ and _____, (1989c) "Product Development and International Trade," *Journal of Political Economy*, December 1989, *97*, 1261–83.

_____ and _____, (1989d) "Quality Ladders in the Theory of Growth," National Bureau of Economic Research Working Paper No. 3099, September 1989. (*Review of Economic Studies*, forthcoming.)

_____, _____ and Razin, A., eds., *International Trade and Trade Policy*, Cambridge, MA: MIT Press, forthcoming.

Judd, Kenneth, "On the Performance of Patents," *Econometrica*, May 1985, *53*, 567–85.

Krugman, Paul R., "The Narrow Moving Band, the Dutch Disease, and the Competitive Consequences of Mrs. Thatcher: Notes on Trade in the Presence of Dynamic Scale Economies," *Journal of Development Economics*, October 1987, *27*, 41–55.

_____, "Endogenous Innovation, International Trade and Growth," *Journal of Political Economy*, forthcoming, 1990.

Lucas, Robert E. Jr., "On the Mechanics of Economic Development," *Journal of Monetary Economics*, July 1988, *22*, 3–42.

Maddison, Angus, "Growth and Slowdown in Advanced Capitalist Economies: Techniques of Quantitative Assessment," *Journal of Economic Literature*, June 1987, *25*, 649–98.

Pasinetti, Luigi, *Structural Change and Economic Growth*, Cambridge: Cambridge University Press, 1981.

Romer, Paul M., "Increasing Returns and Long-Run Growth," *Journal of Political Economy*, October 1986, *94*, 1002–37.

_____, "Endogenous Technological Change," *Journal of Political Economy*, forthcoming, 1990.

Solow, Robert M., "Technical Change and the Aggregate Production Function," *Review of Economics and Statistics*, August 1957, *39*, 312–20.

[30]

ECONOMIC INTEGRATION AND ENDOGENOUS GROWTH*

Luis A. Rivera-Batiz and Paul M. Romer

In a world with two similar, developed economies, economic integration can cause a permanent increase in the worldwide rate of growth. Starting from a position of isolation, closer integration can be achieved by increasing trade in goods or by increasing flows of ideas. We consider two models with different specifications of the research and development sector that is the source of growth. Either form of integration can increase the long-run rate of growth if it encourages the worldwide exploitation of increasing returns to scale in the research and development sector.

I. INTRODUCTION

Many economists believe that increased economic integration between the developed economies of the world has tended to increase the long-run rate of economic growth. If they were asked to make an intuitive prediction, they would suggest that prospects for growth would be permanently diminished if a barrier were erected that impeded the flow of all goods, ideas, and people between Asia, Europe, and North America. Yet it would be difficult for any of us to offer a rigorous model that has been (or even could be) calibrated to data and that could justify this belief.

We know what some of the basic elements of such a growth model would be. Historical analysis (e.g., Rosenberg [1980]) shows that the creation and transmission of ideas has been extremely important in the development of modern standards of living. Theoretical arguments dating from Adam Smith's analysis of the pin factory have emphasized the potential importance of fixed costs and the extent of the market. There is a long tradition in trade theory of using models with Marshallian external effects to approach questions about increasing returns. More recently, static models with fixed costs and international specialization have been proposed that come closer to Smith's description of the sources of the gains from trade [Dixit and Norman, 1980; Ethier, 1982; Krugman, 1979, 1981; Lancaster, 1980]. There are also dynamic models with fixed costs and differentiated products in which output

*Conversations with Robert Barro, Gene Grossman, Elhanan Helpman, and Danyang Xie about their work on related issues have been very helpful, as were comments by Ray Riezman and Robert Staiger on earlier versions of this paper. The work of the second author was supported by NSF grant #SES88-22052, by a Sloan Foundation Fellowship, and by the Center for Advanced Studies in the Behavioral Sciences, which received support from NSF grant #BNS87-00864.

The Quarterly Journal of Economics, May 1991

grows toward a fixed steady state level [Grossman and Helpman, 1989a].

Recent models of endogenous growth have used these ideas to study the effects that trade can have on the long-run rate of growth. (See, for example, the theoretical papers by Dinopoulos, Oehmke, and Segerstrom [1990]; Feenstra [1990]; Grossman and Helpman [1989b, 1989c, 1989d, 1989e, 1990]; Krugman [1990, Ch. 11]; Lucas [1988]; Romer [1990]; Segerstrom, Anant, and Dinopoulos [1990]; and Young [1990]. Backus, Kehoe, and Kehoe [1991] present both theoretical models and cross-country empirical evidence that bears on their models.) These models permit a distinction between a one-shot gain (i.e., a level effect) and a permanent change in the growth rate (i.e., a growth effect) that is extremely important in making an order of magnitude estimate of the benefits of economic integration. Conventional attempts to quantify the effects of integration using the neoclassical growth model often suggest that the gains from integration are small. If these estimates were calculated in the context of an endogenous growth model, integration might be found to be much more important.

The papers written so far have already demonstrated, however, that the growth effects of trade restrictions are very complicated in the most general case. Grossman and Helpman [1989b, 1989c, 1989e, 1990] have been particularly explicit about the fact that no universally applicable conclusions can be drawn. There are some models in which trade restrictions can slow down the worldwide rate of growth. There are others in which they can speed up the worldwide rate of growth.

To provide some intuition for the conjecture described in the first paragraph, that trade between the advanced countries does foster growth, we narrow the focus in this paper. We do not consider the general case of trade between countries with different endowments and technologies. Instead, we focus on the pure scale effects of integration. To set aside the other "comparative advantage" effects that trade induces in multisector trade models, we consider integration only between countries or regions that are similar. Therefore, we do not address the kinds of questions that are relevant for modeling the effects that trade between a poor LDC and a developed country can have on the worldwide rate of growth.

In the early stages of our analysis of integration and growth, it became clear that the theoretical treatment of ideas has a decisive effect on the conclusions one draws. In many of the existing models, flows of ideas cannot be separated from flows of goods. In others, flows of ideas are exogenously limited by national boundaries regardless of the trade regime. In either of these cases, economic integration can refer only to flows of goods along cargo networks. We consider a broader notion of integration, one that assigns an effect to flows of ideas along communication networks.

Flows of ideas deserve attention comparable to that devoted to flows of goods, for public policy can influence international communications and information flows to the same extent that it influences goods flows. Governments often subsidize language training and study abroad. Tax policies directly affect the incentive to station company employees in foreign nations. Immigration and visa policies directly limit the movement of people. Telecommunications networks are either run by government agencies or controlled by regulators. Some governments restrict direct foreign investment, which presumably is important in the international transmission of ideas. Others have made the acquisition of commercial and technical information a high priority task for their intelligence agencies.

Although these are the only ones we consider, it should be clear that flows of goods and flows of ideas are not the only elements in economic integration. Under some assumptions about nominal variables and the operation of financial markets, economic integration will also depend on monetary and institutional arrangements. The growth models we consider are too simple to consider these effects. It should also be clear that economic integration is not synonymous with political integration. Firms in Windsor, Ontario, may be more closely integrated into markets in the United States than they are to markets in the neighboring province of Quebec. Moreover, the notion of full economic integration does not entail the abolition of citizenship distinctions that have taken place in Germany's reunification.

The structure of the paper is as follows. Section II lays out the basic features of the production structure on which all arguments rely. It describes preferences, endowments, and the nature of equilibrium under the two specifications of R&D. Section III describes the equilibrium for both models in the closed economy and complete integration cases, and illustrates the scale effects that are present. Section IV presents the three main thought experiments concerning partial integration. Sections V and VI describe the general lessons that can be learned about the relation between the scale of the market and growth and discuss limitations of the models, extensions, and the relation to other models of endogenous growth.

II. SPECIFICATION OF THE MODELS

A. Functional Forms and Decentralization in the Manufacturing Sector

The specification of the production technology for the manufacturing sector is taken from Romer [1990]. Manufacturing output is a function of human capital H, labor L, and a set $x(i)$ of capital goods indexed by the variable i. To avoid complications arising from integer constraints, the index i is modeled as a continuous variable. Technological progress is represented by the invention of new types of capital goods.

There are two types of manufacturing activities: production of consumption goods and production of the physical units of the types of capital goods that have already been invented. A third activity, research and development (R&D), creates designs for new types of capital goods. This activity is discussed in the next section.

Both manufacturing activities use the same production function. Let $x(i)$ denote the stock of capital of type i that is used in production, and let A be the index of the most recently invented good. By the definition of A, $x(i) = 0$ for all $i > A$. Output Y is assumed to take the form,

$$(1) \qquad Y(H,L,x(\cdot)) = H^\alpha L^\beta \int_0^A x(i)^{1-\alpha-\beta} di.$$

Since the production function for manufacturing consumption goods is the same as that for manufacturing units of any type of existing capital, the relative prices of consumption goods and all types of existing capital goods are fixed by the technology. For simplicity, we choose units so that all of these relative prices are one. Fixed prices imply that the aggregate capital stock $K = \int_0^A x(i)\, di$ is well defined, as is aggregate output Y.

In this specification one unit of any capital good can be produced if one unit of consumption goods is forgone. This does not mean that consumption goods are directly converted into capital goods. Rather, the inputs needed to produce one unit of consumption are shifted from the production of consumption goods into the production of a capital good. Since inputs are used in the same proportions, it is easy to infer the allocation of inputs between the different production activities from the level of output of those activities. Because all the outputs here have the same production function, the consumption sector and all of the sectors producing the different capital goods can be collapsed into a single sector. We can therefore represent total manufacturing output as a function of the total stock of inputs used in the combined manufacturing sectors and can describe the division of inputs between sectors by the constraint $Y = C + K$. For one of the models of R&D described in the next section, we can use this same observation to combine the research sector and the aggregate manufacturing sector into a single sector describing all output in the economy. In the other model the R&D and manufacturing sectors must be kept separate.

There are many equivalent institutional structures that can support a decentralized equilibrium in manufacturing. For instance, the holder of a patent on good j could become a manufacturer, producing and selling good j. Alternatively, the patent holder could license the design to other manufacturers for a fee. Formally, it is useful to separate the manufacturing decision from the monopoly pricing decision of the patent holder, so we assume that patent holders contract out manufacturing to separate firms. It is also easier to assume that the patent holder collects rent on its capital goods rather than selling them. For analytical convenience, we therefore describe the institutional arrangements in the following, slightly artificial way. First, there are many firms that rent capital goods $x(i)$ from the patent holders, hire unskilled labor L, and employ skilled human capital H to produce manufactured goods. Each of these firms can produce consumption goods for sale to consumers. It can also produce one of the capital goods on contract for the holder of the patent. All of the manufacturing firms have the production function given in equation (1), which is homogeneous of degree one. They are price takers and earn zero profit. Manufacturing output is taken as the numeraire.

The firm that holds the patent on good j bids out the production of the actual capital goods to a specific manufacturer. It purchases physical units of the good for the competitive price, by normalization equal to one. The patent holder then rents out the units to all manufacturing firms at the profit-maximizing monopoly rental rate. It can do this because patent law prohibits any firm from manufacturing a capital good without the consent of the patent holder. The patent is a tradable asset with a price of P_A that is equal to the present discounted value of the stream of monopoly rent minus the cost of the machines. It is easy to verify that this set of institutional arrangements is equivalent to other arrangements. For example, the equivalent licensing fee for each unit of capital sold by a licensee is the present value of the stream of monopoly rent on one machine minus the unit cost of manufacturing it.

B. Functional Forms and Decentralization in R&D

We consider two specifications of the technology of R&D that permit easy analytic solutions. Each specification captures different features of the world, and neither alone gives a complete description of R&D. We use both of them because they help us isolate the exact sense in which economic integration can influence long-run growth. As the example in the next section shows, it would be easy to come to misleading conclusions about integration and growth if one generalized from a single example.

The first specification of the technology for producing designs for new capital goods assumes that human capital and knowledge are the only inputs that influence the output of designs:

$$(2) \qquad \dot{A} = \delta H A,$$

where H denotes the stock of human capital used in research. The stock of existing designs A is a measure of general scientific and engineering knowledge as well as practical know-how that accumulated as previous design problems were solved. (See Romer [1990] for additional discussion of this specification.) New designs build on this knowledge, so we refer to this type of R&D process as the knowledge-driven specification of R&D. This specification imposes a sharp factor intensity difference between R&D and manufacturing. Neither unskilled labor nor physical capital has any value in R&D. Because of this difference, the resulting model must be analyzed using a two-sector framework.

A useful polar case is a technology for R&D that uses the same inputs as the manufacturing technology, in the same proportions. If H, L, and x_i denote inputs used in R&D and B denotes a constant scale factor, output of designs can be written as

$$(3) \qquad \dot{A} = B H^\alpha L^\beta \int_0^A x(i)^{1-\alpha-\beta} di.$$

This specification says that human capital, unskilled labor, and capital goods (such as personal computers or oscilloscopes) are productive in research. But in contrast to the previous specification, knowledge per se has no productive value. Access to the designs for all previous goods, and familiarity with the ideas and know-how that they represent, does not aid the creation of new designs. We refer to this as the lab equipment specification of R&D.

As noted above, the growth model with the knowledge-driven specification for R&D has an unavoidable two-sector structure. The production possibility frontier in the space of designs and manufactured goods takes on the usual curved shape. In the lab equipment model the production functions of the goods and R&D sectors are the same, so the production possibility frontier is a straight line. If the output of goods is reduced by one unit and the inputs released are transferred to the R&D sector, they yield B patents. Thus, the price P_A of a patent in terms of goods is determined on the technology side as $P_A = 1/B$. Since capital goods and consumption goods have the same production technology, we integrated them into a single manufacturing sector in the last section. In the lab equipment model we can go farther and aggregate manufacturing and research into a single sector. Let H, L, and $x(i)$ denote the entire stock of inputs available in the economy at date t. Then we can express the value of total output $C + \dot{K} + \dot{A}/B$ in terms of the total stock of inputs,

$$(4) \qquad C + \dot{K} + \frac{\dot{A}}{B} = H^\alpha L^\beta \int_0^A x(i)^{1-\alpha-\beta} di.$$

The model's symmetry implies that $x(i) = x(j)$ for all i and j less than A. We can therefore substitute $K/A = x(i)$ in equation (4) to obtain a reduced-form expression for total output in terms of H, K, L, and A:

$$(5) \qquad C + \dot{K} + \dot{A}/B = H^\alpha L^\beta A (K/A)^{1-\alpha-\beta}$$

$$= H^\alpha L^\beta K^{1-\alpha-\beta} A^{\alpha+\beta}.$$

The knowledge-driven and lab equipment specifications of the R&D sector lead to different assumptions about how equilibrium in the R&D sector is decentralized. In the knowledge-driven model, output of designs is homogeneous of degree two. By Euler's theorem it is not possible for both of the inputs A and H to be paid their marginal product. We make the assumption that A receives no compensation. Holders of patents on previous designs have no technological or legal means of preventing designers of new goods from using the ideas implicit in the existing designs. The stock of A that can be put to use, with no compensation, by any individual researcher is therefore the entire stock of knowledge about previous designs, provided that there exists a communication network that makes this information available. The equilibrium is one with knowledge spillovers or external effects in the R&D sector (but not in the manufacturing sector). In this case, we can describe research as if it were done by independent researchers who use their human capital to produce designs, which they subsequently sell.

In the lab equipment model, output of designs is the same, homogeneous-of-degree-one production function as in the manufacturing sector. As is the case for the manufacturing sector, the equilibrium is one in which patents convey market power but in which there are no other entry restrictions. There are no external effects and no knowledge spillovers. There is free entry into both R&D and manufacturing. The only restriction is that no one can manufacture capital of type i without the consent of the holder of the patent on good i. In this case we conceive of R&D as being undertaken by separate firms that hire inputs, produce patentable designs, and sell them for a price P_A.

III. BALANCED GROWTH AND INTEGRATION

The description of the technology given so far represents output as a function of the inputs $H, L, K,$ and A, and specifies the evolution equations for K and A. To facilitate the simple balanced growth analysis that we undertake, the stocks of L and H are each taken as given. Increases in either L or H could be accommodated if we undertook the more complicated task of solving a nonlinear system of differential equations with growth rates that vary over time.

The calculation of a balanced growth equilibrium for each of the two specifications of the R&D technology can be summarized in terms of two linear relations between the rate of growth and the interest rate that hold along a balanced growth path. One relation comes from the conditions of equilibrium in production and the other from preferences.

As shown in the Appendix and as illustrated in Figure I, the interest rate implied by equilibrium in the production sector is decreasing in the rate of growth of output for the knowledge-driven model:

(6) $$r_{\text{technology}} = (\delta H - g)/\Lambda.$$

The term in the denominator depends only on the production function parameters, $\Lambda = \alpha(\alpha + \beta)^{-1} (1 - \alpha - \beta)^{-1}$.

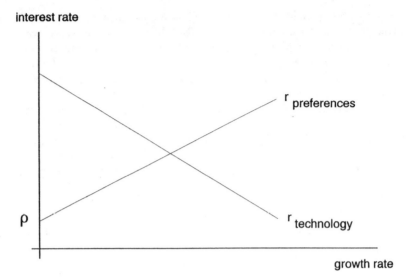

FIGURE I
The Balanced Growth Equilibrium in the Knowledge-Driven Model

The corresponding expression for the interest rate from the lab equipment model is shown in the Appendix to be a function of the production parameters and the stock of H and L. It does not, however, depend on the rate of growth:

$$(7) \qquad\qquad r_{\text{technology}} = \Gamma H^\alpha L^\beta,$$

where Γ is defined by $\Gamma = B^{\alpha+\beta}(\alpha + \beta)^{\alpha+\beta}(1 - \alpha - \beta)^{2-\alpha-\beta}$.

In the knowledge-driven specification the negative relation between the interest rate and the growth rate arises because an increase in the interest rate reduces the demand for capital goods. The calculations in the Appendix show that an increase in the interest rate reduces the number of units of each capital good that are rented, and thereby reduces the value of a patent. According to the curved production possibility frontier between designs and manufactured goods, the reduction in the price of the patented design causes a shift in human capital out of the production of new designs and into the production of manufactured goods. This shift slows down the creation of technology and thereby slows growth. In the lab equipment model only a single value of the interest rate is consistent with production of both goods and designs. The relative price of patents and final goods is fixed, so the interest rate is technologically determined.

It remains to specify the preferences that provide the other balanced growth relation between the interest rate and the rate of growth. The simplest formulation to work with is Ramsey preferences with constant elasticity utility,

$$U = \int_0^\infty \frac{C^{1-\sigma}}{1-\sigma} e^{-\rho t} dt, \qquad \sigma \in [0, \infty).$$

Under balanced growth the rate of growth of consumption must be equal to the rate of growth of output. Thus, for any fixed rate of growth $g = \dot{C}/C$, we can calculate the implied interest rate from the consumer's first-order conditions for intertemporal optimization:

(8) $$r_{\text{preferences}} = \rho + \sigma g.$$

These preferences yield a positive relation between the interest rate and the growth rate because when consumption is growing more rapidly, current consumption is more valuable compared with future consumption, so the marginal rate of substitution between present and future consumption is higher. Consumers would therefore be willing to borrow at higher interest rates.

There is a parameter restriction that is necessary to ensure that the growth rate is not larger than the interest rate. If it is, present values will not be finite, and the integral that defines utility will diverge. In terms of Figures I and II, the restriction is that the intersection of the two curves must lie above the 45 degree line. This will always be true if σ is greater than or equal to one, since in this case, the $r_{\text{preferences}}$ curve always lies above the 45 degree line. If σ is less than one, the $r_{\text{technology}}$ curve must not lie too far up and to the right.

Because the rate of growth under each specification is determined by the intersection of two straight lines, it can be calculated directly from the relation between r and g determined on the preference side, equation (8), and the relation between r and g determined by the technology, either equation (6) or (7). The balanced rate of growth for a closed economy under the knowledge-driven model of the research sector is

(9) $$g = (\delta H - \Lambda \rho)/(\Lambda \sigma + 1).$$

The balanced rate of growth for the lab equipment model is

(10) $$g = (\Gamma H^\alpha L^\beta - \rho)/\sigma.$$

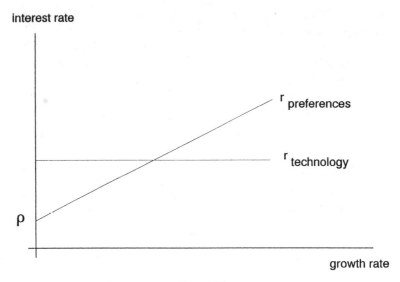

FIGURE II
The Balanced Growth Equilibrium in the Lab Equipment Model

Both of these models have a dependence on scale that is crucial to the analysis of the effects of trade. To see this, consider two economies that have identical endowments of H and L. In the long run these economies will have the same stocks of accumulated inputs as well, so that scale effects offer the only lasting source of gains from trade and economic integration.

Suppose that the two economies are physically contiguous, yet are totally isolated from each other by an impenetrable barrier that impedes the flow of goods, people, and ideas. If these economies evolve under isolation, the balanced rate of growth in each is characterized by Figures I and II and calculated in equations (9) and (10). Now suppose that the barrier is removed, so that the economies are completely integrated into a single economy. The change from two economies with endowments H and L to one economy with stocks $2H$ and $2L$ causes an upward shift in the $r_{\text{technology}}$ curve in both figures. Both the rate of growth and the interest rate increase after complete economic integration takes place, regardless of the specification of the technology for R&D. In both models (even the knowledge-driven model with no knowledge spillovers) the rate of growth is too low compared with the rate that would be selected by a social planner.[1] As a result, one would expect integration to be welfare improving. A full welfare analysis, however, would require explicit consideration of the dynamics along the transition path.

With this discussion as background the examples in the next section are designed to address three questions. First, can free trade in goods between countries induce the same increase in the balanced growth rate as complete integration into a single economy? If not, can the free movement of goods, combined with the free movement of ideas, reproduce the rate of growth under full integration? And finally, what is the underlying explanation for the dependence of the growth rate on the extent of the market?

IV. TRADE IN GOODS AND FLOWS OF IDEAS

In this section we conduct a series of thought experiments about partial integration. In the first two experiments we focus on the knowledge-driven specification for R&D because it permits a sharp distinction between flows of goods and flows of ideas. In the third we consider the lab equipment specification in which ideas have no direct effect on production.

In the analysis of the knowledge-driven specification, we start with two identical, completely isolated economies that are growing at the balanced growth rate. We first allow for trade in goods, but continue to restrict the flow of ideas. To emphasize the distinction between goods and ideas, we assume that trade in goods does not induce any transmission of ideas. For example, we assume that it is impossible to reverse engineer an imported good to learn the secrets of its design. Under these assumptions we show that trade in goods has no effect on the long-run rate of growth. Then in the second experiment we calculate the additional effect of opening communications networks and permitting flows of ideas. We show that allowing flows of ideas results in a permanently higher growth rate.

In the third experiment we consider the effects of opening trade in goods under the lab equipment specification. In this case trade in goods alone causes the same permanent increase in the

1. For the knowledge-driven model, this is shown in Romer [1990]. For an early version of the lab equipment model, this is shown in Romer [1987]. See Barro and Sala i Martin [1990] for a discussion of the optimality of the no-intervention equilibrium and of tax and subsidy policies that can achieve the socially optimal balanced rate of growth in a variety of endogenous growth models.

rate of growth as complete integration. Since ideas per se have no effect on production, the creation of communications networks has no additional effect.

A. *Flows of Goods with No Flows of Ideas in the Knowledge-Driven Model*

In all of the experiments considered here, the form of trade between the two countries is very simple. By symmetry there are no opportunities for intertemporal trade along a balanced growth path, hence no international lending. Because there is only a single final consumption good, the only trades that take place are exchanges of capital goods produced in one country for capital goods produced in the other.

With the knowledge-driven model of research, it is straightforward to show that opening trade in goods has no permanent effect on the rate of growth. In balanced growth the rate of growth of output is equal to the rate of growth of A, $\dot{A}/A = \delta H_A$, which is determined by the split of human capital $H = H_Y + H_A$ between the manufacturing sector and the research sector. Opening trade in goods has two offsetting effects on wages for human capital in these two sectors. Before trade is opened, the number of different types of machines that are used in the manufacturing sector must equal the number that has been designed and produced domestically. Along the new balanced growth path after trade is opened, the number of types of machines used in each country approaches twice the number that has been produced and designed domestically. In their pursuit of monopoly rents, researchers in the two countries will specialize in the production of different types of designs and avoid redundancy, so the worldwide stock of designs will ultimately be twice as large as the stock that has been produced in either country.

With trade in the specialized capital goods, domestic manufacturers can take advantage of foreign designs and vice versa. Ultimately, the level $\bar{x}$ at which each durable is used in each country will return to the level that obtained under isolation. From equation (1) it follows that the increase in A doubles the marginal product of human capital in the manufacturing sector, increasing it from $\partial Y/\partial H = \alpha H_A^{\alpha-1} L^\beta \bar{x}^{1-\alpha-\beta} A$ to $\partial Y/\partial H = \alpha H_A^{\alpha-1} L^\beta \bar{x}^{1-\alpha-\beta} (A + A^*)$, where A^* is the set of durables available from abroad.

For the research sector, opening of trade implies that the market for any newly designed good is twice as large as it was in the absence of trade. This doubles the price of the patents and raises the return to investing human capital in research from $P_A \delta A$ to

$2P_A \delta A$. The knowledge represented by A^* is not available for use in research because flows of ideas are not permitted. Since the return to human capital doubles in both of the competing sectors, free trade in goods does not affect the split of human capital between manufacturing and research. Hence, it does not change the balanced rate of economic growth or the interest rate. In terms of Figure I, opening trade in goods does not change the position of either the $r_{\text{preferences}}$ locus or the $r_{\text{technology}}$ locus.

This result does not imply that free trade in goods has no effect on output or welfare. Consider, for example, the extreme case in which two isolated economies start from completely nonintersecting sets of capital goods A and A^* that have the same measure. Before trade in goods, the home country will use capital at the level $\bar{x}$ for A types of capital goods and the foreign country will use capital at the same level $\bar{x}$ for A^* different types of capital goods. If existing capital is freely mobile, each country will immediately exchange half of its capital stock for half of the capital stock of the other country when trade in capital goods is allowed. Each will then be using capital at the level $\bar{x}/2$ on a set of capital goods of measure $A + A^*$. (Over time, the level of usage will climb back to $\bar{x}$ as capital accumulation takes place because the level of x is determined by r and g, and on the new balanced growth path these are the same as before.) From the form of production in manufacturing given in equation (1), it follows that immediately after trade is opened output in each country jumps by a factor of $2^{\alpha+\beta}$. This is analogous to the kind of level effect one encounters in the neoclassical model and in static models of trade with differentiated inputs in production (e.g., Ethier [1982]). In the specific model outlined here, free trade in goods can affect the level of output and can therefore affect welfare, but it does not affect long-run growth rates.

If the two different economies start from a position with exactly overlapping sets of goods prior to the opening of trade, the timing of the effect on output is different, but the ultimate effect is the same. The level of output at future dates will differ from what it would have been without trade in goods and will generally be higher. But once the transitory effects have died out, the underlying growth rate will be the same as it was prior to the opening of trade in the capital goods.

B. *Flows of Information in the Knowledge-Driven Model of Research*

This second example shows that greater flows of ideas can permanently increase the rate of growth in the knowledge-driven model of research. Once we allow for flows of information, we must make some assumption about international protection of intellectual property rights. In each country we have assumed that patents protect any designs produced domestically. Once ideas and designs created abroad become available, the government could try to expropriate the monopoly rents that would accrue to the foreigners by refusing to uphold their patents. To simplify the discussion here, we assume that neither government engages in this practice. A patent in one country is fully respected in the other. (For a discussion of incomplete protection of intellectual property rights, see Rivera-Batiz and Romer [1991].)

Consider the two identical economies with the knowledge-driven specification of the research sector described in the first experiment. Trade in goods has already been allowed, and this creates the incentive for researchers to specialize in different designs. Over time the sets of designs that are in use in the two countries will be almost entirely distinct, so the worldwide stock of knowledge approaches twice the stock of designs in either country. In the absence of communications links, this means that researchers in each country will ultimately be using only one half of the worldwide stock of knowledge. In the domestic country the rate of growth of A is given by $\dot{A} = \delta H_A A$. In the foreign country it is given by $\dot{A}^* = \delta H_A^* A^*$.

Now suppose that flows of ideas between the two countries are permitted. Research in each country now depends on the total worldwide stock of ideas as contained in the union of A and A^*. If the ideas in each country are completely nonintersecting, the effective stock of knowledge that could be used in research after communication opens would be twice as large as it was before: $\dot{A} = \dot{A}^* = \delta H_A (A + A^*) = 2\delta H_A A$. Even if the allocation of $H = H_Y + H_A$ between manufacturing and research did not change, the rate of growth of A would double. But the increase in the set of ideas available for use in research increases the productivity of human capital in research and has no effect on its productivity in manufacturing. This change in relative productivity induces a shift of human capital out of manufacturing and into research. For two reasons communication of ideas speeds up growth.

Increasing the flow of ideas has the effect of doubling the productivity of research in each country. Compared with the closed economy model, the formal effect is the same as a doubling of the research productivity parameter δ. This would shift the $r_{\text{technology}}$ curve in Figure I upward and lead to a higher equilibrium growth rate and interest rate. The algebraic solution for the balanced growth rate of A (and therefore also of Y, C, and K) can be determined by replacing δ with 2δ in equation (9) to obtain $g = (2\delta H - \Lambda\rho)/(\sigma\Lambda + 1)$.

Doubling the value of the productivity parameter δ has exactly the same effect on the rate of growth of output and designs as a doubling of H. And according to the discussion in Section II, doubling H has the same effect on growth as complete integration of the two economies into a single economy. Flows of ideas and goods together have the same effect on the growth rate as does complete integration. Complete integration would permit permanent migration as well, but since ideas and goods are already mobile and because the ratio of H to L was assumed to be the same in the two countries, migration is not necessary to achieve productive efficiency. For symmetric economies, allowing both trade in goods and free flows of ideas is enough to reproduce the resource allocation under complete integration.

So far, we have considered the additional effect that free flows of information would have if free trade in goods were already permitted. It is useful to consider the alternative case in which flows of information are permitted but flows of goods are not. In this case the results hinge on the degree of overlap between the set of ideas that are produced in each country.

In the absence of trade in goods, there would be no incentive for researchers in different countries to specialize in different designs either before or after flows of information are permitted. Moreover, after flows of information are opened, there would be a positive incentive for researchers in one country to copy designs from the other, and little offsetting incentives to enforce property rights. If the firm that owns the patent on good j is not permitted to sell the good in a foreign country, it has no economic stake in the decision by a foreign firm to copy good j and sell it in the foreign market. (The domestic firm would of course have both the incentive and the legal power to stop exports of the copies from the foreign country.) In the extreme case in which identical knowledge is created in each country, opening flows of information has no effect at all on production.

Alternatively, one could imagine that discovery is a random process with a high variance so that truly independent discoveries would take place in the different isolated countries. In this case, permitting the international transmission of ideas would speed up worldwide growth rates to some extent, even in the absence of trade in goods. With free communication each researcher would be working with a larger stock of ideas than would otherwise have been the case. For example, when the first overland routes to China were opened in the Middle Ages, transportation of goods was so expensive that the economic effects of trade in goods was small. But the economic consequences of the ideas that travelers brought back (e.g., the principle behind the magnetic compass and the formula for gunpowder) were large.

C. Flows of Goods in the Lab Equipment Model of Research

The two previous examples show that there is sometimes a separation between growth effects and level effects. In the first experiment, opening trade in goods had level effects but no growth effects. In the second experiment, opening flows of ideas had both a growth effect and a level effect. (Manufacturing output goes down when H shifts into research, and research output goes up.)

From the first two examples it is tempting to conclude that flows of goods will generally have level effects of the type that are familiar from neoclassical analysis and that it is only flows of ideas that have growth effects. The third example considered shows that this conclusion is wrong. The lab equipment model is constructed so that ideas per se have no effect on production. Hence, permitting international flows of ideas can have no economic effect. Yet we know from the discussion in Section III that complete integration causes a permanent increase in the rate of growth. The experiment considered in this example shows that trade in goods is all that is needed to achieve this result.

Recall that, when trade in goods is permitted in the knowledge-driven model, this increases the profits that the holder of each patent can extract because it increases the market for the good. By itself this increase in the return to producing designs would tend to increase the production of designs, but in the knowledge-driven specification, this effect is exactly offset by the increase in the marginal productivity of human capital in manufacturing.

In the lab equipment specification, opening trade in goods would cause the same kind of increase in the profit earned at each date by the holder of a patent if the interest rate remained constant. But as was noted in subsection II.B, the price of the patent $P_A = 1/B$ is determined by the technology. The only way that the larger market can be reconciled with a fixed price for the patent is if the interest rate increases. A higher interest rate reduces the demand for capital goods, thereby lowering the profit earned by the monopolist at each date. The calculation in the Appendix shows that the required increase in the interest rate is by a factor of $2^{\alpha+\beta}$. When two identical economies are integrated and $2H$ is substituted for H and $2L$ is substituted for L in equation (7), the same increase in r obtains. In each case the higher interest rate leads to higher savings. From Figure II or from equation (10), it follows that this increase in the interest rate leads to the same faster rate of growth as complete integration.

V. SCALE EFFECTS AND GROWTH

In the last example we noted one incorrect conjecture about why tighter economic integration leads to faster growth. From the knowledge-driven model one might conclude that flows of ideas are crucial to the finding that economic integration can speed up growth. But the lab equipment model shows that closer integration can speed up growth even in a model in which flows of ideas have no effect on production. A related conjecture is that knowledge spillovers are fundamental and that increasing the extent of the spillovers is how integrations speeds up growth. The lab equipment model shows that this too is incorrect, for it has no knowledge spillovers.

Finally, one might conclude that it is the increasing returns to scale in the production function for designs, $\dot{A} = \delta H_A A$, that causes integration to have a growth effect in the knowledge-driven model. This conjecture seems to us to come closest to the mark, but it needs to be interpreted carefully. To see why, recall that the production function for designs in the lab equipment model, $\dot{A} = B H_A^\alpha L_A^\beta \int_0^A x_A(i)^{1-\alpha-\beta} \, di$, exhibits constant returns to scale as a function of H, L, and the capital goods $x(i)$. There is, nonetheless, a form of increasing returns that is present in this model. It comes from the fixed cost that must be incurred to design a new good. With integration this fixed cost need be incurred only once. Under isolation it must be incurred twice, once in each country.

To bring out the underlying form of increasing returns, recall from equation (5) that we can substitute $x = K_A/A$ into the expression for $\dot{A}$ and write it as a function of H, L, K, and A that is homogeneous of degree $1 + \alpha + \beta$: $\dot{A} = B H_A^\alpha L_A^\beta K_A^{1-\alpha-\beta} A^{\alpha+\beta}$. Interpreted as a statement about this kind of reduced-form expression, it is correct to say that both models exhibit increasing returns to scale in the production of new designs as a function of the stocks of basic inputs. Consequently, operating two research sectors in isolation is not as efficient as operating a single integrated research sector. To operate an integrated research sector in the knowledge-driven model, two things are required. First, one must avoid redundant effort, that is, devoting resources in one economy to rediscovering a design that already exists in the other. Trade in goods provides the incentive to avoid redundancy. Second, one must make sure that ideas discovered in one country are available for use in research in both countries. Flows of ideas along communications networks serve this function.

In the lab equipment model trade in goods once again provides the incentive to avoid redundant effort. Beyond this, all that is needed to create a single worldwide research sector is to ensure that all types of capital equipment available worldwide are used in all research activities undertaken anywhere in the world. Since ideas do not matter in research, trade in the capital goods is all that is needed.

There is one final point worth emphasizing. Rebelo [1991] offers a general observation about multisector models that is relevant for the experiments considered here. Consider a single-sector model of the form, $C + \dot{K} + \dot{A} = B_0 F_0(K, A)$, where $F_0(\cdot)$ is a homogeneous of degree one function. In this example, K and A can denote any two arbitrary capital goods. If the productivity parameter B_0 increases, the balanced growth rate increases. Consider next a two-sector model in which there is an essential fixed factor L that enters as an input in the homogeneous of degree one production function for consumption and capital of type K: $C + \dot{K} = B_1 F_1(K_1, A_1, L)$. The capital good A, however, is produced by a homogeneous of degree one function $F_2(\cdot)$ of K and A alone: $\dot{A} = B_2 F_2(K_2, A_2)$. In this case a change in the productivity parameter B_1 has no effect on the balanced rate of growth. It has only level effects. In contrast, an increase in B_2 increases the balanced rate of growth.

The connection between Rebelo's observation and our results is as follows. We do not consider changes in technology parameters like B_1 and B_2, but we do induce changes in scale for functions that are homogeneous of some degree greater than one. Increases in scale are analogous to increases in the productivity parameters. In the knowledge-driven model trade in goods exploits increasing returns in the sector that produces C and K, but not in the sector that produces A. It is like an increase in B_1 in Rebelo's two-sector model, and induces only level effects. In contrast, flows of ideas increase the productivity in the research sector that produces A, and are analogous to an increase in Rebelo's coefficient B_2. Finally, trade in goods in the lab equipment model induces a scale effect that is like an increase in B_0 in Rebelo's one-sector model.

VI. LIMITATIONS OF THE MODELS AND EXTENSIONS

As noted in the Introduction, the analysis carried out in this paper takes the form of thought experiments for idealized cases. These experiments reveal the following general insight about the connection between economic integration and the rate of economic growth. In a model of endogenous growth, if economic integration lets two economies exploit increasing returns to scale in the equation that represents the engine of growth, integration will raise the long-run rate of growth purely because it increases the extent of the market. Depending on the form of the model, this integration could take the form of trade in goods, flows of ideas, or both.

This conclusion must be tempered by a large number of qualifications. First, there is no consensus yet about whether the equation that is the engine of growth is homogeneous of some degree that is greater than one in the basic inputs (as it is in both of the models considered here) or instead is homogeneous of degree one (as it is, for example, in the papers by Rebelo [1991] and Lucas [1988]).

Second, as noted in the introduction, we have focused on trade between economies with identical endowments and technologies to highlight the scale effects induced by economic integration. In a general two-sector framework, trade between economies that have different endowments or technologies will induce allocation effects that shift resources between the two sectors in each country. For example, Grossman and Helpman [1990] show that trade between countries that have different endowments or technologies will induce shifts between the manufacturing sector and the R&D sector that can either speed up or slow down worldwide growth. If one wants to take the optimistic conclusions reached in this paper literally, they are most likely to apply to integration between similar developed regions of the world, for example, between North America, Europe, and Japan.

There are many details of R&D at the micro level that have been ignored in all of the analysis. We have assumed that giving participants in the economy an incentive to avoid redundancy in research is sufficient to ensure that no redundancy takes place. We have also assumed that patents are infinitely lived and, implicitly, that the institutional structure avoids patent races. We have not considered the role of secrecy in preserving economic value for ideas. All of these restrictions are very strong. Grossman and Helpman [1989d] show how one element of the microeconomic literature on patents, the destruction of monopoly profits by new discoveries, can be included in an aggregate growth model. Other extensions will no doubt follow.

The functional forms used here cannot be literally correct. For example, in both of our models the output of patents at any date increases in proportion to the resources devoted to R&D. This permits the solution for balanced growth paths using linear equations, but it cannot be a good description of actual research opportunities. We would expect that a doubling of research effort would lead to a less than two-fold increase in R&D output, in large part because of the coordination and redundancy problems at the micro level that we have ignored. Addressing these issues would help reconcile a model in which growth rates increase linearly in H in one case, or as a power of H and L in the second, with a historical record showing that growth rates have indeed increased over time, but not nearly as much as the functional forms used here would suggest. More precision in the definition of the input H that is most important for research would also be helpful in this regard. In terms of their effects on research output, one presumably does not literally want to equate two people holding high school degrees with one person holding a Ph.D. degree.

Perhaps the most interesting limitation of the models considered here is one that it shares with many other models: there is no description of how ideas or information affect the production of goods. Once one admits that ideas per se can influence research output, it is apparent that they can influence the output of goods as well. Presumably this is what learning-by-doing models try to capture with the asumption that some production parameter increases with cumulative experience: producing goods yield both goods and ideas, and the ideas raise the productivity of the other inputs. Formal models in the tradition of Arrow [1962] have not yet addressed the importance of communication networks and information flows. When the learning-by-doing models are used in international trade, it is implicitly assumed that there is a communication network that extends throughout one national economy, yet does not cross national boundaries. Little theoretical attention has been given to the analysis of policy choices that can affect the efficiency of international communication networks and to explaining historical episodes (e.g., the emergence of the textile industry in the United States and of the automobile industry in Japan) that reflect large flows of information from developed industries in one country to developing industries in another.

Given these limitations and qualifications, our only claim is to have formalized, and we hope illuminated, an effect that is potentially important. If the discovery of new ideas is central to economic growth, one should expect that increasing returns associated with the opportunity to reuse existing ideas will be present. If the increasing returns extend to the sector of the economy that generates growth, economic integration will induce scale effects that will raise the long-run rate of growth. And because of the remarkable growth of the exponential function, policies that affect long-run rates of growth can have very large cumulative effects on economic welfare. Many other effects may be present as well, but in future theoretical and empirical work, we argue that scale effects on growth that are induced by economic integration are worth watching out for.

APPENDIX

A. Derivation of Equation (7)

In the lab equipment model the value of total production in manufacturing and research depends only on the aggregate stocks of inputs, not on their allocation between the two sectors:

$$Y + \frac{\dot{A}}{B} = H^\alpha L^\beta \int_0^A x(i)^{1-\alpha-\beta} di.$$

Taking its supply of H and L as given, each representative firm in the manufacturing sector chooses levels of $x(i)$ to maximize profits. Consequently, the first-order condition for the problem of maximizing $Y + \dot{A}/B$ minus total input cost $\int p(i)x(i) di$ with respect to the use of input i yields the economywide inverse demand curve for good i. The rental rate p that results when x units of the capital good are supplied is

(A.1) $p = (1 - \alpha - \beta)H^\alpha L^\beta x^{-(\alpha+\beta)}.$

Input producers choose x to maximize the present value of monopoly rent minus x times the unit cost of each piece of capital, $P_A = \max (px/r) - x$. Using equation (A.1), the first-order condition that determines the number of machines $\bar{x}$ that the holder of the patent on good i rents to manufacturing firms is

(A.2) $$(1 - \alpha - \beta)^2 H^\alpha L^\beta \bar{x}^{-(\alpha+\beta)} r^{-1} - 1 = 0,$$

which implies that $p/r = (1 - \alpha - \beta)^{-1}$. The present discounted value of profit collected by the holder of the patent can then be simplified to

(A.3) $$P_A = \left(\frac{p\bar{x}}{r}\right) - \bar{x} = \frac{\alpha + \beta}{1 - \alpha - \beta} \bar{x}.$$

Since $P_A = 1/B$, this implies that $\bar{x} = (1 - \alpha - \beta)/B(\alpha + \beta)$. Substituting this expression into equation (A.2) yields equation (7) in the text:

$$r_{\text{technology}} = B^{\alpha+\beta}(\alpha + \beta)^{\alpha+\beta}(1 - \alpha - \beta)^{2-\alpha-\beta} H^\alpha L^\beta.$$

B. Derivation of Equation (6)

The demand for the capital goods in this model has exactly the same form as in the lab equipment model, with the qualification that since all of the demand comes from the manufacturing sector, H must be replaced by H_Y. If we use equation (A.1) with this replacement to substitute for p in the expression for P_A, we have

$$P_A = (\alpha + \beta)\frac{p\bar{x}}{r} = \frac{\alpha + \beta}{r}(1 - \alpha - \beta)H_Y^\alpha L^\beta \bar{x}^{1-\alpha+\beta}.$$

Equating the wages of human capital in manufacturing and research yields $P_A \delta A = \alpha H_Y^{\alpha-1} L^\beta A \bar{x}^{1-\alpha-\beta}$. Combining these expressions and solving for H_Y gives $H_Y = (1/\delta), \alpha(\alpha + \beta)^{-1}(1 - \alpha - \beta)^{-1}$ $r = (\Lambda/\delta)r$. Hence, $g = \delta H_A = \delta H - \delta H_Y = \delta H - \Lambda r$.

C. Trade in Goods in Lab Equipment Model is Equivalent to Complete Integration

If the interest rate remained constant, the value of a patent $P_A = \pi/r$ would double when trade in goods between two identical markets is introduced in this model. The monopolist that sells in two identical markets and faces constant marginal costs of production will maximize profits in each market independently and earn twice the flow of profits that would accrue from one market alone. Since the value of the patent must remain fixed at $1/B$ by the specification of the technology for producing patents, the interest rate must increase to restore equilibrium.

As shown above, maximization of profit by the monopolist

implies that p/r is constant, so profit is proportional to $\bar{x}$. To offset the doubling of profit that the opening of trade would otherwise induce, r must increase by enough to make the number of units of capital supplied by the monopolist in each country fall by one half. From equation (A.2) this will happen if r increases by a factor of $2^{\alpha+\beta}$. This is the same as the increase in r that results from doubling H and L when the two countries are combined.

University of California, San Diego
University of California, Berkeley

References

Arrow, Kenneth J., "The Economic Implications of Learning By Doing," *Review of Economic Studies*, XXIX (June 1962), 155–73.
Backus, David, Patrick Kehoe, and Timothy Kehoe, "In Search of Scale Effects in Trade and Growth," Working Paper No. 451, Federal Reserve Bank of Minneapolis, 1991.
Barro, Robert, and Xavier Sala i Martin, "Public Finance in Models of Economic Growth," National Bureau of Economic Research, Working Paper No. 3362, 1990.
Dinopoulos, Elias, James Oehmke, and Paul Segerstrom, "High Technology Industry Trade and Investment: The Role of Factor Endowments," University of Florida working paper, 1990.
Dixit, Avinash, and V. Norman, *The Theory of International Trade* (Cambridge, England: Cambridge University Press, 1980).
Ethier, Wilfred J., "National and International Returns to Scale in the Modern Theory of International Trade," *American Economic Review*, LXXII (June 1982), 389–405.
Feenstra, Robert, "Trade and Uneven Growth," National Bureau of Economic Research, Working Paper No. 3276, 1990.
Grossman, Gene, and Elhanan Helpman, "Product Development and International Trade," *Journal of Political Economy*, XCVII (December 1989a), 1261–83.
____, and ____, "Endogenous Product Cycles," National Bureau of Economic Research, Working Paper No. 2113, 1989b.
____, and ____, "Growth and Welfare in a Small Open Economy," National Bureau of Economic Research, Working Paper No. 2809, 1989c.
____, and ____, "Quality Ladders in the Theory of Growth," National Bureau of Economic Research, Working Paper No. 3099, 1989d.
____, and ____, "Comparative Advantage and Long Run Growth," *American Economic Review*, LXXX (September 1990), 796–815.
____, and ____, "Quality Ladders and Product Cycles," *Quarterly Journal of Economics*, CVI (1991), 557–86.
Krugman, Paul, "Increasing Returns, Monopolistic Competition, and International Trade," *Journal of International Economics*, IX (November 1979), 469–79.
____, "Intraindustry Specialization and the Gains from Trade," *Journal of Political Economy*, LXXXIX (October 1981), 959–73.
____, *Rethinking International Trade* (Cambridge MA: MIT Press, 1990).
Lancaster, Kevin, "Intraindustry Trade under Perfect Monopolistic Competition," *Journal of International Economics*, X (1980), 151–75.
Lucas, Robert E., Jr., "On the Mechanics of Economic Development," *Journal of Monetary Economics*, XXII (1988), 3–42.
Rebelo, Sergio, "Long-Run Policy Analysis and Long-Run Growth," *Journal of Political Economy*, forthcoming (1991).
Rivera-Batiz, Luis A., and Paul M. Romer, "International Trade with Endogenous Technological Change," *European Economic Review*, forthcoming (1991).

Romer, Paul M., "Growth Based on Increasing Returns Due to Specialization," *American Economic Review,* LXXVII (May 1987), 56–62.
——, "Endogenous Technological Change," *Journal of Political Economy,* XCVIII (October 1990), S71–S102.
Rosenberg, Nathan, *Inside the Black Box* (Cambridge, England: Cambridge University Press, 1980).
Segerstrom, Paul, T. C. A. Anant, and Elias Dinopoulos, "A Schumpeterian Model of the Product Life Cycle," *American Economic Review,* (1990), 1077–91.
Young, Alwyn, "Learning by Doing and the Dynamic Effects of International Trade," *Quarterly Journal of Economics,* CVI (1991), 369–405.

Name Index

The International Library of Critical Writings in Economics

The Economics of Defence
Keith Hartley and Nicholas Hooper

The Economics of Business Policy
John Kay

The Balance of Payments
Michael J. Artis

Cost-Benefit Analysis
Arnold Harberger and Glenn P. Jenkins

Privatization in Developing and Transitional Economies
Colin Kirkpatrick and Paul Cook

The Economics of Intellectual Property
Ruth Towse

The Economics of Tourism
Clem Tisdell

The Economics of Organization and Bureaucracy
Peter Jackson

Realism and Economics: Studies in Ontology
Tony Lawson

The International Economic Institutions of the Twentieth Century
David Greenaway

The Economics of Structural Change
Harald Hagemann, Michael Landesmann and Roberto Scazzieri

The Economics of the Welfare State
Nicholas Barr

Path Dependence
Paul David

Alternative Theories of the Firm
Richard Langlois, Paul Robertson and Tony F. Yu

The Economics of the Mass Media
Glenn Withers

The Economics of Budget Deficits
Charles Rowley

Forms of Capitalism: Comparative Institutional Analyses
Ugo Pagano and Ernesto Screpanti